The Coulee Dam showing the power houses and pumping plant which lifts water from Lake Roosevelt (left) to the earth-dammed equalising reservoir (upper right) in the coulee—an abandoned overflow channel. The water is used for irrigation in the Columbia Basin—see Fig. 76. (*Bureau of Reclamation.*)

ADVANCED LEVEL GEOGRAPHY SERIES

BOOK FOUR

NORTH AMERICA

BY

BRIAN CARLSON, M.A.
PRINCIPAL LECTURER IN EDUCATION
CITY OF SHEFFIELD COLLEGE OF EDUCATION

UNIVERSITY TUTORIAL PRESS LTD
9-10 Great Sutton Street, London, E.C.1

ADVANCED LEVEL GEOGRAPHY SERIES

BOOK ONE. AUSTRALIA AND NEW ZEALAND.
Also in Two Parts:
  Part I. AUSTRALIA.
  Part II. NEW ZEALAND.
    By D. C. MONEY, M.A., F.R.G.S.

BOOK TWO. THE MEDITERRANEAN LANDS.
  By HARRY ROBINSON, Ph.D., M.Ed., B.A.

BOOK THREE. SOUTH AMERICA.
  By D. C. MONEY.

BOOK FOUR. NORTH AMERICA.
  By BRIAN CARLSON, M.A.

BOOK FIVE. WESTERN EUROPE.
(SCANDINAVIA, FINLAND, DENMARK, ICELAND, BENELUX, FRANCE, WESTERN GERMANY, EASTERN GERMANY, SWITZERLAND, AND AUSTRIA.)
  By HARRY ROBINSON.

BOOK SIX. MONSOON LANDS.
In Two Parts:
  PART I. GENERAL INTRODUCTION, INDIA, PAKISTAN, CEYLON, BURMA.
    By R. T. COBB, M.A., and L. J. M. COLEBY, M.A., M.Sc., Ph.D.
  PART II. EASTERN ASIA.
    By W. B. CORNISH, B.A.

BOOK SEVEN. AFRICA.
  By W. F. HORNBY, B.A., AND PETER NEWTON, B.Sc.   [*In preparation*

All rights reserved. No portion of the book may be reproduced by any process without written permission from the publishers.
© *Brian Carlson*, 1963, 1965, 1969

Published 1963
Second Edition 1965
Reprinted 1967
Third Edition 1969

SBN: 7231 0500 6

PRINTED IN GREAT BRITAIN BY UNIVERSITY TUTORIAL PRESS LTD, FOXTON NEAR CAMBRIDGE

PREFACE

North America is one of a series of texts specially designed for sixth form students preparing for the General Certificate of Education at Advanced Level and for university entrance. The first part of the book deals with the physical background and this, together with the chapter on the historical geography of the continent, provides a basis essential for the understanding of the contemporary scene. The remainder (and larger part) of the book is devoted to systematic studies of the major regions of North America.

Geography is a dynamic subject, statistics are quickly outdated, and interpretations and emphases change. The tables of figures are as up to date as possible, and have been introduced not only to illustrate the relative economic importance of places but also to provide facts upon which useful exercises can be based. In various places, I have indicated where differences of opinion exist on certain matters, and university candidates may well follow up some of these in works listed in the selected bibliography at the end of the book.

The photographs and maps form an integral part of the book and will repay careful study. As many as possible of the places mentioned have been shown on maps, but the reader should refer frequently to a good atlas. Centigrade equivalents have been given in italics for all Fahrenheit readings, and the notation 30 F.°, etc., has been used to indicate a *range* of temperature.

My thanks are due to friends and colleagues who have helped me in the preparation of this book and particularly to Mr D. C. Money for many useful criticisms and suggestions. The final responsibility for any inaccuracies in the text, however, is mine alone.

I wish also to thank the American Geographical Society, the Geographical Association, and the publishers who have kindly given me permission to quote from works published by them. They are the Oxford University Press (*A Study of History, Vol. 2* by

A. Toynbee), Hamish Hamilton (*Inside U.S.A.* by J. Gunther), Ginn and Co. (*The Oregon Trail* by F. Parkman, and *The Great Plains* by W. P. Webb), and Methuen and Co. (*Canada* by G. Taylor). The American Geographical Society and the Petroleum Information Bureau kindly granted me permission to reproduce Fig. 47 and Fig. 57 respectively. I am grateful to the government departments and private companies which have provided photographs and statistical information. The source of each of the photographs used has been individually acknowledged.

B. C.

NOTE TO THE THIRD EDITION

The present edition has been revised to take account of the latest available statistical information.

B. C.

CONTENTS

CHAPTER		PAGE
I.	PHYSICAL FEATURES	1
II.	CLIMATE	20
III.	NATURAL VEGETATION AND SOILS	54
IV.	THE SPREAD OF SETTLEMENT	76
V.	NEW ENGLAND	100
VI.	MIDDLE ATLANTIC REGION	116
VII.	THE SOUTH	134
VIII.	THE MIDWEST	168
IX.	THE GREAT PLAINS	196
X.	THE MOUNTAIN STATES	215
XI.	CALIFORNIA	240
XII.	PACIFIC NORTH-WEST	257
XIII.	THE ATLANTIC PROVINCES	270
XIV.	THE LAURENTIAN LOWLANDS	291
XV.	THE CANADIAN SHIELD	319
XVI.	THE PRAIRIES	335
XVII.	BRITISH COLUMBIA	355
XVIII.	THE NORTHLANDS	377
XIX.	CANADA AND THE U.S.A.	395
	APPENDIX I	399
	APPENDIX II	400
	FURTHER READING	401
	INDEX	413
	REGIONAL REFERENCES	429

TABLES

TABLE		PAGE
1.	MAJOR SEAPORTS OF THE U.S.A.	129
2.	NEGRO POPULATION OF THE SOUTHERN STATES	137
3.	PER CAPITA INCOME	139
4.	COTTON PRODUCTION BY REGIONS	141
5.	COTTON PRODUCTION IN THE U.S.A.	143
6.	TOBACCO PRODUCTION IN THE U.S.A.	156
7.	RICE PRODUCTION IN THE U.S.A.	162
8.	PRODUCTION OF OIL AND NATURAL GAS	166
9.	ORCHARD AND VINEYARD REGIONS OF THE U.S.A.	178
10.	BITUMINOUS COAL PRODUCTION	181
11.	MAIN LAKE PORTS	184
12.	STEEL CAPACITY IN THE U.S.A.	186
13.	MAJOR CITIES OF THE MIDWEST	188
14.	WHEAT PRODUCTION	208
15.	LIVESTOCK IN PART OF WYOMING AND PART OF IOWA	211
16.	COPPER, LEAD, AND ZINC PRODUCTION	221
17.	POPULATION OF THE ATLANTIC PROVINCES	270
18.	FISH LANDED AND VALUE OF PRODUCTS	277
19.	AVAILABLE AND DEVELOPED WATER POWER IN CANADA	300
20.	MAJOR CANADIAN PORTS	305
21.	CANADIAN IRON AND STEEL INDUSTRY	315
22.	IRON ORE PRODUCTION IN CANADA	315
23.	RESERVES OF SOFTWOOD AND PRODUCTION	326
24.	MAIN MINING CENTRES, CANADIAN SHIELD	329
25.	PRODUCTION AND EXPORT OF CANADIAN WHEAT	346
26.	BRITISH COLUMBIA	365

ILLUSTRATIONS

COULEE DAM	*Frontispiece*
	FACING PAGE
CANADIAN SHIELD	16
MISSISSIPPI DELTA	16
SCOTTS BLUFF, NEBRASKA	17
RIDGE AND VALLEY PROVINCE, PENNSYLVANIA	17
TETON MOUNTAINS AND SNAKE RIVER	32
ATHABASCA GLACIER	32
DEATH VALLEY, CALIFORNIA	33
BRYCE CANYON, UTAH	33
MESAS AND BUTTES IN MONUMENT VALLEY	48
PRAIRIE LANDSCAPE	48
CYPRESS SWAMP, LOUISIANA	49
EVERGLADES	64
SAGEBRUSH	64
YUCCA	65
GIANT REDWOODS	65
NAVAJO INDIANS	96
HOPI VILLAGE	96
DAIRY FARM, VERMONT	97
TOBACCO FIELDS, MASSACHUSETTS	97
LEVEE, LOUISIANA	112
NEW YORK	112
OMAHA, NEBRASKA	113
BATON ROUGE, LOUISIANA	113
TUCSON, ARIZONA	208
MINNEAPOLIS, MINNESOTA	208

ILLUSTRATIONS

	FACING PAGE
COPPER MINE, UTAH	209
COACHELLA VALLEY, CALIFORNIA	209
COACHELLA VALLEY, CALIFORNIA	224
CONTRA COSTA CANAL, CALIFORNIA	224
CORNER BROOK, NEWFOUNDLAND	225
STEEL PLANT, SYDNEY, NOVA SCOTIA	225
OIL WELLS, CALIFORNIA	256
CLEVELAND, OHIO	256
SOUTH BANK OF ST LAWRENCE	257
CANADIAN LOCKS NEAR IROQUOIS	257
SEPT ILES, QUEBEC	272
NIAGARA	272
MINE AND SMELTER PLANT, SUDBURY, ONTARIO	273
ELLIOT LAKE	273
CHURCHILL, HUDSON BAY	352
CANADIAN SHIELD, SASKATCHEWAN	352
MILK RIVER, ALBERTA	353
OKANAGAN VALLEY, B.C.	353
ALUMINIUM SMELTER, QUEBEC	368
KITIMAT, B.C.	368
FORT SMITH, SLAVE RIVER	369
KETCHIKAN, ALASKA	369

NORTH AMERICA

CHAPTER I

PHYSICAL FEATURES

The continent of North America covers an area of over 7 million square miles (Canada, 3,843,100; U.S.A., 2,977,128; Alaska, 590,884) and is exceeded in size only by Asia and Africa. Its latitudinal extent is 58°, from the Florida Keys in the south (25° N.) to the northern shores of Ellesmere Island (83° N.), which are less than 500 miles from the pole. The extreme longitudinal extent is from eastern Newfoundland (53° W.) to the Bering Strait (170° W.), a distance of 4,000 miles. In terms of local time, this is a difference of almost eight hours.

The physical lineaments of the continent are, in outline, quite simple: the complexities of Europe's structural build are missing in America. Even so, there are examples of practically every landform. The various earth movements, such as folding and faulting, and volcanic activity, created the initial land surfaces, which have been worked upon by the different processes of erosion to produce varied and striking topography. Some areas owe their present form to the processes of normal erosion; in large parts of the continent ice has been mainly responsible for the surface features; more restricted areas have developed under arid conditions.

North America can be divided into four major physiographical regions. The north-east is occupied by the Canadian Shield, a glaciated peneplain. In the east is a belt of upland country, the Eastern Highlands, bordered by a coast plain. In the centre, stretching from the Arctic Ocean to the Gulf of Mexico, are the Central Plains, out of which rises a massif of older rocks, the Ozarks. Along the west coast and parallel to it lie the ranges and plateaus of the broad Western Cordilleras (Fig. 1).

THE CANADIAN SHIELD

The vast north-eastern quadrant of the continent is made up of very ancient rocks. Extending over 2 million square miles, the area is one of generally low relief and represents the roots of a former mountain complex. The sediments laid down in the Pre-Cambrian seas were folded, metamorphosed, and split by igneous intrusions. These rocks have been so greatly compressed and deformed, and their texture so altered, that they cannot be dated or classified with

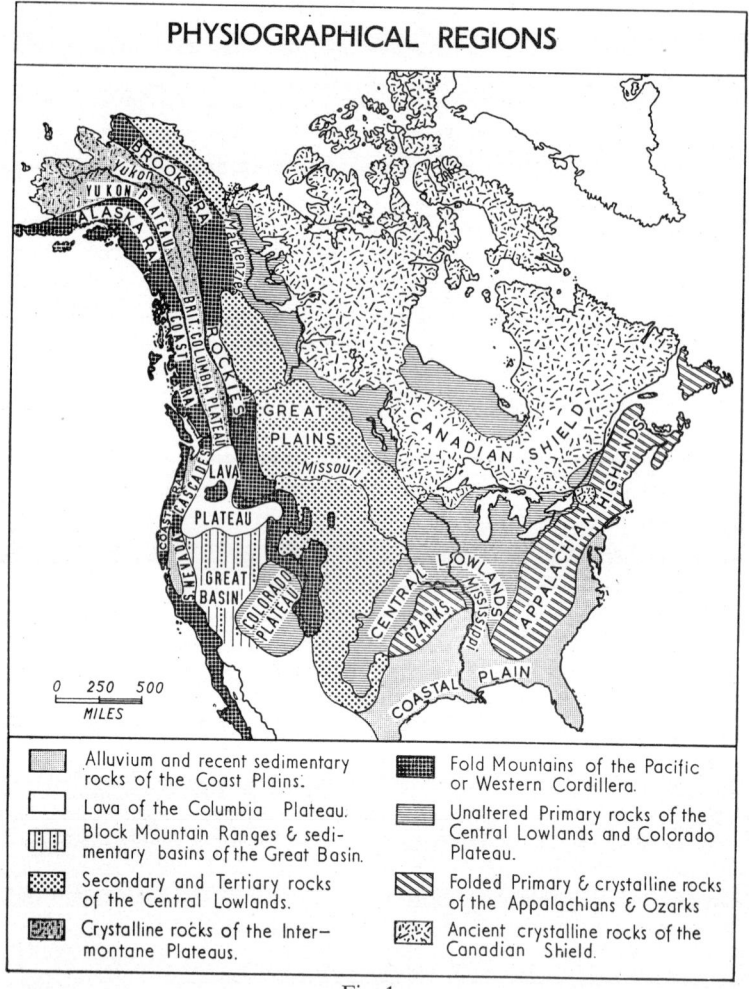

Fig. 1.

any certainty. Subsequent erosion has laid bare the ancient batholiths, schists, and gneisses that occupied the cores of the mountain ranges. It has been estimated that granite rocks occupy over 80 per cent. of the surface area. Unaltered sediments are to be found only on the borders of the Shield, on the southern shores of Hudson Bay, and in minute areas of the interior, where they have been preserved by being down-faulted into the underlying rocks.

This ancient crustal block has withstood the folding of more recent times—the folding which erected first the Appalachians and later the Rockies—but there has been considerable faulting and warping of the crust. The rocks are exposed mainly in Canada but they are also found in the U.S.A. south of Lake Superior. The Adirondacks, too, are really part of the Canadian Shield and are linked to it by a "bridge" of old rock across the St Lawrence Valley (a section where there are numerous islands). Although masked by later sediments, the Shield rocks underlie most of the continent and are exposed at the surface in the Ozarks (St Francis Mountains), in Texas, in the Black Hills of Dakota, and at the bottom of the Colorado Canyon.

The highest parts of the Shield are around its edges: in the centre it has been depressed and is now occupied by the waters of Hudson Bay. The Laurentides, which border the St Lawrence estuary, are more than 2,000 ft high, as are the heights north of Lake Superior. The Torngat Mountains of Labrador reach elevations of between 5,000 ft and 6,000 ft. On the west flank of the Shield the altitude is lower but greater than that of the plains which border it.

From these outer areas, the surface slopes gently downwards, usually only one or two feet per mile, towards the shores of Hudson Bay. From a distance, the sky-line looks monotonously even, but closer inspection reveals an undulating surface with low rounded hills rising 100 ft to 200 ft above the general level of the land. The iron-bearing Mesabi and Penokee ranges near the western tip of Lake Superior are hills of this nature.

The Ice Age

The results of the glaciation of this area are of fundamental importance. There were two main centres of ice accumulation and dispersal and at least one smaller one. It is generally accepted that there were five glacial periods when the ice advanced, with intervening stages when the climate was as warm as, if not warmer than, the present, when the ice retreated. The ice which formed over Labrador and Keewatin (west of Hudson Bay) moved south as far as the present course of the River Ohio and west to the Rockies, where it coalesced with the extensive mountain glaciers.

In the Canadian Shield the work of the ice was mainly of an erosive character. Eskers, till, and moraines cover only small areas, chiefly the former valleys and depressions. Generally speaking, the ice-sheets swept away the superficial deposits and left the exposed rocks polished, grooved, and scratched (see plate facing p. 16). The ice-deepened hollows are now occupied by lakes and marshes, of which there are a striking number. Almost a quarter of the area is water.

The pre-glacial valley system was obliterated and the rivers began to flow anew on a bare, undulating surface. Hollows became

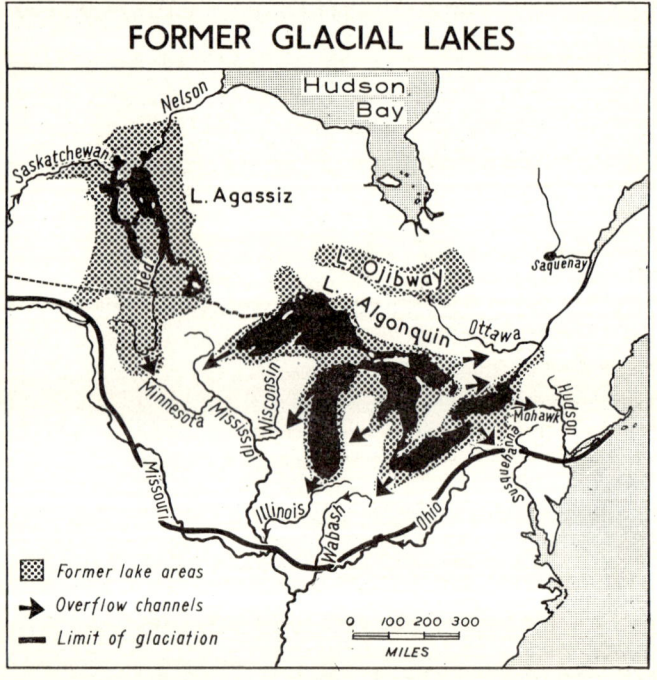

Fig. 2.

lakes and the rivers became spillways between them. Tortuous and tangled streams sometimes expand to form sheets of almost stagnant water and sometimes tumble over rock barriers to form rapids and waterfalls (see plate facing p. 352). Most of the drainage is to Hudson Bay but some streams flow from the edges of the Shield to the Mackenzie, the Great Lakes, and St Lawrence, or to the Atlantic.

Rather different in origin are the lakes which formed along the ice-front. Rivers draining to the north and east were halted by the ice. Water accumulated and rose in level until an escape was found either across the high land to the south or along the ice-front. The Great Lakes are the remnants of a larger sheet of water, *Lake Algonquin*, which at different times overflowed west to the Mississippi, south to the Ohio, and east to the Hudson. These channels were abandoned when the St Lawrence exit was freed from ice. Another pro-glacial lake was Lake Agassiz, which occupied what is now the Red River basin. Most of the water has disappeared; only Lakes Winnipeg, Winnipegosis, and Manitoba remain. The exposed floor of the former lake is now covered with deposits of silt and clay. Similar lacustrine deposits occur in many parts of the Shield, the most extensive in the Clay Belt of Ontario and Quebec, which was formerly covered by the waters of Lake Ojibway (Fig. 2).

The central part of the ice-sheet appears to have attained a thickness of about 10,000 ft and this tremendous weight depressed the crust of the earth. With the removal of the ice, the land began to rise, and this isostatic readjustment is still continuing. Along the shores of James Bay are elevated beach lines of marine clays 500 ft above the present sea level while along the Labrador coast are post-glacial marine terraces 1,500 ft above salt water. Where the ice was thinner, towards the southern edge of the Shield, the uplift has been much smaller. To compensate for the crustal upwarping in the north, there has been some sinking of the land in the south along the Gulf coast.

THE EASTERN HIGHLANDS AND ATLANTIC COAST PLAIN

The Eastern Highlands come directly to the coast in New England, the Maritime Provinces, and Newfoundland. South of New York the coast is backed by a low plain.

The Atlantic Coast Plain

This is a clearly defined region stretching inland from the coast to the Fall Line (p. 6) and from Florida almost to New York, with outlying portions represented by Long Island, the islands off the south coast of New England, and the Cape Cod peninsula. The rocks are mainly soft and unconsolidated sands, gravels, clays, and marls, of Cretaceous and Tertiary age. They dip gently seawards, and continue underneath the sea as a broad continental shelf. The more resistant beds, usually sandstone, but occasionally limestone, have not been eroded as much as the weaker formations and stand out as low, inward-facing *cuestas*. The Coast Plain decreases in width northwards: in Georgia it extends 200 miles from the coast and its inner margin is 800 ft above sea level; in New Jersey it disappears.

In the Florida peninsula, the structure is rather different. In place of the gently dipping beds is a low tabular block of limestone which is partially and irregularly buried under sands. These superficial deposits are extremely porous and underneath them there has occurred extensive solution of the limestone. Much of the drainage is underground, and, in addition, there are numerous sinks and lakelets. In the south is an ill-drained lowland area, Lake Okechobee and the large swampy area known as the Everglades, which are only a few feet above sea level.

The Coastline.—The gentle slope of the Coast Plain continues below sea level and forms the wide continental shelf, which is broadest in the north where the plain itself is narrowest. The coast has emerged over a long period, but there have been minor oscillations of sea level during and since the Ice Age. The rise in sea level, which accompanied the melting of the ice, has caused the coast to be slightly submerged. The effect of this recent submergence is more apparent in the north, where the coast is deeply embayed (*e.g.* Chesapeake and Delaware bays). Farther south are features associated with emergence, which have survived the more recent rise in sea level. Off-shore bars form under the shallow water and migrate landwards. They may become attached to a projecting part of the coast, in which case they form sand-spits. Behind them are marshes and lagoons (called sounds) such as the Dismal Swamp and Pamlico Sound inland from Cape Hatteras, and Indian River along the east coast of Florida. At the southern tip of the Florida peninsula are the Florida Keys, a group of coral islands.

The Fall Line.—Where the weaker sediments of the Coast Plain abut directly against the resistant crystalline rocks of the Piedmont is the Fall Line. This is a zone rather than a line and marks the intersection of the present surface of the Piedmont by an old peneplained surface which has been affected by earth movements and slopes quite steeply to the east. On this surface were deposited the Cretaceous and Tertiary rocks which form the plain. As the land emerged from the sea, the rivers from the "oldland" lengthened their courses and began actively to dissect the rising surface. Erosion was most active along the inner margin of the plain. The softer beds were quickly stripped away to reveal the peneplained surface underneath. Rivers now descend this exposed slope by a series of rapids and small falls (Fig. 3).

THE EASTERN HIGHLANDS

The Fall Line is about 200 miles from the coast and about 800 ft above sea level in Georgia; towards the north it becomes progressively lower and closer to the shore; at Baltimore and Philadelphia it is almost at sea level and near New York it lies off the coast.

The Eastern Highlands

The Eastern Highlands, or Appalachians, extend from Newfoundland in the north-east to Alabama in the south-west. Although they are not particularly high when compared with the Rockies, they form a belt of extremely rugged country which the early colonists found difficult to cross and develop.

The Southern Section.—South of the River Hudson, the highland displays four distinct types of topography (Fig. 3).

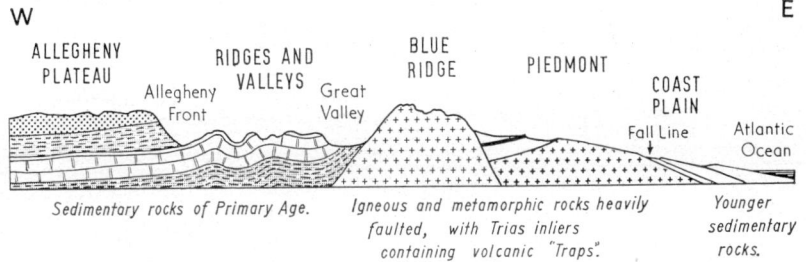

SECTION ACROSS THE APPALACHIANS

Fig. 3.

(i) Lying immediately west of the Fall Line is the Piedmont, which is a low, gently rolling plateau with occasional *monadnocks* (residual hills, usually of more resistant rock) rising 300 ft to 400 ft above the general level of the surface. It is composed of crystalline rocks of Pre-Cambrian age, but in some faulted depressions softer Triassic beds have been preserved. The Piedmont increases in height towards the interior and reaches elevations of over 1,000 ft.

(ii) To the west of the Piedmont is a belt of higher and more rugged country. It is broader and higher in the south where it is known as the Great Smoky Range. Some parts here rise over 6,000 ft. Northwards the zone is narrower and lower but is still recognisable as an upland ridge. Here it is known as the Blue Ridge. The rocks are crystalline as in the Piedmont.

Together, these two regions are known as the *Older Appalachians*. They can be regarded as the roots of a former mountain system which came into existence during the Caledonian mountain-building period (*i.e.* at the time when the mountains of Scotland and Norway were first formed). The other two divisions form the *Newer Appalachians*. They were created later, during the Carboniferous and Permian periods, and are contemporaneous with the Hercynian massifs of Europe.

(iii) The Ridge and Valley Province lies to the west of the Blue Ridge. The Palaeozoic sediments were folded but in a fairly open fashion and the structure is much less complicated than in the Older Appalachians. The topography consists of a series of discontinuous even-crested ridges and valleys arranged in echelon. The ridges rise some 2,000 ft above the valleys and reach summit elevations of 3,000 ft or 4,000 ft. The relationship between the structure and the relief is not a simple one: in some parts the anticlines form the ridges and the synclines the valleys; in other parts the relief has been inverted and there are anticlinal valleys and synclinal mountains.

(iv) Marking the western edge of this province is a pronounced escarpment, the Allegheny Front, which is the eastern limit of the Allegheny Plateau. A similar escarpment is found in the north overlooking Lake Erie. The dominant rock is sandstone of Carboniferous age which contains rich seams of coal. The beds are practically unaltered and dip only slightly westwards. The plateau decreases in height in that direction and merges imperceptibly with the interior lowlands.

Drainage.—On the Allegheny Plateau the drainage is dendritic. Many streams and rivers such as the Cumberland and Kentucky flow to join the Ohio, which itself starts in this region. In parts the plateau is deeply dissected: the valley of the Kanawha, for instance, is 1,000 ft to 2,000 ft below the plateau surface. Because of this, communications are difficult, but in places coal-mining has been made easy as the seams are exposed on the valley sides.

The Ridge and Valley Province has a trellised pattern of drainage. Longitudinal streams follow the valleys for long distances (*e.g.* the Shenandoah) before turning at right angles to cut through the ridges (see plate facing p. 17). River capture which has frequently occurred is responsible for the many wind-gaps. In the south, streams flow southwards to the Tennessee; in the centre, they flow west to the Ohio; in the north, they join the Atlantic rivers such as the Susquehanna and Potomac, both of which have their sources on the Allegheny Plateau. Only in the north, then, do rivers cross all four divisions of the Appalachians. Their valleys provided a routeway inland across the whole system at a point where it is narrowest, lowest, and nearest the coast. This combination of circumstances was of great importance to the early settlers making their way westwards, and has influenced the whole course of development of the U.S.A.

The Northern Section.—North-east of the Hudson Valley, which may be regarded as an attenuated continuation of the Great Appalachian Valley, the highland is more complex. The equivalents of only the Older Appalachians are represented here and the rocks are almost wholly crystalline. There are extensive outcrops of gneiss, schist, slate, quartzite, and granite. As in the Piedmont, fragments of red Triassic rock have been preserved in depressions, the largest of these being the Annapolis-Cornwallis Valley of Nova Scotia and the lower Connecticut Valley of New England.

The highland takes the form of a dissected plateau with an average elevation of 2,000 ft which slopes to the south-east. In the centre of New England, the highland rises above the general level to heights of over 3,000 ft (Mount Washington, 6,288 ft), while over the rest of the plateau there are isolated monadnocks (Mount Monadnock is in New Hampshire). The more elevated western portions of this section—the Taconic Range and the Green Mountains of New England and the Notre Dame Mountains and Shickshock Range of Quebec—are probably an extension of the Blue Ridge element of the southern Appalachians.

Glaciation.—Ice-sheets covered the whole of this northern area and the mark of glaciation lies plainly on the landscape. Many of the features are erosional such as the fiords of Newfoundland and the U-shaped valleys and water-filled hollows of the mainland. Glacial deposits cover a small area only and are of little agricultural use. The drift of southern New England contains a high proportion of boulders. The termination of the ice-sheets is marked by moraines and outwash sands on Long Island and the Cape Cod peninsula. After the ice disappeared, rivers had to develop their courses afresh. There are numerous lakes, abandoned channels, and waterfalls. The water-power resources of New England and the Atlantic Provinces of Canada are a direct consequence of glaciation.

THE CENTRAL PLAINS

The Central Plains extend from the Arctic Ocean to the Gulf of Mexico: they are constricted in the north where the Mackenzie drains a narrow trench between the Canadian Shield and the Rockies; they broaden to the south and reach their widest extent south of the Great Lakes, where the Appalachians and Rockies are almost 1,500 miles apart. This region may be considered as a physical unit less by reason of its altitude, which varies widely, than by its structure and lack of marked relief. Over vast stretches the rocks have been little disturbed and are almost horizontal. In the southern half of this region, the Mississippi collects most of the drainage from the Rockies and the Appalachians. Its affluents provide vast loads of silt and the sudden surges of water which periodically inundate the low-lying flood plains.

The Interior Lowlands

This section of the Central Plains extends from the Appalachians to the Great Plains and from the edge of the Canadian Shield to the Gulf Coast Plain. The Palaeozoic sediments—mainly Carboni-

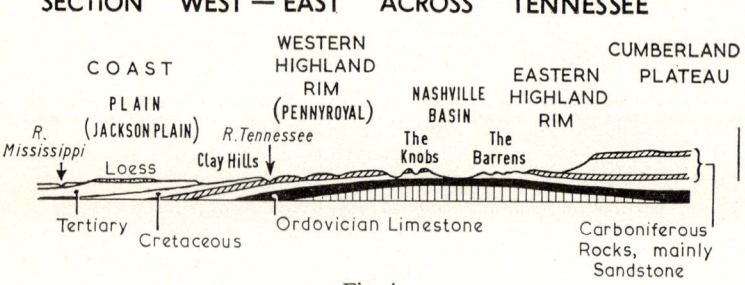

Fig. 4.

ferous sandstones, limestones, shales, and coal-measures—are almost horizontal over large areas. There was, however, some gentle warping of the strata when the whole series was uplifted at the close of Palaeozoic times (*i.e.* when the Newer Appalachians were erected). Where small domes have been formed, as around Lexington in Kentucky, and Nashville in Tennessee, the overlying beds of sandstone have been stripped away by erosion to reveal the softer and more fertile phosphatic limestone underneath (Fig. 4). Where there are broad, saucer-like depressions, as in Michigan and Illinois, upper Carboniferous coal-measures have been preserved.

The northern part of the lowlands was glaciated and the area as far south as the Missouri and Ohio rivers is mantled with a variety of deposits. One small area—the Wisconsin Driftless area—escaped glaciation and has a fairly rugged topography which must have been typical of much of the whole region in pre-glacial times (Fig. 59). Elsewhere, the landscape consists of gently-rolling till plains of subdued relief but diversified by drumlins, moraines, lacustrine plains, and outwash sands. In the areas of newer drift (coextensive with the last ice-sheet) the features are fresh and have been little altered: in the areas of older drift (deposited by earlier ice-sheets which penetrated farther south than the last one) the surface has been much more dissected. Lying outside the glaciated area and mainly west of the Mississippi, are deep and widespread deposits of loess.

The Ozark-Ouachita Uplands

Rising out of the Interior Lowlands is a more rugged region which reaches a height of over 2,800 ft. During the general uplift at the end of the Palaeozoic age, the rocks in this area were domed. The Ozarks are the fairly high plateau-like surface that was formed. Erosion at the apex of the dome has resulted in the exposure of

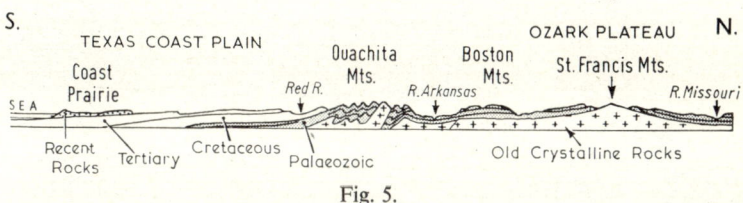

Fig. 5.

Pre-Cambrian crystalline rocks in the centre—the St Francis Mountains. South of the Arkansas Valley, the earth movements were more severe and folding occurred. The Ouachita Mountains, which consist of parallel, even-crested ridges rising 1,000 ft to 2,000 ft above the bordering valleys, bear a close resemblance to the Ridge and Valley Province of the Appalachian system (Fig. 5). The Wichita and Arbuckle mountains are similar but much smaller eroded domes.

The Great Plains

Towards the west, the land rises gradually and almost imperceptibly. At the base of the Rockies it reaches elevations of 4,000 ft. The Great Plains are where the Palaeozoic rocks of the Interior Lowlands are overlain by younger and weaker Cretaceous and Tertiary deposits. The latter are more extensive in the south. The rock waste from the Rockies was spread by the rivers and arranged as broad, thin slabs over the underlying Cretaceous rocks

(Fig. 6). In some parts the eastern boundary of the Plains is marked by an escarpment (the Missouri Coteau and the Break of the Plains); in other parts, the boundary is indeterminate, there being no marked topographic difference between this region and the Interior Lowlands. While much of the Great Plains is little dissected and displays a monotonously even and featureless surface, some areas, such as the Badlands of Dakota and the Sand Hills of Nebraska, are extremely rugged.

Rising conspicuously above the general level of the surface are several isolated mountains. The most pronounced of these are the Black Hills of Dakota which owe their existence to local earth movements. The Palaeozoic and Cretaceous cover was domed and then eroded to expose the crystalline core. The sedimentary rocks

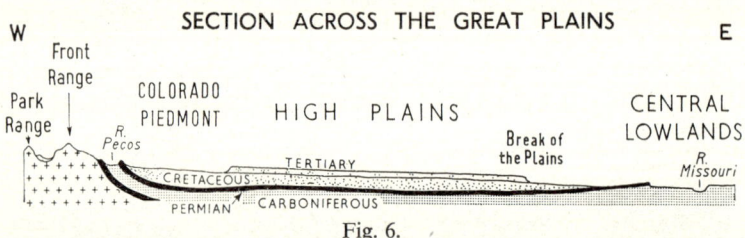

Fig. 6.

now form a series of concentric cuestas around the rugged central uplands.

The Gulf Coast Plain

This is a continuation of the Atlantic Coast Plain and, like it, extends inland to the limit of the Cretaceous and Tertiary rocks. It is rarely less than 300 miles wide and at its inner margin attains heights of 600 ft or 700 ft. The beds dip gently to the sea and continue beneath it to form a broad continental shelf. The oldest rocks come to the surface in the north and the youngest in the south; the parallel bands of rock form a "belted outcrop plain". Strong formations, usually sandstone, form inward-facing cuestas, while the weaker beds, usually clay but occasionally chalky limestone, form the vales and lowlands. The seaward margin of the plain is bordered by salt marshes, lagoons, and sand-spits. Tides are smaller than along the Atlantic coast and the spits and bars tend to be longer. Padre Island, an off-shore bar north of the mouth of the Rio Grande, is unbroken for more than 100 miles.

The coast plain is divided into two halves by the lower Mississippi Valley, a large flood plain 600 miles long and from 50 to 75 miles wide. The silt, which is hundreds of feet deep in places, was deposited during and since the Ice Age in a broad, shallow, gradually sinking structural trough. Practically all the flood plain is below the level of the river which is contained between levees. The flood plain merges imperceptibly into the delta which is growing rapidly. It is estimated that about 2 million tons of sediment are deposited each day and some levees along the major distributaries are extending into the sea at the rate of a furlong or more each year. Between the levees, silt accumulates more slowly and there are many lakes, swamps, sloughs, creeks, and bayous (see plate facing p. 16).

THE WESTERN CORDILLERAS

The western third of the continent is an area of mountain ranges with intervening plateaus, basins, and valleys. At its widest, between San Francisco and Denver, this belt measures about 1,000 miles. The structure is as complex as the relief: practically every type of rock is represented here and examples of almost every structural feature can be found, some of them the most spectacular of their kind in the world. Folding, faulting, and volcanic activity have played their parts in forming an upland surface which has been etched and sculptured by water, wind, and ice.

The whole of the northern part of this region was glaciated. The numerous corries, lake-filled hollows, fiords, etc., are the work of valley glaciers which, at lower altitudes, coalesced to form ice-sheets. The ice has not yet completely disappeared; in Alaska there are extensive ice-fields on the higher parts (as there are in British Columbia) and vigorous glaciers in the valleys (see plate facing p. 32).

Running from north to south in the eastern part of the Cordilleran system is the main continental divide, which, however, does not always follow the highest land (Fig. 7). To the east, most of the streams drain into the Mississippi, Mackenzie, or Hudson Bay. To the west, the rivers flow to the Pacific. In one part of the system, there is a large area of inland drainage.

On the basis of structure and relief, the whole area can be divided into three main physical regions.

The Rocky Mountains

This series of ranges, extending the whole length of the continent from the Brooks Range of Alaska to the Eastern Sierra Madre of Mexico, is the easternmost limb of the Cordilleran system. The present surface has a long history extending as far back as the end of the Mesozoic period when the first generation of mountains was born. These were largely destroyed by subsequent erosion. Renewed uplift at the beginning of the Tertiary period created a second generation of mountains which was also reduced almost to a peneplain. The third and present generation came into being at

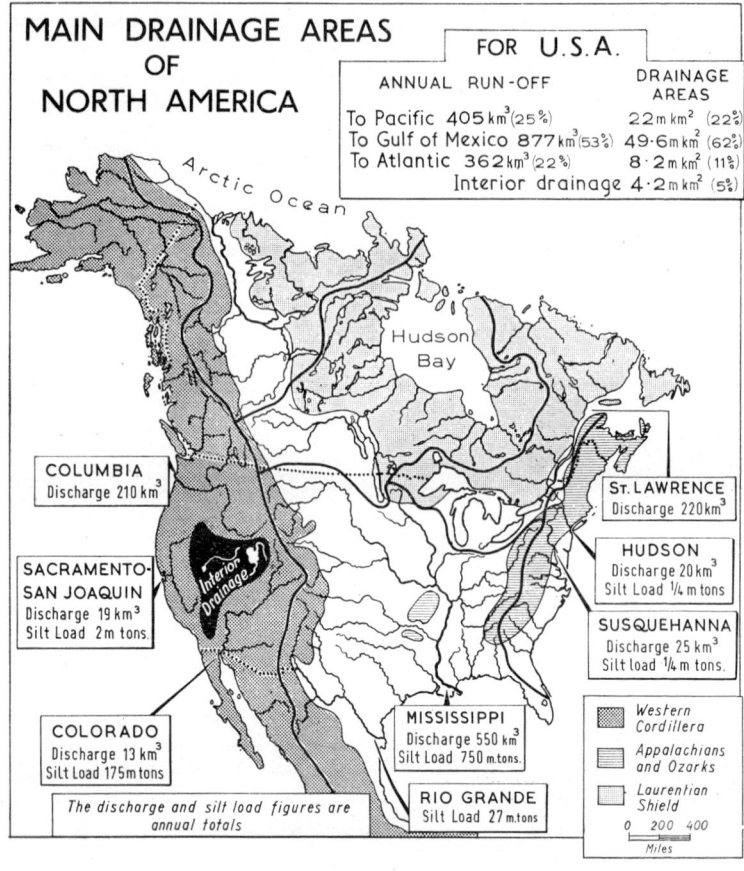

Fig. 7.

the close of Tertiary times. The relatively smooth upland surfaces which exist in some areas represent uplifted peneplains: the higher peaks represent the remnants of the second generation mountains. Although folding in North America was less intense than in Europe, the earth movements were severe enough to contort the sedimentary rocks and allow masses of igneous rock to surge up to the surface.

THE ROCKY MOUNTAINS

This activity led to the formation of mineral veins. In Montana, the folded rocks were thrust eastwards and overlie the younger sediments of the Great Plains (Fig. 8).

Everywhere there is a steep rise of 2,000 ft to 8,000 ft from the Great Plains to the high, serrated, and often snow-capped peaks. There are several heights over 14,000 ft. In spite of the fact that in Colorado there is a zone of foothills—hogsbacks formed by the upturned layers of sedimentary rocks (Fig. 6)—the division between the Plains and the Rockies is one of the most pronounced topographical boundaries in America. The only major break in the whole chain is the Wyoming basin, a feature which has been of great importance in the development of communications. There are

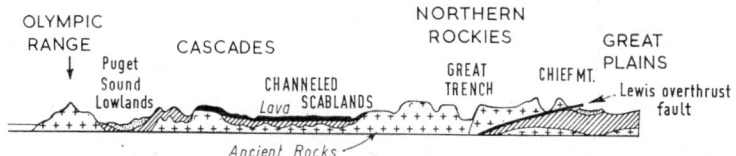

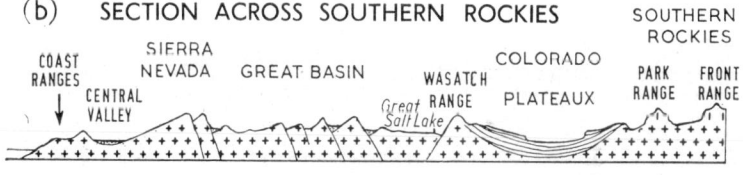

Fig. 8.

several high and narrow passes, some of which are followed by railways. Within the mountains are a few structural depressions known as parks. Volcanic activity has not been on such a large scale here as in other parts of the Western Cordilleras but the Yellowstone National Park in Wyoming displays geysers, hot springs, and boiling mud pools.

The Intermontane Plateaus and Basins

Between the Rockies and the Pacific Mountains is a wide stretch of country with lower altitudes and more subdued relief, but still highly diversified.

The Colorado Plateaus lie in the south-east, immediately west of the Rockies and south of the Uinta Mountains (an off-shoot of the

Rockies). This is an area of horizontal or only slightly warped sedimentary rocks of all ages with some lava sheets The fact that the strata escaped severe folding may be due to the presence near the surface of the underlying rigid crustal block. A fragment of this is exposed at the bottom of the Colorado Canyon. Faulting and erosion have led to the formation of a series of graduated plateaus with an average height of about 7,000 ft. Steep escarpments lead from one plateau surface to the next. The area is very much dissected by the Colorado and its tributaries which have carved deep canyons. In some places dissection has proceeded so far that a former plateau is now represented by widely-spaced mesas and buttes (see plate facing p. 48). In a dry area such as this, the steep slopes are not covered with vegetation or soil and the exposed rocks display a wide variety of striking colours.

The Great Basin, which lies west of the Colorado Plateaus, is not a uniform lowland but a collection of north-south ridges, 10 to 20 miles wide and up to 100 miles long, separated by numerous basins and depressions. The region has undergone severe faulting and each range is a tilted block with one or more steep fault scarps. The basins are filled with detritus carried down from the mountains. The bordering ranges are similar to those of the Great Basin but rise to higher altitudes: the Wasatch Mountains, which attain a height of 10,000 ft, form the eastern limit and present a steep front to the west; the Sierra Nevada on the west have a steep, step-faulted eastern edge and rise to over 14,000 ft (Fig. 8).

Lakes are quite common features of the landscape as the Great Basin is an area of interior drainage. Some are permanent, while others are temporary playas which exist only after periods of heavy rainfall, and usually appear as salt-encrusted flats. The larger and more permanent lakes are to be found mainly at the foot of both the Wasatch Range and the Sierra Nevada. The largest is the Great Salt Lake which is merely the shrunken remnant of the much larger Lake Bonneville which existed during the Ice Age. At that time the waters escaped to the Columbia system: to-day the Great Salt Lake has no outlet. The rivers rise in the better watered mountains and terminate in the lakes. Some are perennial and supply water for irrigation, but many are ephemeral.

The Columbia Plateau lies to the north of the Great Basin and is made up of a great thickness of lava. The flows occurred over a long period at various times and from a number of fissures. Between the different sheets of lava are traces of vegetation and soils. Practically the whole of the intermontane region in these

Above: A small camp on the rocky, boulder-strewn surface of the Canadian Shield north of Schefferville. (*High Commissioner for Canada.*)

Below: The Mississippi Delta looking south from the Head of Passes. Ships entering the river use South Pass, in the centre of the photograph, or South-west Pass on the right. (*U.S. Army Corps of Engineers.*)

Above: Scotts Bluff, Nebraska, a landmark on the old Oregon Trail, rises 700 ft above the general level of the Great Plains. (*Fairchild Aerial Surveys Inc.*)

Below: Part of the Ridge and Valley Province of the Appalachians in Pennsylvania. The steep-sided, wooded ridge separates broad valleys with snow-covered fields. In the foreground is the Susquehanna River which is almost completely covered by ice. (*Fairchild Aerial Surveys Inc.*)

latitudes was buried by lava, in some cases to a depth of 6,000 ft. In the centre of the plateau are the Blue Mountains which rise like an island from the lava sea. Some warping took place after the lava had solidified: in parts the beds are slightly domed and on the edge of the Cascades they are upturned (Fig. 8). A small portion of the plateau in Oregon has interior drainage, but most of the streams are collected by the Columbia and Snake rivers. The surface is scored by several abandoned river channels known as coulees, which carried water from the melting ice-sheets during the Pleistocene period. The Columbia Plateau has more rainfall than the Great Basin or the Colorado Plateau but still depends on the streams fed by the heavier precipitation of the higher ranges for irrigation and hydro-electricity.

The Northern Plateaus.—From about the 43rd parallel northwards, the intermontane region becomes much narrower and north of the international border it is less than 300 miles wide. In its constricted form it continues through British Columbia and the Yukon to western Alaska. In all this region it is composed of old crystalline and metamorphic rocks with occasional beds of lava. Rising above the general level of the plateaus are several mountain ranges.

A significant physical feature is the Rocky Mountain Trench which lies at the western foot of the Rockies. It is a structural depression which can be traced northwards from Montana for about 1,000 miles. In different parts it is occupied by the upper waters of the Flathead, Columbia, Fraser, and Peace rivers.

The Pacific Mountains

The western limb of the Cordilleran system is formed by a double line of mountains separated by a long discontinuous structural depression.

The Inner Ranges include the Sierra Nevada of California, the Cascades of Washington and Oregon, the Coast Range of British Columbia, and the Alaska Range. They are older than the Rockies: they appear to have been formed at the close of the Palaeozoic period (*i.e.* at the same time as the Newer Appalachians) and to have been greatly faulted and tilted by later earth movements. There are large areas of igneous and metamorphic rock. These mountains are high and rugged. The highest peak in North America is Mount McKinley, 20,320 ft, in the Alaska Range. Farther south there are numerous peaks over 10,000 ft high.

Most of the area was glaciated and spectacular glacial features can be seen in the Yosemite National Park (in the Sierra Nevada).

In British Columbia and Alaska, there are still active glaciers. The latest earth movements were accompanied by volcanic activity and a line of volcanoes forms the higher peaks of the Cascades.

The Central Depression is a downwarped part of the crust between the Inner and Outer ranges (Fig. 8). The northern parts are submerged (*e.g.* the Inland Passage and Georgia Strait), but south of Puget Sound there is a series of narrow lowlands (the Willamette Valley and the Great Valley of California). These depressions have thick deposits of sands, gravels, and clays. In the Central Valley they reach a depth of at least 2,000 ft and the floor appears to be still sinking. The depression is not continuous, for in places the bordering highlands coalesce or are linked by transverse ridges and blocks.

The Outer Ranges run more or less parallel to and west of the inner line of mountains. The Coast Ranges of the U.S.A. which reach elevations of 3,000 ft or 4,000 ft, run obliquely to the shore; farther north, this chain is partially submerged and appears above sea level as Vancouver Island, the Queen Charlotte Islands, and the islands off the coast of the Alaska Panhandle. The mountains reappear on the mainland again in Alaska as the Fairweather and St Elias ranges. These are much higher than their counterparts in the south: Mount Elias is over 19,000 ft high.

The summits are the remnants of former peneplains which have been tilted and uplifted. The whole mountain belt is divided into fault blocks, some of which are tilted one way and some another. The structure is complex and this is reflected in the topography. Some of the earth movements have occurred very recently, and the earthquakes of California and volcanic activity in the Aleutian Islands indicates that the region is still unstable.

The Pacific Coast is very different from the Atlantic and Gulf coasts. Nowhere is there an extensive coast plain and in many places the mountains drop straight down into the sea. At a few places spits and sand-bars have been formed but much more common are the newly-cut sea cliffs. Old beach-lines and old sea cliffs at various elevations up to 1,500 ft are evidence of emergence since late Tertiary times. More recently there has been a slight sinking of the land which is responsible for the drowning of the Golden Gate inlet and the fiords along the coast of British Columbia.

The continental shelf is usually very narrow: in places, the steep descent to the ocean depths occurs less than twenty miles from the shore. The platform is widest off southern California, British Columbia, and the Alaska peninsula. At the outer margin of the shelf are a number of submarine canyons similar to those under the waters of the Atlantic Ocean.

The north to south or meridianal alignment of the major structural and relief features is a very important factor in the geography of North America. The effect of this on the climate will be discussed in the following chapter and its influence on the human geography will merit some reference in the regional accounts. The easiest lines of movement run from north to south, but the gradual spread of settlement from the east and the division of the continent into two political units has led to the development of a system of east to west communications and boundaries. Physically, the regions of Canada have more in common with adjacent regions of the U.S.A. than with each other.

CHAPTER II
CLIMATE
General Considerations

1. The general circulation of the atmosphere is the controlling factor in the climate of North America. Large-scale movements of air are governed by the distribution of the areas of high and low pressure. The main pressure areas are:
   (*a*) the semi-permanent "highs" which develop over the oceans in the horse latitudes and strengthen in summer;
   (*b*) the "highs" which occur over the cold northern interior in winter;
   (*c*) the sub-polar "lows" over Iceland and the Aleutians which are most strongly marked in winter and only faintly discernible in summer.

This generalised pattern may not be apparent on daily weather maps and should be regarded as a statistical average of the complicated pressure changes which occur from day to day.

2. As the continent extends over almost 60° of latitude, there is considerable variation in the amount of insolation which places receive and consequently in the temperatures.

3. The longitudinal extent of the land mass is considerable, too, and places in the interior, which are far from the sea, experience extreme temperatures and low precipitation. Around the larger lakes and Hudson Bay, however, these harsh conditions are slightly moderated.

4. The configuration and relief of the continent affects the free flow of air over the land. The Rockies impede or check air movements to the east or west, but in the centre of North America there is no major obstacle to air moving north or south.

5. The high altitudes of the western parts of the continent add to the range of the climatic conditions. Where there is highly accidented terrain, one finds a wide variety of climates within a very small area.

6. Along the coasts are ocean currents which modify the air passing over them and thus influence the climate of the adjacent shores (Fig. 17). The warm Alaska Current is responsible for the

relatively mild winters along the west coast. Air above the warm water tends to be heavily charged with moisture, and if the winds are on-shore then there is usually heavy precipitation. The cold currents (the Labrador Current and the California Current) have their marked effect on the coasts mainly in summer, when the weather is cool and dry. Along the coast of California, the current drifts off-shore and cold water upwells from the depths. Fog is common above the cold waters and above the zone where cold and warm waters mix (*e.g.* above the "cold wall" off Newfoundland and New England in the Atlantic).

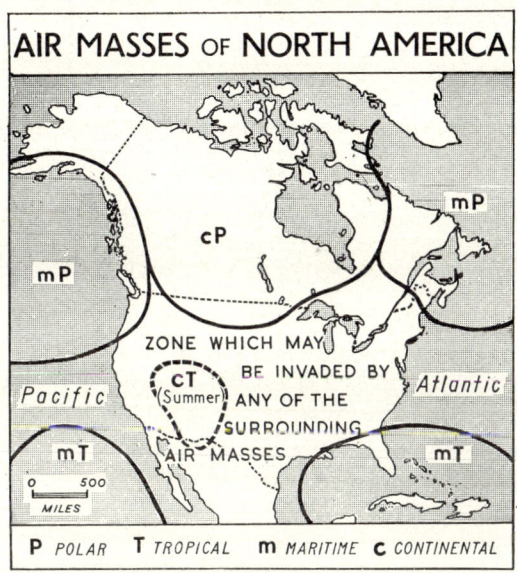

Fig. 9.
The extent of each air mass varies with the seasons and changes almost daily with the passage of depressions (cp. Fig. 11).

AIR MASSES AND ATMOSPHERIC DISTURBANCES

The weather experienced in any part of the continent is due mainly to the air mass which occupies it. The source regions of the air masses where they acquire their particular temperature, humidity, and degree of stability, are the great permanent or semi-permanent high pressure cells. From these source areas, the air moves outwards, its course often being affected by relief features and its characteristics by the surface over which it passes. Warm air moving over a colder land surface (or a cold ocean current) will become cooled, particularly in its lower layers, and so become more stable. Cold air moving over a warmer surface is itself warmed and becomes less stable.*

Areas which experience only one air mass have fairly constant weather: those which are occupied sometimes by one air mass and sometimes by another, have changeable weather. The air masses affecting North America (see Fig. 9) are listed below.

AIR MASSES

Type	Symbol	Source Area	Characteristics
Polar Continental.	cP	Alaska and North Canada.	Very cold, dry, and stable in winter: cool, dry, and stable in summer.
Polar Maritime.	mP	1. North Pacific.	Cool and moist; stable in summer, unstable in winter.
		2. North Atlantic.	Cool, moist, and stable.
Tropical Continental.	cT	South-west U.S.A. and Mexico.	Hot, dry, and unstable: occurs only in summer.
Tropical Maritime.	mT	1. Middle North Atlantic and Gulf of Mexico.	Warm, moist, and stable in winter: hot, moist, and unstable in summer.
		2. Middle Pacific.	Warm, moist, and stable: occurs mainly in summer.

The boundary between two different air masses is known as a *front*. If the characteristics of the two sorts of air are very different, then the front forms a strong discontinuity.

Depressions

Depressions are small atmospheric disturbances. They are born in frontal zone between cold polar and warm tropical air. Once formed they intensify and move eastwards along the front. During their short life of six or seven days, they can travel a distance of over 3,000 miles. Most of the depressions which affect North America originate along the Polar Front in the Pacific Ocean, but some develop over the Prairies and Great Plains. They tend to follow well-recognised tracks. Many enter the continent near Puget Sound and leave it via the St Lawrence Valley or New England, but some take the "southern circuit", especially in winter, across the Gulf states (Fig. 10). Depressions are more frequent

* Air is stable if the lapse rate is less than the adiabatic lapse rate [$5·4$ F.° (3 C.°) for every 1,000 ft in the case of unsaturated air and about 3 F.° ($1·7$ C.°) per 1,000 ft for air saturated with water vapour] and unstable if the lapse rate is greater than this. Unstable air, once forced to rise, will tend to continue rising and thus eventually cause rain: stable air, even if forced to rise, has a tendency to subside.

and more intense in winter, when the air mass differences are greatest. In summer, they are weaker, and, as the Polar Front lies far to the north, take a more northerly course.

Lying as they do along a front, depressions bring changeable weather. Warm air from the south is drawn north in front of the storm centre and cold air is drawn south in its rear (Fig. 11). There is a belt of precipitation where the warm air overrides the cold air along the warm front and another, narrower one, where cold air

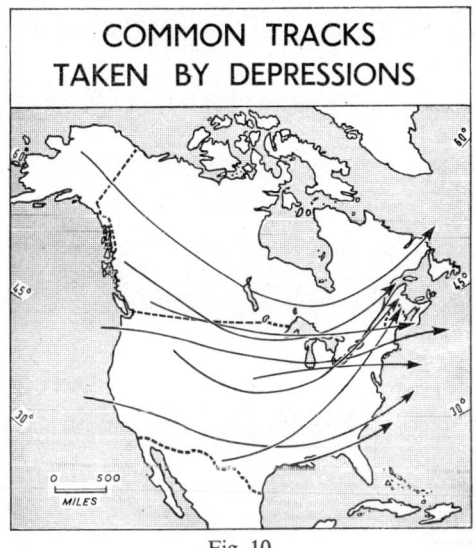

Fig. 10.

thrusting in behind the cold front lifts the warm air off the ground. This often results in severe turbulence and occasionally leads to violent thunderstorms.

Separating the depressions are ridges or cells of high pressure. These anticyclones move more slowly and bring settled weather which is hot and dry in summer and cold and dry in winter.

Hurricanes

These intense cyclonic disturbances are fortunately infrequent and affect only a small part of the continent. Tropical cyclones, or hurricanes, originate over the warm waters of the Atlantic Ocean in latitudes about 8° to 15° N. Once formed, they move westwards and then polewards. Some penetrate the belt of westerlies and,

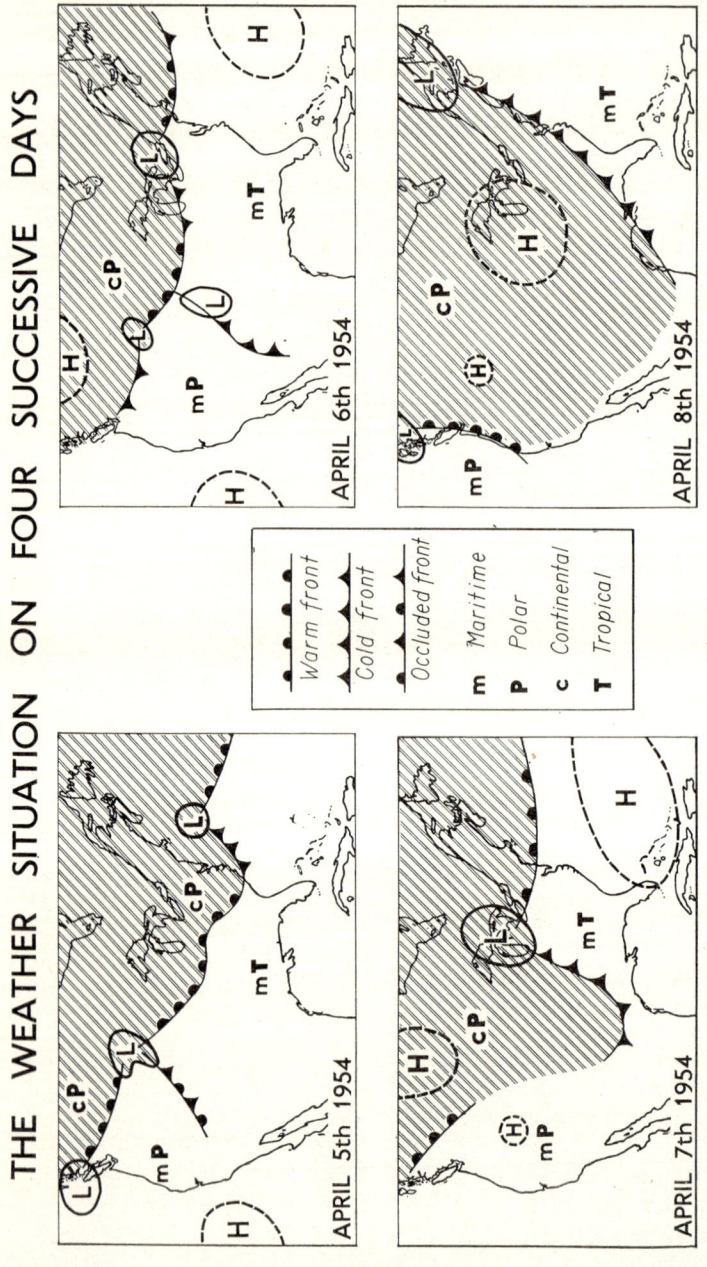

Fig. 11.

Note the development of an anticyclone over the northern Rockies on April 6th and the surge of cP air southwards over the Great Plains and Mississippi Valley on April 7th. On April 8th the anticyclone has moved over the Great Lakes and cP air extends southwards to the Gulf of Mexico and covers almost the whole of the continent.

most of their energy spent, move eastwards as mid-latitude depressions. The fully developed hurricane is an almost circular storm centre of extremely low pressure. The central "eye" is calm, but around it circulate strong winds, which may reach velocities of

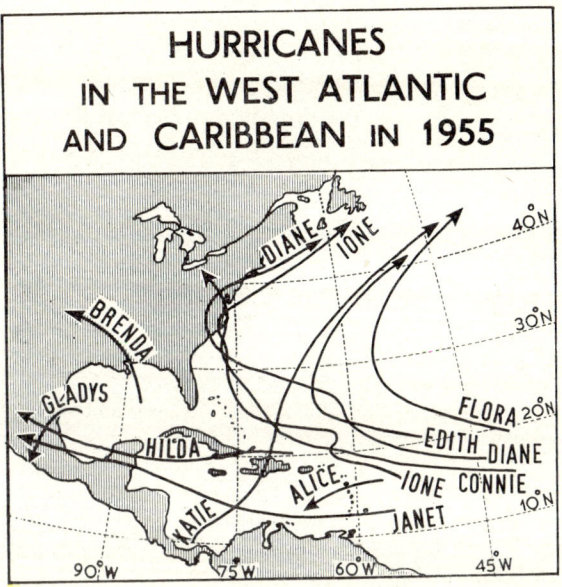

Fig. 12.

Hurricanes are given female names in alphabetical order throughout the year.

Alice—Jan. 2nd-4th.
Brenda—July 31st-Aug. 2nd.
Connie—Aug. 4th-13th.
Diane—Aug. 11th-18th.
Edith—Aug. 24th-31st.
Flora—Sept. 3rd-9th.
Gladys—Sept. 4th-6th.
Hilda—Sept. 12th-19th.
Ione—Sept. 14th-21st.
Janet—Sept. 22nd-29th.
Katie—Oct. 15th-19th.

150 miles per hour. They are most frequent in late summer and autumn.

The U.S.A. experiences an average of five hurricanes a year (Fig. 12). The areas most affected are the Gulf coast, Florida, and the eastern seaboard as far north as New England. The damage to life and property that these storms can cause is immense. In 1900 a hurricane struck Galveston: sea water, driven by the strong winds, surged inland and inundated the low-lying town. 6,000 people lost their lives. To-day, an elaborate warning system keeps coastal towns informed of the movements of these storms, and there were few deaths, although much damage to property, during the progress of the hurricanes Donna in 1960 and Clara in 1961.

Tornadoes

Tornadoes, or "twisters", are small but very intense whirlwinds. Air spirals round the low pressure in the centre with speeds estimated to reach 500 miles per hour. The dark funnel of condensing water, dust, and objects swept up off the ground, is rarely more than one quarter of a mile wide and its life is usually less than ten minutes. During this time, however, it can cut a swathe of destruction twenty-five miles long. Tornadoes appear to be disturbances associated with the cold front of a depression lying over the centre of the continent. They are most frequent in spring and early summer and most common over the Mississippi Valley: they are rarely found over mountainous or forested regions. On an average, Texas, Oklahoma, and Kansas experience over 200 tornadoes each year.

Winter Conditions

The cooling of the continent causes the air to become cold and dense and to accumulate over the interior. This subsiding air is dry and stable and yields little precipitation: the weather is clear but temperatures are very low. Excessive cooling at the surface produces a well-marked temperature inversion. Usually, this cP air is confined to the northern and interior parts of the continent, but on occasions it surges southwards, usually in the train of a depression, and brings freezing conditions to the Gulf coast. There is no marked relief barrier to impede this movement. To the west, the Rockies prevent the cold polar air reaching the Pacific coast except on rare occasions, but the Atlantic coast is less well protected by the Appalachians and frequently experiences cold waves.

Polar maritime air, warmed by the relatively warm ocean, and heavily charged with moisture, impinges on the Pacific coast all the way from Alaska to California (Fig. 13). As it rises over the coastal mountains, heavy precipitation is released. Because of the mountains, these mild, wet conditions do not penetrate far inland. Occasionally, however, this air is drawn over the mountains by a depression lying across the Great Plains. It loses its moisture on the windward slopes and is greatly warmed as it descends the lee-side of the Rockies, reaching the Great Plains several degrees warmer than it was over the Pacific Ocean. This is the Chinook wind which causes a remarkable rise in temperature and rapid snow-melt. Rises of 40 F.° (22 C.°) over a period of twenty-four hours are not unusual at the onset of the Chinook wind.

Over the south-east coast is warm, moist tropical maritime air. Where this air mass meets cold cP air is the Atlantic Polar Front. This is a very marked discontinuity and within a distance of 200 miles the temperature difference may be as much as 60° F. (*33° C.*). The position of the front is not constant: sometimes it lies over the sea, in which case the coastal regions have cold winds from the interior; more rarely, it lies well to the north, and tropical air sweeps inland to the Great Lakes, causing the "January thaws". As the mT air is moving over a colder land surface, its lower layers are cooled and it becomes more and more stable. Precipitation therefore is usually

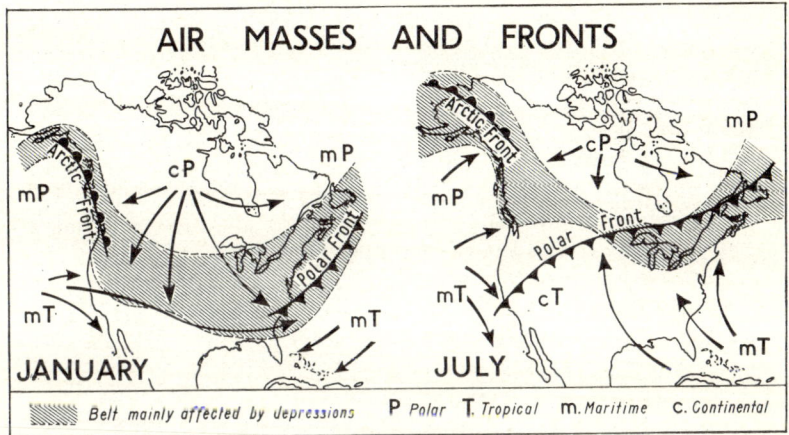

Fig. 13.

light except along the fronts of depressions, where the air rises over the cold cP air.

The general west-to-east movement of air across the continent, which is emphasised by the numerous depressions, means that Atlantic mP air plays little part in determining the weather. It may, however, be drawn over the land by a depression when it brings a "north-easter"—a storm characterised by biting winds and bitter cold—to the north-eastern states.

Summer Conditions

In this season, the continental "high" disappears and the cP air mass becomes less dominant. The temperature and moisture content of the air remains fairly low, but if it moves southwards from its source, heat and moisture are added and it becomes increasingly unstable. In the south-west of the U.S.A. there is intense heating, and the air which subsides in these latitudes becomes hot and dry. This cT air does not travel far from its source but it can bring desiccating conditions to the southern part of the Great Plains.

Over the oceans, the "highs" strengthen and move northwards. The waters of the Pacific are now relatively cool, and the mP air above them is more stable than in winter and yields much less rain. Farther south, mT air is chilled by the cold California Current as it moves landward. This causes fog along the coast but brings very little rain and is responsible for the summer drought of southern California.

Atlantic and Gulf mT air exerts a considerable influence on the climate of North America during this season (Fig. 13). The warm, moist air is drawn into the continent, and, as it moves over the heated land surface, it becomes more and more unstable. It is this weak monsoonal indraft which causes the oppressive heat and thunderstorms experienced over much of the interior. The Polar Front lies well to the north and is not a strongly marked feature. The depressions that move along it are shallower and more infrequent than in winter. Associated with the cold fronts of these weak depressions are tornadoes which appear over the interior in spring and early summer. In late summer and early autumn the coastal areas of the south-east feel the effects of hurricanes.

TEMPERATURES

Fig. 14 shows the mean January and July isotherms. The figures used in the construction of these maps are averages (the monthly average, over many years, of the daily averages) and have been reduced to sea level (by adding 1° F. for every 330 ft or *1° C.* for every 800 ft of elevation). As such, they are abstractions and may differ widely from actual day to day temperatures. Two examples will illustrate this point.

1. New Orleans has a mean January temperature of 54° F. (*12° C.*), but the recorded temperatures on three successive days were:—

    Day 1. Min. temp. 48° F. (*9° C.*)   Max. temp. 70° F. (*21° C.*)
    Day 2.   ,,   ,, 43° F. (*6° C.*)   ,,   ,, 68° F. (*20° C.*)
    Day 3.   ,,   ,, 31° F. (*−1° C.*)   ,,   ,, 43° F. (*6° C.*)

2. Lethbridge has a mean January temperature of 15° F. (*− 9° C.*) but the recorded temperatures on three successive days were:—

    Day 1. Min. temp. 20° F. (*−7° C.*)   Max. temp. 40° F. (*4° C.*)
    Day 2.   ,,   ,, −3° F. (*−19° C.*)   ,,   ,, 29° F. (*−2° C.*)
    Day 3.   ,,   ,, −13° F. (*−25° C.*) ,,   ,, −1° F. (*−18° C.*)

JANUARY CONDITIONS

Deviations from the mean figures are greatest in winter when the air masses show their most violent contrasts. Startling changes of weather can occur if one air mass replaces another. St Louis has experienced temperatures of 74° F. *(23° C.)* and −22° F. *(−30° C.)*, both in January. Also, it is not unusual for the monthly temperature of one year to differ markedly from that of another year. In summer, such fluctuations of temperature are of smaller magnitude, because the difference between the air masses is less marked.

The mean monthly temperatures, then, do not give a true picture of the weather. Nevertheless, they do illustrate broad and marked differences in the climate of the continent.

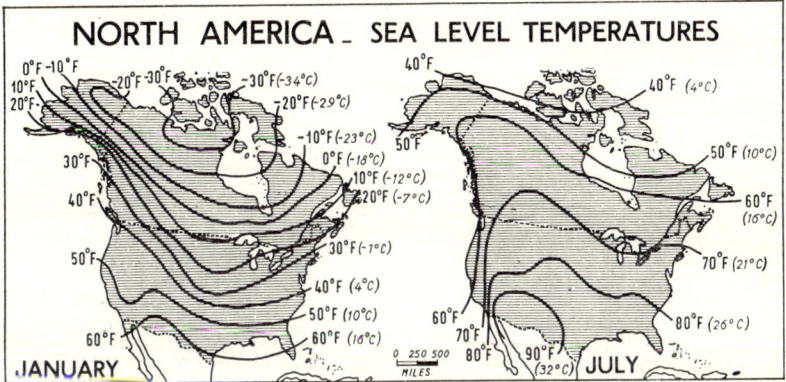

Fig. 14.

January Conditions

The isotherm map for January shows a steep temperature gradient from about 55° F. *(13° C.)* on the Gulf coast [New Orleans, 54° F. *(12° C.)*, Galveston, 54° F. *(12° C.)*], to about −20° F. *(−29° C.)* on the Arctic coast [Coppermine, −19° F. *(−28° C.)*, Aklavik, −21° F. *(−29° C.)*], a decrease of 2° F. *(1° C.)* for every degree of latitude.

Over the centre of the land mass, the isotherms bend equatorwards, and the whole of Canada—except for the Pacific coast—and the north-eastern and interior parts of the U.S.A. have mean monthly temperatures of less than 32° F. *(0° C.)*. The lowest readings occur west of Hudson Bay in Keewatin. The Great Lakes have a slight moderating influence on the temperatures of towns along their eastern and southern shores [*e.g.* Milwaukee on the west coast of Lake Michigan, 19° F. *(−7° C.)* in January; Grand Haven on the east coast, 25° F. (−4° C.)]. Highlands in the interior experience very low temperatures.

Along the coasts, the isotherms swing polewards, but much more noticeably in the west than in the east. This is due to the general west-to-east movement of air over the continent. The Pacific coast receives the full influence of the mild, moist mP air moving across the relatively warm ocean and the harbours of southern Alaska remain ice-free. This moderating effect, however, is closely restricted to the coast: it quickly diminishes inland. The Atlantic coast rarely has onshore winds and the influence of the ocean is slight. The Great Lakes and the St Lawrence estuary are frozen for five months of the year.

	Latitude	Mean Temperature January
West Coast		
Sitka	57° N.	32° F. (0° C.)
Victoria	49° N.	39° F. (4° C.)
San Francisco	38° N.	49° F. (9° C.)
San Diego	33° N.	55° F. (13° C.)
Interior		
Fort Vermilion	58° N.	−10° F. (−23° C.)
Winnipeg	50° N.	−1° F. (−18° C.)
St Louis	39° N.	33° F. (1° C.)
Vicksburg	33° N.	47° F. (8° C.)
East Coast		
Hebron	58° N.	−6° F. (−21° C.)
St John's	48° N.	24° F. (−4° C.)
Washington	39° N.	34° F. (1° C.)
Charleston	33° N.	50° F. (10° C.)

(These are actual, not sea level, temperatures.)

July Conditions

The temperature gradient is smaller than in winter, from about 85° F. (28° C.) on the Gulf coast [New Orleans 82° F. (27° C.), Galveston 84° F. (28° C.)] to about 50° F. (10° C.) on the Arctic coast [Coppermine 49° F. (9° C.), Aklavik 56° F. (13° C.)]—a drop of about 1 F.° for every degree of latitude. This small gradient is due to the long periods of continuous daylight and uninterrupted insolation in high latitudes. Over the land the isotherms bend polewards and there is a great gulf of warmth extending over the Great Plains and Prairies to the Mackenzie basin. The highest monthly temperatures are found in the arid south-west, over the lower part of the Colorado basin.

Over the east and west coasts, the isotherms bend equatorwards. On the Pacific side this effect is particularly marked because the cool California Current and the upwelling of cold water near the shore intensify the moderating influence of the relatively cool ocean. Coastal areas tend to have their highest mean monthly temperatures, not in July, but in August or September [San Francisco, 60° F. *(16° C.)* in September; San Diego, 69° F. *(21° C.)* in August]. Along the Atlantic the southward dip of the isotherms is not so noticeable, except in the north-east on the shores washed by the cold Labrador Current. The temperature gradient is less on the west coast (because the cool current lowers temperatures in the *south*) than on the east coast (because the cold current lowers temperatures in the *north*).

	Latitude	Mean Temperature July	
West Coast			
Sitka	57° N.	55° F.	*(13° C.)*
Victoria	49° N.	60° F.	*(16° C.)*
San Francisco	38° N.	57° F.	*(14° C.)*
San Diego	33° N.	67° F.	*(19° C.)*
Interior			
Fort Vermilion	58° N.	64° F.	*(18° C.)*
Winnipeg	50° N.	67° F.	*(19° C.)*
St Louis	39° N.	79° F.	*(26° C.)*
Vicksburg	33° N.	80° F.	*(27° C.)*
East Coast			
Hebron	58° N.	47° F.	*(8° C.)*
St John's	48° N.	59° F.	*(15° C.)*
Washington	39° N.	77° F.	*(25° C.)*
Charleston	33° N.	82° F.	*(28° C.)*

The Range of Temperature

The well-marked continentality of North America is reflected in the large mean annual temperature ranges (Fig. 15). The smallest difference between the highest and lowest monthly means is found along the coast of California and in southern Florida. The north Pacific coast, and the Gulf coast have mean annual ranges of about 25 F.° *(14 C.°)*. Towards the interior they increase rapidly and reach a maximum of over 90 F.° *(50 C.°)* in the lower Mackenzie basin.

Here again, mean values can be misleading: the only place in the continent that has not experienced frost at some time or another is southern Florida, and there are few places which have not recorded a temperature of 90° F. *(32° C.)* or more. Set out below are the mean annual temperature ranges of towns stretching from the Gulf coast to the interior of Canada. For comparison, the highest and lowest temperatures ever recorded at these places are given alongside.

	Mean Annual Range	Absolute Minimum	Temperatures Maximum
Galveston	29 F.° (*16 C.°*)	8° F. (*−13° C.*)	101° F. (*38° C.*)
Vicksburg	33 F.° (*18 C.°*)	4° F. (*−16° C.*)	107° F. (*42° C.*)
Omaha	55 F.° (*31 C.°*)	−32° F. (*−36° C.*)	114° F. (*46° C.*)
Winnipeg	70 F.° (*39 C.°*)	−35° F. (*−37° C.*)	100° F. (*38° C.*)
Fort Vermilion	74 F.° (*41 C.°*)	−78° F. (*−61° C.*)	98° F. (*37° C.*)
Dawson	81 F.° (*45 C.°*)	−68° F. (*−56° C.*)	95° F. (*35° C.*)

The mean diurnal ranges are of much less magnitude. They tend to be greater during the summer, for in winter, the heating

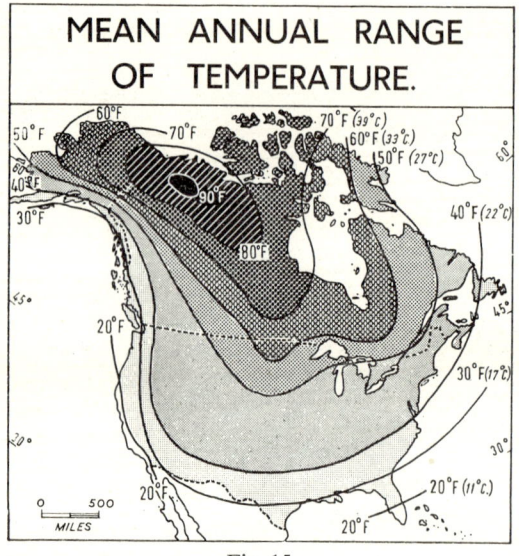

Fig. 15.

power of the sun is relatively small. Where cloudy skies prevail, as over the Pacific coast and the Mississippi Valley, diurnal changes of temperature are small—about 15 F.° (*8 C.°*) to 20 F.° (*11 C.°*)—although the passage of well-marked fronts can cause much larger variations. The northern parts of the continent which experience continuous daylight or darkness for long periods show a difference between daily maxima and minima of 15 F.° (*8 C.°*) or less. The largest ranges are to be found over interior areas where there is little cloud and therefore rapid heating of the surface during the day and rapid cooling at night. In the desert areas of the south-west and in the Central Valley of California, the mean diurnal range in summer is between 30 F.° (*17 C.°*) and 40 F.° (*22 C.°*).

Above: The Teton Mts in Wyoming with the River Snake in the foreground. Note the river terraces. (*Union Pacific*.)

Below: The Athabasca Glacier descends from the Columbia Icefield in the Canadian Rockies. Note the hanging valleys, the tunnel at the snout, the lateral moraine, and the patches of terminal moraine. (*High Commissioner for Canada*.)

Above: Sand dunes in Death Valley, California, the deepest parts of which lie 280 ft below sea level. (*U.S.I.S.*)

Below: Bryce Canyon, Utah, where the multi-coloured rocks have been sculptured into fantastic shapes by the action of wind and rain. (*Pan-American Airways.*)

Frost

As has already been mentioned, there is practically no part of North America which has not at one time or another experienced frost. Fig. 16 maps the *average* frost free season. It is based on the *average* dates of the last killing frost of spring and the first killing frost of autumn. Along the Arctic coast it lasts for under sixty days—fifty-one at Coppermine—but here frosts have occurred in every summer month. In addition, although there might be no frost, the temperatures might not rise high enough for effective plant growth. In Florida and the lower Colorado basin, the growing season is practically continuous but occasional winter frosts do

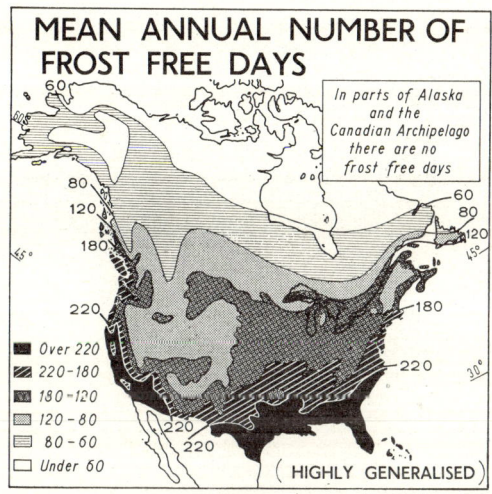

Fig. 16.

occur. In the south, it is the winter frosts that are the farmer's main hazard: in the north, it is the summer frosts which cause most damage.

The pattern in the mountainous areas is extremely complicated: the higher mountain peaks have perpetual frost while the nearby valleys have frost free periods ranging from over 200 days in the south to 80 days in the Yukon.

PRECIPITATION

Mean Annual Precipitation

Generally speaking, the north-west and south-east parts of the continent experience the heaviest precipitation: the lowest amounts are found in the south-west and north-east (Fig. 17). In the northern and elevated parts of North America most of the winter precipitation is in the form of snow. Many areas in the Rockies have falls of over 20 ft every year and considerable tracts of the Sierra Nevada and Cascades have mean totals exceeding 40 ft. In few parts is the precipitation well-distributed throughout the

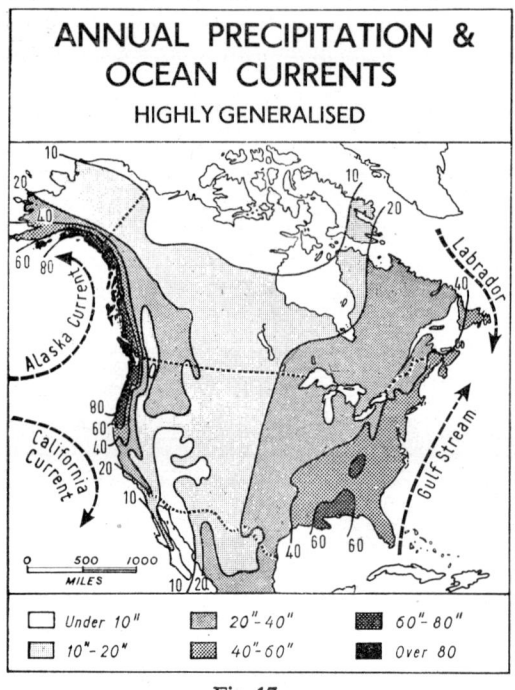

Fig. 17.

year: the seasonal distribution is as important a factor in the climate as the total (Fig. 18).

1. The highest amounts occur along the Pacific coast of Alaska, British Columbia, Washington, and Oregon. Moist mP air rising over the coastal mountains discharges copious orographic rain and there is abundant frontal rain from the many vigorous depressions which come across the ocean. Many windward slopes have over 100 in. and in parts of Vancouver Island mean totals exceed 200 in. By contrast, the leeward slopes are drier (*e.g.* Victoria 27·1 in.). There is a winter maximum, which becomes increasingly marked

towards the south (Sitka has 52 per cent. of its precipitation between November and April, Victoria 73 per cent.).

2. South of about 40° N. on the west coast, the precipitation decreases and the winter maximum is even more marked (San Francisco, 20·2 in., 89 per cent. November to April; San Diego, 10·1 in., 88 per cent. November to April). This is a true Mediterranean regime, where subsiding mT air yields little summer rain and the winter precipitation comes from the depressions which take a more southerly course at this season.

3. Towards the interior, the amounts decrease rapidly. The pattern of precipitation in the intermontane region is very complex,

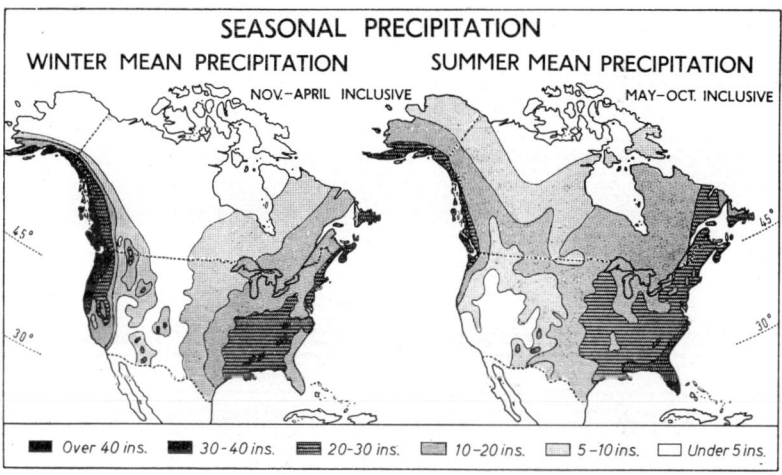

Fig. 18.

and is related to latitude, relief, and aspect. Totals are generally slightly higher in the north, on the elevated parts (up to altitudes of about 5,000 ft) and on the windward slopes. The driest area is in the south-west where a large region has under 10 in. and several stations have under 5 in. (Phoenix, 7·6 in.; Yuma, 3·6 in.).

The seasonal distribution is complicated by the fact that this is a transition area between the Pacific coast with its winter maximum and the Great Plains area with its summer maximum. Some stations in the south-west record double maxima, in winter and late summer.

4. East of the Rockies, precipitation increases once more, but over the Great Plains, amounts are still low (between 12 and 20 in.).

36 CLIMATE

There is a pronounced summer maximum (at Denver, 61 per cent. of the mean total of 14 in., and at Calgary, 76 per cent. of 16·1 in. fall between May and October). In the north, where the ground remains frozen for a long time and the air is slow to warm, the maximum occurs in late summer. The rain comes in heavy downpours associated with the indraft of moist, unstable mT air from the Gulf of Mexico and with the frequent thunderstorms (Fig. 19).

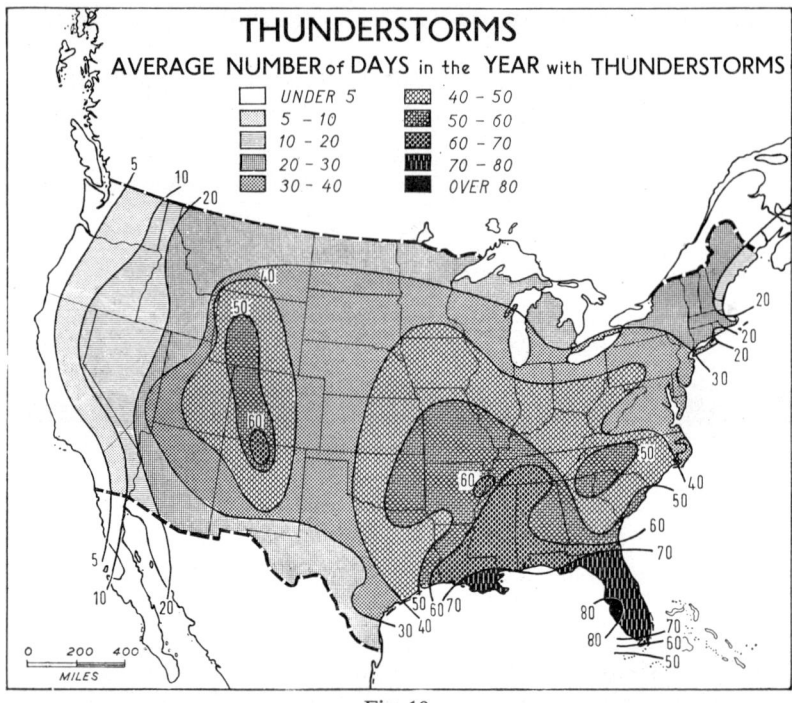

Fig. 19.

5. The south-east of the continent has higher totals. Over 60 in. fall on southern Florida and the more elevated parts of the Appalachians have over 70 in. There is no dry season, but most of the precipitation occurs in summer when the warm, moist mT air invades the land mass. (Miami, 59·2 in., 76 per cent. between May and October; Galveston, 44·4 in., 63 per cent. between May and October; Charleston, 40·3 in., 69 per cent. between May and October.) Places along the Gulf coast and in the South Atlantic states derive some of their rain from hurricanes.

6. The north-east of the continent lies under the influence of stable cP air and has little precipitation (under 10 in.). But higher amounts occur in south-east Canada and the north-east of the U.S.A. Most of the depressions cross the continent here, and there is considerable cyclonic rainfall at all seasons. (New York, 41·6 in., 54 per cent. May to October; St John's, 53·8 in., 44 per cent. May to October; Montreal, 40·8 in., 51 per cent. May to October.)

The Variability of Rainfall

The figures quoted in the preceding section are *average* amounts, *i.e.* the mean annual precipitation computed over at least thirty-five years. As far as the farmer is concerned, however, it is the actual total which matters, not some abstract norm. While an average figure is needed as a yardstick, in order to compare one place with another, it is necessary to know to what extent the precipitation in any year may deviate from the mean. It is the variations that are responsible for the sudden floods and unwelcome droughts.

It seems to be a general principle that variability increases as the mean annual precipitation decreases. The middle Pacific coast, which experiences the highest total rainfall, has the most reliable precipitation, with a deviation of under 10 per cent. (*e.g.* if the mean annual amount is 100 in., the driest year will have over 90 in. and the wettest under 110 in.). The area of greatest variability is the south-west where there is an expected deviation of over 40 per cent. Fig. 20 is a highly generalised map of rainfall variability and there are places where the precipitation is much more unreliable than is indicated. Bismark in North Dakota, for instance, has an average precipitation of 16.2 in., but in four successive years the amounts that fell were:—

1933.	10·7 in.	Deviation	34%
1934.	7·7 in.	,,	53%
1935.	17·9 in.	,,	10%
1936.	6·0 in.	,,	64%

It is in areas where rainfall is marginal for agriculture that variability is most important. Over the Great Plains, where the mean annual amounts range from 12 to 20 in., there is just enough precipitation for farming. If the total falls below the mean in any year, then farming becomes hazardous, and a series of bad years will be disastrous. The problem in areas such as this is aggravated by the fact that there are usually more years with totals below the mean than above it.

38 CLIMATE

Attempts to increase rainfall locally by seeding rain clouds with ice or silver iodide have been made since 1946. It is difficult to evaluate the success of such experiments for there are so many intangible factors to be taken into account. Many farmers object

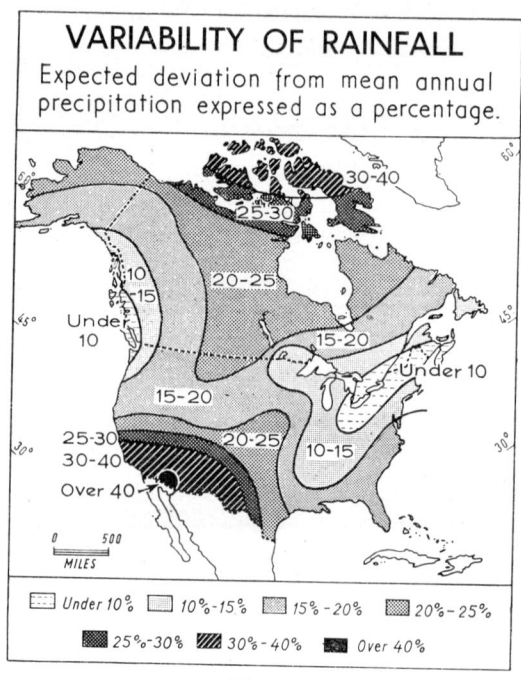

Fig. 20.

If the mean annual precipitation is 50 in., a deviation of 10 per cent. means that the precipitation in any year is expected to be between 45 in. and 55 in. If the deviation is 30 per cent., the precipitation is expected to be between 35 in. and 65 in.

to rainmaking on the grounds that places downwind are deprived of moisture.

Effective Precipitation

The precipitation that falls is disposed of in various ways.

1. Some is evaporated directly from the surface back to the atmosphere. Fig. 21 shows the amount of evaporation that takes place from open tanks constantly replenished with water. In many parts of the country, this figure exceeds the total rainfall, and

is to that extent unreal. But it does suggest that a large proportion of the water that falls is lost and is not available for plant growth.

2. Some water is absorbed by the soil and then subsequently released, either by being drawn to the surface and evaporating, or by being utilised by plants and then transpired.

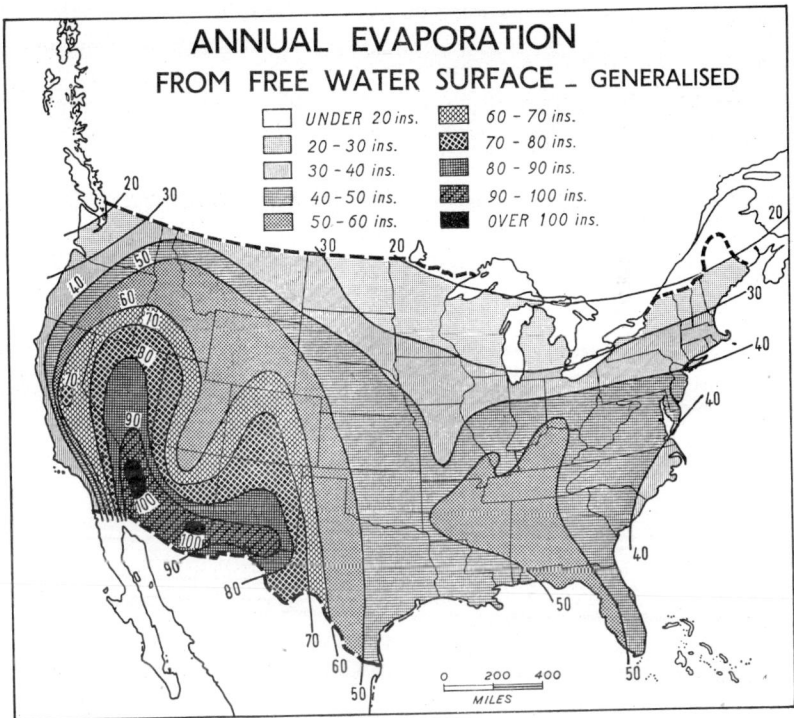

Fig. 21.

It is estimated that (1) and (2) account for 70 per cent. of the precipitation of the U.S.A. Naturally, there will be wide variations from place to place; in deserts, the figure will be higher; in cooler and more humid regions, it will be much lower.

3. Some water enters the soil and percolates through it to form ground water which, in favourable situations, can be utilised for irrigation.

4. Some water enters the soil and sub-soil and moves through it to streams and rivers.

40   CLIMATE

5. The precipitation that is not disposed of in these ways forms the run-off. In the U.S.A. this accounts for an estimated 20 per cent. of the total precipitation, although here again the figure will vary widely from place to place.

Effective precipitation is that which is available for plant growth. The water requirements of plants become greater with increasing heat, and as the evaporation rate increases with heat also, precipitation is less effective in hot regions than in cool regions. In the Arizona desert, 10 in. of rain will support only sparse scrub: the same amount in northern Canada gives rise to dense coniferous

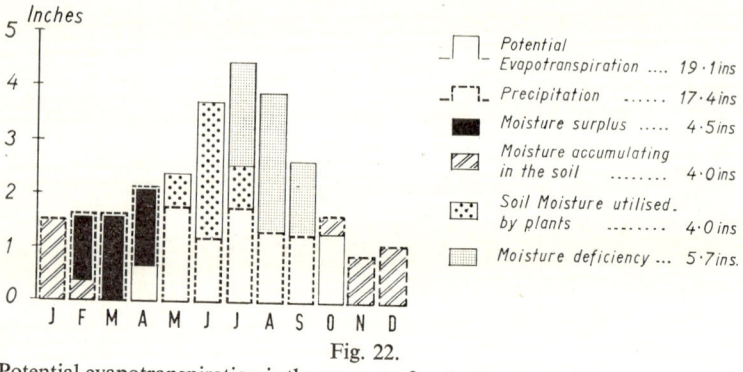

Fig. 22.

Potential evapotranspiration is the amount of water evaporated from the surface and transpired by vegetation, assuming the soil to be constantly moist.

forest. It is estimated that 20 in. of rain in the Canadian Prairies is equivalent to 35 in. in Texas.

In its simplest form, the effectiveness of precipitation for plant growth can be regarded as a function of precipitation and evaporation. It is possible to calculate the effectiveness by dividing the monthly precipitation by the monthly evaporation to give the P/E ratio. The sum of the twelve monthly ratios gives the P/E index. When considering the moisture needs of plants, however, it is impossible to ignore the effects of transpiration as well as evaporation. A more accurate assessment of the effectiveness of precipitation takes into account *evapotranspiration* (combined evaporation and transpiration).

It is not the figures of actual evapotranspiration that are set against precipitation, but those of potential evapotranspiration (*i.e.* assuming plants had all the water they could use and the soil was constantly moist). C. W. Thornthwaite, the American climatologist who introduced this concept, has calculated that the average annual water needs of plants in the U.S.A. vary from less than 18 in. in the high Rockies to over 60 in. in the Arizona desert. Where precipitation falls short of these needs, there is a deficiency of moisture and plants must be adapted to withstand drought. Where precipitation exceeds the potential evapotranspiration rate, there is a surplus of moisture which accumulates in the soil and forms the run-off.

In parts of the south-west of the U.S.A. moisture is markedly deficient in almost every month: in the east, there is a perennial surplus which, in certain areas in the Appalachians, amounts to over 35 in. Elsewhere, there is a moisture surplus in winter and a deficiency of varying length and intensity in summer, when plants need and use most water (Fig. 22). West of the 100th meridian, except for the coast of Washington and Oregon and small areas in the Western Cordilleras, there is insufficient effective moisture for optimum plant growth.

CLIMATIC REGIONS

Fig. 23 shows ten climatic regions into which the continent can be divided.

1. Arctic Climate, under the dominance of Polar and Arctic air masses.

2. Boreal Climate, under the dominance of Polar air masses.

3. Marine Climate of the west coast, under the dominance of maritime Polar air.

4. Sub-tropical Dry-summer Climate of the west coast, under the dominance alternately of Polar and Tropical air masses.

5. Arid and Semi-arid Tropical Climate, under the dominance of Tropical air masses.

6. Arid and Semi-arid Continental Climate, under the dominance of both Polar and Tropical air masses.

7. Humid Continental Climate, under the dominance of both Polar and Tropical air masses, subdivided into Cool-summer and Warm-summer types.

8. Humid Sub-tropical Climate, under the dominance of both Polar and Tropical air masses.

42 CLIMATE

9. Tropical Wet-summer Climate, under the dominance of maritime Tropical air.

10. Highland Climates, with altitude as the dominant control.

Within each region are differences of temperature and precipitation for these climatic elements vary widely from place to place. Nevertheless, there are broadly similar average conditions prevailing

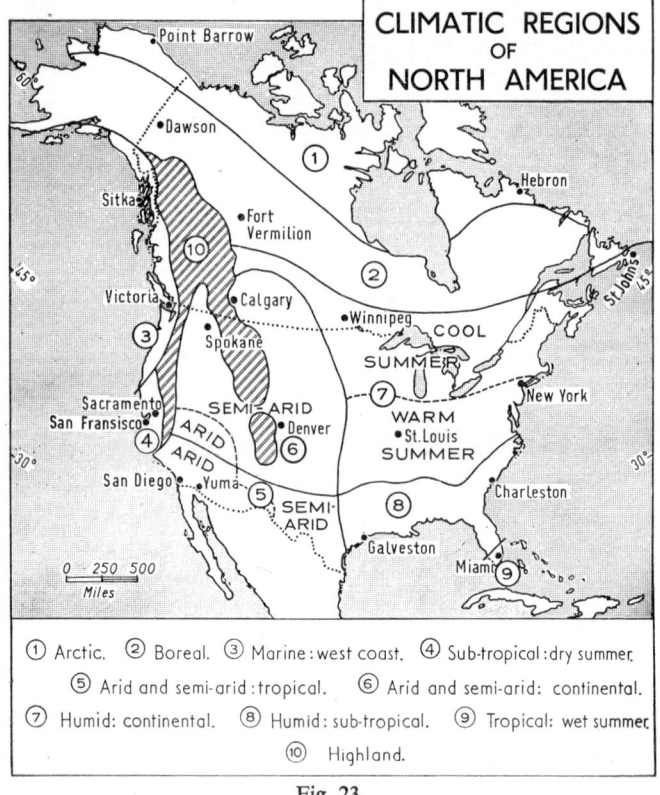

Fig. 23.

over each region which serve to distinguish it from adjacent regions with different sets of conditions. There is no abrupt change from one region to another, but rather a broad zone of transition.

1. Arctic Climate

This climatic region is a belt stretching across the northern part of the continent from Alaska to Labrador. Its characteristics are shown by the following statistics:

		J.	F.	M.	A.	M.	J.	J.	A.	S.	O.	N.	D.	Total
Point Barrow 71° N. 13 ft	°F.	−19	−13	−14	2	21	35	40	39	31	16	0	−15	—
	°C.	−28	−25	−26	−17	−6	2	4	4	−1	−9	−18	−26	—
	in.	0·3	0·2	0·2	0·3	0·3	0·3	1·1	0·8	0·5	0·8	0·4	0·4	5·6
Hebron 58° N. 60 ft	°F.	−6	−5	6	18	32	40	47	48	41	31	20	4	—
	°C.	−21	−21	−14	−8	0	4	8	9	5	−1	−7	−16	—
	in.	1·0	0·7	0·9	1·1	1·6	2·2	2·8	2·8	3·4	1·6	1·1	0·6	19·8

It can be seen that the mean annual temperature range is large, 59 F.° (*33 C.°*) at Point Barrow and 54 F.° (*30 C.°*) at Hebron. During the long, dark winter temperatures are very low with six or more months having mean figures below freezing point. The extreme cold is accompanied by clear skies and long periods of calm. The ground is completely frozen, although the snow cover is usually thin. Hudson Bay remains frozen for nine months of the year and the Arctic Ocean may be ice-bound for an even longer period. In spite of being frozen, the ocean does exercise a slight moderating influence; extreme minimum temperatures occur not on the coast but in central Keewatin. Even in summer the temperatures do not rise very high. It is rare to find a July with a mean temperature of over 50° F. (*10° C.*). The long period of daylight is not enough to overcome the negative effects of the low declination of the sun and the ice-choked polar seas. On a very few days each year the thermometer may rise to 80° F. (*27° C.*), but more usual daily maximum temperatures are about 60° F. (*16° C.*) or lower. Killing frosts are liable to occur at any time.

Annual precipitation is slight throughout the year, usually less than 15 in., and is concentrated in the summer months. At this time eastward-moving depressions take a more northerly course than in winter and bring frontal drizzle and showers. Hebron, lying on the Atlantic coast, has a higher total, but the amount remains small.

2. Boreal Climate

The Boreal Climate is experienced in a broad belt lying south of the Arctic region and extending from Alaska to Newfoundland. This belt reaches farther south on the eastern margin of the continent than on the west, reflecting the effect of continental conditions in a large land mass. For most of the year, the climate is controlled by dry cold and stable Polar air and mean annual ranges of temperature are high.

		J.	F.	M.	A.	M.	J.	J.	A.	S.	O.	N.	D.	Total
Dawson 64° N. 1,062 ft	°F.	−23	−11	4	29	46	57	59	54	42	25	1	−13	—
	°C.	−31	−24	−16	−2	8	14	15	12	6	−4	−17	−25	—
	in.	0·8	0·8	0·5	0·7	0·9	1·3	1·6	1·6	1·7	1·3	1·3	1·1	13·6
Fort Vermilion 58° N. 950 ft	°F.	−13	−5	8	31	48	56	61	57	46	32	10	−6	—
	°C.	−25	−21	−13	−1	9	13	16	14	8	0	−12	−21	—
	in.	0·6	0·4	0·6	0·6	1·1	1·8	2·1	1·7	1·3	0·7	0·6	0·5	12·1

Winter is the dominant season and starts early. Navigation on the northern lakes (Great Bear Lake, Great Slave Lake) may cease as early as October. Six to eight months have mean temperatures below 32° F. (*0° C.*), and at some stations there may be three or four months with means below zero. For long periods the daily maximum temperatures remain below freezing point. Skies are generally clear and conditions are calm but periods of daylight are short and there is excessive radiation. Minimum temperatures often fall very low. The lowest official temperature in North America is −81° F. (*−63° C.*) at Snag in the Yukon.

In the short summers, the days are long and maximum temperatures frequently rise above 80° F. (*27° C.*). Dawson has recorded a temperature of 95° F. (*35° C.*). In spite of the long periods of daylight, there is an appreciable difference between day and night temperatures and the diurnal range is commonly 20 F.° to 30 F.° (*11 C.° to 17 C.°*). The mean monthly temperatures then are not particularly high during this season. The growing period varies with latitude, altitude, and distance from the sea. Generally there are fifty to ninety days but there is always the risk of summer frost. The short duration of the growing season is balanced to some extent by the longer days and certain hardy crops can mature in a very short period.

In general, precipitation is slight: over much of the area it does not exceed 20 in. The pronounced summer maximum is accounted for by the greater frequency of cyclonic storms during this season. A small proportion of the total may be derived from the occasional thunderstorms which yield convectional rain.

3. Marine Climate

This climatic region comes under the influence of maritime Polar air from the Pacific for almost the whole of the year. Only very infrequently is it invaded by modified Tropical or continental Polar air. The region stretches along the west coast from southern Alaska to northern California, but the high mountains lying parallel and near to the coast limit this type of climate to a very narrow belt.

The main characteristics of this region are its mildness and its wetness. Owing to the moderating effect of the maritime air, winters are mild and summers are cool. The mean annual range of temperature is small [23 F.° (*13 C.°*) at Sitka and 21 F.° (*12 C.°*) at Victoria].

		J.	F.	M.	A.	M.	J.	J.	A.	S.	O.	N.	D.	Total
Sitka 58° N. 15 ft	°F.	33	34	37	42	47	52	55	56	52	46	39	35	—
	°C.	*1*	*1*	*3*	*6*	*8*	*11*	*13*	*13*	*11*	*8*	*4*	*2*	—
	in.	7·8	6·7	6·1	5·5	4·2	3·3	4·3	7·2	10·4	12·8	10·2	9·1	87·4
Victoria 49° N. 228 ft	°F.	39	40	44	48	53	57	60	60	56	51	45	41	—
	°C.	*4*	*4*	*7*	*9*	*12*	*14*	*16*	*16*	*13*	*11*	*8*	*5*	—
	in.	4·5	3·0	2·3	1·2	1·0	0·9	0·4	0·6	1·5	2·8	4·3	4·7	27·1

The mean temperatures of the coldest months are above freezing point and this region is from 10° to 30° F. (*6° to 17° C.*) warmer than the average for the latitude. Long periods with overcast skies and the prevailing onshore flow of maritime air keep the diurnal ranges low. Infrequent outbursts of continental Polar air bring short periods of clear, freezing weather. Such conditions are rare because the region is protected to some extent by the Western Cordilleras and also because cP air tends to move eastwards rather than westwards. The mean temperatures of the warmest months vary from about 55° F. (*13° C.*) in the north to about 65° F. (*18° C.*) in the south. Daily maximums do not usually exceed 75° F. (*24° C.*).

Precipitation varies widely within very short distances according to exposure and altitude. Those stations exposed to the onshore winds have high totals (*e.g.* Sitka): those in the lee of mountains have much lower amounts (*e.g.* Victoria). As the precipitation is primarily cyclonic and as depressions are strongest and most frequent in winter then there is a maximum at this season. In summer the Pacific "high" strengthens and moves north: the air is much more stable and tends to subside. Towards the south of this region, the dry summer becomes quite marked, but generally there is adequate rainfall at all seasons. The absence of high summer temperatures means that there is a high degree of precipitation effectiveness. In addition, the precipitation is reliable: great departures from the annual or monthly means are uncommon (Fig. 20). Fog is quite frequent in winter and autumn when warm, moist air from the ocean drifts over the colder land. Vancouver has thirty-seven days a year with fog, and Eureka, in northern California, fifty-one.

4. Sub-tropical, Dry-summer Climate

The chief features of this Mediterranean type of climate are the hot, dry summers and mild, rainy winters. It is really a transitional region, having in summer, the characteristics of the tropical arid area to the south, and in winter, those of the marine region to the north.

		J.	F.	M.	A.	M.	J.	J.	A.	S.	O.	N.	D.	Total
Sacramento 39° N. 71 ft	°F.	46	50	54	58	63	69	73	72	69	62	53	46	—
	°C.	*8*	*10*	*12*	*14*	*17*	*21*	*23*	*22*	*21*	*17*	*12*	*8*	—
	in.	3·8	2·9	3·0	1·6	0·8	0·1	—	—	0·2	0·9	2·1	4·0	19·4
San Francisco 38° N. 207 ft	°F.	50	53	54	55	57	59	59	59	60	60	57	51	—
	°C.	*10*	*12*	*12*	*13*	*14*	*15*	*15*	*15*	*16*	*16*	*14*	*11*	—
	in.	4·4	4·0	3·0	1·1	0·6	0·2	—	—	0·4	0·9	2·1	3·6	20·2

During the summer the region comes under the influence of the air which flows out of the sub-tropical "high". As this air is subsiding, it is stable and gives little precipitation. Monthly average temperatures do not usually exceed 80° F. (*27° C.*), although many stations have recorded absolute maximums of over 100° F. (*38° C.*). The coast is very much cooler than the interior (cp. the figures for Sacramento and San Francisco). This is because of the effect of the cold California current and the upwelling of cold water along the shore. Air moving landward over the cold water is made even more stable and therefore less likely to shed rain. But there is much fog. Almost every afternoon from May to October, fog pours into the Golden Gate. Inland, the clear skies permit rapid heating during the day and rapid cooling at night: the diurnal ranges of temperature at this season are large.

During the winter, the oceanic "high" weakens and moves south. The region is now in the path of the vigorous depressions that move into the continent from the Pacific Ocean. This is the season of

ARID AND SEMI-ARID TROPICAL CLIMATE

maximum precipitation but nowhere are totals very high: stations in the north have greater amounts than those in the south. Winter is distinctly cooler than the summer, but the mean temperature of the coldest month is usually in the high forties (*8° to 10° C.*). However, diurnal ranges are quite large and frosts often occur. Severe frosts are less frequent and are associated with invasions of cold Polar air from the interior. It is on these occasions that orchards suffer most damage.

5. Arid and Semi-arid Tropical Climate

These two types of climate are classed together because they have numerous features in common and differ more in degree than in kind. The semi-arid type is essentially a transition zone around a central arid core. The distinctive characteristic of these climates is, of course, the lack of sufficient rainfall to sustain a dense vegetation growth.

This climate is found in the south-west of North America where the air in the sub-tropical "highs" is subsiding and is consequently very dry and stable. This is the source region of cT air in summer. The desert conditions extend to the west coast, for here mT air which is stable anyway, crosses the cold California Current and the very cold coastal waters and becomes increasingly dry and stable.

		J.	F.	M.	A.	M.	J.	J.	A.	S.	O.	N.	D.	Total
Yuma 33° N. 141 ft	°F.	54	59	64	70	76	85	91	90	84	73	62	55	—
	°C.	12	15	18	21	24	29	33	32	29	23	17	13	—
	in.	0·3	0·4	0·3	0·1	—	—	0·2	0·5	0·5	0·3	0·2	0·5	3·6
San Diego 33° N. 93 ft	°F.	55	55	57	59	61	64	67	69	67	63	60	56	—
	°C.	13	13	14	15	16	18	19	21	19	17	16	13	—
	in.	2·0	2·2	1·6	0·7	0·3	0·1	—	—	0·1	0·5	0·7	1·8	10·1

The cold water off the shore has a pronounced effect on the summer temperatures of stations along the coast. Monthly averages are much lower than in the interior and the highest means tend to occur in late summer or early autumn when the ocean is warmest. Inland, temperatures are very high. The mean temperature of the hottest month is usually about 90° F. (*32° C.*), while daily maximums often exceed 110° F. (*43° C.*). The highest temperature in North America, 134° F. (*57° C.*), was recorded in Death Valley.

Annual ranges are considerable for such low latitudes. The clear skies permit intense insolation in summer and rapid loss of heat by radiation in winter. Coastal stations have much smaller annual ranges. The dry air and lack of cloud is also responsible for the large diurnal ranges, which are greatest in summer and may amount to 30 or 40 F.° (*17 to 22 C.°*).

Precipitation is not only low but extremely variable. Yuma has experienced less than one inch in a year but also over eleven inches in a year. It has an average of only thirteen rainy days annually. Near the coast and the Mediterranean region, precipitation is heaviest in winter but the regime changes to a summer maximum towards the interior. Totals increase towards the moister regions to the north-west and north-east. Fog is prevalent along the coast, San Diego having on the average twenty-two days a year with thick fog.

6. Arid and Semi-arid Continental Climate

The arid and semi-arid types of climate in the middle of the continent differ primarily in degree of aridity and are therefore treated here together. They differ from the arid and semi-arid tropical climate because of their lower temperatures and because they come under the influence of Polar as well as Tropical air. Mountain barriers on the west accentuate the aridity.

This type of climate is found over the intermontane region and the Great Plains of the U.S.A. and where these areas extend into southern Canada. Because of the wide latitudinal spread, there are appreciable differences of temperature but there are several climatic characteristics common to the region as a whole.

		J.	F.	M.	A.	M.	J.	J.	A.	S.	O.	N.	D.	Total
Calgary 51° N. 3,540 ft	°F.	12	15	25	40	49	56	61	59	51	42	28	19	—
	°C.	−11	−9	−4	4	9	13	16	15	11	6	−2	−7	—
	in.	0·5	0·6	0·7	0·8	2·3	2·9	2·6	2·5	1·3	0·7	0·7	0·5	16·1
Spokane 48° N. 1,943 ft	°F.	27	31	40	48	56	62	70	68	59	48	38	31	—
	°C.	−3	−1	4	9	13	17	21	20	15	9	3	−1	—
	in.	1·8	1·4	1·2	1·0	1·2	1·1	0·5	0·6	0·8	1·1	2·0	2·0	14·6
Denver 40° N. 5,272 ft	°F.	30	32	39	47	57	67	72	71	62	51	39	32	—
	°C.	−1	0	4	8	14	19	22	22	17	11	4	0	—
	in.	0·4	0·5	1·0	2·1	2·4	1·4	1·8	1·4	1·0	1·0	0·6	0·7	14·3

Above: Mesas and buttes in Monument Valley on the dry Colorado Plateau in Utah and Arizona. (*Spence Air Photos.*)

Below: Prairie landscape in Canada. Note the large, open, flat fields and the grain elevators along the railway. (*George Hunter.*)

Cypress trees with their swollen bases growing in a Louisiana swamp near the Gulf of Mexico. (*U.S. Forest Service.*)

Everywhere the annual range of temperature is large, a reflection of continental location. For practically the whole of the year, this area is under the influence of continental air masses, Tropical in summer and Polar in winter. A summer day may be uncomfortably like the tropical desert with a maximum temperature of over 90° F. *(32° C.)* and a large diurnal range. In the winter, however, temperatures can fall very low and invasions of cold Polar air bring freezing conditions to even the most southerly parts of the region.

This climatic region has inadequate effective precipitation. Totals of more than 20 in. occur only in small elevated areas such as the Black Hills of Dakota. Elsewhere, they may be much less than this. The arid and semi-arid phases of this climate are differentiated on the basis of precipitation effectiveness: in the arid region, there is sufficient moisture to sustain only desert vegetation, in the semi-arid parts, steppe grassland predominates. The regions are often referred to respectively as mid-latitude desert and steppe. In the Great Plains, spring and summer are the seasons of greatest precipitation, whereas in the intermontane region, there is a tendency towards a winter maximum (cp. Denver and Spokane). Winter precipitation is associated with the occasional depressions which temporarily replace the continental "high". It often takes the form of snow which occurs behind the cold front and is accompanied by high winds (known as blizzards on the Great Plains). In spring, the snow may be melted very rapidly by the warm Chinook winds which descend from the Rockies. Summer rainfall is associated with scattered thunderstorms (which can also produce hail). The mT air from the Gulf of Mexico which invades the continent at this season tends to drift eastwards and so does not bring as much rain to this region as it does to the area farther east. Tornadoes are common in spring and summer.

A characteristic of the precipitation is the great variability. Fig. 24 shows the variations in annual precipitation at Springfield in Colorado over a number of years. The nineteen-thirties and fifties were drier than normal over large areas of the Great Plains, with the result that crops failed and farmers were ruined. It is in areas such as this where the *normal* precipitation is just sufficient for agriculture that the use of statistical averages can be most misleading.

7. Humid Continental Climate

The eastern part of North America between latitudes approximately 35° N. and 55° N. is characterised by large annual temperature ranges, which is the distinguishing feature of a continental regime. In winter, the area is dominated by cold continental Polar air which brings cold, clear weather. In summer, maritime Tropical air invades the region, bringing hot, moist conditions. This is the battle ground of Polar and Tropical air masses and the situation at any instant can be seen from the position of the Polar Front. Depressions move across the area throughout the year, but they are most frequent and vigorous in winter. The weather is changeable: with the passage of a depression, temperatures can drop 60° F. (*33° C.*) or more in twenty-four hours.

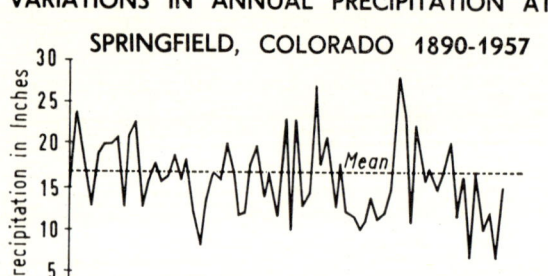

Fig. 24.

There are two sub-regions, the warm-summer and cool-summer types.

(*a*) *Warm-summer Type.*

		J.	F.	M.	A.	M.	J.	J.	A.	S.	O.	N.	D.	Total
St Louis 39° N. 568 ft	°F.	32	34	44	56	66	75	79	77	70	58	45	36	—
	°C.	*0*	*1*	*7*	*13*	*19*	*24*	*26*	*25*	*21*	*14*	*7*	*2*	—
	in.	2·3	2·6	3·5	3·8	4·5	4·6	3·6	3·5	3·2	2·8	2·9	2·5	39·8
New York 40° N. 10 ft	°F.	33	33	41	50	61	70	75	73	67	57	46	36	—
	°C.	*1*	*1*	*5*	*10*	*16*	*21*	*24*	*23*	*19*	*14*	*8*	*2*	—
	in.	3·3	3·4	3·6	3·4	3·1	3·6	4·2	4·2	3·7	3·5	2·5	3·3	41·6

Here the mean monthly temperatures for June, July, and August are near or above 70° F. (*21° C.*). The winters are cold, though less so than places farther north. The frost free season has an average length of 200 days in the south and 150 days in the north. Diurnal ranges in summer are small and nights can be uncomfortably hot.

Precipitation varies from about 20 in. in the north-west to about 50 in. in the south-east. There is no real dry season but most rain falls in the spring and summer, a tendency which is most pronounced at interior stations. This is because of the indraft of unstable mT air at this time of the year.

(b) *Cool-summer Type.*

		J.	F.	M.	A.	M.	J.	J.	A.	S.	O.	N.	D.	Total
Winnipeg 50° N. 760 ft	°F.	−4	0	15	38	52	62	66	64	54	41	21	6	—
	°C.	*−20*	*−18*	*−9*	*3*	*11*	*17*	*19*	*18*	*12*	*5*	*−6*	*−14*	—
	in.	0·9	0·7	1·2	1·4	2·0	3·1	3·1	2·2	2·2	1·4	1·1	0·9	20·2
St John's 48° N. 125 ft	°F.	24	23	28	35	43	51	59	60	54	45	37	29	—
	°C.	*−4*	*−5*	*−2*	*2*	*6*	*11*	*15*	*16*	*12*	*7*	*3*	*−2*	—
	in.	5·4	5·0	4·6	4·3	3·8	3·6	3·8	3·7	3·8	5·4	6·0	5·4	54·6

This region lies north of the warm-summer type and stretches from Newfoundland across the St Lawrence Valley-Great Lakes region to central Alberta. Although maximum temperatures in summer may reach 90° F. (*32° C.*) or even 100° F. (*38° C.*), the mean of the hottest month is usually below 70° F. (*21° C.*). The frost free period is less than 150 days except at some coastal stations. Winters are severe but this climate is distinguished by its summer rather than its winter temperatures.

Annual precipitation is usually less than in the warm-summer type for the area lies farther from the sources of mT air and is dominated by dry cP air for a greater proportion of the year. In the interior a spring and summer maximum is pronounced, but towards the coast the precipitation becomes more evenly distributed throughout the year. The ocean moderates the temperatures and coastal stations have a much smaller range than stations in the interior. Off the coast, fog is common for here the cold Labrador current meets the warm waters of the Gulf Stream.

8. Humid Sub-tropical Climate

The south-eastern part of the U.S.A. is dominated by the maritime Tropical air which flows inland in summer from the sub-tropical "high". The air moves from lower to higher latitudes over a warm ocean current and a heated land surface and in consequence becomes unstable. This is in marked contrast to the mT air from the Pacific high pressure cell which moves southwards, across a cold current and is extremely stable. Along the west coast in these latitudes then there is desert but the east coast has copious rain. In winter the humid sub-tropical region lies in the path of the numerous depressions which cross the continent and bring changeable weather.

The mean temperature of the warmest month is around 80° F. (*27° C.*) but daily maxima may exceed 100° F. (*38° C.*). Diurnal ranges are small and the nights are oppressively hot. The weather is akin to that experienced in a wet tropical climate. The frost free season exceeds 200 days.

		J.	F.	M.	A.	M.	J.	J.	A.	S.	O.	N.	D.	Total
Galveston 29° N. 69 ft	°F.	54	56	63	70	76	82	84	83	80	73	63	57	—
	°C.	*12*	*13*	*17*	*21*	*24*	*28*	*29*	*28*	*27*	*23*	*17*	*14*	—
	in.	3·4	3·0	2·9	3·1	3·4	4·2	4·0	4·7	5·7	4·3	3·9	3·7	46·3
Charleston 33° N. 48 ft	°F.	50	52	58	65	73	79	82	81	77	68	58	51	—
	°C.	*10*	*11*	*14*	*18*	*23*	*26*	*28*	*27*	*25*	*20*	*14*	*11*	—
	in.	2·4	3·0	2·7	2·3	3·0	3·8	6·1	5·6	4·3	2·8	1·8	2·3	40·3

The mean temperature of the coldest month is over 40° F. (*4° C.*) but there are quite wide variations from day to day as Polar and Tropical air masses advance and retreat (p. 27). Frosts are experienced during most winters and on rare occasions cold waves cause a sudden lowering of temperature well below freezing point.

Precipitation is heaviest in the south-east where totals may reach over 60 in. In the west, the annual amount drops to about 30 in. Rainfall is fairly evenly distributed throughout the year with most stations showing a slight summer maximum. Winter precipitation is associated with depressions while in summer there are fewer rainy days but heavier totals from the frequent thunderstorms.

9. Tropical Wet-summer Climate

This climate is experienced only at the extreme southern tip of Florida.

Winters are hot and cold spells are very infrequent, although frosts do occur on rare occasions. For the whole of the year, the region is dominated by maritime Tropical air. In summer and autumn hurricanes pass along the coast and bring heavy rain and high winds.

		J.	F.	M.	A.	M.	J.	J.	A.	S.	O.	N.	D.	Total
Miami 26° N. 5 ft	°F.	68	68	71	74	77	80	82	82	81	78	73	69	—
	°C.	20	20	22	23	25	27	28	28	27	26	23	21	—
	in.	2·5	1·9	2·3	3·4	7·1	7·4	5·3	6·4	8·9	9·0	3·3	1·7	59·2

10. Highland Climates

The higher parts of the Western Cordilleras have been differentiated from the other climatic areas because altitude is the dominant climatic control. There is no highland climate common to the whole area but rather a complex mosaic of innumerable microclimates.

Temperatures decrease with elevation at an average rate of 3·3° F. (*1·8° C.*) per thousand feet, and so uplands are considerably cooler than adjacent lowlands. Aspect plays an important part: southward-facing slopes are warmer than northward-facing slopes. The local climate is also influenced by exposure to winds and the relief itself can generate mountain and valley breezes.

The western highlands in North America act as a climatic barrier and by impeding the movement of cP air westwards and mP air eastwards separate quite different climatic regions. The windward slopes receive most precipitation while the leeward slopes are much drier. Totals tend to increase with elevation but not indefinitely: above about 5,000 ft amounts tend to fall away. At upper levels much of the precipitation is in the form of snow, and the snow cover persists for a long period of time. The lower limit of permanent snow varies with air temperature, aspect, and depth of snow. In the south of the U.S.A. this level is about 14,000 ft, on the 49th Parallel it is under 10,000 ft, and on the Arctic Circle it is about 3,000 ft.

CHAPTER III

NATURAL VEGETATION AND SOILS

In a continent as large as North America there are great contrasts in natural vegetation and soils. These and the climate are closely interrelated. Indeed, the vegetation pattern has been used by many geographers as an index of the climate. The *broad* correspondence of climate, vegetation, and soils is shown in the following table. It must be emphasised, however, that the relationship, although close, is nowhere exact, as factors other than climate are important in shaping the soil and vegetation patterns. Different soils, varying exposure to sun and wind, and changes of slope lead to variations in vegetation, while the nature of the parent rock, the degree of slope, drainage conditions, and the character of the vegetation give rise to different types of soil. Thus within any broad vegetation or soil region there are significant variations. Also, between the regions there are no sharp boundaries but rather a gradual transition from one type to another.

CLIMATE	VEGETATION	SOILS
Arctic.	Tundra.	Tundra soils.
Boreal.	Northern coniferous forest.	Podsols.
Marine West Coast.	Pacific coniferous forest.	Mainly podsols with some grey-brown podsolic soils.
Sub-tropical, Dry-summer.	Mediterranean woodland, Chaparral, and grass.	Chestnut soils and desert soils.
Arid and Semi-arid, Tropical.	(i) Desert vegetation (creosote bush and cacti).	Grey and red desert soils.
	(ii) Mesquite grassland.	Mainly chestnut soils.
Arid and Semi-arid, Continental.	(i) Desert vegetation (sagebrush).	Desert and chestnut soils.
	(ii) Grassland.	Chestnut, chernozem, and Prairie soils.
Humid Continental.	(i) Mixed forest.	Podsols.
	(ii) Hardwood forest.	Grey-brown podsolic soils.
	(iii) Grassland.	Prairie soils.
Humid Sub-tropical.	Mixed forest and southern pine forest with small areas of swamp forest and grassland.	Red and yellow podsolic soils with small areas of bog soils.
Tropical, Wet-summer.	A small area of swamp forest and grassland.	Mainly bog soils.
Mountain.	Mountain coniferous forest with small areas of alpine and desert vegetation.	Complex soil patterns ranging from podsols to desert soils.

NATURAL VEGETATION

Natural vegetation is an expression of the composite physical environment, past and present. All the factors of the environment act collectively and simultaneously upon plants and the action of any one factor is conditioned by all the others. The dominant factor is the climate, though whether it is the means or the extremes of temperature and rainfall that are the main controls is not certain.

Vegetation has not always existed in its present form; it is constantly evolving and as climate has changed in the past, so has the plant cover. The Ice Age led to profound modifications. Certain species which were preserved in the west of North America disappeared entirely from the east. With the amelioration of conditions since the close of the Ice Age, the continent has gradually been recolonised by higher forms of plant life. Such an evolution of the vegetation cover (*e.g.* from lowly tundra plants through coniferous forest to hardwood forest) is known as a "plant succession". The most highly developed type of vegetation that can occur under a given set of climatic conditions is known as a "climax community". This is an association of plants dominated by certain species which, with minor variations, extends over a considerable area. The distinctiveness of the vegetation is derived from the particular plant associations and the species which dominate them.

Variations within the larger plant communities are the result of secondary factors (*i.e.* soil, exposure to wind and sun, and degree of slope). Modification can also occur through the biotic factor. This can operate in a number of ways. The long prairie grasses of Iowa and Illinois, areas where the climate could support forest, are thought to result from overgrazing by bison which has prevented the growth of trees. Other influences are the dispersal of seeds by birds and pollination by insects.

In some parts of the continent there is now little trace of the original vegetation cover. The prairie grasslands have almost entirely disappeared except for some stretches of short grass which occupy the drier areas. Forests have been cleared to make way for agriculture or have been considerably altered by cutting and burning. Inroads into the forests in Canada have been confined to the southeastern part of the country and almost all of the 1,600,000 square miles of original forest remain. In the U.S.A., however, only 700,000 square miles of the 1,300,000 square miles of original forest are left and only 10 per cent. of this area carries virgin forest: the remainder has secondary growth. The destruction of the natural vegetation has been the main cause of soil erosion and increased run-off which leads to flooding.

Fig. 25 shows the main types of vegetation.

Tundra

This type of vegetation is found on the islands of the Canadian archipelago and in a belt of varying width along the north coast of the continent. The southern boundary corresponds approximately

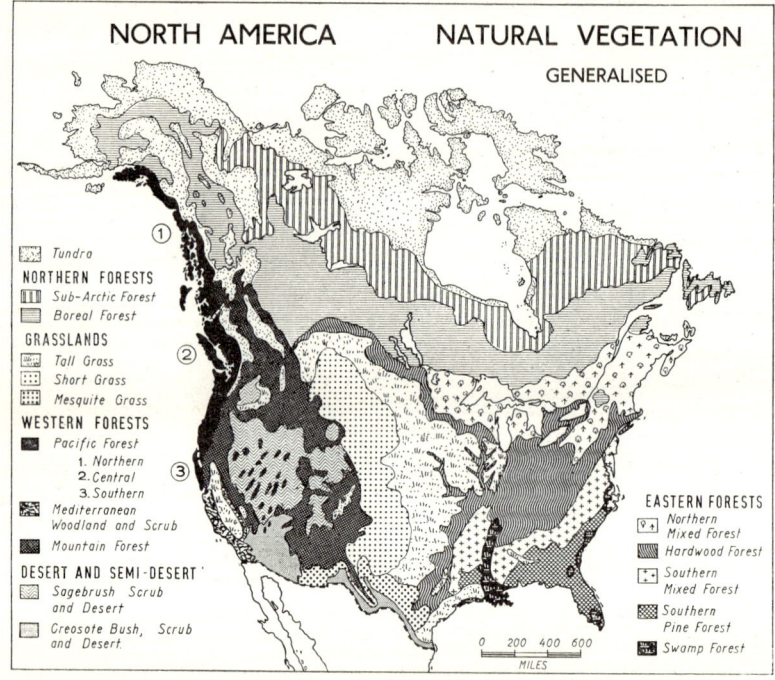

Fig. 25.

with the isotherm of 50° F. (*10° C.*) for the warmest month, which also marks the northern limit of forest. Trees are found in the tundra but in miniature form: dwarf willows, birches, and alders often are less than one foot high. The extreme winter cold, the shortness of the growing season, and the presence of a permanently frozen sub-soil limit the vegetation to hardy, shallow-rooted, and compact plants.

Nevertheless, there is an astonishing variety of species. There are 250 species of mosses, 320 of lichens, and 760 of flowering plants. Almost all are perennial, some running through their life cycle very rapidly, like the purple saxifrage which matures seed within a month of commencing growth, and others requiring many years from germination to first flowering. Leaves are small and roots extend horizontally along the top few inches of soil that thaw in summer. Many of the plants are xerophytic, *i.e.* adapted to withstand long periods of drought, because they are unable to draw water from the soil when temperatures are low.

Plants in the Arctic do not grow haphazardly among one another: those having similar requirements with regard to soil, moisture, and protection from wind grow together in well-defined plant communities. There are four such major plant communities, each capable of subdivision:

  (i) the rock desert characterised by sparsely distributed lichens and mosses;
  (ii) the muskegs or marshes with sphagnum moss and sedges as the dominant species;
  (iii) the seashore with lyme-grass and sea-chickweed;
  (iv) the true tundra with dwarf trees, heathers, berry-bearing shrubs, moss, lichen, and a wealth of flowers (including dandelion, buttercup, primrose, saxifrage, and goldenrod).

The blossoming of the flowers adds much colour to the summer scene: bilberries and crowberries yield their fruits which provide food for the flocks of migratory birds. Common in summer too are the mosquitoes which infest the marshes found above the permafrost (permanently frozen sub-soil). The grasses and mosses provide summer grazing for the caribou and musk oxen.

Northern Forests

South of the tundra is a broad belt of coniferous forest stretching across the continent from Newfoundland to Alaska.

The Sub-Arctic Forest is really an open woodland with a ground cover of lichens. Black and white spruce, tamarack (larch), and jack pine all occur, although the spruces are dominant. The trees are small and widely spaced (see plate facing p. 352). Heights rarely exceed 40 ft and along the tundra margins are much less than this. Sometimes the spruces assume attractive candelabrum shapes. The heaving and sagging of the surface due to the rise and fall of the permafrost level causes the so-called "drunken forest" where the spindly conifers are tilted at precarious angles.

Between the trees, shrubs are occasionally found, including dwarf birches, willows, and aspens as well as Labrador tea and heathers. The lichen floor consists of a carpet several inches thick of purple, orange, green, and grey Cladonia or reindeer moss. On the ill-drained muskegs and marshes, gaunt and stunted spruce and some larch rise from the ground cover of sphagnum moss, sedges, and shrubs.

The Boreal Forest lies to the south of the lichen woodland and is dominated by spruce and balsam fir. This appears to be the climax vegetation and other associations are the result of edaphic (soil) factors. Jack pine is common on sandy or dry soils and larch, together with spruce, on the badly drained lands. Willows and aspens occur along the watercourses and poplars occupy alluvial soils.

The trees are closely spaced and both thicker and taller than those in the sub-arctic forest. In the more gloomy parts of the forest and where there is a thick layer of pine needles, undergrowth is practically absent. Elsewhere, there is a ground vegetation of feather mosses, ferns, and small shrubs such as bunchberry and wood sorrel.

The complete regeneration of a forest area destroyed by fire or human interference takes about 150 years. The plant succession commences with lichens and sorrel and progresses through goldenrod, aspen-birch woodland, and balsam fir to the spruce-balsam fir climax. The southern parts of the boreal forest—in Quebec, Ontario, and latterly in Manitoba—are major lumbering areas. The species found here do not yield good or massive structural timber, but they are suitable, the spruces particularly, for reduction to wood pulp (p. 297).

The controlling climatic factor which determines the nature and extent of the forest seems to be temperature. Precipitation is everywhere adequate for trees under the cool conditions experienced here. There is a long period of physiological drought during the cold season which is induced by the low temperatures. The vertical growth of trees and the width of the annual rings has been closely correlated with July mean daily temperatures.

Western Forests

In the western forests are represented 59 of the 158 genera of arboreal plants found in North America. By far the larger number are conifers; contrasted with the eastern forests, this region is lacking in hardwood trees and the few that are found are small and widely scattered. The nature and extent of the forest varies widely from place to place, the complex patterns reflecting the differences in climate and relief. Precipitation effectiveness increases from south to north, and temperatures from north to south. The upper limit of forest—*i.e.* the tree line—is about 11,500 ft on the southward-facing slopes of the Sierra Nevada, about 7,000 ft in Washington, about 2,500 ft in central British Columbia, and at sea level in the Kenai peninsula of Alaska. In the interior, forests occur only on the mountain slopes and there is a lower limit of tree growth fixed by lack of effective precipitation.

The Pacific Forest is limited to a narrow coastal belt where conditions are mild and humid.

(*a*) In the north, the dominant trees are western hemlock and Sitka spruce. The Tongass National Forest of Alaska consists of 60 per cent. western hemlock and 20 per cent. Sitka spruce; the remaining 20 per cent. includes western red cedar, yellow cypress, lodgepole pine, white birch, and cottonwoods. Under favourable conditions, Sitka spruce may attain a height of 125 ft and a diameter of 4 ft. The dense forest growth rarely extends inland beyond the heads of the fiords (see plate facing p. 369).

(*b*) South of latitude 55° N. Douglas fir replaces Sitka spruce and becomes increasingly dominant southwards. It is associated with western hemlock and western red cedar. The forest stretches inland across the coastal mountains to the windward slopes of the Cascades. Under the mild moist conditions, trees are tall and close together. Many Douglas fir attain a height of over 200 ft and a diameter of 6 ft. Specimens over 350 ft have been measured and foresters claim to have cut one tree measuring 417 ft. The forest is best developed on the Coast Ranges and Olympic Mountains. Here, the great trees, shaggy with mosses and lichens of many colours, are thickly set for mile after mile. Beneath the shade of the lofty branches is a rank growth of young firs, cedars, and hemlocks, and below these a ground cover of ferns, mosses and lichens, and fallen trunks. From a commercial point of view, this forest is of immense importance and produces most of the lumber of North America.

(*c*) "The Redwood Empire" is a relatively small part of the Pacific Forest. It stretches 400 miles from San Francisco to south-west Oregon. The giant redwood (*Sequoia sempervirens*) often forms pure stands but occasionally it is found in association with Douglas fir and western hemlock. The tree flourishes best in moist localities and is restricted to the Coast Ranges, rarely being found more than thirty miles inland. It is thought to derive some of its moisture needs from the coastal fogs. It attains a height of 300 ft or more and a diameter of 16 ft, and forms the densest forest known (see plate facing p. 65). Yields of lumber commonly exceed

250,000 board ft (*i.e.* square feet of boards, one inch thick) per acre. By comparison, stands of Douglas fir yield an average of 40,000 board ft per acre. Undergrowth is generally sparse and consists of ferns and rhododendrons.

Mediterranean Woodland and Scrub occurs on the Coast Ranges south of San Francisco and in the Central Valley of California. The vegetation ranges from clear woods of Garry oak, cypress, and madrona to open scrubland known as chaparral which marks the transition from forest to steppe or desert. In some places chaparral bush thicket is the climax vegetation: in others it represents the underwood remaining after the removal of taller trees.

Owing to the long period of drought which coincides with the season of maximum temperatures when evaporation is most intense, plants are xerophytic and have many protective devices against rapid transpiration. The widely spaced trees are low or stunted with massive trunks and gnarled branches. Underneath is a partial cover of pale, dusty bush vegetation, usually less than 6 ft high, where the foliage is subordinate to the woody parts. Leaves are small and stiff with hard shiny surfaces or a covering of fine hairs, and roots are very long in order to tap underground water during the dry season. Most of the larger plants are evergreen. Between the shrubs are herbaceous and bulbous plants which make a colourful carpet during the rainy season.

The Mountain Forest is very diverse. The simple climatic pattern of temperatures decreasing northwards and precipitation decreasing towards the interior is complicated by the great contrasts in relief which results in a complex mosaic of local climates. The forest is generally confined to the wetter mountain ranges where rainfall exceeds 20 in., except in the north where precipitation is more effective and trees can survive with only 10 in. The interior basins and plateaus are too dry for forest and the lower tree line occurs at about 2,000 ft on the western slopes of the Sierra Nevada and at higher elevations farther inland.

On a climb to the top of one of the mountain ranges, one would pass through several vegetation zones. Each habitat is limited to a particular altitudinal belt by climate, exposure, soil conditions, and rock formations. In the lowlands bordering the range is desert scrub. In the foothills where the precipitation exceeds 10 in. are dwarf piñon, juniper, and cedar which occur in scattered open groves. The piñon grows to a maximum height of about 35 or 40 ft. Its small cones contain a dozen or so small edible seeds which used to be collected by the Indians.

MOUNTAIN FOREST

Above this zone is the true forest. Here precipitation exceeds 20 in. Stands of ponderosa (western yellow) pine occupy areas which have a dry soil or are exposed to the sun. The other dominant trees which have a more limited climatic range than yellow pine are Douglas fir and sugar pine (so called because of its sweet sap). The latter reaches its fullest development on the wet western slopes of the Sierra Nevada. It grows over 200 ft high and has a diameter of 8 to 10 ft. It is found at elevations between 4,000 and 8,000 ft and the stands are interspersed with islands of giant sequoias (*Sequoia gigantea*), relatives of the giant redwood. The fairly open yellow pine-Douglas fir forests of the interior have a ground cover of grasses which provide summer pasture for cattle.

Higher still is the sub-alpine forest consisting of white fir, white spruce, and lodgepole pine. At the highest elevations is Engelmann spruce, a small tree which becomes more and more stunted and gnarled as the tree line is approached. This upper limit of forest growth which is determined by temperature is at about 11,000 ft in the Colorado Rockies and about 6,000 ft on the 49th Parallel.

Above the tree line is alpine flora which is akin to the tundra of Northern Canada. The vegetation consists of sedges, brilliantly coloured flowers such as saxifrage, primrose, and gentian, and meadow grasses. These plants are xerophytic and can

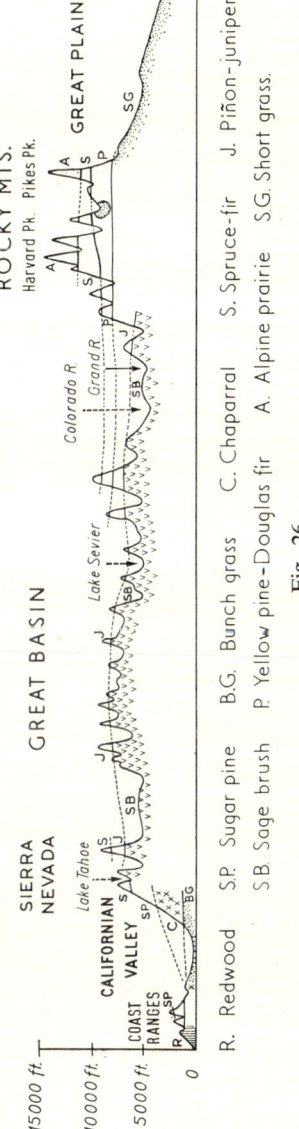

Fig. 26.

withstand the lack of water and the intense insolation of summer. Beyond this zone lies bare rock and, on the higher peaks, permanent snow.

The altitudinal distribution of the vegetation zones in the south of the U.S.A. is shown in Fig. 26.

Desert and Semi-desert

In the interior basins and plateaus of the Western Cordilleras, precipitation is insufficient to support trees except on the higher mountain ranges. It is sufficient to support grass but as the summers tend to be dry with most precipitation occurring in the winter and spring, then shrubs are favoured and vegetation takes the form of desert or semi-desert scrub.

There are very few areas which are completely barren. Indeed, the alluvial fans and bottomlands often carry quite a rich plant cover. Where plants are absent, as in the sand-dune tracts of Death Valley and the excessively saline playas, the reason is to be found in the nature of the soil rather than in the climate (see plate facing p. 33). There are salt-tolerant or halophytic plants, such as saltsage and shadscale but these are restricted to the less saline parts.

The Northern Scrub is found over the northern part of the intermontane region, the Wyoming basin, and occasionally on parts of the Great Plains. The dominant species is sagebrush, which will tolerate mildly saline soils and is adapted to withstand the long droughts caused by low, unreliable rainfall, the intense evaporation, and severe winter frosts. It grows two or three feet high generally and its roots extend fifteen feet or more into the ground. The small, scaly, grey or silvery leaves are often shed if there is a prolonged drought. It is not easily destroyed by fire or grazing and on this account tends to invade adjacent grassy or forested areas (see plate facing p. 64). Other shrubs such as greasewood are occasionally found but the only trees to be seen are willows, alders, and cottonwoods along the watercourses.

The Southern Scrub occurs in the Sonoran Desert where the heat and evaporation are intense and precipitation is very small and irregular. Plants are widely spaced in order to tap underground water from a large area and are adapted in various ways to resist drought and herbivorous animals. Leaves are small and either leathery or hairy. Some plants have no leaves whatsoever, but most have thorns and a few are aromatic. Roots are long and there are various devices for storing water. Many species seem able to absorb the evening dew.

The dominant plant is the creosote bush which can grow 15 ft high but which is usually much smaller than this. It is shrubby and thorny with a strong smell. Animals find it unpalatable. Other shrubs include yucca, mesquite, and cactus (see plate facing p. 65). There are about eighty varieties of cacti, the tallest of which, *e.g.* the saguara cactus, grow to a height of 50 ft. Between the widely-spaced bushes are bulbous plants which flower for a brief period after showers of rain and then lie dormant, often for months on end.

Grasslands

The grasslands occupy the central part of the continent between the western and eastern forests. At its broadest, this treeless belt has a width of over 900 miles. There is a gradation from the luxuriant prairie in the wetter east to poor steppe in the drier west.

Tall Grass Prairie is found in the east where the precipitation ranges from about 20 to about 35 in. Varieties such as bluestem, needle grass, and awned wheat grass may reach a height of 5 ft and develop deep and dense root systems. Among the grasses are many flowering plants which include phlox, violet, cinquefoil, anemone, and crocus. They add much colour to the spring landscape. In the east the grass is interspersed with groves of trees, and along the watercourses, fingers of willows and cottonwoods extend westwards.

Many authorities are unwilling to accept a purely climatic reason for the existence of grassland in a region where the precipitation exceeds 25 or 30 in. They attribute the absence of forest to overgrazing by bison and to fires, either natural or man-made. Both of these factors result in the destruction of seedlings and prevent forest becoming established.

The tall grass prairie pushes westwards in areas of sandy soil as in the Sand Hills of Nebraska where water percolates deeply beneath the surface, but retreats eastwards in clayey areas where water is usually found only in the surface layers.

Short Grass Prairie is found west of the zone between the 98th and 100th meridians. Here the rainfall decreases from about 20 in. to below 12 in. The grasses which grow to a height of 2 ft and have shallow roots, include june grass, spear grass, and western wheat grass. The dominant varieties, however, are grama grasses in the north and buffalo grass in the south. The former complete their life cycle in about 100 days, the latter growing in a hotter region where rainfall is less effective, needs only forty days.

The turf is usually short and felted but towards the west the grass grows in tufts with bare soil between. Where precipitation falls below 12 in. there is an admixture of sagebrush and sometimes prickly pear. Bunch grass, which is akin to the short grasses of the Great Plains, occupies an area of 60 million acres in the Central Valley of California and the Palouse area of the Columbia Plateau.

Mesquite Grassland occurs only in a small area in western Texas. It resembles a short grass savanna. Buffalo grass, dropseed, and the gramas are interspersed with mesquite (a variety of mimosa which grows up to 15 ft high), and in the drier areas, creosote bush and cactus. Here the rainfall varies from 20 to 30 in. annually, but owing to the intense evaporation little of this is available for plant growth. The growing season is long but the rainfall is concentrated in the summer months and the remainder of the year is extremely dry.

Eastern Forests

This forest originally covered the whole of the south-east quarter of the continent, an area of 2 million square miles, but the greater part has been cleared. It extends inland from the Atlantic coast to the Prairies, where rainfall is insufficient for tree growth, and northwards to the boreal forest, into which it merges. There is a large variety of trees—94 of the 158 genera of North America are represented—including both hardwoods and softwoods. Owing to the decrease of temperature northwards and precipitation westwards, and also because of soil differences, the composition and character of the forest changes from one area to another.

The Northern Mixed Forest stretches from the Great Lakes to the Atlantic coast of New England. Here the climate is more humid than in the grass-covered interior and warmer than in the boreal forest zone of Canada. West of the Red River, the northern mixed forest gives way to grassland.

Some trees found in the boreal forest appear in this region —balsam fir, jack pine, spruce, and larch—but they usually occupy the poorer locations such as the wind-exposed Atlantic coast and the higher parts of the Adirondacks and Appalachians. On the lowlands white cedar, red (Norway) pine, hemlock, and white pine are more common. The latter is the monarch of the forest. It grows to a height of 150 ft and its wood is highly prized by lumbermen. Deciduous trees occupy the best land. Often there are pure stands but usually they are intermixed with conifers. The dominant

Above: The Everglades in Florida is a low, badly-drained area covering more than 5,000 square miles. Large areas are covered with saw grass: the remainder, as shown here, consists of jungle and swamp forest. (*U.S.I.S.*)

Below: Sagebrush, two or three feet high, and juniper trees, fifteen to twenty feet high, in the semi-arid plateaus of south-west Colorado. (*U.S. Forest Service.*)

Above: Widely spaced Spanish bayonet or yucca plants which are found in the arid southwest, sometimes attain the size of small trees. The thick, stiff spines contain acrid juices. (*U.S. Forest Service.*)

Below: The giant redwoods of California reach an immense size. The undergrowth consists mainly of ferns with occasional huckleberry. (*U.S. Forest Service.*)

species are yellow birch, maple, ash, beech, basswood, and elm. Oak and chestnut appear only at the southern margin of this forest and are not characteristic.

Much of the northern mixed forest has been cleared to make way for agriculture. In the parts which remain wooded, however, such as New England and southern Ontario, the wide variety of trees adds much colour to the autumn scene.

"Very characteristic of this zone is the autumnal colouring of the leaves of the trees, shrubs, and herbaceous plants. This autumnal colouring lasts a comparatively long time, from about the first week in September to the second week in October, depending upon the dryness of the season. During that period the most splendid display of colours is exhibited, especially in the open mixed woods where underbrush is well-developed. Every shade of yellow, golden bronze, red, and scarlet is mixed in a gorgeous symphony of colours, generally most marvellously modulated by the sombre dark green or bluish-green of the conifers which are dotted among the deciduous trees. No such wealth of colour is ever met with in any other country." Macoun and Malte (*Canadian Year Book*, 1915).

The Hardwood Forest occupies the central and southern portions of the eastern United States. There are small stands of coniferous trees on the higher parts of the Appalachians but these are engulfed by the dense deciduous or broad-leaf forest with its close canopy and shaded interior. The trees include oak, poplar, chestnut, beech, walnut, elm, ash, and birch—species familiar in Europe—as well as hickory, magnolia, tulip trees, and tupelo. Beneath the trees is a rich undergrowth of azalea, laurel, rhododendron, arbutus, dogwood, and vines such as the Virginia creeper.

There are many varieties of oak (some of which are evergreen) and this is the commonest and most widespread tree. It sometimes grows to a height of 150 ft and has a diameter of 6 ft. In the east it is associated with yellow poplar and chestnut mainly, but west of the Appalachians where precipitation is smaller and concentrated in the summer months these two trees tend to be replaced by hickory, which reaches its fullest development in the Ozarks. Gallery forest, usually consisting of alders, willows, and cottonwoods, extends along the watercourses into the drier grasslands. Another westward extension of the hardwood forest occurs in Canada where aspen woods form a narrow crescent around the northern edge of the prairies.

Most of this forest has been cut or burnt and the land brought into cultivation. Extensive wooded areas remain only in the higher and more inaccessible districts.

The Southern Mixed Forest is intermediate between the hardwood forest to the north and the southern pine forest to the south, and consists of species from both. Broadleaf trees occupy the damper and heavier soils while conifers thrive best on the light dry soils.

The Southern Pine Forest is represented by ten species of pine, all exclusively American. Rainfall here is abundant but temperatures are high throughout the year and evaporation is intense. The soils are generally sandy and strongly leached. The dominant tree is long-leaf pine, also known as yellow pine and Georgia pine. It is seldom over 100 ft high and usually has a diameter of 2 ft to 6 ft. Its wood is heavy, hard, coarse-grained, yellowish-brown, and very resinous. It grows best on the dry loose-textured soils of the Coast Plain where it forms open forests with a scanty undergrowth of low bushes and tufted grasses. On moister soils are found slash pine, loblolly pine, and cabbage palms.

The swamps along the coast and in the Mississippi Valley carry thickets of reeds and tupelo, cypress, and red gum trees, which invariably have Spanish moss trailing from their branches (see plate facing p. 49). The Black Belt of Alabama, a crescent-shaped area 300 miles by 40 miles with limestone soils, before being brought into cultivation, was not forested but carried a cover of tall grasses with scattered trees.

SOILS

Soil Formation

Five factors are involved in the formation of mature, virgin soils.

1. The influence of the climate is very pronounced and there is a close similarity between climatic regions and major soil regions. The parent material of the soil is weathered and altered both physically and chemically by temperature and rainfall. When it rains, water enters the soil and moves downwards; during periods without rain, water moves upwards to the surface by capillary action. In humid regions, the predominantly downward movement leads to the removal of soluble materials and the finer clay particles (processes known respectively as leaching and eluviation), from the upper layers. In dry areas, there is little downward percolation but considerable upward movement of water which brings with it salts and bases from the lower horizons. These accumulate in a layer at or near the surface.

2. Vegetation is also of great consequence in soil development. Plants contribute organic matter which is changed into humus by the micro-organisms in the soil—bacteria, fungi, protozoa, etc.

The minerals used by the growing plants are returned to the surface when the vegetation decomposes and then disseminated through the upper layers. The quantity and quality of the humus will depend largely upon the type of vegetation. Leaf litter in forested areas supplies less plentiful and less rich humus than decayed grasses in grassland areas.

3. The texture and chemical composition of a young soil depends greatly upon the parent material but with increasing maturity the characteristics inherited from the bed rock become less important than the characteristics acquired through the operation of the climatic and vegetation factors. It is possible to find very similar soils existing side by side which developed over quite different rocks.

4. The nature of the physical site of the soil may be an important factor. Differences of slope affect the moisture content of the soil and the rate of surface erosion. Soils develop best on rolling and well-drained uplands. There, the removal of old and leached surface material by erosion is balanced by the downward progress of soil-forming processes. Where the slope is steep (and erosion rapid) or the land is level (and drainage is impeded) then the soils remain immature.

5. The formation of a mature soil takes hundreds or even thousands of years. Even when the soil reaches maturity, it does not remain a static and unchanging surface cover but constantly evolves. Thus time becomes an important factor. Some soils at present immature, *e.g.* alluvium, lava, and certain glacial and fluvio-glacial deposits, will, in time, develop profiles and the characteristics of maturity.

Soil Classification

Soils may be classified according to their texture or their chemical reaction, but in most geographical works they are distinguished by the characteristics of their profiles. Because of leaching or lime accumulation, soils display distinctive horizons at different depths from the surface. Any soil which possesses a profile is said to be mature and where this profile reflects the influence of climate and vegetation, then the soil is known as a zonal soil.

Zonal Soils occupy large areas of North America and are described in detail later. There are also two major soil groups which owe their characteristics mainly to factors other than climate and vegetation.

The Intrazonal Soils include those which are quite mature but which reflect the influence of parent rock or poor drainage.

1. Rendzinas are lime-rich soils found overlying the soft limestones and chalks of the Black Belt of Alabama, much of Texas, and eastern Manitoba. 2. Bog and half-bog soils occupy the low-lying seaward margins of the Atlantic and Gulf coast plains from North Carolina to Texas. These are so poorly drained and plants decompose so slowly that thick deposits of semi-decayed vegetation accumulate. 3. Planosols occur on the nearly level stretches of the interior. They have strongly leached upper horizons resting upon a hard clay-pan which has been formed because of the impeded drainage. 4. Saline (solonchak) and alkaline (solonetz) soils are found in a few small areas of the Great Basin where drainage is poor and salts accumulate.

The Azonal Soils are immature and without well-developed characteristics or profiles. 1. Lithosols are very shallow and consist of imperfectly weathered fragments. They usually occur on steep slopes from which any finer soil particles and humus are quickly eroded. They are also found in regions recently scoured by ice-sheets. 2. Sandy soils, such as are found in the Sand Hills of Nebraska, consist of a mass of unconsolidated particles without profile or structure. 3. Alluvial soils occupy large areas in the lower Mississippi Valley and the Central Valley of California and smaller areas along the flood plains of rivers. In time these soils will develop profiles and will then be classified with the appropriate zonal soil. 4. Some glacial and fluvio-glacial deposits are still immature as are the thin lava soils found in the Pacific North-west.

Major Soil Regions

The zonal soils of North America, south of the tundra, fall into two categories.

(*a*) In the humid east are the pedalfers which are rich in iron and aluminium compounds but poor in salts and bases which have been leached out by rain percolating downward through the soil.

(*b*) In the sub-humid and arid west are the pedocals which are characterised by a layer of salt or alkali accumulation at or close to the surface. This is the result of the upward movement of soil water and its evaporation during the long dry periods.

The transition from one soil type to the other coincides with the prairie soils (see Fig. 27), which occupy a zone between the 98th and 100th meridians. This is perhaps the most significant boundary in the U.S.A.

Tundra Soils.—In the treeless regions of the Arctic fringe, the soil profiles show evidence of excessive moisture. This is due to the low rate of surface evaporation, for precipitation is small. During the long period of cold, the soil is frozen and the decomposition of organic matter (of which there is only a small amount) is checked. The sub-soil is permanently frozen and consequently drainage is poor. Under these conditions the soil profile is shallow and consists of a brown peaty layer overlying a boggy greyish horizon which extends down to the top of the permafrost. This

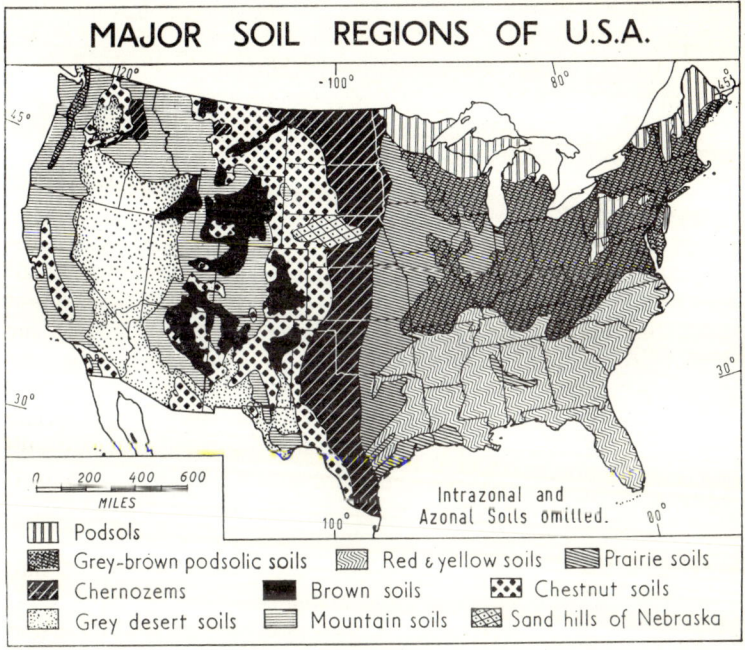

Fig. 27.

lies at a depth varying from a few inches to five or six feet. Often lenses and wedges of ice are found within the soil body.

Podsols are the mature soils of regions having a humid sub-Arctic climate and a vegetation cover of coniferous or mixed forest. Conifers are shallow-rooted and do not draw a large supply of bases to the surface. The resinous pine needles do not yield rich humus and the effect of the long, cold winters and moderately warm summers is to retard bacterial action. Much of the decomposition is accomplished by fungi and the soil is markedly acidic. Beneath shallow surface layers of forest litter and spongy, raw humus is an ashy horizon from which finer particles, colloids, and bases have been leached. The iron and aluminium compounds are rendered soluble by the acidic ground water and eluviated to lower levels. Beneath this leached layer is a brown horizon, again acidic, where the finer soil particles and iron are concentrated. Sometimes this material may be "cemented" together to form a hardpan which impedes drainage and causes bogs and swamps.

Podsols are low in fertility. Under cultivation, the surface film of organic matter is quickly lost and the soil requires lime and fertiliser to counteract acidity and replenish the leached bases. With such treatment, crops suited to the climate, such as potatoes, grass, and oats can be grown, but few areas with podsols have been brought into cultivation.

Grey-brown Podsolic Soils are found in the north-east of the U.S.A. and in the St Lawrence Valley, where the natural vegetation is deciduous forest. The organic material derived from broad leaves contains a certain amount of lime, potash, and other basic elements. Thus the soil is replenished in a way not found in the podsols. The upper horizons, which are slightly acidic, are leached, but are not greatly impoverished or bleached. They have a brown or grey-brown colour. In the lower horizons which are lighter in colour, are concentrated the colloids and bases.

When first cleared for farming, these soils, with their reserves of humus, are quite productive. Under continuous cropping, however, they lose their strength unless carefully managed and well-fertilised. They are suitable for a wide variety of crops and practically everywhere forests have been cleared to make way for agriculture.

Red and Yellow Soils are found in the south-east of the U.S.A. They exhibit the characteristics of both podsols and latosols. The former are found in cool humid regions and are poor in bases, iron, and aluminium. The latter occur in warm or hot humid regions and are low in silica and bases but rich in iron and aluminium. The upper horizon of these podsolic-latosolic soils consists of brown friable clays and loams. Underneath is a deep and compact layer of red or yellow material. The yellow soils are the more strongly leached and occur on the sandy coast plain belt where they carry a cover of southern pine forest. The red soils, which are slightly richer and are preferred by farmers, were formed under hardwood and southern mixed forest.

As the soils are low in calcium and other alkaline substances, their agricultural capacity is not high. However, they are fine-textured and retentive of moisture. Under careful management they can be quite productive. As the temperatures are high for most of the year, organic matter is quickly decomposed and quickly absorbed by the soil. If the soil is not replenished, its structure collapses, it becomes exhausted, and is easily eroded. Because of its fine structure this soil type responds well to treatment with fertilisers.

Prairie Soils are situated between the pedalfers of the east and the pedocals of the west. They occur in a narrow belt where the rainfall is between 25 and 40 in. and where the natural vegetation consists of tall grasses with occasional groves of trees. They are dark in colour and have a fine granular texture, both of which are the result of the abundant organic matter derived from the grass roots. There is no layer of lime accumulation as in the true pedocals, and the soil has no distinct acid or alkaline reaction.

Prairie soils are excellent for agriculture. Their high humus content and good structure place them among the most productive soils in the world.

Chernozem Soils occupy a strip of land from Alberta to Texas where the rainfall amounts to about 20 in. and the natural vegetation consists of mixed tall and short grasses. There is little leaching of the soluble materials and a large proportion of fine particles and colloids remains in the upper horizons. A layer of lime accumulation, three to five feet below the surface, provides an inexhaustible supply of calcium. Grasses are heavy feeders on bases but they return them to the soil quickly and regularly, and the black or very dark brown upper layers are extremely rich in humus.

The soil particles are grouped into granular or crumb-like aggregates and the structure is excellent for crops. Reserves of mineral and organic plant foods are so abundant that the soil will stand cropping for long periods without fertilisation. Towards the south, where the vegetation is less dense and there are more shrubs, the chernozems tend to deteriorate.

Chestnut Soils lie west of the chernozems where rainfall is lighter and short grasses are dominant. Humus is plentiful but not as deep or as rich as in the chernozem soils. The soil is brown in colour and the layer of lime accumulation lies closer to the surface, at a depth of one or two feet.

The chestnut soils are easily tilled and fertile but they lie in a zone where rainfall is low and unreliable. The fact that these soils are regions of stock-raising rather than cultivation is due to a deficiency of rainfall rather than to deficiencies in the soil. Attempts to extend cultivation into this zone may be temporarily successful but usually end in failure.

Brown Soils are very similar to chestnut soils but they occur where conditions are more arid, as in the Wyoming basin, the Colorado Piedmont, and parts of the Colorado plateaus. The vegetation overlying them consists of short grasses and desert scrub. With less humus than the chestnut soils, they are lighter in colour and the alkaline layer lies very close to the surface. Cultivation only takes place where there is irrigation.

Grey Desert Soils develop under a sparse vegetation of widely scattered shrubs. They lack organic matter and are very light in colour. The layer of alkaline accumulation is very close to the surface or even upon it. So abundant are the salts and bases that they are often cemented into a hardpan known as caliche. The soil texture is generally coarse with fragments of the parent rock visible, but there is a large supply of soluble minerals.

Only the fine-textured soils are suitable for cultivation. These are found along the flood plains and terraces of streams and on alluvial fans. Irrigation is essential. Sometimes the concentration of salts prevents plant growth. Generally, those soils which contain calcium are preferred to those which have a predominance of sodium salts.

Mountain Soils.—The pattern of soils in the mountainous west is very complex. On the steeper slopes, soils are immature and well-developed soils are found only on the gentler slopes and at the foot of the mountain ranges. On some slopes it is possible to trace a sequence of soils from desert soils at the base, to prairie soils and podsols at the top. This sequence reflects the variations in rainfall and vegetation with altitude.

Soil Erosion

Even under natural conditions there is a certain amount of soil wastage. The top layers are slowly removed, but at the same time the parent rock underneath is slowly being turned into soil. In some areas this process can be beneficial, for the excessively leached material is transported away to reveal the richer horizons below. Soil erosion, as the term is generally understood, is the acceleration of this natural process through human disturbance of natural conditions.

The rate of erosion depends upon a number of factors, some physical and some human. The physical factors are:

(*a*) the degree of slope, (*b*) the texture and structure of the soil, (*c*) the amount and intensity of the rainfall and the strength of the wind, and (*d*) the nature and density of the vegetation cover.

The human factors are:

(*a*) the removal of the natural vegetation, and (*b*) mismanagement of the land, by overcropping, overgrazing, bad tillage, and monoculture.

The agents of soil erosion are rain and wind. Rain acts in two ways, both of which are most effective in heavy storms when run-off is very great. Gullying is the rapid growth of steep-sided ravines, chiefly along pre-existing hollows. This is most common where the soil consists of softer materials underlying a compact horizon. In heavily eroded areas the dissected surface resembles miniature badlands. Some gullies have attained depths of 100 ft or more in thirty or forty years. They grow rapidly by headward erosion.

Sheet-wash is the removal of the whole of the surface layers of the soil by rain flowing down slopes in a multitude of narrowly-spaced rills. Although less spectacular than gullying, sheet-wash is more widespread and has caused greater damage. Erosion is greater where a widely-spaced crop such as cotton, corn, or tobacco is grown and bare soil is exposed between the rows, than where there is a cover crop such as grass or clover. Where dry-farming is practised and the fields lie fallow in alternate years, there is no vegetation cover to reduce run-off and soil losses are excessive. At one test station in Missouri, 7 in. of soil were lost from bare ground in twenty-four years, while at Spur, in Texas, 40 tons of soil were washed from one acre by 27 in. of rainfall. Overgrazing lessens the protection that vegetation can give to the land. Overcropping reduces the store of humus in the soil which, as a result, becomes less cohesive and more impermeable, thus promoting greater run-off. Also contributing to the more rapid flow of surface water has been the deforestation of watersheds and the ploughing of steep slopes which should have been left under their natural vegetation or under a cover of grass.

Wind erosion affects the ploughed lands and overgrazed grasslands of the sub-humid and arid west. The finer soil particles are lifted by the winds and transported, perhaps very long distances. During drought years losses from exposed soils may be very severe. Three counties in Texas lost fifty million tons of soil in a single day in 1935 by deflation. In the year previous to this, frequent dust storms in the southern Great Plains created the Dust Bowl. The finer material was blown away in great clouds: some fell over the eastern cities and even on ships in the Atlantic Ocean. The heavier particles remained as drifts and hummocks. At its greatest extent, the Dust Bowl covered 16 million acres.

Fig. 28 shows the areas in the U.S.A. which have been seriously eroded. There are, in addition, considerable areas where the soil has been damaged to some extent. About 15 per cent. of the land has been rendered useless for agriculture and over a further 40 per cent. farming has been impaired because of soil losses. Altogether, the U.S.A. is losing some 4,000 million tons of soil every year. The Mississippi alone carries 750 million tons of sediment to the sea annually and the Colorado 174 million tons (see Fig. 7). Much

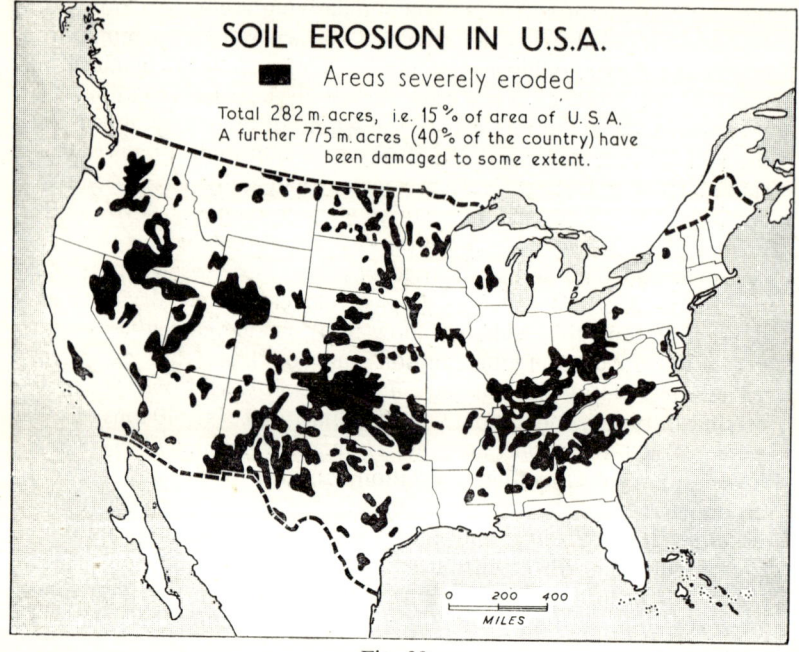

Fig. 28.

material does not reach the sea but buries productive farmland in the river valleys and flood plains, or silts up reservoirs. The cost in terms of abandoned farms, loss of land for crops and livestock, and flood damage, is appalling.

Soil Conservation

In no other continent has soil erosion been so intensively studied. The need for conservation measures has long been apparent but only in the last three decades have they been widely practised. As long as land remained plentiful and cheap, there was little incentive for the farmer to conserve his soil. In fact, one of the characteristics of the development of the U.S.A. has been the reckless exploitation of the natural resources.

The first serious efforts to prevent soil losses and to reclaim eroded land coincided with the inauguration of the New Deal programme in 1933. Farmers were encouraged to form district associations and to co-operate in conservation practices. Information was widely disseminated by state and federal authorities and help and advice was made readily available. The successful work of the Tennessee Valley Authority in restoring the land and rehabilitating the farming population was taken as an example of what could be achieved (p. 147). The movement towards better farming has grown apace, although there was a temporary setback during World War II when much marginal land was ploughed up and sown with crops.

Gullies are being blocked by check dams and by afforestation, and the red gashes which slashed the Piedmont slopes are becoming fewer. The steeper slopes and watersheds are now protected by trees and grasses. The slopes still under cultivation are now being ploughed along the contour, or are terraced so that the flow of water is reduced. Monoculture and the yearly planting of row crops is being abandoned in favour of planned rotations which maintain the fertility and structure of the soil. On some sloping land farmers practise strip farming: intertilled crops such as cotton, corn, and tobacco are sown in strips between belts of cover crops such as grass, clover, lespedeza, and kudzu (p. 155). In drier areas land is being withdrawn from cultivation and restored to controlled grazing. Where dry-farming is still practised, trees are planted to provide shelter-belts and a "trash cover" is left over the soil during the alternate years when the fields lie fallow.

The result of these remedial measures is that much land that was formerly thought to be completely ruined has been made useful again. In some areas the pattern of farming has undergone a great change. Nowhere is this more apparent than in the South, where conservation methods have not only reduced soil erosion but, by leading to more diversified farming, have also contributed enormously to the wealth and stability of the farming community. However, while there can be little doubt that the people of North America are aware of the problem, this awareness has not always been matched by effective action. In spite of the considerable progress that has been made in recent years, it cannot be said that soil erosion has been really conquered.

CHAPTER IV

THE SPREAD OF SETTLEMENT

At the present time, North America supports a population of over 200 million. Except for about half a million Indians, all these people are descended from immigrants who entered the continent during the four and a half centuries that have elapsed since its discovery. The peopling of this land is the result of one of the greatest human migrations in history, and the course of settlement was profoundly affected by the geographical realities examined in the previous three chapters.

Indians

At the time the first Europeans set foot in the continent, the aboriginal population, known to anthropologists as the Amerinds, numbered about one million. These people had made their way into North America from the north-west during an interglacial phase of the Ice Age, when the Bering Strait may have been land. The closing of this land-bridge isolated the Amerinds: they were separated from their racial cousins in Siberia and their development has followed different lines.

But while all Amerinds have similar physical traits which distinguish them from other racial groups, their ways of life differ in different parts of the continent. There is a wide range of environments, from the Arctic tundra in the north, to the humid swamps of Florida or the torrid deserts of New Mexico in the south. The range of activities of a primitive people without knowledge of the wheel, with no domesticated animals except the dog, with only an elementary experience of working metals, with a restricted number of cultivable crops and methods of farming, is bound to be limited. A technically advanced people can apply its techniques to overcome the disadvantages of a particular environment: a primitive people has a simpler and more direct relationship with its habitat.

In the northern parts of Canada, in Alaska and Greenland, lived the Eskimos, a nomadic people whose food, clothing, shelter, and means of transport reveal a very close dependence on the fish and animal life of the sea and tundra. A nomadic life was also characteristic of the Indians living further south in the boreal forests. Tribes such as the Algonquins and Athabascans obtained their food and clothing from the caribou and fur-bearing animals of the forest, and the fish of the lakes and streams. In this area with its poor soils and harsh climate there was little agriculture.

In the Atlantic forests, south of the Great Lakes and St Lawrence, the diet of the Iroquois, Creeks, and other tribes, consisting of fish and game, was supplemented by the fruits of the trees and by maize, beans, and pumpkins. These crops, with tobacco, were grown in small clearings where the trees had been girdled and the undergrowth burnt. The grey-brown earths here are more productive than the podsols developed under coniferous forest and the climate permits a wide variety of plants to be grown. The typical settlement in the east was a large palisaded village.

The open grassy plains of the interior were the home of the Comanche, Pawnee, Cheyenne, and similar nomadic tribes which hunted the bison. Hunting was done on foot until the Indians were able to capture and tame the horses introduced by the Spaniards and allowed to run wild.

Beyond the Rockies in California was a group of Indians with little tribal organisation, who existed by hunting rodents and collecting roots, fruits, wild rice, and acorns. In contrast, the Hopi and Zuna Indians of the south-west, tied to an unfavourable environment of arid plateaus and canyons, lived in permanent stone or adobe pueblos, grew crops of maize, melons, pumpkins, beans, and cotton by means of irrigation, were adept weavers and potters, and had a remarkable social organisation (see plate facing p. 96).

The contact of the indigenous inhabitants and the early settlers was fruitful to both parties at first. The Indians were introduced to new crops, utensils, and techniques, and their legacy to the newly arrived Europeans included the canoe, the forest trail, methods of trapping animals, various items of dress, and maize. Unfortunately, it was soon discovered that the continued existence of traditional Indian ways of life was incompatible with the creation of enclosed and permanently occupied farms. From the fur trader, a temporary inhabitant in the area, the Indian suffered little: indeed, the goods that he brought were eagerly sought. The tribal lands remained intact, except for the almost complete extermination of fur-bearing animals. It was the advent of the farmer that heralded the decline of the Indian. The less numerous and less civilised race retreated before the persistent advance of the farming frontier. As immigration proceeded, the Indians were deprived of their land and either exterminated or pushed westwards. The Seminoles retreated to the swamps of southern Florida, and to-day remain the only tribe that has not signed a treaty with the U.S. Government.

Diseases to which the Indians were particularly susceptible, drink, war, and famine played all too common a part in removing an obstacle to westward expansion. Attempts by the government of the United States to protect the Indians by treaty were nullified by land-hungry settlers and lawless prospectors. In the first half of the nineteenth century, tribes from the area east of the Mississippi were moved to reservations on the Great Plains, which at that time were considered unfit for European settlement. Even this land was not inviolate: the tide of settlement advanced relentlessly and what

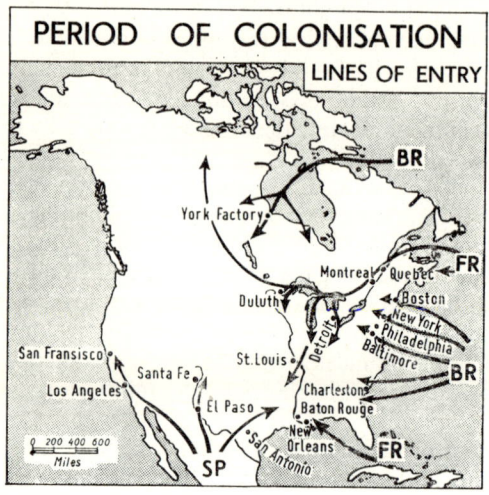

Fig. 29.
This map shows the main lines of entry of the Spanish, French, and British colonists. Some of the early settlements are shown.

was Indian territory eventually became the state of Oklahoma. It is small wonder that the Indians sought to regain by force what they had lost through the abrogation of treaties. There were even despairing attempts by the Indians to break out of the reservations and return to their former homeland.

Not until 1890 was the danger of Indian attack removed. By then the number of Indians in the country had been reduced to about 250,000. In Canada, which was settled later, many of the mistakes made in the U.S.A. were avoided. To-day, the lot of the Indian is in many ways happier than that of the Negro or the Mexican. This is as much the result of a changed attitude of the population as of government action.

COLONISATION

There were three main streams of early colonisation by Europeans (Fig. 29), and some of the differences of customs, religion, systems of land tenure, place-names, and many other cultural features which can be noticed in different areas of the continent, reflect the varying attitudes, habits, and cultures of the colonising peoples.

Spanish

Spanish settlement in the New World followed quickly the discovery (or re-discovery) of the continent by Columbus. The finding of gold and silver led to the occupation of Mexico and the exploration of the land to the north. A force in colonisation almost as potent as the demand for precious metals was religious zeal, the desire to win converts to Christianity. It was this motive primarily which encouraged the Spanish to establish settlements in Florida and on the Gulf coast in the late sixteenth and early seventeenth centuries. They also had a military value. Of all these settlements, however, only Fort Augustine was continuously occupied: the others were abandoned. The missionary work was never very successful owing to the refractory nature of the Indians, and Spain could ill afford to maintain a colony which produced no mineral wealth and could never be self-supporting.

From Mexico, soldiers, prospectors, and priests had pushed northwards into the valleys of the Rio Grande and the Gila. The settlements at El Paso and Santa Fe were contemporaneous with the British and French foundations on the east coast, but two hundred years were to pass before the valley of the Rio Grande was reached from the east. Spain claimed a huge area in North America, but only a fraction was settled and much was unexplored. Sporadic attempts were made to set up new settlements, especially when the British or French seemed about to trespass on what was nominally Spanish territory. It was to counter an imaginary French threat in the lower Mississippi Valley that missions and military stations were established in Texas in the early eighteenth century. Later, in the same century, the Spanish entered California, and in 1769 discovered San Francisco Bay, the only good natural harbour on this inhospitable coast: previous explorations by sea had failed to reveal it. Twenty-one missions were built in the valleys between Los Angeles and San Francisco. The missionaries introduced new crops and began to baptise and educate the Indians; the few Spanish settlers were granted huge tracts of land on which they reared cattle.

Spanish efforts to colonise the south-west can hardly be counted a success. In the course of two centuries, only a few widely-scattered and small settlements were established. The precious metals so eagerly sought remained undiscovered, and agriculture, especially in a sub-humid land, had few attractions for the Spaniards. These settlers, indeed, showed little of the pioneering spirit which motivated the British. The mother country gave little help or encouragement to the new lands. Indeed, it was scarcely in a position to do so as its power was waning and its energies were sapped by a succession of wars in Europe.

Gradually the Spanish lands passed to the United States. The huge area lying west of the Mississippi, but with undefined western boundaries, was ceded to France and later sold to the U.S.A. (1803, the Louisiana Purchase), whilst Florida changed hands in 1819. The Spanish territory in the south-west was transferred to Mexico when that country obtained its independence in 1821. But Mexico was little better placed to govern and develop its territories than Spain had been. Communications with Mexico City were at best tenuous and at worst non-existent. In view of the broken terrain, aridity, and lack of water-points, this is scarcely surprising. Mexico lost Texas in 1836 and the rest of its North American lands, including California, in 1848. It could not hold them in the face of the advancing tide of American settlement (Fig. 30).

French

Unlike the Spanish who pushed into North America from a land base, the French made their entry from the sea at a point where a wide estuary gives easy access to the interior. Shortly after the voyages of Cabot (1497-8), the waters off Newfoundland were being fished by Portuguese, Basques, British, and French, and temporary summer stations were set up on the island to cure and salt the catch. In the years that followed, the St Lawrence was explored and by 1535, Cartier had penetrated as far as the site of Montreal.

It was only in 1608, however, that the first permanent settlement arose. This was Quebec, situated at a point on the river where sailing boats found manoeuvring difficult. Montreal was founded in 1642 and the riverine tract between the two towns was divided into huge estates knowns as seigneuries. The feudal peasants laid out their farms in long strips, running at right angles to the river, and this settlement pattern has persisted to the present day (see Fig. 97 and plate facing p. 257). Montreal lies on the same parallel of latitude as Lyons, but the early colonists found little similarity between their homeland and their new environment. Agriculture did not flourish in this land of short, cool summers and rigorous winters, where the rivers were frozen for four months of the year. The soils of the valley were cultivable but many crops familiar to the settlers could not be grown. Away from the river were vast areas of bare granite and gloomy coniferous forest.

It was in fact from the forest that New France obtained its wealth. Fur-bearing animals abounded, and trapping, together with fishing, employed more men than agriculture. The Indians were encouraged to collect furs and in return were supplied with metal utensils, weapons, and alcohol. The constant search for fresh supplies led French and half-breed trappers and traders to

Fig. 30.

penetrate remote areas. Travel was by canoe and there were few parts that could not be reached by this method of transport. The St Lawrence, although impeded by rapids and falls, led the trappers to the Great Lakes. From these huge sheets of water, and from their tributaries, it was easy to cross narrow stretches of land to other drainage systems. Some of these portages were as little as one mile in length.

Given the will to explore and an easy means of reaching the interior, the French quickly learnt the possibilities of the land. During the seventeenth and eighteenth centuries, trading posts, forts, and missions were established at river confluences, portage points, and other strategic positions. La Salle sailed down the Mississippi in 1682 and as a consequence of his voyage it was eventually decided to occupy the Mississippi Valley. New Orleans was founded in 1718 and a handful of small settlements arose on the Mississippi and its tributaries. Already long-term strategic considerations were evident. The British in New England and the French in the St Lawrence Valley were effectively separated by the Iroquois Indians who occupied the land south of Lake Ontario and along the upper Hudson River. But further afield their interests began to clash. The British Hudson Bay Company set up its first posts on James Bay in 1670, but the belt of French forts and trading posts stretching from the Great Lakes to the Arctic prevented them having any but the slightest contact with the interior. Similarly, the French occupation of the Mississippi Valley was a move to forestall and counter British expansion westwards.

The wide distribution of French place-names testifies to the efforts of the early colonists to extend French dominion over vast areas of the continent. As early as 1671, France had claimed all the land north, south, and west of the Great Lakes. Unfortunately there was never a large enough population to make French claims effective. The primary purpose of French colonisation was trade: agricultural settlement was neglected and at times actively discouraged. In the middle of the eighteenth century when the struggle between Britain and France in Europe had its counterpart in the New World, there were only 70,000 French settlers compared with 1,200,000 in the British colonies.

The superior numbers and resources of the British and their control of the sea resulted in the defeat of France. In 1763, Canada was ceded to Britain and Louisiana (the area west of the Mississippi and south of Canada) to Spain.*

Thus with French claims destroyed and Spanish power moribund, the future of the continent rested upon the efforts of the predominantly British settlers on the east coast.

British

More than a century elapsed after the discovery of the new continent before the British began to take a serious interest in it. At first their eyes were fixed on the Orient and their efforts were directed towards finding a way around America to China, Japan, and the East Indies. The North West Passage was not revealed and it is only in our own generation that a vessel has successfully crossed the Arctic Ocean from the Bering Straits to Hudson Bay.

---

* "Louisiana" became French again in 1800 but was sold by Napoleon to the U.S.A. three years later for $15,000,000.

Colonisation was organised by chartered and proprietary companies, some of them seeking homes for religious dissidents and political refugees. In the opinion prevailing at the time, colonies were to provide raw materials which the mother country was unable to produce itself and in return were to be supplied with manufactured goods. In this way trade would increase to the benefit of both parties.

In the southern colonies, this simple economic system was soon operating. The first permanent British settlement was founded at Jamestown, in 1607, on a small island in the James River. Within a dozen years Virginia was exporting tobacco to Britain. The plantations lined the rivers and each of them was, in effect, a small seaport. A tidewater location was essential while there was such dependence on the mother country for necessities and for marketing the staple crop. Maryland, founded in 1634, followed the example of Virginia and grew tobacco, while North Carolina (1670) concentrated on rice, sugar, and indigo. Georgia was founded much later, 1733, and after initial attempts to grow vines and rear silkworms, turned to cotton growing.

Settlement here was essentially rural, although Baltimore, Charleston, and Savannah were large and important ports. The plantation, worked by negro slaves and white indentured servants, was the dominant unit. Population was sparse but widely spread. Seventy years after the first settlers had landed, the population of Virginia was no larger than that of Stepney parish in London, but the area occupied by plantations exceeded that of England.

The size of the occupied area, which by 1700 included practically all the Coast Plain and Piedmont, can be explained by the largeness of the plantations, and the rapid spread of settlement by the continual search for undeveloped land to replace soils of holdings worn out by the growth of one particular crop year after year.

Besides the growth of staple crops, however, much subsistence farming took place. There were several poor settlers and former indentured servants who occupied only small farms. During the crucial years, the very existence of the inhabitants depended on whether they could support themselves with a minimum of help from the mother country. From the Indians they acquired new crops and methods of cultivation and knowledge of edible forest products. European crops and animals were introduced, but maize, previously unknown to the newcomers, became the dominant cereal.

The picture one gets of the southern colonies, then, is a land of large estates with a scattering of small farms. Towns were rare, except along the coast, and industries absent. In spite of the wide spread of population, many areas remained as forest or swamp.

New England was very different. Its climate did not permit the growth of special crops for the British market. The similarity of this area to the home country can be exaggerated; New England was indeed a "lustier land—a land of hotter summers and colder winters, of brighter sun and more tempestuous rain" (C. O. Sauer in *Climate and Man*). Nevertheless, little would grow here that could not be produced equally well in Britain. The first settlers, who had intended making a more southerly landfall, arrived at Plymouth, on the Cape Cod peninsula, in 1621. They were of sterner metal than those further south, but even so, they derived small reward cultivating a rugged and boulder-strewn land. The townships were planted on the coast, especially on the Boston Lowlands and spread slowly up the river valleys. The settlements were nucleated and frequently the land was held communally and divided into strips.

Fishing soon became a major occupation and this stimulated shipbuilding and trade. Dried and salted fish, together with timber and naval stores, were exported from a great number of ports. With the capital derived from commerce, industries were established to supply the local population and the agricultural areas further south.

The eastern sea-board between New England and the southern colonies was the point of entry for many European peoples. The Dutch had settled on Manhattan and spread up the Hudson Valley, where fur-trading posts were almost as numerous as agricultural settlements. In 1664 this land was ceded to England. Swedes, Finns, and Germans entered the area which was later to be divided among New Jersey, Delaware, and Pennsylvania. This area was intermediate in character between New England to the north and Maryland and Virginia to the south; physically it was more akin to the south, whilst its people had more in common with their northern neighbours. There was both dispersed and nucleated settlement, but slaves and very large estates were absent. Apart from furs, this area produced little for export and farming was mostly of the subsistence sort.

By the mid-eighteenth century, the thirteen colonies had a population estimated at 1,200,000. The settlers were confined to the stretch of country lying east of the Appalachians. These mountains were an obstacle to easy movement, but already trappers, soldiers, and traders had discovered the trails made by Indians and wild animals and were exploring the land to the west, where they came into contact with the French along the Ohio. When the War of Independence started in 1776, settlers were moving into the valleys west of the mountains in defiance of a Proclamation of 1763 which forbade white settlement and reserved the land for the Indians. It was the beginning of a movement which could not be halted. In less time than it took the early settlers to reach the crest of the Appalachians, a vast land had been won and new cities were arising on the Pacific Coast.

WESTWARD MOVEMENT ACROSS THE U.S.A.

Geographical conditions had a pronounced effect on the course of westward movement. Settlers had to face the problems posed by mountain ranges, rivers, thick forests, open prairies, and waterless deserts, and at times a hostile native population. Many of the difficulties could be avoided, but others could be overcome only by greater experience and with the help of new inventions. What would have proved insuperable to the seventeenth century immigrant was made easy for the nineteenth century settler by the development of new techniques and better equipment.

The Appalachians

The thirteen colonies were hemmed in by the Appalachians, a complex upland area, which, however, could be crossed in several places without excessive difficulty. But to penetrate beyond its fastnesses meant untying the link with the tidewater settlements. In fact, the presence of these uplands has been held to be of value in that they restricted the population to the strip of lowland on the east and delayed expansion until the settlement was consolidated. As late as 1800, almost two centuries after the first immigrants arrived, nine-tenths of the population was east of the Appalachians. But the time came when the Coast Plain and Piedmont were unable to offer sufficiently full possibilities to new settlers. Good land became scarce and the settlers followed westwards in the wake of traders, trappers, and frontiersmen.

The nature of the terrain and the pattern of the drainage led to the use of four main routes, each of which soon had a road constructed to carry the increasing traffic (Fig. 31). The easiest routeway through the system is the Hudson-Mohawk lowland, the highest point of which is only 445 ft above sea level, but this route was opened later than others and only after the Iroquois had been pacified. This tribe, the major element of the powerful Confederation of Five Nations, was an effective buffer between the French and

British settlements but eventually yielded its lands between Lakes Erie and Ontario and soon the Genesee Road was carrying a stream of settlers to the west.

The two earliest routes used gaps cut in the Blue Ridge by the Susquehanna and Potomac rivers. Here the coastal plain and Piedmont are narrow and the fertile valleys beyond were occupied by German, Scottish, and Irish immigrants in the mid-eighteenth century. Later settlers pushed on across the Allegheny Plateau

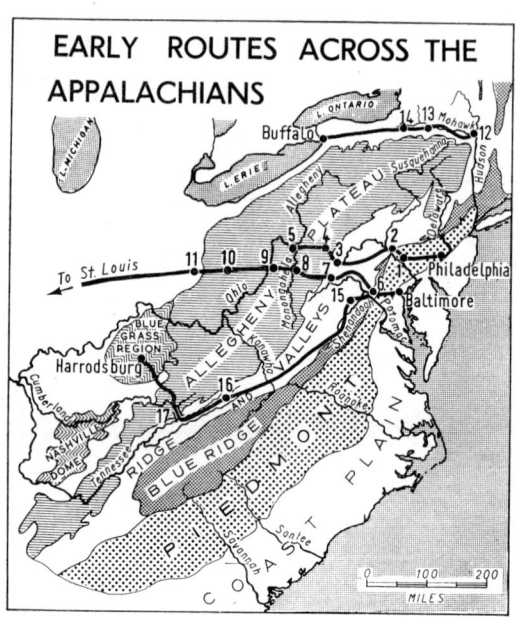

Fig. 31.

Pennsylvania Route: 1, Columbia; 2, Harrisburg; 3, Bedford; 4, Johnstown; 5, Pittsburgh.
Cumberland Road: 6, Harper's Ferry; 7, Cumberland; 8, Brownsville; 9, Wheeling; 10, Zanesville; 11, Columbus.
Genesee Road: 12, Cohoes; 13, Utica; 14, Syracuse.
Wilderness Road: 15, Winchester; 16, Abingdon; 17, Cumberland Gap.

to the Forks of the Ohio (the confluence of the Allegheny and Monongahela, where Pittsburgh now stands). This was the Pennsylvania route, with the Lancaster Pike carrying the traffic in its eastern section. The more southerly route was from Baltimore via the Cumberland Road, Harper's Ferry, and Cumberland to Wheeling on the Ohio below Pittsburgh. In this section of the

Appalachian zone, the divide between rivers draining east to the Susquehanna and Potomac and the tributaries of the Ohio, nowhere presents a serious obstacle to movement. Here the divide is on the Allegheny Plateau: further south it lies in the Ridge and Valley Province or along the Blue Ridge. And so the more northerly valleys were more useful as routeways.

However, the Allegheny Front, a steep escarpment, overlooking the Ridge and Valley Province on the west, is notched by the Cumberland River and this 1,600 ft deep gap was used by settlers on their way to the Blue Grass region of Kentucky. This is a fertile limestone basin in the barren sandstone plateau. The first trail here was blazed by Daniel Boone in 1775, and soon the Wilderness Road was constructed.

South of the Cumberland Gap the streams are longitudinal and flow to the Tennessee, which cuts across the plateau west of Chattanooga and thus provides another gap.

The Gulf Coast Plain is continuous with that along the Atlantic coast and there was no physical obstacle to movement westward from Georgia. As in the extreme north, however, Indians here were hostile. The land was held by the Five Civilised Tribes, among which the Creeks and the Cherokees were extremely powerful, and they were not dislodged until the second decade of the nineteenth century.

With the crossing of the mountains, the "frontier of settlement" began to move westwards with increasing momentum. The "frontier" was a zone separating the settled areas to the east from the unoccupied areas to the west. Generally speaking, this zone had a population density of two to six people a square mile.

The importance of the frontier in American history and thought has been great and the qualities which life on the frontier engendered, the pioneering spirit, self-reliance, individuality, a concentration on material needs, and a denigration of intellectual attainment, have left their mark on modern America. The frontier did not advance at a constant rate: it bulged westward in parts; it engulfed areas unfavourable for settlement; at times it was stationary (see Fig. 33).

Central Lowlands

The convergence of land routes on the Forks of the Ohio quickly led to the rise of Pittsburgh. Both here and at Wheeling, settlers embarked on a great variety of roughly constructed boats and rafts and sailed down the Ohio in search of new farms. The Ohio, flowing in the direction of the advancing frontier, became the highway to the west. A difference of 50 ft between the high-water and low-water levels of the river in some seasons, sandbanks and rapids all impeded navigation. Nevertheless, many flat-boats and keel-boats were to be seen floating downstream, especially in the spring when the crest of the floods facilitated travel. After 1811, steamboats were introduced, and it is a measure of the importance of this river that seventy-six were built here between 1815 and 1819. By 1818 there were 1,200 steam vessels plying for trade on the Ohio and Mississippi. In the early years, however, traffic was almost entirely downstream: powerful crews were needed to bring boats upstream and the journey from New Orleans to Pittsburgh took several months. It was the normal practice of settlers to break up their boats when they reached their destination and use the wood for houses and barns. The frontier advanced at a rapid rate. While some settlers were pushing on to the Mississippi at Cairo, others were penetrating the territory north-west of the Ohio, along the Wabash, Muskingum, and Scioto. South of the Ohio, the Kentucky and Cumberland rivers were the main thoroughfares. Land was cheap. The Federal Government inaugurated surveys whereby the land was divided into townships, each six miles square, and comprising thirty-six sections of 640 acres. Most of the settlers acquired titles to quarter-sections of 160 acres for as little as $1 per acre. The process of peopling this land was helped by land companies which advertised the cheap land in America and Europe. Gradually the landscape was altered and in place of the woodland appeared the characteristic Midwest chequer-board pattern.

By 1820, more than a quarter of the total population of the U.S.A. was west of the mountains, mainly in Kentucky, Tenessee, and the lands along the Ohio and its tributaries. The great problem for the people was finding a market for their produce. It was difficult to transport pork, timber, and grain across the Appalachians, although hogs could be driven to the eastern stockyards. The Mississippi and Ohio became the arteries of commerce and the area became tributary to New Orleans. Unlike the St Lawrence and Great Lakes, the Mississippi and Ohio were navigable the whole of the year and gave access to an expanding market, the southern plantations, and the riverside towns.

Thriving towns such as Cincinnati, Louisville, and St Louis arose on the river banks at strategic points. Industries developed to supply local needs and they were protected by distance from eastern competition. The eastern ports, in an effort to gain some of the trade they were losing to New Orleans, began constructing canals to the interior. Most were abandoned when it was found to be impossible to cross the Appalachian divide, but the Erie

Canal, a 360-mile waterway, using the Hudson-Mohawk gap, was opened in 1825. It was successful from the beginning: in 1826, 19,000 boats used the canal. Other canals connecting the Ohio with the Great Lakes had a brief period of prosperity before they were killed by competition with the railways. Only one of these, the Illinois Canal, which was reconstructed in the present century, is still in use: it links Chicago on Lake Michigan, with the Mississippi.

The frontier in the south started its westward movement later than in the centre and north, but soon the plantation economy was spreading across Alabama and Mississippi. A great stimulus to this expansion was the invention of a cotton gin by Eli Whitney. Its effect was revolutionary: cotton exports jumped from 192,000 lb. in 1792 to 6,000,000 lb. in 1795. The urge for more cotton led to a rapid advance of the frontier in the south.

By 1840, the frontier had crossed the Mississippi: its general course was along the 95th meridian and the Sabine River but many infertile areas in the Appalachians and Ozarks and around the western lakes were unoccupied or very sparsely inhabited. Fingers of settlement were creeping up the valleys of the right bank tributaries of the Mississippi. However, the frontier which had advanced without pause across the Mississippi basin, was now halted and it remained stationary for almost three decades (see Fig. 33).

The West

The Great Plains, upon which the frontier impinged, were thought of as a desert. This open grassland presented formidable difficulties to settlers. The rivers here, unlike those in the east, were useless for navigation except in short stretches by flat-bottomed boats at certain times of the year. The general lack of water, the tough prairie sod, and the shortage of timber, which was to be found only in the valleys, delayed settlement until new methods, techniques, and equipment were introduced.

Nevertheless, while the Great Plains were unoccupied, they were not unknown: thousands of migrants crossed the region before any settlements arose. These people were making their way to the far west, where the opportunities were greater. Fur-trappers had been active in the Rocky Mountains since the mid-eighteenth century and information about the area filtered back to the east. The first official exploration, undertaken by Lewis and Clark in 1804 revealed the nature of what became known as Oregon Territory, and later travellers added to the favourable picture that was drawn.

Western Routes.—Various routes were opened up across the plains during this period, linking the Mississippi-Missouri Valley with the area in the west (Fig. 32).

1. The first to be opened up was the Santa Fe Trail. This started at Independence, near Kansas City, ran west to join the Arkansas Valley, followed it upstream to the mountain front, and then turned south, reaching Santa Fe through a pass in the Sangre de Cristo Mountains. Santa Fe was the entrepôt of the Rio Grande Valley and was in Mexican territory. It was the possibility

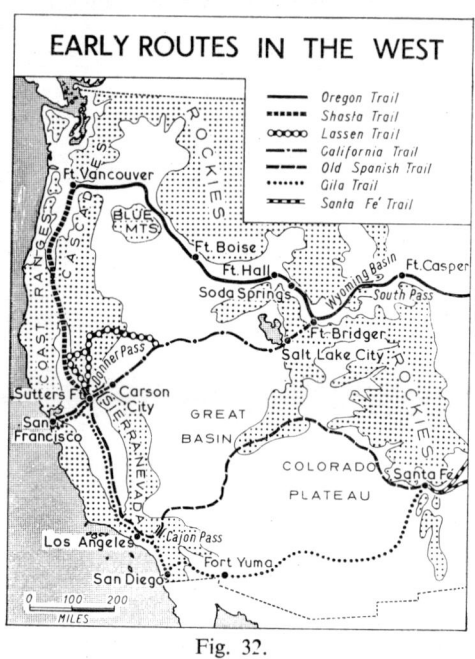

Fig. 32.

of trade that lured the first wagons to make the difficult and dangerous journey in 1822. Thereafter the caravan was a yearly event. American influence increased and the area became part of the U.S.A. in 1848. Santa Fe was connected to San Diego and Los Angeles by the Spanish Trail. This was the easiest route from the Mississippi to the west coast, but it was not much used by settlers: they were making for more northerly regions, and chose shorter, if more difficult routes.

2. The most famous of these was the Oregon Trail, 2,400 miles long and involving a journey of four months. It was used by

thousands of travellers: after 1845, about 10,000 wagons a year rolled westwards to Oregon Territory. The attraction of this region was the well-watered land. Of all places in the U.S.A. this region has a climate most closely resembling that of northwest Europe.

Council Bluffs, which faced Omaha across the Missouri, was the departure point for most expeditions. From here, the route followed the Platte and its northern fork as far as the mountains. Except around the headwaters of the North Platte, and in the extreme south, the Rockies present a steep and high front to the Plains. South Pass, the twenty-mile wide col, separates the North Platte and Colorado drainage systems. It was to the affluents of the Snake that the travellers next made their way. The route followed the Snake for some distance but later left the valley, turning north-west to cross the Blue Mountains and reach the Columbia at Walla Walla. While some immigrants remained in the interior valleys, most sought the lowlands in the Willamette Valley and around Puget Sound.

3. West of South Pass, the route bifurcated and the southern branch went to California, being known as the California Trail. It is estimated that 42,000 prospectors and settlers travelled to the Great Valley and San Francisco in 1849, the year after gold was first discovered. Of all the journeys, this was the most hazardous. The travellers remained close to the Humboldt River as they crossed the desert, but deaths from thirst were not infrequent. The Sierra Nevada were crossed by using the Donner Pass, where an ill-fated party had suffered desperate privation when attempting a winter journey.

Other routes crossed the Great Divide, but none were used as much as the three described above.

Minerals.—Until the middle of the nineteenth century it was primarily the demand for land in the Central Lowlands that motivated the frontier pioneers; afterwards, in the west, the course of settlement was more closely tied to the discovery of minerals. Gold was found in California in 1848 and started the first of many gold rushes. Others followed a decade or so later in Colorado, Idaho, Montana, and Nevada. The last gold rush in the U.S.A. was to the Black Hills of Dakota in 1876, but there were later strikes north of the 49th parallel, notably in the Klondike.

Towns sprang up almost overnight to accommodate the great influx of miners and prospectors. For a time prospecting and panning yielded big dividends, but as the richer and more accessible deposits were exhausted, the claims passed into the hands of large companies. The strong financial resources and mechanical equipment of these groups enabled the mining industry to continue. The erstwhile prospectors and miners either turned to farming or migrated to new mining areas.

It was the minerals that brought the people to western areas, and if irrigation water was available, some at least remained to cultivate the land. Where there was no water or where irrigation was not feasible, the exhaustion of the mineral meant the evacuation of the population. The ghost towns are the mute witnesses of former settlement. In the arid, intermontane area many of the settlements were, and still are, temporary ones, having their *raison d'etre* in the gold, silver, copper, lead, or zinc deposits.

The Civil War in the U.S.A. occurred between 1861 and 1865, but the pace of new settlement did not slacken. Indeed, the west was little affected. It was in the east that the greatest changes were made. The effect of the war on the southern states was little short of devastating: its legacy was one not only of social problems but also of serious economic stagnation. It is only in the last two or three decades that the Old South has been revitalised.

Owing to the war there was an increased demand for materials which stimulated the industries of the northern states, where the presence of raw materials, fuels, sources of power, and capital had already given rise to manufacturing. Along with the expansion of industry went the development of railways, which were to have a profound effect, not only on the war, but on the settlement and development of the west.

Railways

Railway construction had begun in the east in the eighteen-thirties. For the seaboard cities it was imperative that the Ohio Valley should be linked with the east coast so that produce would move to the Atlantic and not the Gulf coast. Also, of course, the rapidly increasing population of the interior created a market that eastern manufacturers wished to exploit. Already industries were rising in the interior because of the lack of good communications and competition. Pittsburgh was soon established as an iron and steel centre.

Between 1830 and 1860, 30,000 miles of track were laid. In the north, six lines crossed the Appalachians, while in the interior and the south short stub lines gave access to navigable water. In the following decades, more ambitious projects led to the linking of the major cities, many of which gained in importance as railway centres by virtue of their position, *e.g.* Chicago, Indianapolis, and Chattanooga.

The first transcontinental railway was opened in 1869, when the lines built east from California met those built west from Omaha, near Ogden in Utah. This was the Union Pacific line, the construction of which was motivated as much by political as economic considerations, for the joining of east and west reduced the separist tendencies of the western states The government had subsidised the Union Pacific Company by granting it 12,000,000 acres of land from the Public Domain, made up of alternate sections for several miles on each side of the track. Other lines were built across the Rockies to Los Angeles and Seattle and received similar aid. By 1890, there were 166,500 miles of track in the U.S.A.

The aim of the railway companies was to open up the empty lands that their lines served. Their eyes were not on large profits from the sale of land, but on expanding freight carriage as the land was peopled. Land was sold very cheaply and the result was the settling of the Great Plains. This vast grassland belt, which the early travellers had found so inimical, had been utilised as a reserve for the Indians. What is now Oklahoma was Indian territory and there were also reserves in what later became Kansas and Nebraska. Here the plain dwellers and the displaced eastern tribes eked out a meagre existence and were often dependent upon the government for food. Outside the true reserves other tribes like the Sioux in the north and the Commanche in the south still hunted the bison, although this means of existence was threatened when professional hunters arrived and began slaughtering the animals in huge numbers, almost to the point of extermination.

The existence of bison augured well for the development of cattle rearing, and this occupation received a fillip when the Civil War led to an increased demand for beef and the railways arrived to transport it to eastern markets. The cattle industry had started in Texas, and after the war, herds were driven north over recognised trails to stock the vacant grasslands or to be sent east. As the railways were pushed westwards practically every railhead became a cattle town. Two of the most notorious were Dodge City and Abilene.

But the railways, as well as making the cattle country, also destroyed it by bringing in settlers. These small farmers displaced the cattlemen who occupied large areas to which they had no claim. Soon the wheat lands of Minnesota, Nebraska, and the Dakotas were pouring cheap grain on to the world markets. (The decline of high farming in Britain coincided with, and was the result of, the opening up of the Great Plains.)

Improved techniques and equipment made the settlement of the Plains a less formidable task than earlier pioneers had envisaged: inexpensive barbed wire appeared at this time and was used to protect the settlers' crops from the unrestricted depredations of the cattle; a new steel plough enabled the tough prairie sod to be broken and the McCormick harvester permitted the grain to be cut easily and rapidly; a new drilling machine, which made possible the cheap construction of wells, overcame one of the serious problems, that of water-supply.

The railway companies advertised the cheap land in European countries and their lines brought to the region thousands of immigrants. The Indians were ousted from their reservations and the last considerable area of the U.S.A. fit for permanent settlement

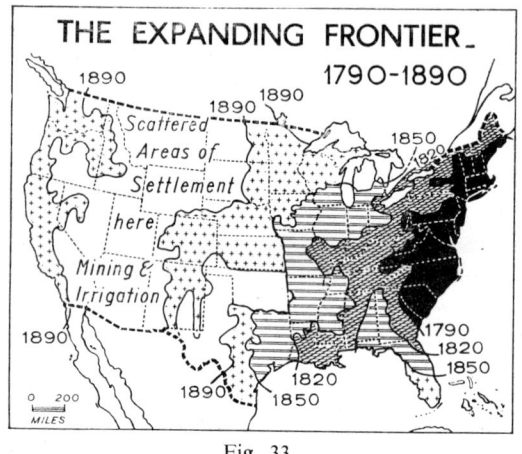

Fig. 33.

was occupied. In fact, rather too many settlers came, for there was an exodus later when a series of dry years exposed the unsuitability of the drier parts of the Great Plains for arable farming. Since that time, the area has experienced a fluctuating density of population, one that increases in wet cycles and decreases in dry ones.

In 1890, it was recognised officially in the government census that the frontier no longer existed (Fig. 33). The era of cheap and plentiful land was finishing. Millions of acres of the public domain had been claimed and occupied by a people not afraid of cutting ties with their homeland or of suffering immediate hardship for future rewards. The U.S.A. still has a considerable area which remains unclaimed, but this lies in the western half of the country where drought and mountainous terrain make settlement unlikely.

IMMIGRATION AND POPULATION

Although the amount of cultivated land has not increased much—there has in fact been a decrease in the acreage harvested during the last thirty years—the population has continued to grow. Until the nineteen-twenties almost unrestricted immigration was permitted and altogether about 30,000,000 people have entered the U.S.A. from Europe. Up to the latter part of the nineteenth century most of the immigrants came from north-west Europe: afterwards they were drawn mainly from the Mediterranean and eastern Europe. While the former group, the Irish, British, Scandinavians, and Germans made their way into the rural parts of the interior, the Italians and eastern Europeans tended to remain in the ports and cities of the north-east manufacturing belt. Some of these national groups have remained unassimilated, but for the majority the U.S.A. has become the melting pot. There are few Americans to-day who cannot claim at least one foreign-born grandparent or great-grandparent among their ancestors. During the last four decades immigration has been restricted: only a certain number of foreigners is permitted to settle in the country. To-day, then, the increase of population in the United States is a natural and internal one, practically unaffected by immigration. The present population of about 200,000,000 is expected to increase at an accelerating rate, but the increase is not, and is not expected to be, uniform over the whole country. The states that show the greatest increase are on the Pacific coast, and the South, particularly Texas, also has gains above the average. This perhaps reflects the increasingly greater opportunities in these regions. The Great Plains show an almost stationary population, although in some states there has been a decrease.

Of all the unassimilated groups in the United States, the pockets of Italians and eastern Europeans in the north-eastern cities, the Japanese and Chinese on the west coast, and the Mexicans in the south-west, it is the 24,000,000 negroes who pose the biggest problem. They were brought in as slaves in the seventeenth century and to-day their descendants account for one-tenth of the total population. For a long time they were confined to the southern states, where their labour permitted the growth and development of the plantation system. In the northern states negro slaves were rare and few were to be found north of Maryland, Virginia, and Kentucky. Naturally, they were, and are, most thickly concentrated in the areas most suitable for the growth of cotton, such as the Black Belt of Alabama, the Piedmont in Georgia and South Carolina, and the bottom lands of the Mississippi, in the state of Missouri. In some *counties* in these areas, they exceed the white population, but in no *state* is there a majority of negroes (Fig. 47). The white population is increasing more quickly and the percentage of negroes in the total population is declining. Segregation, which was widespread in the past, is dying out in spite of the efforts of certain Southerners to maintain it. The federal government refuses to sanction segregation in any form and has used its legal authority to remove discriminatory practices, but the individual states still have legislative measures which hinder, if they do not actually forbid, the negro assuming a position in society equal with the white.

Since the days before the Civil War, when slavery was declared illegal north of the Compromise Line (concurrent with the northern boundary of Missouri), negroes have been leaving the south and moving north. This movement has been particularly marked in the last two or three decades. The industrial cities, New York, Pittsburgh, Detroit, and Chicago have substantial negro populations. More recently there has been a considerable movement to the Pacific states. Hitherto, the negro in the south has been predominantly a rural dweller: in the north his habitation is invariably urban. Now, the increasing industrialisation of the south is leading to a decrease in rural and an increase in urban population and this change affects the negro as well as the white.

THE GROWTH OF CANADA

Canada was peopled much later than the United States. When the land became British in 1763, the population was about 70,000 and was concentrated almost entirely along the 200-mile stretch of the St Lawrence Valley, between Quebec and Montreal, with about ten houses per square mile. The influx of the American Loyalists to the Maritime Provinces and Upper Canada and some Scottish immigrants as well as the natural increase, raised the population to about 600,000 by 1814. Despite the explorations of the French *coureurs de bois* and the expeditions organised by the two great fur companies, the Hudson's Bay Company and the North West Company, which had revealed the lie of the land, there was little movement of settlers to the interior. The Arctic coastlands were known and the west coast had been reached by Mackenzie a decade before Lewis and Clark made their expedition.

INDIANS OF THE SOUTH-WEST

Above: Many of the 60,000 Navajo Indians in Arizona, Utah and New Mexico make a living raising sheep and goats and weaving blanket and rugs. (*Santa Fé Railway.*)

Below: This stone and adobe pueblo of the sedentary Hopi Indians occupies a defensive site the top of a narrow mesa in Arizona. Corn, beans, pumpkins, and melons are grown on y, irrigated fields on the lower ground. (*Fairchild Aerial Surveys Inc.*)

Above: A New England dairy farm near Groton in Vermont. Note the rich pasture, large barn and silo. (*Vermont Development Commission*.)
Below: Tobacco fields in the Connecticut Valley near Northampton, Mass. Note the large curing sheds. The Connecticut Valley produces about one per cent. of the U.S.A. crop. (*Standard Oil Co., N.J.*)

SETTLEMENT OF CANADA

In Canada the Western Mountains have lower passes and are narrower. Fur-trappers penetrated this area and spread southwards into Oregon Territory which was open to both American and British settlement until 1846. In this year the boundary which, east of the Rockies, had been fixed on the 49th parallel in 1818, was extended to the west coast.

Actually, it was the Laurentian Shield, a bleak and forbidding area abutting directly on to Lake Superior and Lake Huron that deterred the extension of the settled area. The magnificent gateway afforded by the St Lawrence was for a long time unused because of this barrier.

In 1867, when the country was reorganised, the population was only 3,500,000: the most densely settled areas were Ontario

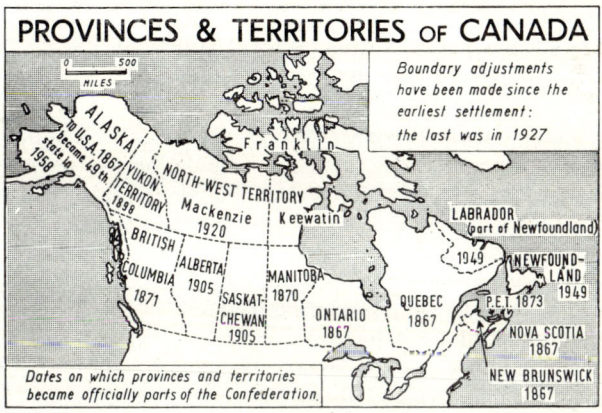

Fig. 34.

(formerly Upper Canada), Quebec (Lower Canada), and the Maritime Provinces. British Columbia had a white population of 8,000 and did not enter the Confederation until 1871 (Fig. 34). Some immigrants and even settlers of long-standing migrated to the U.S.A., where the railways were opening up the western lands and offering greater opportunities than were to be found in the northern dominion.

Within half a century this movement was to be reversed. The building of railways in the east in the middle decades of the century culminated in 1885 in the first transcontinental line. As with similar American railways, the motive was political rather than economic. British Columbia and Manitoba (which was first settled in 1813 and admitted as a province in 1870) were almost isolated from the Canadian east and had good communications with adjacent U.S.A. areas to the south. The Canadian Pacific Railway was necessary if they were to remain Canadian. This line also opened up the Prairies to settlement. Saskatchewan and Alberta became provinces in 1905 and attracted about one-third of their settlers from the nearby states south of the border, where land was becoming scarcer and more expensive. About 70,000,000 acres were given away by the C.P.R., the Hudson's Bay Company, and the Canadian Government. The Prairies became a patchwork quilt of different nationalities, British, American, Irish, Slav, Memnonite, and Douboukhor.

Contemporary with the settlement of the Prairies was the development of the Shield. The exploitation of mineral and power resources has now extended settlement beyond the Arctic Circle. This is the new frontier of North America: on it, the role that the railways played further south has been undertaken by air transport. It is here that the most outstanding changes are likely to occur.

The main social problem concerns the French-Canadians who account for one-third of the total population. They are concentrated in the Province of Quebec, but their rapid increase has led to the migration of these people east into the Maritime Provinces, west into Ontario, and south into New England. For a long time traditional and conservative peasants closely tied to their parish and church, they, like the rest of the Canadians, are moving to the towns and undertaking industrial work. The Eskimos and Indians account for only one per cent. of the population, and the Germans, Ukrainians, Scandinavians, Dutch, Jews, and Poles together between 20 per cent. and 25 per cent.

CONCLUSION

In the three centuries and a half that have elapsed since the first white settlers entered the continent, the face of North America has been considerably altered. Much of the original vegetation has been cleared and the land brought into cultivation; its rivers have been a means of transport and have supplied water for irrigation and power for industry; its mineral resources have been exploited, and have given rise to industries. To serve the farms and towns, a vast and intricate web of roads and railways has been woven across the continent.

This remarkable and rapid development can be attributed to numerous factors, but of these, three are outstanding. First must be mentioned the pioneering spirit of the early settlers and immigrants. They came to America from a variety of motives, but almost all were prepared to endure the most extreme hardships and take the utmost risks for the sake of future freedom, security, and prosperity. Secondly, there was the abundance of cheap or free land which attracted the host of immigrants from Europe during the nineteenth century, and which added impetus to the westward movement of the frontier. The third factor was the improvement of tools and techniques which stimulated the development of agriculture, industry, and communications and made easier the absorption of the increasing population.

Different parts of the continent offered different possibilities to the settlers. The climate, soils, and topography limited the types of farming that could be practised in different areas, and the geology determined whether mining was possible. Nevertheless, the settlers adapted themselves to their environment in different ways, depending upon their cultural background and the tools and techniques at their disposal. The regional differences that may be discerned are a result of both physical and human factors. The remaining chapters of this book are devoted to a study of the major regions of the continent.

CHAPTER V

NEW ENGLAND

Introduction

New England is the smallest and most closely-knit of all the American regions. In its area of about 65,000 square miles live approximately 11 million people. It is a land of bleak winters and warm summers, of forests and lakes, of generally rolling uplands which only occasionally become rugged. In the north, the region retains much of its original appearance with a few small townships of wooden houses surrounded by irregular fields. In the south, the landscape is essentially urban and industrial. To the visitor it often appears to have more in common with parts of Britain than with other regions of the U.S.A.

Its claim to be regarded as an entity is based, not only on its geographical characteristics, but also on its distinctive historical development. Settlement commenced in the seventeenth century and the region quickly became pre-eminent. The early flowering of civilisation here has been attributed to the stimulus of an environment rigorous enough to demand effort and initiative, but not so harsh as to stultify development.

"The optimum climatic area along the North American seaboard has a northern limit at the northern boundary of Massachusetts which corresponds to its southern limit at the more celebrated Mason and Dixon Line. If it is a fact that, beyond the southern boundary of Pennsylvania, the challenge of the physical environment becomes deficient in severity and therefore positively relaxing in its effect on human energies, it is also a fact that, beyond the northern boundary of Massachusetts, the same challenge becomes excessive in severity and therefore repressive. And, in terms of the human response, the effects of repression and relaxation are identical. In areas in which either of these two conditions prevails, the human respondent to the challenge is not stimulated to respond with as great effect as in the optimum area in which the highest physical stimulus is administered by a challenge of mean severity between the relaxing and repressive means." (A. J. Toynbee, *A Study of History*, Volume 2, Chapter 7.)

So pervasive is the sense of the past, that the name itself, New England, has strong emotional overtones. For many people it is the embodiment of the highest American traditions and culture. (Yale and Harvard, two of the oldest and most famous of American universities, are both in New England.) Making allowances for its size and population, it has certainly produced more well-known men than any other region, and has exercised a disproportionate influence on the material and spiritual life of the nation. Massachusetts was the dominant colony until 1776, and the foremost state long after independence was achieved. Its supremacy was challenged only when the U.S.A. became a "continental" as opposed to a "sea-board" power. With the movement of people to the interior, New England lost its pre-eminent position. Whereas once it was the economic and cultural centre of the nation, to-day it suffers from its peripheral position.

Relief

The region comprises six states, Maine, Vermont, New Hampshire, Massachusetts, Connecticut, and Rhode Island. Altogether, they cover an area of 66,608 square miles (*i.e.* slightly larger than England and Wales) or about one-fortieth of the U.S.A. To the east and south lies the Atlantic, while northward the region merges imperceptibly into the Maritime Provinces of Canada. On the west, the boundary is the Hudson-Champlain depression.

This depression can be regarded as a northward extension of the Great Appalachian Valley, and the uplands of New England correspond to the Older Appalachians farther south (Blue Ridge and Piedmont). As noted in Chapter I, the rocks are old and generally resistant to erosion. They were folded during the Caledonian mountain-building period and severely faulted during that and later orogenies. There are large areas of igneous and metamorphic rock which usually form the higher ridges and uplands. The whole area was reduced to a peneplain which was later uplifted—more in the north and west than in the south and east—to form the surface upon which the present features have been carved. There are two upland masses, both trending north to south, the western one comprising the Green Mountains and Taconic Range, the eastern one culminating in the White Mountains. The latter rise to over 5,000 ft, but the general level of the plateau is from 1,500 ft to 2,000 ft (Fig. 35).

Separating the two uplands is the Connecticut Valley, the lower part of which is one of the few areas of extensive lowland in the region. It measures ninety miles by eighteen miles, and is composed of unresistant Triassic rocks with interbedded lava sills, the whole formation being down-faulted into the crystalline complex. There is no real coast plain of young sedimentary rocks as there is south of New York, but along the littoral and extending twenty to forty miles inland is a rolling lowland mantled with glacial drift. The coast itself is indented and there are numerous islands. The rias of Maine and the bays, Boston Bay and Narragansett Bay, are the result of submergence, but raised beaches in Maine indicate some emergence — as much as 300 ft in places—in post-glacial times.

The whole of New England was glaciated by ice-sheets which stretched as far south as Long Island, Nantucket, and Martha's Vineyard. These islands are simply the upstanding part of the terminal moraine. The drift cover on the mainland is not continuous and varies both in constitution and thickness from place to place. It is thickest on the lowlands, where, however, it rarely exceeds thirty feet and gives only poor, boulder-strewn soils.

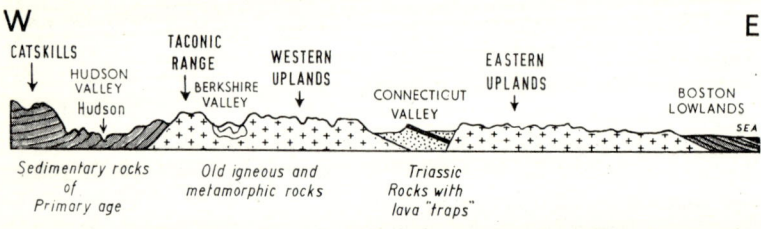

SECTION W. E. ACROSS NEW ENGLAND
Fig. 35.

Around Boston Bay are many drumlins (*e.g.* Bunker's Hill), while on the Cape Cod peninsula are outwash sands. The best soils occur where there were temporary glacial lakes, as in the lower Connecticut Valley. In the north, where little soil remains, are thousands of lakes occupying rock basins and moraine-dammed valleys. Many rivers were diverted from their original courses during this epoch and now follow tortuous paths to the sea. The Connecticut, for instance, leaves its former valley which is cut in Triassic rocks, to cross south-eastwards over much more resistant rock for about twenty-five miles before reaching the sea. Many waterfalls occur, and at these points on the rivers power has been developed.

Climate

The climate of New England has continental characteristics. This is because of the region's location on the east side of the continent in the track of outblowing air from the interior in winter.

New England lies athwart the regular path of the depressions which cross the region at the rate of about two a week. The weather is a succession of storms accompanied by rain in summer and snow in winter with intervening two or three day periods of fair weather which is warm in summer and cold in winter.

The rainfall is distributed evenly throughout the year, and occurs on an average about one day in three. Nowhere does the mean annual total fall below 30 in. Totals are lowest in the north and west: the uplands and the south-east experience over 40 in., while the highest amount, 56 in., falls in southern Connecticut.

NEW ENGLAND

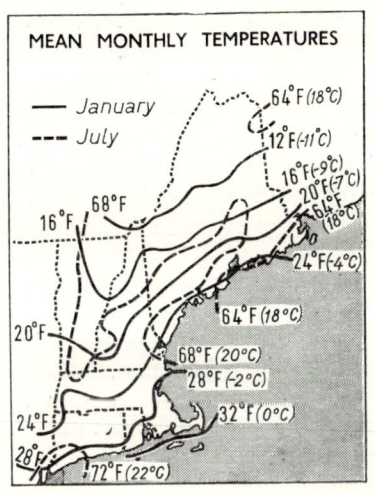 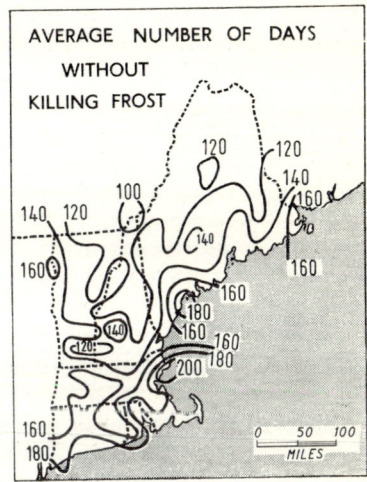

Fig. 36.

Winters are long and severe with mean January temperatures of under 32° F. (0° C.) for the whole region (see Fig. 36). Aroostook Valley in northern Maine has under 10° F. (−12° C.) in this month. Snow lies for more than three months except in the extreme south and along the coast, and because of the snow-melt there are, occasionally, disastrous spring floods. That they are not more frequent is due solely to the numerous lakes which act as reservoirs and regulators.

Summers are short but warm. The mean July temperatures vary from over 70° F. (21° C.) in the south to 62° F. (17° C.) in the north-east. Summer thunderstorms and hailstorms frequently damage crops and sometimes in autumn a vigorous hurricane from low latitudes in the Atlantic might pass along the coast. Fog is prevalent along the coast of Maine, which experiences sixty foggy days a year, but is much less frequent in the south and interior. The growing season, which is measured from the last killing frost of spring to the first killing frost of autumn, ranges from over 180 days in the south-east to under 120 days in the north (see Fig. 36).

Forestry

The natural vegetation of New England is forest, coniferous in the north and mixed and deciduous in the south. When the first settlers arrived practically the whole of the area was covered with trees. The hardwoods provided building materials and fuel, and the land they grew on was gradually cleared to make way for crops and pasture. There are still areas of hardwoods which are extremely colourful in the autumn and attract tourists from the north-eastern cities. Maples are tapped in spring for syrup. But the prize trees were the softwoods. Many New England homes are built of white pine, the most prized tree of all. This wood was in great demand for shipbuilding while the other conifers provided naval stores as well as timber.

Lumbering reached its peak in the first half of the nineteenth century: it declined when stands of white pine were becoming exhausted and other forested regions of the country were being opened up. To-day, about three-quarters of the region is forested, the greatest proportion of wooded land being in Maine, but much of the forest is secondary growth. The remaining stands consist primarily of spruce and fir which are used almost entirely as pulpwood and represent only 5 per cent. of the total reserves of the country and only $2\frac{1}{2}$ per cent. of the country's saw timber.

Present demand exceeds the local supply and half the lumber used in the pulp mills comes from other regions or from Canada. The proportion of local wood used may decrease, for only recently have efforts been made to conserve existing stands and re-afforest cut-over areas. The annual cut, which accounts for about $2\frac{1}{2}$ per cent. of the U.S.A. production, still exceeds the annual growth.

Most of the pulp and paper mills are (*a*) in the north where softwood stands are most extensive, (*b*) near the coast so that sulphur, clay, and soda, and sometimes coal, can be easily imported, and (*c*) on a river (*e.g.* Penobscot, Kennebec, and Androscoggin) to make use of both water and power. There are over fifty paper mills in Maine. The manufacture of thirty tons of pulp requires 100 tons of pulpwood, 120 tons of coal (or its equivalent in electricity), and 3 million gallons of water. Recently, ways have been found of making pulp and paper from hardwood. Finer paper, for which many materials are imported, is manufactured in the Connecticut Valley at Holyoke.

Agriculture

The combination of poor, boulder-strewn soils and short growing season limits the amount of farming that can be carried out and restricts the variety of crops that can be grown. In fact, New England has the lowest amount of improved land per head of population of all the major regions of the U.S.A. Moderately fertile soil occurs only in small patches and the farms themselves are small. Machinery cannot be used on a large scale—although there are mechanical stone-pickers—and the region cannot compete with the fertile and more easily worked lands farther west. During the nineteenth century, many New England farmers abandoned their own homes and moved west to the newly-opened Prairies: others were attracted to the factories and industrial towns then rising in the river valleys The consequence is that to-day the amount of cultivated land is only 40 per cent. of what it was in 1860. There are 7·7 million acres of land in farms (*i.e.* 18·2 per cent. of the whole area), but of this only 5·5 million acres are agricultural land, the remainder being woodland and forest. The decline has increased in pace since 1920.

"Now, for almost a century deserted farms in New Hampshire have been growing up to blueberry pasture, woodland, and forest. The sturdy population that was once evenly distributed over thousands of square miles of the stony upland has slowly and steadily moved down from the hilltops, emigrating to distant places, or lingering yet awhile in the valleys. Large tracts of land have been abandoned or have become the summer homes and playgrounds of well-to-do vacation seekers from the cities." (J. W. Goldthwait, "A Town that has gone Downhill", *Geographical Review*, 1927.)

New England can be regarded as part of the Hay and Dairying Belt which extends from the Atlantic coast westwards to Wisconsin. The cool, damp climate is better suited to grass and fodder crops than to grain. General farming with emphasis on dairying is the common agricultural economy (see Fig. 37). But certain areas are outstanding for milk production. Over 80 per cent. of the farmers of Vermont are dairymen, and in this state are 236,000 of New England's 527,000 milk cows; they are concentrated in the Champlain-Richelieu Valley, the floor of which has small fields of grass and fodder crops, while the hillsides are given over to apple orchards (see plate facing p. 97). Most of the milk is sold fresh to nearby industrial cities of the north-east. On most dairy farms poultry-raising plays an important subsidiary role. In recent years, with the development of quick freezing methods, the number of fowls has increased and there is a flourishing broiler industry.

Agriculture is more intensive in the south: towards the north, farming is more general and less prosperous. The income of

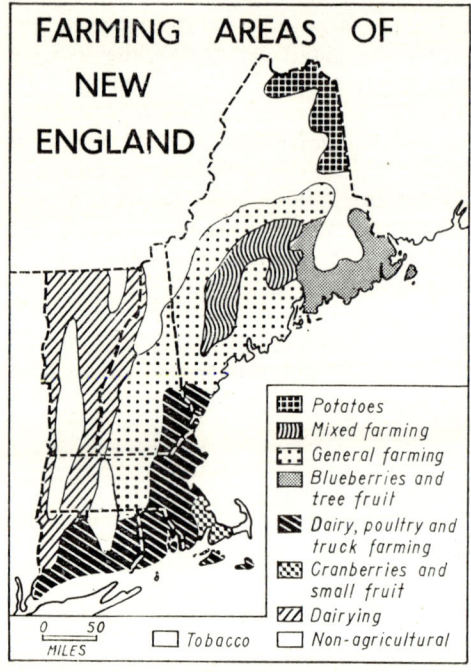

Fig. 37.
Tobacco is grown in the Connecticut Valley.

farmers here is often supplemented by the sale of timber or maple syrup. Many farms have been taken over by city businessmen, either as vacation homes or for part-time farming. The recreation industry in fact is often more important than farming: the cash income from crops and livestock in New Hampshire is about $60 million, while that from tourists is $210 million.

There is a certain amount of specialisation. The valleys of north Maine, particularly the Aroostook Valley, are noted for potatoes which thrive in the light sandy loams under cool, moist skies. This area produces about 13 per cent. of the U.S.A.'s potato crop. The Connecticut Valley produces high quality cigar tobacco (9 million lb. in 1967). Tobacco is grown on the alluvial terraces above the river and in certain districts is covered with cheese-cloth which reduces loss of moisture from the soil and increases the humidity. The soils here, which are derived from Triassic rocks, impart a desirable flavour to the leaves. Large tobacco barns are a common feature of the landscape (see plate facing p. 97). The Connecticut Valley is also noted for vegetables. Small truck farms grow onions, potatoes, sweet-corn, asparagus, tomatoes, cauliflowers, brussels sprouts, and strawberries, both for canning and for sale in the urban centres.

The bogs of Cape Cod peninsula have been utilised for growing cranberries (used in large quantities to make the sauce which garnishes the Thanksgiving Day turkey). Farms average about one acre in size and yield between twenty-five and forty barrels of fruit. Labour requirements are high and there is a large investment per acre for the ground requires careful preparation, and cranberries need careful tending and harvesting. The soils are acidic: they may be deliberately flooded if frost is forecast in order to protect the crop. Along the east coast of Maine are the "blueberry barrens", areas of heavily leached acidic podsols, which produce most of the nation's blueberry crop. A high proportion of the output is canned.

Fishing

Off the coast is one of the most productive fishing grounds in the world. Most of the fishing fleets are based on ports in Newfoundland and the Maritime Provinces. Nevertheless, New England's catch (valued at about $78 million annually), although less impressive than that of its northern neighbours, amounts to one-sixth of the total catch of the U.S.A. Fishing was the cornerstone of the region's prosperity for more than 150 years. It was the trading of fish in return for the products of other regions—especially of the West Indies—which led to the rise of New England as the commercial hub of the nation. Shipbuilding was a natural outcome of fishing and trading.

The main ports are Gloucester, Boston, New Bedford, and Portland, but there are many smaller centres, mostly in Maine where the submerged coast offers several sheltered harbours. The boats, most of which are oil-driven trawlers, fish both inshore and on the banks which extend as a line of broad submarine elevations from Newfoundland to Nantucket. Only about one-fifth of the catch comes from the banks: the rest is netted in New England's own waters. Haddock and cod form the bulk of the catch, but herring, mackerel, and halibut are also landed in large quantities. Formerly much of the catch was salted or dried: now very little is treated in this way. Over one-third is marketed fresh and over one-third is frozen. Shellfish are an important inshore catch, the Maine coast being especially noted for lobsters.

The fishing industry occupies only a small fraction of the population, in all about 18,500 men. It has declined during the present century because of high operating costs, competition from other countries, and lack of modern equipment. Many former fishing ports now derive their prosperity from summer visitors.

The Rise of Industry

The manufacturing industries of the U.S.A. began in New England. In colonial days, the need for domestic equipment led to a primitive sort of industry in the coastal settlements. A wide variety of goods was made (for the early colonists had to be more or less self-sufficient) ranging from pans, horseshoes, and nails to clothing, boots, weapons, and farm implements. More important, however, were fishing and forestry, and as these developed so capital accumulated. These industries stimulated trade and ship-building, thus creating further prosperity. The money was invested in the expanding industries which soon began to supply all the American colonies and which were making New England the workshop of the nation.

About 1750, enterprising industrialists began to harness the power of the rivers for working small mills. In the glaciated valleys were numerous falls and rapids. At practically every water-power site arose a settlement. Unbelievably small falls were utilised but many of the factories did not survive for long. It was in the larger valleys where the greatest falls were found that the towns prospered most. The whole of the Blackstone Valley from Worcester to Providence became virtually one continuous mill village. Lowell and Lawrence were established where there were falls of 32 ft and 26 ft respectively on the Merrimac River. Holyoke is situated where the Connecticut River, diverted from its original course during the Ice Age, drops 70 ft in two miles.

Soon, particular industries came to dominate certain valleys. This is explained by the fact that the valleys are isolated and cut off from one another by rugged uplands. Once a certain industry arose in one centre, it spread to others in the valley by imitation. In the case of some industries, the specialised nature of the finished product created the need for a wide range of semi-finished material and components, and factories were established near the main works to supply these.

With the introduction of the steam engine, the coastal towns became more important, for the coal (and later, oil) had to be brought by sea. Some towns, such as Fall River, had the combined advantage of water-power and a tidewater location. The inland towns were saved from decline when hydro-electricity replaced water-power. Even so, it is estimated that only about 15 per cent. of the industry is based on hydro-electricity; the remainder uses power derived from coal or oil. A marked increase in hydro-electricity production is unlikely for many of the best sites have already been developed. The proportion of developed to potential hydro-electricity is greater in this region than in any other region of the U.S.A. Production in New England is less than one-twentieth of that of the nation. Unharnessed power is available only in Maine where it is less accessible and less needed.

The early start and readily accessible power are two factors which account in large measure for the industrialisation of the region. Even the initially unfavourable factors were, paradoxically, of value. The lack of good agricultural land meant that the inhabitants concentrated more on fishing, lumbering, and trade. Thus there was made available the capital to buy raw materials and equipment. Farmers were only too easily persuaded to forsake their farms for a more prosperous life in the factories. As this region was the point of entry for many of the immigrants, finding labour was never a serious problem.

The inherited fixed capital—factories, workshops, and power plants—and the skill of the working population which derives not only from the workshop, but also from the many technical institutions in the region are the main assets of New England and it is upon these that the future of industry will primarily rest.

Manufacturing

In New England's small area are concentrated 5 per cent. of the nation's population and 9 per cent. of its labour force. The industries are found mainly in the south: apart from the manufacture of pulp and paper, there are few industries north of a line joining Portland and Holyoke. The nine standard metropolitan areas (*i.e.* a town of over 50,000 people, together with its "hinterland", both together having over 40,000 workers in industry) are all in Massachusetts, Connecticut, and Rhode Island.

The largest employers of labour are the industries making machinery (327,000), textiles (168,000), leather (112,000), fabricated metal goods (106,000), and transport equipment (106,000). The total labour force exceeds one and a half million workers, and those not accounted for above are distributed among a wide range of smaller industries.

Textile Manufacturing, one of the oldest industries, remains of considerable importance with 16 per cent. of all the textile mill

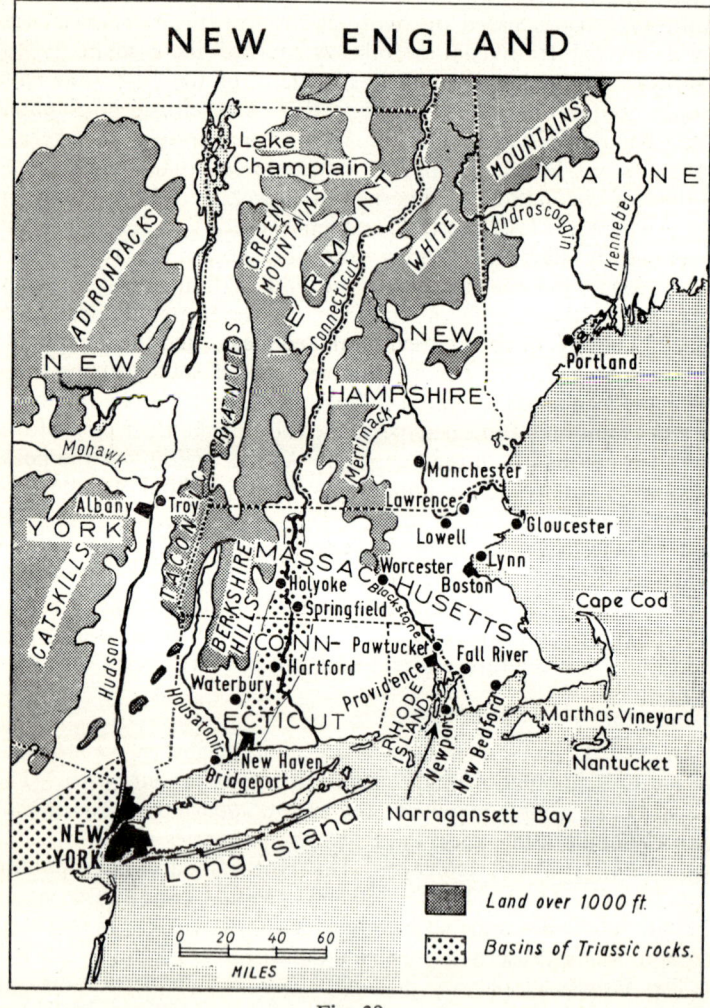

Fig. 38.

workers in the country. The first cotton mill was established in 1790 and others quickly arose at the power sites on the rivers, which also provided soft water for bleaching, dyeing, and washing. To-day the industry is concentrated at Manchester, Lowell, and Lawrence in the Merrimac Valley, and at Worcester, Pawtucket, Fall River, and New Bedford in the Blackstone Valley-Narragansett Bay area.

The raw cotton is shipped from the South, where, before the Civil War, there was no cotton manufacturing. After the war, factories did spring up and by 1924, the South had outstripped New England in the production of cotton cloth. Of the 20·5 million cotton spindles in the U.S.A. at present, 18·3 are in the cotton states and only 2·1 million in New England. The South has more modern factories and more efficient machinery, easier access to raw materials and fuel, and benefits from lower labour and land costs. Since the end of World War II the decline of the cotton industry in New England has been drastic. In 1939, textile mills employed 25 per cent. of the region's labour force: in 1954, the figure was under 12 per cent. Unemployment has become a serious problem in the cotton towns, particularly those which have few other industries. Lowell and Lawrence have been very badly hit by this decline.

Although it was the locally available wool which gave rise to the woollen and worsted industry, almost all the wool is now imported through Boston, the leading wool market of the country. For a long time the proximity of the woollen towns to the large clothing industry of New York and to the large market of the north-east preserved New England as the chief centre of the woollen industry. Now it is declining. Since 1945 New England has lost ground, again to the South, and output has been almost halved.

The Leather Industries are important in the region, for here are concentrated 30 per cent. of all the leather workers in the country. Leather tanning began soon after colonisation and was quickly established as a national industry based on local hides and tan bark. The modern industry is largely concerned with the manufacture of footwear and is located in the towns around Boston. Brockton and Haverhill concentrate on men's shoes and Lynn on women's shoes.

This industry has declined, though not as seriously as the textile industry, in face of competition from other regions, particularly the Midwest. But the decline has been compensated to some extent by the development of rubber industries in the region. These were attracted first by the concentration here of footwear manufacturing. Now, there are, in addition to rubber footwear factories, works producing tyres, and many rubber items for the rapidly growing electrical industries.

It is surprising that the *metal and machinery industries* should be so important in New England, where the necessary raw materials and fuel are lacking. There are only two small steel furnaces in the whole of the region, both on tidewater, at Bridgeport and near Boston. The only blast furnace, at Everett, and a large steel works at Worcester have recently closed. Much of the metal has to be brought from elsewhere in semi-finished form. Nevertheless, there has developed an extremely diverse industry utilising many different metals and turning out a range of products varying from ships and aircraft engines to small instruments and pieces of jewellery. All have this in common: they are highly finished and specialised, use only small amounts of raw material in comparison with their price, and depend to a large extent upon the skill of the workers. This metal-working industry can be traced back to the humble manufacturing of hardware and domestic equipment during colonial times.

Although most towns have some workers in engineering or metal-working, these industries are concentrated in south-west Connecticut and the Connecticut Valley. In the former are the metropolitan areas of Bridgeport, New Haven, Waterbury, and New Britain-Bristol, which produce hardware and small machinery of all sorts for homes, offices, and industry. In the Connecticut Valley are the Springfield-Holyoke metropolitan area which is noted for electrical machinery, particularly refrigerators, and metal goods as well as paper and textiles, and the Hartford metropolitan area which has two dominant industries, the manufacture of aircraft engines and propellors, and office machinery (typewriters, dictating machines, etc.). Hartford is also the insurance centre of the U.S.A. Outlying centres are Worcester, which produces textile machinery, and Providence, which has long been famous for jewellery and silverware.

Special mention must be made of the manufacture of *electrical machinery*. A great deal of development has taken place since World War II and the industry has expanded rapidly since 1939. There are several research and training establishments in New England, particularly around Boston, and these attract new enterprises which develop the new products and processes discovered in the laboratories. Many of these enterprises are small and are located in vacated textile mills. Boston is the chief centre of this

Above: A levee along the Atchafalaya River, a tributary of the Mississippi, in Louisiana, protects low-lying farms from inundation. (*U.S.I.S.*)

Below: New York, looking north, with Jersey City and the Hudson River on the left, Manhattan in the centre, and East River and Brooklyn on the right. See Fig. 44. (*Fairchild Aerial Survey Inc.*)

Above: Part of the stockyards at Omaha, Nebraska, which, after Chicago, is the largest meat-packing centre in the U.S.A. (*Union Pacific.*)

Below: The large oil refinery at Baton Rouge. Note the tankers and barges on the Mississippi and the ill-drained land next to the river. (*Standard Oil Co., N.J.*)

industry and supplies electronic tubes, transistors, radio, and telephone equipment as well as a whole range of electrical apparatus for industry to a rapidly expanding market.

The *chemical industry* has also progressed remarkably since 1939. Again, this development has been largely due to the research work carried out in the region. The labour force remains small but the value of the products (plastics, drugs, etc.) is high. Further expansion seems likely to be limited by lack of power and raw materials. Boston and Springfield-Holyoke are the leading centres.

Industrial Trends

Between the two world wars, industry in New England declined. In most industries the decline was relative, in that as the market expanded New England ceased to maintain its share of the market and lost ground to industries in other regions. In some cases, notably in the case of cotton, the decline was absolute: output dropped, factories were closed, and workers became unemployed.

Just as farming in the region suffered a setback when the West was opened up, so industry declined in face of competition from places in other regions which found themselves better situated for obtaining raw materials, fuel, and power, and for supplying the market. While the market was confined to the eastern seaboard New England remained pre-eminent. To-day, the market extends from the Atlantic to the Pacific and New England, because of its peripheral position, is badly placed to supply it. Transport costs are relatively high and the region lacks raw materials and fuel.

Since 1939 New England as a whole has been prosperous. The gloomy pre-war prognostications of the economists have not materialised. The renewed prosperity has been largely due to the inflow of new industries and the production of new materials. The attraction of the region may be attributed to (*a*) its pool of skilled labour (including the steady output of technicians from the large number of institutes of higher education), (*b*) the presence in the area of several research establishments (especially in the fields of chemistry and electronics), and (*c*) the help offered by local and regional development organisations which seek to expand industries.

The present industrial structure bears little relation to that of the past. In 1919, 40 per cent. of the labour force was employed in the textile and leather industries: to-day, the figure is under 20 per cent. The withering of these industries and the influx of new ones has led to greater industrial diversity, and consequently to greater stability, for one-industry towns are badly hit in times of depression. The textile towns which have few alternative interests are the problem areas in a region of general prosperity. Their revival seems unlikely if, as at present, no government assistance is forthcoming.

In spite of its peripheral position and its lack of materials and fuel, New England in the post-war period has demonstrated its buoyancy and capacity to adapt itself to changing circumstances. How long it will continue to do so will depend upon the relative strength of the factors which attract and those which repel new industries.

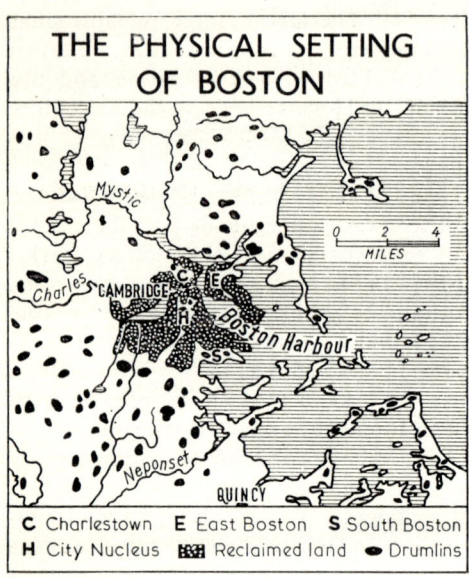

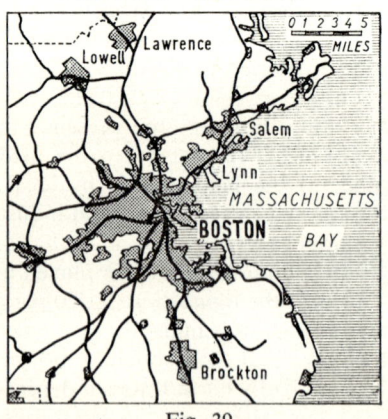

Fig. 39.

Boston

The chief city of New England is Boston (697,000): it participated in the region's prosperity in the past and is sharing its fluctuating fortunes in the present. In the present century it has experienced an influx of foreign-born peoples. Formerly it was the stronghold of the Puritan tradition: now the dominant forces in the city are the Roman Catholic French-Canadians, Irish, and descendants of Central European stock.

Several favourable factors enabled Boston to become the

outstanding port and political centre in colonial times. It arose at a point where several estuaries, notably those of the Charles and Mystic rivers, converge to form Boston Harbour, itself an inlet of Massachusetts Bay (Fig. 39). The harbour is large and deep, and sheltered on its seaward side by an archipelago of drumlins. The core of the city, with its narrow and twisted streets, is a peninsula projecting northwards into the harbour. As it grew, the contiguous area to the south was developed and settlement spread to other peninsulas on the northern side of the harbour. The reclamation of the southern shore of the estuary has still further increased the city's area. Behind the port lay the relatively fertile and extensive coast plain with its thin mantle of boulder clay. This was the area most suitable for settlement and Boston became its centre. The port lies nearer to Britain by the great circle route than any port farther south and was usually the last port of call for ships making the eastward crossing.

During the nineteenth century, however, the disadvantages inherent in its location became apparent. The highly articulated coast hampered the expansion of the city, and even to-day, ferries are the only direct link between the three groups of port terminals. Even more serious was the difficulty of establishing communications with the interior. The two upland masses presented formidable difficulties to railway construction, and by the time Boston was linked with the Hudson Valley by a tunnel through the Taconic Mountains, New York had already established its rail and canal links with the Midwest through the Hudson-Mohawk gap. Thus with trade from the interior being channelled through New York, Boston's hinterland has been restricted to the New England states.

As a consequence, it handles 16 to 17 million tons annually which is only a quarter of the tonnage that New York handles, and it ranks as the eleventh port of the U.S.A. There are thirty miles of docks to accommodate ships drawing up to 40 ft of water. Its imports far exceed its exports, both as regards foreign and coast wise trade. The main commodities imported are coal, oil, wool, and other raw materials. Apart from grain (a winter export from Canada which might be reduced with the opening of the St Lawrence Seaway) there are no bulky materials for export and the outgoing tonnage is only one-tenth of the incoming tonnage.

The continuous built-up area extends over a radius of fifteen miles and carries a population of over 3·2 million, engaged mainly in the textile, leather and electrical industries. Boston is the banking and commercial centre of this area and its influence extends over the whole of New England.

CHAPTER VI

MIDDLE ATLANTIC REGION

Introduction

The Middle Atlantic region stretches from the Adirondack Mountains, southwards to central Virginia and inland to the watershed of the rivers draining to the Atlantic. It coincides with the "Atlantic Slope", and includes the basins of the Hudson, Delaware, Susquehanna, and Potomac rivers. All of these, except the Hudson, rise on the Allegheny Plateau and cross the whole of the Appalachian system, unlike the rivers farther south which cross only a part of it.

Within the region there are marked contrasts of relief between the low Coast Plain and the uplands of the interior. The climate shows smaller variations with a general decrease of winter temperatures and length of growing season towards the interior.

	Mean January Temp.	Mean July Temp.	Growing Season (days)	Precipitation (in inches)
Altoona	28° F. (−2° C.)	71° F. (22° C.)	151	39
Harrisburg	31° F. (−1° C.)	75° F. (24° C.)	204	37
Philadelphia	34° F. (1° C.)	77° F. (25° C.)	211	42

There are contrasts, too, between the heavily populated and highly industrialised seaboard and the practically uninhabited parts of the Allegheny Plateau, between the intensive commercialised farming of the Coast Plain and Piedmont and the poor subsistence agriculture of the remote uplands. In spite of this diversity, however, the Middle Atlantic region has a certain unity by virtue of its position. The ice-free Atlantic coast, which is indented and well-endowed with natural harbours, faces western Europe and was the point of entry of many immigrants. Immediately inland, the Appalachian system is relatively low and narrow, permitting easy contact with the interior along the river valleys.

In the seventeenth century there arose here an assortment of English, Dutch, Swedish, and German settlements which flourished and formed the bases for the colonisation of the interior. The area became wholly British in 1664 and soon achieved primacy in North America which it has maintained to the present day. Within its boundaries are the greatest concentrations of the nation's population (over 30 million people), industry (20 per cent. of the labour force), and commerce. The Midwest and the Pacific Coast are to-day expanding more rapidly than the Middle Atlantic Seaboard, but the pre-eminence of the latter remains unchallenged.

Appalachians

Allegheny Plateau.—The area crossed by the watershed is sparsely populated: to the west lies the industrial region dominated by Pittsburgh; to the east is the Middle Atlantic region which is tributary to the Atlantic ports. The horizontally bedded sandstones and grits of which the Allegheny Plateau is composed, rise to elevations between 1,500 ft and 3,500 ft. The highest parts are in the north, where the Catskills reach a height of over 4,000 ft. The whole surface has been deeply dissected and the rivers often lie 1,000 ft or more below the top of the plateau. Part of the area is forested; the remainder is too rugged, bleak, and infertile for agriculture to be widespread, intensive, or prosperous. The farming economy is generally adjusted to the demand of the great cities for milk, but in the remoter areas communications are so poor that only subsistence farming is possible. Sheep as well as cattle are reared, usually dual purpose animals which provide both wool and meat. Much of the marginal land has been abandoned and has reverted to forest. There is some lumbering and pulp milling.

The northern and eastern edges of the Allegheny Plateau are marked by steep escarpments which road and rail surmount only with difficulty. In the north this cliff overlooks the Finger Lakes, Lake Ontario Plains, and the Mohawk Valley. In the east it is known as the Allegheny Front, and from the top there is a magnificent view eastwards over the series of even-crested ridges and valleys of the Newer Appalachians.

The Ridge and Valley Province and the Blue Ridge.—The rocks here were folded in Hercynian times and have since undergone several cycles of erosion (See Fig. 3). The valleys are invariably of shale or limestone and the ridges of sandstone, grit, or conglomerate. There is no simple relation between the structure and the relief; some of the ridges are anticlines or elongated domes; others are the upturned edges of the eroded synclines. The ridges are short and discontinuous and arranged *en echelon* (Fig. 40). Sometimes they form zig-zag patterns.

The trend of the relief features is from north-east to south-west, but the main rivers cross the region from north-west to south-east, and have cut gaps through the ridges. In a distance of forty miles, the Susquehanna passes through six gorges (see plate facing p. 17). Like the other rivers it must have originated on a higher surface of younger rocks which have since been removed by erosion. The tributary streams do show some adjustment to structure. They occupy the longitudinal valleys, where they are sluggish and meandering, and pass from one valley to another through gorge-like gaps in the intervening ridges. They join the major rivers at right angles and form the trellised drainage pattern. River capture has been common,

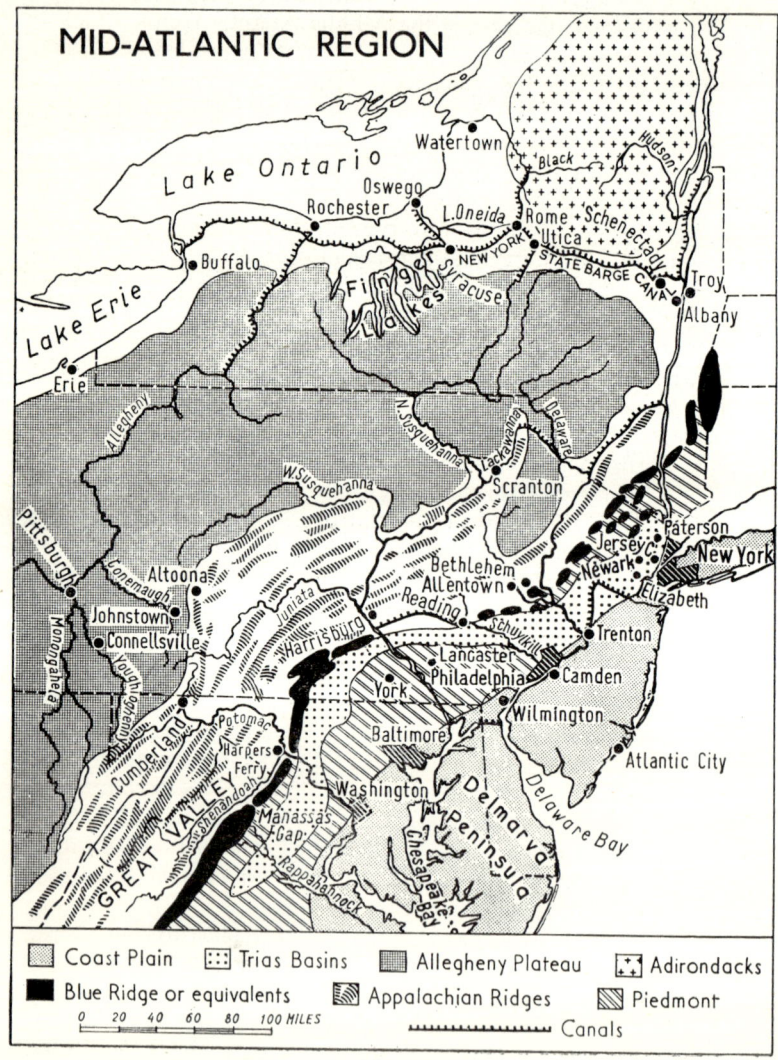

Fig. 40.

particularly in the largest and easternmost of the valleys—the Great Valley—in which flows the Shenandoah. This stream, formerly a minor tributary of the Potomac, extended its headwaters and beheaded rivers flowing across the Blue Ridge to the Atlantic. Several wind-gaps have been left, including the Manassas Gap at Fort Royal and the Rockfish Gap at Waynesboro (Fig. 40). Although these wind-gaps had some importance in the early days of the American frontier, the outstanding routeways across the Blue Ridge followed the water-gaps. Settlers moving west from the coast made for Harrisburg on the Susquehanna or Harper's Ferry on the Potomac. From these gap towns, the routes followed tortuous courses to Pittsburgh or Wheeling on the Ohio, or, from Harper's Ferry, turned south along the Great Valley and then by a series of zig-zags across the whole Ridge and Valley Province, reached the Allegheny Front at the Cumberland Gap, which gave access to the fertile lands of the Kentucky Blue Grass region (Fig. 31).

The Blue Ridge is the easternmost and most continuous of the uplands. Topographically, it is part of the Ridge and Valley Province, but structurally, it belongs to the older Appalachians, where the rocks are more ancient (granites, gneisses, schists, and slates), and have been subject to more intense folding and faulting. Between the Susquehanna and the Schuylkill, the Blue Ridge is a subdued feature, but it gradually becomes more pronounced again to the north-east, and where it is broken by the Hudson at West Point it is about 1,500 ft high (Fig. 40). It continues into New England as the Taconic Range.

The settlement pattern is a reflection of the relief: villages and towns are strung along the roads and railways which follow the narrow, enclosed valleys, rather like the beads on a string. Settlements are most numerous in the broader and more continuous valleys, where farmland is fairly extensive. The valley of the Shenandoah (the Great Valley), which is twenty miles wide, is the most notable of these. The intervening ridges are almost devoid of settlement and carry a forest cover. Occasional wood factories are a legacy of a once flourishing Appalachian lumbering industry.

Farming is confined to the valleys and is best developed where the underlying rock is limestone and the soils consequently more fertile. Formerly, the Shenandoah Valley was a leading wheat-growing area, but competition from the Midwest and the growth of the urban market in the east persuaded the farmers to change to mixed farming with emphasis on dairying. In the less accessible districts beef cattle replace milk cows. Winter wheat is still an important crop in the rotation along with corn, which is usually grown on the alluvial bottom lands, and hay. On the lower slopes of the Blue Ridge and in the Shenandoah Valley, apple orchards are found. They occupy sloping sites with gravelly loam soils and good air drainage which minimises frost damage. The northern part of the Great Valley, a district stretching for twenty-five miles west of Harper's Ferry, is known as the "Apple Pie Ridge" (Fig. 41).

There are clusters of towns suggesting a denser settlement pattern than could be supported by agriculture alone. These are industrial towns and they are grouped in two small areas, along the North Susquehanna and Lackawanna rivers, and along the lower Lehigh. The first of these, a district fifty-five miles by six miles lying around Scranton, is an anthracite mining area. There is no bituminous coal for the seams were contorted, hardened, and their volatile constituents expelled in the intense folding. As the seams lie at angles varying from 10° to 70°, mining is difficult, and the use of machinery almost impossible. Production costs are high and while anthracite is preferred in the cities because it is a smokeless fuel, output has declined steadily from 81 million tons in 1914 to 13 million tons in 1966. The increasing use of oil and natural gas makes a revival of the industry extremely unlikely.

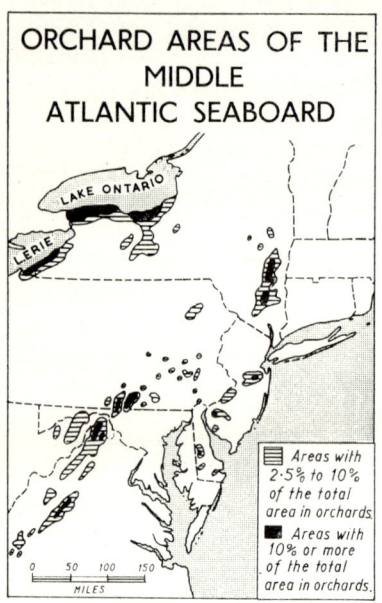

Fig. 41.
Note the concentration of orchards along the shores of L. Erie and L. Ontario, in the Hudson Valley and in the Great Valley of Virginia.

Textile industries, which were introduced into the area to make use of the surplus female labour, continue to flourish.

The towns on the lower Lehigh grew up where magnetite ores occurred. At first these were smelted with locally obtained charcoal, but later coal came down the Lehigh Valley by barge from the anthracite field. Limestone was available close at hand: it was used as a flux and also gave rise to a very important cement industry. (There are about twenty plants in the area.) Now, the local ores are exhausted and foreign ore is imported. The steel produced is used to manufacture mainly railway equipment and motor trucks. Bethlehem and Allentown are the main centres (Fig. 42). The steel industries have tended to drift away from both of these areas to sites better located for receiving ore. The Lackawanna Steel Corporation moved from Scranton to Buffalo at the end of the nineteenth century and before World War I the Bethlehem Steel Corporation set up its main plant at Sparrow's Point, near Baltimore.

Piedmont.—From the foot of the Blue Ridge, approximately 1,000-1,200 ft high, the land slopes down gently to the coast. A marked break of slope occurs along a line joining Philadelphia, Baltimore, and Washington, and this—the Fall Line—divides the Piedmont from the Coast Plain. The Piedmont is composed of metamorphic rocks which are resistant to erosion but which have been peneplained and weathered so that the surface is gently rolling, with occasional hills of very hard rock rising some 400 ft or 500 ft above the general level, and with deep soils of a heavy, clay-like nature. Younger Triassic rocks—mainly sands, grits, and pebbles, together with volcanic beds—fill faulted depressions and have produced lighter reddish soils (Fig. 3).

The Piedmont is a farming area: there is little industry except in the suburbs of the coastal cities which spread on to this region. Mixed farming is common, but emphasis is on dairying, as in most other parts of the north-east where there is such a great demand for milk. Wheat, barley, corn, and legumes (alfalfa and clover) are the crops most commonly grown.

An outstanding agricultural area is along the Susquehanna in the counties of York and Lancaster, where the Pennsylvania Dutch (Dutch = Deutsch = German) have brought European methods and attitudes to farming and created a prosperous farmland, a prosperity which is manifest in the well-kept buildings and equipment. The farm holdings are generally small, averaging about fifty or sixty acres. The fertile limestone soils of Lancaster County are the best in Pennsylvania, and the growing season of 160 to 170 days and the annual precipitation of about 40 in. are adequate for the growth of most mid-latitude crops. More than 90 per cent. of the county is farmland and in some townships over 80 per cent. of the land is in crops.

The main money crop is tobacco, which occupies only a very small acreage as it requires much care and attention and makes heavy demands on labour. It is grown on the best soils which are generously fertilised. Potatoes are extensively grown and in some parts mushrooms, both of which are supplied to the large consuming markets of Philadelphia, Baltimore, and even Pittsburgh.

Dairying, which also has high labour requirements, is important only on those farms which do not grow tobacco. Most farms fatten livestock from Virginia and even from Texas and the western ranching areas. The feed consists of hay, corn, straw, and concentrates: less than 10 per cent. of the land is in pasture. The common rotation practised on most farms lasts four years and consists of tobacco, wheat, clover or alfalfa, and corn.

Coast Plain

The change from the Piedmont to the Coast Plain is marked by the Fall Line, a zone of waterfalls and rapids. Here the older rocks drop under younger sediments which dip seaward at a gentle angle (Fig. 3). There are occasional beds of limestone which form small, inward-facing escarpments, and clay which underlies the strike vales. Most of the rocks, however, are of a sandy nature, and these are often uncleared and uncultivated, like the Pine Barrens of New Jersey, which occupy one-sixth of the state's area. The natural fertility of the soils is extremely low, but in spite of this, the area has become important for truck farming. The numerous cities have created a demand for vegetables, fruit, eggs, and poultry, which the Coast Plain farmers attempt to supply. Delaware alone supplies 60 million chickens to the urban market every year. Tomatoes, sweet corn, spinach, asparagus, cucumbers, peas, and other vegetables, are sent daily to the large cities, the farmer often choosing his market according to the price bulletins broadcast over the radio. The main truck-farming areas are the Delmarva peninsula (the peninsula between Chesapeake Bay and Delaware Bay, comprising parts of DELaware, MARyland, and VirginiA), New Jersey, and Long Island.

The growing season varies in length from 190 days on Long Island to 230 days in northern Virginia, where up to three crops a year can be grown. Spring comes earlier along the coast than in the interior. On the Western Shore of Virginia and Maryland (*i.e.* west of Chesapeake Bay: the coast of the Delmarva peninsula is known as the Eastern Shore) peanuts and tobacco tend to replace the vegetables. The light soils are easily worked and warm up rapidly in spring, but they need heavy fertilisation and marling. Most farmers have a large proportion of their land under a leguminous crop in order to add nitrogen to the soil. Local canning industries, particularly numerous in Baltimore and Camden, were established to absorb part of the produce. But with the increased consumption of fresh vegetables and fruit, and the advent of improved methods of freezing, it seems that smaller and smaller quantities will be available for canning. The canning and freezing plants do not simply absorb the surplus produce: they have contracts with farmers who supply fixed quantities of fruit and vegetables at guaranteed prices. While many truck farmers have such contracts, others prefer to take the risk of making substantial profits or of suffering heavy losses in the highly competitive fresh fruit and vegetable markets of the large cities.

The coast is low and shows evidence of recent changes in level. The lower courses of the rivers have been submerged, which has resulted in the formation of large inlets (*e.g.* Chesapeake Bay, Delaware Bay, and the entrance to New York Harbour). At the same time, the coasts of New Jersey and Delaware have features denoting emergence. There are the lagoons, sand-dunes, and sand-spits which run parallel to the shore. The beaches are the playgrounds of the urban populations. Atlantic City, built on Absecon Island—a spit one mile wide and ten miles long—is the biggest resort; it has 1,000 hotels and caters annually for 15 million visitors. Very different from its glittering artificiality are the run-down settlements on Chesapeake Bay which are the base of operations for crab and oyster fishing. A great number of menhaden are caught off this coast. This fish, which forms the bulk of the total United States' catch, is used primarily as a source of oil, meal for poultry and livestock, and fertiliser.

The Urban Seaboard

The distinctive characteristic of the geography of the Middle Atlantic region is the large urban population, contained for the most part, in the line of towns between New York and Washington. This is one of the greatest agglomerations in the world, for which a new term has been coined—"megalopolis" (Fig. 42). It is the "Main Street" of American geography, a belt less than 250 miles long, with a population of more than 25 million. At this point on the coast, Chesapeake Bay and Delaware Bay penetrate inland to the Fall Line. The cities that developed had the advantage of being ports on sheltered harbours, and also of being at the head of navigation at the foot of the zone of falls and rapids. These, of course, provided water-power and later hydro-electricity. Immediately to the east of the Fall Line is a depression of Cretaceous rocks which was utilised by canals, railways, and roads. To-day, an hourly train service connects New York and Washington, and the air traffic between these two places is the heaviest in the continent. Inland, too, access to the interior along the river valleys was relatively easy. The Pennsylvania Road from Philadelphia, and the Cumberland (or National) Road from Baltimore carried many pioneers to destinations beyond the Appalachians (Fig. 31).

Inevitably, there was competition among the ports for the trade of the interior. New York had the immeasurable advantage of lying at the end of the Hudson-Mohawk gap which provided a

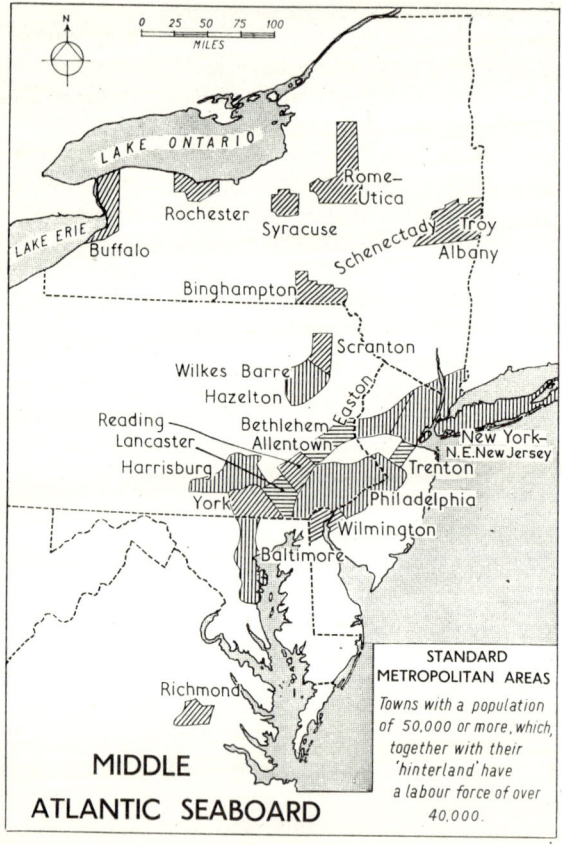

Fig. 42.

lowland route to the west which circumvented the Appalachians. The opening of the Erie Canal established the primacy of the port. Work on canals to link Philadelphia and Baltimore with the Midwest began but was not completed. These ports were revitalised with the advent of railways. They lie nearer to the industrial centres of the interior but even so the lines of the Pennsylvania railway and the Baltimore and Ohio railway have to negotiate much steeper gradients than those of the New York Central, which take a longer but less difficult route through the Hudson-Mohawk Gap.

Philadelphia (2,002,000).—The commission sent by William Penn to select a site for Philadelphia on "a spot that was most navigable, most dry and healthy, and where boats might load and unload without lighterage", performed their task well. The site chosen was eighty-eight miles from the open sea, on a slightly raised terrace of firm ground between the Delaware and Schuylkill rivers. The town was laid out in rectangular blocks and the present city centre still conforms to this grid-like pattern, although later alterations have added numerous cross alleys. As the city grew, and it did so at a very rapid rate, for Pennsylvania was the colony most attractive to settlers from overseas, so it spread, engulfing surrounding villages and extending on to the Piedmont. Until the nineteenth century, when it was surpassed by New York, Philadelphia was the dominant city of the eastern seaboard, and for a short time it was the seat of government.

As a port it ranks second in the U.S.A. (Table 1, p. 129). All but the very largest ships can reach the docks which line the banks of both the Schuylkill and Delaware. A great variety of goods is handled, some from overseas, but most from other ports of the U.S.A. Petroleum heads the list of imports and refined petroleum products the list of exports. Like most large seaports it has diverse industries. Heavy industries such as oil-refining, steel-making, shipbuilding, and railway engineering are located mainly in the southern part of the town. Two modern steel plants here—the mill at Paulsboro and the huge Fairless concern at Morrisville, both on the Delaware—reflect the changing location of the steel industry. This has tended to move coastwards as reserves of American iron ore dwindle. Both plants use ore from Latin America, principally Venezuela, and Canada, and coal from Pennsylvania and West Virginia. Both are more conveniently situated for supplying the eastern seaboard market than are the older works in the Midwest.

Although the area is extremely industrialised there is no really outstanding industry, and emphasis is on consumer rather than capital goods. A list, too long to enumerate in full, would include radios, a wide range of textiles, and the products of the publishing industry. Philadelphia is essentially a commercial city and the hub of a metropolitan district which includes Camden, Trenton, and Wilmington, and which has a population of over 3 million people. Wilmington is the headquarters of the great Dupont chemical concern.

Baltimore (939,000).—This city too has its modern steelworks, at Sparrows Point, which draws its raw materials from the same sources as do the plants at Philadelphia. Other heavy industries on the waterfront include manufacturing fertilisers, smelting copper, and engineering. Here, too, are the largest shipyards in the country. Clothing is an important industry but the canning of fruit and vegetables has declined somewhat in recent years.

Baltimore is situated where the rocks of the Piedmont meet the drowned mouth of the Patapsco River, a three-armed inlet which makes an excellent harbour. This led to the selection of this site for the main town of the colony of Maryland. It handles large quantities of wheat and coal for export, for it is nearer the Midwest than the other Atlantic ports. The imports are also of a bulky nature and include crude oil, fertiliser materials (potash, nitrates, and phosphates), and ores. The main disadvantage of the port is that it lies 180 miles from the mouth of Chesapeake Bay, and circumnavigating the Delmarva peninsula means a long detour for ships crossing the Atlantic. Now the Grand Canal provides a 27-ft channel between Chesapeake Bay and Delaware Bay. It is used by north-bound vessels (Fig. 40).

The city is at the south-eastern limit of the American manufacturing belt. Northwards to Boston is an almost continuous line of industrial cities: southwards, one passes into the more rural South, where industries are fewer—but increasing—and scattered.

Washington (763,000).—In 1790 plans were made for building a federal capital. The seat of government had shifted from city to city and inter-state jealousies made it impossible to choose any existing centre. So a ten-mile square tract of land on the north bank of the Potomac was ceded to the government by Maryland and the District of Columbia was created. A French veteran of the War of Independence, Major L'Enfant, drew up a plan for the new city. It was to have wide avenues on a grid pattern, cut by long diagonal roads radiating from significant points.

The site chosen was near George Washington's home at Mount Vernon, and it had the added advantage of lying near the centre of the area that was inhabited at that time. Fresh water from springs and wells was abundant. Just inland lay the Piedmont and the lowest falls of the Potomac River. Another reason given for choosing this site was that the undulating surface upon which the city would be built provided the slight eminences for the main public buildings. Although alterations were made to the original plan, as the city grew (*e.g.* to make provision for the railways), contemporary Washington stands as a worthy memorial to its founders: its spacious tree-lined streets, its many parks, and its distinctive architecture make it one of the most attractive of American cities. The city is now spreading westwards on to the Piedmont.

Washington's function is to serve as the federal capital. There are no industries. Here are the government buildings (the Capitol, the White House, and the Library of Congress), and museums and monuments (the Museum of Natural History and Ethnography, the Smithsonian Institution, the Lincoln Memorial, and the George Washington Monument). Many of the learned societies have their headquarters in Washington and many of the government and society publications originate here. A great number of hotels cater for the visiting diplomats and the tourists who come in large numbers. During summer, the oppressive heat caused by a combination of high temperatures and high humidity encourages the residents to escape to the cooler shores of Chesapeake Bay or to the interior mountains. It is not only the climate which adds a southern flavour to Washington, but also the high negro population. The cotton fields lie farther south but the problem of racial integration is already becoming apparent.

New York (7,782,000).—New York, at the north-east pole of "Main Street", is the focal point of the whole region, and indeed, in many ways, of the whole of the continent. The importance of the site was first recognised by the Dutch, who in 1621, established their settlement of New Amsterdam on Manhattan Island. The name was changed to New York in 1664 when the territory was ceded to Britain. During colonial times, the small town functioned as a port and was less important than Boston and Philadelphia. It did not confirm its supremacy until early in the nineteenth century when its magnificent harbour and its control of an easy route to the most prosperous part of the interior gave it advantages neither of its rivals could equal. The city is now the largest in North America, and has a population of about 8 million. The standard metropolitan area (cp. Greater London) which extends over a radius of twenty-five miles or more, includes 370 separate municipalities, and has a population of over 13 million.

Where the Hudson reaches the sea the coast is highly articulated with numerous bays containing islands and peninsulas. Manhattan is between the Hudson River, East River (not a river but a strait which is an extension of Long Island Sound) and the Harlem River to the north, which is a natural channel connecting the two. The Hudson was over-deepened during the glacial age and subsequently submerged so that it resembles an arm of the sea. Unlike the Susquehanna and Delaware, it has no falls or rapids: the Fall Line is drowned or obscured by drift on Long Island. It is in fact a strike stream flowing at the eastern margin of a basin of Triassic sediments. These include volcanic sills, the easternmost of which forms a prominent river cliff, the Palisades, overlooking the Hudson (Fig. 43).

Upper Bay, into which the Hudson debouches, is linked to Lower Bay directly through a constricted channel—the Narrows—between Staten Island and Long Island. There is also a more tortuous route to the sea by the Kill van Kull and Arthur Kill (Fig. 44). Lower Bay, with an area of eighty-eight square miles, is partially protected by two sand-spits, Rockaway Beach to the north-

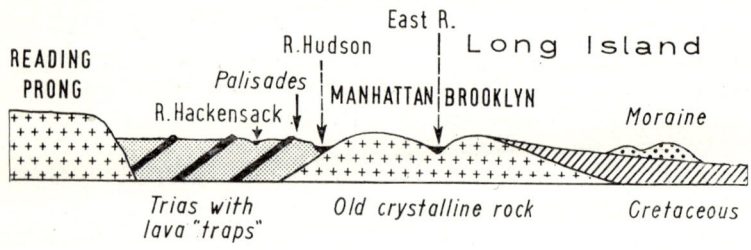

Fig. 43.

east, and Sandy Hook to the south-west. Upper Bay, with an area of fourteen square miles, is much smaller. Here the transatlantic passenger passes the Statue of Liberty and Ellis Island. Every yard of space along the shore is utilised for the accommodation and unloading of ships and the storage and transport of their cargoes. As there is a tidal range of only 4½ ft, ships can enter and leave at any time. Deep water extends close to the shore, making the construction of enclosed dock basins unnecessary. The 770-mile waterfront is lined with finger piers, and is administered by the Port of New York Authority. Shipping is never impeded by ice, but may be delayed, often for long periods, by the frequent fogs.

The port handles more traffic than any other in the world and deals with about half the U.S.A. foreign trade. In addition, it has an enormous volume of coast-wise trade with other American ports. Within the port there is a great movement of goods from

Table 1. Major Seaports of the U.S.A.

Figures in millions of tons (1966).

Seaport	Cargo Loaded		Cargo Unloaded		Total
	Foreign	Coastwise	Foreign	Coastwise	
New York	7·2	17·0	50·0	31·4	105·6
Delaware ports	2·9	7·8	52·7	27·6	91·0
Hampton Roads	36·1	4·7	4·6	1·6	47·0
Houston	10·6	17·6	3·9	2·4	34·5
Baltimore	6·0	1·5	19·4	4·0	30·9
San Francisco	5·6	8·4	6·4	13·2	33·6
New Orleans	20·0	24·9	5·7	2·0	52·6
Los Angeles	4·2	7·0	6·4	5·4	23·0

one shore to another. This is because certain waterfronts specialise in the handling of certain types of ships and cargoes. The large transatlantic liners berth on the Manhattan bank of the Hudson. Here too are found the barges from the Great Lakes. At the East River piers congregate the cargo boats plying between North and South America, unloading their cargoes of tropical foods and beverages and loading manufactured goods. Newark Bay, which has developed rapidly since the war, handles heavy and bulky articles such as timber and coal. Bayonne is principally concerned with the unloading and refining of oil, and it also handles many heavy articles (iron and copper), and rubber.

Owing to the configuration of the coast and the nature of the terrain, settlement has developed along three roughly parallel belts. Communications between them are difficult (Fig. 44).

1. In the east is the cluster composed of the Bronx, Manhattan, Brooklyn, and Queens. The East and Harlem rivers divide these boroughs from one another, but there are many interconnecting bridges and tunnels. There is, in addition, an underground railway. (The "Elevated" ceased to function in 1955.)

2. In the centre and separated from the first group by the Hudson, is a belt comprising Hoboken, Jersey City, Bayonne, and Richmond. The width of the Hudson and the density of the buildings and port installations has made bridge-building difficult and expensive. There is only one bridge and that is some distance upstream, but there are two tunnels under the river for road and rail traffic. Most railways, however, terminate on the New Jersey shore and goods have to be moved by lighters, a slow and expensive procedure. A new bridge being built across the Narrows will link Richmond and Brooklyn but it will do little to relieve the congestion at Jersey City and Manhattan.

130 MIDDLE ATLANTIC REGION

3. West of this belt and separated from it by Newark Bay and the Hackensack Meadows, is a long string of smaller towns which include Perth Amboy, Elizabeth, Paterson, and Passaic.

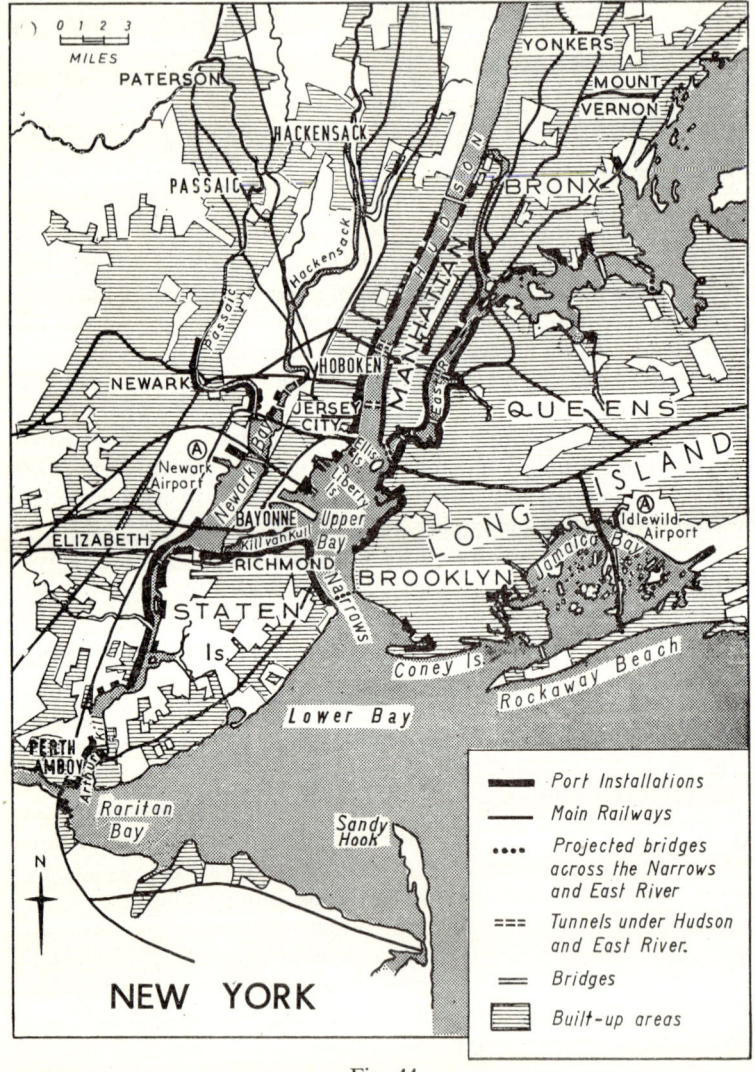

Fig. 44.
Refer also to plate facing p. 112.

It was inevitable that manufacturing industries should arise in New York. Its commercial development stimulates manufacturing just as manufacturing increases commerce. Within the metropolitan area there is a large population which is a concentrated market for consumer goods of all sorts (*e.g.* foodstuffs, house and office equipment, newspapers, furniture, etc.). There is plenty of labour. Most of the dirtiest and lowest-paid work was done by the foreign-speaking immigrants: their descendants do similar work to-day. Until the rise of powerful trade unions wages tended to be low and working conditions poor.

The heavier industries are located along the waterfront, particularly along the New Jersey shore. Here are found the shipyards, the copper refineries, the engineering works, the oil refineries, the railway workshops, and factories making soap, paint, and electrical equipment. Many of the materials for these industries arrive by sea. The textile industries are associated with the towns farther inland, Paterson, Passaic, and Clifton. The main industry of New York, however, is the making of clothes. More than half the nation's output is manufactured in a 200-acre tract on the west side of Manhattan. The factories are numerous but small and unpretentious. Only recently have they been equipped with modern machinery and run along modern lines. The strength of this industry lies, not in producing large quantities of standard articles, but in its ability to create and produce to order small collections of style clothing.

Manhattan is the nerve centre of New York, for here are the financial establishments which guide and control the nation's commerce. What happens on Wall Street has repercussions far beyond the borders of the U.S.A. At the southern tip of the island is a group of skyscrapers housing the shipping lines, the banks, stock markets, and a host of financial institutions. North of this congested area with its narrow, canyon-like streets, is a more open district where the buildings form rectangular blocks which are divided by the "streets" which run from north-west to south-east and the "avenues" which run from north-east to south-west. Broadway runs north to south and cuts diagonally across the other roads. It forms a rough boundary between West Side, the area of clothing factories, Greenwich Village, and the more genteel residences, and East Side, where are found the poor tenements that comprise Chinatown and the Bowery. This is where the immigrants have congregated in their national groups. A big social problem has been caused by the unwillingness or inability of these people to become assimilated. Harlem, in the northern part of Manhattan, is the negro quarter of New York. In the centre of Manhattan is the Midtown district. Here are the theatres, music halls, hotels, and the fashionable shops of Fifth Avenue. This is a district of skyscrapers, but whereas those Downtown (*i.e.* in the south) are citadels of finance, these are the outward symbols of the prosperity and prestige of the business corporations.

Two problems affecting New York have already been briefly noted, the transport problem arising from the nature of the terrain and the social problem arising from the mixed population. Another set of difficulties stems from the mere size of the metropolis, and involves the organisation and efficiency of large service industries. Commuters must be brought daily from the suburbs and distant outlying areas to the centre of the city. At midday in south Manhattan there is little more than one square yard for every person: at night the district is almost deserted. Foodstuffs must be brought great distances; fruit and vegetables come from as far away as California and Florida. Millions of gallons of water are brought daily from the Catskills; the "milkshed" is very extensive, and stretches from New England to Wisconsin.

The Hudson-Mohawk Gap

This valley route is the easiest way of crossing the Appalachians and provides a link between the Great Lakes and Midwest and the Atlantic coast. It was the development of this routeway in the early nineteenth century that added impetus to the growth of New York. The Hudson (Fig. 35) flows south through a structural depression between the Catskills (part of the Appalachian Plateau) and the hills of New England (Green Mountains and Taconic Range). Near Troy it is joined by the Mohawk, which has the Catskills to the south and the Adirondacks—a sparsely populated extension of the Laurentian Shield—to the north. The valley of the Mohawk is an old overflow channel whereby water from the Great Lakes escaped to the ocean when the St Lawrence outlet was still blocked by ice. Other features which resulted from glaciation are the lacustrine plains, the drumlin swarms, the outwash sands, the numerous waterfalls, and the Finger Lakes.

Nowhere does this route rise above 600 ft, and the relief is sufficiently subdued to enable a canal to be constructed. The Erie Canal replaced the Genesee Road along which the early migrants had made their way westwards. Products from the interior began to move to the coast very cheaply. In 1825, the year the canal was opened, the cost of transporting a ton of freight from Buffalo to Albany fell from $100 to $1. Later, railways and modern roads

HUDSON-MOHAWK VALLEY

were built along the same route and the canal traffic declined. Although the original canal was deepened and improved—it is now known as the New York State Barge Canal—the bulk of the freight is still moved by rail or road.

Along the 400 miles of this lowland from New York to Buffalo there is a ribbon of dense settlement. About three-quarters of the people of New York State live in this narrow belt.

Dairying is common in the rural areas and there are extensive orchards along the southern shores of Lake Ontario, around the Finger Lakes and in the Hudson Valley, south of Albany (Fig. 41). Altogether there are almost 200,000 acres of land producing mainly apples, but also grapes, peaches, pears, cherries, and plums.

Farming is subsidiary to industry: this area is highly urbanised (Fig. 42). Buffalo (532,000) is a trans-shipping point for wheat from the Prairies. Along the lakeside are huge elevators and the main industry of the city is flour-milling. The ease of obtaining iron ore and coal has led to the establishment here of an iron and steel industry upon which are based several engineering industries. The main source of power for much of this region is the Niagara Falls (see plate facing p. 272). Rochester (318,000), where the River Genesee tumbles over the Niagara escarpment, is the home of the Eastman Kodak Company. Other towns with specialised industries are Syracuse (chemicals and engineering), Schenectady (electrical engineering), Gloversville (gloves), Cohoes (knitwear), Troy (shirts and collars), and Rome (copper and brass working).

CHAPTER VII

THE SOUTH

GENERAL

Introduction

More than any other part of the United States, the South has long been recognised as a region possessing a highly individual character. Its distinctiveness derives less from its structure and relief, which are extremely varied, than from its climate and its history.

There are perhaps more misconceptions about the South than any other North American region. In romantic novels it appears as a dreamland of trailing Spanish moss, decayed mansions, and old negro retainers, all the nostalgic relics of a splendid past. These images are part of the so-called "magnolia myth": others, given by John Gunther in *Inside U.S.A.*, are "red clay roads curving round unkempt hills and time passing slowly; lazy drawling accents, brides marrying in the evening and the drooping of moss; mouldy lawns and crinolines and broken-down shacks near the railway tracks; afternoons hot as cotton". Yet others are built upon half-remembered and often inaccurate information about cotton plantations, the Civil War, and the River Mississippi. But these images, inaccurate as they are, have shaped not only popular opinion, but also have become embedded in the thought and traditions of many Southerners. The strong regional consciousness of the South is a product of its historical experience and is manifest in a determined adherence to the Democratic Party, a jealous guarding of state rights and, even to-day, a sense of grievance against and distrust of northerners and the central government.

The traditional limits of the South are again a matter of history rather than geography. The Mason-Dixon Line, which follows the boundary between Pennsylvania and Maryland was for long regarded as the northern limit. Westwards, the boundary ran along the Ohio to the Mississippi. To-day, Maryland and West Virginia, which have few "southern" characteristics, are not usually considered as parts of the South. For the purposes of this chapter, the region may be defined as the area lying east of the Great Plains and south of the lower Ohio and Missouri rivers (Fig. 45). It includes the whole of the Gulf Coast Plain, from the Rio Grande to Florida, the lower Mississippi Valley and the Ozarks, as well as the southern parts of the Atlantic Coast Plain and Appalachians. These areas will be described in more detail later in the chapter. First, we must examine those characteristics which are common to the whole of the region, or to large parts of it.

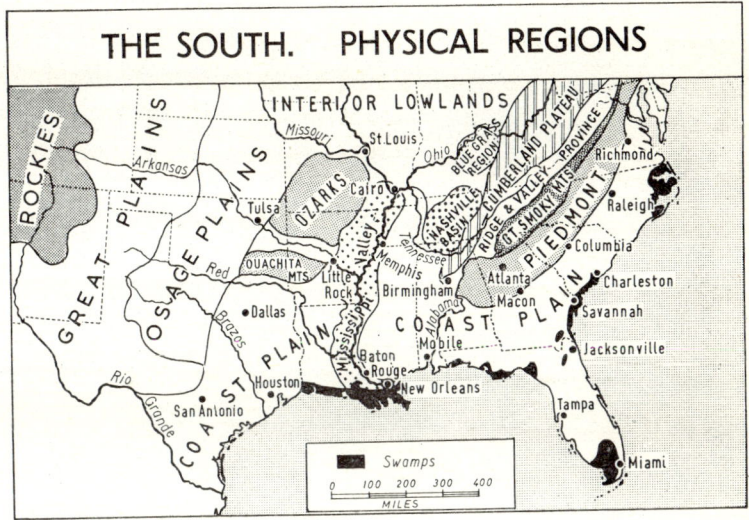

Fig. 45.

Climate

The main features of the climate are summarised in Fig. 46 (see also Chapter II). Only the extreme southern tip of Florida has a truly tropical climate where frost is unknown and the weather is hot throughout the year. Elsewhere the summers are hot with average July temperatures over 76° F. (*24° C.*) everywhere except in the uplands. Much of the region has over 80° F. (*27° C.*) and part of the Rio Grande Valley has 88° F. (*31° C.*). Winters are mild along the Gulf coast, but increase in severity towards the interior. Average January temperatures are above freezing point and reach over 50° F. (*10° C.*) along the south coast, but occasional "northers" bring cold polar air to the whole of the region, except southern Florida, practically every winter. The growing season is long, and this, combined with the high summer temperatures, permits the growth of a large variety of crops.

Precipitation is heaviest in the east where mean annual totals exceed 40 in. and where parts of the Appalachians experience 70 in.

136   THE SOUTH

or more. Totals decrease towards the western boundary of the region and the driest parts here have under 20 in. Although there is no dry period, most of the rain tends to fall during the summer months when there is an inflow of warm, moist air from the Gulf of Mexico. This tendency towards a summer maximum becomes more marked in the west and interior. Over most of the region

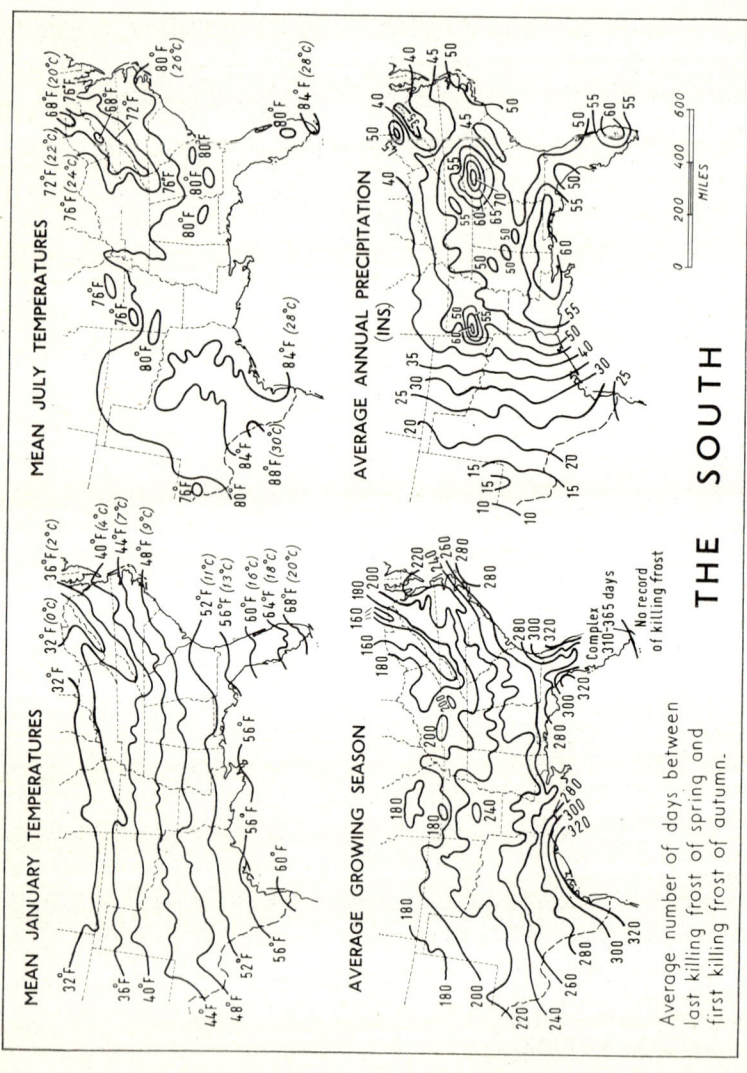

Fig. 46.

amounts are not excessive, but the rainfall is intense and occurs in short, heavy showers. Because of this, run-off is rapid and soil erosion is a severe problem, particularly as a large proportion of the land is tilled and sown with row crops.

Negro Population

For census purposes people of mixed white and negro blood are regarded as negroes, and in 1964, the 20 million negroes in the U.S.A. formed 10½ per cent. of the total population. In most southern states the proportion is higher than this, even though here, as in the country as a whole, it is declining.

TABLE 2

STATE	NEGROES	PERCENTAGE OF TOTAL POPULATION	STATE	NEGROES	PERCENTAGE OF TOTAL POPULATION
Texas	1,187,000	12	S. Carolina	829,000	36
Georgia	1,123,000	28	Virginia	816,000	21
N. Carolina	1,116,000	24	Tennessee	587,000	16
Louisiana	1,039,000	32	Missouri	391,000	9
Alabama	980,000	30	Arkansas	389,000	22
Mississippi	916,000	42	Kentucky	216,000	7
Florida	880,000	18	Oklahoma	151,000	7

As can be seen from these figures, there is no state with a preponderance of negroes, but there are counties within some states where negroes do outnumber whites. The greatest densities are found in the Mississippi flood plain, the Black Belt of Alabama, the Atlantic Coast Plain, and part of the Piedmont in North and South Carolina (Fig. 47). These are areas where the agricultural economy is, or has been until recently, dominated by cotton. There are lesser concentrations in the truck-farming areas of the east coast. Negroes are fewest in the upland parts of the Appalachians and Ozarks, where plantations were never established. There are few in the western parts of the South, which were opened to settlement after the Civil War. The tendency at the moment is for the negro population of the country to become more dispersed. 52 per cent. now live in the eleven states of the old Confederacy compared with 60 per cent. in 1950 and 80 per cent. in 1910. During World War II, many negroes migrated to the north-eastern industrial towns. There are almost a million in New York, and more than half a million in Chicago. In the last decade the negro population of California has increased enormously and now numbers 884,000. Another tendency is for the negro to move from the rural areas to the southern towns.

The psychological effect on the white population of such a large minority has created social problems. State segregation laws and illegal and often violent methods of enforcing white superiority have meant that the negroes have a lower standard of living, poorer health, and more meagre educational facilities than the white population. To-day, conditions are improving slowly: racial discrimination receives no sanction in federal courts, and the lot of the negro, if not equivalent to that of the white, is getting better.

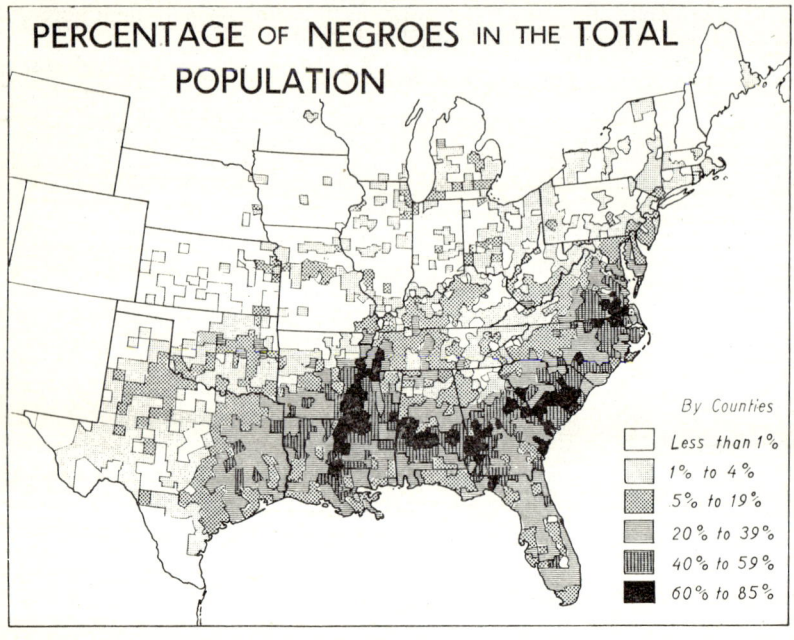

Fig. 47.
(*Reproduced by courtesy of the American Geographical Society.*)

The Civil War

It is impossible to understand the attitude of the people and the development of the South without considering the impact of the Civil War and its aftermath. The war left the South economically prostrate: the "Reconstruction"—a period of military rule which each state experienced before being re-admitted to the Union—left it bitter. During the fighting—which is referred to by the Northerner as the "War of the Rebellion", and by the Southerner as the "War between the States"—the South lost one-quarter of its adult male population. After the war, labour was short and money was practically non-existent. Slavery had been abolished, but the negro had no land or money to buy it. The plantation system collapsed and was replaced by a share cropping system, whereby the labourer gave up a certain proportion of his crop to the landowner—who had no money to pay him—in return for land and implements.

The region remained impoverished for more than half a century, and even to-day *per capita* income is below the national average.

TABLE 3

RANKING OF STATES: PER CAPITA INCOME 1966. (Highest=1; Lowest=50.)

50 Mississippi	42 Louisiana
49 Arkansas	41 Georgia
48 South Carolina	36 Oklahoma
47 Alabama	33 Texas
45 Tennessee	30 Virginia
44 Kentucky	29 Florida
43 North Carolina	25 Missouri

As can be seen, the four poorest states are in the South. The poverty is reflected in numerous ways: housing is often bad, and a large number of homes are without electricity, running water, or effective sanitation; educational facilities are poorer than in other parts of the country, and health standards lower. The poverty of the South, relative to other regions in the U.S.A., is due in part to certain geographical factors. The climate encourages the spread of diseases, particularly malaria, hookworm, and pellagra, which have a debilitating effect upon the people; large areas of land are unsuited to extensive farming, and the high intensity of rainfall contributes to soil erosion and floods; the soils are not, on the whole, fertile and are easily exhausted of nutrient minerals. In part, however, the South has remained impoverished because of the war. Lack of capital prevented the region from developing its resources to the full. After the Civil War, the political and economic power of the country was concentrated in the north-east, and the South, as a possible competitor of the north-east, suffered thereby. Most of the railways are controlled by northern companies, and until recently freight rates in the South (and in the West) were appreciably higher than in the north-east.

To-day, this picture is rapidly changing. During the last thirty years, but particularly since 1939, the South has begun to catch up upon the rest of the U.S.A. Its farming population has decreased by about one-third, while workers in manufacturing increased by over one-half. Great advances have been made in the development of power resources and minerals. Industry has expanded enormously, partly with the help of northern capital and government assistance. The *per capita* income is rising at a faster rate than that of the U.S. as a whole.

Cotton

In the past, the terms cotton and the South were almost synonomous. This crop has played a disproportionate part in the agricultural economy of the region and has influenced very greatly the settlement pattern and the composition and social structure of the population.

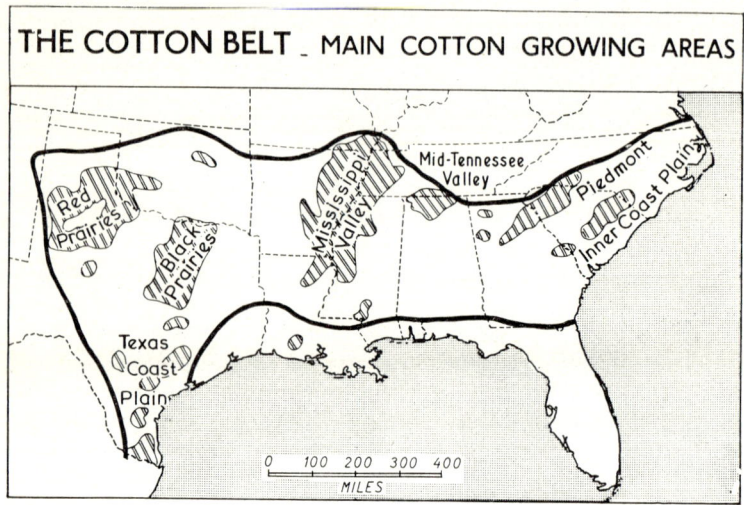

Fig. 48.

Cotton tolerates a wide variety of soils, but it is limited to the southern states by its climatic requirements. It is rarely grown where there are fewer than 200 days free from frosts or where the annual rainfall is under 20 in. (unless there is irrigation), or where the autumn rainfall exceeds 10 in. These requirements define the limits of the Cotton Belt on the north, west, and south respectively. Within the area so defined intensive production is found where the better soils are (Fig. 48):—

1. the Inner Coast Plain, which has rich alluvial soils and is near the cotton manufacturing towns;

2. the Mississippi Valley (the "Delta"), where the extremely rich soils, liable to inundation when the rivers flood, are still productive

after years of continuous cropping, and are not affected by soil erosion;

3. the Black Prairies of Texas with dark, lime-rich soils;

4. the Red Prairies of Texas and Oklahoma, where irrigation is often necessary, but where the boll-weevil is not a serious menace;

5. the Texas Coast Plain (coastal prairies), where cotton is subsidiary to fruit farming.

To-day the Mississippi Valley produces about one third of the U.S.A.'s cotton, and Texas another third. The remaining areas are declining in importance.

TABLE 4
PERCENTAGE OF THE TOTAL COTTON CROP PRODUCED BY THE LEADING DISTRICTS

DISTRICT	1924	1934	1944	1954
Inner Coast Plain	4·68	6·83	6·27	4·75
Piedmont	3·44	4·22	3·60	1·52
Mississippi Valley	12·31	18·65	25·52	23·07
Mid-Tennessee Valley	1·31	2·37	2·39	1·62
Black Prairies	10·47	6·43	5·44	3·17
South Texas	2·54	3·18	2·37	5·49
Red Prairies	11·70	5·15	10·79	12·94
Areas outside the cotton belt	0·81	3·45	3·52	15·02

The remarkable expansion of cotton growing outside the South has taken place in the irrigated valleys of the San Joaquin and Salt Rivers (see p. 246).

Cotton did not become the outstanding crop in the South until the last decade of the eighteenth century, when Eli Whitney invented a gin for separating the seeds from the lint. At the same time, there was a greatly increased demand for cotton goods, which stimulated the production of raw cotton. In 1790, 1·5 million lb. of cotton were produced: in 1810, the figure had risen to 85 million lb. Slavery became even more firmly established, and as the settlers moved west, so did the plantation system. When slavery was abolished and the South was impoverished after the Civil War, the plantation system was replaced by a new form of land tenure. Holdings remained large (the optimum size was thought to be between 800 and 1,000 acres), but instead of the land being worked as a single unit by slaves who lived in a nucleated settlement, it was now divided into plots of thirty or forty acres, each occupied and cultivated by a share-cropper and his family. In return for mules, tools, and seeds, these tenants gave to the owner a proportion of their crop (usually between one-third and one-half). During World War II there was an exodus of rural labour to the towns in both the South and the north-east. This coincided with the development, after much experiment, of an efficient cotton-picking machine. The structure of the plantation is now undergoing a further change. The pattern of separate plots and dispersed settlement is disappearing and in its place is the large unified farm with a small labour force and much machinery.

Cotton is an annual crop. The land is ploughed and arranged in ridges three or four feet apart. Seeds are planted in the furrows and sprout within a week. The plants are thinned and the ground kept free from weeds. In late June or early July the flowers appear and when they fall the boll slowly matures and is ready for picking in late August or early September. The bolls on any one plant mature at different times, but must be picked without delay for, at this stage, rain can seriously affect the quality of the cotton.

Apart from the weather there are other hazards. The boll-weevil first made its appearance in the U.S.A. in 1892 and by 1921 there was no part of the Cotton Belt unaffected by its depredations. Losses now are not as severe as formerly because of the use of powerful insecticides. The insect thrives best in the humid conditions of the east: the western areas are safer and it is significant that these have developed at the expense of those farther east. More serious, however, are the ravages of soil erosion. Thunderstorms occur throughout the year and the augmented run-off, even on gently sloping cultivated land, first strips off the top soil and then becomes concentrated in the rapidly deepening gullies. Cotton and corn—the other major crop—are sown widely apart and do little to halt the flow of water. In Texas, cotton fields suffer one hundred times more damage than comparably situated grass fields. The share-cropping system aggravates the problem for the tenant is usually concerned with getting the most out of land which is not his own. Conservation methods which include terracing, contour-ploughing, strip-cropping, and the planting of cover crops have become more common, and at the same time have helped to diversify the farming, but much land at present cultivated will have to be devoted to forest or grass if soil erosion is to be halted.

Now the heyday of King Cotton is over. In retrospect it might well seem that the decline started after World War I. At this time Europe, the largest market for cotton, was in debt to the U.S.A. and sought its supplies elsewhere. The cotton-growers received only low prices and sought to increase their income by growing more. This simply depressed the price further, and since the Great Depression the acreage sown with cotton has been restricted by the government almost every year. But while the acreage has decreased, the output has not, a fact which can be attributed to better farming methods and the greater use of fertilisers.

TABLE 5

	1924	1929	1934	1939	1944	1949	1954	1959	1967
Millions of acres	39·2	43·2	26·7	22·8	18·9	26·5	18·8	15·1	8·1
Millions of bales (500 lb.)	13·7	14·5	9·4	11·5	11·8	15·4	12·9	14·7	7·6

The U.S.A. produces more than 30 per cent. of the world's cotton. Before the Depression over one-half of the crop was exported: to-day the figure is smaller (4·1 million bales in 1967). This reflects cheaper production in other parts of the world and increasing competition from man-made fibres. The cotton-grower now is not at the mercy of world markets for the government guarantees a minimum price and buys unsold stocks. Amounts paid to farmers by the Commodity Credit Corporation run into hundreds of millions of dollars, and the accumulated stocks number 6·8 million bales. Prices are fixed in relation to the needs of the small cotton farmers in the south-east: they are ridiculously high for the large, efficient, highly mechanised and irrigated farms of the south-west in California and Arizona. Under the stimulus of these price supports, production here has expanded enormously, which has led to further reductions in acreage allotments. These hit the small farmer very severely and may force him out of farming. He has, however, benefited under the soil bank scheme, whereby the farmer is paid not to cultivate his land. It is unlikely that cotton will disappear entirely from the old Cotton Belt, but it seems that production will become concentrated to an increasing degree on larger farms in favoured areas, where efficiency is comparable with that of farms in the western irrigated districts.

On the land freed from cotton cultivation a great variety of crops is being grown. Corn has always been sown widely in the South and the razorback hog is ubiquitous. Certain areas have for a long time specialised in certain crops, such as rice, sugar-cane, fruit, and peanuts. But now, individual farmers everywhere are beginning to broaden their economy by growing soy-beans, sweet potatoes, sorghum, peanuts, and fruit. The acreage under grass and fodder crops has expanded tremendously and parallel with this development has been the great increase in the number of cattle reared. Scientists and breeders have developed new animals—the Santa Gertrudis, Charbray, Brangus, and Beefmaster—all of them containing Brahman blood and capable of enduring the high temperatures and humidity. All are resistant to ticks and many other parasites and pests. Between 1949 and 1956, the number of cattle in the South more than doubled, and the region now has more stock than the whole of the West (excluding the Great Plains). The animals can graze out of doors for the whole of the year and the abundant rainfall ensures adequate feed. The common fodder crops are crimson clover, Bermuda grass, lespedeza, and kudzu, the latter two having been introduced from Asia. As well as providing ample pasture, they also are suitable for covering eroded soils and for preventing further erosion.

In the last three decades the South has witnessed nothing less than an agrarian revolution. Since 1929, the acreage under cotton has decreased by almost four-fifths, and over 30 million acres of land then under crops are now either pasture or forest. There have been great changes in the landscape and in the farming population. The diversification of farming has brought nothing but good to the South.

THE REGIONS

Various regional classifications have been suggested for the South: in the following sections, the region is divided into five simple and broad sub-regions:—

1. The Middle South, which includes the interior highlands and plateaus.

2. The South-east (or Old South), comprising the Piedmont and the Coast Plain east of the Mississippi.

3. Florida.

4. The Lower Mississippi Valley.

5. The South-west (or New South), lying west of the Mississippi and including the Coast Plain and the bordering plains to the north-west.

1. The Middle South

This region lies north of the Cotton Belt but south of the Corn Belt: it coincides, more or less, with the Wheat and Corn Belt or the General Farming Belt. For the most part, it is made up of rugged country with little level lowland. The southern Appalachians and the Ozark-Ouachita Highlands form the eastern and western bastions of the region: in between these lie the plateaus and basins of Kentucky and Tennessee. The Middle South is really transitional, but it appears to have more affinities with the South than with the Midwest.

Appalachians.—There is the same four-fold system here as in the Middle Atlantic region, but each element is on a slightly grander scale (Fig. 45). The Piedmont, because of its lower elevation and relief, is different from the other elements and is considered in the section on the South-east. The Great Smoky Mountains are a continuation of the Blue Ridge: they form a belt of extremely rugged country, 100 miles wide, clothed with forests of oak, chestnut, hickory, and other deciduous trees. They reach a height of over 8,000 ft and form the watershed of streams draining to the Atlantic. There are few passes and communications are difficult. The Ridge and Valley Province is made up of folded Palaeozoic sediments. The ridges, which may be anticlinal arches or the upturned edges of eroded synclines, are discontinuous and separate the long, narrow valleys which are developed on less resistant rocks, usually shale and limestone. The drainage is longitudinal, and the streams are finally collected by the Tennessee or one of the major rivers flowing direct to the Gulf of Mexico. The Cumberland Plateau, composed of Palaeozoic rocks dipping gently to the west, is so heavily dissected as to be barely recognisable as a plateau. Soils here are generally poor, having been developed from sandstones and cherty limestones, and, except on the relatively level land, which occupies only a small fraction of the area, are very thin.

This area has, in many ways, been a remote fastness of the descendants of the original British stock. It was settled during the late eighteenth and early nineteenth centuries, but was largely avoided by later immigrants who sought better lands farther west. The isolation of the people is, in part, responsible for the perpetuation of old ways of speech and old folk songs. Because of the isolation, too, the farming is of a general type where most of the products are consumed on the farm itself. Methods are often out-dated and productivity is low. There is little specialisation except near the towns and relatively little marketing of the farm produce. Corn and winter wheat are the main crops: they are grown on the valley floors and lower slopes. On the upper slopes is forest or pasture, both of which are grazed by cattle and hogs. The density of population is surprisingly high for such an unattractive area (it reaches over 200 per square mile in places), and pressure on the land has resulted in the cultivation of slopes which should have been left wooded. As a result, soil erosion has become a serious problem. A typical hill farm in south-east Kentucky has about ten acres of cultivated land and about three-quarters of this is planted with corn.

There is marked rural poverty throughout the region, which is reflected in many ways: the dirt roads, the unkempt appearance of the shacks that serve as dwellings, the absence of bathrooms, electricity, and mains water, the poor standard of health and education. From the human standpoint, one of the most depressing aspects is the inability of the population to ameliorate their living conditions.

The region is not rich in natural resources, and the development of those that are present has been hampered by the lack of good communications and distance from main markets. The forests which cover much of the area furnish a replenishable source of wealth. Softwoods do occur on the poorer soils, but the majority of trees are hardwoods. The latter have led to the rise of furniture manufacturing at a number of towns, including Chattanooga and Lenoir. Recent research has shown how the hardwoods may also be pulped, and now they, with the softwoods, are treated at the several pulp mills in the Tennessee Valley. The Calhoun plant on the River Hiwassee, in Tennessee, established after World War II by the Bowater Corporation of Britain, handles some hardwood. The company owns several square miles of forest and to date has planted over 70 million trees to replace those cut for pulping (Fig. 54).

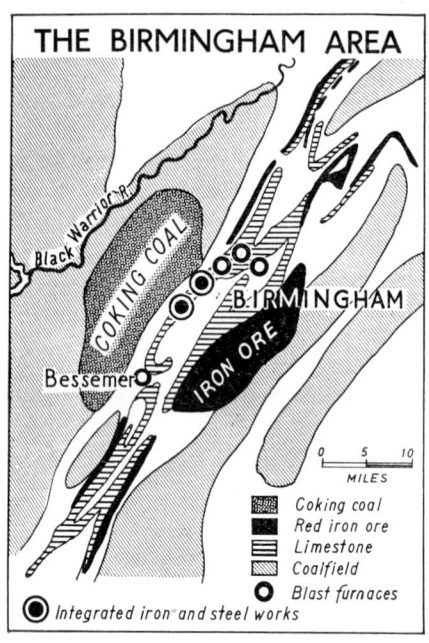

Fig. 49.

Although small quantities of copper and zinc are mined, the main mineral resources of the area are found near Birmingham (341,000), at the southern tip of the Appalachians. Here, in close proximity, are the three raw materials of the iron and steel industry (Fig. 49). To the west of the city is the Warrior coalfield which provides excellent coking coal (production, 14,200,000 tons in 1966);

to the east is Red Mountain with its supplies of iron ore; the limestone and dolomite come from the Birmingham valley. No other American steel manufacturing centre is so favourably placed. Yet Birmingham produces only about one-twentieth of the nation's iron and steel, and lags very far behind other centres in the north (p. 186). Steel production in 1963 was 3,900,000 tons (80 per cent. of capacity). Several factors are responsible for this. The local ore is not of high quality and is usually mixed with high-grade iron ore, imported from Venezuela. Mining costs are high, which tends to offset the benefits of propinquity. Birmingham lies 200 miles from the Gulf coast, and although there is barge traffic on the Black Warrior to within eighteen miles of the city, this long distance has been a drawback. Birmingham must sell its steel in the South, which is not highly industrialised, for the northern markets are dominated by the northern steel centres. However, its position has improved since the ending of the basing-point price system (whereby all prices were based on costs of production at, and transport from, Pittsburgh), and since the equalising of freight rates. (Formerly, to transport identical goods an identical distance cost 39 per cent. more in the South than in the north-east.)

T.V.A.—Part of this poverty-stricken area has been changed out of all recognition by one of the greatest experiments in regional planning ever undertaken. In 1933, under the New Deal programme of the Roosevelt administration, the Tennessee Valley Authority was created to aid in controlling, conserving, and utilising the water resources of the Tennessee basin, an area of 40,000 square miles. There was formidable opposition to the scheme from the seven states involved and the private interests within them. Much of the outcry was silenced by the success of the scheme, but there are still occasional controversies over federal enterprises, which might reduce the powers of individual states and which might compete with private industries. As was inevitable, the activity of T.V.A. influenced the whole economic life of the region, not only within the watershed, but also in contiguous areas.

The Tennessee is formed by the junction of the Holston and the French Broad just above Knoxville (Fig. 50). These and the other tributaries are fed by the heavy rainfall of the Appalachians, which often amounts to more than 80 in. High floodwaters caused periodic devastation in the valleys and went on to swell the Mississippi and caused further havoc. Sixteen dams were built by T.V.A., supplementing the six already in existence (Fig. 50). The heads of water were used to generate hydro-electricity, which in turn attracted industries such as aluminium smelting at Alcoa. During World

War II chemical and munitions factories were established and atomic research was carried out at Oak Ridge. So great has been the demand for power that the Authority has established thermal power stations, which account for 70 per cent. of the electricity it sells.

One of the tasks of T.V.A. was to complete a 9-ft navigable channel as far as Knoxville. Transport on the river has increased fifteen-fold since 1933 and a wide variety of goods is carried, ranging from oil products, crude oil, and coal, to automobiles and fruit. In order to control the river it was necessary for the Authority to

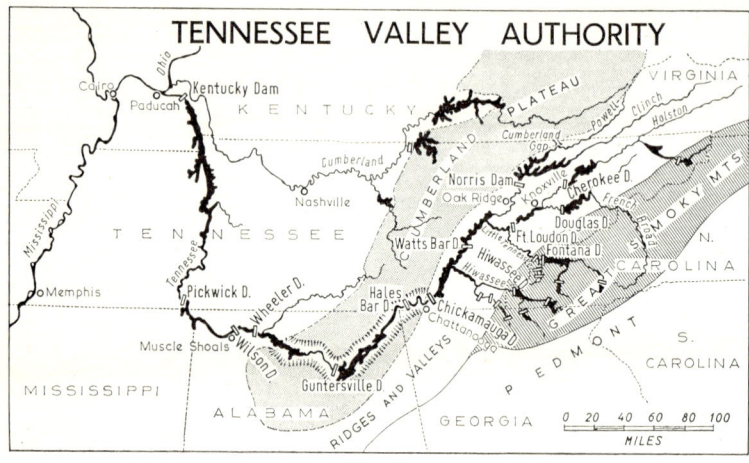

Fig. 50.

The multi-purpose dams (*i.e.* for flood control, power, and navigation) are the Kentucky, Pickwick, Wilson, Wheeler, Guntersville, Hales Bar, Chickamauga, Watts Bar, and Ft Loudon dams on the Tennessee.

Power and flood-control dams are the Norris D. (Powell-Clinch), Cherokee D (Holston), Douglas D. (French Broad), Fontana D. (Little Tennessee), and Hiwassee D. (Hiwassee). All other dams are for water storage and flood control.

see that the watershed was afforested so that the run-off would be retarded and the flood danger reduced. Thus the task of conserving the soil and educating the farmers about the dangers of soil erosion was forced upon the Authority. When work commenced, about one-quarter of the land in the basin had been severely eroded. By means of demonstration farms, propaganda, and financial help, erosion has been halted and much of the damaged land restored. The Authority also makes and sells fertiliser.

The life of the people has been made much easier. Electricity has been brought cheaply to seven farms out of eight, farming has been improved and better communications by road and river have made possible the sale of more farm produce. New industries have been created, towns have grown, and with them the amenities people demand. The reservoirs are now a strong tourist attraction. As an experiment in social and economic planning, T.V.A. has been an immeasurable success. Already it has served as the pattern for similar schemes in other river valleys.

The Interior Plateaus and Basins.—In Kentucky and Tennessee the Cumberland Plateau decreases in height and gives way to a series of low plateaus and basins. General elevations drop from about 1,000 ft along the edge of the Cumberland Plateau to 500 ft or 600 ft, where the older Palaeozoic rocks underlying this area

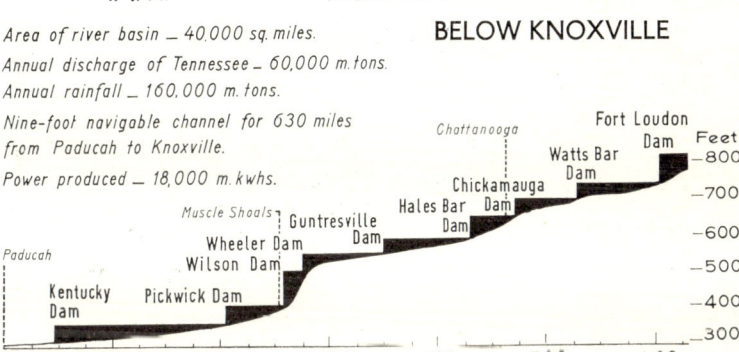

Fig. 51.

disappear under the newer sediments of the Coast Plain which here makes a great embayment northwards into the Mississippi Valley.

The strata are slightly warped and the main structural features are the Lexington and Nashville domes which form parts of a zone of uplift lying west of and parallel to the Appalachians. In both cases the stronger capping rocks have been removed by erosion to reveal the weaker and younger beds in the centre (Fig. 4). In both cases the elevation and relief is less than that of the surrounding area, and they are referred to as basins, but it must be remembered that this appellation pertains to the topography and not the structure.

In Kentucky the phosphatic Ordovician limestone, exposed around Lexington, forms an undulating lowland 130 miles by 130 miles, 300 ft to 400 ft lower than the highly dissected rim, the Kentucky

Knobs, which are made of sandstones and hard cherty limestones of Mississippian (*i.e.* Carboniferous) age. The limestone country shows many of the features of karst topography with sinks, caves, and underground passages. Mammoth Cave, for example, in mid-western Kentucky, has a total explored length of 140 miles. The Nashville basin in Tennessee is smaller (100 miles by 50), but with similar characteristics. The surrounding district is known as the Highland Rim, although that part lying to the west of the basins is sometimes called the Pennyroyal.

The two basins attracted early settlement. Pioneers made their way there either by sailing down the Ohio and up its left bank tributaries, or by using the Wilderness Road which cut through the Cumberland Gap in the Allegheny Front (Fig. 31). To-day they stand out as islands of prosperity in a zone of general farming, and contrast strongly with the poor country around them. The Highland Rim, which has rugged topography, thin soils often exhausted by successive tobacco crops, and poor communications, has large acreages in hay, pasture, and woodland. Winter wheat and corn are grown mainly as feed for the sheep and hogs, and tobacco occupies a small fraction of the area, but the cash returns from the sale of farm produce are small. Some farms have no crops at all and consist of pasture and woodlots.

The soils of the gently rolling lowlands represent the insoluble residue left by the solution of the limestone. They are deep and rich in phosphorus. So naturally fertile are they that they can stand repeated cropping without serious deterioration. Grass grows well and the Blue Grass region (Lexington basin) is traditionally a livestock area, still famous for its horses, but increasingly important for dairy and beef cattle. Blue grass is still grown, but not as much as formerly, because it withstands the hot summers and occasional droughts less well than other varieties such as fescue and ladino clover.

Tobacco is the main cash crop of the two basins. This plant tolerates a wide variety of climates, requiring about 100 frost free days. High temperatures during seeding time are helpful and so is a fairly heavy, evenly distributed rainfall (about 40 to 50 in.), but cold and wet weather can inhibit growth. It grows best on light soils, especially those rich in potassium, phosphorus, and nitrates. The taste of the leaf is, to a large extent, determined by the nature of the soil, and can vary from field to field on the same farm. It is an exacting crop both on the soil and on the labour that is required in its cultivation. For this reason, only a small proportion of the land—usually about 5 per cent., which on most farms amounts to two or three acres—is planted with tobacco. In recent years the federal government has attempted to regulate production by allotting acreages to the farmers and guaranteeing prices. Kentucky and Tennessee produce about 25 per cent. of the nation's tobacco and almost all comes from the Blue Grass region and the Nashville basin (see Table 6, p. 156). It is mainly of the "burley" type which is air-cured and then blended with other types for the manufacture of cigarettes and pipe tobacco.

So much labour is used in planting seed-beds, replanting, weeding, treating plants for diseases and insect pests, plucking buds, harvesting, and curing, that there is little time to devote to the remainder of the farm. Consequently much of the land is under hay (which nowadays often means lespedeza) and feed grains: the common rotation is tobacco, wheat, hay, and corn.

Ozarks.—The Ozark region is very similar to the southern Appalachians, both uplands having experienced similar geological histories. This domed massif lies between the Missouri in the north and the Red River in the south: bisecting it is the Arkansas River. There are three different structural elements (Fig. 5).

1. The Ozarks proper form a dissected plateau rising to over 1,000 ft, composed of little disturbed Palaeozoic rocks which have been removed only in one small area (the St Francis Mountains) to reveal the underlying granite and metamorphic rocks beneath.

2. South of this area, but still north of the River Arkansas, the sandstones, grits, and limestones become thicker and are heavily dissected, forming the rugged Boston Mountains.

3. South of the River Arkansas are the Ouachita Mountains, where the rocks have been folded, giving a landscape of east-west forested ridges and narrow cultivated valleys (cp. the Ridge and Valley Province of the Appalachians). Elevations here are greater than elsewhere in the region and reach over 2,500 ft.

The isolated Arbuckle and Wichita Mountains, lying west of the Ouachitas, are small domes associated with the main Ozark uplift and can be regarded as outliers of the main upland mass.

Much of the land is uncultivated for the soils are thin, cherty, and not particularly fertile. The best land is found in the valleys, particularly in the broad Arkansas Valley, where cotton is grown. Where farming is carried out it is generally of the subsistence type, for the local population is small, and communications with other areas are poor. As in the Appalachians, corn and wheat are the main crops, the former occupying more land than all other crops combined. Animals are reared but cattle are more important than hogs, while sheep are found only on the very rough pastures. Hereford and shorthorn beef cattle are usually sent to the Corn Belt for fattening. More recently fruit growing and dairying have become prominent in the more accessible districts, and there is a significant, if still small, output of apples, strawberries, grapes, tomatoes, and peaches (Fig. 53). Springdale, in Arkansas, is the chief canning centre for fruit and vegetables.

Although much of the region is forested, oak-hickory associations being dominant in the north and oak-pine in the south, lumbering has never been very important: there is even less lumbering now than in the past. The main wealth of the Ozarks lies in its minerals.

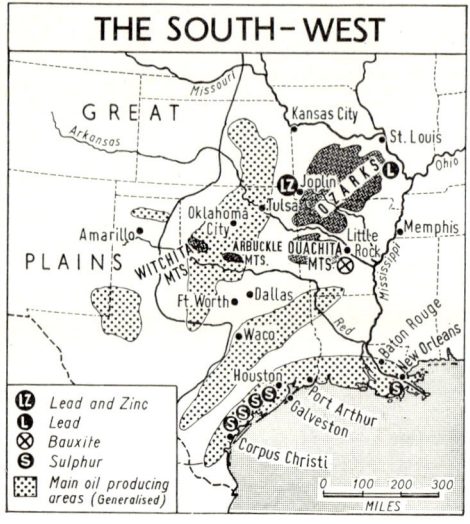

Fig. 52.

The Tri-state area (on the borders of Oklahoma, Kansas, and Missouri) produces zinc and some lead which are processed at Joplin, while in south-east Missouri, around Flat River, sixty miles south-east of St Louis, about 30 per cent. of the U.S.A.'s lead is mined. Some coal is found in the Arkansas Valley, but is not mined to any great extent because of the cheap and plentiful oil and gas supplies in the south-west. More important are the bauxite mines near Little Rock which account for over 90 per cent. of the nation's production (Fig. 52).

As in the Appalachians, the settlers are of old British stock: there are very few descendants of other European immigrants and no negroes. "Frontiersmen, rather than agriculturalists, became the permanent occupants of the area. With the filling up of adjacent regions, the Ozarks became a sort of refuge to the men who clung to the frontier life" (Carl O. Sauer). Population densities remain small and communities are scattered. The general poverty of the region is regarded by some writers as a lack of drive and initiative on the part of the people: more probably it is the result of a harsh and stultifying environment. Other upland regions, e.g. New England and the Appalachians, now derive an income from the annual inflow of tourists, but so far, the Ozarks has not benefited to anything like the same extent.

There are few important towns and the two largest are both on the borders of the uplands and owe much of their importance, not to the Ozark region, but to the contiguous areas. St Louis (750,000) is the regional centre of the northern Ozarks, but in addition, serves a large and prosperous area of the Midwest. Little Rock (107,000) is a centre for the Arkansas Valley and southern Ozarks and it derives some of its importance from the nearby bauxite deposits, but with its negro population and its cotton warehouses it has affinities with the cities of the Mississippi Valley.

2. The South-east

The South-east extends from Virginia to the Mississippi River and comprises two physical regions, the Coast Plain and the Piedmont.

(*a*) The Coast Plain is quite narrow in Virginia and rises inland to about 300 ft. Southwards it widens to over 200 miles and the inner margin reaches elevations of 800 ft in Georgia. The sandstones, clays, and limestones of Cretaceous and Tertiary age dip gently seawards and the more resistant beds form inward-facing escarpments such as the Red Hills and the Pine Hills of Alabama and Mississippi. Much of this area and particularly the sandy tracts remain forested, while along the low-lying and badly-drained coastal areas are extensive swamps with cypress trees and reeds. Dismal Swamp, the largest of these, covers an area of over 2,000 square miles. The coast itself has witnessed many recent oscillations of sea level, the latest of which seems to have been slight submergence, resulting in the formation of long, shallow estuaries. Sand bars and spits which grow southwards in the Atlantic and eastwards in the Gulf of Mexico, wholly or partially enclose lagoons. Off the coast of Georgia are the "sea islands", small mounds of alluvium, which used to produce the high quality sea-island cotton.

(b) The Piedmont rises imperceptibly from the Coast Plain to a height of from 1,000 to 1,200 ft, at the foot of the Great Smoky Mountains. The maximum width is about 125 miles. The surface is broadly rolling and the underlying gneisses and schists are overlain by a thick mantle of sand and laterite, which has accumulated over a long period of time, in a warm and moist climate. Abrupt monadnocks such as Stone Mountain, near Atlanta, rise above the general level of the plateau. The junction of the Piedmont and the Coast Plain is marked by the Fall Line, a zone where rivers descend rapidly to the lower level. These locations, formerly heads of navigation and now power sites, are occupied by a line of towns from Virginia to Alabama (*e.g.* Richmond, Columbia, Augusta, Macon, and Columbus).

Farming.—This region is the "Old South", where the plantation system was born and reached its fullest development. For a long period cotton was the backbone of the economy, but to-day the acreage devoted to the crop has dropped drastically, and intensive production is limited to two small areas, the Inner Coast Plain and the Piedmont of South Carolina and Georgia (Fig. 48). Even here production costs are high when compared with those in the newer lands farther west, for the boll-weevil remains a serious menace and must be held in check by periodic spraying, and yields are low (cp. South Carolina, 419 lb. per acre; Georgia, 422; California, 1,099; Arizona, 1,057), and only maintained by heavy fertilisation.

Elsewhere the reduction of cotton acreages has been accompanied by increasing diversification of agriculture. The Black Belt of Alabama, a fertile area of black earths developed on the Semla Chalk, was once the "type" area of cotton cultivation, but is now mainly a cattle district. In the last three decades, over 16 million acres of land in the South have been taken out of cultivation and replaced with pasture. There are several reasons for this change.

(*a*) The depredations of the boll-weevil.

(*b*) The economic depression of the nineteen-thirties which pauperised many farmers and exposed the dangers of monoculture and dependence on one cash crop.

(*c*) From 1933 onwards the restriction of cotton acreages by the government.

(*d*) The efforts of soil conservationists to persuade farmers to alter the use of their land and government incentives to plant legumes and grasses.

AGRICULTURE   155

(e) The shortage of labour after 1940 (owing to the migration of the rural population to urban centres, both in the South and the northeast), which led to increasing mechanisation and changes in farming practices.

New varieties of grasses and clovers have been introduced, most noticeably lespedeza and kudzu from Asia which combine high fodder value with an ability to cover bare and eroded ground very quickly. This development has been accompanied by a rise in the numbers of beef and dairy cattle, some of them bred specially from Brahman and Zebu stock. Animals can graze out of doors for the whole year and the abundant rainfall keeps the pastures in good condition. In some places supplementary irrigation is used, even though the rainfall may exceed 40 in. annually.

The crop which occupies the largest acreage is corn. It is grown in all parts of the region, but on land which is subject to erosion it is being replaced by crops which offer some protection to the soil. Soy-beans are increasing in importance, and as this crop matures in only 100 days double cropping is possible.

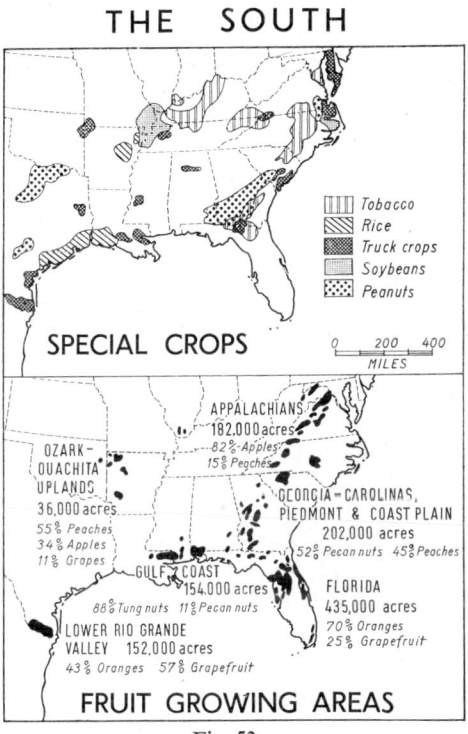

Fig. 53.

Winter small grains are grown widely in the Piedmont and peanuts on many parts of the Coast Plain (Fig. 53). Sweet potatoes and sorghums occupy small acreages in certain localities. A trend towards the greater production of fruit and market vegetables, too, is noticeable (Fig. 53). Truck and fruit farming is helped by the long growing season and the adequate and dependable precipitation. Light sandy soils warm up quickly in the spring and vegetables mature earlier than those grown in the Middle Atlantic region and reach the markets earlier.

The second cash crop of the south-east is tobacco. It is grown on the coast plains of Virginia (known here as "Tidewater"), the Carolinas, and Georgia, and occupies about two or three acres only on each farm as labour requirements are very high. This region produces light, flue-cured tobacco, unlike the Middle South which concentrates on the heavier burley type. The acreage under tobacco and the areas of production have remained stable during the period when great changes have occurred in other parts of the South, and this may be attributed to strict government control of prices and acreage allocations.

TABLE 6

TOBACCO PRODUCTION IN THE U.S.A., 1967

STATE	ACREAGE	PRODUCTION (millions of lb.)
North Carolina	403,000	835
Kentucky	173,000	400
Virginia	70,000	132
South Carolina	76,000	166
Tennessee	58,000	110
Georgia	72,000	150
Maryland	33,000	36
U.S.A.	961,000	1,972

Forest Industries.—The southern forests, predominantly hardwoods on the Piedmont and softwoods on the Coast Plain, are a major resource of the region (Fig. 25). Forests occupy about 55 per cent. of the area of the south-east and in some areas—central Georgia and southern Mississippi for instance—the percentage is much higher. Most of the wooded land is privately owned, large tracts being held by the pulp and paper companies, and only a small proportion is in the hands of the government. On the sandy soils of the Coast Plain there grow large stands of southern pine, the most important of which, commercially, is the long-leaf yellow pine. As well as being cut for timber, these trees formerly provided turpentine and naval stores. Some tapping still takes place, but most of the turpentine now comes as a by-product from the pulp mills. The annual cut is almost as great as in the Pacific states, but in contrast to this area where the forests are being severely depleted, felling in the South does not exceed annual growth. In Georgia alone, 45 million seedlings were planted in one year, and the Bowater Corporation which operates the Catawba mill in

South Carolina as well as the Calhoun plant in Tennessee, has planted over 70 million seedlings.

Emphasis is on the production of pulp wood: the South yields about 42 per cent. of the nation's saw timber, but over 55 per cent. of its pulpwood. There are over seventy pulp mills scattered over the South (Fig. 54), and almost 700 paper and paper-board plants, including a huge works at Rome (Georgia), and a mammoth newsprint works at Childersburg (Alabama). With modern methods, a certain proportion of hardwood can be used in the mills, but softwoods are likely to remain the main raw material if only because their rate of growth is quicker.

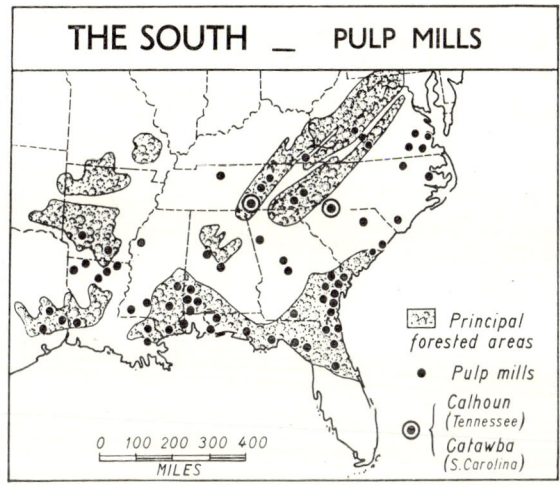

Fig. 54.
See p. 146 and p. 156 for references to Calhoun and Catawba.

Manufacturing.—For long the deprived child of the nation as far as industry was concerned, the south-east is now developing very rapidly. Industrial expansion is rising at a rate nearly 50 per cent. higher than the national average, and manufacturing has drawn ahead of agriculture as a major source of income. This sudden upsurge of industrial development can be attributed to a number of factors.

(*a*) The south-east, although lacking the large oil and gas reserves of the south-west, has local resources which can provide the raw materials of industry once capital is made available.

(*b*) Power is readily available. Hydro-electricity has been developed on the Piedmont and oil and gas are delivered easily from the south-west to all parts of the region, thus permitting industry to be dispersed over a wide area.

(c) The stimulus of war needs led to the establishment of factories here and the influx of capital.

(d) Successful efforts by the various state development commissions to attract capital and industries by granting factory sites, financial aid, and tax concessions.

(e) Reserves of labour in the rural areas which was, or was thought to be, cheaper than that in the north-east.

(f) As the standard of living rises, consequent upon the diversification of agriculture and the spread of industry, so the market becomes greater and attracts even more industry.

The pulp and paper industries have already been mentioned. In addition, there are a large number of factories producing cellulose, chemicals of various sorts, and furniture, all based on the forest resources. Rayon manufacturing has become very important, the mills at Ashville and Roanoke being among the largest in the world. Manufacturing based on agricultural products includes meat-packing and the canning and freezing of fruits and vegetables, as well as two larger, old-established industries, tobacco and cotton. Tobacco is manufactured near where the crop is grown at towns in Virginia (Richmond) and North Carolina (Durham, Reidsville, and Winston Salem). The cotton industry in the U.S.A. started in New England, but during the latter half of the nineteenth century mills were established in the South, and after the end of World War I this region had overtaken New England in the production of cloth. To-day, of the 18·6 million cotton spindles in the country, 17·8 million are located in the South. There are almost 1,000 mills, most of them scattered over the Piedmont in small towns in the rural areas. A dominating feature of the industrial scene is the fact that industries are so dispersed and not concentrated in the large towns. There are in fact no very large cities in the south-east. Most of the ports are small, the largest being Mobile, which has the best natural harbour on the Gulf coast. It has grown quickly since World War II, and now ranks tenth in the U.S.A. Like other south-eastern ports, Mobile ships cotton and lumber, but in addition it has industries, notably shipbuilding, aluminium, for which bauxite is imported, and chemical lime processed from sea shells dredged from the bottom of Mobile Bay. The regional metropolis of the south-east is Atlanta (487,000) which is a rail focus, industrial city, and a commercial and financial centre.

3. Florida

Florida is part of the south-eastern Coast Plain, but it has several unique characteristics and so is best treated as a separate unit. It consists of a low, tabular peninsula extending about 350 miles into the Gulf of Mexico. The underlying rock is limestone which, in the north, contains beds of phosphate. This is quarried and, when processed, is used widely as a fertiliser. Florida produces about one-fifth of the world's phosphate. Where the limestone is exposed at the surface there are displayed features associated with

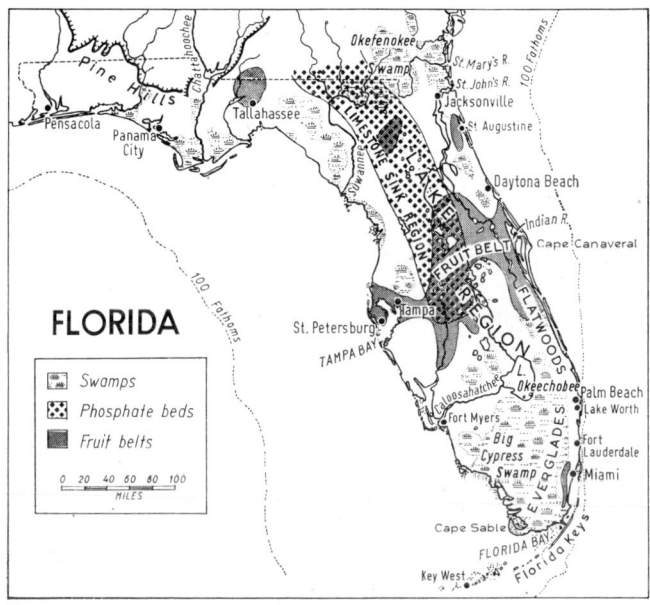

Fig. 55.
(Cape Canaveral is now called Cape Kennedy).

karst scenery, *i.e.* sink-holes, lakelets, and underground caverns (Fig. 55). Elsewhere there is a thin cover of sand. The relief is subdued and nowhere does the land rise over 300 ft, the highest parts being found in the north and centre of the peninsula. In the south is a large, low-lying area with Lake Okeechobee occupying 725 square miles and overflowing westwards, when the level exceeds 20 ft above sea level. Surrounding the lake are the Everglades, an untamed marshland of cypress and gum trees set among wide stretches of saw grass, and harbouring deer, snakes, and alligators (see plate facing p. 64). Living in this fastness are the Seminole

Indians: they retreated here after their conflicts with the encroaching settlers and have never signed a peace treaty with the U.S. government. The south-west coast is fringed with mangrove swamps, but the east coast, equally low-lying, shows a remarkable development of off-shore sand bars, separated from the coastal dunes by long, narrow lagoons (the one north of Palm Beach is known as Indian River). The Florida Keys are a string of sand-covered coral islands lying off the south coast, now joined by a road running from the mainland to Key West, the fishing port and naval base.

These islands have a tropical climate and frost is unknown, but the peninsula itself is sometimes affected by frosts which can cause severe damage to crops, simply because they are so rare and unexpected. In 1927 the whole of the pineapple crop was ruined by an unexpected frost, and there were severe freezes in 1940 and 1957 which caused millions of dollars' worth of damage. Rainfall varies in amount between 40 and 60 in., but as some of the soils are sandy, plants often suffer from lack of water and supplementary irrigation is widely used.

Florida capitalises on its climate. Because the winters are so mild crops ripen early and truck-farming is one of the main agricultural activities. The green bean harvest in Florida takes place in February (cp. May in California), and beans, together with lettuce, cucumbers, potatoes, peas, and tomatoes, as well as fruits such as grapes, strawberries, pineapples, mangoes, and avacados, usually reach the urban markets before the produce of other areas. The soils are not naturally fertile, but with the application of fertilisers, small areas of land can be made productive. The best soils in the state are found along the southern shores of Lake Okeechobee, where about 300,000 acres of peat and silt have been reclaimed and now grow sugar-cane, vegetables, and fodder crops. It is estimated that about 1 million acres here are suitable for agricultural development.

Florida produces about one-third of the U.S.A.'s oranges and two-thirds of its grapefruit (Fig. 53). The orchards lie in the centre of the peninsula between the colder north and the swampy south. The slightly rolling topography promotes air drainage and lessens the risk of frost, while the numerous small lakes have a moderating effect on the temperatures. When frosts are forecast, smudge pots are lit to create smoke screens and lessen the radiation of heat from the earth's surface. Huge fans are also used to stir the lower air and thus prevent frost forming. Another climatic hazard is hurricanes which can cause damage by uprooting trees or by inundating the low-lying areas. Limes, which of all the citrus fruits are most susceptible to frost damage, are grown only in the extreme south.

The great proliferation of holiday resorts is also a result of the climate. Miami (292,000) is the largest, but there are many others, all of them on the east coast which has fine beaches and warm seas. Some are built on the offshore bars which run parallel to the coast for many miles. The resorts cater mainly for winter visitors escaping from the cold of the north-east and Midwest, but there are many summer holidaymakers too. Florida is not industrial, for it lacks power and raw materials and there are few manufacturing cities. Tampa (274,000) handles the shipments of phosphate, while Jacksonville (201,000) is the main port and service centre of the state. There are large military installations at Cape Kennedy, the rocket and missile base. Between the censuses of 1950 and 1960 the population rose by 78 per cent., the greatest percentage increase of any state in the country, and the density of population rose from 51 to 90 per square mile.

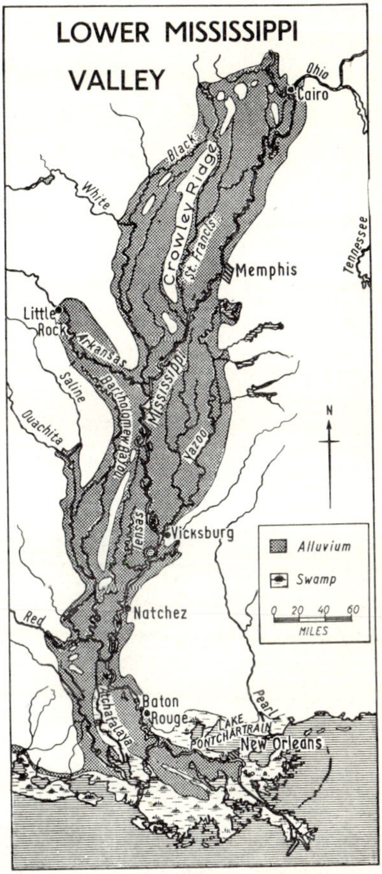

4. Lower Mississippi Valley

Between Cairo and the Gulf of Mexico is a vast stretch of alluvium, 600 miles long and from 50 to 70 miles broad, interrupted by low ridges of Tertiary rock (see Fig. 56).

Fig. 56.

From its confluence with the Ohio, the Mississippi meanders for about 1,000 miles, declining gently at a rate of about 6 in. per mile. The river itself is higher than the land on either side and is enclosed by levees of coarse alluvium and sandy material which have been strengthened to prevent flooding (see plate facing p. 112). Vast areas have been inundated in the past by disastrous floods, and in the back swamps, away from the main river, are oxbow lakes, sloughs, and bayous. Here are the "buckshot" soils of heavy clay. In addition to the material deposited in the Mississippi Valley, the river carries to the Gulf in suspension over 1 million tons of sediment daily, and the "claws" of the bird's foot delta are extending seaward at a rate of 100 yards a year (see plate facing p. 16). Alongside these distributaries are low levees a few feet high, and from one to five miles wide. The depth of sediment in the delta is estimated at 30,000 ft. Mud islands are colonised by marsh plants and gradually become larger, cutting off lagoons from the sea, which are then converted into fresh-water lakes such as Lake Pontchartrain, north of New Orleans. Above the deltaic swamps rise dome-like islands containing salt, sulphur, and oil which usually reach a height of 100 or 150 ft.

The Mississippi Valley is the major cotton-producing region in the U.S.A., and the crop is particularly important in the area that lies between the Mississippi and Yazoo Rivers, the so-called "Delta" (see p. 140). Farther north the farming is more general, with emphasis in recent years on soy-beans. Rice is grown by highly mechanised means and on large farms along the Arkansas River below Little Rock and near the coasts of Louisiana and Texas (Fig. 53). The land in these areas is fairly level and irrigation can easily be carried out. The yields per acre are low but production costs are small: almost half the crop is exported.

TABLE 7

RICE PRODUCTION IN THE U.S.A., 1967

California	360,000 acres	880,000 tons
Louisiana	565,000 ,,	1,100,000 ,,
Arkansas	477,000 ,,	1,075,000 ,,
Texas	508,000 ,,	1,295,000 ,,

Sugar-cane is grown among the Louisiana bayous, but production is low (about 14 per cent. of the nation's requirements) and so expensive that tariff protection is needed. The state has a nine-month growing season and is just inside the northern limit of sugar-cane, but farmers find it safer to plant the crop afresh every year. In the south, also, tung and pecan nuts are grown, and a small area around New Orleans is noted for tomatoes.

Strangely, Louisiana is the foremost fur-producing state in the country. In December, whole families move from farms in the interior or from fishing villages on the coast to the salt marshes where they remain until February trapping muskrat, otter, skunk, and raccoon. The main fur market is New Orleans.

There are few large cities in the Mississippi Valley. The most privileged sites are on the bluffs which rise 100 or 200 ft above the flood plain. Where the river touches the bluff on the east bank, the river towns arose. Vicksburg and Natchez occupy such positions: Memphis (497,000) is larger, for here the railways converge to cross the Mississippi, before continuing westwards, south of the Ozarks. This town has important furniture, chemical, and textile industries: it is a cotton centre, handling over 4 million bales annually. Baton Rouge, at the head of ocean navigation, handles oil and has large refineries and petro-chemical works (see plate facing p. 113).

The outlet for the whole of the Mississippi basin is New Orleans (627,000), founded by the French in 1718, about 110 miles up the river. Its heyday was in the mid-nineteenth century during the steamboat era: at this time it handled more than twice the tonnage of New York. With the development of the railway network and the draining of freight to the east coast and the Great Lakes, the city declined in importance.

At present navigation is possible along 9-ft channels to Minneapolis, Chicago, Pittsburgh, and Knoxville. Oil is the main type of freight, carried on barges pushed by tugs. There is a great deal of trade with other U.S. ports, some of it along the Intra-coastal Waterway, which is a sheltered channel behind the sand bars stretching from the Mexican border to Florida. Foreign trade is mainly with Latin America. Outward shipments include cotton, flour, and petroleum: incoming cargoes consist mainly of sugar, tropical fruits and fibres, and bauxite for the local aluminium works. The docks stretch for four miles along the river and handle about 3,000 vessels each year (see p. 129).

Although it was more or less inevitable that a port should arise near the mouth of the Mississippi, the site of New Orleans has several drawbacks. Most of the buildings are less than five feet above sea level and have to be protected from inundation by an extensive system of dykes and levees; the water-table is high and so houses lack cellars, and graves are above ground level; potable water was scarce and to supply the city purification plants were established along the Mississippi. In spite of these drawbacks and periodic epidemics, the city has continued to grow, but at the same time, has retained much of its French charm and atmosphere, and to-day it is a much-visited tourist centre.

5. The South-west

West of the Mississippi Valley, the South meets the West: cotton growing gradually gives way to ranching, prairies replace forests, and there appears a rawness in the physical and cultural landscape which is absent from the Old South. Although this region extends on to the Great Plains and the Osage Plains (Fig. 45), it mainly comprises the Coast Plain which here displays the same belted topography that is found east of the Mississippi. The swampy, bar-fringed coast is bordered inland by inward-facing cuestas of limestone and sandstone, separated by vales of clay and other weaker rocks. Precipitation decreases westwards and the variations of height, slope, soil, and rainfall combine to produce a great variety of scenery and land-use. Fingers of woodland poke westward along the sandy belts (*e.g.* the Cross Timbers), while the limestone and clay soils are usually covered with prairie grasses (*e.g.* the Black Waxy Prairies and the Grand Prairie). In the extreme south-west, the driest part of the region, mesquite savanna appears.

Agriculture.—Cotton is grown in three areas, the Red Prairies on the Great Plains, the Black Prairies, and the coastal prairies (Fig. 48). Owing to the smallness of the rainfall, irrigation is essential, but on the other hand, the boll weevil is not a serious menace. In the days of Spanish and Mexican rule, there was little farming in the South-west apart from ranching. It was from the western part of the Coast Plain that cattle were driven northwards to stock the Great Plains. To-day ranching is still important in the drier parts of the coastal prairies and on the Osage Plains and the Great Plains. In south-east Texas, where the rainfall amounts to 40 ins. or more, rice is grown by highly mechanised means (see p. 162). The most prosperous farming areas are the irrigated orchards and truck farms along the Rio Grande (Fig. 53). This district has begun to rival Florida and California as a producer of citrus fruit, and in addition, yields melons and dates. It is also a supplier of winter vegetables to the northern urban markets. Double cropping is possible, a cotton or fodder crop following the winter vegetables. The "Winter Garden" district which lies between San Antonio, Laredo, and the Rio Grande is particularly important for onions and spinach. A major problem is the shortage of water and, as well as the storage installations on the Rio Grande, there are an increasing number of dams and reservoirs on the other rivers flowing to the Gulf, especially the Colorado and Trinity rivers.

OIL FIELDS

Oil and Natural Gas.—The drilling of the Spindletop well in 1901 near Beaumont ushered in a period of great prosperity for the South-west. This region is the greatest producer of oil and gas in the nation and has the largest reserves. Oil and gas are commonly found in sandstones and more rarely in limestones and dolomites of various geological ages ranging from Ordovician to Tertiary times. The most productive deposits are in the mid-continental field which lies around Tulsa and Oklahoma City (Figs. 52 and 57). The oil has collected in folds and fault-traps associated with the Ozark-Wichita-Arbuckle uplift. Farther south the reservoirs seem to be

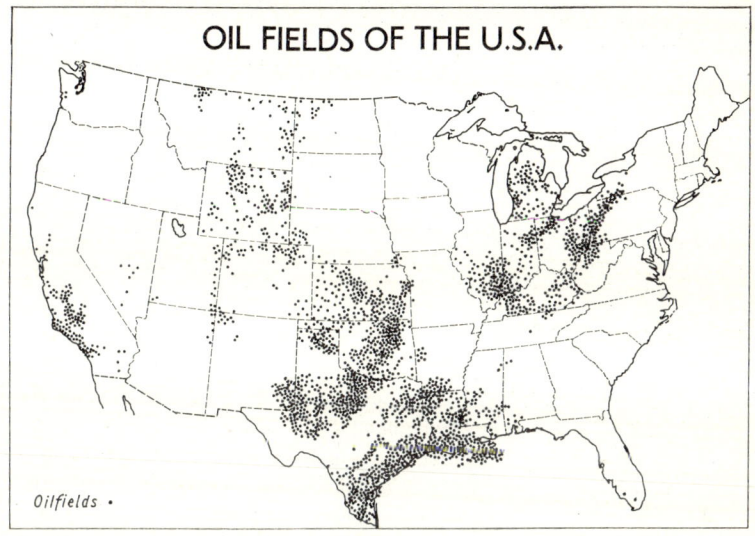

Fig. 57.
The dots indicate oil fields, not the amount of oil produced.

associated with undergound faults lying parallel to the Balcones Fault Escarpment which defines the southern boundary of the Great Plains. Near the coast the oil and gas are found in the salt domes, mounds of salt and sulphur which have been squeezed upwards by compression in the earth's crust. These pools are small and wells have a life of only three or four years (cp. about fifteen years in the mid-continental field). The salt domes occur under the sea also and drilling has begun off-shore. One well lies twenty miles from the coast in over 100 ft of water. The legal controversy as to whether oil found off-shore belongs to the state or the federal government is not yet settled.

Often associated with the oil, but occasionally found separately, is natural gas (methane, butane, propane, and ethane) which is used locally as fuel and raw material, and is piped to the north-eastern cities. An intricate system of pipes of various sizes carries oil to the large urban centres. It is usual for oil to be refined near the market rather than at the source of supply, which is often short-lived, but in the South-west lie six of the country's twelve major refineries. The great upsurge of industry here and the ease of shipping the refined products has probably been responsible for this development. The region is not producing to capacity and many of the wells (altogether there are 197,000 in Texas and over 80,000 in Oklahoma) are shut down two or three days each week to prevent over-production.

TABLE 8

PRODUCTION OF OIL AND NATURAL GAS, 1966

STATE	OIL %	NATURAL GAS %
Texas	35	40
Louisiana	24	30
California	11	4
Oklahoma	7	8
Wyoming	4	1
Kansas	3	5
New Mexico	4	6
U.S.A. total	100	100

Industry.—Over the last two decades the South-west has witnessed a most spectacular development of industry. There are some older industries located in interior cities, *e.g.* meat-packing and aircraft manufacturing at Fort Worth and textiles at Dallas, which is the fashion centre of the South, but modern plants are situated mainly along the coast. Here there is the advantage of a tidewater site with easy access to oil and natural gas which can be used as sources of power *and* as raw materials. In addition there are large reserves of salt in the salt domes along the coast and off-shore, and sulphur, production of which amounts to over 50 per cent. of world output. The deposits lie west of Houston and south of New Orleans (Fig. 52), and the sulphur is extracted by pumping into the ground super-heated water and then drawing to the surface the molten sulphur.

The industries fall into two main categories: those which use the oil and gas as raw materials and comprise mainly chemicals, and those which use the oil and gas as power and comprise mainly metal-smelting concerns. Since the beginning of World War II over seventy-five chemical plants have been built, many of them financed by the government. These included factories producing synthetic rubber which was needed so urgently after the Japanese had overrun south-east Asia and cut off supplies of natural rubber. Practically all the wartime plants have been converted to peacetime production. The largest installations are the Dow plants at the mouth of the Brazos River (Freeport-Velasco) and the Dupont works on the Sabine River (Orange). The others are clustered around Houston (twenty-seven plants along the Houston Ship Canal), Corpus Christi, and Beaumont-Port Arthur, close to the refineries.

The metal-smelting plants include the Sheffield steel works on the Houston Ship Canal which has a capacity of 3 million tons annually (p. 186), a tin smelter at Texas City, a zinc smelter at Corpus Christi (there is another at Amarillo in the Texas Panhandle), an antimony smelter at Laredo, and a new aluminium works at Port Lavaca. In addition, magnesium is extracted from sea water at Freeport.

Industrial development has occurred without a notable increase of population, additional labour being drawn from the local rural surroundings. In spite of the great increase in factories, it is still true to say that the South-west's economy is based mainly on the extraction of oil and gas and the production of cotton and beef. The continued expansion of industry here is linked with the oil and gas reserves: without this base the whole economic structure will crumble.

Houston has experienced a phenomenal growth: in 1900 it had a population of 63,000; in 1960 it had over 930,000. The original settlement, founded in 1836, was the first capital of the Republic of Texas. Its growth was slow until the beginning of the present century when oil was discovered. It is now important as an oil centre, a focus of trunk railways, and a port (see p. 129). Houston is linked to the sea by the fifty-eight mile long Ship Canal, the banks of which are lined with industrial concerns, and it now handles much of the trade formerly handled by Galveston, together with much additional freight arising out of the agricultural and industrial development of the South-west. The bulk of cargoes consists of oil and oil products, but there is an increasing trade in cotton, newsprint, and tropical products. Along the coast runs the Intracoastal Waterway which provides a sheltered nine-foot channel for 1,100 miles from the Rio Grande to Florida and which will ultimately be extended to New York.

CHAPTER VIII

THE MIDWEST

Introduction

The Midwest grew out of the "Territory North-west of the Ohio"—the lands which Britain had decided to reserve for the Indians, but which were opened to settlement after the War of Independence. Fur-trappers had traversed the area prior to this and French fur posts had been established along the St Lawrence-Mississippi routeway. At first, settlement in the area was slow, and in 1800, nine-tenths of the population still lived east of the Appalachians. During the nineteenth century the movement gathered momentum and by 1820 about one-quarter of the population lived west of the mountains. The recognised routes were overland from the east coast by the valleys of the Potomac and Susquehanna to Pittsburgh or Wheeling on the Ohio (Fig. 31). From these expanding towns a great variety of craft carried settlers down the main river and then up the many tributaries. A later route followed the Hudson-Mohawk Valley to the Lake Erie plains. The frontier moved rapidly down the Ohio Valley but more slowly across the plains between the Ohio and Great Lakes. It was not until 1860 that the westernmost parts of the Midwest were settled. A great variety of people came here: there were the religious sects such as the Memnonites; the social reformers like Robert Owen who founded New Harmony; the various nationalities from Europe who left their native place-names on the map and introduced new methods of farming.

The land that these groups occupied formed part of the Public Domain which the government auctioned or sold to individual farmers or private companies. Before sale the land was carefully surveyed under instructions laid down by the Ordinance of 1785. These instructions were that the whole area was to be divided into townships, each six miles square, and the land was to be sold in multiples of one square mile (a section). Later acts reduced the minimum size of the holding to a half-section, and later to a quarter-section. For as little as $1.25 an acre, and with several years to pay the total sum, settlers could obtain some of the richest farm land in the U.S.A. Certain sections in each township were reserved by the government for financing schools and public roads. Thus was inaugurated a system which was to determine the landscape pattern all the way across the Mississippi basin from Ohio to Nebraska (Fig. 58). Here are the monotonously regular square fields, straight roads crossing each other at right angles, evenly-spaced farmsteads, and every twenty or thirty miles almost identical country towns. The Ordinance also made provision for eventually dividing the territory north-west of the Ohio into five states and admitting each of them to the Union once its population reached 60,000. In this way Ohio became a state in 1803, Indiana in 1816, Illinois in 1818, Missouri in 1821, and Michigan in 1837. Of the

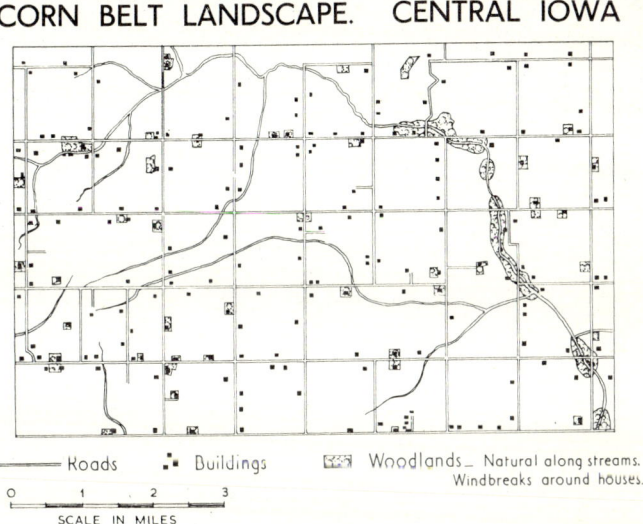

Fig. 58.
The chequerboard pattern with its dispersed settlements is characteristic of much of the Midwest.

other states Iowa was admitted to the Union in 1846, Wisconsin in 1848, and Minnesota in 1858.

The farming potentialities of the region were quickly recognised but the lack of good communications hindered progress. At first New Orleans at the end of the Mississippi-Ohio system served as the outlet. Later, railways linked the area firmly with the Great Lakes and the east coast ports. Not all the settlers were prospective farmers. In Michigan and Wisconsin the forests of mixed hardwoods (oak, maple, and birch) and conifers (white pine and red pine) were savagely exploited. During the seventies and eighties of the nineteenth century when lumbering was at its peak, this area provided much of the nation's timber. By 1900, the forests were practically exhausted, and while lumbering is still carried on, the region has not regained its former importance. Minerals, too, attracted the immigrants: the lead deposits at Galena (Wisconsin) were discovered in the eighteen-twenties, but were exhausted within thirty years; more important were the copper ores in the Keweenaw peninsula, and the iron ores of the "ranges" around Lake Superior.

To-day the Midwest is one of the richest parts of the country. It has about one-quarter of the total population of the country, its soils are productive, and its farms are prosperous. Owing to the proximity of large masses of iron ore and coal which can easily be moved along a great inland waterway and a dense railway network, and the presence of a large market, industries have grown apace both in numbers and variety. Foreigners often appear to regard the Midwest—perhaps unfairly—as the embodiment of materialism, where culture is neglected and where cash is the yardstick of success. The former isolationism and the present blatant commercialism are attributed sometimes to the rawness of a young and expanding society which has not yet had time to develop spiritual values, and sometimes to the persistence of the frontier spirit. Faced by hostile Indians and an untamed environment, the pioneer had to be a practical man, self-reliant and independent. He had no time to develop cultural interests and he tended to distrust and despise those who did have them. So runs the argument. This materialist ethos is commented upon so often and by so many writers that one cannot ignore it; on the other hand, it should be noted that the cultural amenities of the major cities seem in no way inferior to those of comparable cities in other parts of the world. It has been stated many times that if a distinctive American culture is to evolve, it will develop in the Midwest.

Physical Features

From the Allegheny Front in the east, the land slopes gently towards the Mississippi: in some places the western edge of the Allegheny Plateau is marked by a low escarpment; in others it merges imperceptibly into the Central Lowlands (Fig. 59). West of the Mississippi the land rises slowly to the Missouri Coteau, a long escarpment which marks the eastern edge of the Great Plains. The underlying rocks are almost horizontal. They are of Palaeozoic age and cover the whole surface except the north, where they thin out and disappear, giving way to the ancient igneous and metamorphic rocks of the Canadian Shield which here extend south of Lake Superior. However, the sedimentary rocks are only rarely exposed: almost everywhere there is a cover of glacial drift of variable thickness brought and left by the Pleistocene ice-sheets.

The last ice-sheet (of the Wisconsin glaciation) was not as extensive as earlier sheets and so there remains a southern area of older drift and a northern area of younger drift. The main effect of the ice was to smooth and lower the upstanding parts of the surface and to fill with drift the basins and valleys. The relief therefore is subdued—especially in the area of newer drift where the streams have not had time to dissect the surface to any significant extent. The surface features are diverse: drumlin tracts, long, low,

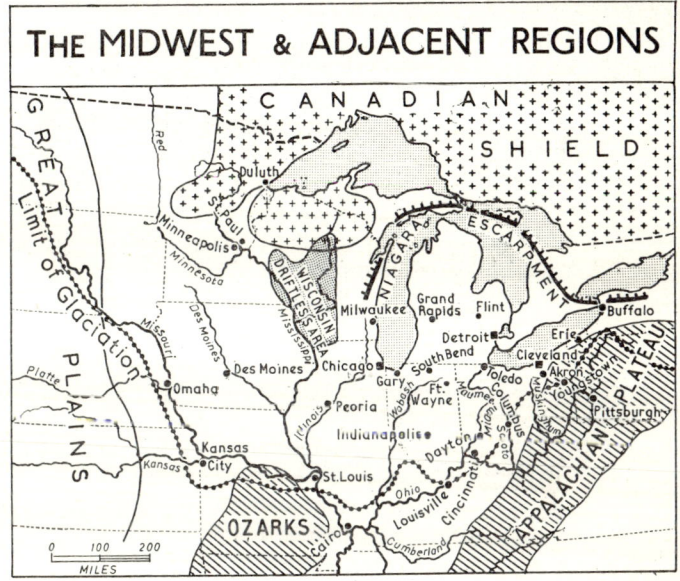

Fig. 59.

morainic ridges, and sinuous eskers alternate with the extensive till plains. In Minnesota there are many lakes and marshes which occupy hollows in the glaciated surface. The drainage pattern of the area was upset by the successive glaciations. The Great Lakes occupy over-deepened ice-basins, and the numerous overflow channels (Fig. 2) have been utilised as routeways for roads, railways, and canals. The Ohio was diverted from its pre-glacial valley near Cincinnati, and the Mississippi at Rock Island. The Missouri, which had formerly flowed to Hudson Bay, skirted the edge of the ice-sheet and took a completely new course south-eastwards to the

Mississippi. During the closing stages of the Ice Age, many of the lakes occupied larger areas than they do now. When the waters receded they left fertile lacustrine clays (Fig. 2), particularly significant in the Red River Valley (formerly Lake Agassiz) and along the southern shores of the present Lake Erie. Also dating from the Pleistocene period are the deposits of loess which stretch across Nebraska, Iowa, Missouri, and Indiana. This wind-blown sand (probably derived from the tundra waste which surrounded the ice-sheets) has often been picked up and redeposited by the rivers. Almost in the centre of the region is the Wisconsin Driftless area which was between the lobes of ice following Lake Michigan and the Mississippi Valley and thus escaped glaciation. The terrain is more rugged and dissected than the surrounding areas and may be typical of the pre-glacial scenery of the Midwest.

After the Ice Age as the climate became progressively milder, the region was colonised by vegetation. The first arrivals were the lowly tundra plants which were later replaced by coniferous forests. These in turn gave way to deciduous forests but only in the south. The early settlers found pine stands on the crystalline rocks of Minnesota and north Michigan, and hardwood forests in Ohio and Illinois. Between lay a zone of mixed forest. In the western areas were oak glades and prairies where the tall grasses sometimes attained a height of five feet.

The soils are generally immature, but unleached and rich in soluble plant foods, especially in the area of newer drift, and vary a great deal within short distances. The boulder clay is usually fertile, whereas the sandy moraines and eskers remain uncultivated. Where the soils have developed under coniferous forest they are acidic and lacking in humus. These ashy podsols are much less fertile than the grey-brown earths which are found under the hardwood forests. The best soils are those rich in the humus derived from the prairie grasses. Some of these have been cropped for over a century without loss of structure or fertility. The Midwest has the highest percentage of first-class land of all the regions of the U.S.A.

Climate

The climate of the Midwest is of the Humid Continental type (see Chapter II). Precipitation falls throughout the year but tends to be concentrated in the summer months when there are torrential thunderstorms. Amounts vary from over 40 in. in the east to about 20 in. in the west, and nowhere need agriculture be seriously impeded by lack of water.

In the southern half of the region summers are hot [*e.g.* mean July temperature at Chicago, 74° F. (*23° C.*), at St Louis, 79° F. (*26° C.*)], and the weather is frequently enervating because the high temperatures are associated with high humidity. Inhabitants find the heat of summer nights particularly uncomfortable. Farther north, the summers are only warm [*e.g.* mean July temperature at Duluth, 66° F. (*19°C.*)]. Winter temperatures are extremely low for these latitudes (which are the same as those between the Balearic Isles and Paris). Duluth has five months below freezing point,

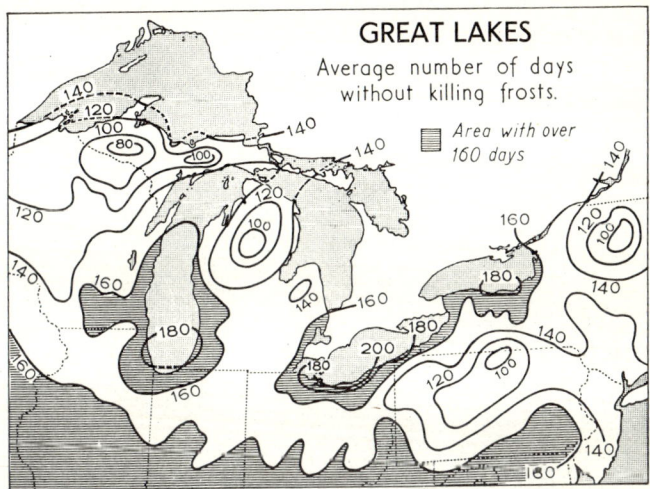

Fig. 60.
The effect of the Great Lakes on the incidence of frost is very marked.

St Paul four, and Chicago three. The mean January temperature at St Louis, which lies near the southern border of the Midwest, is 32° F. (*0° C.*). The shores of the Great Lakes are frozen for four months of the year (the centres do not freeze) and there is no navigation from December to March.

Although this region lies in the path of depressions, the weather is dominated by the continental high pressure in winter and the indraft of warm, moist air from the Gulf in the summer. This accounts for the summer maximum of precipitation and the wide annual temperature range. The growing season varies from under 80 days in parts of the north to over 180 days in the south (Fig. 60).

Agriculture

The Midwest is the main agricultural region in North America: nowhere else is there such an extensive area of intensive farming. Land which was bought by the early settlers for $1.25 an acre can be resold at prices running into hundreds of dollars per acre. While economic considerations are important in determining the type of farming, physical factors exert a dominating influence. The soils become poorer towards the northern, eastern, and southern margins

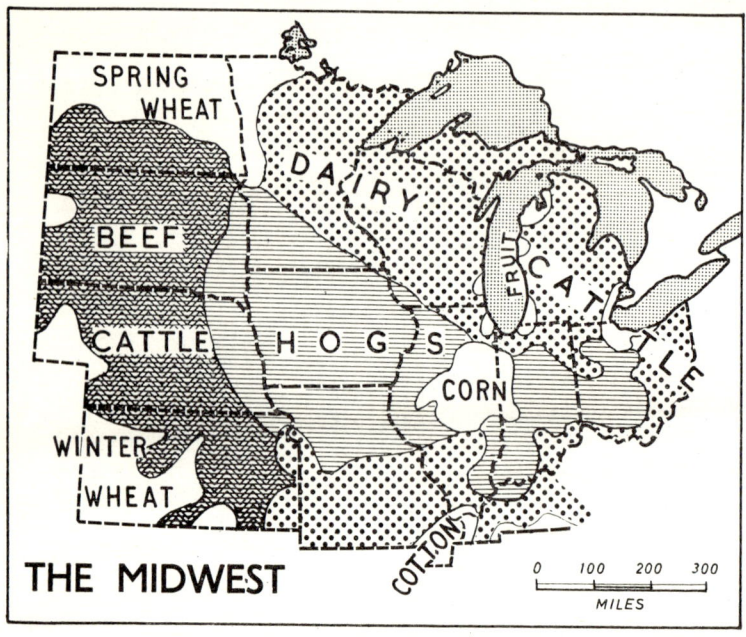

Fig. 61.

In the shaded areas more than half the farm income is derived from livestock and livestock products. In the unshaded areas crops provide more than half the farm income. The main crops and animals are indicated.

of the region and specialised farming is often replaced by general farming or forestry; the shortening of the growing season towards the north and the increasing aridity towards the west limit the types of crops that can be grown on these margins. The core of the Midwest is divided between two agricultural regions, the Corn Belt in the south and the Hay and Dairying Belt in the north (Fig. 61).

Corn Belt.—Corn (maize) is widely grown in the U.S.A., but nowhere so intensively or in such great quantities as on the Corn

CORN BELT

Belt. It is a tall crop, growing six feet or more in height, and it requires a growing season of at least 130 days. For the crop to ripen, high summer temperatures of 70° F. (*21° C.*) or more are essential, while for fast growth the night temperatures of over 55° F. (*13° C.*) are considered ideal. The amount of rain falling in July can affect the yield of the crop very much: with about 5 in. a bumper crop is likely; with less than 3 in. the situation becomes critical. Yields are heavy (much heavier than those of the small grains: *e.g.* the *average* yields per acre in the U.S.A. are corn 4,400 lbs., wheat 1,500 lbs., barley 2,400 lbs., and oats 2,900 lbs.). Owing to the development of a new hybrid corn, they are becoming heavier. Hybrid corn, which is less susceptible to disease than ordinary corn, has to be pollinated by hand. However, the extra yields are worth the greater labour. As with other crops, there are years when production exceeds demand and the government offers subsidies to farmers to reduce their acreages under corn.

Only in central Illinois and north central Iowa is corn grown mainly as a cash crop; significantly these two areas have the best soils in the Midwest. Elsewhere on the Corn Belt it is grown for animals: in fact, a more accurate name for the area would be the Meat Belt (Fig. 61). The commonest animal is the hog which can convert corn into meat more efficiently than any other animal. It requires about 5 lb. of grain to add 1 lb. of live weight—an increase which can occur in twenty-four hours. Young pigs are ready for slaughter after about eight months. About three-quarters of the country's hogs are on the Corn Belt. Beef cattle too are reared, and a typical farm might have 30 hogs, 20 cattle, and about 100 chickens. In the past, many cattle were brought from the Great Plains for fattening before slaughter, but this practice is now declining. Corn-fattened animals are still valued more highly than those fed on peanuts, oil seeds, sorghums, or other fodder.

The farms are usually about 160 acres (*i.e.* a quarter section or half-mile by half-mile), of which one-third or one-half is planted with corn. Other crops such as wheat, oats, barley, hay, and clover occupy smaller acreages and are used for fattening the animals. A crop which has gained in importance recently is soy-beans: oil can be extracted from the beans and has a variety of uses, while the vegetable matter is nutritious animal fodder. To maintain the fertility of the land great amounts of fertiliser are used and a crop rotation system is followed. The common four-course rotation is (i) corn, (ii) corn or soya, (iii) oats, (iv) hay. Almost every farm is highly mechanised: there seems to be a machine for every conceivable job. Even so, not all the corn is harvested; hogs and cattle are often turned loose in the fields to eat the crop as it stands.

In spite of the general prosperity of the Corn Belt, agriculture is not without its problems. Because farming is so commercialised, the producer is tied very strongly to a market economy (unlike the subsistence farmer who is less at the mercy of the consumer). In recent years there has been a tendency to over-produce and the federal government buys the agricultural surplus at agreed prices, a surplus which occasionally cannot be disposed of in national or international markets and consequently must be written off as a total loss. Another problem is soil erosion, for, although the land is flat or gently rolling, the rainfall occurs in short but heavy showers and run-off is accelerated. A partial answer to this problem would be to replace some of the land in grain by grass or cover crops.

The Corn Belt landscape, which stretches for 1,000 miles from central Ohio to eastern Nebraska, is essentially a rural one. The flat or gently undulating land is marked off in squares, each differently coloured according to the crop that is growing. Farmsteads appear to be widely spaced along the straight roads and consist of wooden farmhouses, huge red barns, shining metal silos, machine sheds and garages, and usually windpumps. Surrounding each farmstead may be a windbreak. The small villages with their banks, petrol stations, elevators, cold-storage plants, shops, and offices perform only a minimum of service functions. Many of the consumer goods are not bought locally but are obtained from mail-order houses in the large cities.

Farming activities on the Corn Belt have given rise to many industries, the most important of which is meat-packing. Large stockyards and abattoirs handle about 130 million animals every year. The greatest centre is Chicago with stockyards covering an area of over one square mile; others are St Louis, Omaha, St Paul, Kansas City, and Sioux City (see plate facing p. 113). The huge statue of a Hereford steer in Kansas City symbolises the importance of the meat-packing industry in this town.

Hay and Dairying Belt.—Almost as prosperous as the Corn Belt farms are those found farther north in the states of Minnesota, Wisconsin, and Michigan (Fig. 61). Swiss, German, and Scandinavian immigrants took over the lands cleared of their original forest cover and found the short growing season and cool summer more suitable for grass and hay than for other crops. Small grains—wheat, oats, and barley—are grown to supplement the animals' feed. In this climate corn does not ripen but it is grown and cut green to make silage. Much winter feed is needed, for the cattle are stall-fed during the severe winter cold. Soils are generally inferior to those in the Corn Belt and are used more advantageously in farming practices that place less emphasis on grain and cash crops. Dairying became commercially important only in the early years of the present century when a changing public taste and the increasing population of the country created a demand for milk and dairy produce. The use of refrigeration and the ever improving motor transport enabled this expanding market to be supplied.

There is some degree of specialisation: fresh milk comes from the areas closest to the towns; butter is made in the more remote areas where the cream content of the milk is high (usually where the grass-hay diet is liberally supplemented with concentrated grain feeds); cheese is processed from milk which has an average or low cream content. Powdered and condensed milk are also produced. To-day, partially dehydrated milk is sent in glass-lined tanks in express trains to cities as far away as Miami, in Florida, and Boston. At the destination, water is added to form reconstituted milk. Large surplus stocks of butter and cheese are stored in refrigerated warehouses.

The most important state is Wisconsin which has over 2 million dairy cattle out of the 15 million in the U.S.A., and where the farmers derive over half their income from the sale of dairy produce. The scenery is reminiscent of the Corn Belt with farms of similar sizes (120 to 160 acres carrying herds of 20 or 30 cattle), and similar collections of barns, silos, and other outbuildings. The main difference is that most of the land is sown with grass and not with crops. However, there are small areas where the farmers produce potatoes, peas, beans, and sweet corn, all of which yield better here than in the warmer Corn Belt, exemplifying the tendency of plants to grow best, not over the whole area that has adequate temperatures, but towards their cooler limits.

The northern parts of Minnesota and Wisconsin comprise the crystalline rocks of the Laurentian Shield which have only a thin cover of poor soils. Here dairying is still the predominant farming activity, but farms are fewer and less prosperous and often separated by extensive uncultivated areas. Some of the farms here have been abandoned.

Fruit Farming.—Certain areas adjacent to the Great Lakes are important for fruit growing. Here are found the hardy deciduous fruits, apples, cherries, and peaches, as well as grapes. Formerly almost every farm in the Midwest must have had a small orchard which received little attention but supplied the farm with fruit. It was the growth of the cities and the changing diet of the people

THE MIDWEST

which increased the demand for fruit and led to certain areas specialising in the production of high quality fruit for this expanding market.

The main orchard and vineyard areas lie along the eastern shore of Lake Michigan (171,000 acres) and the southern shores of Lake Ontario (101,000 acres) and Lake Erie (62,000 acres). Smaller, but still important, regions are the Door Peninsula (12,000 acres) and the valleys of the Finger Lakes (24,000 acres), (Fig. 62).

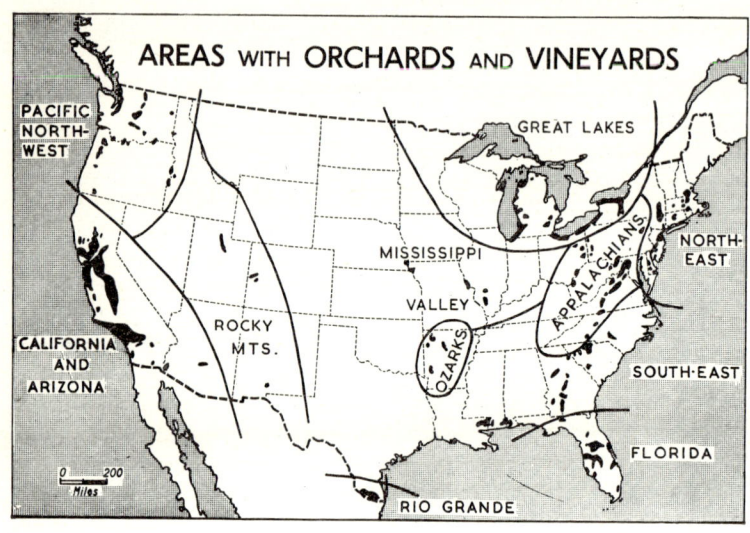

Fig. 62.

TABLE 9
ORCHARD AND VINEYARD REGIONS OF THE U.S.A.

Area	Acreage	Area	Acreage
California and Arizona	1,523,000	Florida	557,000
Great Lakes	338,000	South-east U.S.A.	309,000
Appalachians	255,000	North-west U.S.A.	253,000
Rio Grande Valley	152,000	North-east U.S.A.	134,000
Mississipi Valley	46,000	Ozarks	36,000
Colorado and Utah	41,000		
		Total U.S.A.	3,621,000

The orchards are located on light, well-drained soils such as those on the limestone escarpment of the Door Peninsula and the sandy moraines and till plains of Michigan, Ohio, and New York State. The land is usually sloping so that there is air drainage and the danger of frost is reduced. By far the most important factor, however, is the presence of large bodies of water. The fruit is grown on the eastern and south-eastern sides of the water masses so that the winter winds, blowing mainly from the west and north, pass over the relatively warmer waters of the lakes. Winter temperatures on the eastern side of Lake Michigan are about 10 F.° (6 C.°) higher than those on the west. Dormant trees (especially apple trees) can withstand very low temperatures (depending upon a number of factors such as the age of the tree, the time of the cold spell in relation to the end of summer, and the beginning of dormancy) but, naturally, the less exposed sites are preferred. The eastern shores also have rather heavier falls of snow and cloudier skies. The critical time is April or May when the trees are bearing blossom and are most vulnerable to attack by frost. Here again the lakes serve a useful purpose in delaying blossoming time (for by now the waters are relatively cooler than the rapidly warming land surface) for a fortnight or three weeks when the incidence of frost is much lower.

The Grape Belt stretches for fifty-five miles along the southern shore of Lake Erie and varies in width from two to five miles. Over 5 per cent. of the area is in vineyards, most of which are situated on old beach ridges where the soils are well drained. The growing season exceeds 170 days (cp. 150 on the plateau immediately to the south) and temperatures are modified by the lake as described above (Fig. 60). Farms average fifty to seventy-five acres, of which ten to twenty are planted with vines. Concord grapes are grown, most of which are used in the manufacture of grape juice. The number of vines is less than in the past (15 million now as against 25 million in 1930) but production is greater (now about 80,000 tons).

Industry

The Midwest is the western half of the Manufacturing Belt (Fig. 66) which stretches from Milwaukee and St Louis to the east coast. Within this belt is found just under half the population of the country and almost three-quarters of the industry. The basis of manufacturing on such a large scale is the availability of power and raw materials, an adequate labour force and market, and superlative communications.

Power

(a) *Coal.*—There are three coalfields which serve the Midwest. Two are peripheral—the Appalachian Coalfield and the Western Interior Coalfield—and one is close to the core of the region—the Central Coalfield (Fig. 63). The Appalachian field is the largest and the greatest producer. With only minor breaks it extends 800 miles from Pennsylvania to Alabama, and it coincides with the

Allegheny Plateau. The strata is horizontal or only gently folded into shallow basins and low domes. The coal seams are thick—the Pittsburgh seam has an average thickness of six feet—and close to the surface. Mining is concentrated in three main areas, western Pennsylvania-eastern Ohio, West Virginia-Kentucky, and around Birmingham in Alabama (Fig. 63).

Coal was first exploited in Pennsylvania where the Monongahela, Youghiogheny, Allegheny, Connemaugh, and other streams are incised below the level of the Allegheny Plateau and the coal seams are exposed on the valley sides. Thus by means of adits, the coal could be easily brought to the valley side and from there taken downstream by railway or barge. As all the streams focus upon

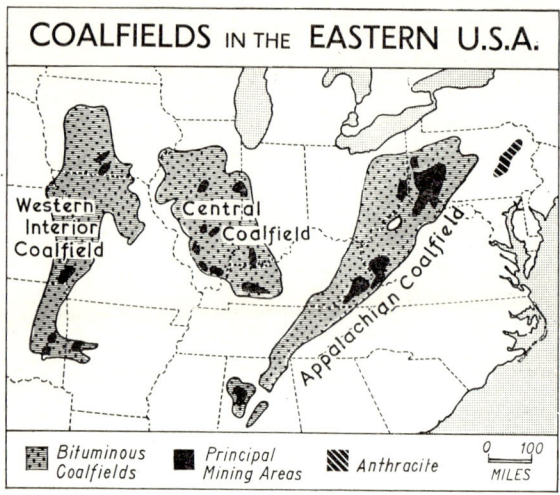

Fig. 63.

Pittsburgh, this city became the collecting centre of the region. To-day, the mining and transport methods are still the same, although recently open-cast mining has been started in northern Pennsylvania and motor transport is used for hauling coal short distances. Generally speaking, the harder coals with a higher carbon content are found in the eastern part of the coalfield, and softer types with a greater percentage of volatile material and ash are found towards the west. The valuable coking coal is found in the east around Connelsville. Formerly some of the Pennsylvania coal moved to other parts of the U.S.A. and abroad: now it is almost all used locally.

COAL

In West Virginia and Kentucky mining started later, but to-day the output is greater than in Pennsylvania.

TABLE 10

BITUMINOUS COAL PRODUCTION IN 1966

STATE	AMOUNT (m. tons)	STATE	AMOUNT (m. tons)
West Virginia	149·7	Ohio	43·3
Kentucky	93·2	Virginia	35·6
Pennsylvania	81·4	Indiana	17.3
Illinois	63·6	Alabama	14·2

Total U.S.A. 534·0

National production declined after 1945 owing mainly to the railways switching to diesel power, but has started to rise again in recent years. The largest markets for the coal are the electricity utilities (these are expected to use about twice as much coal in 1975 as they are using now) and the steel industry. Coal supplies about 27 per cent. of the total energy consumed in the country (cp. oil 32 per cent., natural gas 37 per cent., water-power 4 per cent.).

Mining conditions in West Virginia and Kentucky are similar to those farther north except that the plateau here is more deeply dissected and the valleys narrower. The seams outcrop high on the valley sides and chutes are necessary to convey the coal to the railways alongside rivers such as the Kanawha and Big Sandy. The main producing areas are around Fayetteville and Pocahontas. As there has been little industrial development in this region, much coal moves by rail to the Midwest manufacturing centres or to Hampton Roads for shipment to home and overseas markets (p. 129).

The coal seams in the Central field have been preserved in a shallow basin: they are exposed on the edges but lie deep underground in the centre. Most mines are around the edges (Fig. 63). The coal is of a poor quality and although the field is nearer to Chicago than other fields, production is hampered because of the competition of higher quality coal from West Virginia. The Western Interior Coalfield yields only poor quality coal and here production is low because there is no large local market and also because of keen competition from nearby oil and natural gas.

(b) *Oil and Natural Gas.*—Oil production is of historical rather than immediate interest in the Midwest. The first oil well in the country—"Drake's Folly"—was drilled near Titusville (Penn.) in 1859, and until the end of the nineteenth century Pennsylvania was the leading producer. Production has declined during the present century and some wells are worked only one day each week in order to allow the oil underground to collect at the foot of the drill hole. That production has not ceased completely is due to the fact that the oil is of high quality, free from impurities, and capable of yielding good lubricants. Small quantities of oil are produced in other areas of the Midwest: of these south-east Illinois is the most important (Fig. 57). The refining was carried out at Chicago, Toledo, and Cleveland: to-day these refineries which are well placed to supply the large local market, use oil from the Gulf and Mid-continental fields (see Chapter VII). Natural gas is obtained locally but only West Virginia produces a significant amount. Most of this is piped to Pittsburgh. The bulk of the gas used is sent to the Midwest from Texas and Louisiana, and there is a dense network of pipelines to carry both oil and gas, but some oil travels up the Mississippi and Ohio by barge.

(c) *Hydro-electricity.*—The fairly level nature of the terrain precludes the large-scale development of water-power. There are some small hydro-electricity stations in Michigan and Wisconsin, but the only major development is the harnessing of the water of the Niagara Falls (see plate facing p. 272). An agreement between Canada and the U.S.A. allows each country to use 65,000 cu. ft per sec. of water. Niagara was the first major hydro-electric establishment in North America and the cheap power attracted chemical and metallurgical industries to the Niagara Valley and the surrounding area. Further power installations are being added, and those completed in 1964, have a capacity of 2·2 m. kW (*i.e.* enough to supply the total needs of a city the size of Chicago). Electricity is transmitted distances of 200 miles or more.

Minerals.—In the rocks of the Laurentian Shield which extend into the U.S.A., west and south of Lake Superior, are large masses of iron ore. The pockets of haematite which are covered by a varying thickness of boulder clay (10 to 150 ft) are known as ranges, although they are not upstanding ridges. There are six ranges and they produce almost 80 per cent. of all the iron ore in the U.S.A. (1967, 64 million of the 84 million tons). The greatest of these is the Mesabi Range extending north-east to south-west through Hibbing (Fig. 64). The ore is obtained by open-cast mining methods and accounts for about 40 per cent. of the country's total output. On the other ranges, where the iron ore is covered by a thicker over-burden, underground mining is necessary. The iron content of the ore is high (over 50 per cent.) and the ore formerly mined had a higher percentage. Reserves are dwindling rapidly

IRON ORE

and increasing use is being made of an inferior ore, taconite, which contains only 20-35 per cent. iron and a large amount of silica. It is found associated with the haematite of the Mesabi and Marquette ranges, but before shipment it is beneficiated (*i.e.* concentrated), to avoid transporting an unnecessary amount of useless rock. Production of iron ore in this district, and in the U.S. generally, has fallen since the mid-nineteen fifties. At the same time stocks held at mines have increased, exports have fallen, and imports have risen.

In view of the eventual exhaustion of the range ores, U.S. companies have acquired complete or partial control of some of the more recently opened mines in Canada. North of Lake Superior,

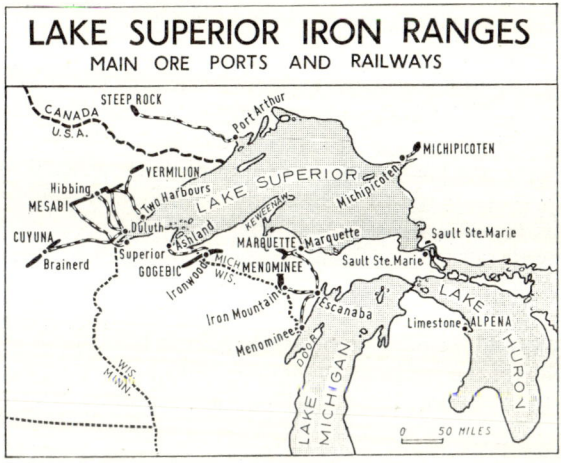

Fig. 64.

iron is found near Michipicoten and at Steep Rock. In the latter area, the ore lay under a lake which had first to be drained before mining could commence. This ore now feeds the U.S. furnaces and so does much of the ore from Schefferville (Quebec). The opening of the St Lawrence Seaway is expected to lead to an increase in the use of ore from this area.

Two other minerals are exploited in the Lake Superior region. Copper is found in the Keweenaw Peninsula, but is less important now than in the past (production amounts to about 6 per cent. of the U.S. output). Near Alpena, limestone is quarried and sent to the steel centres where it acts as a flux in the blast furnaces (Fig. 64).

The Great Lakes.—The main coal supplies lie south of Lake Erie: the iron ore mines are around Lake Superior, 700 miles away.

To make steel, the two raw materials must be brought together. Fortunately, between the two mining areas stretch four of the five Great Lakes. They came into existence during the Ice Age (Chapter I) and needed only minor modifications to enable large ships to sail from Buffalo on Lake Erie to Duluth at the head of Lake Superior or Chicago at the southern tip of Lake Michigan. The greatest undertaking was the construction of the Soo Canals at Sault Ste Marie where the waters of Lake Superior drop twenty feet to Lake Huron. A canal was built here in the eighteenth century, but the first of the present five canals (four on the U.S.A. side and one on the Canadian side), dates from 1855, soon after the discovery of iron ore. Traffic through the canals varies from year to year, depending mainly upon economic circumstances. In busy years the canals handle more ships than the Suez and Panama canals combined.

Very little needed to be done to make the channel between Lake Huron and Lake Erie navigable. (For the St Lawrence Seaway, see p. 305.) Vessels carrying over 20,000 tons of cargo ply between Duluth and Buffalo or intermediate ports for the eight months of the year (April to December) when the Great Lakes are not closed by ice. Bulky goods can be moved very cheaply. It costs more to rail the ore from the ranges to the ports than to ship the ore ten times the distance in freighters. All the ranges lie close to the lake side and loading is both easy and efficient. Piers project into the lake and the ore is tipped from the trucks above down chutes to the holds of the freighters lying alongside. The faster ships can make up to thirty trips during the ice-free period.

TABLE 11
MAIN LAKE PORTS
Cargo Handled in Millions of Tons, 1966

	IN	OUT	TOTAL
Duluth-Superior	4·9	41·4	46·3
Toledo	6·6	27·8	34·4
Detroit	31·9	1·0	32·9
Chicago	14·6	12·1	26·7
Cleveland	23·5	0·5	24·0
Buffalo	17·2	1·0	18·2

Total freight on Great Lakes 386·7

Eighty to ninety per cent. of the traffic passing through the Soo Canals is eastbound. The main cargo is iron ore with wheat coming a long way behind. Small quantities of other grains, wood, and oil are also carried. Westward traffic is light and consists mainly of coal and limestone. Much of the coal transported on the

Great Lakes does not pass through the Soo Canals (whereas almost all the iron ore does), but is delivered to Lake Michigan ports. Toledo is the main coal-shipping port.

Iron and Steel Industry.—The presence of iron and coal in the region and the easy means of transporting one to the other has led to the rise of a great iron and steel industry. The main centres are on the Appalachian Coalfield and on the lake shores. It was at Pittsburgh that the smelting of iron first started: here both the ore and coal were obtained locally. There was little competition from the older-established industry on the eastern seaboard which was cut off from the interior by the Appalachians. So Pittsburgh began to supply the rapidly growing Midwest market. The site of the town at the confluence of the Allegheny and Monongahela was ideal for collecting coal from the mines located along these rivers, but space for expansion was rather limited and the iron industry spread to surrounding towns such as Johnstown, Youngstown, and Wheeling. Even so furnaces line the two rivers for a distance of almost thirty miles upstream from Pittsburgh. When the Lake Superior ores were discovered, the industry was already well established. To-day the Pittsburgh area produces about 37 per cent. of the U.S.A. steel output (p. 186).

The lakeside centres fall into two groups, an eastern group along the shores of Lake Erie, and a western group on Lake Michigan and Lake Superior. Buffalo, Cleveland, Toledo, and Detroit all lie where incoming ore meets outgoing coal. When Lake Superior ores began to arrive in quantity to feed the Pittsburgh furnaces, these centres developed firstly as ports to handle ore and coal, and secondly as industrial cities processing the materials they handled. More recently batteries of coke retorts have been built and the by-products are used in many newer industries.

The other lakeside group includes the Chicago-Gary-Indiana harbour area which is fast becoming the greatest steel producing area in the continent. This industrial cluster lies midway between the ore ranges and the Appalachian Coalfield (the nearer Central Coalfield does not produce good coking coal). The furnaces lie along the shores of Lake Michigan where land is available for expansion (the steel plant at Gary was erected on uninhabited sand-dunes) and water is plentiful (65,000 gallons of water are needed to make one ton of steel). There is a tendency for industries to be located more and more with regard to the market than to the source of power or raw materials. It is because Chicago is in a good position to supply the interior market that it is developing so quickly. Other steelworks are located at Sault Ste Marie and Duluth, but these are smaller than the other lakeside centres. Both places take advantage of the cheap coal which is brought westward at preferential rates on the returning ore freighters. The whole of the lakeside region produces about 35 per cent. of the U.S.A. steel output.

TABLE 12
STEEL CAPACITY IN THE U.S.A., 1959

	(m. tons)			(m. tons)
U.S.A. total	147·6			
Pittsburgh and surrounding centres	53·7	including—Pittsburgh		18·3
		East Ohio		13·6
		Towns on Ohio and tributaries		13·2
		West Pennsylvania		4·6
Great Lakes	51·4	including—Chicago-Gary		26·9
		Detroit		7·9
		Buffalo		7·2
		Cleveland		5·4
		Lorain		2·6
Atlantic Seaboard	20·6	including—Baltimore		8·3
		Bethlehem		3·9
		Morrisville		2·6
South	8·4	including—Birmingham		5·4
		Houston		3·0
West	10·0	including—Fontana		2·9
		Geneva		2·3

Production is invariably less than these figures. In 1966 it amounted to 134·1 million tons.

The steel feeds numerous industries both in towns already mentioned and in others which do not actually make steel. Some of these industries will be noted in connection with the cities described in the following section.

Major Cities

Original settlements in the Midwest arose at points where *local* topographical features offered some advantages. The site might be a sheltered creek or river mouth on one of the Great Lakes (*e.g.* Cleveland and Duluth), a firm level terrace along one of the rivers (*e.g.* Cincinnati), a river confluence (*e.g.* St Louis and Pittsburgh), or a portage point (*e.g.* Fort Wayne). Those settlements which developed more quickly than their neighbours did so by virtue of their superior situation when viewed in a *regional* setting and their control of major routes. Almost every large city was in turn a fur-trading post or fort, an outfitting base and jumping-off point for the migrants moving west, and a commercial centre for the surrounding district. The very factor which made a settlement important for fur-trading (accessibility) also contributed to its growth as a commercial nucleus. It is not without significance that every town is on a lake or river. In most cases this is because in the eighteenth and early nineteenth centuries water transport was the main method of moving goods and people: in other cases, the settlements grew up where a major road crossed a river (*e.g.* the extension of the Cumberland Road from Wheeling to St Louis crossed the Muskingum at Zanesville, the Scioto at Columbus, the Miami at Dayton, the White River at Indianapolis and the Wabash at Terre Haute).

The table on p. 188 gives the dates of the establishment of the major towns and their growth from 1850. All the towns are

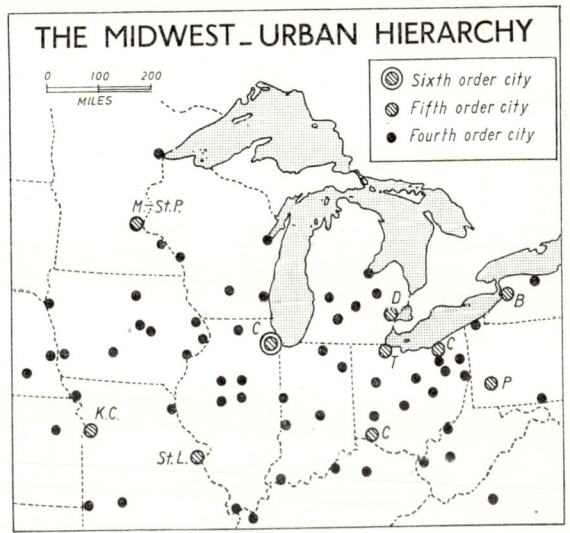

Fig. 65.

A suggested classification of the major cities in the Midwest. The one sixth order city can be regarded as the regional capital, the nine fifth order cities as major market and commercial centres, and the fourth order cities as commercial centres with a more limited sphere of influence.

important commercially and some (especially those experiencing phenomenal growth) are important industrially too (Fig. 65).

Most of these cities fall within the American Manufacturing Belt, the most productive industrial area in the world. It is impossible to treat in detail all the different industrial activities and their locations. In the following pages only the major manufacturing areas are discussed (Fig. 66).

Chicago-Milwaukee Area.—This area occupies the western and south-western shores of Lake Michigan and includes satellite towns

THE MIDWEST

TABLE 13

THE MAJOR CITIES OF THE MIDWEST

Population in thousands. See also Fig. 66. The drop in population of some cities between 1950 and 1960 reflects a movement of people from the central area to the suburbs.

CITY	ESTABLISHED	1850	1900	1950	1960
On River Ohio					
Pittsburgh..	1754	68	452	676	604
Cincinnati..	1788	115	326	503	503
Louisville..	1778	43	205	369	391
On the Lakes					
Chicago ..	1803	30	1,699	3,620	3,550
Detroit ..	1701	21	286	1,849	1,670
Cleveland..	1796	17	382	914	876
Milwaukee	1795	20	285	637	741
Buffalo ..	1790	42	352	580	532
Toledo ..	1833	4	132	303	318
On River Mississippi					
St Louis ..	1764	78	575	856	750
Minneapolis	1819	—	203	521	483
St Paul ..	1841	1	163	311	313
On National Road					
Indianapolis	1820	8	169	427	476
Columbus ..	1812	18	126	375	471
Dayton ..	1796	11	85	243	262

and cities (thirty-nine in all) extending a short distance inland. Heavy industries predominate, practically all manufacturing being based upon the primary iron and steel industry at the southern tip of Lake Michigan. The type of product tends to vary with distance from the steel mills, becoming progressively lighter the farther one goes from Chicago-Gary. Other industries are based upon the agricultural produce of the surrounding area or serve the farming, industrial, and domestic markets. Chicago is the metropolis of this area and holds a dominating position, Milwaukee (cars, machinery) and South Bend (sewing machines) being the most important subsidiary centres.

Chicago (3,550,000).—It is the greatest city in the Midwest and the second largest in the country. The original site was at the southern tip of Lake Michigan which extends southwards into the fertile agricultural land of the interior, where the mouth of the Chicago river offered shelter to lake shipping. Bordering the lake is a lacustrine plain varying in width from four to twenty miles and this is backed by a series of moraines. Behind Chicago these are breached by two overflow channels (the Chicago Portage and the Calumet Sag) through which waters from the pro-glacial lake made their way to the Des Plaines and then to the Mississippi. Several canals have been built, utilising these valleys, and to-day there is a nine-foot channel linking Lake Michigan to the Gulf coast. About 20 per cent. of Chicago's water-borne commerce uses this canal: the remainder is carried in the lake freighters.

However, it is not primarily as a port that Chicago is important. Its rapid growth coincided with the spread of the railway network. At first it was a convenient terminal point for the short stub lines which served the shipping on the Great Lakes. Later it became a terminal point for lines from the east and eventually the point

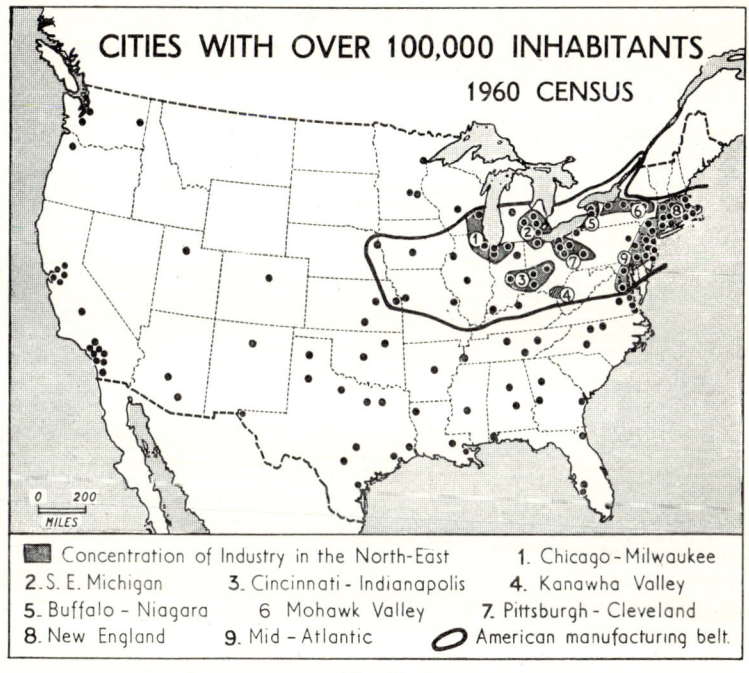

Fig. 66.

of departure for the lines which penetrated the western prairies, the Great Plains, and the Rockies (Fig. 67). Over 1,800 trains a day (passenger and freight) enter or leave Chicago by the forty different lines which reach the city. It is essentially a railway terminus, for until recently there was not one through-route.

As is natural where routes converge, commerce has developed. Chicago is one of the large grain markets of the country, situated as it is near to the Corn Belt and the Spring Wheat Belt, but the meat-packing industry is even more important. The stockyards cover more than a square mile and handle millions of cattle and hogs each year. Its position in the centre of a large and prosperous market has also enabled Chicago to become an industrial town. It is estimated that the city and its suburbs have over 10,000 factories. The iron and steel industry has already been noted and because of its proximity engineering concerns have arisen. Two of the leading manufactures are railway equipment and agricultural machinery, both of which owe a lot to early inventors who established workshops in the city. Pullman made railway coaches and McCormick produced here the first combine harvester. A great variety of other manufactures includes clothing, leather goods, and electrical equipment. Gary, which is contiguous with Chicago but across the state boundary in Indiana, was, in effect, the creation of the U.S. Steel Company. In 1906 this concern built its huge steel plant on the hitherto uninhabited lake shore. Much oil and natural gas is sent by pipeline from the south-west to refineries in the Calumet district.

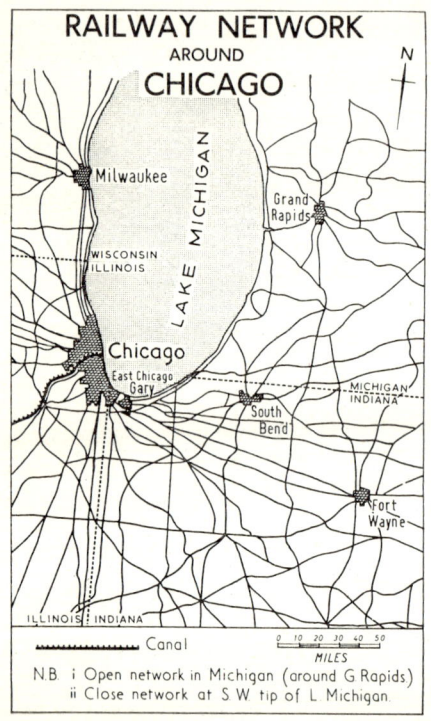

Fig. 67.

The very rapid growth of Chicago from an isolated fort (Fort Dearborn) in 1803 to second city of the nation in 1890 has been held responsible for the congestion of the industries along the Calumet (south of the Loop—the central core and business area of the city) and the great social contrasts between rich and poor. The former live along the opulent Gold Coast, the latter in sordid slums near the factories. The great number of foreign immigrants imposed a severe strain on the city administration, itself notorious for political graft. There are Polish, German, Jewish, Slav, Swedish, and Italian communities, and a negro population of almost half a million.

South Michigan Area.—Manufacturing activity in this area is almost entirely concerned with the production of automobiles. There is a small output of steel but not enough to feed an industry which absorbs one-fifth of the U.S. steel production. Around Detroit are rings of towns (an inner ring including Pontiac and Ann Arbor, and an outer ring including Flint, Lansing, and Toledo) which manufacture the hundreds of different components for the assembly lines. Many of these towns depend entirely on the automobile industry and are severely hit in periods of depression. This industry is one of the first to suffer when financial conditions become stringent. In fact, car sales provide a sensitive barometer of economic prosperity.

Automobile manufacturing became concentrated in this area in the early part of the present century, but to-day it is becoming more and more dispersed. Assembly lines are being established nearer the markets (*e.g.* California) and they use locally-manufactured components or those made in the South Michigan area.

Detroit (1,670,000), the centre of the industry, is situated at one of the few narrow points of the Great Lakes system (cp. Sault Ste Marie). The importance of the site on the St Clair River was recognised by the French, who, in 1701, established a fort there. The early settlement was isolated from the areas to the south and south-east by the Black Swamp along the Maumee River. Thus it was not until well on in the nineteenth century that Detroit progressed beyond the stage of being a fur-trapping and timber-collecting post. Then it became the jumping-off point for settlers moving into Michigan, and shared with other lakeside towns in the development of the iron and steel industry. To-day it is recognised as the automobile centre of the U.S.A., a position it owes in no small measure to Henry Ford who established his first modern factory there. Other manufacturers were attracted to the area and the present position is that the three largest companies, General Motors, Ford, and Chrysler, have their main plants in Detroit. In and around the city have sprung up factories manufacturing the numerous different components which feed the assembly lines. While the rise of the industry is the result of human rather than geographical factors, there is the added advantage that Detroit is centrally placed with regard to the densely populated areas of both Canada and the U.S.A. Other industries include the manufacture of pharmaceutical goods, copper and brass articles, paint, and rubber.

A large proportion of foreign-born people and second and third generation descendants of immigrants live in Detroit. The negro population numbers over 300,000.

Cincinnati-Indianapolis Area.—Although remote from the Great Lakes and lacking power and raw materials, this area, which extends from central Ohio to central Indiana, is dominantly industrial. It is strategically located with respect to the Ohio River and lies between the coalfields to the east and the productive farmlands to the west. Crossing it are the old Erie-Ohio canal and the National Road which ran from Wheeling to St Louis. There are two main centres, each with its cluster of satellite towns. Indianapolis (476,000) is a focus of railways and has many diverse industries including the canning of vegetables, meat-packing, and the manufacture of automobile parts. It is a commercial and banking centre for much of Indiana. Cincinnati (503,000) functioned first as a supply point for western settlers and later as a market, meat-packing centre ("Porkopolis"), and port. It remains a gateway to the south and has excellent rail facilities. It is a commercial and financial centre for the middle Ohio Valley and manufactures machine tools, soap, chemicals, automobile and aircraft parts, and electrical goods. The surrounding towns (Dayton, Hamilton, Springfield) concentrate, like Cincinnati, upon precision machinery and high-value manufactures (*e.g.* refrigerators, calculating machines).

Kanawha Valley.—The "Chemical Valley" stretches for a distance of sixty miles along the River Kanawha in West Virginia. Chemical industries always tend to cluster together because any one branch will tend to use the by-products of others. Manufacturing became established here during World War I and it has expanded and intensified ever since. The closely-spaced plants use the local coal, natural gas, and hydro-electricity. Among the more important products are synthetic rubber, sulphuric acid, many brands of anti-freeze, various alcohols, soda, ammonia, and chlorine. Rayon and nylon are manufactured here and a large range of ferro-alloys. The main town is Charleston (86,000), which occupies a restricted site in the narrow, steep-walled valley.

Cleveland-Pittsburgh Area.—This is the country's outstanding iron and steel producing district, and it supplies a large area with raw and semi-finished steel for secondary industries. It is strategically located for heavy industry since it lies between Lake Erie, over which move iron ore and limestone, and the North Appalachian Coalfield, and is centrally placed in the densely populated Manufacturing Belt. Although iron and steel is the dominant industry in Pittsburgh and Cleveland, the two main cities, and Canton, Youngstown, Wheeling, and Johnstown, there is also the manufacture of electrical machinery, automobiles, machinery, aircraft parts, chemicals, glass, and textiles. Akron is the main rubber manufacturing centre in the U.S.A.: the first factory was erected in 1870 by Goodrich, although this town possesses no geographical advantages not shared by many Midwestern centres.

Cleveland (876,000) is the third largest of the Midwest cities. It is the foremost of the many centres that line the southern shores of Lake Erie. It arose on the right bank of the Cuyahoga River (Cuyahoga is an Indian word meaning "crooked"), the estuary of which afforded shelter to lake shipping. The development of the port has been somewhat hampered by the lack of berthing space (see plate facing p. 256). In normal years about 14 million tons of iron ore are unloaded, partly for local use and partly for shipment to Pittsburgh and other inland steel centres. Cleveland has invested heavily in Labrador ore, and with the opening of the St Lawrence Seaway the importance of the port is likely to increase.

More important than its site, which is not superior to many similar river mouths along Lake Erie, is its situation in relation to the Appalachian Plateau and the Ohio drainage. The Mohawk routeway, continued westwards, skirts the plateau and naturally focuses upon Cleveland. South of the city the edge of the plateau trends southwards and so routes can splay out. There are good connections with Pittsburgh and towns in the Ohio Valley. The Cuyahoga Valley leads to the watershed between drainage to the lakes and drainage to the Ohio. A canal was built across this area following the valleys of the Cuyahoga and Scioto to link the city with the Ohio.

Its nodality made Cleveland an important commercial centre: its position with easy access to lake-borne iron ore and Pennsylvanian coal made it an industrial town. While steel-making is the greatest industry, manufacturing is more diverse than that of Pittsburgh, and a great variety of metal and electrical goods are produced as well as automobiles. Oil-refining is a major industry: oil supplies formerly came from Pennsylvania, but are now brought from the Texas-Louisiana-Oklahoma area. Textiles are important and there are many smaller industries, including paint and chemicals.

Pittsburgh (604,000) had its origin as Fort Duquesne, a French post at the "Forks of the Ohio", *i.e.* where the Allegheny and Monongahela unite to form the main river. To-day, this site is the hub of the city and is known as the Golden Triangle. Pittsburgh functioned as a military post, outfitting base for the migrating settlers, and river port, but quickly became the centre of a flourishing iron and steel industry based on local ores and an abundance of good coking coal which was easily mined in the valleys of the Allegheny,

Monongahela, and Youghiogheny. These rivers and their sheaves of tributaries focus naturally upon Pittsburgh, and coal moved along rivers, canals, and railways which followed the valleys to this ideally-placed collecting centre. Later, Minnesota ores, transported cheaply on the Great Lakes, replaced inferior local ironstones, and furnaces and steel plants soon occupied every available piece of lowland in the valleys.

Almost one-half of the city's industrial workers are engaged in primary metal production, while a further third produce machinery and metal goods of all kinds. The words Pittsburgh and steel are almost synonymous, although the hegemony of the city has declined and is declining as steel production increases, not only in other parts of the Midwest, but also in the West, the South, and along the Atlantic coast (p. 186). Pittsburgh is cramped for space; not only have industries spread up the valleys of the Allegheny, Monongahela, and Youghiogheny, but also the city has had to build high and there is an imposing group of tall buildings, including the "cathedral of learning", the forty-two-storey university. Formerly notorious for the thick pall of smoke which formed an umbrella over the city, it is now one of the cleanest of heavy industrialised centres, owing to the smoke-abatement policy recently carried out. In spite of increasing competition, Pittsburgh, by virtue of its pool of skilled labour and the enormous investment that has gone into its heavy industries, seems to have an assured industrial future.

Cities of the Western Margins.—Along the interior margin of the Midwest lies a belt of cities which are partly industrial and partly commercial in character. They are transitional between the predominantly industrial centres of the Manufacturing Belt and the predominantly commercial cities of the Great Plains. They are important mainly for livestock and grains, especially Omaha (302,000) and Kansas City (508,000), and their trade territories extend almost to the Rockies. In addition, Kansas City benefits from the local exploitation of oil and natural gas, and has aircraft and automobile industries. The two largest cities are Minneapolis-St Paul and St Louis.

Minneapolis-St Paul (796,000) are twin cities, the centres of which are only ten miles apart on opposite sides of the Mississippi. St Paul was established at the effective head of navigation where the Mississippi rejoins its pre-glacial valley. Above St Paul, the river flows in a post-glacial valley and the profile is irregular. Minneapolis grew up on the St Anthony Falls which supplied power for the earliest industry, saw-milling (see plate facing p. 208). With the destruction of the native forests, Minneapolis developed other interests (although saw-milling is still important), and with the coming of the railways which opened up the rich wheat lands of the Red River Valley and the Dakotas it rose to eminence as a flour-milling centre. St Paul is the centre for the dairying and meat industries. Thus while St Paul is a regional centre for the area to the east and south, where it competes with other large Corn Belt cities, Minneapolis serves the area to the north and west where cities are fewer and its trade area, in consequence, is much greater.

St Louis (750,000) has had its boundaries unaltered since 1876 and in consequence the population figure given is smaller than that of the built-up area. About twenty miles below the confluence of the Mississippi and Missouri, a low terrace on the west bank afforded a convenient site for a French trading post (1764). It became a focal point for trade along the Missouri and its tributaries. Later it was important as a crossing place of the north-south artery, the Mississippi, by the great east-west migration route along the Ohio and lower Missouri. Its importance grew during the steamboat era and with the coming of the railways, St Louis became the natural bridging point of the Mississippi. Twenty-seven lines now converge on the city. Its central position in the Mississippi basin, midway between the 49th Parallel and the Gulf of Mexico, and between the Appalachians and the Great Plains has made it a great commercial centre. St Louis is an industrial city, too, manufacturing the products of the farms (meat-packing, flour-milling, leather-working) and using coal from the Central and Western Interior Coalfields to make a wide variety of metal goods, chemicals, and electrical equipment. The city itself is in Missouri and east of the river in Illinois is East St Louis, where many of the industries are located.

CHAPTER IX

THE GREAT PLAINS

Introduction

To the early travellers moving across the central part of the U.S.A. the Great Plains posed a set of unusual problems. Here there were conditions which the settlers had never encountered before. The earliest arrivals left records which coloured the attitude of those following in their wake.

"It combines within its frightful and extensive territory the Steppes of Tartary and the moving sands of Africa" (1816).

"In regard to this extensive section of the country, I do not hesitate in giving the opinion that it is almost wholly unfit for agriculture and, of course, uninhabitable by a people depending on agriculture for their subsistence" (1821).

On the maps of the continent, until well past the middle of the nineteenth century, the words Great American Desert were printed across the Great Plains. Indeed, for a brief period camels were used in western Texas as a means of transport. The luckless experiments made to settle in the region did little to dispel the prevailing beliefs, and the migrants came to regard the Plains as 400 miles of waste to be crossed before they could reach the Rockies and the humid forested lands of Oregon or the gold-fields of California. Several decades elapsed before a new approach was made, conditions were understood more fully, and methods were found of coming to terms with the environment.

The western margin of the Great Plains is firmly marked by the front of the Rockies: the eastern boundary is less definite. But somewhere between the 97th and 100th meridians, there occurs a series of changes in natural conditions and consequently in the cultural landscape so that this *zone* is one of the most significant boundaries in the U.S.A. There are changes in—

(*a*) climate, from the humid east to the sub-humid and semi-arid west;

(*b*) vegetation, from long grass and wooded glades to short grass;

(*c*) soils, from pedalfers to pedocals;

(*d*) farming, from humid agriculture to dry farming, ranching, and irrigation;

RELIEF AND STRUCTURE

(*e*) settlement, from a relatively dense population and large settlements to a sparse population with few sizeable towns.

Surface Features

The Great Plains are not low: on the west where they meet the abrupt rise of the Rockies they have an elevation of 5,000 ft or more; from here they slope gently eastwards to an elevation of about 1,500 ft. The underlying rocks are almost horizontal over most of the area, but where they meet the Rockies they have been upturned and the more resistant beds form hog-back ridges (Fig. 6). During Tertiary times the eastward-flowing rivers brought eroded material from the mountains and spread it over the older rocks, forming a level slab of sands and pebble beds. Erosion by wind, water, and (in the north) ice has produced surface features which vary from district to district and several different types of terrain can be seen (Fig. 68).

In the south is the Edwards Plateau, a limestone tableland from which the overlying Tertiary cover has been removed. There has been remarkably little dissection of the exhumed surface. The southern boundary of the Edwards Plateau, and of the Great Plains, is the Balcones Fault Escarpment which overlooks the Texas coast plain. Lying north of the plateau are the High Plains where the Tertiary beds present a monotonously level, treeless surface broken only by occasional broad river valleys. To guide travellers across part of this featureless surface, the Staked Plains, routes were marked with stakes or buffalo bones. The eastern boundary here is the Break of the Plains where erosion of the Tertiary slab has left a low, ragged escarpment. On the west, too, these beds have been removed by the River Pecos and the longitudinal tributaries of the Arkansas and Platte rivers, and the underlying Cretaceous and Permian beds are exposed. This scarped vale at the foot of the Rockies is known as the Pecos Lowlands in the south and the Colorado Piedmont farther north. In Nebraska the wind has brought sand and loess—probably derived from the wide river beds which are incompletely covered for most of the year—and spread it across the land, forming sand-dunes in some parts. Beyond the Pine Ridge which marks the northern limit of the Tertiary rocks is the Missouri Plateau.

The land here is rolling rather than flat and in the northern portion is covered by a mantle of glacial drift. The rivers flow in a north-easterly direction and many of them are sunk in deep valleys. Rising abruptly from the Plains is a crystalline mass, the Black Hills of Dakota, which can be regarded as an outlier of the

Rockies. The rocks were domed owing to the intrusion of igneous material from below and the overlying sedimentaries were stripped away from the central crystalline core, leaving a series of concentric cuestas around it. Between the Black Hills and the Pine Ridge are the Badlands. This is an area where horizontal rocks of unequal resistance have been sculptured by occasional torrents and

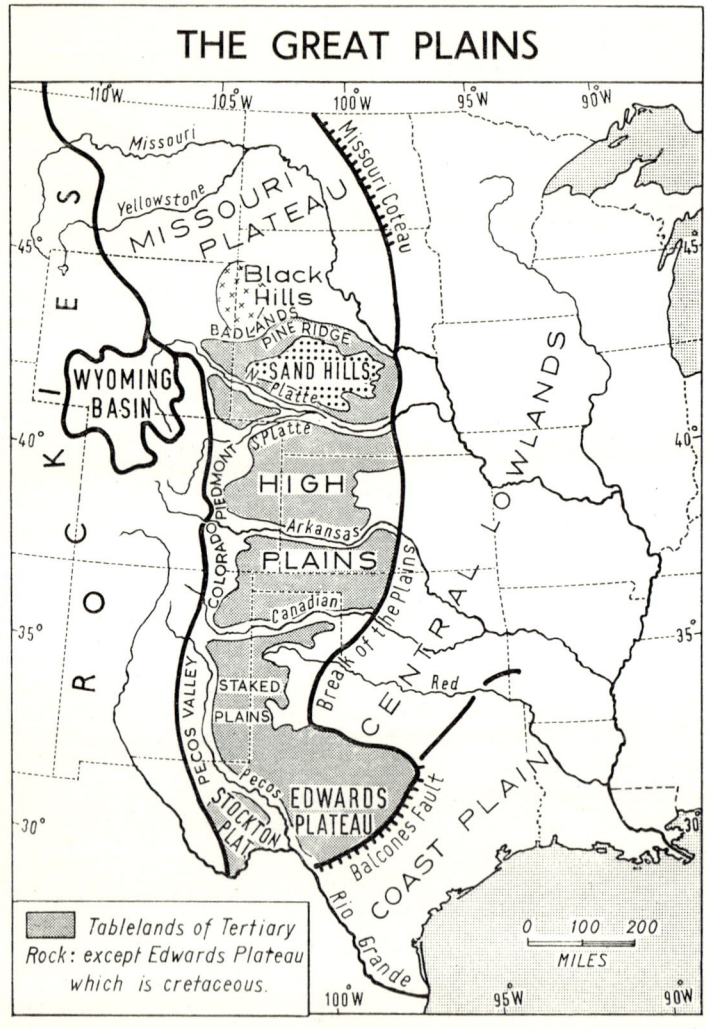

Fig. 68.

CLIMATE

the wind into many fantastic shapes. The name was given to the area by the early travellers who found the rugged terrain very difficult to cross. The eastern limit of the Missouri Plateau is the Missouri Coteau, an escarpment which drops sharply to the Central Lowlands.

Physiographically then, there are three well-defined boundaries: the Rockies in the west, the Balcones Fault scarp in the south, and the Missouri Coteau in the north-east. Elsewhere the Great Plains merge into the Central Lowlands, and, apart from the Break of the Plains, which is not a significant topographical feature, no sharp physical division can be made.

Climate

It is the climate of the Great Plains which is the dominating influence on man and consequently the most pronounced factor in the geography of the region. The main features have been described in Chapter II: in the following paragraphs the distinctive characteristics are recapitulated (Fig. 69).

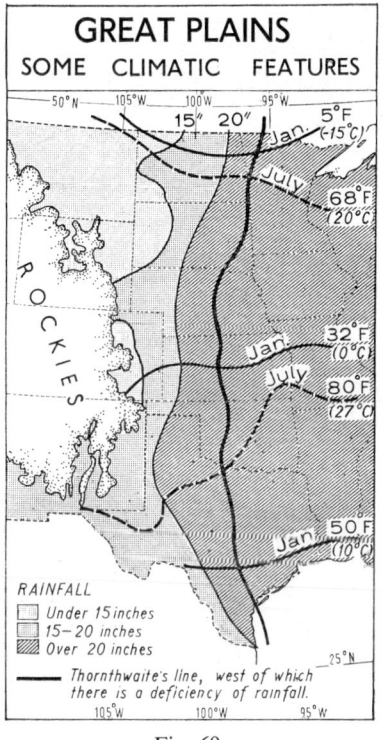

Fig. 69.
Rainfall is deficient when potential evapotranspiration exceeds precipitation. See p. 41.

1. There is a very large mean annual range of temperature, as is natural in an area in middle latitudes which is remote from the sea. In January, temperatures along the Canadian border average 0° F. ($-18°$ C.) and the cold Polar continental air which lies over the region occasionally surges southwards to bring freezing conditions to the Gulf coast where temperatures are normally over 50° F. (*10° C.*). The North Platte is ice-covered from November to March. Spring comes suddenly and the temperatures rise rapidly to reach 80° F. (*27° C.*) in Texas in July and almost 70° F. (*21° C.*) in North Dakota.

2. Precipitation is light, another characteristic of continental climates. Few parts have more than 20 in. and large areas have under 15 in. Summer is the wettest season, for at this time moist air is drawn into the interior from the Gulf of Mexico. Denver has 13·4 in. of rain a year and almost 70 per cent. of this falls in the six summer months. Evaporation is intense and consequently there is a water deficiency (Fig. 70 and Fig. 22). Rainfall decreases towards the west and as it does so becomes less reliable. Totals,

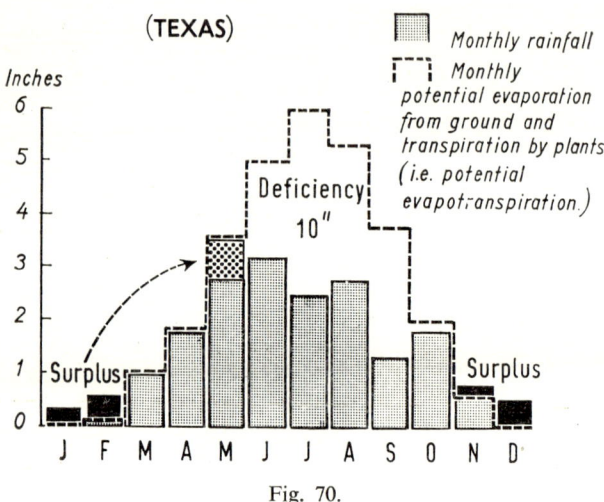

Fig. 70.

During the winter months there is a water surplus, some of which is held in the soil and used in summer. The overall deficiency, equivalent to 10 in. of rain, restricts vegetation and run-off.

averaged over a number of years, mean little for amounts in successive years can vary extremely widely (see p. 37). It is the unreliability of the rain and the variability from year to year that have caused so much agricultural distress on the Plains. The rain comes in the form of torrential downpours associated with thunderstorms. Occasionally summer precipitation is in the form of huge hailstones, which can do enormous damage to growing crops, and farmers often insure themselves against such a contingency. Rainfall is more "effective" in the north where temperatures are lower and evaporation not so intense: 20 in. of rain on the Canadian border is equivalent to 30 in. in Texas.

3. One climatic feature of the Plains which cannot be ignored is the wind. Velocities are high, for there are few obstructions on the open level plains. In summer hot winds limit corn growing and sometimes destroy wheat which is more resistant to desiccation. The Chinook wind which is warmed adiabatically as it descends from the Rockies causes rapid snow-melt in spring. The Norther and the blizzard are bitterly cold winter winds. Another hazard is tornadoes which occur especially in summer. During their brief existence they cut swathes of destruction through the countryside. Apart from the direct effect of the winds on the land, there appears to be a psychological effect on human beings, which has been commented upon by several writers. It appears that the monotonously strong and constant winds are responsible for the high proportion of irritability and nervousness found among the inhabitants of the region.

Vegetation and Soils

Because the rainfall is so small, trees do not flourish except along the watercourses and the dominant vegetation is grass. In the east are the long grasses (Prairie grassland) consisting of bluestem, bunch, and needle grass. The slightly heavier rainfall here permits the grass to grow tall, up to 3 ft, and develop long roots. Westwards these species are gradually replaced by shorter grasses (Plains grassland), the main types being grama and buffalo grass. Whereas the long grass tends to grow in bunches, the short grass (except in the very dry areas where it is tufted) forms a continuous mat on the surface, which protects the soil from erosion by wind and rain. The grass is drought-resisting, and in summer is cured into hay as it stands, a favourable feature which enabled the early ranchers to winter their cattle out of doors. Where rainfall becomes markedly deficient, sagebrush and desert vegetation replace the short grass. In the south the grasses are interspersed with mesquite, yucca, and prickly pear (see plate facing p. 65). The only extensive area of forest is on the Black Hills of Dakota, a humid island in a sub-humid plain (Fig. 71).

The soils which have developed under this vegetation are pedocals (rich in lime), unlike the pedalfers of the eastern states (where the salts and bases have been leached out by the heavier rainfall). In the pedocals a layer of calcium carbonate occurs somewhere between the surface and the water-table. As the rainfall decreases so the layer comes closer to the surface. Roughly coextensive with the long grass are the chernozem soils, which are black in colour and very rich in humus. The zone of lime accumulation lies well over two feet deep. Where short grass appears there are the dark brown (chestnut) soils. The humus content is not so great and the carbonate layer may be only twelve inches below the surface. In the more arid parts the soils are a lighter colour, as the alkaline salts rise very close to ground level and humus becomes scarce. Immature soils (*i.e.* recent soils without a fully developed profile, where the parent rock is more important than the climate and vegetation), are found in the Sand Hills of Nebraska and the drift-covered Missouri Plateau.

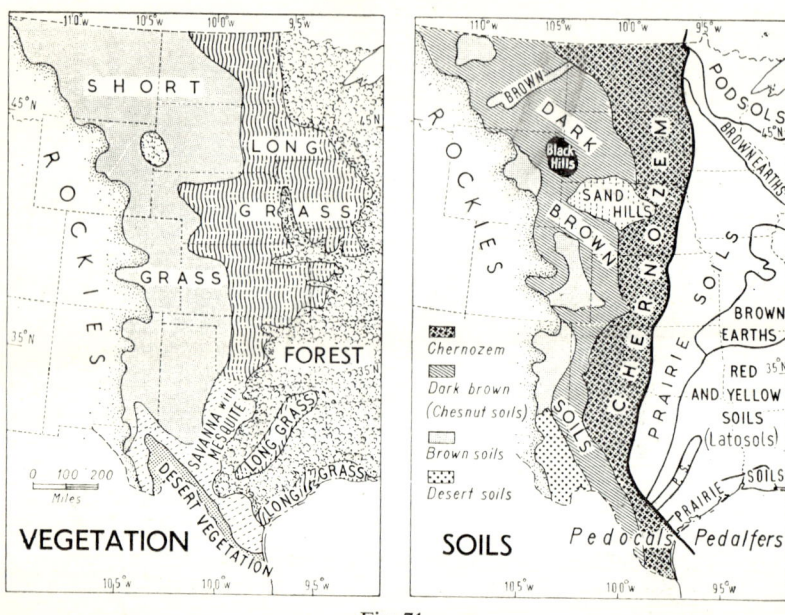

Fig. 71.

Rivers

Except in the south where the Pecos flows parallel to the Rockies before joining the Rio Grande, the Great Plains are drained by a series of eastward-flowing streams. Those in the north, the Yellowstone, Cheyenne, Platte, and Kansas are collected in turn by the Missouri. Farther south the Arkansas and Red River both collect a sheaf of tributaries before joining the Mississippi. Whereas in the past these streams were depositing their load across the Plains in the form of huge, coalescing fans, now they are engaged in deepening and widening their valleys, *i.e.* removing the material they formerly deposited. Erosion is not very effective for the streams are few, have little water for much of the year, and are often choked by silt and sand. Rainfall is slight and evaporation so intense that the discharge of the rivers is often less than 5 per cent. of the precipitation. Some of the rivers such as the Cimarron and Canadian dry up altogether. The valleys are broad and the rivers shallow and braided.

"For league after league, a plain as level as a lake was outspread beneath us; here and there the Platte divided into a dozen thread-like sluices . . . . Two lines of sand-hills, broken often into the wildest and most fantastic forms flanked the valley at a distance of a mile or two on the right and left; while beyond them lay a barren, trackless waste, extending for hundreds of miles to the Arkansas on the one side and the Missouri on the other. . . . . The river itself runs through the midst, a thin sheet of rapid, turbid water, half a mile wide, and scarcely two feet deep. Its low banks are of loose sand, with which the stream is so heavily charged that it grates on the teeth in drinking." (Francis Parkman, *The Oregon Trail*, Chapter 6.)

Although the water level is normally very low, particularly at the end of summer, the torrential summer showers can cause sudden floods during which the rivers may alter their beds and banks. Where these rivers are boundaries (*e.g.* the Red River and the Rio Grande), the frequent and sudden alterations of course lead to prolonged discussions over the territorial changes.

The early migrants found the rivers to be unsuitable for navigation. Only the Missouri was used and then only the lower part of the river by specially built vessels. A more important use has been the development of irrigation along the Piedmont where the streams debouch from the Rockies. Some irrigated areas cover only a few acres: others, as along the Arkansas and Platte rivers, extend for miles. However, the supply of water is limited and already water is being brought through tunnels from the western side of the Rockies to part of the Colorado Piedmont. There are parts of the Missouri Plateau where irrigation is practicable.

The Missouri flows for almost 2,500 miles to its confluence with the Mississippi near St Louis. Its basin, which covers 516,000 square miles or one-sixth of the U.S.A., includes all the northern Great Plains, part of the northern Rockies, and a fraction of the Midwest. Since the success of T.V.A. attempts have been made to inaugurate a similar scheme for the Missouri Valley in order to increase the amount of irrigated land, improve navigation, control flooding, harness power, and improve agriculture by eradicating soil erosion. The upper part of the basin with annual rainfall of under 15 in. is short of water, while the lower part with 30 in. or more is subject to severe periodical floods.

The river is in the joint charge of the Bureau of Reclamation (which is primarily interested in irrigation and hence concentrates on the upper portion of the Missouri) and the U.S. Corps of Engineers (which is primarily concerned with navigation and flood control and consequently operates mainly down river). Each body has produced a plan to develop the Missouri basin, the Sloan Plan by the Bureau of Reclamation and the Pick Plan by the Engineers.

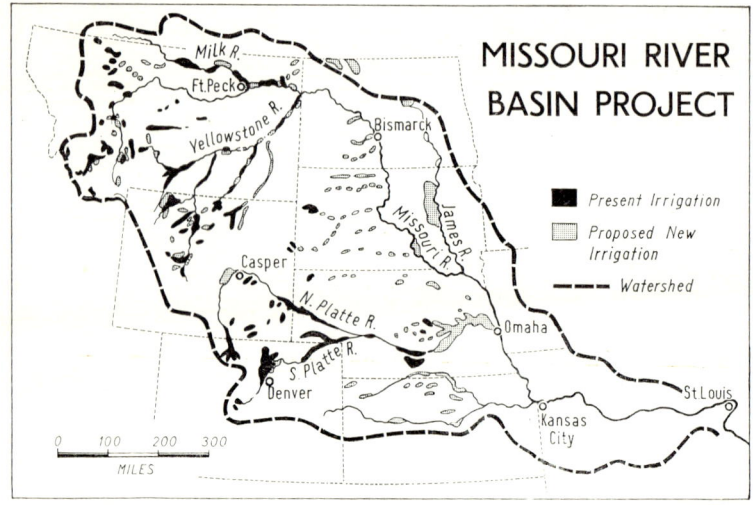

Fig. 72.

As an uneasy compromise, these plans were merged in the Pick-Sloan Plan which is now being put into operation by the Missouri Valley Administration. The plan (Fig. 72) envisages the construction of 150 reservoirs, and the irrigation of 5 million acres of land in addition to the 5 million already irrigated. A nine-foot navigation channel to Sioux City already exists and this can be extended, while the construction of levees will reduce the danger of flooding. If fully harnessed, the river and its tributaries could produce about 10,000 million kilowatt hours of hydro-electricity annually. The Department of Agriculture has produced a parallel programme for agricultural development.

Since 1944, when work started, the basin has been developed project by project as funds have been made available by Congress. While there can be no doubt that the Pick-Sloan Plan will bring enormous benefits to the Missouri basin, many people regret the fact that, owing to political controversy and the complications of a federal system of government, a truly regional plan was not adopted.

The Human Occupance

It has already been noted that the first travellers to cross the Plains were unfavourably impressed by the conditions, and that their reports coloured the beliefs and attitudes of the intending settlers.

"For two centuries American pioneers had been working out a technique for the utilisation of the humid regions east of the Mississippi River. They had found solutions for their problems and were conquering the frontier at a steadily accelerating rate." (W. P. Webb, *The Great Plains*, Introduction.)

"In the first half of the nineteenth century we see the advance guard of this moving host of forest home-makers emerge into the new environment where there are no forests, no logs for cabins, no rails for fences, few springs and running streams." (*Ibid.*, Chapter 5.)

The result was a complete, though temporary, breakdown of the ways of pioneering. The almost total absence of forest and the scarcity of surface water led many pioneers to regard the region as a desert, although geographers to-day classify it as sub-humid or semi-arid rather than arid. The settlers crossed the uninhabited Plains on their way to the familiar forested environment of Oregon and settlement had to wait for the invention of new apparatus and techniques (see plate facing p. 17).

Meanwhile the bison that roamed the Plains were being slaughtered for their hides by professional hunters, and the Indians, who saw their means of existence being wiped out, were being pacified by military units. The first developments in the actual settlement of the area took place in the south. Cattle from the coast plains of Texas spread north and west on to the higher and drier lands. Cattlemen, finding that the animals could endure the extreme climatic conditions provided that water was available, occupied the river banks and assumed control over the Public Domain as far as the local watershed. Over this open range roamed the increasing herds and marketing the animals was a serious problem until the railways began to penetrate the Great Plains. This happened after the Civil War and coincided with a great demand for meat in the expanding industrial cities of the north-east. Soon the whole of the area from Texas in the south to Montana in the north consisted of vast "estates" devoted to the production of beef steers. A round-up was held once a year for sorting out the branded cattle, branding the calves, and selecting steers for the market. They were driven over recognised trails such as the Chisholm Trail to the nearest rail-head. Until the railroad was pushed farther west, each of these rail-head stations enjoyed a brief but hectic period of prosperity and notoriety, none more so than Abilene in Kansas.

However, the "cattle kingdom" did not last long: its decline was ushered in by the invention of barbed wire. At last the intending homesteader had a fence to protect his crops from the depredations of the half-wild cattle. The cattleman found barbed wire useful too, for he could segregate his stock and improve the quality of his animals. The advent of the cultivator meant a reduction in the size of the cattleman's holdings: the fenced ranch replaced the more extensive open range. Just as barbed wire was used by both homesteader and rancher, so too was the wind-pump, which began to appear on the Plains in large numbers from the mid-eighteen-seventies. These cheap and often crude contraptions could raise water from depths too great to be tapped by the hand-hauled bucket. The rancher was no longer restricted to the river-side and the homesteader had water for domestic purposes and for irrigating the small garden which surrounded his prairie-sod dwelling.

Barbed wire, the wind-pump, and new machinery (particularly the steel plough and reaper) permitted the pioneer to settle on the Great Plains, but he found that increasing aridity towards the west imposed a limit to the area that could be profitably cultivated. Owing to the variability of the rainfall, this boundary fluctuates widely from year to year. However, the settlers continued to move farther and farther west, and the influx reached its peak in 1886. Then in the eighteen-nineties came a series of dry years and an exodus of those settlers who had insufficient financial backing to maintain themselves during the lean period. The subsequent history of the Plains has been marked by periodic advances and retreats. In Nebraska the wheat crop has failed disastrously (*i.e.* over one-third of the planted area was not harvested or yielded less than two bushels of wheat per acre) in 1893, 1894, 1899, 1917, 1923, 1932, 1934, and 1941. Yields per acre of wheat at the Colby Experimental Station in Kansas have varied from 0 (1935 and 1936) to 46·3 (1947) bushels, with an average over three decades of

18 bushels. All over the Plains a severe setback coincided with the great economic depression of the early nineteen-thirties. Steinbeck's *Grapes of Wrath* gives a vivid impression of conditions here at this time.

The zone of instability is found in the central strip of the Plains: in the east the cultivator is less at the mercy of unreliable rainfall and fluctuating markets, while in the west, the grazier reigns supreme. In between is a transitional area, where a mixed economy based firmly on livestock would seem to be the most stable type of farming. Unfortunately, the temptation to concentrate on more profitable wheat cultivation has proved hard to resist.

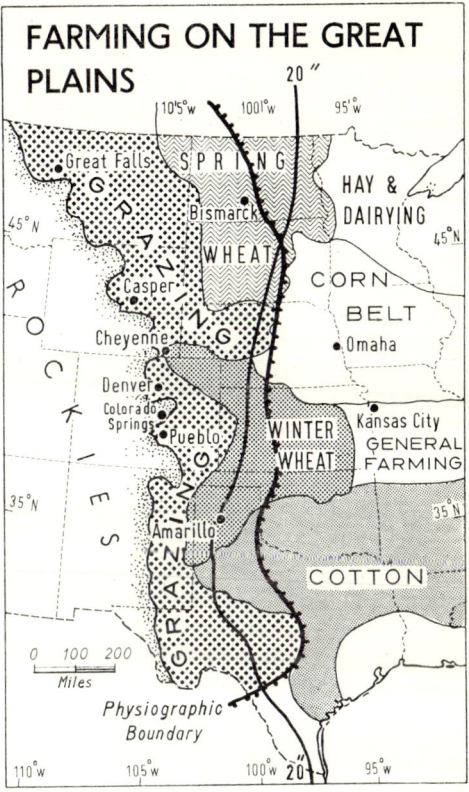

Fig. 73.

Agriculture

Within the Great Plains are found three distinct types of land use: there are the western areas devoted to grazing livestock, certain small areas where irrigation is possible, and the eastern areas forming parts of the different crop belts. In the six Plains' states about 133 million acres are dry farmed, 234 million grazed, and 9 million irrigated. Cotton has spread into a small section of the southern Plains and corn has a foothold in the central portion, but the crop of the Plains *par excellence* is wheat (Fig. 73).

Spring Wheat Belt.—This belt extends from the fertile lacustrine soils of the Red River Valley, where the rainfall is over 20 in., westwards across North Dakota into Montana, where it is less than

15 in. As the rainfall decreases and cultivation becomes more precarious, so the size of farms increases: holdings of less than 320 acres are rare.

Table 14

Wheat Production, 1967

	Million Acres	Million Bushels	Annual Yield in Bushels per Acre
Kansas	11·1	221·6	20·0
Nebraska	3·3	88·1	26·5
Oklahoma	5·2	88·7	17·0
Minnesota	1·0	33·8	32·1
Texas	3·3	53·2	16·0
Colorado	1·9	38·3	19·5
Montana	4·7	119·1	25·2
South Dakota	2·6	73·1	27·7
North Dakota	7·9	176·8	22·2
U.S.A. total	59·0	1,311·7	25·8 U.S.A. av.
U.S.A. exports	—	750	—

The wheat grown is a hard variety (although soft wheat, which is not so suitable for bread-making, can be found in the more humid parts of Minnesota), resistant to rust and drought and capable of ripening in a short growing period. Winters are harsh, with five months below freezing point, and the snow-cover is too thin to protect autumn-sown varieties. Summers are warm with mean monthly temperatures over 60° F. (*16° C.*) for three months or more. There is maximum precipitation in the months of May, June, and July. The level nature of the surface permits the large-scale use of power-driven machinery, which is essential anyway because of the size of the farms and the lack of labour. The chernozem and chestnut soils are extremely fertile. The main hazard is drought and over most of the area farmers allow the land to lie fallow every second or third year, when it is classed by the Department of Agriculture as "cultivated fallow" (see p. 210).

Other crops which enter into rotations include oats, barley, rye, and flax. In the more humid parts corn (for silage), hay, sugar beet, and potatoes are also grown. The present tendency is for farming to become more diversified, especially in the east where the Spring Wheat Belt adjoins the Hay and Dairying Belt. Farther west diversification becomes difficult for there are few crops suited to the dry conditions.

The landscape is one of large fields, dispersed farmsteads, and every few miles a small town with a few hundred people. In these small centres are the tall elevators and government storage bins

Above: Tucson, Arizona, lies in the valley of the Santa Cruz, which is dry for most of the year and is almost completely surrounded by mountains. It is a popular winter resort and the centre of a productive irrigated area. (*Southern Pacific*.)

Below: The St Anthony Falls, in the left foreground, provided power for the first flour mills at Minneapolis. A new lock, shown under construction, will allow river traffic to use the upper Mississippi. (*Minneapolis Chamber of Commerce*.)

Above: The scale of the workings at the Bingham copper mine in Utah is shown by the size of the railway trucks and excavators. The pit is almost 2,000 ft deep. (*Union Pacific.*)

Below: Young plants in the irrigated Coachella Valley, California, are protected from the sun by paper cones. In the background are date palms with their fruits enclosed in paper bags. (*U.S.I.S.*)

where surplus grain is stored. Sometimes the surplus is so large that wheat is kept on the ground under canvas. The grain is moved by rail to Minneapolis, the main milling centre of the region, or by rail and lake to centres farther east for milling or export.

Winter Wheat Belt.—The core of this belt lies in Kansas but it extends into the contiguous states, principally Oklahoma and Texas. It is separated from the Spring Wheat Belt by the Sand Hills of Nebraska, which is a grazing region. Farms are large, averaging about 400 acres in central Kansas and increasing in size westwards. The natural hazards are insufficient rainfall, summer hailstorms, the blasts of hot air that occasionally come from the south-west, the plagues of grasshoppers that frequently devour the growing crops, and the incidence of rust and smut. The farmer, too, is very much at the mercy of the market, for he relies almost entirely on his wheat. Sorghums, alfalfa, and barley are grown, but at any one time occupy no more than a quarter of the land. The cultivation of sorghum has increased very much in recent years; it is particularly suited to the area for it remains dormant during drought, has a low transpiration rate, is resistant to desiccation, and matures very quickly. It can, therefore, be planted in the early summer as a catch crop if the autumn-sown wheat has failed. About 13 million acres are planted with sorghum, mainly in Kansas, Nebraska, and the Oklahoma and Texas Panhandles; production amounts to about 700 million bushels a year.

In the western parts of the belt, the landscape often appears deserted for some farmers do not live on their holdings but travel to them only to sow and harvest their crops. This is known as suitcase farming, and the farmers who practise it may have holdings in both the Spring Wheat Belt and the Winter Wheat Belt. In the former area, wheat is sown in spring and harvested in August: in the latter, it is sown in autumn and harvested in June. Here we find farming on a highly commercial scale: labour requirements are very small, every operation being mechanised. Aircraft and helicopters are now almost as essential as ploughs, tractors, seeders, and combines. Harvesting is a highly organised business. Custom operators, owning as many as fifty combines, move them from place to place on trucks, starting in Texas in early June and finishing in North Dakota and Montana in August. On their return journey southwards, the operators may also harvest and thresh the sorghum crop. The machines are fitted with headlights and generally work day and night. The cultural landscape is very similar to that of the Spring Wheat Belt. The main milling centres are Topeka, Wichita, and Oklahoma City. Exports, which do not account for the whole of the surplus, move out through the Gulf ports.

To overcome the problem of inadequate precipitation the farmers have evolved a system of dry farming where wheat is grown in alternate years. In the intervening year, about one-quarter of the rain that falls can be "stored" in the ground. This is achieved by constantly harrowing the surface to reduce capillary action and so prevent the water rising and evaporating. The crop is sown in the following year and has the benefit of the annual rain, plus the water conserved in the soil. It will be readily seen that this constant pulverising of the surface increases the risk of soil erosion, particularly in a region such as this where rainfall is torrential and winds are strong. In the spring of 1934 a large part of Oklahoma was reduced to a "Dust Bowl". The area affected covered 16 million acres. During the winter months fine particles of soil were whisked away hundreds of miles and even out over the Atlantic. The heavier particles, not caught up in these "black blizzards", remained as drifts and hummocks, which often attained heights of 20 ft. The whole atmosphere was choked with dust: in some areas people had to wear protective face-cloths when out of doors. The vegetation was coated and made unfit for the cattle.

To-day the farmers are less prone to leave the soil bare. Eroded tracts are grassed, and where the "cultivated fallow" system is still used, the ploughing is done along the contours or at right angles to the prevailing wind. The previous year's stubble (the "trash cover") is allowed to remain in the soil. In 1956 the Soil Bank Scheme was introduced, whereby farmers were paid to stop cultivating marginal land. In this way the soil would be conserved and the over-abundant wheat crop reduced. It was hoped that over a number of years the wheat acreage would drop from 60 million to 35 million acres. But there has been only a slight decrease in the area cultivated (although payments under the Soil Bank Scheme in 1959 amounted to $19 million in Kansas and $41 million in Texas), and over production has resulted in large surpluses which are stored in elevators, government depots, and even under canvas. Between 1933, when it started its work of buying stocks and making loans to farmers in order to support prices, and 1963, the Commodity Credit Corporation has made a loss of $1,373 million on wheat and flour alone. In 1963 the stockpile of wheat totalled 1,000 million bushels: by 1967 this figure had fallen to under 200 million bushels.

Livestock.—The drier western parts of the Plains and certain areas of more rugged relief, such as the Black Hills of Dakota, the Nebraska Sand Hills, and the Flint Hills of Kansas are not cultivated but are used as grazing grounds for cattle and sheep. There is a northern and a southern grazing area separated by the Winter Wheat Belt. The decrease in temperature northwards accounts for minor differences between the two areas, but they have many characteristics in common. Farms are large, ranging from 2,000 to over 100,000 acres as the carrying capacity of the short grass is small. The drier the area, the more acres each animal needs to derive sufficient food. In the northern Plains, ranches average about 4,000 acres and carry about 140 head of cattle. In the following table a comparison is made between a county in Wyoming and one in Iowa.

TABLE 15

LIVESTOCK IN PART OF WYOMING AND PART OF IOWA

	Natrona Co. East Central Wyoming	Carrol Co. West Central Iowa
Percentage of land in crops	0·6	63·1
Livestock units per square mile	13·8	116·1
Acres per animal unit	46·4	5·5
Number of animals to every acre of cropland	3·4	0·28

A livestock unit is equivalent to 1 horse, 1 cow, 5 swine, 7 sheep, or 100 poultry.

In Natrona Co. the animals are cattle and sheep: in Carrol Co. cattle and hogs.

It can be seen that in Wyoming cultivation is negligible and it is the livestock which are the main source of income.

Water is obtained from watercourses and wells operated by wind-pumps. On the drier land, sheep tend to replace cattle, and in Texas angora goats are reared for their mohair. A system of transhumance is practised whereby the animals are taken to mountain pastures—generally leased from the government—in the summer and return to the Plains in the winter (see plate facing p. 353). In the north some protection for the animals is necessary, for the winters are very severe, and supplementary winter fodder is needed. Corn is brought from the Corn Belt and cotton seed from the Cotton Belt; the irrigated lands supply hay, alfalfa, and sugar beet pulp. In dry years fodder has often to be supplied in the summer, too. It is customary to fatten the cattle before they are slaughtered; some are taken to the Corn Belt, but this practice is decreasing.

Even the grazing lands are not free from soil erosion. Where the mat grass gives way to separate tufts, the rain and wind attack the exposed soil. Erosion is accelerated if over-grazing takes place, for this reduces the protective vegetation cover. The problem is not so serious in the grazing areas as it is in the cultivated regions.

Irrigation.—It was stated earlier in the chapter that the rivers of the Plains are widely spaced and have only a small discharge. This restricts the amount of water available for crops. Practically every stream has been tapped for irrigation water but some of the irrigated areas are extremely minute. Along the rivers North Platte, South Platte, and Arkansas there has been considerable development. At present about 5½ million acres are under irrigation in the Missouri basin, a figure that can be doubled when plans for developing the rivers are fully implemented (Fig. 72).

Irrigation projects are under four types of ownership and management: (*a*) mutual irrigation companies where every farmer is part of the organisation, (*b*) privately-owned companies which construct all facilities and sell services to water users at a profit, (*c*) irrigation district movements which depend upon private capital for construction works but involve some measure of public support, and (*d*) federal irrigation districts, organised and financed by the Bureau of Reclamation, which sells land and water to settlers on easy terms. While there are many examples of the third type in the Great Plains, most schemes, including the most successful belong to either the first or fourth types.

Water is much scarcer in the southern part of the Plains and it appears that more water is taken out of the ground than is being replaced naturally. In Texas there are 2½ million acres of land on the Great Plains irrigated by underground water, devoted mainly to the growing of cotton which in this area needs over 9 in. of water in addition to the average rainfall. Nebraska has more than 10,000 wells irrigating an area of 600,000 acres. A similar acreage in Colorado is irrigated by water from the River Gunnison, which is taken through a thirteen-mile tunnel through the Front Range. This is the Colorado-Big Thompson Project which is being undertaken by the Bureau of Reclamation.

Farms are small, for land and water are expensive and labour requirements are heavy. In western districts the economy is closely linked with that of the surrounding ranches; farther east there is more concentration on cash crops. Alfalfa occupies the largest acreages. Up to eighty tons of water are needed to produce one ton of alfalfa. Hay is another fodder crop. The main cash crop is sugar beet, which is one of the most efficient users of irrigation water as it transpires less than alfalfa; it is suited to a fairly short growing season. This crop yields extra fodder in the form of pulp. So much fodder is produced that fewer cattle are now being sent to the Corn Belt for fattening. Other crops include potatoes and a large variety of fruits and vegetables.

Industry and Towns

Of the minerals found in the Great Plains by far the most important are oil and natural gas. The Mid-continental field extends into this region and there are other productive fields in the Permian basin area of west Texas, the Panhandle of Texas, and Oklahoma, and the Williston basin of North Dakota, which was first tapped in 1951. Minor fields occur in Colorado, Montana, and Wyoming (see Table 8, p. 166). In the Panhandle of Texas there are several refineries and catalytic cracking plants, and many petro-chemical plants using oil and natural gas as power and raw material to turn out a variety of industrial products. Cheap gas has also led to the establishment of zinc smelters at Amarillo (138,000) and Dumas, the ores coming from the Rockies in Colorado, New Mexico, and Arizona.

Another mineral is potash, a large deposit of which occurs over a tract 70,000 square miles in area, along the boundary between Texas and New Mexico. It is more expensive to mine than German potash and so mining is restricted. Most of the U.S. potash is derived from the salt lakes of the Great Basin. The high quality deposits of the Plains are looked upon as a strategic reserve upon which the country can draw in time of need.

The coal and lignite beds that underlie much of the Plains are not actively exploited. Despite the severe winters of the Dakotas and Montana, there is little mining of the thick lignite beds, while the low-grade bituminous coal is strip-mined only in a few areas for local use. The most important of these are the Judith basin (Montana), the Powder River district (Wyoming), around Denver (Colorado), and in the Raton Mesa area on the borders of Colorado and New Mexico. From the latter field coal is sent to the iron and steel plant at Pueblo (91,000) which has the capacity to produce 1,800,000 tons a year. The iron ore is obtained from the Rockies and from southern Wyoming.

Metallic minerals are found only in association with the old crystalline rocks of the Black Hills. The only one of importance is gold which was first discovered in 1874 when this upland area was part of the Sioux Reservation. The largest gold producer in the U.S.A., the Homestake Mining Company, operated continuously from 1876 until World War II, during which period production exceeded $440 million. The mine was reopened after the war and to-day South Dakota is the leading gold-mining state in the country.

Other industries are based on the agricultural products of the region and include flour-milling, meat-packing, and sugar-refining. It seems doubtful whether there will be much expansion of industry on the Plains, except in the oil and gas areas of the south, for the population is thinly spread and the market is small. The Great Plains produce only a fraction of the goods consumed there, and consume only a small fraction of the foodstuffs and minerals produced. It is a zone of transit and lies athwart the transcontinental railways. The only north-south route follows the base of the Rocky Mountains and links the piedmont cities—Pueblo, Colorado Springs, Denver, Cheyenne, and Great Falls. These are commercial rather than industrial, and exemplify the tendency of cities to arise on or near the boundary between different physiographical regions. The largest is Denver (494,000).

CHAPTER X

THE MOUNTAIN STATES

There are eight mountain states. The eastern tier—Montana, Wyoming, Colorado, and New Mexico—have within their borders most of the Rocky Mountains; they also include the western portions of the Great Plains. The western tier—Idaho, Nevada, Utah, and Arizona—occupy the intermontane plateaus and basins; this physiographic region extends beyond the boundaries of these states into the Pacific states—California, Oregon, and Washington (Fig. 74).

The dominating characteristic of this area is the sparsity of the population. None of the eight states has more than twenty people per square mile: Colorado has seventeen and Nevada less than three. Certain areas have never been settled: over three-quarters of Utah and four-fifths of Arizona are still Public Domain land. The adverse factors in the environment are the ruggedness of the terrain and lack of water. For a long time the area was a negative region—to a certain extent it still is—a stretch of unattractive land separating the Mississippi basin from the Pacific coast, which could only be crossed with great difficulty and hardship. Settlement came with the discovery of minerals, with the utilisation of surface and underground water for irrigation, and with the extension of the ranching system from the Great Plains.

THE ROCKIES

The Rockies were born at the close of the Mesozoic era and the beginning of Tertiary times, when more than 20,000 ft of sediments were subjected to the Laramide earth movements. In some places the thick sedimentary rocks were unable to bend; they were shattered by faults and the huge blocks slipped up, down, and sideways along fault planes. In other places the strata were more flexible and were bent into folds, sometimes with considerable distortion. Erosion began as soon as the mountain tops appeared above sea level, and by the middle of the Tertiary period, uplift had ceased and the highland had been almost obliterated. Then mountain-building forces were renewed and a second generation of mountains came into existence. This uplift was accompanied by further faulting and by volcanic activity. Lava spread over the

Yellowstone Plateau, the San Juan Plateau, and the basin of the Snake River (Fig. 74). Subsequent erosion lowered the summits and detritus filled the valleys and basins. Eventually a peneplain was formed with monadnocks rising above it along the axes of the major ranges. The whole area was raised yet again in late Tertiary times and the present mountains were created. It is the sculpturing of this surface by water, wind, and ice that has produced the land forms visible to-day.

The features are bold and rugged with extensive areas rising above 9,000 ft. In Colorado there are fifty-two peaks rising above 14,000 ft, although nowhere in the whole system is a height of 15,000 ft attained. The most common geological structures are the anticlinal arch and the large faulted crust block, the former being more widespread in the south, the latter in the north. The rivers, except for the Rio Grande, show little adaptation to structure. Most of the streams are superimposed and where they cross resistant beds or mountain ranges there are deep and spectacular gorges. The major divide in the continent follows the Rockies (Fig. 7), but it does not always coincide with the higher crests.

The climate varies considerably according to altitude and latitude. In an area of such marked relief it is difficult to generalise, for there is a vast mosaic of numerous, small, local climates where slope and aspect play an important part. However, one might say that the winters are long and cold except in the lower, southern valleys, and the growing season is short, rarely being longer than three months. Summers are mild, for the altitude tempers the heat one associates with interior regions. Precipitation is heaviest in the north and on the higher ranges, with amounts reaching 40 in. or more in some places. The Montana valleys receive 15 to 20 in., while the southern valleys and the Wyoming basin have under 10 in.

Because the climate varies considerably in quite short distances, the vegetation pattern is complex and comprises many types of plant associations. On the drier lowlands is sagebrush which gives way at slightly higher elevations to juniper and piñon trees (Fig. 26). The true forests occur where the rainfall is near or over 20 in. and extend over an altitudinal range of 6,000 ft. Stands of Ponderosa (yellow) pine occupy areas which have a dry soil or are exposed to the sun. The other common trees are Douglas fir, white fir, white spruce, and sugar pine. Where the virgin forest has been cleared or burnt, the affected area is colonised by lodgepole pine. At the highest elevations is Engelmann spruce which assumes a more stunted and gnarled appearance as the growing season becomes shorter, the winds more destructive, and the snow-cover much thicker. The tree line is at about 11,000 ft in Colorado and 6,000 ft on the 49th Parallel. Above the forest is a cover of Alpine flora consisting of brilliantly-coloured flowers—primroses, saxifrages, and forget-me-nots—with meadow grasses. Beyond this zone lies bare rock and, on the higher peaks, permanent snow.

Southern Rockies

The Southern Rockies lie to the south of the Wyoming basin and can be regarded as two main series of ranges running north to south, connected at intervals by transverse ridges. The eastern limb comprises the Laramie Range, the Front Range, and the Sangre de Cristo Mountains; to the west of and parallel to these are the Park Range, the Sawatch Range, and the San Juan Mountains (Fig. 74). South of Santa Fé the line of the mountains is continued by only small, discontinuous ranges which eventually link up with the Eastern Sierra Madre of Mexico. Between the ranges are a number of basins known as "parks" which are at elevations of 7,000 to 9,000 ft, and almost completely enclosed by highland. The soils are generally fertile but the rainfall is meagre and farming, apart from ranching, is dependent upon irrigation.

The Rio Grande rises in the San Juan Mountains, where it is fed by melting snow and then flows southwards through the San Luis Park. Between Santa Fé and El Paso the river passes through at least eight basins which are separated by narrow gorges. These basins were once occupied by lakes and are the areas of farming and settlement. The largest city, Albuquerque, is situated in one of these basins. Much of the irrigation water is derived from the Elephant Butte Reservoir, which also regulates the flow of the river and produces power.

Mining is important in the Southern Rockies but less so now than in the past. Gold was discovered in 1859 near where Denver now stands. Mining towns such as Central City were set up in the nearby Rockies and on them converged settlers from the east, their wagons emblazoned with the words "Pike's Peak or bust". Many of these settlements were ephemeral. A mining camp would arise within a few week of the initial discovery. Sooner or later the ore would be exhausted. Then the population either drifted away, in which case the camp became a ghost town, or turned to agriculture for a living. Some mining centres have experienced remarkable vicissitudes: the population of Leadville (Colorado) in 1877 was 200; in 1879 the number had leapt to 15,000, and there were thirty mines and fourteen smelters operating in and around the town; the centre declined and in 1950 it had only 4,000 people, but continued to produce lead, zinc, and manganese. The mining settlement at Climax, 11,000 ft above sea level, produces over 90 per cent. of the world's molybdenum. Gold is mined at Cripple Creek.

Wyoming Basin

The Wyoming basin is where the Southern Rockies sink beneath the thick cover of Tertiary deposits. This area, 6,500 to 7,500 ft high, is really a series of basins separated by short ranges which project through the Tertiary floor. They were once completely buried and are now being gradually exhumed. The aridity of the area is apparent from the intermittent streams, scattered salt lakes, and sparse vegetation. The growing season lasts only four months and cultivation is subordinate to stock-rearing (see Table 15, p. 211). Sheep are more important than cattle. The farms are large and the population is small. There are no minerals apart from coal and oil, and these are exploited only on a small scale. It was across the Wyoming basin that the nineteenth century pioneers made their way to the Pacific coast. The Oregon Trail followed the North Platte to this lowland embayment and South Pass gave access to the Snake basin. The Union Pacific, first of the transcontinental railways, followed this route. The fact that no other transcontinental line uses this, the easiest of the Rocky Mountain passes, is a commentary on the lack of freight and traffic.

Central Rockies

The Central Rockies extend from the Wyoming basin to the Yellowstone Plateau. The ranges, although still mainly associated with anticlinal structures as in the Southern Rockies, have a less regular alignment. The Teton Range, which displays some of the grandest glaciated scenery in the U.S.A. (see plate facing p. 32), the Wasatch Range, and the Uinta Range run in different directions (Fig. 74). The Yellowstone Plateau is made of volcanic rocks; the accumulated lava and fragmented debris is over 1,000 ft thick in places and buries a rugged underlying topography. There are several volcanic peaks, hot springs, active geysers, boiling mud pools (known as paint pots), and a petrified forest. The Yellowstone River has cut a remarkable gorge, 1,000 ft deep in the plateau, and in this gorge are the spectacular Yellowstone Falls, where the river falls more than 300 ft over a vertical mass of hard lava.

In between the mountains are small lowlands. One of the largest of these is the Big Horn basin, which is really, like the Wyoming basin, an embayment of the Great Plains. Underground water is available for irrigation and there are reserves of oil and natural gas.

Northern Rockies

The Northern Rockies are lower and broader than the area to the south. The system is more broken by valleys, particularly those opening to the Snake Plateau in the south and the Missouri Valley in the east. In Montana, almost 20 per cent. of the area is

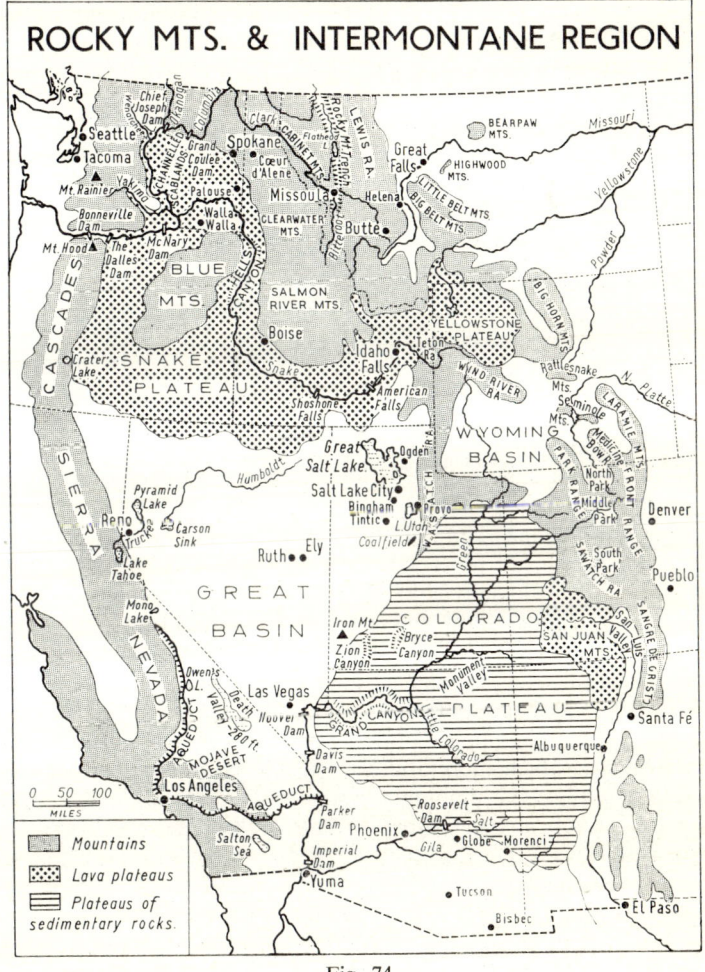

Fig. 74.

valley lowland. A notable feature is the Rocky Mountain Trench which is tectonic in origin and extends far into Canada (Fig. 8); in Montana it is occupied by Lake Flathead and the Bitterroot River. Farther west is the similar but smaller Purcell Trench, with Lakes Pend d'Oreille and Coeur d'Alene. In Montana, the Lewis Overthrust Fault carried folded strata about fifteen miles eastwards, over the undisturbed sediments of the Great Plains. Faulting is also much in evidence in the Purcell Range, an upthrust block with several minor horsts. The Salmon River Mountains are the dissected remnants of an old granite batholith. Glaciation has been much more active in the Northern Rockies than farther south; erosion features are well-displayed in the Glacier National Park, where there are still seventy-five glaciers.

The reports of the Lewis and Clark expedition of 1804 publicised the main features of the area, but even before this the ground had been fairly thoroughly explored by the fur-trappers. Modern development started with the discovery of gold in 1862 at Virginia City in the Madison Valley and later at Helena and Butte. These places were connected to the Pacific and the eastern cities by the transcontinental railways which utilised the numerous valleys on both sides of the Divide. After the gold was exhausted, silver and lead were mined, but the most important mineral now is copper. Butte is the main centre and it accounts for about 8 per cent. of the nation's production.

"By night it has a certain inferno-like magnificence. By day it is one of the ugliest places I have ever seen. The mine dumps, heaps of slag that nobody removes, line the hills; there is hardly any vegetation since the fumes from the open hearth smelting in the old days seared and poisoned the living green; the frowsy streets are faced with slovenly and dilapidated ancient tenements . . . The gallows frames show where the mines are and underneath are not less than 2,700 miles of winzes, shafts, and tunnels; the town sits crazily on a shaky and sagging crust of ore." (J. Gunther, *Inside U.S.A.*, Chapter 11.)

The ores are complex and are associated with metamorphic rock which is much more abundant in the Northern Rockies than in other parts of the mountain system. Silver, zinc, and gold are by-products of copper mining. The high-grade ores occur at depths of from 2,000 to 5,000 ft. Most of the mining is carried out by the Anaconda Company which also operates a smelter at Anaconda and a refinery at Great Falls on the Missouri.

The other major mining area in the Northern Rockies is around Coeur d'Alene (Idaho). The minerals, lead, zinc, and silver are associated with a small granite massif and were first exploited in 1882. About 20 per cent. of the U.S.A. lead output comes from this district. It is smelted at Bradley (Idaho) and East Helena (Montana). Zinc is refined at Kellog (Idaho), Anaconda, and Great Falls.

TABLE 16
STATES PRODUCING SIGNIFICANT QUANTITIES OF COPPER, LEAD, AND ZINC
(Figures for 1967 in tons.)

	COPPER	LEAD	ZINC
Arizona	498,000	5,000	15,000
Utah	168,000	54,000	35,000
Montana	71,000		3,000
Nevada	47,000		
Michigan	58,000		
New Mexico	75,000		22,000
Idaho		59,000	55,000
Colorado		23,000	53,000
Washington		3,000	22,000
Missouri		150,000	
Illinois			20,000
New York			72,000
Tennessee			110,000
Virginia			19,000
U.S.A.	950,000	311,000	546,000

There is little agriculture, although more than in the Southern Rockies, for there is a greater area of lowland and the rainfall is slightly heavier. Some general farming with emphasis on dairying is carried out near the mining centres. The rearing of sheep and beef cattle is more widespread and more suited to the terrain and climate. In the valleys of the Bitterroot, Flathead, and Kootenay, where irrigation is practised, fruit, alfalfa, and cereals are grown. Lumbering is another occupation of this region but the area is not easily accessible and is far from the markets. Transportation of a product of such bulk and low value is both difficult and expensive. Local demand is small and the yearly cut represents only a small fraction of the country's timber production. Saw mills are located at convenient collecting points such as Missoula (Montana) and Coeur d'Alene (Idaho).

Summary

The significance of the Rocky Mountains in the geography of North America is two-fold. At all times the mountains have been a barrier, for while the trend of the ranges is from north to south, the main routes run from east to west. The transcontinental lines sought the easiest paths through valleys and passes and helped to open up the region. However, settlement has been generally repelled. The presence of minerals and timber has led to the establishment of settlements, but many of these are transitory. The small, permanent population is swollen by the influx of tourists, both in summer and in winter. Modern roads have opened up many areas where the scenic attractions and features of interest have become national parks and monuments. Only agriculture, which is not an extractive industry like mining and lumbering, has given rise to stable settlement. Grazing is possible over practically the whole of the region, although the carrying capacity of the land is very low; cultivation depends on irrigation and the areas that can be irrigated are small and scattered. There seems to be little scope for extending the cultivated area and there seems little likelihood of the population increasing to any marked extent.

THE INTERMONTANE REGION

This area can be divided into three distinct physical units, but it has characteristics which are common to all of its parts. The climate varies as is natural where there is such a marked latitudinal and altitudinal range, but everywhere there is deficient rainfall. The climate was fully described in Chapter II. Here it will suffice to recapitulate the main conclusions.

1. There is a general increase in mean monthly temperatures from north to south.

	January	July
Spokane (Washington)	25° F. ($-4°$ C.)	70° F. ($21°$ C.)
Salt Lake City (Utah)	29° F. ($-1°$ C.)	78° F. ($26°$ C.)
Phoenix (Arizona)	51° F. ($11°$ C.)	91° F. ($33°$ C.)

The growing season on the Canadian border is under 120 days and snow lies for thirty days or more on the lowlands. In the extreme south, years may pass without a killing frost and snow is extremely rare.

2. Rainfall decreases from north to south: everywhere it is deficient for normal agricultural activities.

Phoenix 7·12 in. (48 per cent. in summer). Spokane 14·92 in. (33 per cent. in summer). As well as being low, the rainfall is unreliable.

Phoenix: Average annual precipitation, 7·12 in. Highest 19·73 in. Lowest 3·03 in.

Evaporation is intense: the evaporation rate for Yuma (Arizona) is 120 in. a year and the relative humidity is always low (27 per cent. at 6 p.m. and lower still in the afternoon).

3. Relief has a great effect on both temperatures and rainfall: a map showing isotherms or isohyets bears a marked resemblance to a relief map. In a region of such accidented terrain, wide variations are experienced in short distances. The mountain ranges stand out as humid islands.

The vegetation pattern, like the climate, is complex. The driest and hottest area in the south is desert (Fig. 25). Vegetation is sparse, the dominant plant being the creosote bush which is thorny and aromatic: animals find it unpalatable. Other shrubs include the yuccas (see plate facing p. 65) and about eighty varieties of cacti. After the rains there appear carpets of flowers which lie dormant for the remaining ten or eleven months of the year. In the northern part of the region where it is not as dry or as hot, sagebrush is more common. This plant tolerates saline soils and is adapted to withstand the unreliable rainfall, the intense evaporation, and severe winter frosts. It grows two or three feet high and its roots extend three or four times this distance into the ground. The small grey or silvery leaves are often shed if there is a prolonged drought. It is not easily destroyed by fire or grazing and on this account tends to invade adjacent areas of grass or forest. The only trees to be seen are the alders and cottonwoods along the watercourses. At higher elevations there is the same sequence of vegetation as is found in the Rockies: junipers (see plate facing p. 64) and piñons at lower levels being replaced upwards by Ponderosa pine, Douglas fir, and Englemann spruce (Fig. 26).

The population is very small: large areas are empty or have only occasional ranches. The whole area is cut off from the more densely peopled parts of the country by the Rockies on the east and the Sierra Nevada and Cascades on the west. The only lowland outlet—one which is not used to any significant extent—is the Gulf of California.

Columbia-Snake Plateau

The Columbia-Snake Plateau occupies the northern portion of the region. It is a huge lava tableland covering an area of over 200,000 square miles. The lava issued from a number of vents and fissures to bury the underlying topography to a depth of 5,000 ft in some places. There were several emissions and between them quiescent periods when vegetation flourished and rivers spread alluvial deposits. Layers of decayed vegetation and silt are intercalated among the lavas. The Blue Mountains, which rise to 9,000 ft, were not completely covered: lava rises to a height of 7,000 ft on the slopes and the way the beds are tilted suggests that some uplift occurred after the lava had been poured out. In other places are shallow anticlines and synclines, where the volcanic beds have been folded. Both the Columbia and Snake are deeply incised in the plateau, the latter flowing through Hell's Canyon (where the Rockies and Blue Mountains approach most closely), which has dimensions similar to those of the Grand Canyon but which lacks its spectacular appearance.

The drainage was temporarily altered during the Ice Age when lobes of ice diverted the rivers into new channels known as coulees. The most striking of these is the Grand Coulee, a gash 800 ft deep and from $1\frac{1}{2}$ to $4\frac{1}{2}$ miles wide, which carried the swollen waters of the Columbia to a point lower along its course (Fig. 76). The whole area between the Columbia and Snake is scored with similar sand-choked spillways and is known as the Channelled Scablands (Fig. 8). Loess, which dates from the Ice Age, overlies much of the plateau. Both loess and weathered lava give extremely fine soils, porous but retentive of moisture.

The Palouse area of south-east Washington (the Inland Empire) has over 12 in. of rainfall and dry farming is practised. The terrain is undulating with whale-back hills of loess and volcanic dust aligned north-east to south-west. The steepness of these hills necessitates the use of special machinery. Ploughing is done along the contours but in spite of this and also the low intensity of the rainfall, erosion has become a serious problem.

Half the cultivated land lies fallow each year, every field producing a crop in alternate years. Wheat occupies four-fifths of the harvested land (Fig. 75) and the only other important crop is peas which need less water than wheat, and being leguminous, add nitrogen to the soil. Under bunch grass vegetation the lava and loess soils developed deep profiles and became rich in humus. To maintain the structure and fertility crop rotations should be used, but there are few crops which can endure such dry conditions.

"This is undulating country and the wheat planted along the hills in eccentric rings and ovals, climbs up one slope and down another. And the colours! The whole rippling landscape . . . might have been the palette of an artist painting sunsets. The colours are fantastically variegated because the wheat, planted at different times, is ripening at different stages of growth: they run from a deep red-copper, through a buttery chrome to gamboge, to fawn. . . . But these are not the only colours. Look at the browns and greens. The deep sienna brown is just bare earth. This is because half the acreage must be left fallow each year in this dry part of the world. The green stripes and pools may be mustard,

IRRIGATION IN CALIFORNIA

Above: Date palms (light foliage), citrus groves, mainly grapefruit, and truck crops in the Coachella Valley, California. The Coachella branch of the All-American Canal can be seen in the left foreground. (*Bureau of Reclamation.*)

Below: The Contra Costa Canal irrigates the San Joaquin Valley. In the background are the Coast Ranges and Mt Diablo. Note the arid nature of the uncultivated land. (*Bureau of Reclamation.*)

Above: The pulp and paper mills at Corner Brook, Newfoundland, near the mouth of t[he] Humber River. About one-third of the pulpwood is floated down the river, the remain[der] being brought by rail or by sea. (*Bowater Paper Corporation.*)

Below: The iron and steel plant on the waterfront at Sydney, Nova Scotia, uses local c[oal] and iron ore from the Wabana mines on Bell Island, Newfoundland. (*Canadian Natio[nal] Railways.*)

COLUMBIA-SNAKE PLATEAU

tumbleweed, or thistle. . . . We passed pools of platinum—oats and barley. We passed pools of emerald—alfalfa, planted in the gullies to hold the top soil down, to check wind erosion. . . . Above all we saw the fallow pools, dead brown except for green weeds and trash. . . . There were other things besides wheat. This is all lava country and we saw basalt buttes and outcroppings of scab

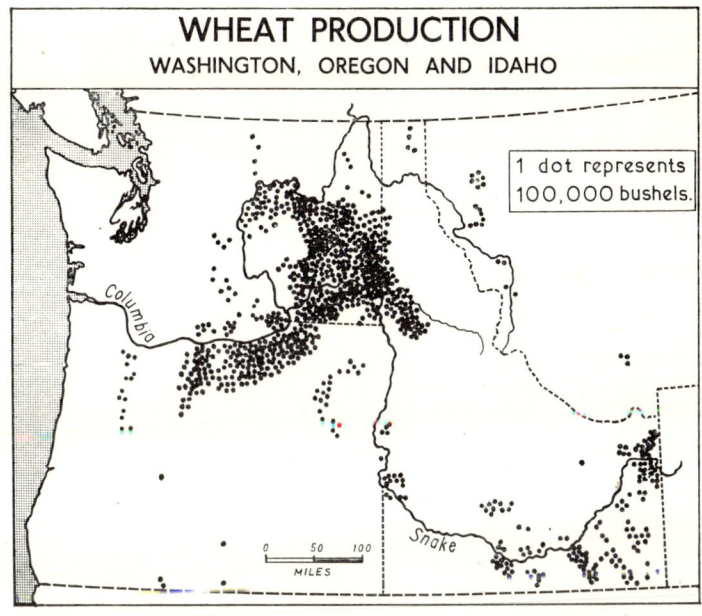

Fig. 75.

	ACRES OF WHEAT (in millions)	PRODUCTION (in millions of bushels)
Washington ..	2·9	118
Oregon ..	1·0	32
Idaho ..	1·3	57

rock. The squat shining towers carrying electricity to the farms still strode along our route. Every once in a while came a house, which forms a kind of self-contained island in the ocean of wheat, a pool of dark green cottonwoods and poplars, a windmill, the house always painted white, the barn always painted red." (J. Gunther, *Inside U.S.A.*, Chapter 9.)

Irrigation.—Outside the Palouse area farming in the region entails irrigation. Altogether in the Columbia basin there are about 4·5 million acres of irrigated land and the long-term plans of the Bureau of Reclamation envisage the addition of another 4 million acres. There are three main irrigated areas (Fig. 81).

1. On the eastern flanks of the Cascades are the "Apple Valleys". In the Yakima Valley are 61,000 acres of irrigated land and 2 million apple trees; the Wenatchee Valley has 30,000 acres and 1·5 million trees; and the Okanagan Valley 13,000 acres and about 500,000 trees (see plate facing p. 353). The growing period of 200 days is relatively long and there is a high amount of sunshine. Both these characteristics are favourable for fruit growing but it is the careful organisation of growing, inspecting, advertising, and marketing that has really raised these valleys to the forefront of fruit growing districts (see Fig. 62 and Table 9). Apples occupy about half the orchard areas and other fruits include pears, plums, cherries, and even peaches and grapes. Altogether fruit occupies about 60 per cent. of the irrigated land, usually the gentle slopes which are less susceptible to killing frosts. The remaining land grows potatoes, sugar beet, hops, beans, and alfalfa. Dairying and poultry raising are increasing in importance.

2. Another string of irrigated tracts lies along the Snake River in Idaho. About 2 million acres altogether are devoted to growing apples, potatoes, sugar beet, beans, and peas. A common feature of the landscape around Boise is the fruit cellar, an earth-covered structure for storing apples during the winter. Alfalfa is important here and with the pulp and tops of sugar beet provides supplementary feed for the cattle and sheep reared on nearby ranches.

3. The largest scheme is the Columbia Basin Reclamation Project which is not yet complete (Fig. 76). Water is derived from the 150-mile long Lake Roosevelt which is dammed by the Grand Coulee Dam. From behind the dam water is lifted 280 ft to the Grand Coulee channel and is stored in an equalising reservoir (see Frontispiece). A network of canals leads the water over the "Big Bend" area, where 1,200,000 acres will ultimately be irrigated. The present increment is about 70,000 acres every year. Since 1952 the region has been producing an increasing quantity of alfalfa, sugar beet, potatoes, and vegetables. The Bureau of Reclamation has experimental farms in various parts of the project area to discover the types of farming best suited to the conditions.

As well as providing vast quantities of water for irrigation, the Columbia and its tributaries are harnessed for power. There are over twenty large installations on the Snake River and seven on the Spokane, but the greatest developments have taken place on the Columbia itself. The Grand Coulee Dam, the Chief Joseph

Dam, the McNary Dam, the John Day Dam, the Dalles Dam, and the Bonneville Dam provide (or will provide when fully in operation) a block of power unequalled by any other river (Fig. 88). The capacity of the generators at Grand Coulee alone is 2·5 million kilowatts. The Columbia basin possesses about 35 per cent. of the potential hydro-electric power of the nation and of this over 75 per cent. is still untapped.

Mining is not important in this region and the main settlements are simply service centres of different sizes. The simplest settlement is the crossroads hamlet with filling station, bank, cinema, and drug store. Wenatchee, Yakima, Walla Walla, and Boise are true market towns, serving their respective farming districts. The capital of the Inland Empire is Spokane (182,000), which lies at the meeting point of five transcontinental and twelve branch lines. There are flour mills, meat-packing plants, an aluminium refinery, banks, stores, and a stock exchange, but the main function of the town is commerce—"a funnel for outgoing products and a spray nozzle for incoming goods".

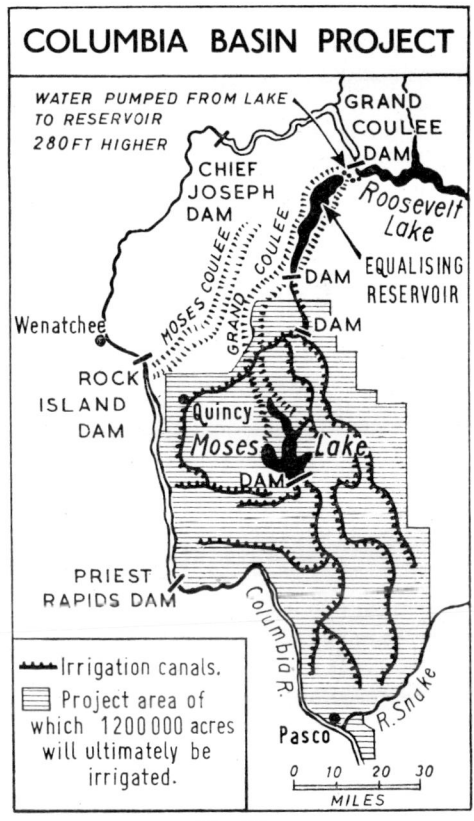

Fig. 76.

Great Basin

The Great Basin covers 400,000 square miles and lies between the Wasatch Range in the east and the Sierra Nevada in the west. Both these ranges are tilted blocks with their steep faulted edges facing one another across the basin (Fig. 8). In between are a number of smaller ranges, fifty to seventy-five miles long and five to fifteen miles wide, arranged *en echelon* with their axes running from north to south. Some attain a height of 10,000 ft, but altitudes are usually lower than this. The steep faces which are scarred by canyons and arroyos are the result of faulting. Fresh scars running horizontally across some slopes are evidence of very recent earth movements. Between the ranges are basins (bolsons) which are gradually being filled with detritus from the mountains. Except in the south where the Colorado flows into the Gulf of California, drainage is internal. Streams rising in the better-watered highlands have only short courses and a short life. Some are lost in the sands and gravels which form fans at the foot of the mountains; others continue to the centre of a basin, where, after a period of rain, there might be a temporary playa lake. More usually the surface is simply of cracked clay or encrusted with salt. The longest river is the Humboldt which flows for 200 miles before losing itself in either Lake Humboldt or the Carson Sink, according to the volume of water in the river. In summer it often disappears underground. Permanent lakes are found at the edges of the Great Basin, at the base of the Wasatch and Sierra Nevada. Unless they have an outlet (to another lake) they are excessively saline. They are remnants of much larger bodies of water which existed during the Ice Age. At that time Lake Bonneville covered a great area and its surface was 1,000 ft above the level of the Great Salt Lake, its shrunken remnant. The old shore lines and former river deltas can be seen at various elevations on the slopes of the Wasatch Mountains. In the west the former Lake Lahontan is now represented by a few scattered lakes at the foot of the Sierra Nevada.

Livestock.—Much of this land is valueless. The ranches found here are large for every animal requires a large area to find sufficient herbage. In parts of Arizona, where the rainfall is under 10 in., seventy-five acres are required to support one steer. Both cattle and sheep are reared, the latter occupying areas of rougher terrain and poorer pastures. Almost everywhere some form of transhumance is practised: in summer the animals move up the mountain slopes to high pastures which are often under government control. Three-quarters of the Public Domain are leased by the federal government to graziers. This land consists of scrub and light forest and the number of animals each operator is allowed to pasture is strictly regulated to prevent erosion and deforestation. On the permitted grazing districts of Nevada which cover an area of 47·6 million acres (*i.e.* almost as much as the whole of the British

Isles) there is forage for about three million animal units (*i.e.* one cow or five sheep) each month. In the southern parts of the region, cattle and sheep can graze out of doors the whole of the year: farther north, winter shelter and supplementary fodder are needed. There has grown up a close relationship between the ranchers and the farmers of irrigated land, who grow hay, alfalfa, and roots for the animals. Formerly many animals were shipped to California or the Corn Belt for fattening. Recently a far higher proportion of the cattle and sheep have been slaughtered locally, especially at Salt Lake City and Ogden.

Irrigated Areas.—Cultivation is restricted to the irrigated areas which occupy only a pitifully small fraction of the total area. Only 3 per cent. of Utah is farmland and the percentage for Nevada is even smaller. Water from streams and underground sources is utilised in a number of areas (Fig. 81).

1. For a distance of 130 miles along the base of the lofty and snow-capped Wasatch Range, stretches the Salt Lake Oasis. The width of the belt of intensely cultivated orchards and farms varies from two to eighteen miles. The Mormon settlers arrived here in 1847, and within ten years had brought into cultivation an area almost as large as that which exists to-day. Numerous streams issue from the canyons in the mountains (*e.g.* River Weber, Bear River) and on the alluvial fans at the mouth of each is a city or village. Dispersed settlement is rare in Utah. Between the settlements are the small plots that resemble gardens rather than farms. Sugar beet and potatoes occupy much of the land and are grown in rotation with wheat and alfalfa. There is also a large production of tomatoes, onions, and lettuce. The orchard crops, particularly apples and peaches, are grown at higher elevations on the ancient deltas of Lake Bonneville, where the soil is of a coarse texture and heats quickly, and there is less danger from frost. On the lowest parts of the slope towards the Salt Lake, the soil is heavier and often waterlogged and saline. This land is used as pasture for sheep and cattle. Dairying is important and the milk that remains after local needs have been met is sent to Colorado and California.

2. Hundreds of miles to the west, at the foot of the Sierra Nevada, are some irrigated tracts along the rivers Truckee, Carson, and Humboldt. The largest of these is the Reno Oasis. Farms are larger than in Utah and cultivation is not so intensive. Alfalfa, wheat, and vegetables are grown and there is some dairying.

3. One of the largest irrigated areas occupies what was entire desert before the present century in an alluvial depression near

the mouth of the Colorado River (Fig. 77). Both the Imperial and Coachella Valleys lie in California, but belong geographically to the Great Basin. A series of dams on the Colorado (Hoover, Davis, Parker, and Imperial) control the flow of water. Before the river was regulated, floods periodically inundated the Salton Sea, which lies below sea level. The last occasion was in 1905 (after

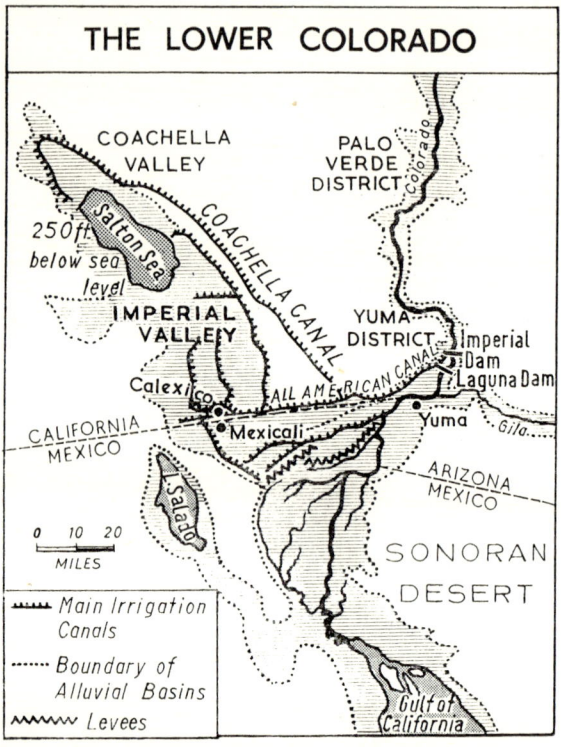

Fig. 77.

some land had been brought under cultivation), and it was not until 1907 that the area was sealed off by the construction of levees.

The All-American Canal which replaced the older Alamo Canal running partly through Mexican Territory, started to deliver water to Imperial Valley in 1942. The Coachella Branch (see plate facing p. 224) was completed in 1946 and irrigates the area north of the Salton Sea. Together these valleys constitute one of the most prolific agricultural regions in the world. 1,250,000 acres are under cultivation, and as there is an almost continuous growing season (frost being practically unknown), two or more crops can be grown in a year. In Imperial Valley the main field crops are cotton, alfalfa, and sugar beet. All these are heavy users of water: alfalfa requires one inch of water every three days in midsummer, while the fields of sugar beet are irrigated twenty times or more during the growing season. Also important are the winter vegetable crops, particularly lettuce which can be sent to the eastern markets when supplies are unobtainable from elsewhere. Agricultural production in 1959 was valued at $137 million, lettuce contributing $20 million to this figure. The population of Imperial Valley is about 70,000. In the smaller Coachella Valley, grapefruit, grapes, and vegetables (notably lettuce and carrots) figure highly in production, but the special product of the area is dates which occupy almost 5,000 acres (see plates facing pp. 209 and 224).

Along the lower Colorado are two small irrigated areas. These are the Palo Verde district (55,000 acres) which produces alfalfa, melons, and vegetables, and the Yuma district (15,000 acres).

4. Two tributaries of the Colorado, the Salt and Gila, have been dammed at certain points (*e.g.* the Roosevelt Dam on the Salt River) and large areas around Phoenix and Tucson have been brought into cultivation (see plate facing p. 208). The rivers are so closely regulated that the Gila has no discharge to the Colorado. Of the water used, only one-quarter is supplied by the rivers: the remainder comes from wells sunk in the sands and gravels which fill the basins. The abstraction of water from these underground sources has lowered the water-table by amounts up to 60 ft. Further lowering is inevitable and it is difficult to see how irrigation on such a scale can continue. The Central Arizona Project, if carried out, will alleviate the situation. It envisages the damming of the Colorado at Bridge Canyon and the diversion of over 1 million acre-feet of water to the Salt and Gila valleys by means of tunnels and canals (Fig. 78). At present about 725,000 acres around Phoenix are irrigated and grow alfalfa, sugar beet, vegetables, and cotton. Cotton growing has expanded rapidly in recent years; the more intensive cultivation in a dry climate which inhibits the activities of the boll weevil, results in yields per acre being five times those in Texas.

Mining and Industry.—The miners and prospectors enjoyed a brilliant but brief period of prosperity in the Great Basin. In Nevada alone there are 400 ghost towns which bear witness to a vanished prosperity. The most remarkable town was Virginia City, which arose near the Comstock Lode, possibly the richest mineral deposit in the world. In its heyday the city had 40,000 inhabitants: at present it has 800. The mining of precious metals is not important to-day and interest is centred upon the base metals (Table 16, p. 221).

At the eastern edge of the Great Basin, at the base of the Wasatch Range, are a number of mining towns. The largest are Bingham, thirty miles south-west of Salt Lake City, which produces copper (see plate facing p. 209), and Tintic, sixty miles south of Salt

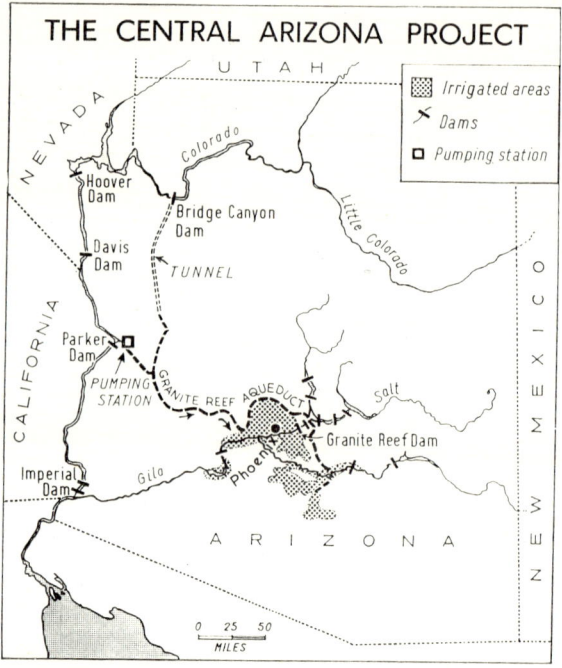

Fig. 78.

Lake City, which has lead and silver mines. Near both is the Garfield smelter. Copper is mined also in eastern Nevada at Ely, Ruth, and Yarrington (Fig. 74). It was not until the advent of the railways and new techniques that copper mining flourished. The ores are low-grade, often averaging less than one per cent. metal. To extract the metal locally, or transport it in its natural state would have been very expensive. Mining became feasible with the invention of a process for cheaply concentrating the ore. In the Arizona Highlands are a number of towns—Bisbee, Morenci, and San Manuel

—which together produce almost one-third of the nation's copper. A problem here, as in the districts described above, is the fluctuating price of the metal. At times mining becomes uneconomic and the discovery of richer ores in other parts of the world is a serious threat to the continuation of the industry. A recent addition to the list of minerals is uranium which is mined at Ambrosia Lake (New Mexico), about eighty miles west of Albuquerque.

In Utah there are fifty-four coal-mines and the state is practically the only one in the West which produces significant quantities of coal (about 5 million tons annually). Iron ore too is mined and the presence of the two in close proximity has led to the establishment of a huge integrated steelworks (capacity 2·3 million tons) at Geneva, near Provo (Utah). This supplied essential war materials during World War II and now caters for the expanding western market.

Industries are few in number and are usually concerned with the processing of local produce. The largest towns are all in irrigated areas and on the transcontinental railways, where they can collect and distribute goods. The greatest is Salt Lake City (189,000), centre of the Salt Lake Oasis and headquarters of the Mormon church. Railways from east of the Rockies pass through here on their way to Puget Sound, San Francisco, and Los Angeles. The mining concerns have offices in the city; the banks and shops serve and equip miners, ranchers, and farmers of a large area. There are local industries, railway yards, sugar refineries, and meat-packing factories, but the prosperity of the city is firmly founded on commerce. Some towns in Nevada, particularly Reno and Las Vegas, owe their size to the gambling and divorce laws which are less stringent in this state than elsewhere.

The Colorado Plateaus

These are vast tablelands between the Southern Rockies to the east, the Uinta Range to the north, and the Wasatch Range to the west (Fig. 74). The whole region covers an area of 130,000 square miles and presents a variety of scenery almost unequalled anywhere in the world. Upon a crystalline base which is exposed at the bottom of the Grand Canyon, are great thicknesses of sedimentary rocks which range in age from Palaeozoic to Tertiary times. This has been a remarkably stable area, and although uplift has occurred, there has been little deformation of the rocks. The strata is almost horizontal for long stretches, although there are domes and basins of small amplitude. Long faults have resulted in the vertical displacement of the beds and the separation of the region into several plateaus of different elevations.

The most striking features are due to differential erosion. The varied beds offer different resistances to the attack of wind and water. Weaker rocks yield readily to erosive forces and are rapidly removed, and so the overlying stronger rocks are undermined. Angular cliffs are produced, and with the continuous weathering are forced to recede. Where a whole series of strata has been removed from a more resistant base a stripped plain is left. Frequently isolated remnants of the old plateau rise above this monotonous surface; they are called mesas if they have a recognisably flat summit and buttes if they are pointed or rounded. Monument Valley, on the borders of Arizona and Utah, is a wonderful example of such scenery (see plate facing p. 48).

Large areas are trenched by sheer-walled canyons with depths that measure thousands of feet. These contribute to the ruggedness of the region and make many places inaccessible. Precipitation is usually in the form of infrequent but torrential downpours and run-off is rapid, especially as there is no dense vegetation cover to protect the land. After a storm a valley, which for most of the year is dry and sand-choked, is filled by a raging torrent with great erosive power. Most of the canyons exhibit the "cliff and bench" profile which is the result of alternating bands of hard and soft rock. In some areas, *e.g.* Bryce Canyon, the sculpturing of these varying beds by water and wind has resulted in many fantastic land forms (see plate facing p. 33). Just as striking as the features themselves are the colours, for in a region of prevailing aridity there is little soil or vegetation to obscure the rock. Sandstones appear in a large range of whites, yellows, and reds, while the shales are predominantly blue, purple, yellow, or chocolate. Almost every tint is visible in the Painted Desert of north-eastern Arizona.

On the bordering ranges and on the higher parts of the Colorado Plateaus, precipitation exceeds 30 in., but this figure drops rapidly with decreasing altitude, and the drier parts have under 5 in. The vegetation is arranged in altitudinal zones with drought-resistant scrub, consisting of yucca, mesquite, and creosote bush in the dry valleys, and conifers on the wetter and cooler highlands (Fig. 79).

This is a negative region; there is little mineral wealth and only small pockets of cultivable land. Lowland is scarce and the rivers so unreliable and deeply incised that irrigation is impracticable. Because of the great amount of dissection this is a very difficult region to cross. In the last few decades, however, the building of roads has enabled tourists to savour without discomfort the outstanding scenery. Tourism is an increasingly profitable industry: it brings an income of over $150 million to Arizona annually.

Perhaps the most interesting facts about the human geography of the Colorado Plateaus are supplied by the Indians. The 60,000 Navajo who occupy a large reserve in the centre of the region, are traditionally stock rearers (*i.e.* since they acquired sheep from the early Spanish settlers), while the Hopi and Pueblo Indians are cultivators who, over the centuries, have developed a distinctive culture (see plate facing p. 96). Their pueblos, built of stone and adobe, are situated in defensive positions, usually on the tops of mesas. They grow corn, squashes, beans, tobacco, and cotton on the damp patches of soil beneath the spring lines on the lower slopes of the mesas. They carry out their work as they have done for generations, but they are not completely unaffected by the white men who flock to the region to witness their religious ceremonies and snap up their artefacts. In the Indian reservations there is considerable pressure on the land and the federal government is making efforts to move some of the surplus population on to new irrigated lands.

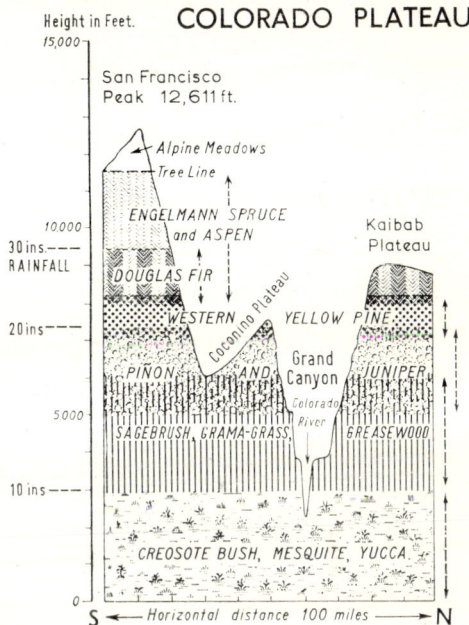

Fig. 79.
Note the very great vertical exaggeration.

River Colorado.—The Colorado is a snow-fed river which rises in the Colorado Rockies and flows for 1,450 miles in a general southwesterly direction to the Gulf of California. For most of its course it crosses the Colorado Plateaus where it collects its main tributaries, the Green, San Juan, and Little Colorado. Practically all the streams follow tortuous paths and are entrenched in deep canyons. The most spectacular of these is, of course, the Grand Canyon, which is 135 miles long and in places over 5,000 ft deep and less than five miles wide. It appears to have inspired a volume of descriptive writing achieved by no other natural feature.

Below Boulder Canyon the river enters the Great Basin and tends to decrease in volume; the only major tributary here is the Gila, which, since its waters have been utilised for irrigation, now has no discharge to the main stream. For the last eighty miles of its course the Colorado passes through Mexico and splits into a number of distributaries, the channels of which are constantly changing. Before it was controlled the Colorado fluctuated enormously in volume and the discharge varied from 3,000 cu. ft

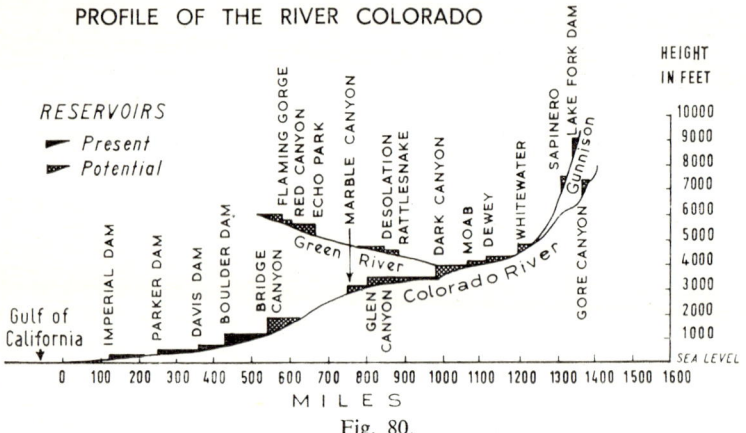

Fig. 80.

per sec. to 200,000 cu. ft per sec. Its regime now regulated, it flows at the rate of 21,000 cu. ft per sec.

The drainage area covers 244,000 square miles and includes within its boundaries seven states. The division of the water among the states has proved to be a subject of acrimonious dispute. Arizona, Nevada, and California in the lower part of the basin, where the shortage of water is most acute, have been allocated a total of 7·5 million acre-feet annually. California draws heavily on this supply: a 139-mile aqueduct takes water to the Los Angeles area for domestic, industrial, and irrigation uses, and this has recently been extended to San Diego; further quantities are taken by the All-American Canal to Imperial Valley and the Coachella Valley. These developments have been possible only since the construction of the multi-purpose Hoover (Boulder) Dam. Arizona uses less water for small irrigation schemes at Palo Verde and Yuma, but wishes to draw upon large amounts for the Central Arizona Project (Fig. 78). California wishes to safeguard future supplies for its rapidly developing population and industries.

The Colorado below Boulder Canyon is strictly controlled; the Hoover Dam stores a quantity of water (29 million acre-feet in Lake Mead), greater than the average annual discharge, and also provides about 1·3 million kilowatts of hydro-electricity. Dams on the river above the Hoover Dam (work has already started on the Glen Canyon and Flaming Gorge Dams) will provide additional storage facilities, a greater degree of flood-control, more water for irrigation, and more power (Fig. 80).

Irrigation in the Intermontane Region

It might be convenient at this point to summarise the factors involved in the development of irrigation in the Intermontane Region (Fig. 81).

(*a*) In the areas where irrigation is necessary, precipitation is small and unevenly distributed throughout the year. The rivers have irregular regimes and some form of control and water storage is essential. This entails the erection of dams and reservoirs, a process which often necessitates government aid.

(*b*) The siting of reservoirs is important. Most rivers drain terrain which has little vegetation, they have steep gradients, and carry large loads. Dams built across their courses will trap the silt. The Colorado is depositing about 200 million tons of material every year in Lake Mead, behind the Hoover Dam. It is estimated that the lake will be completely filled with silt by the year 2380.

(*c*) Where a dual-purpose dam is built, *i.e.* one which stores water for both irrigation and hydro-electricity, then the problem of water control arises. Farmers want a lot of water during the growing season; the power house engineers require a steady flow throughout the year.

(*d*) The reservoirs and canals lose water through evaporation. In the dry south-west, where the relative humidity is low, losses can be serious.

(*e*) Once water has been brought to the land it must be removed, otherwise the water-table will rise and the land will become saline.

(*f*) Where underground water is used there is the danger of lowering the water-table to such an extent that the cost of raising water becomes prohibitive.

(g) Extensions of the irrigated area become progressively more expensive for the easiest schemes are tackled first and the more difficult left until later.

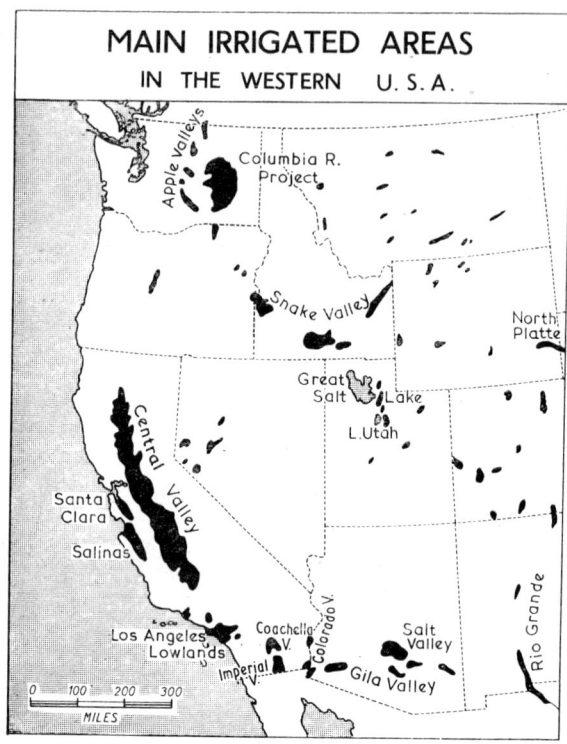

Fig. 81.

STATE	ACRES OF IRRIGATED CROPLAND	IRRIGATED CROPLAND AS PERCENTAGE OF TOTAL CROPLAND	PERCENTAGE OF THE TOTAL U.S.A. IRRIGATED AREA
California	7,387,000	66	22
Colorado	2,685,000	37	8
Idaho	2,577,000	56	8
Montana	1,875,000	20	6
Wyoming	1,470,000	64	4
Oregon	1,384,000	34	4
Arizona	1,154,000	94	3
Utah	1,062,000	72	3
Washington	1,007,000	19	3
New Mexico	732,000	48	2
Nevada	543,000	77	2
U.S.A.	33,211,000	9	100

(h) Where a river flows through two or more states and particularly if adjacent states recognise different water rights, there is often a dispute over the division of the waters. California and Arizona have been engaged for many years trying to reconcile their individual claims to the water of the Colorado River.

(i) Once all the physical problems have been resolved, there sometimes remains the problem of finding suitable markets for the produce. The smaller and more remote districts cannot always compete with the larger and more favourably placed areas.

CHAPTER XI

CALIFORNIA

Introduction

California extends over four physical regions and within its boundaries is a remarkable diversity of relief, climate, and resources. In the south-west is part of the Great Basin, which is described in Chapter X, with two extensive areas below sea level, Death Valley and the Salton Sea. Immediately to the west is the high, rugged, and unbroken Sierra Nevada with the highest peak in the U.S.A., Mount Whitney, 14,696 ft. Parallel to this range and separated from it by the low-lying and almost featureless Central Valley, are the Coast Ranges which drop steeply to the ocean and form an inhospitable shore-line. The climate, too, varies greatly: in some parts of the state precipitation exceeds 100 in. and in others is below 5 in.; while some areas experience constant heat, there are others which have continuous cold.

The human geography of California is also full of contrasts. The Spaniards, who entered the region from the south and established a chain of missions, pueblos (agricultural villages), and presidios (military posts) stretching from San Diego to San Francisco, left a legacy in the form of place-names and styles of architecture. They introduced European crops and methods of irrigation. When California passed under Mexican rule, ranching spread over the Central Valley. As late as the eighteen-forties, however, the white population numbered only 5,000. The rapid development of the state and its resources began with the discovery of gold in the Sierra Nevada foothills in 1848. A flood of miners, prospectors, and speculators poured into the state and mining dominated the economic scene until the easier deposits were worked out and the remainder passed into the hands of large companies. Then began a farming era; most landholders concentrated on wheat-growing (an activity well-suited to the Mediterranean climate) but towards the end of the nineteenth century fruit and truck farming became possible on a large scale and on the lowland areas of California rose vast commercial enterprises for the production of these commodities. The amount of capital investment in irrigation and equipment has been tremendous. In the present century the discovery of oil and the rise of industries (particularly since 1939) have added greatly to the wealth of the state.

The population at the 1960 census numbered 15·7 million and had increased by almost 50 per cent. in a decade. California is now, by population, the largest state in the U.S.A. and has thus become important politically as well as economically. The average age of its inhabitants is rather higher than that of the country as a whole, and this reflects the attraction to the region of large numbers of retired people from the east and Midwest, who find the climate congenial. Many of the people living there were born outside the state; some came during the depression of the thirties, and others during the war years. In addition there is a considerable population of Chinese and Japanese descent and a yearly influx of Mexicans who work in the orchards and fields during harvesting times. The negro population has grown rapidly during the last decade and now numbers almost 900,000. The population and industries continue to increase at a rate greater than that of the country as a whole. While this to some extent is due to the region's rich resources, it can be attributed also to its location on the Pacific coast. American interests (and commitments) in the Pacific have risen sharply since 1939, and this is reflected in corresponding developments in California.

Climate

California extends over eleven degrees of latitude (33° N. to 42° N.) and is one of the regions of the world which experiences a Mediterranean type of climate. Rainfall is deficient in summer: both total precipitation and the length of the wet season decrease southwards. Red Bluff, in the north of the Central Valley, has an average annual total of 25 in.; Bakersfield, in the south, has 6 in. But the windward slopes of the Coast Ranges and the Sierra Nevada have amounts that in places exceed 100 in. (Fig. 82). By contrast, the leeward slopes are dry and the rain-shadow areas in the south-west have under 5 in. and are truly arid.

Summer temperatures are highest in lowlands cut off from the sea by the mountain ranges. Average July figures are over 88° F. ($31°$ C.) in the south-west and over 80° F. ($27°$ C.) in those parts of the Central Valley which are not opposite the break in the coastal mountains at San Francisco. Along the coast the cold waters of the California Current chill the air moving landwards. In addition to the cold current there is also an upwelling of very cold water near the shore. These have the effect of delaying the warming of the land in spring and summer and in consequence, summer temperatures are low for the latitude and occur late in the year, *e.g.* San Diego, 70° F. ($21°$ C.) in September, and San Francisco, 60° F. ($16°$ C.) in

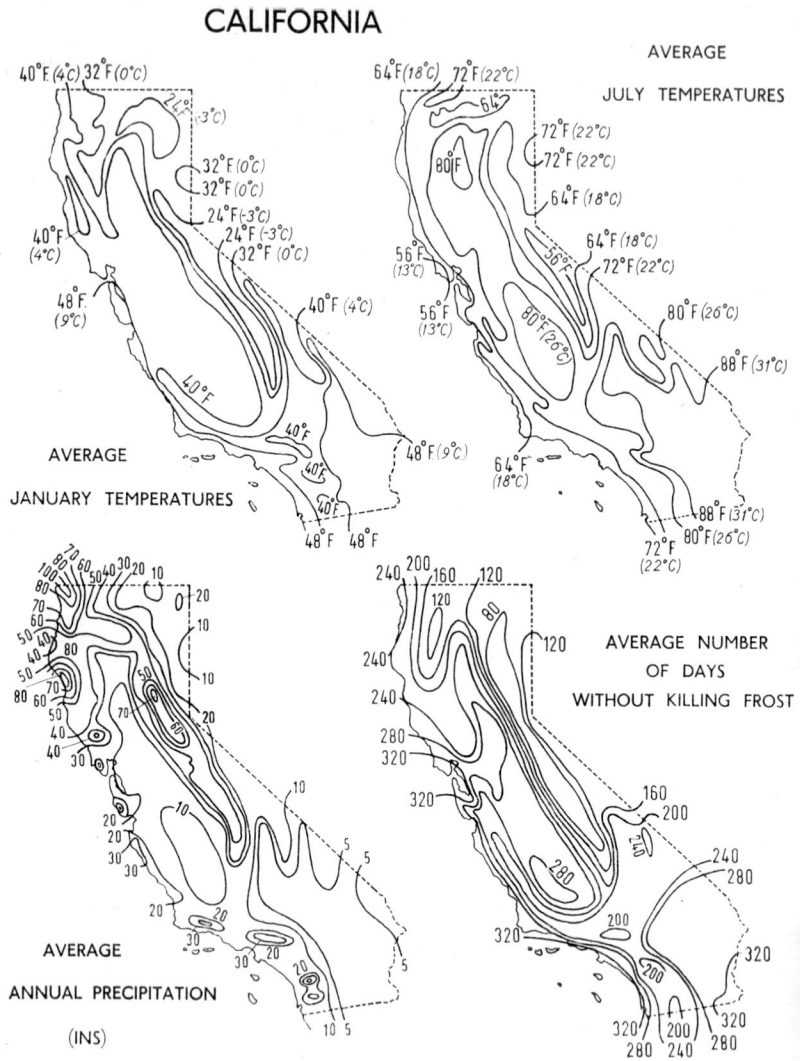

Fig. 82.
The Climate of California.

September [cp. Sacramento, 75° F. *(24° C.)* in July]. Fog and low cloud are prevalent along the coast due to the cooling of the air.

Winter temperatures vary from over 48° F. *(9° C.)* along the coast south of San Francisco and in the Great Basin to well below freezing point in the highlands (Fig. 82). In the Central Valley, January averages are generally between 40° F. *(4° C.)* and 48° F. *(9° C.)*. At this season the region lies in the path of depressions which bring most

Fig. 83.

of the precipitation. Frosts are rare along the coast, but can be disastrous to fruit and truck crops in the interior, if no protection is given. In the interior and towards the north, the growing season is shorter, while on the higher parts of the Sierra Nevada there is continuous frost and permanent snow.

Sierra Nevada

This massif is a huge tilted block, 400 miles long and fifty to eighty miles wide (Fig. 83). The structure is complex, with folded sediments, igneous intrusions, and local faulting. Mount Shasta and Lassen Peak are active volcanoes. The range presents a steep face to the east; in places there are drops of 8,000 or 10,000 ft from the high peaks which reach 14,000 ft to the floor of the Great Basin. Lakes Mono, Owens, and Tahoe occupy benches between step faults along this edge. The gentler western slope is dissected by many canyons and displays magnificent examples of glacial erosion (*e.g.* in the Yosemite National Park). In the north the Sierra Nevada merges into the Klamath Mountains, while in the south it curves to join the Coast Ranges in the vicinity of the Tejon Pass.

Because it is so high and unbroken, the range acts as a most effective barrier to climatic influences and to communications. Rain-bearing winds from the Pacific shed most of their moisture as rain or snow on the west-facing slopes. Many rivers rise here, fed by the rain and melting snow, and they descend rapidly to the Central Valley. Their waters are impounded for use in irrigated districts and to produce hydro-electricity. Precipitation and run-off decrease southwards and so most of the reservoirs and power plants are located in the northern half of the area. For a distance of 175 miles in the southern part of the Sierra Nevada there is no road across the range and there is only one railway in a distance of 300 miles. The higher passes are blocked by snow for eight to ten months of the year and the Donner Pass, which is used by both road and rail, is kept open only with great difficulty.

The western slope of the highland shows a striking relationship between climate and natural vegetation. At the foot of the range, conditions are so arid that the land supports a grass cover which is green for only a few weeks each year. With increasing altitude and precipitation, dry oak and chaparral appear which in turn are replaced by forests of pine, fir, cedar, and sequoia. Yellow pine occupies the land 3,000 to 4,000 ft high, sugar pine and sequoia the intermediate slopes, and red fir the land 7,000 to 9,000 ft high, where there is a thick winter snow mantle. Above this zone are subalpine species of lodgepole pine, white pine, and mountain hemlock. The tree line is found at about 11,000 ft on southward-facing slopes, but as low as 7,500 ft on those facing north (Fig. 26).

In the whole of California there are about 17 million acres of commercial forest, and most of this area lies in the Sierra Nevada. The annual cut of 6,500 million board feet comprises about one-seventh of the nation's lumber. Much of the wood is used within the state, some of it for making the packing cases for fruit and vegetables. It appears that the existing forests are being depleted, for the estimated annual growth is only 3,500 million board feet.

A great deal of the wooded area is open to controlled grazing during the summer season, while on the foothills ranching is common. Both the forests and the areas above the tree line have a recreational value.

The gravels of rivers in the Klamath Mountains and the northern Sierra Nevada (*e.g.* the Feather, Yuba, and American) are dredged for gold which has been washed down over millions of years from "Mother Lode". The foothills remain a major source of the metal even though California is no longer the leading gold-producing state. There is a small production of mercury and platinum.

The Central Valley

The Central Valley is a geosynclinal trough which has been sinking since Tertiary times. It is filled with a great thickness of sediments, mainly sands and clays, and has a surface mantle of alluvium. The height rarely exceeds 400 ft, although there are occasional protuberances above the rather monotonously level surface. These are small faulted blocks, salt domes, and volcanic hills. The lowland which covers an area 400 miles by 50 is almost completely enclosed by the Sierra Nevada, the Coast Ranges, and the Klamath Mountains. The only break in the mountain rim is behind San Francisco where the two main rivers join and flow to the sea. The northern part of the valley is drained by the Sacramento and the southern and larger part by the San Joaquin. The tributaries of these rivers descending the slopes of the Sierra Nevada have built large alluvial fans at the foot of the highlands. These have coalesced and the whole of the western part of the valley can be thought of as a large bajada. In the south the Lake Tulare basin has been separated from the San Joaquin Valley by a fan built by the King's River.

Agriculture.—Before the Gold Rush there was little farming in this region. Patches of cultivated land could be found around the missions and villages, but almost all the land in the Central Valley that was occupied was divided into huge ranches, which were owned by Mexicans. Even after the heavy immigration during the mid-nineteenth century, farming continued on extensive lines with wheat fields replacing the cattle ranches. Modern intensive farming began in the last two decades of the century after the introduction of refrigeration, irrigation, and reduced freight rates on the railways. The western third of the valley remains predominantly ranching country but the remainder is a rich and varied agricultural empire.

A traverse along the 400 miles of the Central Valley from north to south will show how intensive the farming is and how bewildering is the variety of crops (Fig. 84). In the north are many fields of grain, mainly barley which has replaced wheat as the principal cereal, and acres of winter pasture for cattle and sheep. As one moves southwards, orchards of deciduous fruits appear and become more numerous as the acreages under grain and grass decrease. Prunes, pears, peaches, and apples are most common, but around Corning there are olive groves. The 360,000 acres devoted to rice growing are found along the lower Sacramento where the heavy clay subsoils and the ease of irrigation encourage the cultivation of this crop (Table 7, p. 162). The rice is of an inferior quality and much is exported to Hawaii and Puerto Rico.

South of Sacramento is the rich delta area where thousands of swampy acres have been reclaimed by dikes and levees for the production of vegetables. Among others grown here are asparagus, celery, spinach, lettuce, carrots, and melons. Many of the truck-farmers are Nisei—*i.e.* American-born Japanese. Because of the nearness of this area to San Francisco and its neighbouring cities there are a number of dairy and poultry farms.

In the San Joaquin Valley irrigation becomes much more important, as the summers are both drier and warmer than farther north. The deciduous fruits give way to peaches, apricots, figs, and walnuts. Fresno is the centre of a rich vine-growing area and among the vineyards can be seen the large trays of grapes being dried into raisins under the hot sun. Here, too, are found the first orange groves. Navel oranges are grown because they are more resistant to the dry heat of summer and the occasional frosts of spring and winter than the Valencia oranges (the main type grown around Los Angeles). In the southern part of the valley, the dominant crop is cotton which has increased in importance in recent years (p. 141). It depends heavily on irrigation and needs about 24 in. of water in addition to the normal rainfall every year. Olives, too, are grown in the south, but there are only small amounts of land here devoted to alfalfa and grains.

There are certain distinctive features about the farming in the Central Valley and these are summarised below.

1. The high temperatures and large amounts of sunshine favour the growth of a great variety of fruits and vegetables if water is available for irrigation. However, in spring particularly, measures are necessary to protect the crops against occasional frosts. Small plants such as tomatoes and asparagus are covered by paper cones or sheets of plastic; the orchards have "smudge pots" or wind

machines spaced at intervals to provide air turbulence. The daily temperatures are widely publicised and closely scrutinised, and some farmers have installed automatic warning signals which sound an alarm when the temperature drops to a critical level. The weather, in fact, is a matter of great concern; interest is shown even in the winter snowfall on the Sierra Nevada, for on this may depend the availability of irrigation water during the following summer.

2. Farming is specialised; although agriculture in the valley is very varied, individual crops are grown in highly localised areas. The farmer is very much at the mercy of distant markets, quite frequently on the eastern seaboard, and dependent upon seasonal labour for harvesting his crop. There is a large force of migrant workers, largely braceros from Mexico, which moves across the state during the year. The existence of this group raises several social problems.

3. Because of the emphasis on fruit and vegetable crops, whether for canning, freezing, or immediate sale, on small and specialised farms, some sides of agriculture have been neglected. This is particularly the case with regard to stock feeds and livestock. There are to-day about 5 million cattle in California, but this number is insufficient to meet the needs of an expanding population, and stock for fattening and slaughter are brought from the mountain states and Texas. Hogs are brought from as far away as the Corn Belt. California is drawing upon an ever-widening area for its meat and milk.

4. One must picture the fruit and truck farms as factory-like concerns for the production, processing, and marketing of special crops. The producer has to sell his fruit, vegetables, or wine in highly competitive, distant markets, and must rely on cheap production, good transport, attractive packaging, and successful advertising. Sometimes the farmers belong to large-scale co-operative concerns; sometimes they work through marketing agencies which are empowered to enforce high standards and which are in a position to obtain the highest possible prices from buyers and favourable freight rates from the railway companies; sometimes they have contracts with very large firms, usually canners or processors, which effectively control the output of each individual farmer. Much use is made of machinery. The rice fields are seeded by aircraft which also spray the cotton plants to defoliate them immediately before the harvest. Vacuum machines are used to pick up nuts from the ground, and there are devices for shaking fruit and nuts from trees. The larger concerns, with their multi-harvesters, carefully-regulated production schedule, high rate of

investment, and central packaging depots, exemplify the success of industrial methods applied to agriculture.

Irrigation.—Altogether, there are about 7 million acres of irrigated land in California and between 60 per cent. and 70 per cent. of this is located in the Central Valley (Fig. 84). Irrigation first became important in the eighteen-eighties and led to the replacement of extensive wheat cultivation by intensive fruit and truck farming. Water is drawn from surface streams and from underground sources. Because of the irregular regime of the

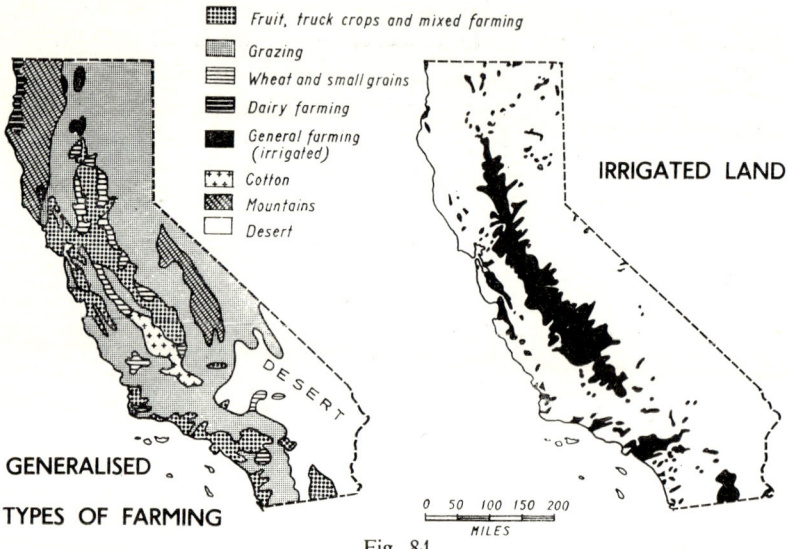

Fig. 84.

rivers, storage reservoirs are necessary, and there is an intricate network of channels to lead water to the fields. Where underground water is used, the water-table has often been lowered and pumping becomes more difficult and expensive.

Irrigation is most essential in the south but this is the region where water is most scarce. The Central Valley Project, inaugurated in 1935, is an attempt to overcome this problem (Fig. 85). Water from the Sacramento Valley, where supply exceeds demand, will be taken by canal and aqueduct across the delta southwards to the San Joaquin Valley. The rivers are to be regulated, which will prevent flooding and also keep the delta free from incursions of salt water. The project will entail the construction of forty-eight dams and twenty large canals (see plate facing p. 224). Some of these works have been completed for some time (*e.g.* the Shasta Dam, the key structure on the Sacramento, was finished in 1937). A more recent plan envisages the building of over 260 dams during the next

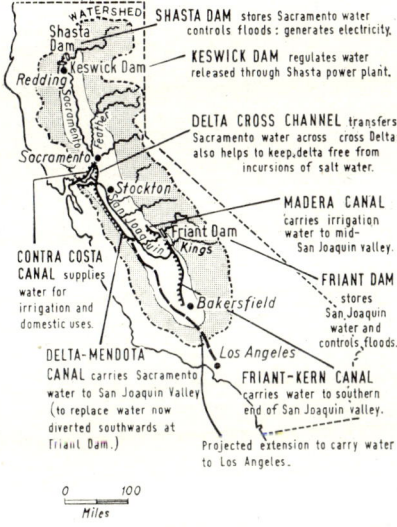

THE CENTRAL VALLEY PROJECT
Fig. 85.

The Sacramento Valley has ⅔ of the water but only ⅓ of the agricultural land. Before regulation, the river flooded in winter and was low in summer.

The Delta Region. Before the rivers were regulated, salt water invaded this area in summer when the rivers were low.

The San Joaquin Valley has ⅔ of the agricultural land but only ⅓ of the water. This area can be fully utilised only if water is brought from the Sacramento Valley.

100 years, and the extension of the aqueducts to the Los Angeles area by 1971.

Mining and Industry.—Because of the recent nature of the rocks which fill the Central Valley, there is little mineral wealth apart from great reserves of oil (see plate facing p. 256). This is found in the south of the San Joaquin Valley, where twenty-three fields produce most of California's output (Table 8, p. 166). The centre of this oil-producing district is Bakersfield. Natural gas is more widespread and is piped from the lower Sacramento Valley and the San Joaquin Valley to the San Francisco and Los Angeles areas.

Most of the manufacturing in the region is concerned with the processing of agricultural products, although in recent years factories turning out agricultural machinery have been established. Besides the multitude of small plants producing cellophane wrappers, packing cartons, and crates, etc., there are over 400 wineries, several sugar beet factories (mainly in the Sacramento Valley), and a number of meat-packing plants.

The Coast Ranges

These uplands rarely exceed 4,000 ft and drop steeply to the coast; they are, however, a real barrier to movement and are crossed by only a few, narrow, winding roads. The ranges extend the whole length of the state, from the north, where they merge into the Klamath Mountains, to the south, where they become more broken and less regularly aligned. In only a few places is there a coast plain (*e.g.* around Los Angeles). The folded sediments have been subjected to much faulting, some of it of very recent date. A notable fracture and line of weakness is the San Andreas Fault, movement along which was responsible for the earthquake that devastated San Francisco in 1906. The presence of old shore-lines, sometimes 1,000 ft or more above present sea level, indicates a general uplift of the area. There is no true continental shelf and water close to the shore is often thousands of feet deep. The sea bed is scored with submarine canyons. The ranges run diagonally to the coast and form bold cliffs and headlands between which are shallow bays on to which open fault-guided valleys such as those of the Salinas, Santa Ynez, and Santa Clara. The only natural break in the whole system is at San Francisco, where local submergence has created the Golden Gate and San Francisco Bay.

North of San Francisco, the Coast Ranges are clothed with giant redwoods and stands of Douglas fir, and lumbering is an important occupation (see plate facing p. 65). To the south, precipitation (under 20 in. except on a few west-facing slopes) is insufficient to support true forest and the natural vegetation is chaparral. This is an association of evergreen shrubs such as scrub oak, chamise, and holly-leaved cherry. Usually there are dense thickets, 3 to 10 ft high, but occasionally open chaparral is found where isolated shrubs are interspersed with coarse grass.

Cultivation is almost entirely restricted to the valleys where the soils are richer and deeper, and irrigation is possible. Here, as elsewhere in California, there is a great amount of specialisation.

THE COAST RANGES

The valleys of the north (*e.g.* Klamath, Russian, Sonoma) with fairly heavy and reliable precipitation, concentrate on dairying (Fig. 84). Immediately to the south of San Francisco is the Santa Clara Valley which is rapidly becoming urbanised. It is noted for the production of prunes and apricots, although there are also fields of pears, walnuts, vines, and vegetables. Watsonville, in the centre of the Pajaro Valley, is a name associated with apples. The Santa Maria and Santa Ynez Valleys are large producers of vegetables and flower seeds. The largest of the Pacific valleys is that of the Salinas (the "Salad Bowl") which produces lettuces from April to December. The cool summers and high incidence of fog (due to the cold current off-shore) are favourable for the growth of this crop.

California's coastline is over 1,000 miles long and off-shore there is a great variety of fish, with temperate species in the north and semi-tropical types in the south. Although the continental shelf is so narrow, there is an abundance of fish food because of the upwelling of waters near the shore which brings mineral salts near to the surface. California is the leading fishing state in the U.S.A. Fishing boats based on Los Angeles ("Fish Harbor"), San Diego, San Francisco, Eureka, and Monterey bring back to the canneries (which absorb over 90 per cent. of the total catch) large quantities of sardines and tuna. Tuna clippers operate in waters south of the equator and as far west as Hawaii. The crews of all the boats are dominantly Italian, Yugoslav, Portuguese, Japanese, and Scandinavian, or the American-born descendants of these nationalities.

San Francisco (743,000) is the centre of a Standard Metropolitan Area with a population of 2,700,000. It is a colourful and cosmopolitan city built on the northern tip of a hilly peninsula overlooking the Golden Gate to the north and San Francisco Bay to the east. The entrance to the bay, through the Golden Gate, is less than one mile wide (Fig. 86) and is spanned by a modern bridge. This is the only natural break along the whole coast south of Puget Sound.

The harbour is deep, sheltered, and almost tideless; the peninsula on which the city stands is lined with piers, warehouses, and shipyards. There is seventy-eight miles of berthing space, and vessels of many sorts dock here, ranging from the fishing boats at Fisherman's Wharf to the large liners at the Embarcadero. Blunt-nosed tugs push strings of barges up the Sacramento and San Joaquin rivers to Sacramento and Stockton. In 1966, the port handled 33·4 million tons of cargo (cp. 23·0 million tons at Los Angeles), the greater part of which was coast-wise traffic. Outgoing cargoes consist primarily of oil and oil products, grain, canned fruit, vegetables and fish, and cotton. The main imports are coffee, tropical fruits, vegetable oils, and sugar. San Francisco is the nearest U.S.A. port to the Far East and Hawaii and there are important trading links with these areas and Australia.

Opposite the Golden Gate is the mouth of the Sacramento-San Joaquin which provides a lowland route to the Central Valley. Almost directly in line with this gap is Donner Pass which affords the easiest crossing of the Sierra Nevada. Railways terminate on the eastern side of the bay at Oakland (367,000), Berkeley (111,000), Richmond (72,000), and Alameda (61,000). Train ferries cross the bay and there is a long road bridge which uses one of the islands, Yerba Buena Island, as a "stepping stone".

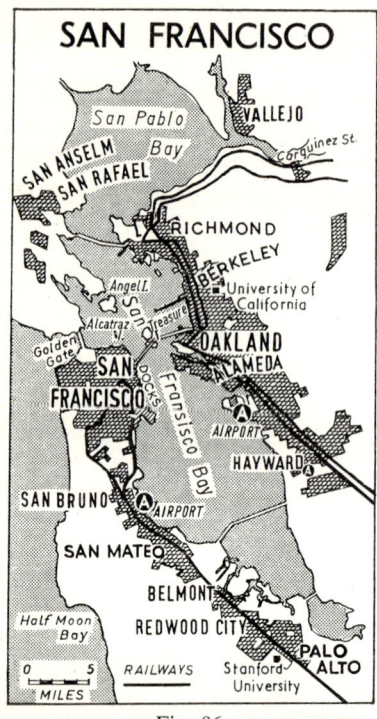

Fig. 86.

Since 1939 the bay area has witnessed a tremendous industrial expansion. There is no local coal or iron (although in spite of this there are four small steel plants), but oil and gas are available from the Central Valley and hydro-electricity from the Sierra Nevada. Many of the industries, *e.g.* the canneries and the factories producing tin-plate, glass, and card and paper containers, are directly related to the products of farming and fishing. Other, and usually newer, industrial activities include oil-refining (mainly at Richmond) and the manufacture of chemicals, and engineering. San Francisco also functions as the commercial and banking centre of a large part of the West.

The growth of the city is impeded by the rugged nature of the peninsula (many of the smaller hills were removed as the city spread), and most of the recent developments have taken place outside the city limits along the shores of the bay, where land is level and relatively cheap, and in the cities on the eastern shore.

These are responsible for an increasing proportion of the area's industry and also are favoured residential districts, as they are less foggy and warmer in summer than San Francisco itself. The future of industrial growth is not assured for already there are signs of shortages of oil, water, and hydro-electric power.

Southern California

South of Point Conception, the Coast Ranges become more broken and less regularly aligned. The region is a jumble of faulted blocks, some, like the San Gabriel Mountains, heavily dissected with deep canyons and peaked crests, others, like the San Bernadino Mountains, less sculptured with rounded crests and high level plateaus (Fig. 83). The islands found off the shore are the undrowned portions of faulted blocks on the continental shelf. The lower mountains are deeply covered with debris from the upstanding blocks. Intermittent streams lose themselves in the alluvial fill and rarely reach the sea. Except where the Los Angeles lowlands reach the sea, the coast is steep and abrupt, making communications difficult. Inland, too, travel is hampered by the lack of gaps in the encircling mountains. The main routes use the San Gorgonio Pass to Imperial Valley, Cajon Pass to the Mojave Desert and the east, and the Tejon Pass to the San Joaquin Valley.

The southern parts of these coastal ranges are particularly broken and inaccessible and consist of a complex of faulted blocks of various sizes and elevations. Along the western edge of this bulwark are marine and alluvial terraces which form a sort of coast plain about ten miles wide. However, this terraced plain is traversed by many deep canyons which have separated the area into numerous mesas. The only harbour is San Diego where a wide, shallow, lagoon-like bay is nearly enclosed by a long sand-bar.

Los Angeles.—The largest area of lowland lies around Los Angeles and here is found one of the greatest urban concentrations on the continent and one of the most intensively farmed and prosperous regions in the world. As precipitation exceeds 20 in. only on the surrounding mountains, irrigation is essential. Some water is drawn from the short streams that descend quickly to the Pacific, some is brought from the Colorado, some travels by aqueduct from Owen's Lake, and the remainder comes from underground sources, particularly the alluvial and gravel fans at the foot of the ranges. Much of the land is devoted to orange and lemon groves, but there are also fields of peaches, apples, grapes, celery, tomatoes, and lettuce. Most of the farms are smaller than ten acres and the farmers usually belong to marketing organisations which sell the fruit fresh, canned, or frozen. Because of the nearness of a large urban population, dairying has become important. The land around the city is arid and mountainous and the animals occupy feed lots within the metropolitan district. All fodder is purchased and up to 250 animals are kept on a ten-acre plot. These are milk "factories" rather than farms. With the rapid spread of the urban area, the amount of cultivated land is decreasing.

The centre of Los Angeles lies in the midst of this productive plain fifteen miles from the sea. Founded by the Spaniards in 1781 on the Los Angeles River (which provided water for irrigation), the city's growth was slow until the eighteen-eighties when the transcontinental railway arrived and oil was first discovered. It then expanded rapidly in all directions and absorbed the surrounding, satellite settlements—the "nineteen suburbs in search of a city". The built-up area reaches the coast at San Pedro and Long Beach, where there is a fine artificial harbour. The city area is 453 square miles, the largest of any city in the U.S.A., and the population is over 2,500,000 (for the Standard Metropolitan Area, it is 6,700,000).

Several factors are responsible for the phenomenal growth of Los Angeles, among them the attractiveness of the Mediterranean climate, which drew retired people from the populous east, the rapid development of industries and the demand for a large labour force, and the "glamour" of the city as the centre of film-making. The motion picture industry grew up here because of the sunny Mediterranean climate and the great variety of scenery to be found within a small area—mountains, desert, tropical vegetation, and sea coast. Although much "shooting" now takes place indoors, the industry is firmly entrenched in Hollywood and the surrounding centres to which it has latterly expanded, *e.g.* the San Fernando Valley. The Mount Palomar telescope is located in this area where cloud is infrequent.

Oil was first discovered in the eighteen-eighties, but it was not until after World War I that production on a large scale began. The output of the Los Angeles region is slightly less than that of the San Joaquin Valley (see plate facing p. 256). Altogether, California has over 41,000 oil wells (some of them lying off-shore) and produces about 950,000 barrels daily, which amounts to about 12 per cent. of the U.S.A. output (Table 8, p. 166). Much of the oil is refined on the coast and in the past some was exported to Alaska and the Far East. To-day there is a deficiency of oil and extra supplies are imported. The Bay Area of San Francisco has become a more important refining centre than Los Angeles. Both oil and the natural gas, which is found associated with it (but in insufficient quantities so that large amounts have to be piped from Texas), are used as fuels and as raw materials in the numerous chemical industries.

Two of the largest employers of labour are the aircraft and automobile industries. The assembly of aircraft parts began in the inter-war period and by 1939 this area was producing about one-third of all the U.S.A.'s aeroplanes. This remarkable concentration seems to have been due to the warm, sunny climate which rarely inhibited flying and made the heating of large hangars unnecessary, and to the availability of sites near airports. The "technical climate" is favourable, for in California are many institutions of higher education. During the war the industry was dispersed over interior cities because of vulnerability to attack from the Pacific, but since 1945 it has returned to its home area. The industry occupies over one-quarter of all manufacturing workers in the Los Angeles area and three-quarters in San Diego (573,000), where aircraft and missiles are made. As a manufacturing centre of automobiles, Los Angeles ranks second to Detroit. Many of the parts are sent from eastern cities and assembled here (prefabricated articles of all kinds are received for assembly in this region), and over half a million vehicles are produced each year.

There is one car for every 2·2 persons in Los Angeles and some authorities attribute the prevalence of smog in the city to the exhaust gases rather than to other industrial waste. Smog has become very much more common in recent years and it seems paradoxical that the city which owes its growth mainly to its climate should now experience the same sunless conditions as the valley-sited industrial centres of the east. The occurrence of smog can be correlated with the existence of a temperature inversion, due to the inflow of stable maritime air at high levels over this semi-enclosed lowland. The fumes are trapped in the lower atmosphere and form a pall on about seventy days each year.

Both coal and iron are absent, but during World War II a large steel plant was established at Fontana, fifty miles east of Los Angeles, to supply plates for shipbuilding. The coal comes from Utah, 800 miles away, and the iron ore from Eagle Mountain, 160 miles distant. There is a large amount of local scrap which feeds the furnaces. The plant has a capacity of 2·9 million tons annually, and much of the production is used in the oil industry and the canning factories. Consumption of steel in California amounts to about 5 million tons annually, and extra supplies are brought from the Mountain States plants at Geneva and Pueblo, as well as from the Midwest.

Los Angeles, including San Pedro and Long Beach, is an important commercial and fishing port, handling about 40 million tons of cargo each year, and about 5,000 ships. Most of the trade is coast-wise but the port also shares with San Francisco the Latin American and Pacific Island trade. The port lies nearer the Panama Canal than San Francisco but farther from the Far East. The outgoing shipments include oil and oil products, cotton (Los Angeles ranks as a major cotton-exporting port), canned fish, fruit and vegetables, and machinery. Incoming cargoes comprise oil, rubber, lumber, tropical foodstuffs, chemicals, and newsprint.

The major problem facing Los Angeles is the shortage of water. Local resources from wells and streams are much too small to meet the needs of such a large city which is expanding so rapidly. Extra supplies were first sought in the Sierra Nevada and a 240-mile long aqueduct was constructed to bring water from two of the lakes, Mono and Owens. Later a 400-mile long aqueduct was led from the Colorado River and this carries over 1 million acre-feet of water annually, most of which is used outside the urban area. Local sources supply about 26 per cent. of the city's needs, the Owens-Mono aqueduct about 70 per cent., and the Colorado aqueduct only about 4 per cent. There is a long-standing interstate dispute between California and Arizona about the future uses of the waters of the Colorado River. According to recent plans, Los Angeles should be receiving water brought from the Sacramento River by a 700-mile long aqueduct by 1971. At present, in years with under average precipitation, there is some curtailment of irrigation water and power supplies.

Above: There are more than 36,000 oil wells in California, mainly in the Los Angeles area and the southern part of the Central Valley. They produce about 12 per cent. of the U.S.A.'s oil. (*U.S.I.S.*)

Below: Cleveland is situated where the Cuyahoga River enters Lake Erie. Note the large freighters which bring iron ore, and the special bridges. (*Fairchild Aerial Surveys Inc.*)

THE ST LAWRENCE

Above: French-Canadian farms, each with a water frontage, on the south bank of the St Lawrence between Trois Rivières and Quebec. (*Canadian Pacific.*)

Below: The Canadian Locks near Iroquois. To the left is the dam which controls the flow of water from Lake Ontario. See Fig. 103. (*Aerofilms.*)

CHAPTER XII
PACIFIC NORTH-WEST

Introduction

The Pacific North-west, which lies west of the Cascades and between the borders of California and Canada, is the only truly humid region in the whole of the American West. As such, its development has been distinctive and the present economy differs from that of the other western states. Because the area east of the Cascades falls within the hinterland of the Pacific ports, and because there are firm economic links between this area and the Pacific North-west, it is impossible to describe the latter without reference to the former (which was more fully described in Chapter X).

The population of the three north-western states is 5,589,000 (Washington, 3,050,000; Oregon, 1,826,000; Idaho, 713,000). Of this number, over three-fifths live west of the Cascades on one-fifth of the area (Fig. 87). The area was explored during the early years of the nineteenth century (the Lewis and Clark Expedition, 1804-5), and it was during this period that fur-trappers began to enter the region. At first this territory was jointly controlled by the U.S.A. and Britain. Missionaries and settlers followed in the wake of the trappers, most of them making their way across the continent along the Oregon Trail. Their numbers increased during the eighteen-forties, and in 1846 the boundary between the U.S.A. and Canada was fixed along the 49th Parallel. This represented a compromise between British claims to the area north of the Columbia and American insistence upon a boundary along the parallel 54° 40′ N.

Growth during the following decades was slow, due to the constant Indian wars and the distance of the North-west from the east. The arrival of the transcontinental railways after 1880 was a great stimulus to agricultural and industrial development. The Northern Pacific reached the coast in 1883, the Union Pacific in 1884, the Great Northern in 1893, and the Chicago, Milwaukee, St Paul, and Pacific in 1909 (Fig. 89). Now began the active exploitation of the forests and fisheries and increasing immigration (cp. population in 1880, 282,000; in 1910, 2,140,000). However, until World War II the region remained an economic dependency of the U.S.A., providing basic materials and foodstuffs and shipping in manufactures. After 1939 there was a great influx of industries, partly because of the abundant cheap power, and partly because of the region's location on the Pacific coast. Since 1945 development has slowed down, although there has been no great recession as there was after World War I, and the rate of population increase is slightly less than that of the country as a whole (cp. U.S.A. 19 per cent.; Washington, 20 per cent.; Oregon, 16 per cent.; Idaho, 13 per cent; California, 49 per cent.).

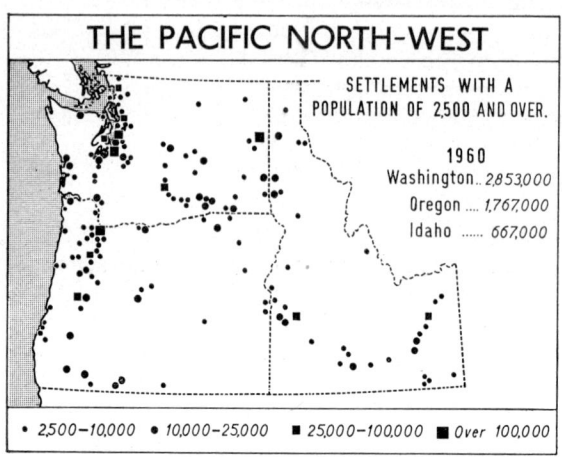

Fig. 87.
The Distribution of Population.
About three-fifths of the inhabitants of the three states live west of the Cascades.

Physical Features

Three major physical regions can be distinguished: they are the northward extension of similar features in California.

The Coast Ranges form a belt of country about fifty miles wide and reach elevations of almost 4,000 ft in the south, where they merge into the Klamath Mountains, and over 1,500 ft in the north. The rocks are gently folded sedimentaries, mainly sandstones and shales with some igneous intrusions. There are two to five ranges running parallel to the coast and not diagonally to it as in California. The coast plain is more continuous too, but it is rarely more than three miles in width. Marine terraces are evidence of emergence but recent submergence is suggested by the drowned estuaries of the Umpqua, Rogue, and Coos rivers (Fig. 88). Along the coast are southward-growing spits and dunes which have blocked some of the smaller streams and formed lakes.

Between the Chehalis River and Juan de Fuca Strait are the Olympic Mountains which have a diameter of sixty miles and reach an elevation of 7,915 ft in Mount Olympus. The topography is rugged and the radial valleys show marked glacial features. All the coastal mountains are heavily forested with spruce, hemlock, and cedar associations on the windward slopes and Douglas fir on the slightly drier eastern slopes. Only the higher parts of the Olympic Mountains lie above the tree line.

The Puget Sound-Willamette Valley Trough is a narrower and less continuous extension of the Central Valley of California, from which it is separated by the Klamath Mountains (Fig. 88). The average width is thirty-five miles. The southern portion is drained by the Willamette and the central part by the Cowlitz, both tributaries of the Columbia. The northern third is partially drowned under the waters of Puget Sound. Rising from the alluvial floor of the Willamette Valley are low hills, a few hundred feet high, of sandstone and basalt, and along the foot of the Cascades is a series of alluvial fans. The northern part was covered by a lobe of the ice-sheet which was joined by small valley glaciers descending from the Cascades and Olympic Mountains. The shores of Puget Sound, which was submerged during the post-glacial rise in sea level, are plastered with drift, and south of

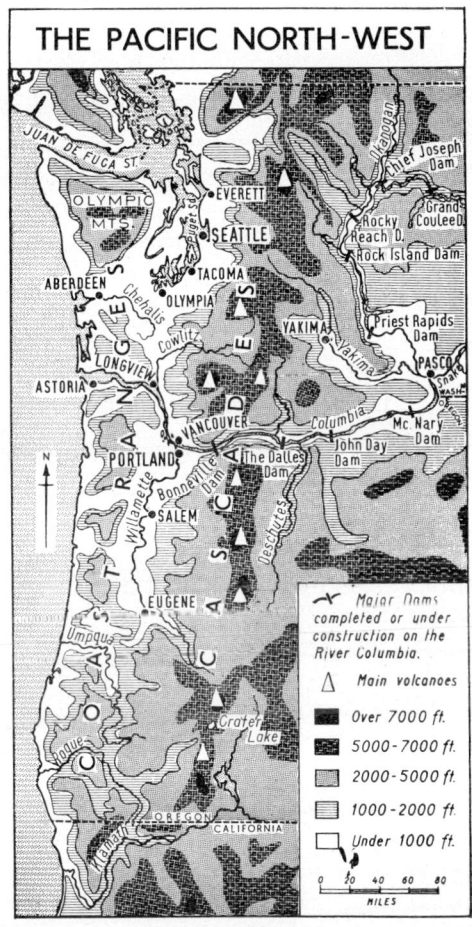

Fig. 88.

Olympia, there is a terminal moraine with southward-spreading outwash sands. This area is low and marshy.

The Cascades are a dissected plateau 500 miles long with a width of fifty miles in the south and 100 miles in the north. Older rocks are exposed in the west, and the topography is extremely rugged; in the east the lava which covers the slopes gives rise to less dissected country. The southern portions, too, which are primarily of extrusive rocks, are smoother than the north which has large areas of sedimentary rocks and granite batholiths. There are over 120 volcanic peaks in this mountain system, the major cones, like Mount Hood and Mount Rainier, rising some 3,000 to 4,000 ft above the level of the plateau. Another interesting volcanic feature is Crater Lake in the south of the Cascades, which occupies the sunken caldera of an extinct volcano. The upland was severely glaciated and there are many erosional features. Lake Chelan is eighty-eight miles long and occupies a glacially-deepened trough on the eastern side of the Cascades which descends below sea level. Many small glaciers still exist on the higher peaks, particularly on the northern flanks, but they seem to be shrinking.

The Cascades act as a barrier both to climatic influences and to communications. The interior is dry and has extremes of temperature, while the western side has copious precipitation and more moderate temperatures. The only major break in the system is where the Columbia cuts through its gorge at The Dalles and is followed by the main lines of communication. Several high passes farther north are utilised by roads and railways, but most are closed during the winter months.

River Columbia

The industries in the coastal towns of the Pacific North-west and the agriculture of the interior are almost completely dependent upon the waters of the Columbia and its tributaries. The river rises in Canada and flows 1,214 miles to the sea; in the 600 miles of its lower course which lie in the U.S.A., it drops 1,300 ft. The drainage basin covers an area of 259,000 square miles, of which 220,000 lie in the U.S.A. The average annual discharge amounts to 180 million acre-feet, 37 million being contributed by the Snake and 22 million by the Willamette. This represents eight times the flow of the Colorado and twice that of the Nile. Some of the more remarkable physical features, such as the Snake Canyon, the drainage diversions, and the coulees were described in Chapter X. In the next paragraphs are discussed the four major uses of the river and its tributaries.

The system does not carry a large volume of traffic. There is a 35-ft channel to Portland, which can be negotiated by large vessels, and a 27-ft channel between Portland and Bonneville. Above the dam here, a 14-ft channel exists as far as The Dalles and vessels drawing less than 7 ft can proceed upstream to Pasco. On the Willamette, an 8-ft channel has been created between Portland and Oregon City. Altogether there are about 600 miles of navigable waterways carrying about 3 million tons annually. The upstream traffic consists mainly of oil and oil products, while logs and wheat make up the bulk of the seaward-bound cargoes.

In the Columbia basin there are about 4·5 million acres of irrigated land, almost all of it lying east of the Cascades (see Chapter X and Fig. 81). The most notable areas are the valleys of the Snake, Yakima, Wenatchee, and Okanagan, and the Big Bend area of central Washington (the Columbia Basin Project). Without irrigation there would be very little farming in this dry area. Nearer the coast the river fisheries are important and will be described later in the chapter.

Utilisation of water for the generation of electricity is unusually important in the North-west. The numerous power stations have a combined capacity of almost 10 million kilowatts, which is less than one-quarter of the potential hydro-electric power of the region. The earliest developments took place at rapids and waterfalls (*e.g.* Oregon City on the Willamette), but the recent large power houses are sited below huge dams which store the water and regulate the flow of the river. While in the past much of the power was harnessed by private interests, the latest developments have been sponsored and carried out by federal agencies, the Bureau of Reclamation and the Corps of Engineers. The electricity is sold by the Bonneville Power Administration. The Bonneville (0·5 million kilowatts) and Grand Coulee (2·5 million kilowatts) schemes are now working to full capacity (see Frontispiece). Other installations with their present and ultimate capacities are at the Chief Joseph Dam, 1 million kilowatts (ultimately, 1·7 million kilowatts), the McNary Dam, 1 million (1·4 million), the Dalles Dam, 0·8 million (1·7 million), and the John Day Dam, 1·3 million (ultimately 2·2 million kilowatts) (Fig. 88).

The electricity is the cheapest of any produced in the U.S.A., and there are plans to transmit surpluses to California under the Pacific Northwest-Southwest Intertie System. The region, it is estimated, has between 35 and 50 per cent. of the potential hydro-electric power in the country and much of this is still unharnessed. But there are certain handicaps. Because the high water of the

Columbia occurs in summer, due to the melting of the mountain snows, and the low water in winter when power needs are usually greatest, storage works become essential. The river is incised in many places along its course and this makes the construction of dams and reservoirs relatively easy. But already the U.S.A. is looking across the border to British Columbia for further sites. Under a recent agreement the U.S.A. will finance the building of reservoirs and dams in Canada north of the 49th Parallel, which will regulate the flow of the river and produce more power. Future developments in British Columbia are likely to be influenced almost as much by power demands in the U.S.A. as by local needs (see Chapter XVII).

Climate

The marine climate of this region was described in Chapter II and below are listed only the main characteristics.

1. Temperatures decrease from the coast inland during the winter and increase in summer. The mean annual range along the littoral is quite small—from over 40° F. *(4° C.)* in January to under 60° F. *(16° C.)* in July—but in the interior the continental effect is very marked—the Middle Snake Valley has mean January temperatures of about 25° F. *(− 4° C.)* and mean July temperatures of over 75° F. *(24° C.)*.

2. Precipitation is heaviest on the coast where annual totals of over 100 in. are experienced. Parts of the northern Cascades, too, receive over 100 in., although this is mainly in the form of snow. At elevations of 3,000 ft and over, snowfall amounts exceed 400 in. The snowline is found at about 8,000 ft. Between the Coast Ranges and the Cascades, amounts are from 40 to 50 in. Portland, for example, has 44 in. East of the Cascades, precipitation is drastically reduced and the rain-shadow effect of the mountains lying athwart the prevailing winds is very marked. Yakima has only 7 in. annually, but totals increase gradually away from the immediate lee slope to over 20 in.

3. Most of the precipitation occurs during the winter months when depressions are numerous and intense. Summer drought is only apparent in the southern parts of the Willamette Valley; elsewhere (except, of course, in the interior) summer rainfall, although smaller than winter amounts, is sufficient for most forms of agriculture.

4. Within such a small area, the growing season varies enormously. The frost free period is longest along the coast and lower Columbia Valley and amounts to over 240 days. It is about

AGRICULTURE

140 days in the Palouse area and about 120 days in the middle Snake Valley. On the higher parts of the Cascades, frost is likely to occur at any time (Fig. 16).

5. From the above it is evident that the Cascades are an important climatic divide, perhaps the sharpest in the continent. To the west marine influences are dominant: to the east they are markedly absent.

Agriculture

In the Pacific North-west there are four easily-recognised types of agriculture: general farming is common west of the Cascades, irrigation farming takes place in the valleys of the interior, wheat is produced by dry-farming methods in the Palouse, and ranching occupies the remaining parts of the Columbia Plateau. The interior region was described in Chapter X, and attention here is concentrated upon the humid lands in the west.

A large proportion of the land is high, rugged, and forested, and agriculture is confined to the central lowlands and the coastal valleys. Altogether about 4 million acres are under cultivation. This is a mellow and restful landscape, with small diversified farms, and it contrasts strongly with the starkness of the interior and the colourful opulence of southern California.

On the lowlands around Puget Sound, dairying is the main activity, particularly on the dyked and reclaimed tidal flats, and here are found over one-half of the milk cows in Washington. The rainfall is between 30 and 50 in., and pastures are maintained in good condition even in the two driest months, July and August, for most farms occupy alluvial soils which permit water seepage to the surface. Holdings are invariably under 100 acres, and usually about half that size. Oats and other fodder crops are grown on half the acreage and used to make silage (some grain and alfalfa come from eastern Washington), the remaining land being pasture and hay. A potato patch and an orchard may occupy a small area on each farm. About fifteen or twenty cattle are kept and usually some poultry. Most of the milk is absorbed by the large coastal settlements, and the needs of these places has led to the rise of truck farming. Peas, beans, cabbages, cauliflowers, and rhubarb are grown both for local consumption and for dispatch to other parts of the country. There are many canning and freezing plants in this area.

The Willamette Valley experiences cooler winters and warmer summers than the Puget Sound lowlands. Rainfall totals are smaller and the summer drought is more marked, particularly in the south.

Many farmers have introduced sprinkler irrigation for their pasture and cash crops. General farming is more common than in the area farther north; there is slightly less dairying and more land under small grains and corn (which is cut green for silage because summers are not hot enough to ripen the crop). There is more orchard land, too, producing prunes, apples, cherries, and strawberries (Fig. 62 and Table 9, p. 178). Hops are an important crop, occupying over 20,000 acres, and an even larger area carries walnut and hazel trees (the latter producing filberts). Several farms specialise in growing flowers, flower seeds, and bulbs. Truck farming is found around Portland and there is a large output of cabbage, kale, mustard, and potatoes.

The coastal valleys such as those of the Rogue, Umpqua, Coos, and Chehalis are the wettest of the farmed areas and as grains do not ripen easily here, dairying is predominant. Much hay and practically all the feed grains come from outside the area. As in the Puget Sound lowlands, farms often have areas of uncleared or half-cleared land. Stump pastures provide inferior grazing, but because reclamation costs are heavy, improvements are carried out only slowly. While some of the milk is sold fresh in the north-western cities, much is made into cheese.

Forestry

Commercial forests (*i.e.* those where tree growth is relatively rapid, and which are so located that the timber can easily be extracted) cover more than 45 million acres in the Pacific North-west, *i.e.* about 80 per cent. of the total forested area. Apart from their commercial value, the forests protect watersheds from erosion, provide grazing for sheep and cattle, particularly east of the Cascades and serve as areas for recreation. Densest stands are found west of the Cascades, and it is in this region that most lumbering takes place and that most of the forest industries are located.

There are two main forest associations, the spruce-hemlock type on the northern Coast Ranges and the Douglas fir type on the southern Coast Ranges and the western slopes of the Cascades. The latter also occurs farther east, but is subordinate to Ponderosa pine. The principal species in the spruce-hemlock type are western hemlock (about 60 per cent. of the trees), Sitka spruce (about 11 per cent.), and western red cedar (about 16 per cent.). All these are moisture loving and flourish under the heavy precipitation and moderate temperatures that prevail in the Coast Ranges. Over much of its extent, Douglas fir constitutes 90 per cent. of the timber volume. It grows to a great size and is the most prized tree in the region. The Willamette Valley was not thickly wooded when the first settlers arrived, and what timber there was quickly disappeared under the farmer's axe. It is the upland slopes which provide the lumber.

The first saw mill was established near Vancouver as early as 1827, but the logging industry did not really get under way until the last two decades of the nineteenth century, when the timber reserves in the eastern parts of the country were becoming exhausted. Most of the lumber was shipped to its destination, but the advent of the railways permitted shorter hauls across land and also stimulated production through the demand for wood for the construction of bridges, etc. To-day lumbering is highly mechanised, and transport by rail or road finely organised. Wood moves to one of the 3,500 saw mills or fifty pulp mills. Logs float down the Willamette River and there is some coastal movement of timber along the shores of Puget Sound, where many of the large mills are situated. Industries connected with wood, including pulp, paper, hardboard, plywood, turpentine, etc., give employment to over half the factory workers in the two states.

The region produces about half of the nation's softwood (cp. one-third from the South), and about 17 per cent. of its pulpwood. It has the richest and most accessible store of timber in the continent, if not in the world. Wasteful exploitation of the forests in the past has now been partially replaced by a policy of "wise use" (*i.e.* the conservation of existing reserves) and the reafforestation of cut-over areas. Sometimes seed trees are left standing and regeneration occurs naturally; sometimes nursery-raised seedlings are planted by hand. Helicopters are occasionally used to seed some areas. Nearly half the privately owned forests are now managed as tree farms where the conservation and regrowth of timber are carefully carried out and where stringent precautions are taken against damage by fire and pests. Nevertheless, the annual cut, which averages about 7,000 million board feet in Oregon and about 3,500 million board feet in Washington, still exceeds the net annual growth, which amounts to 4,000 million board feet and 3,000 million board feet respectively in the two states.

Fishing

The coastal and off-shore waters of the North-west, as well as the rivers and lakes, offer a variety of marine habitats. The rich fish pastures flourish here where cold and warm currents intermingle and nutrient salts for the plankton are abundant. Along the rugged littoral and the shores of the numerous islands in Puget Sound and the Inland Passage of British Columbia are sheltered waters for spawning. With such an ideal and diverse environment, it is not surprising that commercial fish are caught in great numbers and in great variety.

Salmon provide the bulk of the catch, both in weight and value. There are five different species, all of which spend the greater part of their lives in the sea and then migrate up the rivers to their own birthplace to spawn. Sockeye, or red salmon, weighs from 4 to 10 lb., and is the ideal cannery fish from the standpoint of size and colour. Once it provided the whole of the American pack, but now it accounts for only about a quarter of it, the remainder being supplied by the other species—the Chinook or king salmon, coho or silversides, humpback or pink, and chum or keta salmon. Salmon congregate in the coastal waters in spring and summer prior to moving upstream, and they are caught by purse seiners and in traps.

Most of the catch is canned. The first cannery was established in 1866 and production increased very rapidly as further plants were built on tidewater sites. The industry reached its peak before World War I and has since declined. Production now amounts to about three-quarters of a million cases (of 48 lb.) annually (cp. Alaska's output of 3·5 million cases). The decline is due to over-fishing and to the pollution of the streams. By a joint treaty, both Canada and the U.S.A. now regulate fishing in order to conserve stocks. The damming of certain rivers, too, has cut off some of the spawning grounds, although modern dams (*e.g.* the Bonneville and McNary dams, but not Grand Coulee) have ingenious fish ladders to enable the salmon to negotiate the barrier. Artificial propagation is increasingly practised.

Other varieties of fish caught in large quantities include tuna (albacore), the bulk of which is canned, halibut, which is sold fresh or frozen, herrings, and pilchards. In addition, crabs and shrimps are taken from coastal waters and oysters are cultivated on the shallow tidal flats of Puget Sound.

Nearly every harbour has a fishing fleet but more vessels are based at Seattle than at any other port. Fisherman's Terminal here can accommodate 1,000 vessels, some of which range as far as Alaska. Apart from the scores of canneries there are in the North-west a number of fish reduction plants which produce oil, fish-meal, fertiliser, etc. Astoria is a leading canning and processing centre, but the majority of the products of fishing, whether fresh, frozen, or canned, pass through Seattle warehouses.

Cities and Industries

Although more people are engaged in manufacturing than in agriculture, fishing, and mining combined, by both criteria commonly used to measure industrial activity, *i.e.* number of persons employed in manufacturing, and value added by manufacture, the Pacific North-west is below the national average. And it remains so, in spite of the spectacular progress made since 1939.

Industrial activity is dominated by the processing of the products of the forests, farms, and the sea. Mills and factories using timber employ over half the workers in the region, and while they are found in all parts of the area, tend to be concentrated in the Puget-Willamette lowlands. Food processing which includes canning, milling, and freezing, is the second major industry.

The region is not well endowed with minerals. There are several small coalfields, but only a few in the Puget Sound lowlands are exploited, *e.g.* at Bellingham, and production amounts to little more than 200,000 tons annually. There are no significant deposits of oil or metallic minerals, although the region can draw upon the non-ferrous metals of the interior at Coeur d'Alene. Small steelworks at Seattle and Vancouver (Washington) use a very high proportion of scrap. Natural gas is now imported from British Columbia in increasing quantities, and provides an additional form of power, but the main resource is water-power (see p. 261). Hydro-electricity is available in large quantities at low rates and has attracted several industries, the most important of which is the aluminium industry.

Alumina (processed bauxite) is brought almost 3,000 miles by rail from the Gulf coast for reduction in one of the six plants, all of which have been established since 1939. Three are situated on the lower Columbia at Vancouver, Longview, and Troutdale, and one at Tacoma. The remaining two are in the interior near Spokane and Wenatchee. Although there are a number of fabricating industries, most of the finished aluminium moves to California and the Midwest. The major local consumer is the large Boeing aircraft works at Seattle. The aluminium industry, which accounts for 53 per cent. of all factory workers, uses one-fifth of all the hydro-electricity generated in the Pacific North-west, and there are fears of future power shortages. This factor might hamper the expansion of the industry, as might the fact that the distance from the markets and raw materials is so great. Electrical energy is also used in large quantities at the two atomic plants in the interior—Hanford (near Richland) and Arco (Idaho).

Industrial development in the North-west is handicapped to a certain extent by distance from the main markets in the eastern half of the country and heavy freight rates. The strongest stimulus to further expansion is likely to come from the growth of population in the area, and the increasing market for its products in California.

Seattle (557,000) dominates the coastal lowland around Puget Sound that contains a number of cities such as Everett, Bellingham,

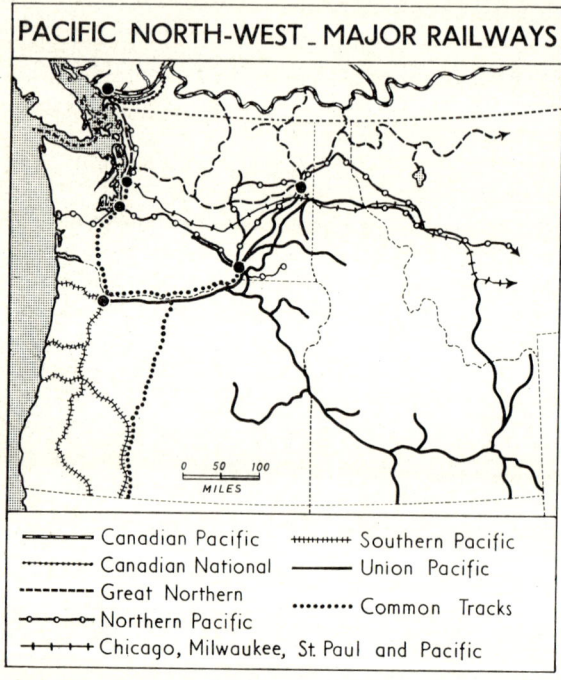

Fig. 89.
Note the concentration of routes at Spokane, Pasco, Portland, Tacoma, and Seattle.

and Tacoma. It is situated between Elliot Bay to the west, which offers ample anchorage and a large dock frontage, and Lake Washington to the east which is joined to the sea by a canal. In the middle of the city is Lake Union which provides additional port facilities. The settlement grew up on a series of low hills of glacial debris, leaving the lower and less favoured sites for railways and industries. The buildings are scattered and somewhat unco-ordinated because of this. Expansion to the east is restricted because of Lake Washington, and Seattle has grown northwards and southwards.

Lumber industries dominate the industrial scene, but there are important shipyards, engineering plants, and aircraft works in addition to numerous food processing factories. As a port, Seattle handles about 12 million tons annually and ranks twenty-third among the ports of the U.S.A. It became the gateway to Alaska in 1897 when the gold rush started and still manages much of the trade of this outlying state. Seattle is the nearest U.S.A. port to Japan on the great circle route, and there are shipping links with this country and other Pacific islands. However, it is the farthest point on the west coast from the Panama Canal and has less trade with eastern U.S.A. and Latin America than either San Francisco or Los Angeles. It handles the products of the interior with which it has good railway communications (Fig. 89), and exports mainly lumber and timber products.

Tacoma (147,000) was the original terminus of the Northern Pacific Railway, and before 1900 was a serious rival of Seattle, which lies nearer the open sea. The city claims to be the "lumber capital of the world" and wood industries (including over a dozen furniture factories) are predominant, but there are also a copper refinery, an aluminium smelter, several flour mills, and engineering works and chemical plants. Tacoma's hinterland is much smaller than that of Seattle and the port handles under 4 million tons annually.

Portland (373,000) is the oldest and most mature city of the North-west. It was the terminus of the Oregon Trail and later of a transcontinental railway. The settlement arose on the Willamette, fourteen miles above its confluence with the Columbia and 113 miles from the sea at the head of ocean navigation. There is a 35-ft channel to the coast, but navigation is occasionally handicapped by a bar across the mouth of the river. Small craft can sail up the Columbia through the gorge cut through the Cascades at The Dalles. This valley also provides a lowland route to the interior, which is followed by roads and railways. The port handles slightly less cargo than Seattle and ranks twenty-fourth in the U.S.A. The main exports are lumber, paper, and wheat.

Portland acts as a trade centre for the Willamette Valley and part of the Columbia Plateau, but its hinterland is smaller than that of Seattle and consequently its growth has been less rapid and its general economic importance is not so great. However, there are lumber, textile, and aluminium industries; shipbuilding, which was important during World War II, is no longer carried on.

CHAPTER XIII

THE ATLANTIC PROVINCES

Introduction

This region comprises Newfoundland and the Maritime Provinces—Nova Scotia, New Brunswick, and Prince Edward Island (Fig. 90). Situated on the periphery of the continent and facing western Europe, the Atlantic Provinces witnessed the earliest landfalls and welcomed some of the first settlers. Historically, the region has tended to look seaward, partly because of the rich fishing grounds off the coast and partly because trading links have been mainly with overseas countries rather than with the rest of Canada.

The region forms part of the Appalachian system. The commonest features of the landscape are the long ridges of moderate elevation and broad low plateaus; lowlands are few in number and limited in extent. Glaciation has deprived the land of its best top soils. Agriculture is restricted to certain areas with favourable soils and even here, the cool, moist climate prevents the cultivation of many crops. While the natural resources—the forests, the fisheries, and, to a certain extent, the minerals—have been widely exploited, there has been no corresponding development of manufacturing.

As a consequence, population densities remain small, most settlements being situated along the coast or in the interior valleys (Fig. 91). The overall density of population is about twenty per square mile, but figures vary from province to province as shown in the table below.

TABLE 17
POPULATION OF THE ATLANTIC PROVINCES 1965

PROVINCE	AREA	POPULATION 1901	POPULATION 1965	DENSITY
Newfoundland[1]	143,045	221,000	498,000	3·4
Prince Edward Is.	2,184	103,000	108,000	49·1
Nova Scotia	20,402	460,000	761,000	38·0
New Brunswick	27,835	331,000	624,000	22·3
Canada	3,560,238	5,371,000	19,703,000	5·5

[1] Including Labrador.

Although this region had its share of the early settlers, later immigrants were attracted to the richer lands farther west. Even the indigenous inhabitants have drifted away: between 1921 and

1955, 212,000 people (*i.e.* over 20 per cent. of the 1921 population), most of them young and enterprising, left for other parts of Canada. In 1871, the Atlantic Provinces had over 20 per cent. of the population of Canada: to-day the figure is 10 per cent. With the shift of attention to the interior, the region has become something of a backwater and has lagged behind the rest of the country in development and prosperity. While the towns continue to expand, the rural areas are being depopulated.

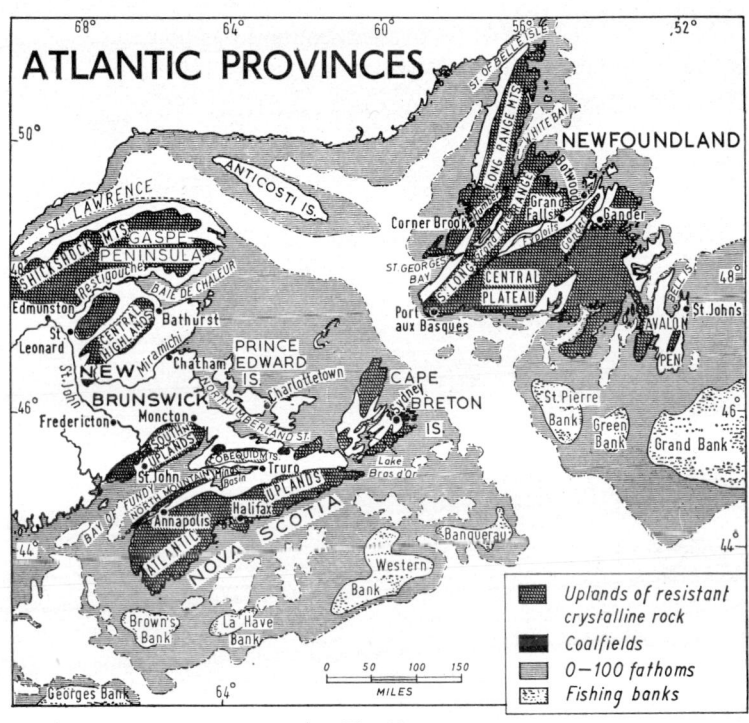

Fig. 90.

NEWFOUNDLAND

Newfoundland was first discovered by John Cabot in 1497, although it was possibly known to European fishermen before this date. The richness of the off-shore fisheries was quickly realised and soon, fishermen from many parts of western Europe were making annual trips to the Grand Banks. Summer stations were established on the mainland to dry and preserve the catch, and their names testify to the number of nations taking part—English

Harbour, Frenchman's Arm, Spaniard Bay, Portuguese Cove, Biscay Bay, Port aux Basques, and Harbour Breton. For many years no country laid claim to the island and it was not until 1583 that England took possession. It has been estimated that about 1600 there were 10,000 fishermen and 200 ships from Britain engaged annually in the fisheries.

The first permanent settlement was established in 1610 at Cupids in Conception Bay, but subsequent colonisation was very slow. About 1650, the total population of the island was only 2,000. Permanent settlement was actively discouraged as prejudicial to the interests of the fishing fleets. Restrictions were placed upon

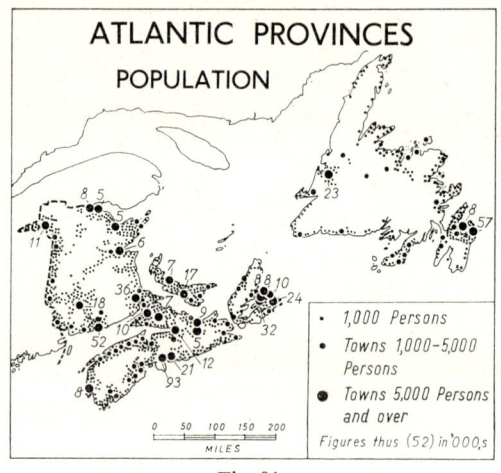

Fig. 91.

Note the concentration of population along the coast and in the river valleys.

house building and land cultivation, and fines were imposed on captains returning to Britain with less than full crews. At the beginning of the nineteenth century, when Massachusetts had a population of almost half a million, Newfoundland had under 25,000 inhabitants.

To-day, Newfoundland has a population of almost 500,000 and the average density is about three people per square mile. The figure is higher along the coast where almost all the settlements are found (Fig. 91) and in the Avalon Peninsula which has over 40 per cent. of the population (with almost half of this number in St John's). The typical settlement is the small fishing village, usually situated at the head of some cove with its fish flakes (drying

Above: Iron ore is brought 357 miles by rail from Schefferville to the terminal at Sept Iles. (*National Film Board of Canada.*)

Below: The Niagara Falls. Goat Island separates the American and Canadian Falls. One of the power stations which utilises the 167 ft head of water lies in the gorge near the foot of the Canadian Falls. (*Canadian National Railways.*)

Above: The International Nickel—Frood mine and smelter plant at Sudbury. See Fig. 1 (*Aerofilms.*)

Below: Uranium was discovered at Elliot Lake in 1950. This photograph taken in 19 when the population was about 25,000 shows the planned town. Since then the populati has declined and the settlement is becoming a ghost town. (*High Commissioner for Canad*

platforms), kitchen gardens, and infrequent small fields of potatoes and vegetables.

There are over 1,000 such settlements and most suffer from lack of transport facilities. There is no recognisable road network outside the Avalon Peninsula and only one railway crosses the island (from St John's to Port aux Basques), and this has a narrow gauge with only four short branch lines (Fig. 92). Many villages depend upon communications by sea, but large parts of the coast are icebound during the winter months. There is, however, a large airport at Gander, which, because Newfoundland is the point in North America nearest to western Europe, handles a considerable amount of the trans-Atlantic traffic. The island is also the terminus of fourteen ocean cables.

The harsh environment and the poverty of the interior has resulted in considerable emigration. Newfoundland, which was a dominion apart from Canada, suffered greatly during the depression years of the nineteen-thirties and voluntarily acceded to government by a commission from London in 1934. With increasing prosperity during and after World War II, the country, with its dependency, Labrador, voted to become a confederate part of the larger dominion.

Physical Features

Newfoundland is composed of old rocks. Archean and pre-Cambrian formations constitute the basement of the island and appear at the surface over large areas (Fig. 92). There are no deposits younger than Carboniferous, except for thin and scattered occurrences of glacial moraine. In the west, the archean and pre-Cambrian rocks are mainly granites, schists, and gneisses, but in the Avalon Peninsula slates, quartzites, and sandstones are more common. The grain of the country is from north-east to south-west and is strikingly shown on the geology map. The island is the northernmost part of the Appalachian system and the structural trends are the same as those of the Maritime Provinces and New England. The Palaeozoic sediments occupy the downfolds and have been preserved during successive planations. Ordovician sandstones, shales, and limestones are found in the valleys of the Gander and Exploits rivers and around White Bay, while Carboniferous rocks outcrop in the Humber Valley and around St George's Bay. These Palaeozoic areas provide the best farming lands in Newfoundland.

Elevations are nowhere very great: more than half the island lies under 1,000 ft and only a few summits rise over 2,000 ft (Fig. 92). Three plateau levels, representing old erosion surfaces, have been recognised. The oldest is found at a height of about 2,200 ft in the Long Range; the second level, at 1,300 ft, is confined to the western part of the island also; the youngest is a sloping surface 500 to 1,000 ft high, declining gently to the east and north.

A large proportion of the surface is rocky and barren, having been swept bare of soil during the Ice Age. There are many lakes and a few depositional features. The removal of the ice-sheet has resulted in the submergence of coastal areas. The highly articulated 6,000-mile long coast conforms to the NE.-SW. trend of the rocks. Raised beaches are due to isostatic readjustment: the north coast of Belle Isle is estimated to have risen 500 ft since Pleistocene times.

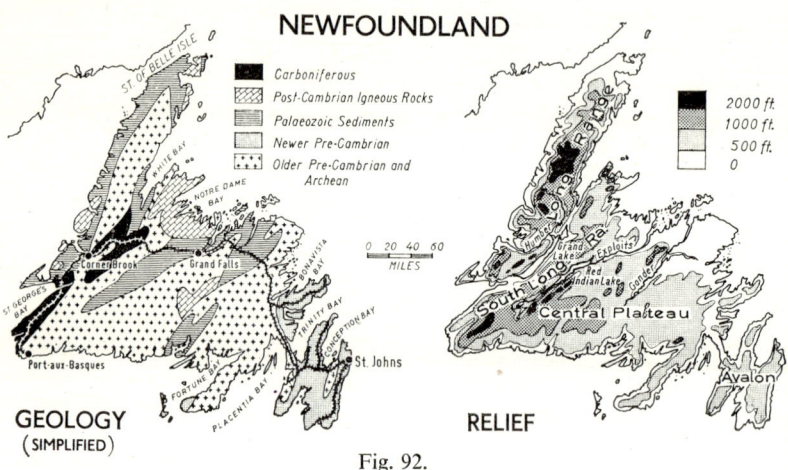

Fig. 92.

Off the south-east coast of Newfoundland are the Grand Banks, an upraised portion of the broad continental shelf, which are composed of material from the ice-sheets and melting icebergs. Rivers are short (the Exploits is 200 miles long and the Gander 100) and occupy the downfolds, which pitch towards the north-east. This is the main direction of flow, although the Humber, which occupies the faulted depression between St George's Bay and White Bay, east of Long Range, flows to the south-west and reaches the sea through a deep gorge at Humbermouth. The rivers draining to the south coast are short and rapid.

Climate and Vegetation

The two main factors in the climate of Newfoundland are the dominance of eastward-moving continental air masses and the presence off the coast of the cold Labrador Current. Temperatures generally are low for this latitude and extreme (Fig. 93). In January, the mean monthly temperature is under 25° F. (−4° C.) everywhere except for a small strip along the south coast, while in July, mean monthly temperatures rise over 60° F. (*16° C.*) only in a small area. The mean annual range is over 40 F.° (*22 C.°*) for a large part of the island. Owing to the Labrador Current, springs and summers are retarded: at St John's, August is warmer than July (see p. 51). The growing season is short and nowhere exceeds 150 days. Precipitation is greatest in the south-east which experiences over 50 in. annually: no place has under 30 in. There is no dry season but precipitation tends to be concentrated in the winter months when depressions (leaving the continent by the St Lawrence Valley) are most frequent and intense. Much of the

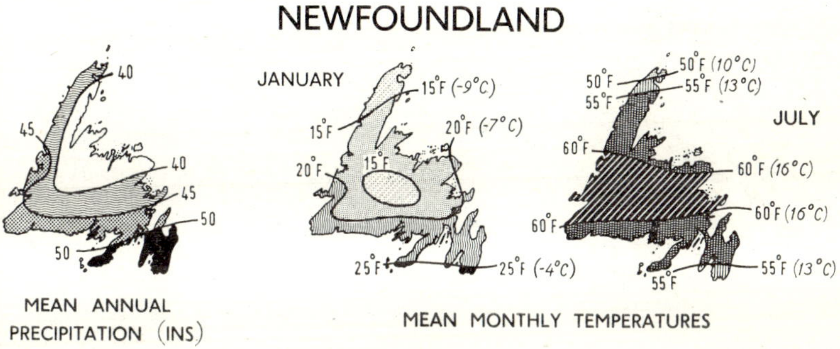

NEWFOUNDLAND

MEAN ANNUAL PRECIPITATION (INS.)

JANUARY

JULY

MEAN MONTHLY TEMPERATURES

Fig. 93.

winter precipitation is in the form of snow and amounts are often high (*e.g.* the average annual snowfall at Corner Brook is 164 in.). Occasionally in winter comparatively warm air from the south crosses the cold land surface and sheds its moisture as rain which freezes on contact with the ground. During one of these "glaze storms" great thicknesses of ice can accumulate and cause considerable damage.

Along the "cold wall" where the waters of the Labrador Current meet the Gulf Stream, fog is frequent. St John's experiences thirty-seven foggy days a year and Cape Race 188. The Grand Banks have even more. Fog is most frequent in summer at a time when the iceberg menace to shipping is greatest. Ice starts to form along the northern coasts in December and gradually spreads southwards. It reaches its greatest extent in March when only the south coast is open and the entrance to St John's harbour is kept free by ice-breakers. The twelve-mile wide Strait of Belle Isle is ice-bound from December until June.

The climate is inimical to the growth of deciduous trees and examples (red maple and yellow birch) are found only around St George's Bay. Coniferous forest, or taiga, covers about half the island but not all this is of commercial value. The productive forests occupy the basins of the Humber, Exploits, and Gander rivers. On the valley bottoms and ill-drained lands, black spruce is the dominant species. The well-drained slopes carry a mixture of balsam fir, white spruce, white pine, and white birch. The tree line is about 1,200 ft and above this level forest is replaced by reindeer

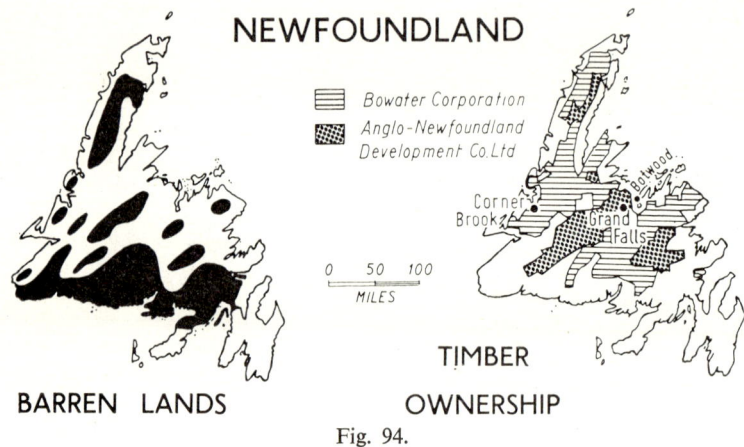

Fig. 94.

moss (*cladonia*), lichens, and sphagnum bog. These associations are also found on lower land and altogether occupy about half the surface area (Fig. 94). Soils are generally thin and heavily leached. Large areas are barren rock and only in the valleys are deeper soils found, but these are podsolic in character.

Fishing

The fishing industry dominates the lives of the people and employs almost one-third of the working population. The basis of the industry is the rich sea pastures of the continental shelf. Plankton flourishes in the cool, shallow waters which are rich in minerals and carbon dioxide. The smaller fish which feed on the plankton are themselves food for the cod.

Cod accounts for well over half the total catch (which is valued at about $33 million annually) and cod fishing takes place in three well-defined areas.

(*a*) About three-quarters of the catch is derived from the shore fisheries. Small, power-driven boats (dories) based on the numerous coves and harbours fish the seas within six miles of the coast. The cod are landed and are cured on the wooden flakes or drying platforms that are a feature of almost every village. This air drying takes three weeks.

(*b*) About one-eighth of the catch is taken in Labrador coastal waters between June and October. Each year, about 4,000 men and their families migrate to the mainland shore bases and follow the shoals in large schooners.

(*c*) Another eighth is taken from the Banks. Schooners and trawlers make three voyages a year between March and September and salt or freeze the catch until it can be landed. Most of these vessels are based on St John's. The government is attempting to increase the importance of this branch of the cod fisheries by subsidising the construction of large, modern, and more efficient vessels.

TABLE 18
FISH LANDED AND VALUE OF PRODUCTS (1964)

PROVINCE	MILLION LBS.	$ MILLION
Newfoundland	583	21·9
Prince Edward Island	38	5·6
Nova Scotia	427	40·9
New Brunswick	234	10·2
British Columbia	773	48·3
All Canada	2,345	145·1

The traditional outlets for the dried and salted cod are the Mediterranean countries and Latin America. To-day, an increasing proportion of the catch is marketed fresh or frozen in other parts of Canada and the U.S.A. There are over a dozen quick-freezing plants in Newfoundland and the more modern ships are fitted with refrigerators. There seems to be little danger of the fisheries being depleted for there is a closed season during winter when the seas are frozen and this coincides with the time the cod spawn.

Herring are caught along the west coast and salmon along the east coast. The lobster fisheries of the south coast and Notre Dame Bay are valuable. There are canneries in Fortune Bay and

Notre Dame Bay and some live lobsters are flown to the U.S.A. Whaling, which ceased in the nineteen-thirties, was revived during World War II and seals are still hunted on the ice off the northern shores in March.

Forestry

Forestry occupies a smaller proportion of the population of Newfoundland than fishing, but the value of its products is much higher. Almost 10,000 men are employed in the woods, most of them during the winter when there is very little fishing or farming, and a further 4,000 in the two large paper mills. Practically the whole of the productive forest (and parts of the non-productive forest also) is controlled by the two paper companies that operate on the island—the Anglo-Newfoundland Development Company, with 7,500 square miles, and the Bowater Corporation, with 11,000 square miles (Fig. 94). A three-mile wide belt along the coast is reserved as Crown land, from which householders have the legal right to cut up to 2,000 cu. ft of wood a year for domestic use. There are about 1,000 small saw mills providing timber for fuel, boat-building, local construction, and pit props, but most of the wood that is cut is destined for the paper works.

The Anglo-Newfoundland Development Company was established by Lord Northcliffe in 1909 and a paper mill was built at Grand Falls to provide paper for the *Daily Mail*. At the site of the mill there is a 125-ft head of water on the Exploits River which generates about 70,000 h.p. Grand Falls is linked to Botwood, its port twenty-two miles away, by rail, and between these two centres is Bishop's Falls, a subsidiary site of the company. Corner Brook (now the second largest settlement in Newfoundland with 23,000 inhabitants) was established in 1923 on a deep water site near the mouth of the Humber River and on the trans-island railway (see plate facing p. 225). The port is frozen in winter and during this season paper is exported through Port aux Basques. Corner Brook also ships wood to the corporation's mills in Britain. Much of the wood is cut in the Humber Valley, for it is in the valleys that the productive forest is found, and about one-third of the mill's requirements is floated down the river. A further third is brought by rail and the remainder along the coast by barge. The corporation has built a power plant on Deer Lake which generates over 165,000 h.p. Production amounts to over 300,000 tons of newsprint annually.

Recent economic developments in Newfoundland are due in no small measure to the work of these two companies which have provided employment for thousands of people, established their "company towns", built hundreds of miles of roads, and harnessed over half of the island's hydro-electricity. They maintain their own fire protection services, but have not yet begun reafforestation. Since 1910, only 13 per cent. of the productive forest has been cut over and much of this has been regenerated naturally. Fires, however, can cause severe losses: in 1961 Newfoundland lost the equivalent of ten years' supply of pulpwood when one million acres were burnt over.

Mining

Several minerals, including gold, silver, nickel, and chromium, are known to exist but not in deposits capable of exploitation. There are nine seams of coal, one of them four feet thick, in the Carboniferous rocks around St George's Bay, but the rock structure is unfavourable to mining. Limestone, fluospar, gravel, and brick clay are quarried on a small scale in several localities but major mining developments are found at only two places, Buchans and Baie Verte.

Ores containing copper, lead, and zinc were discovered near Red Indian Lake in 1907, but it was not until 1927 that mining commenced. The ores are concentrated at Buchans and sent by rail to Botwood from where they are shipped to the U.S.A. and Western Europe. Production amounts to over 1,000 tons a day. Bell Island, about six miles long and two miles wide is composed of Ordovician sandstones and shales which dip gently to the north-east. Within these beds are three layers of haematite which outcrop on the island. Mining started here in 1895 and was quickly extended two miles or more under the sea bed. The ore is low grade with a high silica and phosphorus content. Production costs were high, and faced with strong competition from the Labrador and imported S. American ores, production ceased in 1966. About half the ore fed the furnaces at Sydney, Nova Scotia: the rest was exported to Europe and the U.S.A. Important deposits of asbestos are now being developed around Baie Verte, together with copper and zinc.

Agriculture

Farming plays a minor part in the economy of the province and is supplementary to the other primary industries. Almost all the 2,000 farms are under fifty acres and are operated on a part-time basis. There has been a decrease both in the amount of farmland and in the number of farms during this century. In 1911, there were 233,000 acres of farmland, of which 113,000 carried crops or improved pasture: to-day there are under 70,000 acres, only 30 per cent. of which is improved land (Fig. 98).

The two main handicaps are the shortness of the growing season combined with cool summers, and the lack of fertile soil. Much of the farming is concentrated on the Avalon Peninsula where the frost free period is between 100 and 140 days in most years and where the underlying pre-Cambrian sediments yield better soils than the crystalline rocks of the interior and the west. Here too, are most of the people in the island and a market for milk, potatoes, and vegetables. The only other major farming area is the depression lying between White Bay and Port aux Basques. Carboniferous rocks provide the best soils on the island. As in the Avalon Peninsula, emphasis is on dairying, and over half the cultivated acreage is under hay or pasture. Within this area, most farms are to be found in the Codroy Valley, west of Port aux Basques, and the middle and upper Humber basin.

Elsewhere, agriculture is represented only by kitchen gardens. Potatoes, carrots, turnips, and cabbages are grown on very small plots, and in favoured locations there may even be a small output of strawberries, gooseberries, and currants. Locally, the gathering of blueberries is an important part-time occupation. The Newfoundland government has attempted to encourage agricultural development. Soil surveys have been inaugurated and bonuses are granted for land clearing: financial assistance is available to farmers trying to improve their livestock. But the amount of improved farmland continues to decrease and the prospects of full-scale commercial farming developing are extremely remote.

THE MARITIME PROVINCES

This region comprises the peninsulas and islands that form the provinces of Nova Scotia, New Brunswick, and Prince Edward Island. The first settlement was established by the French at Port Royal (Annapolis) which became the centre for the drained and cultivated tidal marshes of Acadia. Most of the early settlements were located along the coast of the Bay of Fundy, although there was some forest clearance in the interior, particularly in the Annapolis-Cornwallis Valley. When Acadia was ceded to Britain in 1713, the population numbered about 15,000. Cape Breton Island with its powerful fortress at Louisbourg remained in French possession until 1758, when, during the Seven Years War, it too passed under British control. During this period over 6,000 settlers were evicted from their lands because they were thought to be a menace to British interests. Many returned later when conditions were more settled.

From the mid-eighteenth century onwards, there was sporadic immigration. Halifax was founded in 1749 to counterbalance the power of Louisbourg, and four years later, a party of Germans established Lunenburg. The number of immigrants from Britain, particularly Irish and Scots (Gaelic is still the mother tongue of some communities in Nova Scotia), was augmented after the American War of Independence by Loyalists entering the region from New England and New York State. Several settlements were established in unfavourable areas and were later abandoned. The pattern of settlement which is visible to-day crystallised in the early nineteenth century (Fig. 91). Rural areas had their maximum population in the eighteen-eighties: after this decade, they lost people to the towns and to the more fertile western parts of Canada which were being opened up by the Canadian Pacific Railway. New immigrants were attracted to these developing lands and the Maritime Provinces became "the region that was passed by".

The present population numbers over one and half million, of which one-fifth is French-speaking. Almost all are Canadian-born and this region has the lowest proportion of recent immigrants of all regions of Canada. Every province has experienced periods of alternate population increase and recession. In Prince Edward Island there has been an absolute decline since the beginning of the century, while in New Brunswick there has been a constant but irregular increase. In Nova Scotia there has been an overall increase but in some years there have been temporary decreases.

Relief and Structure

The major physical features of the Maritime Provinces are a complex of low, rounded plateaus and ridges set amid undulating lowlands. The uplands, composed of old and resistant rock—usually crystalline or pre-Cambrian—form part of the Appalachian system and trend from north-east to south-west. They are separated by valleys in which the less-resistant sediments—Permo-Carboniferous and Triassic—have been preserved. The region takes the form of a large synclinorium with its main axis running NE.-SW. along the Bay of Fundy.

A traverse across the grain of the country from the St Lawrence to the Atlantic shore of Nova Scotia would reveal a series of gigantic ridges and furrows (Fig. 95). In the Gaspé Peninsula, which lies outside the Maritimes proper, are the Shickshock Mountains, culminating in Mount Jacques Cartier (4,160 ft). To the southeast, these uplands drop to a low, ice-smoothed plateau drained by the River Restigouche and opening to the Baie de Chaleur (Fig. 90). The next upland is the Central Highlands, a granite batholith rising out of the Devonian slates. The sky-line is at about 2,000 ft, but the surface is deeply dissected by rivers and has rising above it some relic mountains (*e.g.* Mount Carleton, 2,700 ft). Between the Central Highlands and the Southern Uplands is a triangular lowland

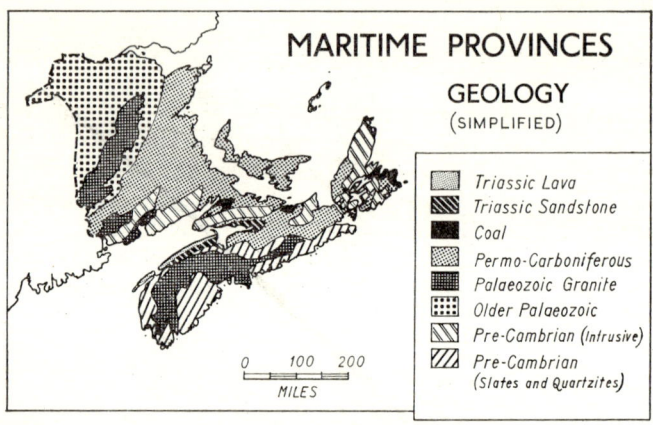

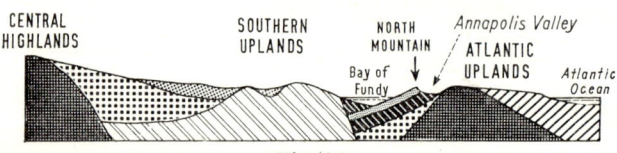

Fig. 95.
Compare with Fig. 90.

of Permian and Carboniferous rocks which extend under Northumberland Strait and form the low surface of Prince Edward Island. The Southern Uplands are a complex of ridges, some of them of pre-Cambrian rock and some granitic, separated by short rivers such as the Kennebecasis. They extend across Chignecto Bay as the Cobequid Mountains.

The Bay of Fundy occupies a depression floored by Triassic rocks. The south-eastern shore is a long, narrow, volcanic sill intruded in these rocks which forms North Mountain. Parallel to the ridge is the Annapolis-Cornwallis Valley which, again, is underlain by red rocks of Triassic age. Eastern Nova Scotia is composed of igneous and pre-Cambrian rocks, which form the Atlantic Uplands. The highest elevations are found in South Mountain, and from there the surface slopes gently to the ocean. Cape Breton Island has a central core of pre-Cambrian intrusive rocks, partially drowned under the waters of the Bras d'Or. On the western, southern, and eastern flanks of the island is a crescent-shaped outcrop of Carboniferous rocks, in which coal is exposed around Sydney.

The general height of the uplands decreases from north-west to south-east, at an average rate of about 10 ft per mile. The present summits are thought to be the remnants of a peneplain formed in Cretaceous times and since then uplifted, tilted, and heavily dissected. As can be seen from the map, there is a close relationship between the structure and the major coastal features: peninsulas coincide with outcrops of resistant rocks and the bays are the drowned vales of younger sediments. Much of the coast was drowned during the post-glacial rise in sea level and along southern Nova Scotia are many rias such as are found in Maine. The whole of the Maritime Provinces were covered by ice during the Pleistocene period and much of the surface has been scraped bare or covered with a thin layer of glacial drift. Waterfalls and rapids interrupt the courses of many rivers (*e.g.* Grand Falls and the Reversing Falls on the St John) and there are many lakes.

Most of the rivers are short and follow the structural depressions. The longest is the St John which is transverse to the grain of the country and cuts through a number of ridges, at which points the valley becomes gorge-like. Some rivers have been harnessed for the generation of hydro-electricity but many sites are still unused. In fact, more electricity is produced in thermal power stations (1·7 million kWh. as against 1·2 million kWh.) for coal is available locally. It has been suggested that the tides of the Bay of Fundy, which rise to over 30 ft everywhere and exceed 50 ft in the Minas basin, could be harnessed for the production of electricity.

Climate

Although few places lie more than thirty miles from the sea, the climate has marked continental characteristics. The general movement of air in these latitudes is from west to east and so air reaching the Maritime Provinces has usually had a previous history over the continent.

During the winter, the cold, continental Polar air mass is dominant and mean January temperatures are very low [e.g. 8° F. (−13° C.) at Edmundston and 23° F. (−5° C.) at Annapolis]. The Gulf of St Lawrence and the northern coasts are ice-blocked but Halifax and St John remain open and handle all Canada's Atlantic trade between December and April. Mean July temperatures show much less variation from place to place and over almost the whole of the region lie between 60° F. (16° C.) and 65° F. (18° C.). The lowest readings occur in the highland areas and along the south-east coast where air is chilled by contact with the cold Labrador Current. Here, the onset of summer may be delayed several weeks because of the moderating effect of this body of water. At this time, too, the coast of Nova Scotia and the Bay of Fundy experience heavy fog on as many as 100 days a year.

The growing season varies considerably over the region. Prince Edward Island and the southern coasts experience 140 frost free days or more, but in the northern interior of New Brunswick, where the uplands rise over 1,000 ft, less than sixty days on the average can be expected each year without frost. Mean annual precipitation which is distributed fairly evenly throughout the year is heaviest in the south-east (over 50 in.) and least in the north-west (under 35 in.). In the latter area, snowfall is heavy (100 to 120 in.) and is important in lumbering activities.

Agriculture

Because of the preponderance of thin, infertile soils that are found on the crystalline uplands, and the coolness and shortness of the growing season, agriculture in the Maritime Provinces is neither widespread nor intensive and occupies only a marginal role in the economy. The sale of farm products accounts for less than 5 per cent. of the total for all Canada. In many areas, farming is a part-time occupation only (in conjunction with fishing and forestry) and even in districts where conditions are most favourable, agriculture is of the subsistence type. Corn and wheat do not grow well, but oats, hay, potatoes, and other root crops are suited to the climate. These occupy over three-quarters of the cropland. Dairying would seem to be the type of farming best suited to the conditions, but the lack of large local markets is a severe handicap, and only around the urban centres can it provide adequate standards of living.

In all three provinces, farms average between 100 and 150 acres, but not all the farmland is used. About 60 per cent. of the 1,000,000 acres of farmland in Prince Edward Island is cropland or improved pasture, the remainder being woodland or waste. 30 per cent. of New Brunswick's 3,000,000 acres of farmland are improved, and only 20 per cent. of Nova Scotia's 2,700,000 acres. Almost everywhere large quantities of fertiliser are needed to maintain yields and winter fodder has to be brought from other parts of Canada. Many upland farms have been abandoned (cp. New England), and efforts by the provincial governments to introduce settlers and open up areas to cultivation have had only limited success.

The uneven distribution of farming land is shown on Fig. 98 and the main farming areas are described below.

1. The most important area is Prince Edward Island which is almost fully occupied and cultivated. Of this province, Jacques Cartier said in his diary over 400 years ago that "all the said land is low and plaine and the fairest that may possibly be seen, full of goodly medowes and trees". There are about 9,000 small-holdings on the rich, red Permian soils, which are fertilised with seaweed and mussel mud, growing seed potatoes and apples, and rearing dairy cattle on the hay, oats, and fodder crops. Hogs and poultry are adjuncts of the dairying industry. (It might be mentioned also that poultry-keeping is a gruesome adjunct of fur-farming.) Fur-farming was started in 1914 but after an initial period of great prosperity has experienced fluctuating fortunes as fashions have changed.

2. The middle St John Valley is a noted potato-growing area (just across the Maine border is Aroostook Valley), while downstream around Fredericton is a fertile orchard and dairying district.

3. On the eastern and southern shores of the Bay of Fundy are the dykelands, where silts and clays, carried by the strong tidal currents were reclaimed in the seventeenth century by the French Acadians. Initially, grain was grown in rotation with hay, but in the eighteenth and nineteenth centuries the lands were given over entirely to growing hay and fattening beef cattle. During the present century many of the dykes and drainage channels have been neglected and agriculture has suffered. Since World War II, some co-operative efforts have been made to restore the dykelands.

4. One of the most productive agricultural districts of the region is the Annapolis-Cornwallis Valley, an area eighty-five miles long by ten to fifteen miles wide underlain by red Triassic rocks. It is separated from the Bay of Fundy by North Mountain which affords some shelter from northerly winds. For many years the valley has been noted for apples, producing between one-third and a half of the Canadian crop, but in face of the declining British market farmers are concentrating more on dairying and poultry raising. Farms vary in size from 20 to 140 acres and are arranged

in strips across the valley. Orchards, totalling about 35,000 acres in all, occupy the middle slopes which are well drained and relatively free from frost, with meadow and hay on the lower parts and forest and pasture above. The value of commercial fruit produced in various provinces in 1961 was Newfoundland $240,000; Prince Edward Island $396,000; Nova Scotia $4 million; New Brunswick $1·4 million; Quebec $5·8 million; Ontario $24 million; British Columbia $17·7 million.

Forestry

Even after centuries of occupance, Nova Scotia and New Brunswick remain largely forested. Some upland areas are too rocky and cold for trees and some lowlands (including almost the whole of Prince Edward Island) have been cleared, but it is estimated that forest covers more than four-fifths of the area. In northern New Brunswick is the true boreal forest with white spruce and balsam fir on the drier soils and black spruce and tamarack on marshy sites as the dominant species. Farther south is the Acadian forest consisting mainly of conifers such as red spruce, white spruce, hemlock, and white pine, with an admixture of hardwoods such as maple, yellow birch, beech, and ash.

The exploitation of the forests began in the eighteenth century, the main purpose being to provide naval stores and timber for shipbuilding. In the present century pulpwood is by far the most important product. The annual cut amounts to about 300 million cubic feet, while reserves are estimated at 24,000 million cubic feet. Regeneration often takes place naturally but sometimes seedlings are planted in deforested areas.

Forestry occupies 40 per cent. of the industrial employees of New Brunswick and 20 per cent. of those of Nova Scotia. Lumbering is mainly a winter occupation, and is often carried out by part-time farmers. The main logging areas are in northern and central New Brunswick (Fig. 109). There are hundreds of small saw mills producing lumber, but most of the wood is floated down the rivers (especially the Restigouche and Miramichi), or sent by rail, to the large pulp and paper mills situated on navigable water or on a railway. The largest mills (Fig. 99) are at Edmundston, Dalhousie, Bathurst, Atholville, all in New Brunswick, and Liverpool in Nova Scotia.

Fishing

Off the coasts of the Maritime Provinces lie 200,000 square miles of shallow ocean (Fig. 90). As in Newfoundland, fishing is carried on both on the banks and inshore. The deep-sea fishing fleets, formerly consisting of the traditional schooners, each with seven to ten dories, but now with an increasing number of modern trawlers and draggers, are based primarily on Halifax or Lunenburg, and to a lesser extent on Yarmouth, Canso, and North Sydney. Cod makes up most of the catch, the remainder consisting of haddock, hake, pollock, herrings, and sardines (the latter being canned at Black's Harbour, N.B.).

Inshore fishing is performed within twelve or fifteen miles of the home harbours which are most numerous along the indented coast of Nova Scotia. Small motor boats are used and the catch is landed daily. Lobsters are taken in Northumberland Strait and have a value exceeding that of the total cod catch. Some are shipped alive by rail and truck to distant parts of Canada and the U.S.A.: the remainder are canned in the 125 canneries that line the shores of the strait. Pictou is the main centre. Oysters are cultivated in the Bay of Fundy and along the shores of Prince Edward Island, where the mud from old oyster beds is dug up and used as a fertiliser.

Formerly over 60 per cent. of the fish was sold dried or cured, but in recent years only one-third has been marketed in this form (mainly in the Caribbean islands and Latin America). The ports are less isolated than those of Newfoundland and a bigger proportion of the catch is sold fresh. The fisheries give employment to about 15,000 men and there are about 350 fish curing and packing plants along the coast (see Table 18, p. 277).

Mining and Industries

The industrial development of the region has been retarded and a large proportion of the manufacturing is accounted for by the processing of local resources—timber and fish. There is, however, some mining and a large iron and steel industry. Associated with the Carboniferous rocks of Nova Scotia are deposits of high quality coal. The most productive field is on Cape Breton Island, where the build consists of a series of alternating anticlines and synclines aligned NE.-SW. The Carboniferous rocks are preserved in the synclines while older rocks are exposed on the eroded anticlines. All the formations dip to the north-east and it is along a thirty-mile stretch of the north-east coast that the coal is found. There are seven workable seams with a total thickness of about 40 ft. Owing to the dip of the seams, they pass under the sea and some of the tunnels extend over two miles from the coast. Here there is a real danger of the workings being flooded.

Other mines are located around Inverness on Cape Breton Island, and near Pictou (Fig. 90). Those around Springhill, south-east of Amherst, were closed in 1958 after a series of tragic accidents. The coastal situation of the main coalfield is an advantage but, generally speaking, the mines are deep, labour costs are high, and there is a low output per worker. In consequence, there has been a decline in production in recent years, in spite of government subsidies. The increasing use of oil and natural gas in the St Lawrence Valley has hastened the decline. Production amounts to about 5 million tons annually.

Within sight of the collieries at Sydney (34,000), are batteries of coke ovens, three blast furnaces, and ten steel furnaces (Table 21, p. 315) all operated by the Dominion Steel Company, which also controlled the Wabana iron mines on Bell Island in Conception Bay, Newfoundland (see plate facing p. 225). Most of the ore was derived from this source, which is 400 miles from the furnaces, but is now imported from Brazil and Labrador. Limestone, which is used as a flux, also comes from Newfoundland. The seaboard location of the plant and the proximity of raw materials means that production costs are low, but the industry is hampered by the distance from large markets. Some steel is used in the Maritime Provinces for shipbuilding (at Halifax), for railway equipment (at New Glasgow) and rails (at Sydney), and some is sent by water to Quebec and Montreal for processing: beyond these points transport costs become excessive and competition is felt from the lakeside steel industries of both Canada and the U.S.A. A tariff barrier prevents export to the U.S.A. The works operate at less than full capacity (which is slightly under one million tons of steel) and account for about one-tenth of Canadian steel production.

The crystalline rocks of the region have yielded traces of metallic minerals, mainly lead, copper, and zinc, but until recently they have been mined only at Buchans in Newfoundland. Within the last decade, however, important deposits of these minerals together with manganese have been discovered in New Brunswick and mining has now started in the Bathurst-Newcastle area.

There is a group of industries based on imported materials. These are usually found in the larger seaports, especially Halifax (198,000) (see Table 20) which has shipyards, an oil refinery, and several small factories processing imported tropical products, and St John (102,000), where, apart from shipbuilding and paper-milling, sugar refining, and the processing of tea, coffee, and spices are important.

The Maritime Provinces and New England

Comparisons are often made between the Maritime Provinces and New England. Both areas are similar in size, the former covering about 50,00 square miles and the latter about 65,000 square miles. Both lie within the Appalachian system and so have a large proportion of high, rugged terrain with only a limited amount of lowland. They have a similar climate (the Humid Continental, Cool Summer type), but New England is slightly warmer in both winter and summer and has a slightly longer growing season. There is little difference in the vegetation of the two regions: both have a cover of mixed forest, although the Maritime Provinces have a greater proportion of conifers and fewer hardwoods. Both regions are on the periphery of the continent.

The similarities are most prominent in the physical geography of the two areas. When one considers the human geography there are significant differences. New England has almost seven times as many inhabitants as the Maritime Provinces and while this can be explained partly in terms of the physical differences, it seems to be mainly due to human factors.

Commercial farming is much more developed in New England. Both regions have large areas of negative land and abandoned farms, but while the Maritime Provinces have the advantage of a larger area of lowland, New England has the longer growing season and, more important, has a larger local market which has stimulated the development of dairy farming and truck farming. New England is much more heavily industrialised, although it is almost completely lacking in resources (more so than the Maritime Provinces which have reserves of coal). These industries arose very early in the colonial period and were financed by money derived from trade in fish and forest products. They supplied the needs of a large part of the growing Atlantic communities during the eighteenth and early nineteenth centuries before industries arose in other parts of the U.S.A. New England had the benefit of an early start and has maintained its industrial momentum, unlike the Maritime Provinces which, being more remote from the main settled parts of Canada, lacked the markets so necessary to the development of industry.

The fact that New England formed the political and economic core of a newly independent nation, while the Maritime Provinces were merely an outlying part of a sparsely populated dependent territory is of great significance. Many immigrants entered the U.S.A. through the New England states: some settled there and contributed to the region's growth. The Maritime Provinces, however, lay outside the main line of entry into Canada, which was along the St Lawrence.

Arnold Toynbee (see quotation on p. 100) has suggested that the stimulus to civilisation was much greater in New England than in the

Maritime Provinces. Other writers have suggested that but for the accident of the international boundary, the Maritime Provinces could be as densely populated as New England for, as part of the U.S.A., they would have tariff-free access to a large market and greater financial backing for the development of their resources. This may be doubted, however, for Maine, the state nearest to the Maritime Provinces, is as little developed as they are. It has a population density of thirty-one per square mile as against twenty-eight per square mile in Nova Scotia, New Brunswick, and Prince Edward Island.

CHAPTER XIV

THE LAURENTIAN LOWLANDS

This region is a narrow belt of varying width stretching over 600 miles from Lake Huron, along the St Lawrence to a little below Quebec, and covering an area of about 35,000 square miles. It derives its unity from the fact that it is the most densely populated part of Canada with over 25 per cent. of the country's inhabitants. In Quebec province there are only eight people per square mile,

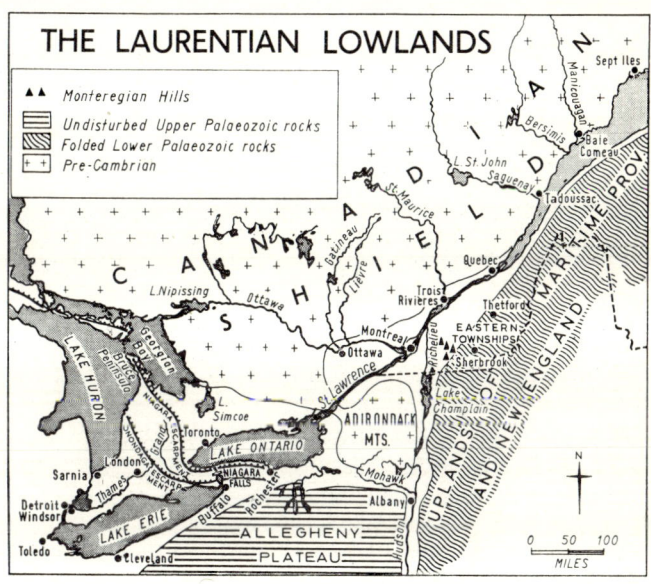

Fig. 96.

The band of pre-Cambrian rock north of Lake Ontario divides the Laurentian Lowlands into two parts, the St Lawrence Valley and the Ontario Peninsula.

whereas in the lowlands the figure is 120. Another unifying factor is the navigable waterway which threads the lowlands and is the lifeline of the region.

The lowlands are broken into two parts by a narrow band of resistant pre-Cambrian rock (the Frontenac Axis) which crosses the St Lawrence in the Thousand Isles section to link the Canadian Shield with the Adirondack Mountains. Down-stream from this "bridge" is the St Lawrence Valley, a long strip of lowland, narrowly confined between the Shield and the Appalachian system. Upstream is the Ontario Peninsula, a triangular-shaped lowland bounded by Lakes Ontario, Erie, and Huron, and the edge of the Shield (Fig. 96).

Historically, as well as physically, there is some justification for regarding this region as two distinct units. The bridge of pre-Cambrian rock is a pronounced economic and cultural divide.

ST LAWRENCE VALLEY

Introduction

The wide Gulf of St Lawrence led the early French explorers to the heart of the continent. The earliest settlements were trading posts (*e.g.* Quebec, founded in 1608; Trois Rivières, 1634; and Montreal, 1642). Later, settlers acquired land along the rivers for farming. By 1763, when the territory was ceded to Britain, there was an almost unbroken ribbon of settlement from Quebec (population at that time about 9,000) to Montreal (about 6,000). Large blocks of land had been granted to landlords (seigneurs) who undertook to establish settlers (Fig. 97). These seigneuries took the form of long strips which extended a long way inland from a narrow front on a navigable waterway. The individual farms in the seigneurie were laid out in a similar fashion: each was a mile or more long and had a width of about 600 ft. When the riverside was fully occupied, a second line, or *rang* was established further inland (see plate facing p. 257).

During this settlement period there crystallised the landscape pattern which has persisted until the present day and which is so characteristic of French Canada. The villages consist of long strings of houses along roads which run close to the river or between two *rangs*. The focal point of each settlement is the parish church, for the influence of the Roman Catholic priest has always been very strong. The French-Canadians have been successful in maintaining their distinctive culture in spite of British rule and the wave of immigration. This is due in no small measure to the concentration of this group in one province, which, under the federal constitution, can legislate for the preservation and maintenance of its language, school system, and religion. In the past, the French-Canadians have felt a strong attachment to their land and their parish: their outlook has tended to be rural and even parochial. In recent times, however, coincident with the rapid growth of industry and towns, these ties have been loosened. This group has a high birth-rate—23 per 1,000—and there has been movement from the rural areas to the

EARLY SETTLEMENT

towns and also to other regions, especially the Eastern Townships (see Fig. 96), the Maritime Provinces, and New England.

In the years following the transfer of the land to Britain, there was little further settlement, although the French-Canadian population continued to increase. The next wave of immigration occurred after the War of American Independence when the Loyalists left their New England homes to settle under British rule in the Eastern

LAURENTIAN LOWLANDS

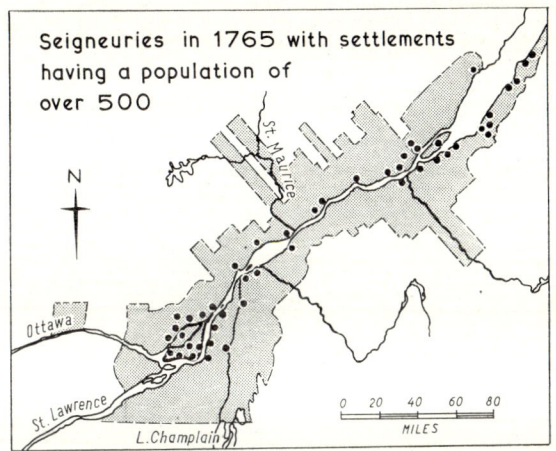

EARLY SETTLEMENT IN THE ST. LAWRENCE VALLEY

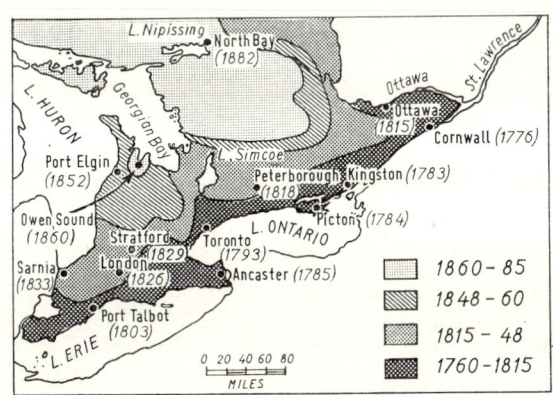

THE SETTLEMENT OF THE ONTARIO PENINSULA

Fig. 97.

Townships. The woodland was cleared and farms established, but after the opening up of the Prairies, many of these were abandoned or were taken over by French-Canadians. By 1831, the St Lawrence Valley had a population of about half a million: of these, four-fifths were French-speaking. To-day, the proportion of French-speaking people is the same in a total population of about 5 million. Another million French-Canadians live in the other provinces. In New Brunswick, in fact, over 40 per cent. of the population is French-speaking.

Physical Features

Underlying the St Lawrence Valley are shales, limestones, and sandstones of Palaeozoic age. These rocks are more or less undisturbed and are separated from the folded sediments (of the same age) to the south by a faulted belt of shattered rocks. This folded zone, an extension of the Appalachians, stretches from Lake Champlain to the Gaspé Peninsula. Overlooking the valley on the north side is the steep front of the Canadian Shield which is composed of ancient pre-Cambrian rocks. The rise in sea level which occurred as the ice-sheets were melting caused the valley to be flooded. Marine sands, clays, and silts were deposited over an area which stretched as far as Lake Ontario. The Champlain Sea penetrated up the Saguenay Valley into the Lake St John basin, and also up the valley of the Ottawa River. Following the delayed isostatic readjustment of the earth's crust, which occurred after the removal of the ice load, the area rose above sea level.

The plain is low and flat and rarely exceeds 200 ft in height, but in the south, its uniformity is broken by the Monteregian Hills, a line of eight denuded igneous intrusions. These are Mounts Johnson (875 ft), Brome (1,755 ft), Shefford (1,775 ft), Yashama (1,470 ft), Rougemont (1,250 ft), Beloeil (1,437 ft), St Bruno (712 ft), and Mount Royal (769 ft), which lies in the heart of Montreal.

The valley is widest between Ottawa and Lake Champlain, a distance of 120 miles. Downstream from Montreal the bordering uplands close in. The lowland strip on the right bank is only fifteen miles wide opposite Quebec and downstream from there continues merely as a narrow riverside terrace. Below Quebec on the north bank there is no lowland, settlements are few, and the railway which follows the cliff foot terminates at Murray Bay (La Malbaie). Jacques Cartier described the riverside thus: "It is appalling and rugged rock and stone, for along the whole of the north shore I saw not even a cart-load of soil. It seems most likely to me that here is the land God gave to Cain."

Climate

The climate of the St Lawrence Valley is a Humid Continental type with cool summers.

		J.	F.	M.	A.	M.	J.	J.	A.	S.	O.	N.	D.	Total
Montreal 46° N. 187 ft	°F.	12	14	25	41	56	65	69	65	58	46	34	20	—
	°C.	−11	−10	−4	5	13	18	21	18	14	8	1	−7	—
	in.	3·8	3·0	3·5	2·6	3·1	3·5	3·8	3·4	3·7	3·3	3·5	3·7	40·9
Quebec 47° N. 250 ft	°F.	10	11	22	37	51	61	67	63	55	43	30	16	—
	°C.	−12	−12	−6	3	11	16	19	17	13	6	−1	−9	—
	in.	3·4	2·8	3·1	2·3	3·1	3·5	4·0	4·0	3·6	3·4	3·2	3·2	39·6

Winters are long and severe with temperatures well below freezing point and, on the bordering uplands, below zero. Ice forms on the rivers in mid-December and the St Lawrence is closed to shipping from then until mid-April. During this season, the region comes under the dominating influence of continental Polar air which lies over the centre of the land mass, but the passage of many depressions along the St Lawrence corridor as they make their exit from the continent brings changeable weather and heavy falls of snow. The thick snow cover tends to delay the advance of spring.

The frost free season lasts for about 120 to 130 days for most lowland stations but exceeds 150 days upstream from Montreal. Summer temperatures are fairly high and are often associated with a high relative humidity which is unpleasant for city-dwellers. Precipitation varies between 35 and 40 in. and is distributed quite evenly throughout the year except for a slight tendency towards a maximum in late summer and early autumn. Progressing up the valley, winters become milder and shorter, summers warmer and precipitation lighter.

The relatively large annual range of temperature and the tendency for most precipitation to fall during the summer half of the year are indications of continental conditions. Although this region lies close to the coast, the general west to east movement of air, which has acquired continental characteristics before reaching the St Lawrence Valley, means that marine influences are slight. The presence of the cold Labrador Current off the coast tends to intensify the continental conditions.

THE LAURENTIAN LOWLANDS

Agriculture

As an employer of labour and source of wealth, agriculture has fallen, and continues to fall, behind manufacturing. Almost all the farmland in Quebec (16 million acres out of a total area of 380 million acres) is to be found in the valley of the St Lawrence and its tributaries (Fig. 98). Outside this area, soils are absent or very thin and the climate is too rigorous for the cultivation of crops. Even in the lowlands there are large tracts of sandy or ill-drained land which remain as forest or waste. Of the 16 million acres of farmland, only about half is cropland or improved pasture, the remainder being wooded, rough pasture, or waste. Around

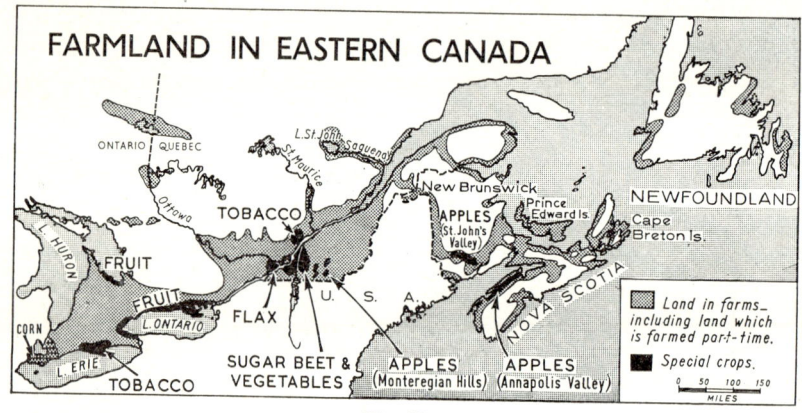

Fig. 98.

Montreal about 75 per cent. of the occupied land is improved, around Quebec about 60 per cent., and in the Lake St John region about 50 per cent.

The St Lawrence Valley can be regarded as an extension of the Hay and Dairying Belt of north-eastern U.S.A. Maize and wheat do not ripen (although they may be sown and harvested green for silage), and cultivation is limited to the growth of oats, barley, buckwheat, root crops, and hay. Sixty per cent. of the cropland is under hay and a further 20 per cent. under oats. The region has over a million dairy cattle—about one-third of the Canadian total. Approximately 40 per cent. of the milk is marketed fresh, about 50 per cent. is made into butter, and the remainder is made into cheese and other dairy products. Hogs are an important adjunct of dairying and poultry are kept on most farms. The

AGRICULTURE

average Quebec farm occupies 125 to 170 acres and has a herd of fifteen to twenty cattle.

There is a certain amount of specialisation. Around the cities are market gardens which often have a considerable area under glass. The Ile Jésus, Laprairie, and Napierville supply Montreal with vegetables. The chief crops include tomatoes, sweet corn, peas, cabbage, and cauliflower. Tobacco is grown on the sandy plains around Joliette in the Assomption Valley, flax on the Soulanges Plain between the Ottawa and St Lawrence, and sugar beet in the Richelieu Valley. In the last-named area are about 5,000 farms and 340,000 acres of cropland. The gravel soils on the flanks of the Monteregian Hills carry apple orchards.

On the more marginal land, part-time subsistence agriculture is common, many of the farmers devoting a large proportion of their time to fishing (*e.g.* along the South Shore and North Shore below Quebec) and lumbering. An important product of the forest is maple syrup, the area of largest production being the Eastern Townships.

Forestry

Although most of the forest which is dominantly hardwood has been cleared from the St Lawrence Valley and the Eastern Townships, there remain large stands of softwood in the Appalachians and Gaspé Peninsula and particularly on the Canadian Shield. The commonest species are black and white spruce, balsam fir, white and red pine, jack pine, and tamarack (larch). Of the 365,000 square miles of forest in the Quebec part of the Shield, 126,000 are accessible and yield over 1,000 million cu. ft of lumber and pulpwood annually.

Most of the forest is Crown land which is leased to timber and pulp companies. They are obliged to adhere to a scientific programme of forest exploitation based on the principle of sustained yield. The private forests have been more recklessly exploited but now the provincial government provides free seedlings from nurseries to replant cut-over areas. It is hoped that ultimately 10 million seedlings will be planted annually on privately owned forest land. Small woodlots on many of the farms provide a surprisingly large amount of timber. Some forest depletion occurs because of fires, disease, and the depredations of insect pests such as the larch sawfly and the spruce bud worm.

About twice as much wood is cut for pulp as for lumber. There are about 1,500 saw mills which give employment to 10,000 men but fifty-six pulp and paper mills employing almost 30,000 people.

Cutting is estimated to employ about 40,000 men during the winter months (Fig. 109).

There are two methods of obtaining the fibrous material from which paper is made. The older method is purely mechanical: logs are forcibly pressed against a rapidly rotating grindstone and converted into fibrous shreds. Most paper is now made by the chemical method: chips of wood are digested with various chemicals (sodium sulphate, sodium sulphite, or sodium hydroxide) which destroy the non-fibrous portions and leave the fibres in a purer form than the mechanical method does. After the fibres are washed and bleached, the pulp is fed on to a fine wire screen and then through rollers. The soft sheet of wet paper is then treated with heat and pressure.

The pulp and paper mills are located at places with access to timber and power and good transport facilities. They are large and

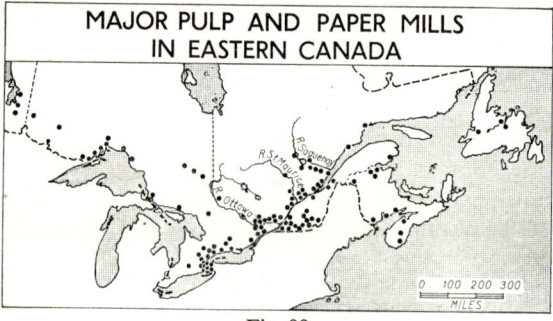

Fig. 99.

Note the concentration of mills around the Niagara Falls and in the St Lawrence Valley.

expensive plants and must be permanent, unlike the saw mills which can migrate with the lumber camps. They consume great quantities of electricity and a large volume of water. For these reasons, they tend to be situated near the mouths of the tributaries of the St Lawrence where they collect the logs floated downstream from the Shield, use the water of the river itself for various processes, and draw upon the power generated at falls where the rivers cross the edge of the Shield. Along the St Lawrence Valley there are good railway facilities for transporting the finished pulp or paper. Fig. 99 shows the distribution of the main mills in eastern Canada. In the St Lawrence region they are concentrated in four areas:

    1. the St Maurice Valley, with mills at Trois Rivières, Shawinigan, Grand'Mère, and La Tuque;

2. the Lake St John area, with mills at Kenogan, Jonquière, Port Alfred, Riverbend, and Dolbean;
3. the Ottawa Valley, with mills at Gatineau, Hull, Buckingham, Masson, and Kipawa;
4. the Montreal area with mills at St Jerome, Lachute, Mont Rolland, Joliette, and Beauharnois.

The annual production of pulp amounts to about 5 million tons and about 80 per cent. of this is processed into paper. (Production in Canada is over 13 million tons of pulp and over 8 million tons of paper.) Almost 80 per cent. of the pulp and paper exported goes to the U.S.A. and most of the remainder to Great Britain.

Industries and Towns

The province of Quebec produces about 30 per cent. (by value) of Canada's manufactures, and most of the manufacturing industries are located in the St Lawrence Valley. This area lacks coal, oil, and metallic minerals which, however, are found on the Canadian Shield and are largely refined and processed in the lowlands at Montreal and Quebec. It does have large deposits of asbestos and the district around Thetford in the Eastern Townships produces over a million tons annually (equivalent to almost half the world's output). The asbestos is found in veins a few inches thick and up to 100 ft long in serpentine, a basic igneous rock intruded into the Devonian sediments of the Appalachian system. After the rock is crushed and the fibres sorted, the waste is dumped in huge pyramids beside the quarries. About 10 per cent. of the asbestos is processed in Canada, the remainder being exported mainly to the U.S.A.

Major factors accounting for the development of industries in the St Lawrence Valley are (i) the minerals and forest resources of the Shield, (ii) the availability of large amounts of hydraulic power, (iii) location on a navigable waterway, the funnel through which goods enter and leave the country, (iv) a stable labour force which is also an expanding market for manufacturing goods, and (v) the inflow of American capital.

Hydro-electricity.—On its way to the sea, the St Lawrence collects sheaves of tributaries. Those on the right bank are relatively unimportant and only on the St Francis in the Eastern Townships are there power plants (with a total capacity of about 100,000 h.p.). Those on the left bank rise on the Canadian Shield where the annual precipitation amounts to between 35 and 40 in. They pursue sluggish and tortuous courses through lakes and muskegs, except where they are interrupted by short sections of falls and rapids. When they reach the steep faulted edge of the Shields, they drop rapidly with a greatly steepened gradient to the St Lawrence Lowlands. Along this marked break of slope are numerous power sites. The innumerable lakes act as reservoirs, regulating the flow of water, and, in addition, many large dams have been built to enlarge storage capacity and increase the head of water available.

Quebec has 51 hydro-electric stations with an installed capacity of 12·8 million h.p. and a further 2·5 million h.p. is under construction.

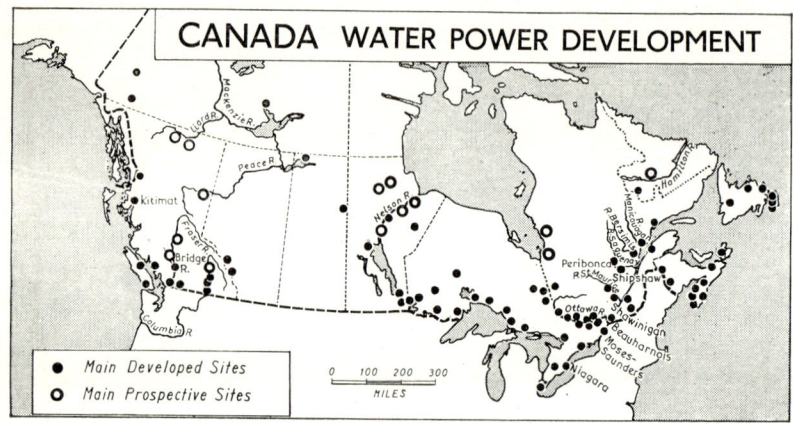

Fig. 100.

TABLE 19

AVAILABLE AND DEVELOPED WATER POWER, 1963

PROVINCE	INSTALLED CAPACITY in million h.p.	POWER AVAILABLE at ordinary six-monthly flow in million h.p.
Atlantic Provinces	1·0	3·8
Quebec	12.8	23·7
Ontario	8·0	7·7
Prairie Provinces	1·5	12·0
British Columbia	3·7	19·4
Canada	26·7	69·5

NOTE.—1. Figures in the last column are based on the volume of water which can be expected to be available for generating purposes for at least six months in the year. Installed capacity may exceed these figures.
2. Ontario has developed most of its available power.
3. The greatest reserves of power are in Quebec and British Columbia.

Most of the power has been developed by private corporations. By far the largest of these is the Aluminium Company of Canada

(Alcan) which operates five plants on the Saguenay and Peribonca rivers with a total installed capacity of 3 million h.p. (Fig. 101). Lake St John (the level of which was raised by the building of a dam) and Lake Kenogami act as reservoirs and there are power

THE SAGUENAY VALLEY AND THE SHIPSHAW SCHEMES

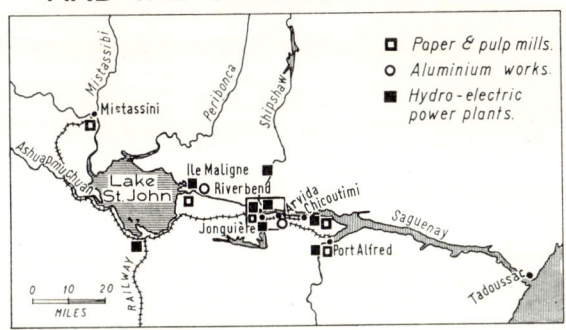

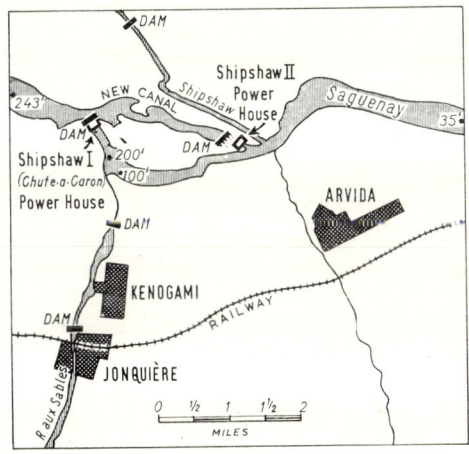

Fig. 101.
The rectangle on the upper map locates the area shown on the lower map.

houses at Ile Maligne, Chute-a-Caron (Shipshaw I), Kenogami, Chicotimi, and on the New Canal (Shipshaw II). The Shawinigan Water and Power Company operates seven plants on the St Maurice River with an installed capacity of about 1·8 million h.p. The largest of these are at Shawinigan, La Tranche, La Tuque, and Grand'Mère. The power feeds local industries and is distributed over a wide area of the St Lawrence Valley and Eastern Townships. Other private concerns have established plants on the Ottawa River and its tributaries, the Gatineau and Lièvre, and the Manicouagan River near Baie Comeau.

Over 4·5 million h.p. has been developed by the Quebec Hydroelectric Commission, which was formed in 1944. It has undertaken seven major schemes, some of which are not yet completed. The Beauharnois scheme on the St Lawrence Seaway has an installed capacity of about 2 million h.p., a figure that will ultimately rise to about 2·3 million h.p. Two schemes on the Bersimis River, 200 miles downstream from Quebec, yield a total of 2·2 million h.p., and one on the Ottawa River at Carillon, 800,000 h.p. Work has started on a 3·6 million h.p. plant on the Manicouagan, and on another on the Outardes.

Manufacturing.—The largest users of electricity are the pulp and paper industry, described on p. 298, and the aluminium industry. Together, they absorb over 80 per cent. of Quebec's power. To produce one pound of aluminium requires 10 kW. of electricity and with its great power needs the industry is restricted to areas where electricity is both plentiful and cheap, *i.e.* at water-power sites. As the bauxite has to be imported from British Guiana, Jamaica, and West Africa, proximity to navigable water is another prerequisite. The first smelter was opened at Shawinigan (32,000) in 1900, but further development was slow until World War II, when a sudden surge of industrial expansion raised Canada to the forefront of the aluminium producing nations. The Aluminium Company of Canada (Alcan) has smelters at Ile Maligne and Arvida (both of which derive power from the Saguenay), La Tuque and Shawinigan (both on the St Maurice), and Beauharnois on the St Lawrence with the capacity to produce 600,000 tons. In addition, the Canadian British Aluminium Company has a new smelter at Baie Comeau, using power from the Manicouagan River with a capacity of almost 200,000 tons (see plate facing p. 368). Total production of aluminium in Canada amounts to almost 1 million tons.

There are several other important industries in this region. Montreal, with its access to local power and its superlative location for the assembly of materials, has become the centre of a manufacturing district. Shipbuilding is a major industry at Sorel, and here too is a smelter for refining the titanium mined at Lake Allard in the eastern part of the Canadian Shield. Aircraft are manufactured at Longueuil, textiles at St Hyacinthe, and electrical equipment at Beauharnois. The industries of Montreal and its satellite towns are extremely diversified and include oil-refining, meat-packing, and the making of clothes, in addition to those previously mentioned. Quebec is a much smaller industrial centre and its manufactures are less varied. They include the manufacture and processing of leather, paper, textiles, and food products. In the Eastern Townships are a dozen thriving centres such as Granby, Magog, and Megantic, which produce textiles and paper. The largest of these towns is Sherbrooke (75,000).

Quebec (265,000), the historic capital of Lower Canada, lies where the St Lawrence widens from less than a mile to ten miles. At this point, at the head of the estuary, navigation for sailing vessels became difficult and Quebec became the terminal for ships crossing the Atlantic. Steamers, however, can proceed upstream without hazard and when the St Lawrence was deepened in 1870, and large vessels could reach Montreal, Quebec lost its pre-eminence as a port. Large modern docks can accommodate the largest liners and the trade of the port is by no means negligible (see Table 20, p. 305). Numerous ferries cross the river and the lowest bridging point is about seven miles upstream from the city.

Quebec is built on and around an elevated platform of Palaeozoic rocks. The southern edge drops steeply to the St Lawrence: this was the cliff that Wolfe's men scaled to reach the Plains of Abraham (the summit of the platform) in 1759. To the north, and between this platform and the edge of the Shield, is a broad depression formerly crossed by the St Lawrence and now drained by the River St Charles. The upper town, which includes the Parliament Buildings, Laval University, and the main hotels (the most striking being the Château Frontenac), occupies the eastern end of the plateau: the lower town, with its factories, warehouses, and railway yards, was once crowded in the space between the east end of the cliff and the river but it has now expanded into the valley of the St Charles. Here, on the waterfront, are found the major industries which are concerned with paper and pulp, leather, and textiles. Quebec is the capital of the province and the religious centre of French Canada.

Montreal (2,436,000) lies midway along the St Lawrence Valley at the meeting point of routes from the western lakes (via the Ottawa Valley), the lower lakes (via the St Lawrence Valley), New York (via the Hudson-Champlain-Richelieu Valleys), and the ocean (via the lower St Lawrence Valley). It has become the largest city in Canada, far outstripping its older rival, Quebec, simply because the roads and railways focus here in the most densely populated part of the dominion. Montreal is built on the easternmost of three islands which lie in the St Lawrence (Fig. 102). The original settlement was on a terrace near the harbour and it grew towards the lower slopes of Mount Royal, the volcanic relic, 769 ft high, which dominates the island. To-day the city occupies practically all the island as far as Back River (Rivière des Prairies).

Just above the harbour are the Lachine Rapids which for a long time made Montreal the effective head of navigation for large ships. The early canals which were constructed to by-pass the rapids could handle only small vessels. In spite of the fact that its harbour

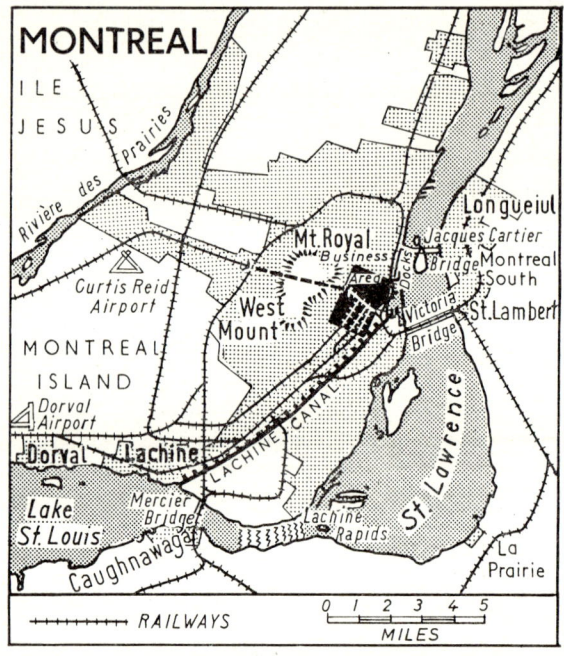

Fig. 102.

is closed by ice for four months of the year (December to April), Montreal is the leading Canadian port.

As the St Lawrence is tideless above Trois Rivières, enclosed docks are unnecessary. Alongside the wharves are cold storage plants, elevators, oil refineries, and ship repair yards. A wide variety of vessels enters the harbour, including ocean liners, barges, and freighters specially built to use the Great Lakes-St Lawrence canals. The effect on Montreal of the opening of the St Lawrence Seaway is discussed in the following section.

Almost 5,000 factories are located in and around the city, for not only is Montreal the centre of the largest market in Canada, but it is also in a good position to distribute goods to other parts of the country. Power is available locally, and raw materials can be easily assembled. In addition to the heavy industries found along the waterfront, there are railway shops and factories preparing food, clothing, leather, and chemicals.

TABLE 20

MAJOR CANADIAN PORTS 1965—CARGOES IN MILLIONS OF TONS

PORT	FOREIGN		COASTWISE		TOTAL
	Loaded	Unloaded	Loaded	Unloaded	
Montreal	4·9	7·7	4·2	5·0	21·9
Sept Iles	16·7	0·6	1·2	0·2	18·7
Port Arthur	3·8	0·3	11·8	1·1	17·0
St John	1·5	2·7	1·1	0·4	5·8
Vancouver	9·3	2·1	4·7	4·4	20·5
Hamilton	0·2	7·8	0·5	1·7	10·3
Halifax	2·9	4·0	2·1	0·5	9·5
Toronto	0·3	3·8	0·2	1·5	5·8
Sault Ste Marie	0·2	3·7	0·3	1·2	5·4
Quebec	1·7	1·4	0·2	3·0	6·3

THE ST LAWRENCE SEAWAY

From the Atlantic Ocean to the head of Lake Superior, a distance of 2,200 miles, there is a continuous waterway to the heart of the continent. To make this waterway fit for navigation has been the dream of North Americans since the eighteenth century. The earliest recorded improvement dates back to 1700, when a canal eighteen inches deep was constructed near Lachine (Fig. 102).

Lake Superior is 602 ft above sea level and the water drops 23 ft down the St Mary's River to Lake Huron. The first of the Soo Canals was constructed here round the Sault Ste Marie Rapids in the middle of the nineteenth century shortly after the discovery of iron ore in Minnesota. To-day, there are five canals (see p. 184). The drop from Lake Huron to Lake Erie, along the St Clair and Detroit rivers, is quite a small one of only seven feet. At this point only dredging was necessary to make the passage navigable. Between Lake Erie and Lake Ontario there is a difference of 326 ft; the steepest part of this descent is where the Niagara River tumbles vertically 167 ft over the Niagara Escarpment (see plate facing p. 272). The recession of the falls from their original position at the scarp face has led to the formation of a gorge seven miles long. This barrier to navigation was overcome by the Welland Canal, which has been periodically modernised and now has a depth of 27 ft.

The St Lawrence proper starts at the exit of Lake Ontario where the level is 246 ft. Between this point and Montreal, 189 miles downstream, where the level is 22 ft, is a turbulent stretch of water. Numerous rapids made navigation impossible and the early French explorers avoided this route and followed the Ottawa Valley to the

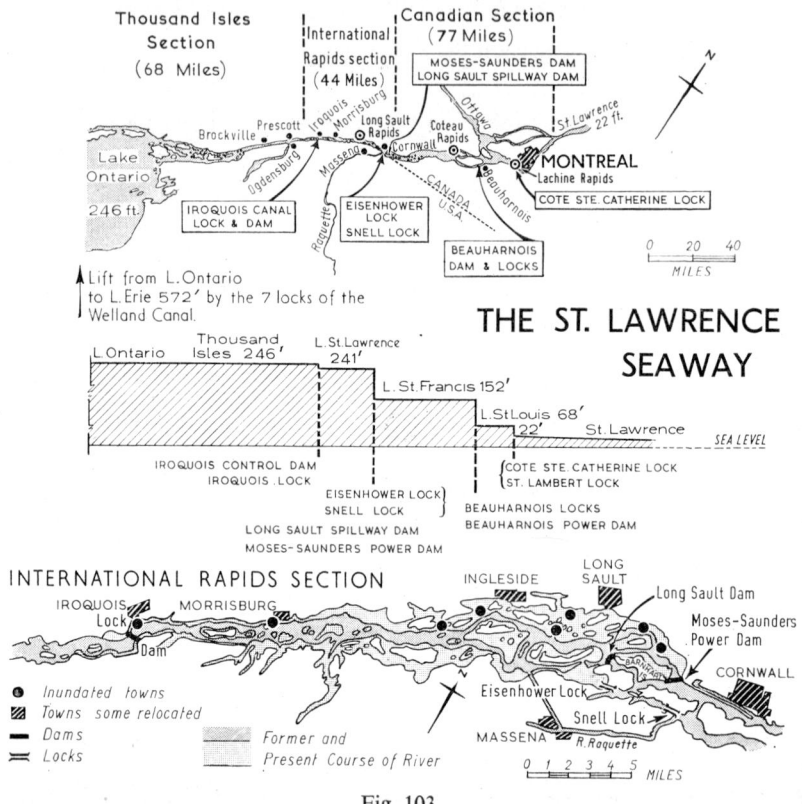

Fig. 103.
The upper map shows the St Lawrence Seaway, the middle diagram is a profile of the Seaway, and the lower map shows the changes in the International Rapids section.

interior. Minor improvements were made in the eighteenth and nineteenth centuries, and between 1876 and 1908 a series of locks and canals was built to circumvent the rapids and create a 14-ft channel which allowed passage to the smaller lake freighters. Ocean vessels larger than 3,000 tons could proceed no farther than Montreal.

THE ST LAWRENCE SEAWAY

The idea of a deep seaway was first mooted in 1895 but a decision to start construction was not taken until 1951. In the section between Lake Ontario and Montreal, the St Lawrence forms the boundary between Canada and the U.S.A. For a variety of reasons, the U.S. withheld its support of the scheme. Only the realisation that Canada would go ahead alone, that extra electricity which the scheme would provide was needed in New York State, and that Labrador iron ore would soon be needed to replace the dwindling stocks of Lake Superior ores decided the U.S. to co-operate.

The scheme (Fig. 103) involved the construction of seven large locks to replace the twenty-two old ones in order to create a 27-ft channel between Montreal and Lake Ontario (a 30-ft channel already existed between Montreal and Quebec). The Lachine Rapids were by-passed by a new ten-mile lock and canal system on Montreal Island. Between Lake St Louis and Lake St Francis are the Beauharnois locks which lift vessels 84 ft. The most difficult part of the river was the International Rapids section between Prescott and Cornwall. The four stretches of rapids were drowned by building the Moses-Saunders and Long Sault Dams at Cornwall to raise the water level. A new dam at Iroquois controls the flow of water from Lake Ontario into Lake St Lawrence (see plate facing p. 257). In all, 34,000 acres of land were flooded and the inundated roads, railways, and settlements (seven in number) were relocated. In addition, existing bridges had to be raised to allow a passage to larger ships. The seaway was officially opened in 1959.

As yet, it is rather early to assess the success of the scheme. It was hoped that there would be an increase of traffic generally and especially of grain shipments outwards (from Port Arthur and Fort William) and of iron ore shipments inwards (from Sept Iles to the steelworks on the shores of Lake Michigan and Lake Erie). During the first eight years of operation the volume of cargo carried doubled, but it seems safe to assume that for some time the lake freighters will continue to handle most of the cargoes, for they can carry up to 25,000 tons whereas the ocean-going vessels, because of their different build, can carry only 9,000 tons. The fees collected from ships that used the seaway were less than had been expected. These tolls are to pay off the cost of the scheme, which amounted to $470 million (an additional $650 million was spent developing power), within fifty years. The charges are 4 cents on the ship's tonnage plus 40 cents per ton on bulk cargo, and 90 cents per ton on general cargo. These tolls, the difficulty of manoeuvring ocean-going vessels in confined waters, and the necessity of using pilots, has deterred many European shipowners from entering upon direct trade with lakeside ports. It is likely that for a long time a very large proportion of the traffic will be between lake ports, as hitherto, and not between them and ports on the St Lawrence or overseas. In 1964 direct overseas trade amounted to 15 million tons; 51 million tons of cargo passed through the Welland Canal.

A great handicap to increased traffic on the seaway is the freezing of the waters from December to April. Various ways of preventing this have been suggested, ranging from blowing air through perforated pipes on the bed of the river, to generating heat by means of thermo-nuclear explosions, but none seem to have any immediate practicability.

More importance can be attached to the hydro-electric power developments. Indeed, it was the possibility of obtaining more power which seems to have been the prime motive for carrying out the scheme. Ontario, with seventy power stations had already developed most of its potential power sites (see Table 19, p. 300). The accelerating growth of manufacturing was leading to a demand for more and more power. This will be met from the output of the Moses-Saunders Dam (1·2 million h.p.) which is equally divided between Canada and the U.S.A. The Beauharnois scheme in Quebec is wholly Canadian and provides another 2 million h.p.

THE ONTARIO PENINSULA

Settlement in the Ontario Peninsula occurred much later than in the St Lawrence Lowlands. Some forts and trading posts were established by the French (*e.g.* Fort Cataraqui, now Kingston, in 1673; Fort Niagara in 1678; and Fort Rouillé, now Toronto, in 1749), but the population remained small, and there was practically no agriculture. The attention of the French was directed southwards to the Ohio and the Mississippi (where Fort Dusquesne, now Pittsburgh, St Louis, and New Orleans were founded), and northwestwards to the fur-yielding forests of the Canadian Shield. The Ontario Peninsula lay between these lines of movement and remained a neglected area. After 1763, the forts on the lakes and rivers were taken over by the British but for twenty years no serious efforts were made to bring in new population. During and after the War of American Independence, some Loyalists entered the area but by 1791, the population had reached only 25,000, most of whom were established in the Niagara Peninsula.

The turn of the century saw increased immigration. Tracts of land were granted to military veterans and land companies disposed of large areas to Germans from Pennsylvania and an ever increasing number of English, Scots, and Irish settlers. The frontier of settlement advanced from the shores of the lakes in a north-westerly direction (Fig. 97). By 1851 there were almost 1 million inhabitants, a number which was to be doubled during the next thirty years. Ontario (Upper Canada) was united with Quebec (Lower Canada) in 1867 when the country received a federal constitution and dominion status. In the last two decades of the nineteenth century, gains were smaller for this was the period when settlement of the Prairies was proceeding apace. Rapid growth was resumed after World War II, and the present population of Ontario exceeds 6 million, almost 90 per cent. of whom live in the peninsula, where the density is over 100 per square mile.

Physical Features

The Ontario Peninsula is a triangular area lying between the edge of the Canadian Shield and Lakes Huron, Erie, and Ontario. The underlying rocks, which are of Palaeozoic age, dip gently to the south-west and the more resistant beds form cuestas (Fig. 96). On the northern border and rising some 50 ft or 100 ft above the pre-Cambrian rocks of the Shield is the Trenton Escarpment which is made of Ordovician limestone. Across the middle of the peninsula is the more prominent Niagara Escarpment, formed by resistant Lockport dolomite of Silurian age resting upon much weaker red shale. This feature rises from 200 ft to 1,000 ft above the surrounding plain and forms the two transverse "barbs" of the triangle, the Bruce Peninsula and the Niagara Peninsula. The Onondaga Escarpment of Devonian limestone farther south is not a conspicuous feature.

Practically the whole of the underlying rock is covered by a mantle of glacial deposits of varying sorts (Fig. 104). The drift geology is complex and gives rise to a number of land-forms.

1. About one-third of the peninsula is covered with till. This may take the form of boulder clay, silt, or sand and, in parts, includes small tracts of lacustrine clays. The till plains reach a maximum height in south-west Ontario, where they rise above 1,700 ft and form an undulating surface—the "Ontario Island"—cut by deep spillways now occupied by the tributaries of the Thames and Grand rivers. Drumlin swarms are common in certain parts of the region and give rise to "basket of eggs" topography. More than 7,000 drumlins have been counted; most of them are found in the area between Lake Ontario and Georgian Bay.

2. West of the Niagara Escarpment, the till plains are partially encircled by the Horseshoe Moraines, rugged areas of unsorted

boulders, sand, and other glacial debris. East of the Niagara Escarpment is the Oak Ridge Moraine, an eight-mile wide belt of rugged country rising to 1,300 ft which constitutes the watershed between rivers draining to Lake Ontario and those draining to Georgian Bay.

3. The clay plains which border the lakes were formed during the period when the ice-sheets were retreating and the present lakes were much more extensive than they are now. These lacustrine sediments are thickest and most widespread in the extreme south-west of the province, in the Niagara Peninsula, at the head of

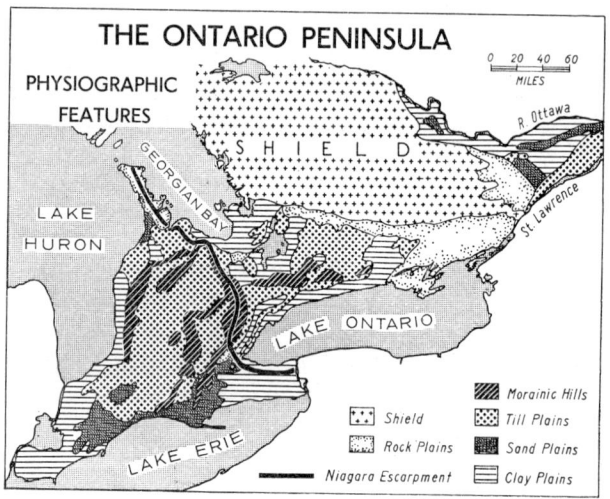

Fig. 104.

Georgian Bay, around Lake Simcoe, and along the northern shores of Lake Ontario.

4. Along the northern shores of Lake Erie are plains of sand which are coextensive with the former deltas of the Thames and Grand rivers. The constitution of the sand varies considerably: in some areas it is coarse and in others very fine.

Climate, Vegetation, and Soils

Peninsular Ontario is the southernmost part of Canada and is the warmest area in the country in summer. The mean July figures exceed 70° F. (*21° C.*) in the south and south-west and do not fall below 65° F. (*18° C.*) in the rest of the region. In winter, temperatures everywhere are below freezing point. The January isotherms tend to run parallel to the shores of the lakes which have a moderating effect on the climate. January figures are highest in the south-west (over 24° F. or −4° C.) and lowest around Lake Simcoe (under 18° F. or −8° C.). The water bodies also have the effect of delaying the onset of winter and thus extending the growing season of places along their shores. Windsor has an average frost free period of 170 days, Toronto 150 days, and the uplands of the south-west interior under 130 days.

Precipitation is lighter than in the St Lawrence Valley, with mean annual totals ranging from 30 in. to 40 in. It is heaviest on the western sides of the "Ontario Island". There is no pronounced wet or dry season, but there are occasional and sporadic heavy falls of rain, which, if they occur at the time of the spring snowmelt, can cause floods.

		J.	F.	M.	A.	M.	J.	J.	A.	S.	O.	N.	D.	Total
Toronto 44° N. 379 ft	°F.	22	22	29	41	53	63	68	67	59	47	36	26	—
	°C.	−6	−6	−2	5	12	17	20	19	15	8	2	−3	—
	in.	2·9	2·6	2·7	2·4	3·0	2·8	3·0	2·8	3·2	2·5	3·0	2·9	33·9

The original vegetation, of which less than 10 per cent. remains, consisted of dense forest. Everywhere the dominant trees were broad-leaved hardwoods with occasional conifers which increased in numbers towards the north. On the till plains, sugar maple, beech, walnut, and oak were the most numerous species, while on the imperfectly drained clay plains, elm, ash, and yellow birch were more common. The sand plains originally supported fine stands of white and red pine, and these trees were also found on the morainic uplands together with tamarack, spruce, and balsam fir.

Soils are generally immature and vary according to the underlying rock, but they tend to have the characteristics of grey-brown earths. The morainic hills have sandy soils with featureless profiles and drainage is excessive. The impeded drainage of the clay plains has led to the formation of half-bog soils. On the gently rolling and well drained surface of the till plains, the soils are developing profiles very similar to those of the grey-brown earths.

Agriculture

Almost all the 140,000 farms and 20 million acres of farmland in Ontario are found in the peninsula (Fig. 98). This is the foremost agricultural area in Canada and the value of the produce (about one-third of the Canadian total), is one and a half times that of the 103,000 farms (on 62 million acres) of Saskatchewan. There are few areas which are not utilised and these include mainly the steep slopes of the Niagara Escarpment, the limestone plains with their shallow soils, and some of the marshy and sandy tracts. Before the opening of the Prairies, the Ontario Peninsula was the main wheat-growing area of Canada, but now, cash grains, with the exception of corn, are relatively unimportant. Most farms are mixed, but there is a considerable amount of specialisation where soils, climate, and proximity to markets are favourable (Fig. 105).

In the extreme south-west, where the summers are hot and the growing season lasts seven months, corn will ripen and it is grown

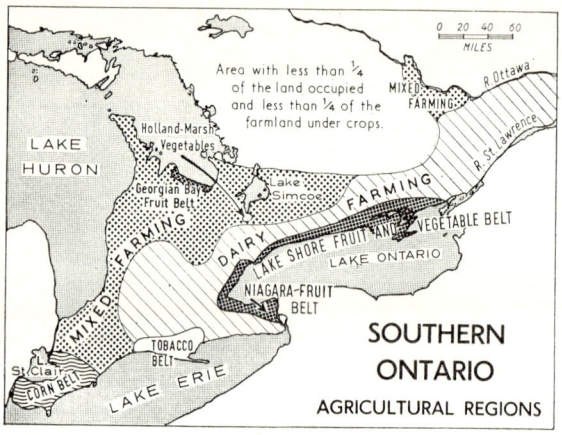

Fig. 105.

as a major crop. Harvests here are a fortnight earlier than along the north shore of Lake Ontario. Elsewhere it is commonly cut green for silage, although new hybrid varieties which grow well under cooler conditions, are now being grown outside the Corn Belt of Kent and Essex counties. The beds of the old lake provide very fertile soils, but sometimes irrigation is necessary because of the light rainfall. Other major crops are sugar beet and tomatoes.

The Tobacco Belt of Norfolk and parts of the adjacent counties along the northern shores of Lake Erie produces 90 per cent. of Canada's tobacco, as well as small quantities of fruit and vegetables. The light sandy soils require heavy fertilisation, and farmers also generally practise a three course rotation consisting of tobacco, rye (which is ploughed into the soil to supply humus), and either clover, soy beans, or alfalfa (which add nitrogen to the soil). Because of their lightness, these soils are easily eroded by the wind and there has been considerable afforestation to prevent this happening. Irrigation water is drawn from streams, ponds, and wells, and delivered to the tobacco plants by gravity feed or by sprinklers. Distinctive features of the farming landscape are the large curing barns and the glass nurseries. The chief marketing centres are Simcoe and Delhi.

In the mid-nineteenth century almost every peninsula farm had its orchard, but now the commercial production of fruit is restricted to lakeside sites where the presence of large bodies of water reduces the incidence of frost and retards blossoming (thus making damage from any late spring frosts less likely). Peaches grown near the lake shore, for instance, ripen a week later than those grown two miles inland. Apples, plums, and pears are grown around Collingwood in the Georgian Bay Fruit Belt, where the lakeshore plains are loamy and well-drained. The more extensive belt along the north shore of Lake Ontario has many fields of vegetables and small fruits as well as apple orchards. The Niagara Fruit Belt lies along the southern shore of Lake Ontario in the counties of Lincoln and Wentworth. Orchards of peaches and cherries occupy the clay and loam soils which form the narrow strip of country, two to six miles wide, between the lake and the foot of the Niagara Escarpment. Grapes, too, are widely grown, but do particularly well on a narrow belt 100 to 500 ft wide at the base of the escarpment. Fruits are the chief cash crops, but only about one-fifth of the farmland is in orchards. Several varieties of vegetables are grown, and here, as along the north shore of Lake Ontario, are many canneries. Much good farmland in this belt has been taken up by roads and the fast growing suburbs, particularly around Hamilton and St Catharines.

South of Lake Simcoe are peaty marshes, 7,000 acres of which have been drained and reclaimed. On these rich soils of the Holland Marsh, Dutch, German, Japanese, and Italian farmers grow crops of lettuce, onions, carrots, celery, and potatoes, which are marketed in Winnipeg, Toronto, Montreal, Quebec, Halifax, and many smaller cities. Only about one-third of the Holland Marsh has so far been drained; the part nearer Lake Simcoe will probably be reclaimed when there is a greater demand for vegetables.

The Dairy Belt extends eastwards from the Western Uplands across the Frontenac Axis into the Ottawa Valley. It coincides with the most densely populated zone. Heaviest concentrations of dairy cattle are found in Oxford county, north of Lake Erie. As the winters are severe and cattle must be kept indoors for long periods, large quantities of fodder must be grown, and large acreages are devoted to oats, clover, turnips, and mangels. Increasing quantities of fresh milk are supplied to the cities and there is an important output of cheese and powdered and condensed milk. Hogs, fed largely on skim milk, are a prominent side-line on most farms.

In the remaining parts of the peninsula, which generally have poorer soils and rougher topography and are farther from the large urban centres, mixed farming is common. Most of the land is under pasture or fodder crops (hay, clover, alfalfa, oats, turnips, etc.). Some dairy cattle are kept but beef cattle are more numerous, while the poorer lands carry sheep. In addition, most farmers rear hogs, chickens and turkeys.

Industry and Towns

Virtually one-half of Canada's manufacturing capacity is found in the Ontario Peninsula. By Canadian standards, this region is very densely populated and, with one-third of the country's inhabitants, provides a large local market and a pool of labour which attracts newer industries. Industrial development has also been influenced by the region's location near to the heart of the continent which means that it is well placed for supplying the national market and contiguous regions of the U.S.A. to the south. Transport facilities are excellent: not only does peninsular Ontario lie on the Great Lakes waterway, but also it has the finest railway network in Canada.

There are few important raw materials found locally, apart from the agricultural produce which is processed in the numerous creameries, canning plants, meat-packing factories, etc. Minerals obtained are those used mainly in the construction of roads and buildings and only rarely in manufacturing. Within easy reach, however, are the abundant resources of the Canadian Shield. Some wood is brought south to be manufactured into pulp and paper, but far more important are the minerals which are brought into the peninsula for refining (Fig. 110). Nickel and copper are smelted at Port Colborne (15,000) which is situated on Lake Erie near the entrance to the Welland Canal. Radium is purified at Port Hope (8,000) on Lake Ontario and cobalt, nickel, and silver at Deloro. A minute quantity of oil (less than one per cent. of Ontario's needs) is mined around Petrolia, but large amounts are brought by pipeline from Alberta to refineries at Sarnia (55,000), Clarkson, and Port Credit. Sarnia is the main oil-refining centre and is now

IRON AND STEEL

important for synthetic rubber and chemicals. Natural gas, too, has entered the province and supplements the power derived from small local wells and hydro-electricity plants.

Practically all the water-power has been developed by the provincial government. The Hydro-electric Power Commission of Ontario, or Ontario Hydro, was created in 1907 and now operates seventy power plants with a capacity of over 8 million h.p. (Table 19, p. 300). Seven power houses, five on the River Niagara and two on the Welland Canal, utilise the 326 ft drop of water from Lake Erie to Lake Ontario and together produce over 2·5 million h.p. The recently completed Moses-Saunders Dam on the St Lawrence yields 1·2 million h.p. and a further 1 million h.p. is derived from the River Ottawa. Smaller plants are located on the Madawaska, Mississippi, Muskoka, and Trent rivers. There are very few remaining sites where power can be developed and Ontario Hydro purchases hydro-electricity from Quebec Province. It has also built two large thermal power stations which produce over 1 million h.p.

TABLE 21
CANADIAN IRON AND STEEL INDUSTRY 1959

	STE MARIE	HAMILTON	SYDNEY	TOTAL
Coke ovens	251	251	114	616
Blast furnaces	7	6	3	16
Capacity ('000 tons)	1,553	1,897	680	4,130
Steel furnaces	14	23	10	47
Capacity ('000 tons)	1,120	2,800	936	4,856

TABLE 22
IRON ORE PRODUCTION, 1965

PROVINCE	MAIN AREAS	PRODUCTION (million tons)
Labrador	Schefferville	12·7
Quebec	Gagnon (Lac Jeannine)	15·5
Ontario	Marmora, Steep Rock, Michipicoten	8·0
British Columbia	Texada Is., Quinsam Lake	2·0
Canada		39·8

The proximity of this region to the densely populated U.S. Midwest, and, at the same time, its separation from it by an international boundary (and tariff barrier), has been of great significance.

The car industry, centred on Detroit, has spread across the border to Windsor (217,000), Oshawa (80,000), St Catharines (97,000), and Hamilton (298,000). The ease of obtaining coal from Pennsylvania and West Virginia, and iron ore from the Lake Superior ranges (and now from Schefferville) has led to the rise of an iron and steel industry at Hamilton, which is on the shores of Lake Ontario and admirably placed for assembling the necessary materials. More than half of Canada's steel is made here and it is used in various engineering industries both in Hamilton itself and in the surrounding towns (see Fig. 106). There is also a large steel plant at Sault Ste. Marie.

Manufacturing is characterised by its diversity; in Ontario there are almost 150 manufacturing centres, which, among them, produce almost every type of consumer article. Important industries not

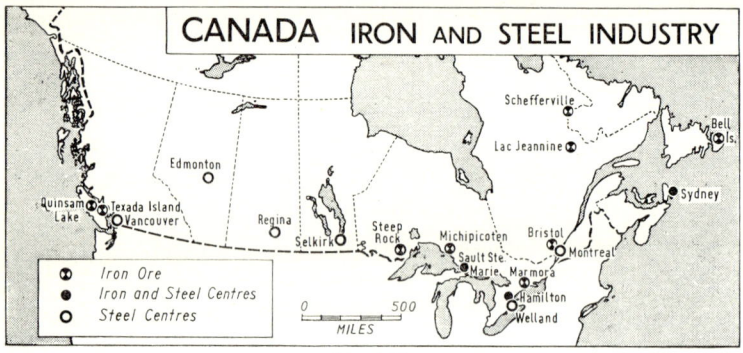

Fig. 106.

already mentioned include locomotives, aircraft, machinery, and agricultural equipment, rubber goods, metal goods, chemicals, and textiles and clothing. Fig. 107 shows the value of manufactures in the fifteen major industrial centres of the Ontario Peninsula.

Recent developments have been spectacular; over 3,000 new industries have been established since 1945 and the labour force has increased by over half a million. By far the larger majority of the immigrants who enter Canada settle in southern Ontario and Quebec, and not in the pioneer lands of the north and west. The imbalance in the distribution of the nation's population seems to be growing rather than lessening.

The major cities of this region can conveniently be classified in two groups: those in the basins of the Thames and Grand rivers, and those on the seaway. The former group includes London 200,000 (locomotives, electrical apparatus, chemicals, and textiles),

Chatham, 23,000 (motor parts, metal goods, fertilisers, and textiles), Kitchener, 98,000 (rubber goods, furniture, clothing, machinery, and electrical apparatus), Galt, 34,000 (metal goods, textiles, shoes, and chemicals), Brantford, 60,000 (machinery, hardware, and textiles), and Guelph, 53,000 (boiler machinery, electrical apparatus, and leather goods). These cities grew up on streams which could be used for transporting logs and developing power for grist and saw mills. Unfortunately, the valleys are subject to flooding, a danger which has been increased by the destruction of the original forests, and which, in spite of conservation measures, has not yet been overcome. Paradoxically, these towns also suffer from a shortage of water, for, with their expanding populations and industries, they

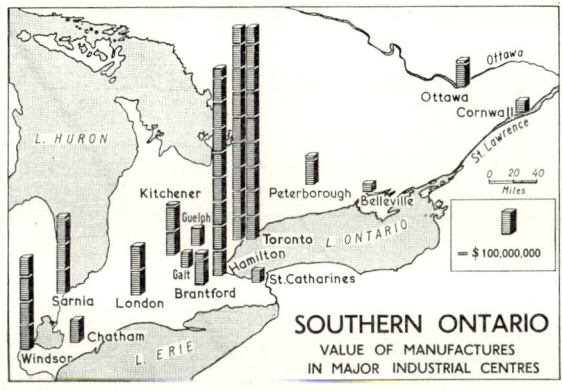

Fig. 107.

have drawn heavily on underground supplies. Reservoirs have been created on the headwaters of the tributary streams and these both augment supplies and help to control flooding, but it seems likely that before the end of the century, the cities will be drawing upon the waters of Lake Erie.

The cities on navigable water include Sarnia, 55,000 (with its oil refineries, grain elevators, and chemical works), Windsor, 217,000 (automobile works and chemical plants), St Catharines, 97,000 (automobile parts, chemical works, farm machinery, and electrical appliances), Hamilton, 298,000 (furnaces along the waterfront, heavy machinery, textiles, electrical equipment, and rubber goods), Oshawa, 80,000 (cars, textiles, glass, and metal works), and Belleville, 32,000 (machinery, radios, and cement). There is no major settlement on the north shore of Lake Erie for here the water is shallow, storms are frequent, wave erosion is rapid, and first-class harbours are lacking. Urban settlement is densest around the western end of Lake Ontario, the so-called "Golden Horseshoe". Suburbs are spreading rapidly and are consuming much of the best agricultural land, particularly in the Niagara Fruit Belt.

Toronto (1,900,000) is the largest city in the region and the second largest in Canada. It originated in 1793 as York, a trading post at the terminus of the overland route from Georgian Bay and Lake Simcoe. Before this date, two temporary French forts had occupied the site. Here was the best natural harbour on Lake Ontario, a small bay, sheltered by a sandy hook, with a depth of 24 ft. To-day, the port handles almost 5 million tons of freight annually, most of it inbound (see Table 20, p. 305). The harbour is now deep enough to accommodate ocean-going vessels.

Inland from the harbour lies the Iroquois Plain, a three-mile wide littoral of sandy material deposited under the waters of an enlarged Lake Ontario. Behind this plain is an old cliff line and then an undulating till plain. The early settlement occupied the coastal plain and did not spread beyond the old cliffs until after 1900. Expansion to the east and west was prohibited for a time by two deep ravines cut by the Don and Humber rivers. The present built-up area extends well beyond the city limits (which enclose an area of thirty-four square miles).

Many railways focus on Toronto and make it a route centre second in importance only to Montreal. The railways and shipping bring in a wide variety of raw materials to feed the industries served by the power from the Niagara power houses and a large thermal plant. There are over 4,000 factories in the city, located mainly on the waterfront and along the railways. Recently, the tendency has been for new plants to be located in nearby towns away from the congested sites where land values are high. An interesting example of this is the erection of an oil refinery together with modern port facilities at Clarkson, sixteen miles from the centre of Toronto. Among the diverse industries are meat-packing and the manufacture of textiles, clothing, chemicals, aircraft, electrical apparatus, machinery of all sorts, rubber goods, and metalware.

Toronto is an important banking and commercial centre, not only for the Ontario Peninsula but also for a large part of Canada, and it has the largest university in the country. The city itself is an important geographic factor in the region; many of the other centres measure the advantages and disadvantages of their locations by reference to their distance from Toronto.

CHAPTER XV
THE CANADIAN SHIELD
Physical Features

The north-eastern quadrant of North America is a vast expanse of ancient resistant rocks covering an area of 2 million square miles (Fig. 1). This is the Canadian Shield, the boundaries of which are defined where the ancient rock complex disappears under later sediments in the south and west. In detail, the structure is exceedingly complicated and the pre-Cambrian sediments which have been rent by igneous intrusions and highly metamorphosed by heat and pressure cannot be precisely dated.

Long before Cambrian times, great thicknesses of lavas and sediments accumulated and were folded into mountains. In their roots, a tremendous volume of superheated rock became fluid and formed granite and other igneous rocks. The ancient mountains were reduced by erosion and their granite cores exposed. The surrounding seas encroached on the resulting lowlands and the whole cycle of deposition, volcanic activity, mountain building, and denudation began again and was to be repeated many times in the 3,000 million or 4,000 million years that elapsed before the start of the Cambrian period. As a result of this long and complex history, the Shield to-day consists mainly of granite and granite-gneiss (estimated to cover 80 per cent. of the surface area), with relatively small areas of highly contorted sediments and volcanic material scattered throughout it. The prevalence of igneous and metamorphic rock accounts for the numerous metallic deposits. Since the close of pre-Cambrian times, the Shield has remained a stable unit, sinking at times, and subject to some faulting, but solidly resistant to the mountain-building forces of later periods.

The Shield takes the form of a huge basin or saucer with the depressed central part occupied by Hudson Bay. Along the southern shores of this sea is the only extensive area of undisturbed Palaeozoic sediments (Fig. 1). This low-lying swampy plain is underlain by poor-grade deposits of soft coal and veneered with recent marine silts and sands. The raised rim is seen most strikingly in Labrador, where the Torngat Mountains rise to over 6,000 ft, and in Baffin Island, where some peaks are over 9,000 ft high. It is still apparent, although lower, farther south where the Laurentides (reaching 2,000 ft) overlook the St Lawrence estuary. In the west, the rim is less pronounced: it is marked by a line of large lakes—

Great Bear, Great Slave, Athabasca, and Winnipeg—which occupy the furrow between the edge of the Shield and the escarpment of overlying sedimentary rocks. In the south-west are the remnants of the pro-glacial Lake Algonquin, which occupy a similar furrow, over-deepened by ice-sheets during the Pleistocene Age.

Most of the local relief is less than 200 ft, but although the sky-line everywhere seems level, the traveller on the ground has a strong impression of rough and rugged terrain. Lakes and muskegs are separated by low but numerous steep-sided ridges and knobby monadnocks.

Perhaps the most significant chapter in the geological history of the region has been the last one, the Ice Age. There were several centres of ice dispersion: from each, the ice-sheets moved outwards and coalesced. Much of the soil was stripped away and there remain large areas which are completely bare and sterile (see plate facing p. 16). Some of the drift filled hollows and valleys but most was taken outside the boundaries of the Shield. The pre-existing drainage pattern was obliterated and the retreat of the ice revealed a surface spangled with an enormous number of lakes, occupying ice-deepened hollows or moraine-dammed depressions, and chaotic river systems. The water spills from one lake to another along tortuous courses; long stretches of sluggish water are interrupted by abrupt rapids and falls, some of which are harnessed for hydro-electricity (see plate facing p. 352). The present drainage pattern is extremely intricate and the early voyageurs found it possible to travel the length and breadth of the region in canoes by using short portages. The water parting, as to be expected from the structure, lies close to the outer edge of the Shield (Fig. 7), and most of the water drains eventually to Hudson Bay. In the south-east, however, several long rivers break through the encircling rim and descend rapidly to the St Lawrence Valley. Some of these streams have been harnessed to produce hydro-electricity, but there is still a very large amount of untapped power (Fig. 100). The Churchill Falls scheme will produce over 5 million kW. when completed. North of Lake Superior, the divide is low and it has been possible to divert some small northward-flowing rivers into the lake in order to increase the amount of water flowing through the St Lawrence power houses.

During the retreat of the ice, melt-water, impounded between the ice-front and the land sloping up to the divide in the south, formed temporary lakes. The sites of these are marked by layers of clay and silt, which provide the only cultivable soils in the Shield (Fig. 98). Several small pockets exist close to the northern shore of

Lake Huron; the largest area is the Clay Belt of Ontario and Quebec which was submerged under the waters of Lake Ojibway (Fig. 2). Another result of the withdrawal of the ice has been the upwarping of the land. The uplift has been greatest around Hudson Bay where evidence from raised beaches indicates a vertical movement of 600 ft. Uplift appears to be still in progress.

Climate

For practically the whole of the year continental Polar air overlies the region. In winter, the land cools quickly and excessively for the daylight period is short and the sun is low in the sky. The mean January temperatures decrease from 10° F. ($-12°$ C.) in south-east Labrador and the northern shore of Lake Superior to $-25°$ F. ($-32°$ C.) in central Keewatin, which is the coldest part of the continent. In summer, the land mass warms up more rapidly than the sea and the temperature gradient in July is from 65° F. ($18°$ C.) around Lake Superior to 45° F. ($7°$ C.) along the Arctic coast. The Labrador coast remains cool—below 55° F. ($13°$ C.)—and this is the result of the cold Labrador Current (see p. 31). Tundra vegetation makes a southward salient along this coast. Precipitation is nowhere very heavy, and tends to be concentrated in the summer months when depressions are more frequent. The south-eastern fringes of the Shield have over 35 in. and the whole of the north-western area under 20 in. About one-third of the precipitation falls as snow.

Cochrane can be taken as a typical station in the southern part of the Shield. It lies near the 49th Parallel, but the mid-year temperatures compare unfavourably with those of Prairie stations (*e.g.* Winnipeg, see p. 51). Figures are significantly lower in March, April, May, and October, and the frost free season lasts only seventy-five days.

Cochrane 49° N. 800 ft		J.	F.	M.	A.	M.	J.	J.	A.	S.	O.	N.	D.	Total
	° F.	0	1	15	32	47	58	63	59	51	38	22	8	—
	° C.	−18	−17	−9	0	8	14	17	15	11	3	−6	−13	—
	in.	1·6	1·0	1·0	1·8	2·3	2·3	3·7	3·5	3·3	2·2	1·8	1·5	26·0

Humans in this region must adapt their methods and techniques to this rigorous climate. The Eskimos in the north have found suitable food, clothing, and shelter but their cultural standards are simple and their needs few. Early travellers and later immigrants adopted their diet and articles of dress but faced entirely new problems when they came to establish mining settlements. The long period of cold and darkness means that living conditions can be comfortable only at great expense. Heating is difficult in the tundra area where there is no wood, coal, or oil. Fuel has to be brought long distances by inadequate means of transport. Measures have to be taken to make safe the foundations of houses and underground pipes in this region where the sub-soil is permanently frozen (the permafrost or *tjaele*). Transport difficulties will be described later in the chapter.

Much remains to be learned about this climate and its effect on humans. Little yet is known about the psychological effect of the long winter darkness. The effect of low temperatures too will not be fully understood until more research has been carried out, linking temperature with the relative humidity and winds. A recent concept to be investigated quantitatively is wind-chill, which is based on the principle that the stronger the wind, the greater its cooling power. It has been found that with a wind speed of less than 5 m.p.h. temperatures of $-20°$ F. are not harmful, whereas with a wind speed of 20 m.p.h. frost-bite can occur when the temperature is $10°$ F.

Vegetation

Extending across the Shield as latitudinal bands are three large vegetation zones (Fig. 25). The dominant influences are the short growing season and long, severe winters. In the north is the tundra, a treeless zone with a wide variety of lowly plants (see p. 56). All are short-lived and pass through their annual cycle of growth extremely rapidly. On the drift covered areas grasses, sedges, many berry-bearing shrubs, heather, and flowers such as Arctic poppy and dandelion are found. The rocky areas have more scattered plants, the dominant ones being lichen and ferns. Early attempts to correlate vegetation and climate led to the suggestion that the tundra was to be found north of the July isotherm of $50°$ F. However, in the field, it has been found that the southern limit of this type of vegetation corresponds with this isotherm only very loosely. So far, no relationship between climate and vegetation has been discovered and it would seem that many climatic factors, apart from temperature, must be taken into account. There is also the fact that the vegetation is changing consequent upon the retreat of the ice-sheets and has not yet achieved stability.

As one moves south from the tundra, trees begin to appear; at first they are small and scattered but become taller and denser as the Great Lakes are approached. The northerly forest belt consists of spruce, tamarack (larch), and willow. This is the sub-Arctic or transitional boreal forest (see p. 57). The true boreal forest* has extensive stands of spruce (particularly on the poorly drained land), jack pine (on the dry, sandy areas), balsam fir, white pine, and hemlock. In the extreme south hardwoods become more common but aspen, willow, and birch can be found in the far north as well. The southern limit of the coniferous forest corresponds fairly closely, though not exactly, with the isopleth of places having six months with a temperature in excess of 43° F.

In the north of Canada the ground is permanently frozen (Fig. 129). Only a surface layer, varying from a few inches to three feet, thaws in the summer. Water cannot percolate through the underlying frozen layer, which is thought to be 1,000 ft or more thick in some places, and remains on the surface. Summer marshes which attract millions of mosquitoes (and consequently birds) carry a cover of sedges and sphagnum. These water-loving plants are found also on the infilling lakes or muskegs which are so common on the Shield. Eventually, they are replaced by tamarack and aspen and later by spruce.

Fur-trapping

White settlement first penetrated the Laurentian Shield in search of furs. The French voyageurs, the first arrivals, found a sparse population of Algonquin and Cree Indians (two to five per 100 square miles). They were migratory hunters, and were quickly induced to provide pelts in return for weapons, clothing, utensils, and drink. Most of the trapping to-day is done by Indians and half-breeds (known as Metis and Chippewas). The British arrived after 1670 when the Hudson's Bay Company was granted exclusive rights to trade in Prince Rupert's Land (the western hinterland of Hudson Bay). Trading posts were located on the shores of the bay and trappers brought in their pelts. As trade became more competitive and as the nearest hunting grounds were over-trapped, posts were established in the interior. Hudson's Bay Company to-day operates 200 trading posts (see Fig. 108). Some were taken over from the North West Company which, in the late eighteenth and early nineteenth centuries was its most serious competitor. Many of the present posts are not solely or even primarily engaged in the fur trade.

For centuries furs were the only resource of interest to Canadians. It was a profitable interest, for until after 1800 the value of pelts

---

* The whole of the forest belt is often referred to as the *taiga*. Some writers, however, restrict the use of this term to the sub-Arctic forest only.

exported exceeded the value of any other commodity. The fur-bearing animals, the most important of which are beaver, mink, marten, fox, and ermine inhabit the forest regions, although some are found in the tundra. The trapper works a fifty-mile fur line in winter when the furs are thickest (and in some cases white); food is short (thus the animals take the bait more easily) and travel over the frozen ground is relatively easy. A beaver pelt is worth about $13, a white fox $15, and a mink $16. In some areas the number of fur-bearing animals has been severely depleted and the provincial governments now have imposed controls. Trappers must obtain licences and, in addition, trapping of certain species is forbidden if they are in danger of extinction.

Fig. 108.
The Hudson's Bay Company operates about 200 trading posts in northern and eastern Canada.

The demand for furs fluctuates as the fashions change. There does not appear to have been any marked decline in recent years. A major change has been the introduction of fur-farming. Animals, particularly mink, silver fox, nutria (coypu), and chinchilla are kept in captivity: their pelts form an increasing proportion (now 60 per cent.) of the total. Trapping is declining and in some areas there has been a reduction of one-third in the number of registered trappers. Ontario and Manitoba are the main fur-producing states, the value of the pelts being about half that of Canada as a whole.

Forestry

Lumbering is confined to the boreal forest where the trees are larger, more closely packed, and more accessible than in the sub-Arctic forest (Fig. 109). Almost the whole of the forest area is owned by the Crown and administered by the provincial governments. Large companies which usually control both the cutting and processing of wood lease tracts of land from these governments. Lumbering in the Shield is a winter occupation (whereas in British Columbia it takes place throughout the year) and the lumbermen usually have other jobs during the summer. After the logs are cut, they are transported across the frozen ground to the ice-covered rivers on which they are stacked to await the spring thaw. On the rivers that drain southwards to the St Lawrence the logs move downstream to mills in the St Lawrence Lowlands. North of the divide, mills are located at points where railways cross main rivers (Fig. 99).

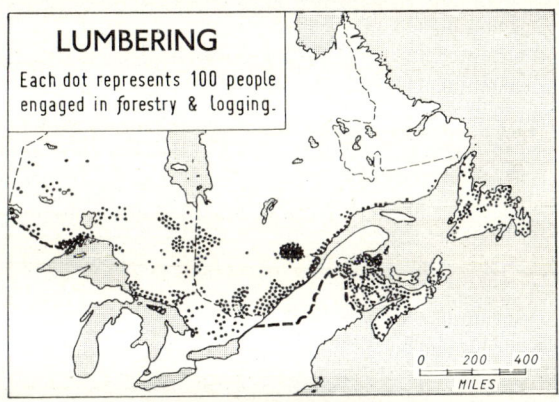

Fig. 109.
Note the concentration of lumbering activities in the more accessible parts of the Canadian Shield.

There are few trees in eastern Canada that produce good timber: the most prized wood was white pine, but there are few remaining stands of this tree left. The Pacific coast produces most of the country's timber and has tended to gain in importance as the timber trees in the east have been cleared. However, there are on the Shield vast reserves of pulpwood; white spruce has long fibres which make it particularly suitable for paper, while black spruce is favoured for making rayon. Even the hardwoods such as poplar, aspen, and white birch, which are frequently found in the boreal forest, can be processed to yield pulp.

The largest areas of productive forest lie in Quebec and Ontario, although there are smaller reserves in Manitoba and Saskatchewan. The problem of conservation is not yet serious and may be rendered easier of solution because the forests are state-controlled. Nevertheless fires are responsible for large annual losses of valuable timber

TABLE 23

ACCESSIBLE COMMERCIAL RESERVES OF SOFTWOOD AND PRODUCTION (1963)

Figures in cubic feet equivalents.

AREA	RESERVES	CUT
Atlantic Provinces	32,000,000,000	380,000,000
Quebec	42,000,000,000	914,000,000
Ontario	51,000,000,000	535,000,000
Prairie Provinces	41,000,000,000	217,000,000
British Columbia	302,000,000,000	1,621,000,000
Canada	474,000,000,000	3,671,000,000

It has been estimated that in the last 100 years five times as many trees have been burned as cut. Active measures are being taken to prevent and control fires. The burnt-over areas are colonised by the less valuable species. In the boreal forest trees require about 100 years to mature fully and lately some concern has been expressed because it is thought that felling exceeds regeneration. The present trend is for lumbering to shift to the less accessible areas as the older areas are cleared. Aerial photography is being used increasingly to discover the most promising areas for development.

Agriculture

Farming has made only very small inroads on the Shield. The climate is unfavourable to many forms of agriculture: the long winters, short growing season, high and irregular incidence of frosts, and the rather heavy summer and autumn rainfall all restrict the number of crops than can safely be grown. Even the long summer days do little to compensate for these climatic disabilities. Over much of the area soils are completely absent. Such soils as are found are usually podsolic and infertile or are waterlogged and must be drained before agriculture can take place. There are several patches of better soil developed on the clays which occupy the beds of former glacial lakes (Fig. 98).

The Little Clay Belt around Lake Timiskaming, a relic of the glacial Lake Barlow, is a fairly well-developed mixed farming area. Other clay areas in the Sault Ste Marie-Sudbury Basin-North Bay Trough support pockets of agriculture. In the Thunder Bay district, behind Port Arthur and Fort William, are about 400,000 acres of agricultural land, three-quarters of which is occupied. A similar area in the Rainy River district has a rather larger proportion of occupied land. In all these regions, hardy vegetables and potatoes are grown but most fields are sown with hay, oats, and barley which feed beef and dairy cattle and hogs. The produce finds a limited market in the local lumbering camps and mining settlements. Farming in the Lake St John area has been described on p. 296.

The largest of these agricultural areas is the Clay Belt of Ontario and Quebec which lies midway between the Great Lakes and Hudson Bay (Fig. 98). Lake Abitibi occupies a small part of the belt and is the shrunken remnant of the glacial Lake Ojibway. The level stretches of whitish clay, overlain by peat are broken by low, rocky ridges and sandy eminences. The total area of the Clay Belt is 14 million acres, but only about 5 million acres appear to be suitable for cultivation. Before farming can be started the forest must be cleared, the peat removed, and the land drained. The most favourable areas are those near rivers where the peat cover is thinnest and drainage is better. Many settlers who take plots of 160 acres often do so for the timber that the land carries rather than with any idea of bringing the land under the plough. Settlement first started in 1912 when the Canadian National Railway from Quebec penetrated the region. However, attention was attracted away from farming possibilities to mining which started after the discovery of rich mineral deposits in the Clay Belt. The present mining population is a market for the local farm produce (milk, butter, cheese, and vegetables). Without this market it is doubtful whether there would be any farming at all for the costs of long-distance transport are prohibitive. It has been estimated that only 5 per cent. of the area is occupied by farmers and some of the farm land has recently been abandoned.

Mining

The Laurentian Shield is one of the richest metalliferous regions in the world. There is no coal or oil for the rocks are very ancient. The rich metal ores are derived from hot gases and liquids which percolated along cracks and fissures and cooled in the form of mineral veins. These are found in the igneous and metamorphic rocks which form such a large part of the Shield.

Because of its size and lack of good communications, the area has been difficult to explore and survey. In recent years aircraft have been used and knowledge has greatly increased. The discovery of minerals is made easier by the fact that much of the surface is bare of soil and the rocks are fully exposed.

Although some minerals were discovered and exploited before 1900, most of the mines have come into operation only in the present century, several of them only in the last decade. Development is proceeding apace and within the last decade the value of the minerals produced has more than doubled. Many more mineral occurrences are known but are not worked at all. More detailed surveys seem likely to reveal further occurrences. In many cases mining will only come about when means of transport become available. If the demand for a particular mineral is great enough communications will be provided (*e.g.* the 357-mile railway from Sept Iles to the iron-ore deposits at Schefferville and the branch lines to Manitouwadge, Chibougamau, and Lynn Lake).

The main mining centres and minerals are shown on the accompanying map (Fig. 110) and Table (Table 24).

Fig. 110.

The following points might be noticed.

1. For a long time the output of gold was greater in value than that of any other mineral. Mining was first started in 1903 at Cobalt and reached its zenith here in 1911. Most of the mines are now closed. The main producing area to-day is the Porcupine district (Fig. 111) around Timmins (27,000). The first mine was opened in 1909 and the present landscape is one of large shaft-heads set among piles of tailings, and sparse forest. There are several farms, for this is part of the Clay Belt, supplying the mining settlements with dairy produce, vegetables, and poultry. Other

MINING

TABLE 24. MAIN MINING CENTRES

	Nickel	Cobalt	Copper	Lead	Zinc	Silver	Gold	Uranium	Titanium
Taltson Lake	—	—	—	X	—	—	—	—	—
Eldorado-Uranium City (Beaverlodge)	—	—	—	—	—	—	—	X	—
Rankin Inlet	—	—	X	—	—	—	—	—	—
Lynn Lake	X	X	X	—	—	—	—	—	—
Thompson Lake	X	—	—	—	—	—	—	—	—
Porcupine	X	—	X	X	X	X	X	—	—
Sudbury	X	X	X	—	—	X	X	—	—
Kirkland Lake	—	—	—	—	—	X	X	—	—
Cobalt	—	X	—	—	—	X	—	—	—
Sept Iles	—	—	—	—	—	—	—	—	X
Allard Lake	—	—	—	—	—	—	—	—	X
Coppermine	—	—	X	—	—	—	—	—	—
Port Radium	—	—	—	—	—	X	—	X	—
Yellowknife	—	—	—	X	X	—	X	—	—
Sherridon	—	—	X	—	—	—	—	—	—
Flin Flon	—	—	X	X	X	—	—	—	—
Red Lake	—	—	—	—	—	—	X	—	—
Long Lac	—	—	—	—	—	—	X	—	—
Noranda-Rouyn-Val d'Or	—	—	X	X	X	X	X	—	—
Chibougamau	—	—	X	—	—	—	X	—	—
Elliot Lake	—	—	—	—	—	—	—	X	—
Bancroft	—	—	—	—	—	—	—	X	—
Pine Point	—	—	—	X	X	—	—	—	—

Small quantities of manganese, chromium, tungsten, platinum, and magnesium are also produced.

centres producing gold are Kirkland Lake, Yellowknife, Red Lake, and Noranda (11,000). Ontario mines 60 per cent. of Canada's gold and Quebec 25 per cent. While the price of gold has remained remarkably steady for many years, the costs of production are constantly rising, and many mines with high operating costs are kept going only by government assistance.

2. To-day, copper and nickel are both more

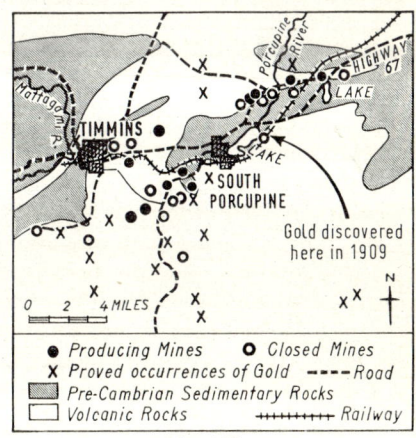

Fig. 111.

important than gold. Near Sudbury both these metals as well as silver, platinum, and gold are obtained from complex ores (see plate facing p. 273). The area is a boat-shaped structural depression measuring thirty-six miles by sixteen, with pre-Cambrian rocks in the centre surrounded by a scarped ring of irruptive rocks (Fig. 112). The ores are found near the base of these rocks, and were first exposed in 1883 in a railway cutting during the construction of the Canadian Pacific Railway. Because of the fortuitous presence of the railway, mining quickly commenced. The mines and smelters

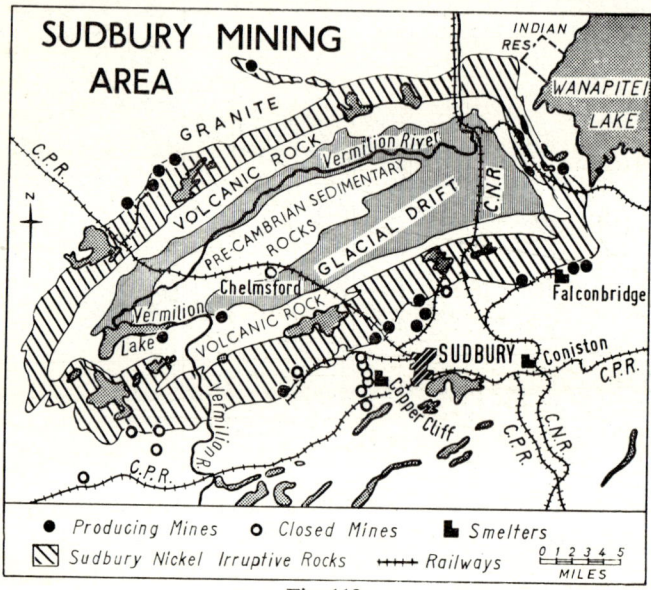

Fig. 112.

employ about 15,000 men. Sudbury (85,000) itself is a short distance from the mines and smelters (at Copper Cliff, Coniston, and Falconbridge). Some of the smelted nickel is sent to Port Colborne on Lake Erie for further refining. On the lower central part of the basin, inside the high scarp, are about 500 farms which grow hay, oats, and potatoes, and rear dairy cattle.

Other important centres for copper are Rankin Inlet, Coppermine, Lynn Lake, Thompson Lake, Porcupine, Flin Flon, Noranda-Rouyn-Val d'Or, Manitouwadge, and Chibougamau. In the last-named place, which lies 150 miles east of the Clay Belt, copper was discovered over fifty years ago, but it was not until a branch of the C.N.R. was constructed in 1957 that mining started. Nickel, as well as copper, is increasingly important at Thompson and Lynn Lake where mining operations commenced in 1954. The population and even the buildings were transferred here from Sherridon, 147 miles to the south, where mining had declined. The concentrated nickel ore is sent to Fort Saskatchewan for refining.

3. In terms of value, uranium is of much less importance than in the years succeeding 1945. When production reached its peak in 1958 there were twenty-three mines in existence: they were concentrated in the Eldorado-Uranium City (Beaverlodge) area, the Elliot Lake (Blind River) area (Fig. 110), at Bancroft, and at Port Radium. The deposit in the Blind River district was discovered in 1950 and the town of Elliot Lake was founded in 1955. By 1959 the population had risen to over 25,000. Some of the ore is milled locally before being sent to nuclear plants at Chalk River in the Ottawa Valley, Toronto, Hamilton, and Rolphton. Canada's needs of uranium are small and most of the output is exported, 80 per cent. going to the U.S.A. and 15 per cent. to Britain. The extremely rapid exploitation of the uranium occurrences was due in large measure to the demands of the U.S.A. The discovery of large reserves in New Mexico (p. 233) has not only halted expansion in Canada but has also caused the closing of some mines. The contracts placed with Canadian companies will expire in 1970 and may not be renewed. In early 1961 the population of Elliot Lake dropped to 12,000 and it is expected to drop still further. The town which had been planned as a model mining community with a hospital and ten schools is in the process of becoming a ghost town (see plate facing p. 273). Only four uranium mines were operating in 1966 and production amounts to about 3,500 tons. Some uranium is now exported to Japan.

4. Iron ore is to-day the most important mineral mined. The small amount of mining which takes place at Michipicoten and Steep Rock (where a lake was drained to allow mining operations to take place) is controlled by U.S. companies (Table 22, p. 315, and Fig. 64). The largest deposit of iron ore is at Schefferville (3,000), near the boundary between Quebec and Labrador. Mining commenced when it was realised that the reserves of ore in the Lake Superior ranges were nearing exhaustion. The ore, which can be mined and transported only during the summer months, is sent by the 357-mile railway (completed in 1954) to Sept Iles and thence up the St Lawrence to lakeside smelters (see plate facing p. 272). In competition with Mesabi ore it is severely handicapped by high transport costs (cp. $6.40 a ton from Schefferville to Lake Erie; $3.11

a ton from Mesabi to Cleveland). The ore is rich with an iron content exceeding 50 per cent. and the reserves, estimated at almost 400 million tons, are very large. Further deposits have been discovered north of Schefferville in the Ungava Trough; these, no doubt, will be exploited if and when the need arises. Production is not constant but fluctuates according to the demands of the U.S.A. In recent years the average annual output has been about 12 million tons. New deposits are now being worked at Gagnon and Wabush Lake. Beneficiated ore will be shipped from Port Cartier (Shelter Bay) 193 miles by rail from Gagnon.

Transport

The exploration of the Shield and the maintenance of settlements are dependent upon transport. The development of communications is made difficult by the climate and the nature of the terrain. For the early pioneers the canoe was the most suitable form of transport in summer. To travel the length and breadth of the Shield on the maze of waterways involved only a few short portages across the low and narrow watersheds. During winter, a variety of methods was used. Snow-shoes, skis, and dog-sleighs are each particularly suited to different types of terrain. Amundsen, the famous explorer, covered the 800 miles between Point Barrow and Nome in Alaska on skis in sixteen days.

Winter is in fact the best time for land travel, for in summer the surface is marshy. Nowadays there are mechanised forms of transport, usually a type of snow tractor with a diesel engine. Some of these machines can haul loads of over 100 tons. They must, however, keep to recognised trails; rocky ground which might have only a thin snow cover can be a hazard.

The use of aircraft has revolutionised life in the north. Planes fitted with either skis or floats can operate in either winter or summer, although in the brief spells when lakes are thawing and freezing landing is impossible. There is an increasing number of airfields—many constructed for military purposes—and the amount of air traffic might be quite high. Goose Bay in Labrador was the point of departure for the thousands of Americans ferried across to Britain during World War II. Frobisher Bay on Baffin Island is a military post and a possible important refuelling point on future trans-polar air routes.

The real mainstay of the communications is still the railway system (Fig. 110). The first line (the C.P.R. in 1883) was built to link the two Canadian seaboards and strengthen federal bonds. Mining arose because the line crossed a rich metalliferous zone.

The Grand Trunk line (now C.N.R.) was built later and followed a more northerly course across the Shield. It, too, led to the opening of mines and the development of farming on the Clay Belt. Many branch lines have since been constructed to outlying centres (*e.g.* Lynn Lake and Chibougamau) or to other main lines. The line to Churchill was built in 1929 to expedite wheat shipments from the Prairies but outgoing cargoes have never been large and incoming cargoes always extremely small. The annual shipments of wheat now average about 20,000,000 bushels which is only a small fraction of the total. The number of ships handled during the twelve weeks when the port is free from ice is invariably less than fifty (see plate facing p. 352). Freezing starts towards the end of October and the harbour ice, which attains a thickness of about five feet, extends up to seven miles from the shore. In late June the ice begins to break up and drifts with the currents to the North Atlantic. During July Hudson Strait still has drifting ice and the route into the Bay is not open until August. The other Hudson Bay terminal is at Moosonee, a smaller settlement which cannot handle ships with a draught greater than 12 ft.

Good roads are still few in number, although they are increasing rapidly. The Trans-Canada Highway skirts the southern edge of the Shield. Short feeder roads lead to some of the mining centres not on the railway (*e.g.* Red Lake). The Mackenzie Highway links the Great Slave Lake with the Alaska Highway and the railway system (p. 386). The most northerly settlements such as Yellowknife and Coppermine still await good roads.

Three of the largest settlements in the Shield owe their existence mainly to transportation factors. Sault Ste Marie (43,000) at one of the two "detroits" of the Great Lakes has an iron and steel industry based on lake-borne ore and coal (Table 21, p. 315). Port Arthur and Fort William (together about 90,000) are terminals handling the bulk of wheat shipments from the Prairies. They are located on the lakeside site nearest to the Prairies. In 1965, the combined ports, which have a waterfront extending over thirty-seven miles, shipped 9 million tons of wheat. Huge grain elevators have a storage capacity of 93 million bushels. Other installations are the storage and transit sheds, the iron-ore docks (for Steep Rock ore), shipyards, aircraft, and automobile works, four pulp and paper mills, and an oil refinery.

Conclusion

Settlement in the Shield is increasing at a marked rate and the northern frontier is on the march. This is not a steady expansion from the settled southern areas but a leap-frog movement across intervening barren tracts to spots of mineral wealth. It is the possibility of finding and exploiting minerals that attracts the population, but the pace of expansion is limited by the amount of capital available, by the means of transport in existence, by the speed with which knowledge of the Shield is increased, and by the demands of the world markets.

The present focus of attention on the north has been seen as a counterbalance to the pull of the U.S.A. to the south.

"As the mining industry grows it should act as one of the most powerful unifying forces of the country. Moreover, since the growth is mostly in the north, it pulls Canada towards the north; it gives the north a vital role in making Canada a distinct entity. For a very long time the parts of Canada have been considered, geographically, as but extensions of American regions ... But in the Shield, Canada has something distinctive; something to all intents and purposes its own. And as the Shield changes from being a negative area in Canadian life, to becoming a very positive one, it may well be regarded as the Canadian heartland, giving Canada its true significance as a separate country. Since the bulk of this heartland lies to the north, its pull upon the nation will help to balance the pull to the south which has been apparent in its history heretofore."
J. W. Watson in *Geography*, 1954.

Against this assessment must be set other facts. Mining populations are, in the long run, transitory, for all mineral deposits are eventually exhausted or abandoned as uneconomic. Lumbering, the other dominant occupation, is seasonal and does not attract a large or permanent population. Truly permanent settlements in the Shield based on agriculture are few and small. The region looks south for many of its needs, its capital, and its inhabitants. Many of its products go south for processing. And while the Shield is developing rapidly and is playing an increasingly important part in the economic life of the nation, the development of the Ontario and Quebec lowlands has been even more rapid. It is this area which is the core of the country; as far as one can see, its preeminent position is unlikely to be usurped.

CHAPTER XVI

THE PRAIRIES

Physical Features

The Prairies are formed of little disturbed sedimentary rocks lying between the ancient crystalline complex of the Canadian Shield on the east and the contorted sediments of the Rockies on the west. The region is at its broadest along the 49th parallel where it stretches a distance of 800 miles: at the latitude of the Peace River District, the width narrows to 400 miles. The lowland continues northwards as a tapering belt to the shores of the Arctic Ocean, where, at the mouth of the Mackenzie River, it is 100 miles wide. Although similar in structure, this northern area is not part of the Prairies.

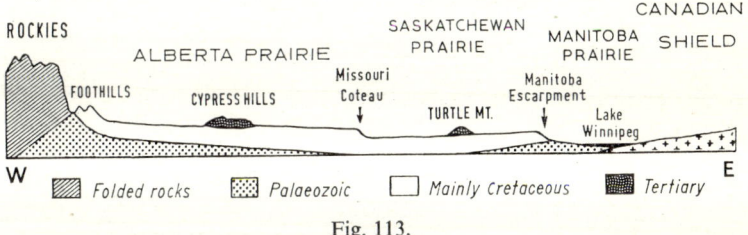

Fig. 113.
See also Fig. 114.

The rocks are almost horizontal but the lowlands are not featureless. The land rises to the west in a series of three great "steps" (Fig. 113). The lowest, flattest, and smallest area is in the east where the ancient rocks of the Shield pass under the Palaeozoic sediments of the Red River basin and Lake Winnipeg lowlands. Only rarely are these rocks exposed, for there is a thick mantle of glacial drift overlain by the silts laid down in Lake Agassiz, an ice-dammed lake which covered the lowlands for several centuries during the later stages of the Ice Age. The lacustrine silts are 10 ft thick at Winnipeg and even thicker in some other parts of the plain. Lakes Winnipeg, Winnipegosis, and Manitoba are the shrunken remnants of this former extensive sheet of water. The soils developed from these deposits are generally fertile, particularly in the Red River Valley, but there are several negative areas coinciding with marshy districts and sand hills.

THE PRAIRIES

The western boundary of the Manitoba Lowland is a steep escarpment of Cretaceous rocks rising from about 800 ft—the level of the plain—to over 2,000 ft. The scarp itself is very irregular and is broken by rivers such as the Pembina, Assiniboine, Swan, and Red Deer which flow to the Manitoba Lowland. The crest is a series of isolated hilly areas: from north to south these are the Pasquia Hills, Porcupine Mountain, Duck Mountain, Riding Mountain, and Pembina Mountain (Fig. 114). Upon these hills,

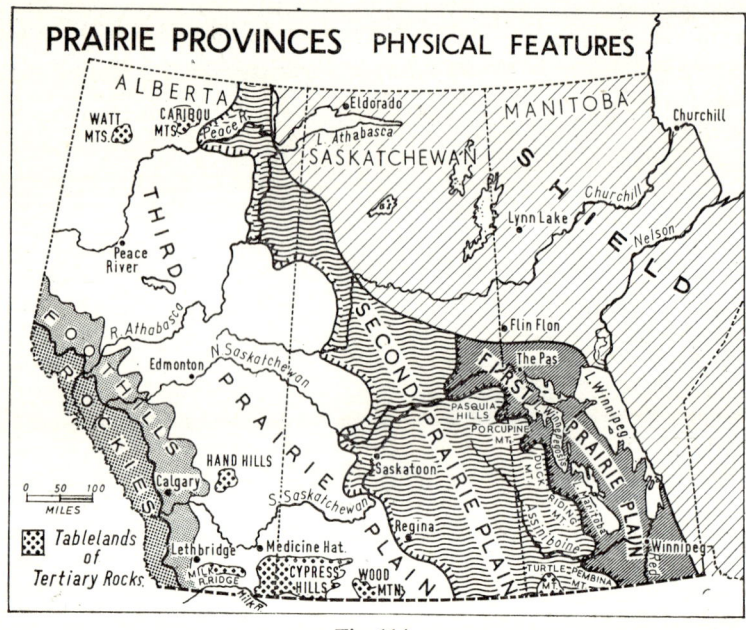

Fig. 114.
See also Fig. 113.

which are the remnants of a Tertiary erosion surface, are extensive patches of rough moraine with small lakes, while on the lower slopes of the scarp are sandy beaches and gravel deltas which mark the fluctuating shore of the former lake. The Second Prairie Plain, or Saskatchewan Prairie, is the dip slope of this thick Cretaceous formation, which is, however, almost entirely concealed under glacial deposits of various sorts. The relief is subdued and in some areas are flat clay plains which represent the floors of glacial lakes. There are still a number of small lakes occupying shallow depressions. Rising 700 ft above the plain is Turtle Mountain, a mesa of Tertiary rocks.

This plain is separated from the third level by the Missouri Coteau, a lower and less abrupt feature than the Manitoba Escarpment. The crest is mantled with morainic debris and reaches elevations of about 2,500 ft. From here, there is a gradual slope upwards to about 4,000 ft at the foothills of the Rockies, where the sedimentary beds are upturned and the topography is much rougher. The Third Prairie Plain, or Alberta Plateau, has bolder relief than the other levels. Rising above the plateau surface are the Cypress Hills, Wood Mountain, Caribou Mountain, and other hilly areas of Tertiary sediments. In the drier parts, these rocks have been severely dissected and form "badlands". Such an area occurs along the Red Deer River in Alberta (not to be confused with the Red Deer River which breaks through the Manitoba Escarpment in the eastern Prairies), where fossil beds with the skeletons of dinosaurs and other extinct reptiles have been exposed.

The North and South Saskatchewan rivers are the major streams crossing the Prairies: they take the drainage from a wide area to Lake Winnipeg, whence the water goes to Hudson Bay via the Nelson River. Run-off water also reaches Hudson Bay via the Churchill River. In the extreme south, a small area lies in the catchment basin of the Milk River, which is tributary to the Missouri, while in the north, a rather more extensive area is drained by the Athabasca and Peace rivers which carry water to the Mackenzie. The valleys are marked topographic features; they are wide and often deeply incised. Between them, the rolling surface of the interfluves has indeterminate drainage with many small lakes and intermittent streams. Parts of southern Saskatchewan and Alberta, with a total area of 36,000 square miles, have interior drainage. Glacial spillways, or coulees, formed when the drainage was disarranged during the Ice Age, are to be found in parts of the Prairies, particularly on the watershed between the Saskatchewan and Missouri systems.

Climate

More than anything else, perhaps, it is the climate and the direct consequences of the climate on vegetation and soils which give the Prairie region its characteristic unity. The main features are summarised on Fig. 115. This is a region situated in the interior of a continent in northern latitudes. Winter temperatures are low: January averages decrease from little more than 15° F. ($-9°$ C.) in south-west Alberta to under $-20°$ F. ($-28°$ C.) in north-east

Manitoba. The relative mildness of the south-west reflects to only a small extent nearness to the moderating influences of the Pacific; much more significant are the occasional Chinook winds which sweep down from the Rockies and raise the temperatures 20 F.° (*11 C.°*) or 30 F.° (*17 C.°*) in a few hours. In years when the Chinook is persistent, winter days are characterised by warmth and sunshine. In 1907, Calgary had a January temperature of 26° F. (*−3° C.*) whereas the January of 1906, which experienced few Chinook winds, had a temperature of only − 6° F. (*− 21° C.*).

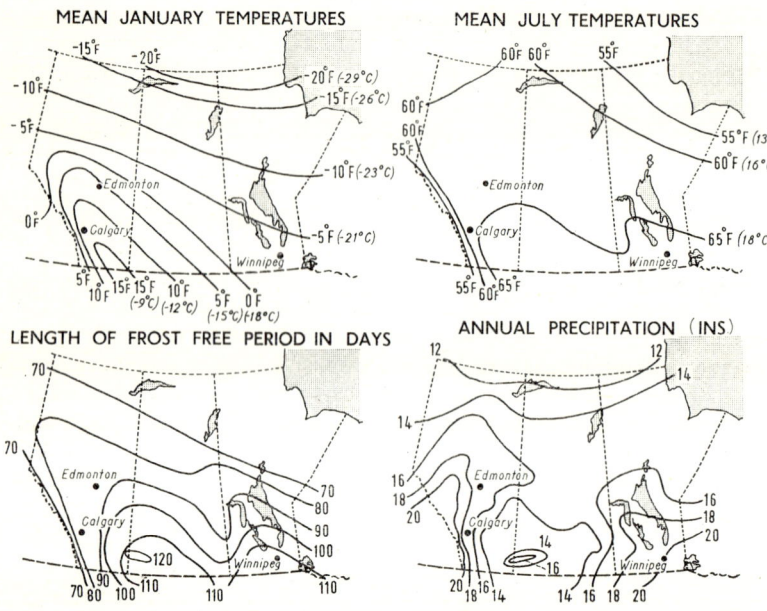

Fig. 115.

The July temperature gradient is much smaller, from about 70° F. (*21° C.*) in southern Alberta to under 50° F. (*10° C.*) along the shores of Hudson Bay. A great "gulf" of summer warmth, which is the distinctive feature of the Prairie climate, extends north-westwards across the continent towards the Arctic Ocean, between the Shield and the Rockies. The annual range is very large and the rapid rise and fall of the temperatures means that spring and autumn are of short duration. The *average* frost free period is 120 days in the south but little more than sixty days in the north.

Frosts, however, can be experienced at any time of the year, even in July. Summer hailstorms, which develop as a result of local atmospheric instability, are a hazard for the wheat farmer.

Precipitation is light: it is heaviest in the extreme south-east and south-west, where totals exceed 20 in. The amount decreases towards the centre of the Prairies and the north. There are large areas with less than 15 in. Fortunately for the farmers, most rain falls during the summer months.

	Total Precipitation	Percentage, May-October
Winnipeg	20 in.	72
Saskatoon	14 in.	79
Edmonton	18 in.	74

Here, as on the Great Plains, totals can be misleading, for the precipitation is unreliable and varies greatly from year to year.

PRAIRIE PROVINCES

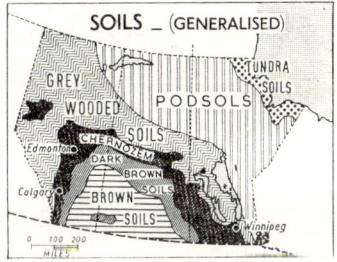 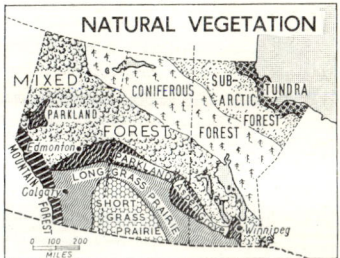

Fig. 116.

Medicine Hat, one of the driest parts of the Prairies, has a mean annual rainfall of 12 in. but totals have varied from 7 in. to 18 in. In places such as this, where the total, for agricultural purposes, is marginal, such fluctuations can be disastrous. According to Thornthwaite's formula (p. 41), Saskatoon has a moisture deficiency of $6\frac{1}{2}$ in.

Vegetation and Soils

The Prairies are fairly clearly defined by the vegetation (Fig. 116). The boreal forest, which extends across the continent as a broad belt, covers the northern two-thirds of the Prairie Provinces. This region is not part of the Prairies and is considered in other chapters. Farther south, the precipitation is heavier but less effective because of the more intense evaporation and the vegetation cover consists of grass with an increasing admixture of trees as the boreal forest is approached.

The short grass prairie, or true steppe, occurs in the more arid parts of southern Saskatchewan and Alberta (the area designated Palliser's Triangle, see p. 342). Characteristic species are blue grama grass, common spear grass, June grass, and western wheat grass. The short tufts are widely spaced with bare soil between the plants, but the root systems are very extensive and invade practically the whole of the soil mass in search of water. Among the grasses are found pasture sage and opuntia (prickly pear cactus).

Extending as a crescent around the short grass prairie, from south-west Manitoba to south-west Alberta, is a belt of taller grasses, which often attain a height of three feet or more. The common species are northern wheat grass, green spear grass, and rough fescue. In spring, the sudden blossoming of many flowers, *e.g.* cinquefoil, anemone, and crocus, adds colour to the landscape. Along the streams and in natural depressions, small groves of willow, poplar, and various shrubs occur.

Separating the true prairie from the boreal forest is the "Parkland" or aspen grove belt. Here, the tall grasses are interspersed at frequent intervals with small "bluffs" or groves of trees, which indicates an increased moisture supply. Aspen, poplar, and willow are the trees most frequently found.

Coextensive with the short grass prairie is a zone of brown soils which cover an area of about 32·5 million acres, one-quarter of which is classed as potentially arable land. The surface layer of these soils is light both in colour and texture and its organic content is rather low. It has a shallow profile with a layer near to the surface where lime or salt has accumulated. Under cultivation, it tends to lose its texture and becomes susceptible to erosion by wind. Where the surface relief is greater, there is danger of erosion by rain-water.

The dark brown soils coincide fairly closely with the tall grass prairie. With moister conditions, the vegetation cover is thicker and the humus content of the soils is greater than in the brown soil zone. The profile is deeper and darker with the lime layer at a depth varying from 10 to 18 in. These soils extend over 35 million acres, 60 per cent. of which is regarded as potentially arable land.

The richest soils of all are the chernozems found under the tall grasses of the "Parkland" belt. They cover an area of 42 million acres, and of the area classed as arable land (30 million acres) 90 per cent. is now in use. A true black soil has a deep profile with a surface layer 12 to 15 in. deep. The horizon of lime accumulation lies 15 to 30 in. below the surface. Soil profiles vary throughout the belt and along the northern border are degraded or leached chernozems where forest seems to have invaded the grassland. An outlier of black soils, separated from the main belt by grey wooded soils, is found in western Alberta in the Peace River District.

The grey wooded soils which have a leached upper layer and, at the same time, a zone of lime accumulation at the base of the profile, are not naturally fertile and very little of the area has been brought under cultivation.

The Settlement Pattern

The development of the Prairies has taken place almost entirely during the present century.

"In the span of a single lifetime, the Prairies were transformed from a fur-trading empire to a fully settled modern agricultural community comprised of multiples of quarter sections (160 acres) of farm lands and many small urban distribution centres of a few hundred people dispersed along a network of over 19,000 miles of railways and characterised largely by clusters of towering grain elevators at six-to-eight-mile intervals." *Official Handbook of Canada,* 1959 (see plate facing p. 48).

The northern tracts of Manitoba and Saskatchewan formed part of the trapping territory of the Hudson's Bay Company but fur-trapping did not, of course, extend over the grassland area. The first agricultural settlement was established in 1812, when a stretch of land along the Red River was purchased from the Hudson's Bay Company by the Earl of Selkirk, who undertook to bring in farmers. This embryonic colony remained small for a long time and suffered severe vicissitudes. As transport facilities were extremely poor, the settlers had to be self-sufficing. Their early efforts were almost unavailing owing to the plagues of grasshoppers which devoured their crops, the floods of the Red River which inundated their settlement, and attacks by Indians and Metis. Nevertheless, the colony maintained a precarious foothold on the doorstep of the Prairies until the advent of the railways. In 1870, the settlement had a population of about 12,000, and the district which the Earl of Selkirk had purchased became the province of Manitoba.

As exploration of the Prairies proceeded, widely differing estimates of the possible value of the land were made. Many of the investigators fell into the same error as their forerunners in the U.S.A. had done two or three decades earlier, and suggested that the treeless short grass prairie was a semi-arid area unfit for agricultural settlement (see p. 196). Captain Palliser's estimate, which was made after his travels across the Prairies between 1857 and 1860, was one of the most publicised and least unrealistic. (The boundary of his "semi-arid desert", known as Palliser's Triangle—it is in fact a pentagon—is superimposed on the land-use map, Fig. 117.)

Full scale settlement commenced after the railways penetrated the region. The Canadian Pacific Railway was completed in 1885, and had been built primarily to strengthen federal bonds. Until this time what settlements there were in western Canada had been forced to seek outlets for their produce in the U.S.A. A railway had connected Winnipeg with St Paul and Chicago since 1878, and until 1885 Manitoba had stronger connections with the U.S.A. than with Canada. After this date, however, branch lines from the trunk railway soon spread over the open grasslands and immigrants poured in, many of them from eastern Europe. The land had already been surveyed on the American pattern (see p. 168) and divided into townships of thirty-six square miles. Settlers could obtain a free claim to a quarter section (160 acres) of the Public Domain, which was the land remaining after reserves had been set aside and grants made to railway companies. The C.P.R. had obtained 25 million acres as a subsidy. The company sold its land, which was arranged in alternate sections for several miles on either side of the track, very cheaply in order to encourage settlement and thus increase traffic and freight. As the Public Domain was free, this land was occupied first, and the land that had to be purchased was taken up later. Thus the early settlement pattern was rather loose and the lack of integration made the provision of roads, schools, and other services expensive.

In the pre-motor age, farmers tended to live within ten miles of a railway or siding, for it was found to be uneconomic to haul wheat a greater distance. In some cases, settlement preceded the railway, but this was only in the confident expectation that the line would pass nearby. If it did not come, the hamlet usually moved to a more favourable location. As the railways needed to be about twenty miles apart, with stations or sidings every seven or ten miles, a close railway mesh developed, so close in fact that after 1931, some lines became uneconomic and were abandoned. With the advent of motor transport, distance was no longer so important, but the pattern of settlement had already been established. Between 1911 and 1931, the settled area increased very little, except in the Peace River District.

The present population of the three provinces is about 3 million, *i.e.* about 17 per cent. of Canada's population. Most people live in the southern half of the area where the density is about eight people per square mile (cp. over 100 per square mile in the Ontario

Peninsula). Population increased rapidly until 1931 and then more slowly until the post-war boom in Alberta. In Saskatchewan the population actually declined and in spite of post-war increases has not yet reached the 1931 figure. Rural densities appear to be decreasing, for there is little space left which will support pioneer farms, and there is a tendency for present holdings to become larger. The increases are being largely felt in the towns, particularly in Edmonton and Calgary, which are rapidly becoming industrialised. It would seem that the pioneering stage is over, and a second stage, the development of industrial cities, is beginning.

Agriculture

About one-third of the provinces is occupied farmland, two-thirds of which is improved. One-third of the working population gains employment from the land. Owing to the particular combination of soils and climate, this region has become a wheat farming area *par excellence* with ranching and mixed farming of subsidiary importance.

Ranching.—Cattle ranching spread northwards from the Great Plains of the U.S.A. during the last quarter of the nineteenth century. The earliest record is of a herd entering the Wood Mountain area in 1874. Very large ranches were established over a wide area. With the arrival of the cultivator, however, the cattle-men withdrew from the more humid parts and ranches were reduced in size. Ranching is still the dominant farming activity in the dry, short grass prairie and on the areas of rougher terrain such as the Cypress Hills and the foothills of the Rockies (Fig. 117). There are about 200 ranches, which have an average size of about 10,000 acres. Most of this land is leased from the provincial governments. The carrying capacity of the prairie is low, and as many as forty acres may be needed to support one animal. Herds number from 200 to 500 cattle, usually Herefords which can stand the harsh winter conditions better than other breeds. Some land cannot be used for grazing because it is too far from water. Supplementary feeding is necessary during the three winter months: some of the fodder is obtained from the irrigated farmlands in Alberta. Some cattle are sent to feed lots in Ontario for fattening before slaughter, but about 1 million are handled by the prairie abattoirs every year. Calgary, Edmonton, and Winnipeg are the main meat-packing centres (see plate facing p. 353).

On the very poor lands some sheep are reared.

Wheat.—In the more humid parts of the Prairies, ranching was replaced by commercial wheat farming. Wheat is quite suited to a short but sunny growing season and light summer rainfall. It is necessary to plant the crop in spring for the harsh winters and lack of a thick snow cover prohibit autumn sowing. The product is hard with a high gluten content, and is more suited for bread-making than the bulky and starchy grains of wetter and milder climates. The soils, particularly the chernozems, are deep and rich; they do not appear to lose much fertility even after years of cropping, but once ploughed, they are susceptible to wind erosion.

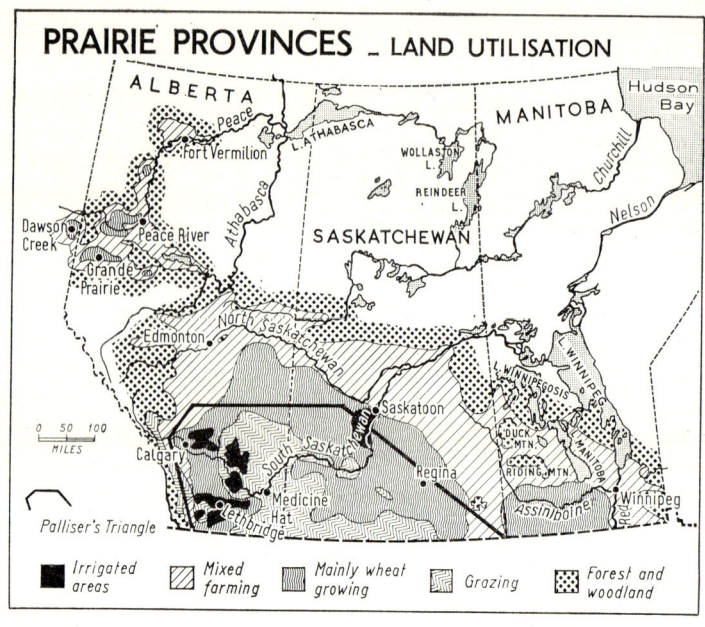

Fig. 117.

The level, or gently rolling nature of much of the terrain favours the use of large-scale farm machinery.

The key to the development of wheat farming is the railways. They brought in the settlers; they carried out the produce. Wheat was the only crop capable of bearing the transport charges. The export of large quantities of cheap wheat after the eighteen-nineties, had great repercussions on farming in Britain and Denmark, where land formerly devoted to wheat was sown with pasture and fodder crops.

The prairie pioneer was fortunate in that some of the problems that confronted him had already been tackled and solved in the

U.S.A. (p. 205). The main Canadian contribution to the development of the sub-humid lands was the breeding of new strains of wheat. None of the varieties known to the early settlers was very well suited to the short growing season, which exceeds 120 days only in the extreme south-east. The first successful strain to be developed was Red Fife, which extended the wheat growing area northward and westward from the Manitoba Lowland. In 1904, the Marquis strain was introduced. This ripened a week earlier than Red Fife and could be grown on the limits of the present settled area. Later varieties included Garnett and Reward which combined the ability to mature early with resistance to rust (a fungoid growth on the stems and leaves of plants). Marquis has now been largely replaced by rust-resistant varieties such as Thatcher, Selkirk, and Manitou. Durum wheat, used to make macaroni, is less resistant to drought, more susceptible to rust, and matures rather later than other varieties. It is grown mainly in south-west Manitoba. The boundary of wheat cultivation has been pushed far to the north and the limit now is set not so much by the shortness of the growing season but mainly by the poor soils and the thick forest cover.

Hazards which the wheat farmer must face, apart from rust and early autumn frosts, are insect pests, summer hail, and drought. Many farmers now insure their crop against loss through hailstorms. Drought is a more pervasive danger. An annual rainfall total of 12 in. can be regarded as the minimum that safety allows, and it is estimated that every additional inch up to 18 in. leads to an increased yield of $2\frac{1}{2}$ bushels per acre. The wheat output in Saskatchewan in 1928, a rainy year, was 321 million bushels (yielding at the rate of 23 bushels per acre); in 1927, a dry year, it was 36 million bushels ($2\frac{1}{2}$ bushels per acre). Average yields are not high by European standards, amounting to 23 bushels per acre compared with 46 in Britain, but are steadily increasing. There has been a rise of four bushels per acre in each of the last three decades, due mainly to the use of new disease-resisting and high-yielding varieties, increasing mechanisation, and stricter control of noxious weeds by chemicals. Farmers can now seed and harvest crops more rapidly and so reduce the risk of losses because of inclement weather. Increasing production, however, poses the problem of how to dispose of larger surpluses.

Farming is extensive, and although yields per acre are low, output per worker is high. Dry farming is practised over large areas. During the year when the land lies fallow, the farmer tries to conserve as much moisture as possible in the soil; in favourable circumstances this might amount to as much as 40 per cent. of the rainfall. In the drier parts, *i.e.* south-west Saskatchewan and south-east Alberta, wheat and fallow alternate in successive years; there is no alternative crop. Where it is more humid, there are usually two wheat crops after each year of fallow. Only large farms can operate successfully under this system and there has been a tendency for farms to increase in size as the smaller units are absorbed by the larger and more successful farms. In the last fifteen years, over 60,000 farms have disappeared in this way.

Because the crop yield varies so widely from year to year owing to the vagaries of the weather, and because foreign demand for wheat fluctuates so much, government aid is made available to farmers, although not on such a lavish scale as in the U.S.A. All wheat is marketed through the government-controlled Canadian Wheat Board. The farmer is paid a fixed price (determined annually) for his wheat when he delivers it to a country elevator. He receives more if the Board sells the crop at a price above this guaranteed minimum. There is also a system of deficiency payments which, in 1960, amounted to $41 million.

TABLE 25
PRODUCTION AND EXPORT OF CANADIAN WHEAT

	1956	1957	1958	1959	1960	1961	1962	1968	1964	1965	1966
Production (million bushels)	573	370	369	413	490	283	557	723	600	648	840
Exports (million bushels)	261	316	295	278	354	353	358	331	594	400	583

Exports are mainly to China, U.S.S.R., western Europe, and Japan. Between 150 million and 170 million bushels are consumed within Canada annually and the remainder forms the "carry over". In 1966, this accumulated surplus amounted to 325 million bushels or about a half year's entire crop. Some is stored in specially built elevators but much lies in the open, protected by tarpaulins. The acreage under wheat fluctuates, in 1965 amounting to 27·8 million acres.

There are several routes by which wheat for export reaches the ocean terminals. The rail route to Vancouver (which is an ice-free port) is increasingly important and carries an average of over one-third of the total. The route to Churchill (open for twelve weeks every years—see plate facing p. 352) carries a very small amount (see p. 333). Most of the exports move through Winnipeg to the huge elevators at Port Arthur and Fort William. The need to convey as much wheat as possible to the coast before the lakes freeze means that there is an enormous amount of rail and lake traffic. Between mid-September and mid-December, trains laden with wheat leave

Winnipeg at the rate of one every twenty minutes. From Port Arthur and Fort William, freighters take the grain to Montreal or Buffalo and it is trans-shipped and exported from Montreal (closed by ice for four months of the year), St John, Halifax, or New York (all of which are ice-free). The St Lawrence Seaway now permits ocean-going vessels of up to 9,000 tons to penetrate to the head of Lake Superior. If these were to replace lake freighters, perhaps a few cents could be saved on every ton of grain, as there would be no need to trans-ship the cargo at Montreal or other intermediate ports, but so far, there has been little change in the established methods of transport (p. 307).

Mixed Farming.—The cash return from wheat is high but the risks are great; dependence on one crop means that during a bad year there is very little farm income. In addition, the fallow period which is necessary in many parts of the wheat belt increases the danger of soil erosion. Diversification of agriculture, not only leads to more stable conditions, but also is less destructive of the soil.

Mixed farming is carried on chiefly in the "Parkland" belt and it is spreading very slowly into the coniferous forests—the pioneer fringe. In these cooler regions with their shorter growing season, farmers raise livestock in addition to growing grain. Oats, barley, and rye are grown as fodder crops, but usually two-thirds of every farm is devoted to hay and alfalfa. Now, some farmers are growing sunflowers for ensilage: the seeds are used as poultry feed. Vegetables, apart from potatoes, are not generally important.

Cattle and hogs are very important. More beef cattle are reared in this belt than in the ranching areas. Dairying is of significance only near the large towns such as Winnipeg, Calgary, and Edmonton.

Peace River District.—This block of land in north-western Alberta and adjoining parts of British Columbia covers an area of about 25,000 square miles. It is separated from the mixed farming area of central Alberta by about 150 miles of forest and muskeg, and includes both open prairie and parkland.

The railway from Edmonton reached Grande Prairie in 1915 and settlers moved in. Although it lies about 8° farther north than the Ontario-Quebec Clay Belt (p. 327), the Peace River District, by virtue of its better soils, warmer summers, and drier weather is the more attractive pioneering area. During the prolonged drought in the southern Prairies during the nineteen-thirties, thousands of farmers moved north to this area where rain is more effective. To-day, farmlands occupy over four and a half million acres, about half of which is cropland. There are about 8,500 farms and a total population of 60,000. Wheat is an important cash crop, especially in the darker soil areas. The growing season of 100 days is short, but summer days have as much as twenty hours of sunlight. Barley growing has increased with the introduction of Olli and other varieties suitable for northern latitudes. The region has become noted for the purity of its seeds and is the main seed-growing area of the country for clover, alfalfa, and flax seed. Mixed farming occupies two-thirds of the area, mainly on the grey wooded soils.

The most pressing need, a direct link with the Pacific coast, has recently been met (1958) by the construction of a new railway from Prince George to Dawson Creek by way of Pine River Pass. Wheat now travels direct to Vancouver instead of going the longer journey via Edmonton. The Alaska Highway has increased the prosperity of the district and more recently, pioneer farming has developed along the Mackenzie Highway, which runs from Grande Prairie to Hay River on the Great Slave Lake.

Irrigation.—In the drier part of Alberta, around Calgary, and Lethbridge, about 1 million acres of farmland have been irrigated. There are fifteen major projects, the most important of which are shown on Fig. 118. They use the waters of the Bow, Oldman, Belly, and St Mary rivers, all of them tributaries of the South Saskatchewan. Storage works are not essential, though desirable, for these streams are fed by the Rocky Mountain snows and have their maximum flow in summer.

In 1898, a group of Mormon pioneers came from Utah to the St Mary Valley and used the water of the river to irrigate their land. Later projects were undertaken by the C.P.R. The largest, the Eastern Irrigation District, lies west of Medicine Hat and between the Bow and Red Deer rivers. Precipitation amounts to about 12 in. annually, while evaporation from a free water surface is 33 in. The project was designed to serve 400,000 acres but no more than 90,000 acres were irrigated in any one year. Since the scheme was taken over by the Alberta government in 1935, the area under the ditch has increased.

The South Saskatchewan Project will, when complete, add an additional 500,000 acres to the irrigated area. It is estimated that there are another 3 million acres of irrigable land in the southern part of the Prairies but their utilisation would involve tapping the waters of the North Saskatchewan which flows far to the north.

An average farm in an irrigation district consists of about 230 acres, of which about 120 acres are irrigable. The farmer usually raises beef and dairy cattle and poultry. Grain and fodder crops are grown and yields are high, with 50 bushels of wheat per acre (cp. 18 elsewhere in Alberta), 100 bushels of oats (cp. 48), and 70 bushels of barley (cp. 37). Alfalfa, a major fodder crop, requires about 18 in. of irrigation water annually. Special crops, such as sugar beet, potatoes, tomatoes, vegetables, and soft fruits are grown in many districts but are most important around Lethbridge (35,000). They are marketed in the Prairie provinces.

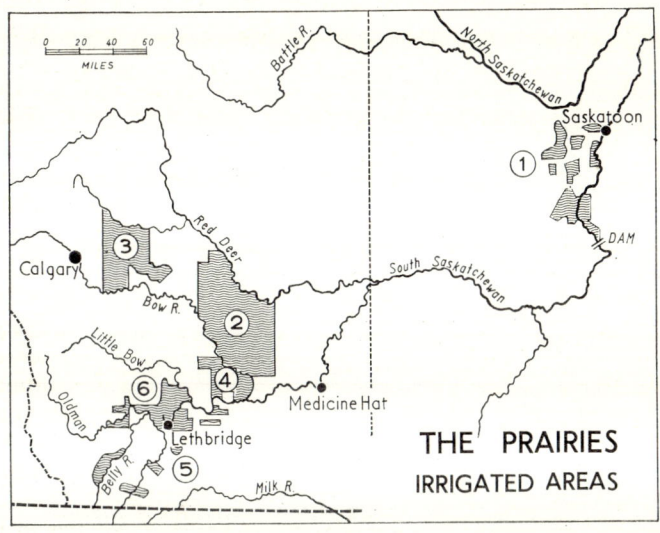

Fig. 118.

1. South Saskatchewan Irrigation Project   500,000 acres
2. Eastern Irrigation District   250,000 ,,
3. Western Irrigation District   50,000 ,,
4. Canada Land   130,000 ,,
5. Lethbridge District   100,000 ,,
6. Lethbridge Northern District   100,000 ,,

Industries and Towns

The Prairies are still primarily agricultural, although industry is becoming increasingly important. The value of manufactures of all three provinces is only one-seventh of that of Ontario. Most of the manufacturing takes the form of processing local materials, and there are several flour mills, meat-packing plants, canneries, and oil refineries.

Coal.—There are large reserves of coal and lignite (some 98,000 million tons) in the Cretaceous and Tertiary rocks which cover an extensive area of the Prairies. The poorer coal, together with lignite is found in Saskatchewan where Estevan is the main mining centre. Practically all the output is absorbed by a local steam electricity plant. Farther west the quality of the coal improves and in the Alberta foothills, where folding has occurred, anthracite is found, as at Banff. Mining is confined to a few sites only, *e.g.* Lethbridge, Edmonton, and Drumheller on the plains and Crow's Nest Pass in the Rockies (Fig. 119). At Edmonton, the coal-bearing formations are over 1,000 ft thick with fourteen seams having an aggregate thickness of 60 ft. At Crow's Nest Pass, six seams with 57 ft of coal are found in 277 ft of coal measures.

Production has never been large and was mainly used to supply the railways with fuel. Now, diesel engines have completely replaced steam locomotives. The abundance of oil and gas locally, too, has led to a decline in coal production. A major outlet in recent years has been Japan, which ships quantities of coking coal from Crow's Nest Pass and Fernie, just across the border in British Columbia. The federal government assists the cost of transport to Vancouver at the rate of $5 per ton.

Oil and Gas.—It is only in the last decade that Canada has become one of the main oil-producing countries in the world. Oil was first discovered in the Turner Valley, twenty-five miles south-west of Calgary, in 1914. Other small fields were tapped in the inter-war years but production remained small.

The present boom started with the discovery, in 1947, of large reserves at Leduc, twenty miles south-west of Edmonton. The successful strike followed 123 unsuccessful bores which cost the exploring company $23 million. In the following years several new fields were brought into production, the two main ones being Pembina and Redwater (Fig. 119). There are over 14,000 wells in Canada, of which about 10,000 are in Alberta (spread over sixty producing fields). This province accounts for 66 per cent. of the Canadian oil output, and Saskatchewan for 28 per cent.

Refineries have been built at Calgary, Edmonton, Winnipeg, Regina (137,000), and Moose Jaw (35,000). Some oil is piped over 2,000 miles (partly through U.S.A. territory) to refineries at Sarnia, Toronto, and Montreal; some goes 700 miles by trans-mountain pipeline to Vancouver.

Often associated with oil, but sometimes found in separate fields, is natural gas. Alberta produces 80 per cent. of the total and British Columbia and Saskatchewan account for practically all the rest. This, too, is piped to eastern Canada (as far as Montreal), and westwards to Vancouver and the Pacific states of the U.S.A. About one-third of the natural gas is exported to the U.S.A. at

OIL AND NATURAL GAS

present and the Canadian Government has recently approved the export of much larger quantities over the next twenty-five years (an average of 261,000 million cu. ft annually; the 1966 production was 1,100,000 million cu. ft, equivalent to 45 million tons of coal). In 1961 a 1,100-mile pipeline between Alberta and California was completed. Natural gas supplies about 15 per cent. of Canada's energy.

Canada is the third largest consumer of oil in the world and production is not yet sufficient to meet needs. The huge reserves are sufficient for this purpose, but these are located in the western

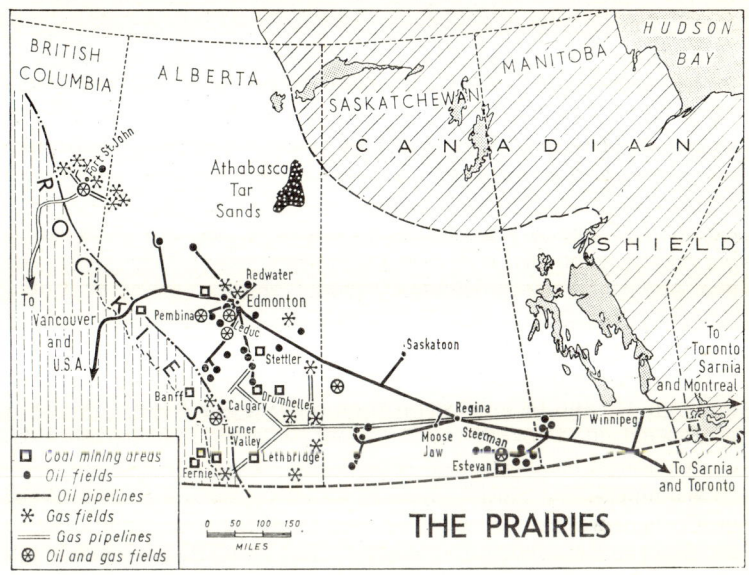

Fig. 119.

half of the country, while much of the refining capacity is in the east (*e.g.* at Montreal and Halifax). For these refineries it is cheaper to ship crude oil from Venezuela or the Middle East than to transport it from the Prairies. In 1966, 350 million barrels of oil were produced in Canada. One-third of the output was exported (to U.S.A.); 40 per cent. of the oil used in Canada is imported. The aim of the Canadian Government is to increase home production and to achieve this it is prepared to place restrictions on imports.

An additional source of oil is the Athabasca tar sands along the lower Athabasca River around Bitumount (Fig. 119). The oil-impregnated sands, which also contain sulphur and various metals, are about 200 ft thick and cover an area estimated at between 10,000 and 30,000 square miles. Their existence was first recorded in 1778 by a traveller who noticed the oil oozing into the rivers and saw Indians using it to waterproof their canoes. Some oil has been produced experimentally, but so far no means has been found of extracting it economically.

A recently exploited source of wealth is potash. Underlying an area of about 100,000 square miles in Saskatchewan are thick beds of rich (about 25 per cent.) K_2O, which dip gently towards the south-west. Mining takes place near Esterhazy, Saskatoon, and Lanigan, and new mines are planned. Production amounts to about 15 per cent. of the world total.

Winnipeg (510,000).—This city is the largest and oldest of the Prairie settlements. A French post, Fort Rouge, was erected at the confluence of the Red and Assiniboine Rivers in 1738, on a site which was, and still is, exposed to flooding. This early settlement served as a centre of the fur trade and it was the scene of open and bitter rivalry between Hudson's Bay Company and the North West Company. The city assumed its present name in 1870 when it became the capital of the newly-created province of Manitoba. At this time it had 200 inhabitants. It was a meeting point of trails— otherwise a trading post would never have been established there— and its function as a route centre was confirmed during the railway age. As Winnipeg lies in the narrow gap between Lake Winnipeg on the north and the 49th Parallel on the south, it became the point of concentration for all traffic to and from western Canada. Its description as the "Gateway to the West" is not exaggerated.

Winnipeg is primarily a market which operates to exchange the products of western Canada with the rest of the world, but it is also an important manufacturing centre. The agricultural produce has given rise to food processing industries, while the proximity of oil and gas (from the Prairies), coal (from the U.S.A.), and hydro-electricity (from the Winnipeg and Nelson Rivers) means that there is ample power for consumer industries. There are important printing and clothing factories, and along the railway marshalling yards are rolling stock works. The three oil refineries at Winnipeg can handle about 30,000 barrels daily.

Edmonton (420,000).—If Winnipeg is the "Gateway to the West", Edmonton is the "Gateway to the North". It extends along the North Saskatchewan River, although buildings tend to avoid the flood plain which lies entrenched 150 ft below the level wooded prairie. Like almost all the other major cities of Canada, it originated as a fur-post. Its growth from 1808 until the twentieth century

Above: Winter at Churchill. Hudson Bay is frozen for nine months of the year. Note the elevator and loading bins, the ice-bound ships and the very long shadows. (*National Film Board of Canada.*)

Below: The subdued surface of the Canadian Shield in northern Saskatchewan with Lefty's Falls in the foreground. (*Saskatchewan Government Photo.*)

Above: Hereford steers on their way to summer pasture ford the Milk River in southern Alberta. (*National Film Board of Canada.*)

Below: Apple orchards in the Okanagan Valley, British Columbia. Note the crops between the rows of fruit trees and the river terraces. (*Canadian Pacific.*)

was slow, for it was not on the route of the C.P.R. and was served only by ox-cart and a steamer service on the North Saskatchewan. The arrival of the railway in 1891 led to increased settlement in the surrounding area. To-day, Edmonton is served by eight railroads. It became a jumping off point first for the Peace River district and later for the Yukon to which it was linked by the Alaska Highway. It became the provincial capital in 1905 and now, with its rich oil and gas fields, its coal seams which are exposed in the valley sides, and its developing food-processing and chemical industries, it is one of the most rapidly growing cities of the dominion. The oil refineries, petro-chemical plants, steel, and cement works are located on the eastern side of the town.

Calgary (355,000).—Calgary lies where the Prairies meet the Rocky Mountain foothills. The original site of the settlement was on a flat terrace at the confluence of the Bow, Elbow, and Nose rivers. West of the city is the Kicking Horse Pass through which the railway runs to Vancouver. Calgary is not as old as Edmonton. It was founded as a police post in 1875 but its growth was rapid, especially after 1883, the year in which the C.P.R. arrived. It became the centre for the ranches, wheat farms, and irrigation districts round about. The discovery of oil in the Turner Valley in 1914 made Calgary the oil centre of Canada, a position it has now lost to Edmonton. Coal is available nearby. In and around the city are over 300 factories, its industries including oil-refining, meat-packing, flour-milling, railway-engineering, and the manufacture of chemicals.

The Prairies and the Great Plains

In many ways the Prairies resemble the adjacent lands south of the 49th Parallel, but there are some significant differences.

1. The growing season is shorter in the north, and low temperatures and the shortness of the growing season become as important for the farmer as low rainfall. In Canada the spread of wheat cultivation was somewhat retarded until new, quick-maturing varieties were introduced. The frontier in Canada is to the north, and not, as in the U.S.A. to the west.

2. The Prairies were opened to settlement much later than the northern plains of the U.S.A. and some of the mistakes made south of the border were avoided in Canada; occupation of the land was more orderly and less experimental for a technique of pioneering dry and treeless areas had already been developed.

3. Whereas the frontier moved across the U.S.A. without a break and there was a continuous settled area immediately behind the pioneering zone, the frontier in Canada leapt across the barren Shield. Prairie settlers were isolated from the occupied areas in the east by a large expanse of uninhabited forest and waste. The existence of this negative area represents a costly lengthening of the export route, for the railways pick up little traffic or freight across the southern stretches of the Shield. The sense of isolation experienced by Prairie settlements in the past encouraged political fission, a tendency which was dispelled by the arrival of the transcontinental railway. To-day, this isolation is encouraging the development of manufacturing.

4. Because it is a more compact unit and also, perhaps, because it acts as a base for the human attack on the Northlands, the Prairie region is a more "positive" and coherent area than the Great Plains, which, in some respects, is a mere fringe of the more densely populated and developed eastern U.S.A.

5. The different economic settings must also be noted. The U.S.A. is much more densely populated and industrialised than Canada. Agricultural produce from the Great Plains is absorbed mainly by the home market; any surpluses are relatively small and agricultural aid from government is lavish. The sparse population of Canada cannot absorb all the produce of the Prairies, an outlet for which must be sought in world markets which are notoriously unstable. The farmers are cushioned against economic disaster but they cannot hope for the benefits their neighbours in the U.S.A. enjoy.

CHAPTER XVII

BRITISH COLUMBIA

British Columbia is a province of marked geographical contrasts. Its complicated relief features include lofty and rugged mountains, open plateaus, narrow trenches, and steep-walled fiords. The luxuriant forests of the mild and humid coast are very different from the semi-desert vegetation of the dry interior valleys or the alpine flora on the higher ranges. These changes of vegetation are

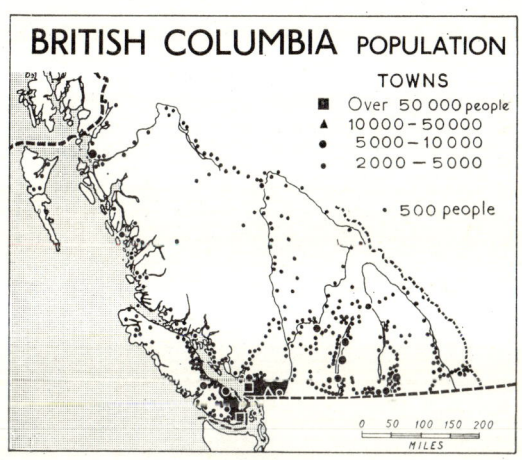

Fig. 120.
Note the concentration of population in the lowlands of the south-west and in the interior valleys of the south.

a reflection of variations in climate. The greatest precipitation in Canada is experienced in British Columbia and also the lowest.

These physical contrasts help to explain much about the nature and location of agriculture and other primary industries, and the distribution of population. The average density is four people per square mile, but this figure is meaningless for three-quarters of the population live within ninety miles of Vancouver on a mere fraction of the total area (Fig. 120). The occupied area is about 7,000 square miles out of a total area of 360,000 square miles.

Over 90 per cent. of the province is too high, steep, or rocky for farming or close settlement, but about one-third has, and is capable of sustaining, commercial forest. The geological structure is favourable to the occurrence of a wide variety of minerals. Economic development is handicapped not only by physical conditions but also by the province's location on the western margin of the country where it is separated by long distances and high mountains from the densely populated areas in the east. British Columbia's outlook on the Pacific could be an asset, but trade with Asian countries has never been large and most of the shipping is directed through the Panama Canal to Atlantic ports. The lack of a large local population and the distance from the main markets of eastern Canada has retarded the growth of manufacturing. Only those products which can bear relatively high transport costs are shipped out of the region.

There are many similarities between British Columbia and the states of the Pacific North-west in the U.S.A. Both have similar environments and resources, and both suffer by their position on the periphery of the continent. The parallels are so close that many writers are tempted to think that, in its main essentials, the growth of British Columbia will faithfully mirror that of the more fully developed states south of the 49th Parallel.

Physical Features

The relief consists of a number of mountain ranges trending from north-west to south-east, and separated by plateaus and trenches. In the extreme north-east and covering about one-tenth of the provincial area is a portion of the central plains (Fig. 121).

The Island Ranges.—These are similar in character and build to the Coast Ranges of the U.S.A., but in Canada they are broken and partially submerged. The upper parts form the line of islands that lies off the coast. There are some areas of intrusive rocks dating from Jurassic times, but the uplands consist mainly of metamorphic rock and have rounded summits. On Vancouver Island, the mountains rise steeply from the rocky, inhospitable coastline to reach heights of 7,000 ft. Towards the north-west elevations diminish and in the Queen Charlotte Islands no summit rises above 4,000 ft. The mountains take the form of individual blocks, separated by narrow valleys and dropping precipitously on the Pacific side to a rocky and irregular shore.

The Coastal Trench.—The off-shore islands are separated from the mainland by a structural depression which is a continuation northwards of that occupied by the Sacramento and San Joaquin rivers in California and the Willamette and Cowlitz rivers in Washington and Oregon. North of Puget Sound most of the trench is

PHYSICAL FEATURES

submerged, but there are emerged portions on the eastern side of Vancouver Island, in the lower Fraser Valley, and on north-eastern Graham Island.

On Vancouver Island the lowlands have an average width of eight miles but are rarely continuous and take the form of small

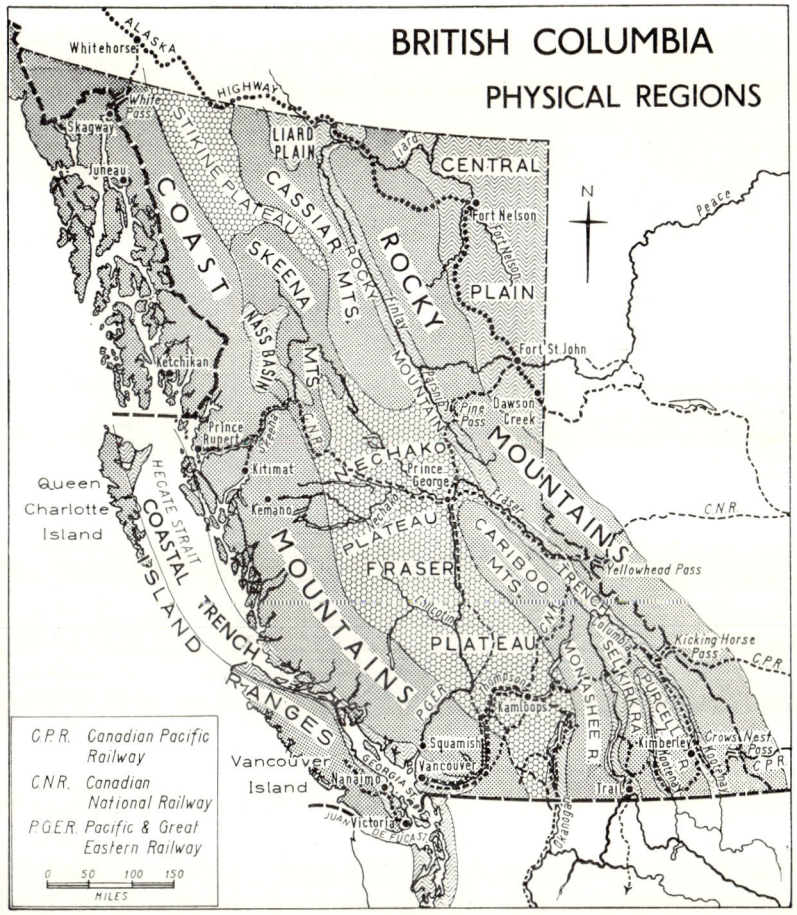

Fig. 121.

basins separated by eastward-projecting spurs of the Island Ranges. The lower Fraser Valley is a triangular area less than 1,000 ft in elevation and consisting mainly of the recent river delta which is below 50 ft, and an older raised delta or terrace at an elevation of

200 ft. The level plain of north-eastern Graham Island covers an area of 2,000 square miles. It is generally below 200 ft, but is interrupted by a few residual volcanic hills.

The Coast Mountains.—South of the Fraser River, these mountains consist of three ranges, the innermost of which rises to an elevation of 8,000 ft and is the highest. They are known as the Cascades and are a continuation northwards of the ranges of the same name in the U.S.A. North of the Fraser they are known as the Coast Mountains (but are not connected in any way with the Coast Ranges of the U.S.A.). They are a solid wall of granite with large areas over 10,000 ft and peaks rising to over 13,000 ft. The lowest area is the Skeena Saddle which is only 4,000 ft above sea level. Here, the Skeena River has cut a deep valley. The whole mountain mass has been greatly dissected by the rivers which are generally transverse to the trend of the ranges and are incised in deep, canyon-like valleys. The Fraser and Skeena Valleys are important because they are the means by which communications link the coast and the interior.

Fiords indent the coastline: they vary in width from one to three miles and some penetrate as much as eighty miles inland. They bear witness to the great amount of erosion performed by mountain glaciers during the Ice Age. To-day, there are still permanent ice-fields on the higher parts in the north.

The Interior Uplands.—Lying between the Coast Mountains and the Rockies is a region of extremely diversified topography. The Interior Uplands comprise a series of plateaus, basins, and mountain ranges (Fig. 121).

The plateaus are underlain by metamorphic rocks which usually give subdued relief features, but in places there is a superficial cover of lavas or sedimentary rocks. In the Nechako Plateau which has a general elevation of about 2,500 ft large sections were flooded by glacial and post-glacial lakes and are now covered by thick deposits of lacustrine clays. The Fraser Plateau is higher, rising to 6,000 ft in the south. It is greatly dissected and the Fraser River is entrenched 4,000 ft below the plateau surface between Lillooet and Hope.

Rising above the plateaus are several mountain ranges formed mainly of granite or of lavas. These include the Cassiar and Skeena mountains in the north and the Cariboo Mountains, Monashee, Selkirk, and Purcell ranges in the south-east. All have a north-west to south-east trend. The southern ranges, where some peaks exceed 10,000 ft, are separated from one another by deep structural trenches which are occupied by rivers and lakes. Along the sides of these depressions are series of terraces: there are six on each side of the Okanagan Valley. They are thought to have been formed during the closing stages of the Ice Age when the glaciers were waning. Detritus from the exposed hillsides collected along the edges of the valley glaciers and formed terraces. As the ice retreated to lower levels, so successive terraces were formed. The highest terraces therefore are the oldest.

The Rocky Mountain Trench.—This is one of the most remarkable structural features of the Cordilleran system. The detailed geology is not yet fully known for till covers the bedrock to a considerable depth. It runs parallel to and immediately west of the Rocky Mountains for a distance of 1,000 miles from Lake Flathead (Montana) to the Liard Plains. The width varies from two to ten miles and the general height is above 2,000 ft with the mountains rising 6,000 ft or more very steeply on either side. For almost its entire length it carries rivers: those in the north eventually break through the Rockies into the central lowlands and drain to Hudson Bay or the Arctic Ocean; those in the south eventually turn west to flow across the Interior Uplands to the Pacific. From north to south there are the Liard and its tributary the Kechika, the Finlay and Parsnip, both of which are tributaries of the Peace River, the upper Fraser, the upper Columbia, and the Kootenay. The watersheds are insignificant features. Only two miles separate the Kootenay from the head of the Columbia at Canal Flat. An early canal built across the intervening gravel flat has long been disused.

Railways have made use of this lowland corridor. The two C.P.R. lines which cross the Rockies by the Kicking Horse and Crow's Nest passes are linked by a branch line running along the trench. The C.N.R. line, after crossing the Yellowhead Pass follows the Fraser along the trench for over 200 miles before turning west to Prince George (and then Prince Rupert or Vancouver).

The Rocky Mountains.—East of the great trench lie the Rockies which form the eastern rampart of the cordilleras. They extend from the 49th Parallel to the Liard Valley and form a belt of extremely rugged country, varying in width from twenty-five to seventy-five miles, and rising to over 10,000 ft in several places. Large glaciers are conspicuous especially between Banff and Jasper where the Columbia ice-field is situated (see plate facing p. 32.)

The Rockies were built by strong compressive forces which originated to the west of the Rocky Mountain Trench. Pre-Cambrian, Palaeozoic, and Mesozoic sediments were severely folded and faulted, and great thrust faults carried the contorted sediments over the soft, little-disturbed Cretaceous shales of the interior plains. Subsequent erosion has created in most places a bold, eastward-facing escarpment. In some of the synclines coal-bearing rocks have been preserved, especially in the south near Crow's Nest Pass, and in one or two locations, the intense folding has changed the coal to anthracite. Very little igneous activity accompanied the earth movements and in consequence the Rockies have few metallic minerals; these are found associated with the igneous intrusions of the Coast Mountains and the Interior Uplands.

There are several passageways through the Rockies. In the north the continental divide lies well to the west of the mountains across the Interior Uplands and the Rockies are breached by both the Liard and Peace rivers. In the south, where the divide follows the crest, there are no river gaps but four narrow passes, all of which are followed by railways (Fig. 121). These are Pine Pass, 2,850 ft, Yellowhead Pass, 3,700 ft, Kicking Horse Pass, 5,388 ft, and Crow's Nest Pass, 4,459 ft.

Climate and Vegetation

The climate of British Columbia is extremely diversified, more so than any other province in Canada (Fig. 122). Not only is there regional diversity because of the latitudinal spread of the province and the trend of the mountains athwart the prevailing westerly winds, but also there are marked local variations because of the mountainous nature of the land. Climatic differences found in a few thousand feet on a mountain slope may be as great as those extending hundreds of miles latitudinally. Depending upon exposure to sun and prevailing winds, two slopes of one mountain may exhibit very different climatic characteristics at comparable elevations.

The Coast.—The coastal belt is characterised by mild and very wet winters and cool, foggy summers. Annual precipitation is heavy and many stations record over 100 in. Henderson Lake has experienced over 250 in. in several years. Most of the rain falls in autumn and winter but normally there is no deficiency of moisture in summer. Over the Insular and Coast mountains, much of the precipitation is in the form of snow and in some years as much as 30 ft of snow has accumulated on protected slopes by the end of winter.

The average January sea level temperatures are usually above freezing point and the annual temperature range is small. Only in exceptional circumstances does continental Polar air invade

CLIMATE

this region and displace the mild, moist maritime Polar air from the Pacific. Average July temperatures are below 60° F. (*16° C.*), except in certain sheltered eastern lowlands where they may be two or three degrees higher. Sea fog and low stratus clouds are common in summer.

The Victoria-Nanaimo Lowlands on the leeward side of Vancouver Island have smaller amounts of precipitation than are

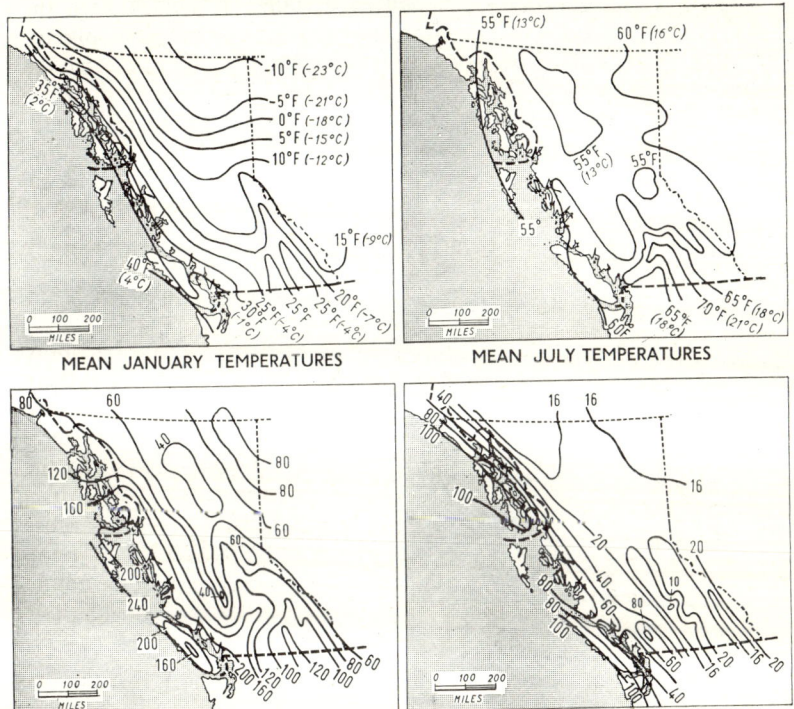

Fig. 122.

experienced elsewhere along the coast. Victoria has 30 in. and Vancouver 60 in. (Fig. 123). There is a water deficiency of 5 to 10 in. during the summer months (p. 41). Temperatures are similar to those experienced along other parts of the coast but the summers are slightly warmer and sunnier. The figures for Vancouver are tabulated below and may be compared with those for Victoria on p. 45.

Vancouver 49° N. 45 ft		J.	F.	M.	A.	M.	J.	J.	A.	S.	O.	N.	D.	Total
	°F.	36	38	42	47	54	59	63	62	56	49	48	43	—
	°C.	2	3	6	8	12	15	17	17	13	9	9	6	—
	in.	8·6	6·1	5·3	3·3	3·0	2·7	1·3	1·7	4·1	5·9	10·0	7·8	59·8

Under these climatic conditions the forest is dense and luxuriant. There are few deciduous trees but their number is increasing for they tend to colonise cut-over areas. Of the conifers, which predominate, western hemlock and red cedar are the most numerous species (Fig. 124). They thrive best in the wettest areas where they reach heights of 150 ft or more. Douglas fir tends to occupy drier areas where some specimens attain a height of 250 ft and have a diameter of 9 ft. On the Queen Charlotte Islands Douglas fir is replaced by Sitka spruce and the northern limit of red cedar lies in the southern part of the Alaska Panhandle. The tree line

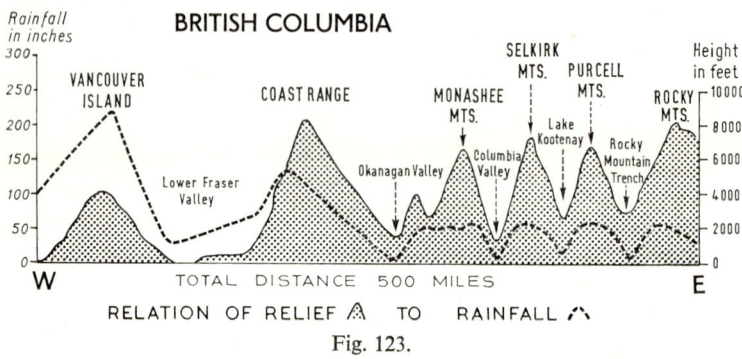

Fig. 123.

declines only very gradually from 5,000 ft in the south to 4,000 ft in the Queen Charlotte Islands. Above the forest limit is tundra and higher still permanent snow.

The Interior.—The interior is cut off from marine influences by the Coast Mountains and its climate has continental traits. Even so, it is less extreme than the climate of the Prairies. Winter temperatures are from 10 F.° to 20 F.° (*6 C.° to 11 C.°*) lower than on the coast. The Kootenay valleys experience a mean January temperature of about 23° F. (*— 5° C.*), while in the northern parts of the plateaus figures are under 0° F. (*— 18° C.*). The mean July temperatures in the south rise to over 70° F. (*21° C.*) with maximum readings of over 100° F. (*38° C.*) on some days. In the north they rarely exceed 60° F. (*16° C.*).

Precipitation on the lee side of mountains and in the valleys is slight but windward slopes usually have totals exceeding 40 in. (Fig. 123). The southern valleys experience less than 15 in. and in some areas less than 10 in. There is a tendency for most rain to fall in summer, a characteristic of continental climates, but some places show a double maximum.

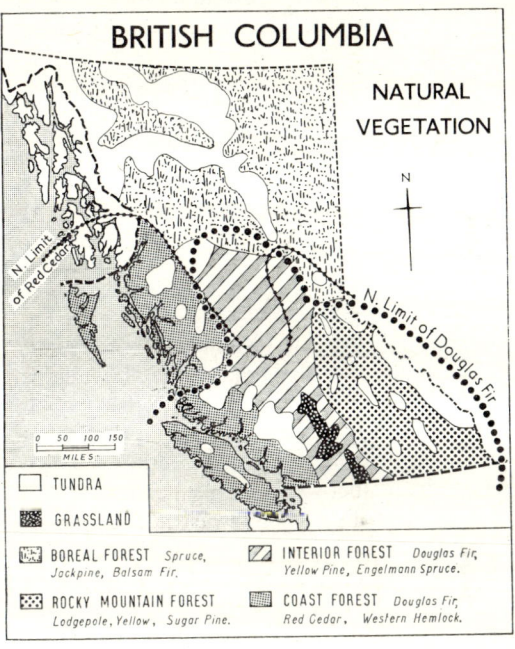

Fig. 124.

		J.	F.	M.	A.	M.	J.	J.	A.	S.	O.	N.	D.	Total
Kamloops 51° N. 1,160 ft	°F.	23	26	38	50	58	64	70	68	58	45	35	28	—
	°C.	*−5*	*−3*	*3*	*10*	*14*	*18*	*21*	*20*	*14*	*7*	*2*	*−2*	—
	in.	1·0	0·8	0·3	0·4	0·9	1·2	1·1	1·1	0·8	0·6	1·0	0·9	10·1

Precipitation increases slightly towards the north (Fig. 122) and is more effective there because of the less intense evaporation. Parts of the Nechako Plateau are among the best-watered areas of the interior, for the low Skeena Saddle in the Coast Mountains offers an easy passage to the moisture-laden Pacific air.

Where the precipitation exceeds 12 in. there is generally a cover of forest, except on the higher peaks which have tundra vegetation. The forest is densest on the better-watered ranges and comprises stands of Douglas fir, red cedar, and western hemlock. On the drier lowlands the forest is open and park-like; ponderosa pine (western yellow pine) and lodgepole pine are, with Douglas fir, the dominant species. At higher elevations these are replaced by Engelmann spruce and alpine fir. The trees decrease in size and the timber line becomes lower as one goes northwards and the northern part of British Columbia has true boreal forest with white spruce, balsam fir, and jack pine.

In the southern valleys and basins where the rainfall is under 12 in. the forest or woodland is replaced by natural grassland. Indeed, in the Okanagan Valley and the Thompson Valley, below Kamloops, the bluebunch wheat grass and spear grass is interspersed with desert vegetation consisting of sagebrush and cactus.

Human Geography—General Features

The development of British Columbia did not really start until 1858 when placer gold was discovered in the alluvial deposits of the Fraser Valley near Hope. Before this time fur-trapping and seal fishing had been the occupations of the handful of settlers who had first arrived at the end of the eighteenth century. The coast, which was the scene of rivalry between Spanish, Russian, American, and British navigators and fishermen, was not accurately surveyed until 1793.

Gold mining enjoyed only a brief spell of prosperity; it declined after 1863 and in its wake came the expansion of lumbering, salmon fishing, farming, and the mining of base metals. The two original colonies on Vancouver Island and the mainland were united in 1866, and five years later British Columbia joined the dominion on the understanding that a railway would be constructed to link the Pacific coast with eastern Canada. This was completed in 1885 and marked another milestone in the development of the province. The population jumped from 50,000 in 1881 to almost 400,000 in 1911 and to 1,600,000 in 1961. During the last forty years the population has increased more rapidly than in any other Canadian province.

The following table of selected statistics summarises the economic geography of British Columbia and forms the basis for a brief examination of the main characteristics of the human geography.

Table 26
British Columbia

		As Percentage of Canada
Area	360,000 square miles	10
Population (1968)	1,900,000	9
Area in Farms (1961)	4,500,000 acres	2½
Improved Farmland (1961)	1,300,000 acres	1
Cash Income from Sale of Farm Products (1967)	$170,000,000	4½
Mineral Production (1967)	$392,000,000	7½
Products of Fisheries (1965)	$98,000,000	33
Products of Saw Mills (1964)	$578,000,000	68
Products of Pulp and Paper Mills (1964)	$440,000,000	22
Selling Value of all Manufactures (1967)	$3,086,000,000	10
Hydro-electricity (1964)—		
Potential at six-month flow	19,400,000 h.p.	30
Developed	3,700,000 h.p.	14

Forestry

From the figures given above it is apparent that much of the wealth of British Columbia is derived from its forests. About half the working population depends directly or indirectly upon the forest resources. About 70 per cent. of the province is forested but only half of this area is considered to be of commercial value and much of it is, under present conditions, virtually inaccessible.

The main lumbering areas lie near the coast for here the trees reach their greatest size, the penetrating fiords allow easy access to the stands, and transportation is relatively simple. Logging takes place all the year round, in contrast with eastern Canada where it is a winter occupation.

The expense of hauling logs long distances has restricted the exploitation of forests on the Nechako Plateau and the interior ranges, but as the coastal forests are depleted so these areas are increasing their output, which at present amounts to 14 per cent. of the total for the province.

Douglas fir and red cedar provide strong and durable timber and account for 40 per cent. and 20 per cent. respectively of the annual cut. Western hemlock, which accounts for another 20 per cent. of the cut provides timber for certain types of constructional work, but it is not as highly prized as Douglas fir and red cedar, and much of it is cut for pulping. British Columbia cuts more timber than any other province (Table 23 on p. 326) but, in contrast with eastern Canada, only a small proportion—about 20 per cent. in fact—is destined for the pulp mills. The bulk of the timber is handled by about 1,200 saw mills which are concentrated on

Vancouver Island and around Vancouver—New Westminster on tidewater. In the interior, most saw mills and processing works are located along the railways. The largest saw mill and plywood factory in the interior is at Kelowna in the Okanagan Valley.

The pulp and paper mills absorb about 14 per cent. of the cut and, in addition, utilise the chippings and waste from the saw mills. There are 20 mills, all located on the coast within easy reach of cheap hydro-electricity (Fig. 125). The plant at Powell River is one of the largest in the world. Port Edward, near Prince Rupert, is the site of a large cellulose factory which provides the basic materials for cellophane, celluloid, plastics, and rayon.

There are two problems facing the forest industries of this region. Firstly, along the coast the annual cut exceeds replacement and the provincial government which owns 90 per cent. of the forest lands

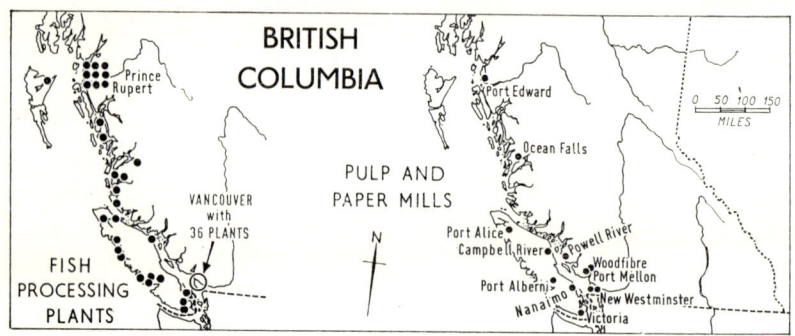

Fig. 125.

is concerned to reverse this situation. This could be done by practising selective cutting in place of clear cutting, using the interior forests in order to prolong the life of those on the coast and by increasing the amount of artificial reafforestation. Secondly, there is the problem of finding customers for the timber. To-day the U.S.A. is by far the best customer and it takes about 70 per cent. of the products. A large amount is supplied to Japan, too, but Britain, which before the war took 27 per cent. of the region's timber, now takes only 5 per cent.

Mining

Mineral production tends to fluctuate from year to year, depending upon world political and economic conditions. Industrial and trade recessions, and the discovery of rich, easily developed supplies in other parts of the world can lead to curtailed output, whereas stock-piling and industrial advances can stimulate production. It is rare, however, for all minerals to be affected adversely in any one year.

Apart from small quantities of coal which is mined in the Cretaceous rocks near Fernie and Crow's Nest Pass in the Rockies and on Vancouver Island near Nanaimo and Courtenay, asbestos, which is now coming in increasing quantities from McDame in the Cassiar Mountains, in the remote northern part of the province, and oil and gas in the Peace River District, practically all the minerals

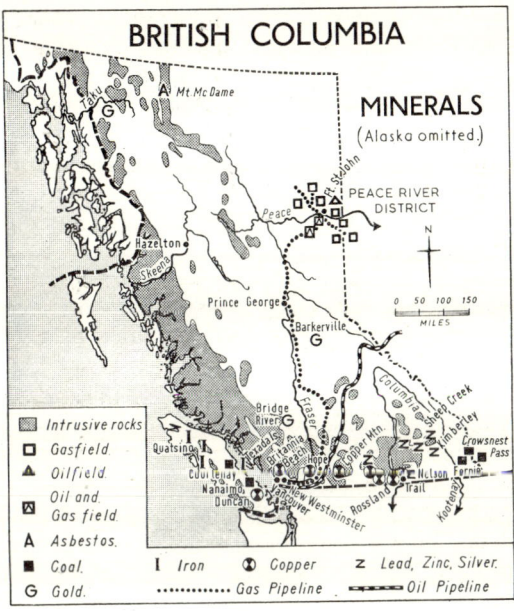

Fig. 126.

are metallic. By their nature, they are found in association with igneous and metamorphic rock and occurrences are most numerous in the Coast Mountains and the interior ranges and markedly absent in the Rockies (Fig. 126).

British Columbia produces almost all Canada's lead and about half its zinc. These metals are usually found associated with one another and with silver. Mining takes place in the Selkirk and Purcell mountains, and the largest producer is the Sullivan mine at Kimberley, which came into operation in 1923 and has, since that time, yielded a great amount of both lead and zinc. Here a tunnel is driven into the mountain side along an ore body which reaches a maximum thickness of 240 ft. The ore is crushed and then concentrated. The refining is carried out at Trail. A new iron and steel plant has been erected at Kimberley which makes use of iron recovered from the huge piles of tailings.

Gold is now of minor importance and accounts for less than 10 per cent. of British Columbia's mineral production. It was the gold rush of 1858 which first attracted miners to the region. After the deposits at Hope were exhausted the miners moved along the Cariboo Trail to Barkerville in the Cariboo Mountains. This settlement has now become a ghost town (and a tourist attraction). The most important mining areas now are at Bridge River, and Tulsequah on the Taku River in the far north.

The production of copper has declined; it is mined at Copper Mountain and Britannia Beach. Iron mining, however, is becoming increasingly important and a considerable proportion of the output is sent to Japan. The main areas of production are Quinsam Lake on Vancouver Island and Texada Island. The mining of molybdenum is becoming increasingly important.

Trail is one of the main smelting centres in Canada. It commenced operations in 1895, drawing mainly upon copper ore from Rossland, where mining has now ceased. Now it produces mainly lead and zinc with small quantities of tungsten, silver, and antimony. The installations are on a narrow terrace on the west bank of the Columbia River. From the waste gases and gangue a wide range of fertilisers and other chemicals is produced. The works derive their power from electricity plants on the Kootenay. The other large smelter in the province at Kitimat uses imported bauxite to produce aluminium (see plate opposite).

Some oil and natural gas are produced in the Peace River District, the latter moving by pipeline to Vancouver and Washington (see p. 350). Asbestos is mined at Cassiar in the north of the state.

Fishing

The income from fishing is only half that from agriculture but British Columbia is the main fishing province in Canada (Table 18, p. 277). The continental shelf is not very wide and there are no extensive banks as there are off Newfoundland or the shores of north-west Europe, but there are many inlets and sheltered waterways which provide good fishing grounds, safe harbours, and excellent sites for canneries. Halibut, which is sold fresh in eastern Canada and the U.S.A., and herring, which is canned or made into meal, are more important than cod or sole. In recent years there have

Above: The recently completed aluminium smelter at Baie Comeau on the north bank of the St Lawrence in Quebec. (*George Hunter.*)

Below: The township of Kitimat, which lies at the head of the Douglas Channel on the coast of British Columbia. Electricity for the aluminium smelter comes from Kemano fifty miles away. (*High Commissioner for Canada.*)

Above: Fort Smith on the Slave River is the effective head of navigation in the Mackenzie Basin. Note the river steamers, the Hudson's Bay Company store, and the vegetable garden. (*High Commissioner for Canada.*)

Below: Ketchikan in the Alaska Panhandle is a fishing port and a large pulp and lumber producing centre. (*U.S.I.S.*)

been increased catches of tuna. Whaling is still carried out in the waters west of Vancouver Island and in Queen Charlotte Sound.

The wealth of the fisheries, however, lies in the salmon catch which accounts for about 60 per cent. of the value of all fish landed. There are five different species, pink (or humpback) salmon, chum (or dog or keta) salmon, coho (or silver) salmon, chinook (or king or spring) salmon, and sockeye (or red or blueback) salmon. The last-named is the most prized because of its tender, red flesh. Fishing is a seasonal activity and is confined to the late spring and summer months when the mature salmon, after two to six years in the ocean, return to the rivers and coastal waters to spawn. Purse seines, gill nets, traps, and trolls are used to catch the fish as they converge on the river mouths. The main fishing areas are the Fraser River and Georgia Strait. While some salmon are sold fresh, mainly in the U.S.A., or smoked or frozen, over two-thirds of the catch is canned at the numerous canneries along the coast (Fig. 125), and sold mainly in Britain.

The salmon catch varies widely from year to year; runs appear on the Pacific coast in two and four year cycles, depending upon species. The danger of depleting stocks by over-fishing has been overcome by government intervention. An international fishing commission determines the length of the fishing season and fixes quotas. There are, however, other hazards, for with increasing industrialisation rivers are becoming polluted and dams are being erected to harness power. Fish ladders can be built around the dams, as at Bonneville in the U.S.A., but it seems that the full development of the Fraser River may be delayed because the salmon fisheries are so profitable. It was along this river that a landslip near Hell's Gate, resulting from the construction of a railway in 1913, prevented salmon reaching their spawning grounds and reduced the catches in succeeding years. Finally, in 1946, the obstruction was removed. Since then catches have been large: in 1958 over 19 million salmon returned to the upper Fraser, of which 15 million were caught.

Because British Columbia depends so much on exports, changing market conditions can affect the fishing industry. Importing countries may impose quotas or competing exporters may undercut world prices. Exports to the United Kingdom have declined since 1939 because of the post-war dollar shortage.

Agriculture

The area in farms is pitifully small and of this area, only one-quarter is actually cultivated. The terrain is extremely rugged with three-quarters of the land over 3,000 ft and there are few areas with gentle slopes and fertile soil. The climate, too, greatly restricts the extent of the farming areas. The northern parts, which have some favourable land and soils, are too cold for most types of agriculture; the western parts are too rugged and very wet; the interior areas are dry and in most parts irrigation is essential if crops are to be grown.

The most important farming area is the lower Fraser Valley which has rich, deep, alluvial soils associated with the post-glacial deltas and old lake bottoms. The very low areas, usually under 10 ft, yield heavy crops of vegetables and small fruits, when drained and dyked to prevent flooding. Most of the land is under grass which remains green throughout the year in the moist, cool climate. Alfalfa, hay, and corn (for ensilage) are grown also and are fed to a large number of dairy cattle. The milk and dairy produce find a ready market in the large settlements in the lowlands. Poultry and hogs are found on most farms, the latter feeding upon the skim milk.

This type of intensive mixed farming is also found on the eastern lowlands of Vancouver Island where the soils are generally fertile and rainfall is lower than on the mainland. In addition to specialised vegetable crops such as lettuce, celery, and potatoes, there is a large output of strawberries and loganberries. Flower seeds and bulbs are grown in the Saanich Peninsula. Together, the lower Fraser Valley and the eastern lowlands of Vancouver Island have about 35 per cent. of the cultivated land in British Columbia.

In aggregate, a relatively large proportion of the cultivated land is found in the southern valleys of the interior. Of these, the Okanagan Valley, with 15 per cent. of the province's cultivated land, is the most prosperous (Fig. 127). For a distance of 130 miles northwards from the U.S.A. border, the terraces and old deltas of whitish silt which fringe the lakes are planted with vegetables and fruit. This belt is only two miles wide in the south, but it broadens to six miles at Kelowna and to twelve miles in the north. Rainfall is slight: the southern tracts have only 10 in., but totals increase northwards. In the south, it is impossible to farm without irrigation but in the north mixed farming is possible without it. The winters are relatively mild and the long, hot, sunny growing season favours the growing of fruit and vegetables. Altogether there are about 2 million fruit trees, about half of which are apples growing mainly in the central part of the valley. Peaches and apricots which are more susceptible to frost than apples are concentrated in the south. Some irrigation water is drawn from the River

Okanagan, the remainder being led through pipes and flumes from the small mountain streams. The present trend is for farming to become more diversified; dairy farming has been introduced and vegetables and small fruits are displacing apples (see plate facing p. 353).

The other valleys are not quite so well developed. There are some irrigated tracts along the Arrow Lakes in the Columbia

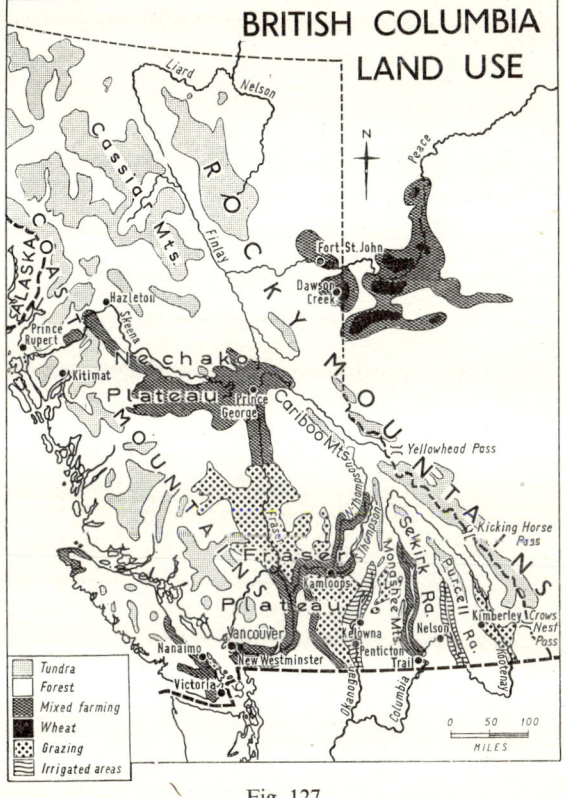

Fig. 127.

Valley and in the South Thompson Valley, but the moister climate is not so suitable for fruit-growing. The farther east one goes the less important fruit becomes and the greater the emphasis on mixed farming and grazing. In the Rocky Mountain Trench the winters are long and severe and prohibit fruit-growing, although they do not prevent the cultivation of wheat. On the fringes of the cultivated areas cattle and sheep are reared.

The main grazing area is the Fraser Plateau where the topography is rough and the rainfall is light. Both sheep and cattle are reared on the grassy or lightly forested land and are driven to the alpine pastures in summer. In winter, the herds and flocks shelter in the valleys where there are small patches of irrigated land growing fodder. Farther north, on the Nechako Plateau, the relief is more subdued and the rainfall more effective. There is in fact a danger of too much rain in late summer, and summer frosts are an additional hazard. The soils are rather thin and poor and require careful management. The Canadian National Railway opened up this area and along its course from Smithers to Prince George arose a belt of mixed farming. The low temperatures limit the crops to hay, roots, and oats which are fed to cattle. In some parts farming is still of a subsistence standard.

The largest block of cultivable land in the province lies in the Peace River District (p. 347).

Hydro-electricity

British Columbia is poorly endowed with coal (although it has more than some provinces) and the annual production amounts to only 2 million tons, but it has huge reserves of water-power, second in Canada only to those of Quebec (Table 19, p. 300). The heavy precipitation feeds a large number of swift streams which pursue tumultuous courses down the steep mountain slopes. However, run-off is extremely rapid: a less steep surface would allow more water to be stored in lakes and in the ground. Precipitation is heaviest in winter and to develop sites storage dams must be built to ensure an even flow of water. Many of the best sites are a long way from the manufacturing towns and in rugged country difficult of access. Only about one-fifth of the potential power has so far been harnessed.

The developed sites are mainly in the south, near the settled areas. There are a number of small stations on Vancouver Island but most of the plants are along the lower Fraser and the lower Kootenay. One of the largest and most recent developments is the Bridge River Scheme near Lillooet, where the plant has a capacity of 700,000 h.p. (Fig. 100). Some power passes by submarine cable from the mainland to Victoria on Vancouver Island.

Large blocks of power are available on the middle Fraser, between Prince George and Hope, on the Peace River where it breaks through the Rockies near Hudson Hope, and on the Columbia. Development of the Fraser may be delayed because of the importance of the salmon fisheries but work has started on the construction of a large dam on the Peace River at Portage Mountain, near Hudson Hope, which will produce about 2·3 million kilowatts.

For many years there have been discussions between Canada and the U.S.A. about the best way of utilising the waters of the Columbia River, which rises in the Canadian Rockies and flows 1,214 miles to the Pacific. With its large volume, fairly regular regime, relatively steep gradient, and small silt load, it is an ideal river for the development of hydro-electricity. It is already almost fully harnessed in the U.S.A. and by an agreement signed in 1964, Canada and the U.S.A. are to co-operate and jointly finance the development of the Canadian section of the river. Three large reservoirs will be built (at Mica Creek, the outlet of the Arrow Lakes, and on the River Kootenay), which will double the present storage capacity of 13 million acre-feet, and regulate the flow through the U.S.A., thus permitting extra electricity to be produced at the eleven main dams. New dams are to be built in Canada at Mica Creek, Downie Creek, Revelstoke Canyon, and Murphy, which will produce a total of about 4·5 million kWs. of electricity. The payment that the U.S.A. will make to Canada for the extra power to be produced at its own dams, and for the benefits of additional flood control, will partially pay for the construction of the reservoirs and dams north of the 49th Parallel. Work started in 1964 and the three reservoirs are expected to be completed by the early nineteen-seventies. The power surplus to British Columbia's requirements is expected to be sold to the U.S.A. and may be used in California (see p. 260). There can be no doubt that the Columbia River Project will confer enormous benefits on both countries.

The largest hydro-electric plant in British Columbia is at Kemano, which lies well away from the main settled area. A large dam, the Kenney Dam, was constructed across the Nechako River and from the head of the 150-mile reservoir it created, a ten-mile tunnel was driven through the Coast Mountains to an underground power house at Kemano. The effective head of water is 2,600 ft and over 1 million h.p. is produced. When the scheme is finally completed, the capacity of the power station will be $2\frac{1}{2}$ million h.p. The electricity is sent overland for fifty miles to Kitimat, now a town of 10,000 inhabitants at the head of the Douglas Channel, where a large aluminium smelter has been in operation since 1954. It uses processed bauxite from Jamaica and produces about 200,000 tons of aluminium annually. The final capacity is expected to be 300,000 tons (see plate facing p. 368). A similar scheme now mooted would involve the diverting of water from the Teslin and Atlin rivers, both tributaries of the Yukon, into the River Taku to provide power for a smelter at Tulsequah.

These latest developments and plans seem to suggest that the development of the northern part of the province, as in the Canadian Shield, is likely to proceed under the aegis of the mining companies and smelting corporations.

Industries and Towns

Manufacturing is not strongly developed in British Columbia; most of it is concerned with the processing of primary products (timber, fish, minerals, and foodstuffs). There are about 100,000 employees in manufacturing industries and almost half of these are in factories or mills turning out wood products or pulp and paper.

The western market is too small for the development of large-scale consumer industries, and the distance from the main settled area of Canada (it is over 2,500 miles to the Laurentian Lowlands) means that western manufacturers cannot compete there, except in products peculiar to the west, because of high transportation costs.

Vancouver (384,000).—Most of the manufacturing is in and around Vancouver and New Westminster (38,000). The whole metropolitan district has a population of over 940,000. The core of Vancouver, where the settlement first developed less than 100 years ago, is a silt ridge rising 120 ft above sea level between Burrard Inlet on the north and False Creek on the south (Fig. 128). Burrard Creek is a fiord backed on the north side by the high Coast Mountains. It provides a fine, ice-free, sheltered harbour, and its southern shores are lined with docks capable of accommodating fifty-two ocean-going liners (p. 305). Here, too, are the grain elevators which handle the wheat from the Prairies, and the oil refineries which receive oil from Alberta. The oil pipeline from Alberta and the gas pipeline from the Peace River District both terminate here.

A smaller industrial section fringes False Creek, where the saw mills and timber works are mostly to be found. Other industries in Vancouver include meat-packing, food processing, sheet metal production, and a little shipbuilding. Recently, manufacturing has spread to the banks of the Fraser River and a new industrial estate on Annacis Island has factories belonging to twenty different companies. This is an area of deltaic alluvium which has hitherto been avoided by industries.

Vancouver was the obvious choice as the terminus of the trans-continental railways and consequently as the outlet for the Prairies. It occupied a firm site, north of the marshy delta and could make use of the Fraser Valley as a routeway to the interior. It possessed a fine harbour opening on to the Pacific and much of its early trade was with the Orient. The opening of the Panama Canal permitted Vancouver to compete more easily in European markets and was a fillip to trade. Exports continue to consist mainly of primary goods such as lumber and wheat but large quantities of pulp and paper are also exported. Imports include rubber, aluminium ore, sugar, and beverages. The present tendency is for Vancouver to tap more and more of the products of the interior; its hinterland is increasing in area and importance. Around the city are concen-

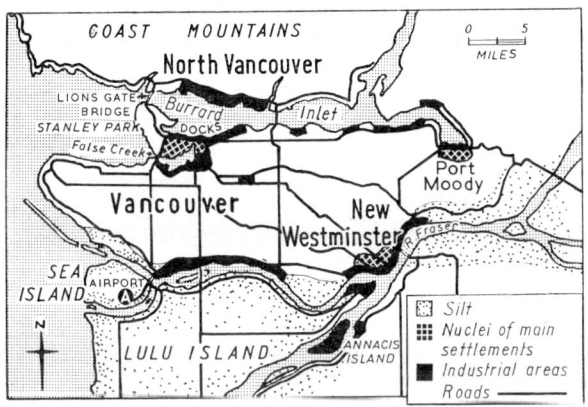

Fig. 128.

trated most of the farming, fishing, lumbering, and manufacturing in British Columbia.

Other Cities.—Apart from Greater Vancouver, cities are small and function as market or industrial towns. Victoria (173,000), the second largest settlement, has a small, sheltered harbour and is a minor port with shipyards, lumber mills, machine shops, and a paint factory. Prince Rupert (12,000) was founded in 1906 on Kaien Island as the future terminus of the C.N.R. which arrived there in 1913. The site was laid out to accommodate a population of 50,000. It is a port of call for ships going to Alaska and the Orient, and it has a grain elevator and fish processing plants. Kitimat (10,000) which was also planned for 50,000 inhabitants is the site of a new aluminium smelter. It is joined to the main C.N.R. line by a branch line forty miles long.

Nanaimo (14,000) on Vancouver Island, Penticton (14,000), Prince George (14,000), Kelowna (13,000), Kamloops (10,000), and Vernon (10,000) are all market centres for surrounding agricultural areas and have industries connected with foodstuffs and timber. Trail (11,000) is a metal refining town and owes its importance to the nearby deposits of lead, zinc, and copper.

CHAPTER XVIII

THE NORTHLANDS

This region occupies a large part of North America. Politically, it includes Alaska and the Yukon, and the North-west Territories (Mackenzie, Keewatin, and Franklin) which lie north of the 60th Parallel. Geographically, however, it is more extensive than this and may be defined as (*a*) all those areas which lie north of the limit of continuous settlement, (*b*) all those areas north of the southern limit of discontinuous permafrost (Fig. 129), or (*c*) the area embracing the Tundra and Sub-Arctic Forest (Fig. 25)—*i.e.* the Sub-Arctic

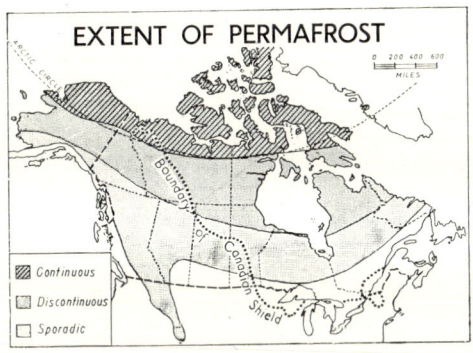

Fig. 129.

region, which has less than four months of the year with temperatures over 50° F. (*10° C.*), and the Arctic region, which lies north of the July isotherm of 50° F. (*10° C.*) and thus has no month reaching this temperature. Using any one of these criteria, the Northlands is seen to include practically all Labrador and the northern parts of Quebec, Ontario, Manitoba, Saskatchewan, Alberta, and British Columbia, as well as the territories mentioned above.

The outstanding characteristic of the region is its coldness. Winters are long, dark, and severe practically everywhere except along the southern coasts of Alaska, while summers are short and generally cool, although the hours of daylight are long and daily maximum temperatures may be quite high. Frost is liable to occur even in the summer months. At Fort Smith, the last frost of spring has never been earlier than mid-May and the first frost of autumn has never been later than the end of September. It is not uncommon, however, for the last frost of spring and the earliest frost of autumn both to occur in July. Because of the cold, all the northern areas and most of those in the south are regions of permafrost (p. 57).

A distinction can be made between the cordilleran area in the west and the lower area in the east. Each of these two major divisions can be subdivided: the former into Alaska and the Canadian North-west, and the latter into the Arctic Archipelago and the Canadian Shield. The last-named area has already been described in Chapter XV.

Alaska

Alaska was purchased by the U.S.A. from Russia in 1867 for $7,200,000. At this time the population consisted of a few Eskimos, Aleuts, and Indians, and a handful of Russian fur traders and fishers who lived in scattered posts such as Sitka and Kodiak. There was much objection to the acquisition, and for some time the territory was regarded as an expensive and burdensome addition to the Union. After three decades of oblivion came an influx of settlers in search of gold, drawn thither by news of the Klondike discovery in the neighbouring Yukon. Gold-mining in Alaska has not been as important or as spectacular as in the Yukon. Nevertheless, the value of gold produced has paid for the territory a hundred times over, and the present annual output, which is less than it was formerly, exceeds the original purchase price.

In the early years of the present century fishing began on a large scale and more recently there have been limited developments in lumbering and agriculture. Alaska has been well to the forefront in American minds since 1940 because of its strategic location *vis-à-vis* Japan and Russia. Vast amounts of money have been poured into the area to establish military and scientific bases, to extend communications, and to explore and tap the resources. The territory became the 49th state of the Union in 1958. The present population is 248,000 including about 44,000 Eskimos and Indians.

Physical Features.—Alaska exceeds every other American state in area. From the compact peninsula, two long "fingers" of land project outwards: one, comprising the Aleutian Islands extends to the west into the northern Pacific; the other, the Alaska Panhandle, stretches southwards as a narrow coastal belt with off-shore islands into the temperate zone. The build of the state is accounted for by the extension north and west of the physical units of British Columbia. The core is the Yukon Plateau, an extension of the intermontane plateaus farther south (Fig. 130). It is drained by the Yukon and its tributary the Tanana, and the shorter Kuskokwim. To the south is the large arc of the lofty Alaska Mountains which continue the line of the Coast Mountains. They include the highest peak in North America, Mount McKinley, 20,320 ft. The range decreases in elevation in the Alaska Peninsula and is partially submerged to form the Aleutian Islands where there are eighty volcanoes. Along the southern coast and extending across the Kenai Peninsula and Kodiak Island are the St Elias Mountains, which have much in common with the Island Ranges of British Columbia. Both the Alaska Mountains and St Elias Mountains have extensive snowfields and large glaciers. On the north, the Yukon

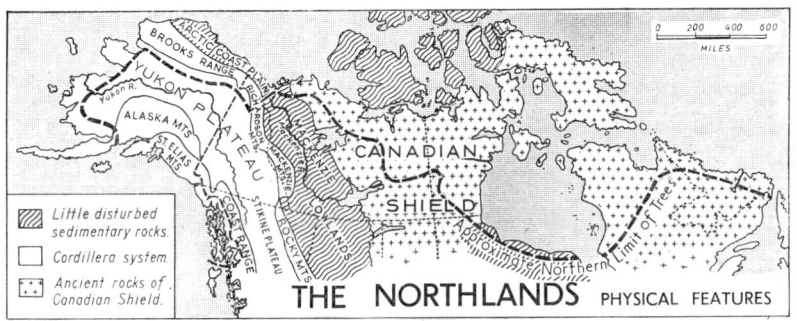

Fig. 130.

Plateau is bordered by the Brooks Range, an extension of the Rockies, and beyond that lies the low Arctic slope.

Northern Coastlands.—The northern coast is the most inhospitable inhabited part of Alaska. The climatic figures for Point Barrow (see p. 43) show that there are only three months in the year when the temperature is above freezing point and that the precipitation is under six inches. The Arctic Ocean is frozen for almost the whole of the year and even the Bering Sea is open to shipping for only seven or eight months.

Most of this region is a lowland plain with slight relief. The surface is diversified by stone polygons, circles or strips which are the result of frost-thaw action, and numerous lakes and swamps. When the top few inches of ground thaw in the summer, water cannot escape because of the underlying permafrost and remains on the surface. Few parts are without a vegetation cover of some sort and what might seem a rock-strewn, barren flat from the air, often turns out on closer inspection to be a veritable rock garden.

As an adaptation to the short Arctic summer, practically all tundra plants are perennial and develop the following year's flowering buds before the onset of winter. Some require many years from germination to flowering and many do not depend on seed production for their propagation but reproduce vegetatively. There is an amazing variety of plants—250 species of mosses, 330 of lichens, and 760 of flowering plants which include dandelions, primroses, saxifrages, poppies, heathers, and rhododendrons. All are low and shallow-rooted.

Most of the 40,000 Eskimos, Aleuts, and Indians in Alaska live in this area and there are minute pockets of white settlement associated with the meteorological stations, radar posts, and airfields. The Seward Peninsula has a small population of miners who are served by Nome, the main port on the west coast. This settlement how has 1,900 inhabitants, a marked decline from the 20,000 who populated the town in 1900 at the height of the gold-rush (Fig. 131).

Before the coming of the Russians and Americans, the Eskimos had successfully adapted themselves to their harsh environment; for a people of limited technology their success was startling. To-day, some still live as their ancestors did but few have been untouched by white civilisation. Many have found work in military camps, trading posts, mines, and canning factories. An attempt to induce the Eskimos to become herders instead of hunters, and thus make their existence less precarious, has had mixed success. Reindeer were imported at the end of the nineteenth century and their numbers multiplied to such an extent that by 1932 there were over 600,000. Since then the number has decreased drastically to under 30,000.

The decline has been attributed variously to the unwillingness of the Eskimos to discipline themselves to an ordered existence, to the lack of markets for venison, and to the poor transport facilities. Estimates have been made of the potential use of land for grazing. In the delta grasslands and best lichen woodland, the carrying capacity of the land is put at sixteen reindeer per square mile. This compares favourably with the number of cattle per square mile in Arizona and New Mexico. It is thought that there is enough grazing land in Alaska for about 2 million reindeer. Cultivation is impossible in this northern region and herding seems to be the only feasible means of livelihood at present. The exploitation of oil has begun (Fig. 131). There are about 80 producing wells and plans to build an oil pipeline.

ALASKA

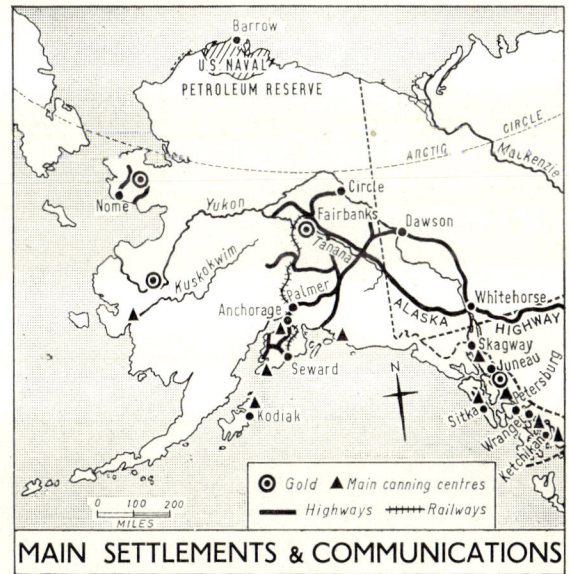

Fig. 131.

Central Plateaus.--The Yukon Plateau carries a light forest vegetation consisting of white spruce, balsam fir, and white birch, with a large admixture of heather and lichens. The trees are small and seldom exceed six inches in diameter. The best timbered areas are the valleys of the Yukon, Tanana, and Kuskokwim where there are level benches and alluvial terraces (Fig. 131). The rougher parts of the plateau and the isolated mountain ranges are covered with sparse woodland or tundra.

The Yukon is navigable for three months of the year for a distance of 2,000 miles from the shifting delta sands to Whitehorse in the Yukon. In 1898, when the gold fever was at its height, sixty shallow-draught stern-wheelers plied along its length: to-day there is not one. Fairbanks, which lies at the head of navigation on the Tanana was founded in 1902 when gold was found in the vicinity. It is now the terminus of the Alaska Highway and the 420-mile Alaska Railroad (from Seward), the capital of the state, and the seat of a university. It serves as a centre for the whole of the plateau region.

Around Fairbanks, in the Tanana Valley, is one of the two agricultural areas in Alaska. Winters are harsh, with mean January temperatures of $-12°$ F. ($-24°$ C.), and the growing season is very short. Only on the sheltered, south-facing slopes does this period exceed 100 days. The important climatic factor, however, is the summer warmth with mean July temperatures of $63°$ F. (*18° C.*). There are long periods of sunshine owing to the length of daylight, and most of the 11 in. of rain falls during the growing period. Potatoes, oats, peas, and other vegetables are grown by the thirty or forty families engaged in agriculture. The cropland amounts to only 2,400 acres. Clearing the land for cultivation is expensive and costs the prospective settler $100 to $200 per acre. Production is limited to the amounts that can be consumed locally for the lack of transport facilities makes marketing a difficult problem.

Authorities differ on the future prospects of farming on the Yukon Plateau. Some see little chance of further development: others are quite optimistic.

"Many species of berries, wild flowers, and shrubs carpet the interior and the immense fertile lowlands are as well suited to agriculture as are the uplands to grazing. Large scale agriculture has to date been confined to the Tanana Valley, but in future will probably spread over the entire region."—*Geography of the Northlands*, Ed. Kimble and Good, Chapter 14.

Southern Coastlands.—The other agricultural area is the Matanuska Valley which lies between the Alaska and St Elias mountains and reaches the sea at Cook Inlet. Dairying is the main activity for the short growing season permits the growth of only small grains, hay, and potatoes. The long, harsh winters enforce a lengthy period of stall-feeding and six acres are needed to provide enough fodder for one animal. Vegetables and soft fruits, especially strawberries, are grown and in the prolonged summer daylight reach prodigious sizes. It is not uncommon for cabbages to weigh 40 lb. and be as big as medicine balls. The valley was colonised in 1935 by 200 families from the Midwest. At present there are under 200 farms with about 9,000 acres of cultivated land. In the whole of Alaska the total cropland amounts to under 12,000 acres, but the area in farms exceeds 420,000 acres. Estimates place the amount of cultivable land in the valley at 50,000 acres.

The main market for the agricultural produce is Anchorage (30,000), the largest settlement in Alaska. It lies on the Alaska Railroad and is becoming the hub of the Alaska road system. It is proposed shortly to improve the sea approaches to allow large ships to dock there. In 1940, Anchorage became the headquarters of the Alaska Defence Command and this contributed to its growth and importance. Since the war it has become an important staging post on the transpolar air routes. French, Dutch, and Scandinavian aircraft touch down at the airfield on their way to the Orient. The importance of aircraft in the internal communications of the state, where there are only two railways and few good roads, can be gauged from the fact that there are twelve airlines and over 300 airfields.

In the Kenai peninsula, south of Anchorage, large reserves of oil and natural gas have recently been discovered, and there is good quality coal in the Matanuska Valley around Palmer.

The Panhandle.—The southern coast which has just been described and the Panhandle are the most accessible parts of Alaska. The ports here are ice-free and communication is maintained all the year round with Seattle. Freight rates, however, are exceptionally high and this hampers the economic development of the state.

The shores are washed by the warm North Pacific current and are exposed to the eastward moving depressions. The maritime Polar air which impinges on this coast brings mild winters and heavy precipitation. Juneau, which experiences the full effect of the sea's moderating influence, has a January temperature of 28° F. ($-2°$ C.), a July temperature of 58° F. (*14°* C.)—which is lower than that at Fairbanks in the interior (p. 382)—and an annual precipitation of 91 in.

Agriculture is not important here for the summers are cool and very damp, and there is little lowland. Along the northern part of the Panhandle is the Tongass National Forest which covers an area of 25,000 square miles. The dominant trees are Sitka spruce and western hemlock, both of which reach great sizes. The mountain slopes are clothed in forest to a height of 3,500 ft and few parts lie more than two and a half miles from navigable water. The growth cycle lasts about eighty years and there appears to be no reason why the forest cannot be continuously "farmed". Alaska's first pulp mill was recently established at Ketchikan. A newer one at Sitka was financed partly by Japanese money and it supplies pulp for Japan's rayon and paper industries (see plate facing p. 369).

Ketchikan is the centre of Alaska's most lucrative industry, salmon fishing. Herring, cod, and halibut are caught also, and there is a strictly regulated amount of sealing off the Pribilof Islands in the Bering Sea, but these pale into insignificance beside the value of the salmon catch, which far exceeds that of British Columbia. The five species which are commercially important (p. 369) ascend the mountain streams after varying lengths of time at sea. They are caught in the Cook Inlet, around Kodiak Island, and particularly in the maze of waterways of the Alexander Archipelago. Here are numerous deep-water sites for canneries, which operate during the summer months and close during the winter. Many of the 108 canneries are controlled and financed from Seattle or San Francisco, where much of the white and Filipino labour is hired before being flown north for the three summer months. About 15,000 to 20,000 men are employed annually in salmon canning.

The present pack is about 3·5 million cases (each containing forty-eight one-pound cans) worth about $60 million. This is much less than in pre-war years when the pack occasionally amounted to 8 million cases. The recent decline can be attributed to increasing competition from Japan and Russia, and the depletion of stocks, particularly of sockeye (red) salmon, the species most prized for canning.

Behind the Inland Passage, the innermost channel of the intricate maze of waterways separating the islands from one another and the mainland, the coast is highly indented with long fiords, known in Alaska as "canals". From Skagway at the head of the Lynn Canal a narrow-gauge railway runs 111 miles across White Pass to Whitehorse on the Yukon. It follows closely one of the routes taken by the gold seekers at the turn of the century. (The other route lay over Chilkoot Pass.)

About one-fifth of Alaska's white population (170,000 altogether) lives in the Panhandle, mostly in the larger settlements such as Juneau, Sitka, Ketchikan, and Wrangell. Here are the important forest reserves, the richest salmon runs, and occasional pockets of minerals (*e.g.* gold at Juneau). Reserves of water-power are immense but are at present almost completely unharnessed. In spite of the exciting potentialities of this region, it is not developing as quickly as the Anchorage area which has the advantage of a more central position.

The Canadian North-west

Physical Background.—The Canadian North-west comprises two distinct physical areas, the Cordillera and the Mackenzie Valley. The grain of the mountainous country is from south-east to north-west and the various physical elements link up with similar features in British Columbia (where the grain is NNW. to SSE.) and Alaska (where there is a general east to west trend). On the south are the high peaks of the St Elias and Coast Mountains (Fig. 130). Inland from these is the complicated series of low ranges and highly dissected, elevated tablelands of the Yukon Plateau. The Rockies, which form the easternmost limb of the Cordillera, terminate at the Liard basin but their line is continued by the Mackenzie and Richardson mountains. The Franklin Range is an outlying portion of this system (Fig. 132).

To the east of the Cordillera is a narrow lowland of relatively undisturbed rocks, an extension northwards of the Central Plains which is drained to the Arctic by the Mackenzie River. This lowland becomes more and more constricted towards the delta of the river as the ancient crystalline rocks of the Canadian Shield, which forms the eastern boundary, project farther westward.

The coastal highlands shut off North-west Canada from the Pacific and moderating climatic influences. Consequently, the region has a severe continental climate with very cold winters and, for its latitude, quite warm summers. At Dawson, 64° N., the January mean is $-17°$ F. ($-27°$ C.) and the July mean is 60° F. ($16°$ C.), but maximum and minimum temperatures vary consider-ably from the mean; a winter temperature of $-81°$ F. ($-63°$ C.) has been recorded, whilst on several occasions in summer the thermometer has registered 95° F. ($35°$ C.). However, throughout the summer there is always the possibility of an invasion of cold Arctic air, and no part is immune from occasional summer frosts.

During the winter when cold, stable air covers the whole of the northern part of the continent, precipitation is slight and most of the rainfall occurs during the passage of weak cyclonic disturbances in summer. Everywhere totals are low, often under 10 in., and vary considerably from year to year.

Permafrost underlies much of the area and is responsible for the large number of swamps and muskegs (Fig. 129). Some of the effects on building operations have already been noted (p. 322).

Fig. 132.

In turn, the interference of man often leads to a change in permafrost conditions. The removal of vegetation, particularly mats of moss and sphagnum, which acts as an insulator, leads to a drop in the level of summer permafrost while the erection of buildings often causes the sub-soil to thaw. Aklavik, which was on a western distributary of the Mackenzie, had to be relocated recently because of slumping due to the melting of the permafrost. The new settlement (called Inuvik) was established on insulated rafts on gravels on the eastern side of the Mackenzie, thirty-three miles away.

The permafrost is thought to be responsible for pingoes, small circular mounds which are common in the Mackenzie delta. Unfrozen water is trapped between the permafrost layer and the frozen surface and the fine silt and clay that it saturates is squeezed up by the surrounding ice rather like a kind of ice-volcano.

On Fig. 130, the tree line is shown. This is not a definite boundary but a broad zone of transition where trees of the Sub-Arctic forest become fewer and smaller until they finally disappear and are replaced by the tundra vegetation of the Arctic coast. The

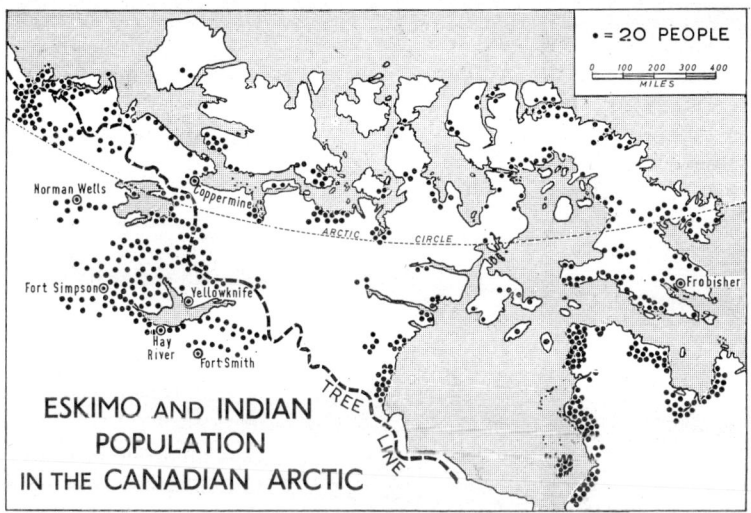

Fig. 133.
Most Indians are found south of the tree line and most Eskimos north of it.

tree line is perhaps the most significant boundary in the Northlands for it separates *potential* farmland from the barren cold desert. It also marks the approximate divide between Eskimos and Indians (Fig. 133). It will be seen that much of the North-west lies south of the tree line, whereas most of the eastern Northlands lies in the tundra zone. The timber itself, which includes black spruce on the muskegs, white spruce on the richer valley and terrace soils, and lodgepole pine and jack pine on the drier lands, has little economic importance. Some is cut for fuel but the trees are too small, too widely scattered, and too remote from markets to be significant.

Economic Development.—The first white people to enter the area were the fur-trappers. Their widespread searches for fresh hunting grounds brought them to the North-west towards the end of the eighteenth century and a few trading posts were established in strategic positions in the Mackenzie basin. They were followed—in the latter half of the nineteenth century—by the religious groups which founded missions, schools, and churches. Later still, the Yukon was opened up by miners and prospectors who poured into the area after the discovery of gold in the Klondike Valley in 1898. In this year over 30,000 prospectors crossed from the Alaska Panhandle into the Yukon via White Pass, a route which was to be quickly followed by the railway from Skagway to Whitehorse, or Chilkoot Pass. At the beginning of the present century, Dawson, near the Klondike, had a population of almost 40,000; this number rapidly dwindled to a few hundred as the placer deposits were worked over and exhausted. At the present time, huge dredges excavate about $2 million worth of gold every year. Lead, zinc, and silver are mined at Mayo, and low-grade coal has been mined sporadically to serve local needs. Other mineral deposits are present but transport costs prohibit the exploitation of all but the most valuable ores.

The area stagnated until World War II when the strategic implications of the Northlands were recognised and the government undertook the construction of defence bases and roads and inaugurated an intensive search for minerals. The boom has not continued since the war but the region has not relapsed into its pre-war state. The Alaska Highway (Fig. 135), which was constructed during the war, has improved communications enormously. It passes through Whitehorse, which as railhead and head of navigation on the Yukon quickly became a focal point. It has replaced Dawson as capital of Yukon Territory. Its population rose rapidly to 15,000 but since 1945 this has declined to 5,000. Oil was discovered at Norman Wells in 1920 but production was extremely small until the war when further wells were drilled and a pipeline was built across the Mackenzie Mountains to a refinery at Whitehorse. Since the war the pipeline has been abandoned and production restricted.

In the face of severe physical and climatic handicaps, farming is practically non-existent. There are only four farms in the Northwest Territories and the farming population of the Yukon is only fifty. However, there are many small garden plots where hardy vegetables flourish and grow to enormous sizes during the long summer days. It has been estimated that there are about 300,000 acres of potential arable land in the area, but this is widely scattered and for the most part is to be found on the discontinuous river terraces.

THE CANADIAN NORTH-WEST

Transport.—Transport is perhaps the greatest problem of the Northlands. Both the Yukon and the Mackenzie are navigable for long stretches but on the former shipping has almost completely disappeared. The Mackenzie is still used but with difficulty and for, at most, four months of the year. Floods are likely to occur on the upper part of the river in May and June, when the lower reaches are still frozen, and again in September, when the ice has re-formed on the delta but not on the upper course. In between these dates, the level of the river often drops dangerously low, exposing rapids and snags which are hidden at high water. The Mackenzie is navigable for 1,700 miles, from Tuktoyaktuk on the delta to Waterways which is connected by rail with Edmonton. Rapids occur on the Slave River above Fort Smith and necessitate a sixteen-mile portage of goods and passengers from one steamer to another (see plate facing p. 369). Navigation on the Athabasca, Peace, and Hay rivers is also interrupted by rapids (Fig. 132).

Since the war, diesel tugs have replaced the old stern-wheelers: they push strings of up to five barges. Most of the freight moves downstream to Yellowknife, Norman Wells, and the small fur-trading posts, police stations, and defence stations. Some freight is trans-shipped at Inuvik and Tuktoyaktuk and taken by schooner to Eskimo settlements, missions, and weather stations along the Arctic coast. There is little upstream freight, for the few settlements cannot provide enough furs or minerals to fill the barges and so freight charges are high.

In 1958, an American submarine powered by atomic energy crossed the Arctic Ocean under the ice pack. Its journey may point the way to the future use of large submarine freighters carrying oil and other minerals from the northern coasts and islands to ports farther south.

Only two good roads cross this vast area—the Alaska Highway, which runs from Dawson Creek to Whitehorse and then into Alaska, and the Mackenzie Highway, which links the road system of the Peace River District with Hay River on the Great Slave Lake. In 1960 the Great Slave Highway linking Hay River and Yellowknife was opened to traffic (Fig. 132).

Transport by air has become very important since the war; areas opened up by "bush" pilots are now served by recognised airlines. In addition to the military airfields, there are over fifty civilian airports, a quarter of which are on land (mainly in the Yukon) and the remainder on water. Planes fitted with floats or skis can land here throughout the year except during the short periods when ice is forming or breaking up. At the present time, aircraft are the only really effective link between the small and widely scattered communities.

Population.—The population of Yukon Territory and the Northwest Territories (*i.e.* Mackenzie, Keewatin, and Franklin) numbers about 41,000, of whom about one-quarter are Eskimos and one-fifth Indians. The former live along the coast in the tundra areas, the latter in the forest lands. Both are actively engaged in the fur trade which is the main source of wealth in the region (Fig. 108). As in Alaska, an attempt has been made to introduce reindeer herding. In 1929, 6,000 animals set off from Alaska but only 2,400 survived the long journey which lasted several years. A count in 1952 showed that there were almost 8,000 disease-free reindeer and the experiment appears to have been initially successful. Further progress will depend upon how many Eskimos can be induced to forsake their traditional ways of life (or their new jobs on airfields and in mining settlements), and take up herding. It has been stated that the Canadian Northlands could support about 40 million head of reindeer.

White settlement is still in its "outpost" stage. There are only nine communities with a population in excess of 500 and in these life revolves around the mine, or the airfield, police station, store, mission, and school.

"At Hay River there used to be a large Anglican Mission and church, with a three-storey school and a hospital. To-day only the hospital is in use, though the Catholic Mission seems to be flourishing. Several hundred Indians live in the settlement in huts and tents during the summer; and early in July they collect for the 'Treaty Money' (five dollars a head) which is distributed by the government agent at this time of the year. . . .

"Fort Providence had much the same appearance as Hay River, though the cut-bank (river bank) was considerably higher, and showed the remains of a former ancient 'oxbow meander' perched up above the present river. Here were two Catholic churches, a huge three-storey school for the Indian children, and a large barn. . . . At intervals along the cut-bank were the neat buildings of the Hudson's Bay store, the radio engineers, and at the further end of the settlement the cluster of buildings belonging to the Mounted Police. The white folk are distributed somewhat as follows. There are four priests and a dozen sisters at the Catholic Mission, five members of the staff at the new airport, four at the wireless station, five at the store, and two police officers. Two white trappers make this their headquarters when they are not trapping. There is also a small store owned by a Syrian, giving a total of about forty white folk at Fort Providence."—G. Taylor, *Canada*, Chapter 11.

The Arctic Archipelago

The Arctic islands spread over 20° of latitude—62° N. to 83° N.—and cover about 500,000 square miles of tundra and ice. Many of the islands are little known and most are unexplored. The attention of European navigators was focused upon this area between the seventeenth and nineteenth centuries when various

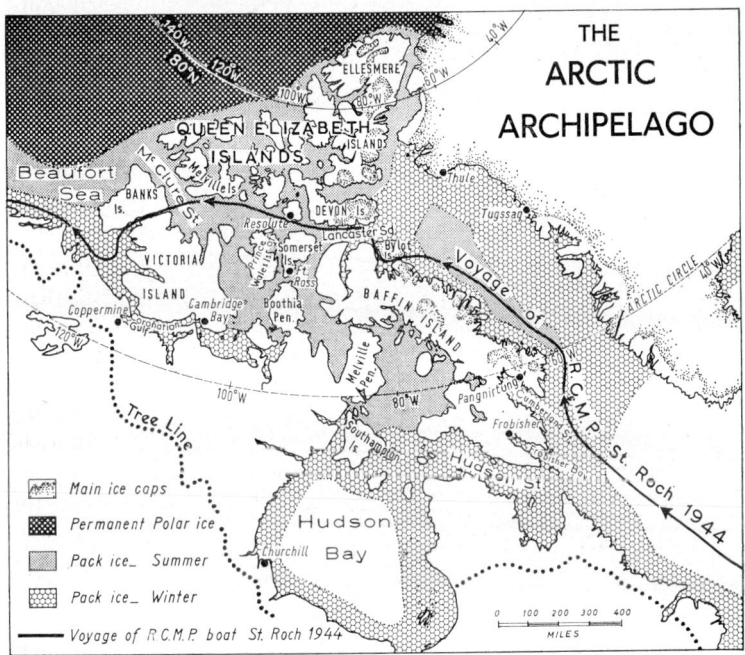

Fig. 134.

unsuccessful attempts were made to discover a north-west passage. The channels and straits separating the islands from one another and from the mainland are locked in ice for the greater part of the year; some in the far north are perennially ice-bound. The first crossing from the Bering Sea to the Atlantic was made by the Royal Canadian Mounted Police boat, St Roch. It took over two years to make the westward trip (1940-42) but the return journey in 1944 from Lancaster Sound to the Beaufort Sea took only eighteen days (Fig. 134).

The archipelago is a depressed part of the Canadian Shield. Over practically the whole of Baffin Island the ancient granites and gneisses are exposed at the surface and in the north form a belt of high, rugged country rising to over 7,000 ft. In the other islands the basal complex of crystalline rocks is hidden beneath a cover of Palaeozoic sediments which become progressively younger towards the north-west. These sediments give rise to plateau-like land forms except in Ellesmere Island where they have been folded and produce steep and rugged mountains rising to 10,000 ft. Some of the islands are known to have seams of coal, outcrops of which are easily recognisable because of the lack of vegetation and top soil. Parry's expedition in 1820 used coal found on Melville Island and a well recently drilled here has tapped a rich reservoir of oil.

Ellesmere Island, Devon Island, and Baffin Island have extensive ice-caps and smaller patches of ice are found on some other islands. The climate is truly Arctic with average July temperatures everywhere under 50° F. (*10° C.*), and average January temperatures below − 20° F. (*−29° C.*) for most of the region. The flora that exists under these conditions is really quite remarkable. Trees are virtually absent but there is a wealth of grasses, moss, flowers, and other tundra vegetation (p. 380) which supports musk ox, caribou, and hares. Upon these prey wolves, foxes, and rodents. The seas are very rich in plankton, and although fish life is not prolific, there are large numbers of seals, walrus, and whales. The larger species of whale were almost exterminated during the nineteenth century (numbers are now slowly increasing), but the smaller white whales are still hunted by Eskimos.

The 3,000 Eskimos in the archipelago are less touched by civilisation than those in other parts of the Northlands, but some have abandoned hunting, fishing, and trapping to take up work as guides, dog-drivers, and stevedores or as servants and labourers in stores and on airfields. They live on the coasts for fishing is one of the main means of livelihood, but their settlements are also located where game is most plentiful. Greatest concentrations are found along the shores of Baffin Island and Victoria Island (Fig. 133).

The white population numbers only 300 and is essentially non-permanent. These transient workers staff the airfields at Frobisher and Resolute, the hospital at Pangnirtung, the small number of police posts, and weather and radar stations which are scattered so widely and so sparsely over the archipelago.

Agriculture in this region is virtually impossible. Some minerals are known to exist and it is likely that more will be discovered when the region is surveyed more fully, but the difficulties of mining seem insuperable. This is the most remote and also the most isolated of all the regions of Canada. As long as better placed and better known areas farther south still await development, it is unlikely that any large scale attempt will be made to settle and exploit the archipelago.

Conclusion

It is apparent that the Northlands is an underdeveloped region. Only 200,000 people inhabit the vast area which extends from the Bering Sea to the Atlantic Ocean. Farming has made small headway and estimates of the agricultural possibilities vary widely. Some authorities are quite optimistic (see p. 382). Professor G. Taylor suggests that the southern parts of the Mackenzie basin could grow oats and barley and carry a farming population of about five people per square mile, that the northern parts are not unsuited to root crops and could support about one person per square mile, while the tundra and mountains are unlikely to support any agricultural settlement at all. Other authorities are less sanguine: they think that agriculture will not be important, not only because of the physical handicaps, which are extremely severe, but also because of the lack of transport and local markets and the decline of the pioneering spirit. There are few pioneers to-day with the large amount of capital necessary to clear the land and buy equipment. Few people are willing to become subsistence farmers (for without a market there could be no immediate sale of farm produce) and few are willing to live in isolated farmsteads (isolated because the good land is found in widely scattered patches) in an isolated region without the amenities of life which are commonplace farther south. If the pioneering spirit is moribund, and there are no signs that it is not, then it would seem that agriculture is unlikely to provide a firm economic base upon which successful settlement can be established.

Development is much more likely to be founded upon the mineral wealth of the Northlands. Many minerals are known to exist and it is highly probable that others still await discovery, but only those which can bear the heavy cost of transport are being exploited (*e.g.* radium, uranium, and gold). To tap the remainder—and to develop the water-power resources—much better communications than those already existing will be necessary. A great amount of capital will have to be made available, and most of this will almost certainly have to come from the government. Both the U.S.A. and Canada are well aware of the strategic importance of the Northlands which look across the Bering Sea and Arctic Ocean to the shores of the U.S.S.R. During the war money was spent on roads and military bases, and in post-war years radar stations have been established (*e.g.* the chain of Distant Early Warning stations— the D.E.W. Line) as part of the continental defence system (Fig. 135). It is doubtful whether these establishments will lead to *permanent* settlement in the region.

The north of the U.S.S.R. carries a much larger population than the north of North America. The figures are 29,700,000 and 1,600,000 respectively for equivalent climatic areas. (These areas include parts lying south of the Northlands as defined at the begin-

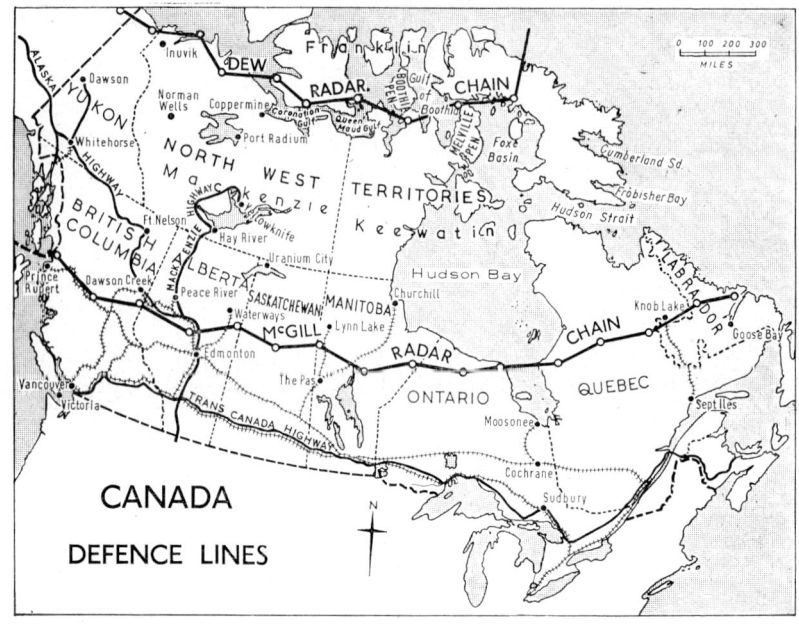

Fig. 135.

ning of this chapter.) The greater development in the Old World has been due to a forceful government policy which has employed both inducements and coercion to bring in settlers and which has been expensive in both human and economic terms. It must be remembered, however, that Siberia has had a much longer history of settlement than the American Northlands. Neither Canada nor the U.S.A. is likely to adopt a policy such as the U.S.S.R. has employed but without some government sponsorship, control, and financial assistance, the development of the Northlands seems certain to remain slow and haphazard.

CHAPTER XIX

CANADA AND THE U.S.A.

In conclusion, we may sum up the main characteristics of North America and note the broad similarities and differences of the two countries into which it is politically divided.

1. In the three and a half centuries that have elapsed since the first European settlements were made, North America has risen to the forefront in world affairs. The peopling of the continent involved one of the greatest migrations in human history. Millions of Europeans sought political and religious freedom in the New World and a chance to improve their lot. The predominance of Anglo-Saxon immigrants has meant that English is the common language. Most of the other immigrants went into the "melting pot" and emerged with a new language and culture, but some, notably the French-speaking peoples of Canada and smaller groups such as the Puerto Ricans in the U.S.A., have not been completely assimilated and retain their own ways of life, and in some cases, their own languages.

2. The division of the continent between two countries has introduced a certain dichotomy in human relations. The boundary between them runs from east to west and had led to the perpetuation of the east-west lines of communication which developed as settlement spread across the continent from the east coast. However, the major physical divisions run from north to south, and the easiest natural routeways are in this direction too. Some regions of Canada have more in common with adjacent parts of the U.S.A. than they have with other Canadian regions. But, conditions on both sides of the international boundary are not identical because of climatic, historical, and political differences.

3. Regional differences in both countries tend to be accentuated. Not only do Canada and the U.S.A. cover large areas, but both have a wide variety of terrains, climates, and natural resources which promote regional diversity. Both have federal constitutions and each state or province enjoys a large measure of autonomy, which is another factor accentuating regional differences. In spite of this, however, there seems to be a sameness about American cities and ways of life that is paradoxical.

4. Both countries are well endowed with natural resources. There are large areas of fertile land, which, because of climatic

differences, can produce a wide range of agricultural products. There are large areas of forest, great reserves of water-power, and rich mineral deposits. There are few materials that the continent does not produce and in the production of many it leads the world.

Imports fall into three categories. The largest group consists of foodstuffs from tropical areas, *e.g.* coffee, tea, cocoa, bananas, pineapples, etc. The second group consists of raw materials which are lacking in North America or are produced in only small quantities and must be supplemented, *e.g.* jute, wool, tin, and rubber (although the invention of synthetic rubber, made from oil, has greatly lessened the U.S.A.'s dependence on Asian natural rubber). The third group includes materials produced in great quantity in North America, but in insufficient amounts to meet the huge demand, *e.g.* copper and oil.

5. In both countries, but particularly the U.S.A., many of the resources have not been wisely used. Soil erosion resulting from misuse of the land has destroyed millions of acres of cropland and partly ruined more. Forests have been devastated and rivers polluted. During the formative years of the countries' growth, the vast areas held only a sparse population and immediate development took precedence over long-term progress. Individual enterprise was encouraged and any attempt to regulate economic activity was restricted. To the frontiersman there seemed to be inexhaustible amounts of land, timber, and minerals, and this belief became part of the national psychology. When it was ultimately realised that the resources were being squandered, this same national psychology hindered conservation measures, and the efforts of the central government to intervene in order to regulate the use of soils, forests, water, and minerals have often, but not so much in recent years, been tentative and ineffective. In Canada, where settlement was later, where the exploitation of resources was on a smaller scale, and where the government kept a stricter control of land, the mistakes have been less serious.

6. In both countries the economy is wasteful. Agricultural production exceeds demand and almost every year there is a carry-over surplus of wheat, maize, cotton, butter, and other produce which cannot be disposed of economically in world markets. Production increases yearly because of increasing mechanisation, the development of new strains of seeds, and the use of powerful insecticides. Agricultural production in the U.S.A. has doubled in the last thirty years. In order to meet the problem the governments of both countries are encouraging farmers to take some land out of

cultivation and are at the same time offering them price guarantees and subsidies.

The productive capacity of American industries is tremendous, as was amply demonstrated during World War II. With its unrivalled array of resources, the U.S.A. has become the leading industrial country of the world and Canada is rapidly becoming a manufacturing country of the first rank. Together, they produce over half the world's manufactured goods. But recurrent periods of boom and slump mean that production fluctuates and is frequently less than capacity.

7. There is a great amount of trade between the two countries: each is the major trading partner of the other. The U.S.A. is the leading trading nation in the world but the trade per capita is quite small. Canada, which ranks as the fourth largest trading nation, has the highest trade per capita of all nations. The nature of the trade of each country differs; Canada exports mainly raw and semi-processed materials and imports mainly manufactured goods. The U.S.A. imports mainly raw materials and exports mainly manufactures. Of Canada's exports, over 60 per cent. go to the U.S.A. (comprising wood pulp, newsprint, timber, and minerals) and from that country it receives 80 per cent. of its imports (machinery, vehicles, iron and steel in various forms, and electrical apparatus). In spite of being a member of the Commonwealth, Canada has only a limited amount of trade with Great Britain, which takes 12 per cent. of Canada's exports and supplies 7 per cent. of its imports. There are fears in Canada that if Britain joins the European Common Market the exports will be reduced below this figure.

8. Canada is very much the junior partner in North America. Its population is only one-tenth that of its southern neighbour and it is less wealthy and much less developed. U.S. influence on Canadian life and economy is very strong and is accentuated by the fact that about three-quarters of Canada's population lives within 100 miles of the long and easily crossed border between the two countries. In recent years, much U.S. capital has been invested in Canadian industries, particularly in the primary products such as iron ore, pulp, oil, and gas, reserves of which are becoming depleted south of the 49th Parallel. Also subsidiary manufacturing companies are being established to circumvent Canadian tariff barriers and tap the expanding market. Well over one-quarter of all industries in Canada are controlled by U.S. concerns; in manufacturing industries the proportion is about one-half and in the primary mineral resource industries it is about two-thirds.

Without American capital Canada would certainly not have made the rapid progress it has done since the war. At the same time, many Canadians are aware of the threat to their economic independence and stability. In any case, Canada's economy is less buoyant than that of the U.S.A. Its two major weaknesses are that it is so dependent on the U.S.A. as a market for exports and supplier of imports and that it relies on its exports of raw materials to such a large extent. Trade cycles in the U.S.A. rarely fail to influence the Canadian economy. In addition, the nature of the Canadian climate means that there is much seasonal unemployment in winter, particularly, but by no means wholly, in the northern parts of the country where mining activity and transport are curtailed.

9. A century ago the U.S.A. was in a position similar to that of Canada to-day. It exported foodstuffs and raw materials and imported manufactured goods. In the last hundred years, its population has increased sixfold and it has become the greatest industrial country in the world. Canada still has only half the population that the U.S.A. had in 1861 and although the number of secondary manufacturing industries based on primary products is increasing rapidly, it seems likely that Canada's development will not parallel that of the U.S.A., but will be much slower and closely related to economic conditions of its neighbour.

APPENDIX I

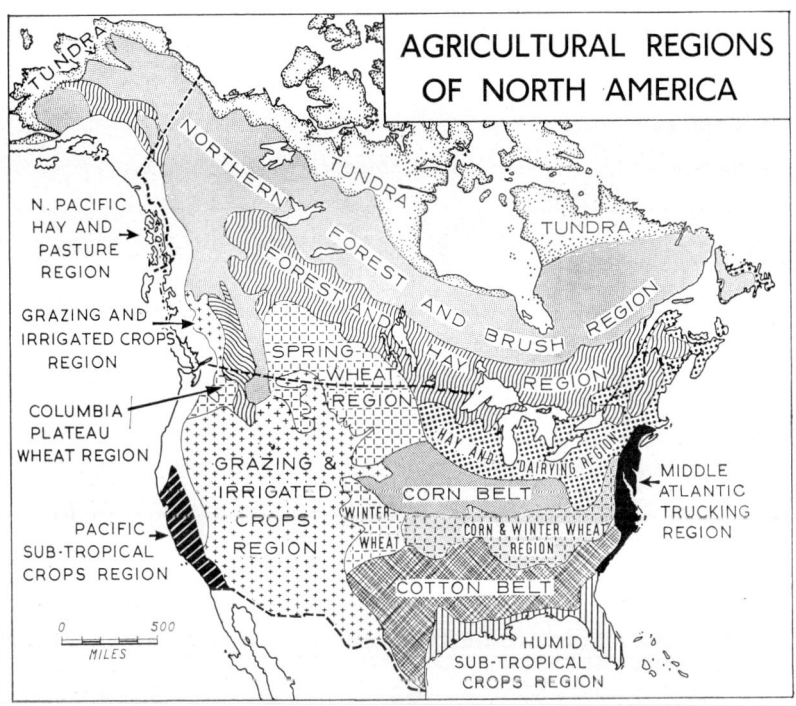

This map gives a highly generalised picture of land-use in North America and is still useful despite the fact that considerable changes have occurred since the boundaries of the regions were defined over thirty years ago. The greatest differences are to be found in the Cotton Belt and Corn Belt (see pp. 140-4 and pp. 174-6).

	U.S.A.		CANADA	
Total area	1,902	million acres	2,282	million acres
Farmland	1,120	,,	174	,, ,,
Corn	60·4	,, ,,	0·7	,, ,,
Wheat	59·0	,, ,,	28·2	,, ,,
Hay	64·7	,, ,,	12·7	,, ,,
Oats	15·8	,, ,,	8·6	,, ,,
Barley	9·2	,, ,,	6·0	,, ,,
Cotton	8·0	,, ,,		
Soy-beans	39·7	,, ,,	0·2	,, ,,
Fruit	4·7	,, ,,	0·2	,, ,,
Vegetables	3·6	,, ,,	0·2	,, ,,

APPENDIX II

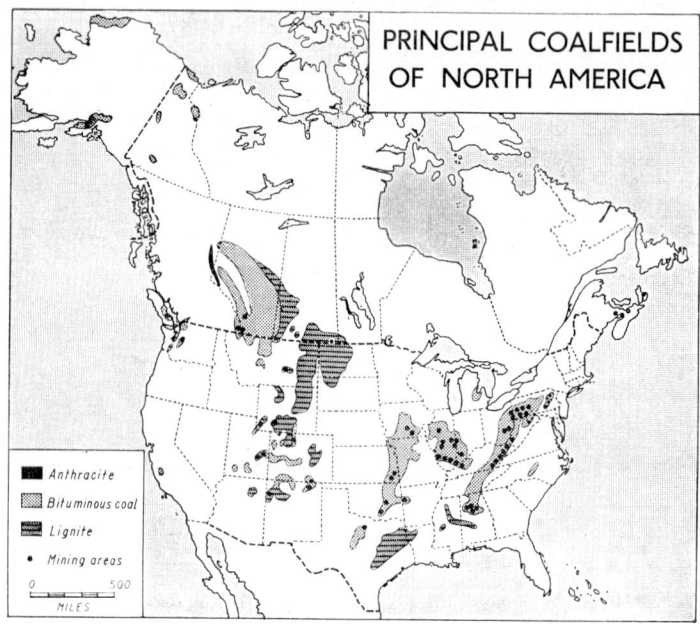

The U.S.A. produces annually over 500 million tons of bituminous coal and lignite, about 80 per cent. coming from the Appalachian Coalfield and about 15 per cent. from the Central Coalfield (see Fig. 63). Under 15 million tons of anthracite are mined annually. Canada produces under 12 million tons of bituminous coal and lignite, Nova Scotia accounting for 35 per cent., Alberta for 30 per cent., and Saskatchewan (where only lignite is mined) for 17 per cent.
In both countries production has declined since World War Two.

FURTHER READING
GENERAL

1. *Amérique Septentrionale (Géographie Universelle, Vol.* 13), H. BAULIG.
2. *Anglo-America.* W. H. PARKER.
3. *North America.* J. H. PATERSON.
4. *North America.* G. J. MILLER, A. E. PARKINS, and B. HUDGINS.
5. *North America.* L. R. JONES and P. W. BRYAN.
6. *North America.* J. W. WATSON.
7. *The Regional Geography of Anglo-America.* C. L. WHITE and E. J. FOSCUE.
8. *Anglo-America.* E. B. SHAW.
9. *North America.* J. W. WATSON.
10. *The United States and Canada.* W. R. MEAD and E. H. BROWN.
11. *L'Amérique.* J. GOTTMAN.
12. *American Resources.* J. R. WHITAKER and E. A. ACKERMAN.
13. "Agricultural Regions of North America." O. E. BAKER, *Econ. Geog.*, **2-9**.
14. *The Agricultural Regions of the United States.* L. HAYSTEAD and G. C. FITE.
15. *American Agriculture, Geography, Resources and Conservation.* E. HIGBEE.
16. *Regional Studies of the U.S.A. and Canada.* K. R. SEALY and H. REES.
17. "The Railroad Pattern of the United States." E. J. ULLMAN, *Geog. Review*, **39**, p. 242.
18. "American Orchard and Vineyard Regions." C. W. OLMSTEAD, *Econ. Geog.*, **32**, p. 189.
19. *Inside U.S.A.* J. GUNTHER.
20. *Statistical Abstract of the United States.* U.S. Bureau of the Census.
21. *Canada Yearbook.* Canadian Government Bureau of Statistics.
22. *A Regional Geography of Canada.* D. F. PUTMAN and D. P. KERR.
23. *Canada: A Study of Cool Continental Environments and Their Effect on British and French Settlement.* G. TAYLOR.
24. *Patterns of Canada.* W. J. MEGILL.
25. "The Pattern of Canada's Post-war Growth." J. W. WATSON, *Geography*, **39**, p. 163.

FURTHER READING

CHAPTER I

Physical Features

1. *Physiography of Eastern America.* N. M. Fenneman.
2. *Physiography of Western America.* N. M. Fenneman.
3. *The Physiographic Provinces of North America.* W. W. Atwood.
4. *The Evolution of North America.* P. B. King.
5. *Glacial Geology and the Pleistocene Epoch.* R. F. Flint.
6. *This Sculptured Earth: the Landscape of America.* J. A. Shimer.
7. "A Bird's-Eye Cross Section of the Central Appalachian Mountains and Plateau, Washington to Cincinnati." J. L. Rich, *Geog. Review*, **29**, p. 338.

CHAPTER II

Climate

1. *Climatology.* A. A. Miller.
2. *Climates of the Continents.* W. G. Kendrew.
3. *The Restless Atmosphere.* F. K. Hare.
4. *Our American Weather.* G. H. T. Kimble.
5. *Climate and Man.* Yearbook of Agriculture. U.S. Dept. of Agriculture 1941.
6. "Air Mass Climatology." A. A. Miller, *Geography*, **38**, p. 55.
7. "The Climates of the Earth." C. W. Thornthwaite, *Geog. Review*, **23**, p. 433.
8. "An Approach Towards a Rational Classification of Climate." C. W. Thornthwaite, *Geog. Review*, **38**, p. 55.
9. "Measuring Potential Evapotranspiration." R. C. Ward, *Geography*, **48**, p. 49.

CHAPTER III

Natural Vegetation and Soils

1. *Soils and Man.* Yearbook of Agriculture. U.S. Dept. of Agriculture, 1938.
2. *Soil.* Yearbook of Agriculture. U.S. Dept. of Agriculture, 1957.
3. *Grass.* Yearbook of Agriculture. U.S. Dept. of Agriculture, 1948.

4. *Trees.* Yearbook of Agriculture. U.S. Dept. of Agriculture, 1949.
5. *Conservation of Natural Resources.* G. H. SMITH.
6. *The Soils that Support Us.* C. E. KELLOGG.
7. *Soil Conservation.* H. H. BENNETT.
8. "The Geographical Relation of Soil Erosion to Land Productivity." H. H. BENNETT, *Geog. Review*, **18**, p. 579.

CHAPTER IV

THE SPREAD OF SETTLEMENT

1. *Atlas of the Historical Geography of the United States.* C. O. PAULLIN.
2. *Historical Geography of the United States.* R. H. BROWN.
3. *Geographic Influences in American History.* A. P. BRIGHAM.
4. *American History and its Geographic Conditions.* E. C. SEMPLE and C. F. JONES.
5. *The Exploration of Western America.* E. W. GILBERT.
6. *Discoverers and Explorers of North America.* J. B. BREBNER.
7. *Westward Expansion.* R. A. BILLINGTON.
8. *The Course of Empire.* B. DE VOTO.
9. *The Oregon Trail.* F. PARKMAN.
10. "Types of Rural Settlement in Colonial America." G. T. TREWARTHA, *Geog. Review*, **36**, p. 568.
11. "Population Maps of the Colonies and U.S.A., 1625-1790." H. R. FRIIS, *Geog. Review*, **30**, p. 463.

CHAPTER V

NEW ENGLAND

1. *The Economic State of New England.* A. A. BRIGHT and G. H. ELLIS.
2. *The Rural Economy of New England.* J. D. BLACK.
3. "The Changing Industrial Patterns of New England." R. C. ESTALL, *Geography*, **46**, p. 120.
4. "The Empty Areas of the North-eastern United States." L. E. KLIMM, *Geog. Review*, **44**, p. 325.
5. *New England: A Study in Industrial Adjustment.* R. C. ESTALL.
6. "Hinterland Boundaries of New York City and Boston in Southern New England." H. L. GREEN, *Econ. Geog.*, **31**, p. 283.

CHAPTER VI

MIDDLE ATLANTIC REGION

1. "Megalopolis, or the Urbanisation of the North-eastern Seaboard." J. GOTTMAN, *Econ. Geog.*, **33**, p. 189.
2. "Communications in the Port of New York." G. J. FULLER, *Geography*, **44**, 128.
3. "The Southern Anthracite Region." E. W. MILLER, *Econ. Geog.*, **31**, p. 331.
4. "The Philadelphia Iron and Steel District." C. J. SHARER, *Econ. Geog.*, **39**, p. 363.

CHAPTER VII

THE SOUTH

1. *The South: its Economic-Geographic Development.* A. E. PARKIN.
2. *The South-eastern United States.* J. F. HART.
3. "Cotton goes West in the American South." F. J. HART, *Geography*, **44**, p. 43.
4. "Recent Industrial Development in the Gulf South." J. J. PARSONS, *Geog. Review*, **40**, p. 67.
5. "The Geography of Natural Gas in the United States." J. J. PARSONS, *Econ. Geog.*, **26**, p. 162.
6. "The Florida Tropics." R. B. CARSON, *Econ. Geog.*, **27**, p. 321.
7. "Florida's Human Resources." S. DE R. DIETTRICH, *Geog. Review*, **38**, p. 278.
8. "Problems of Florida's Water Resources." R. B. MARCUS and D. MOOKHERJEE, *Geography*, **47**, p. 368.
9. "The Distribution of the Negro Population in the United States". W. C. CALEF and H. J. NELSON, *Geog. Review*, **46**, p. 82.
10. "Land Occupance in the South-east." M. PRUNTY, *Geog. Review*, **42**, p. 439.
11. "Recent Expansion in the Southern Pulp-Paper Industries." M. PRUNTY, *Econ. Geog.*, **32**, p. 51.
12. "The Renaissance of the Southern Plantation." M. PRUNTY, *Geog. Review*, **45**, p. 459.
13. "The Human Geography of the Cotton Belt." F. G. MORRIS, *Geography*, **34**, p. 146.
14. "Why American Industry moves South." J. H. PATERSON, *Geography*, **39**, p. 139.
15. "The Burley Tobacco Region of the Mountain South." L. DURAND and E. T. BIRD, *Econ. Geog.*, **26**, p. 247.

FURTHER READING

16. "Land Use in the Blue Grass Region." R. W. JOHNSON *Econ. Geog.*, **16**, p. 315.
17. "The Rice Country of South-west Louisiana." L. C. POST, *Geog. Review*, **30**, p. 574.
18. "Dairying in the South." H. HATCHER, *Econ. Geog.*, **20**, p. 54.

CHAPTER VIII

THE MIDWEST

1. *The North American Midwest.* J. H. GARLAND.
2. *Midwest at Noon.* G. HUTTON.
3. *The Great Lakes.* H. HATCHER.
4. *Industrial Activity and Economic Geography.* R. C. ESTALL and R. O. BUCHANAN.
5. "The Major Milksheds of the North-eastern Quarter of the U.S." C. DURAND, *Econ. Geog.*, **40**, p. 9.
6. "The American Dairy Region." L. DURAND, *Econ. Geog.*, **23**, p. 32.
7. "Agricultural Land Use in Iowa." H. L. SMITH, *Econ. Geog.*, **25**, p. 190.
8. "The Agricultural Geography of the Dakotas." R. R. RAWSON, *Geography*, **25**, p. 6.
9. "Changing Patterns of Cropland Use in the Middle West." J. C. WEAVER, *Econ. Geog.*, **30**, p. 1.
10. "Crop Combination Regions in the Middle West." J. C. WEAVER, *Geog. Review*, **44**, p. 175.
11. "Livestock Units and Combination Regions in the Middle West." J. C. WEAVER, P. H. LEVERETT, and B. L. FENTON, *Econ. Geog.*, **32**, p. 237.
12. "A Functional Classification of Cities in the United States." C. D. HARRIS, *Geog. Review*, **33**, p. 86.
13. "Changing Patterns of Coal Production in the Eastern Interior Field." H. G. ROEPKE, *Econ. Geog.*, **31**, p. 234.
14. "The Geographical Significance of Recent Changes in Mining in the Bituminous Coalfields of Pennsylvania." G. F. DEASY and P. R. GRIESS, *Econ. Geog.*, **33**, p. 283.
15. "The Mining of Taconite, Lake Superior Iron Mining District." C. F. KOHN and R. E. SPECHT, *Geog. Review*, **48**, p. 528.
16. "Industrial Inertia—a Major Factor in the Location of the Steel Industry of the United States." A. RODGERS, *Geog. Review*, **42**, p. 56.

17. "Water—a Neglected Factor in the Geographical Literature of Iron and Steel." C. L. WHITE, *Geog. Review,* **47**, p. 463.
18. "Economic Development of the Great Kanawha Valley." L. M. DAVIS, *Econ. Geog.,* **21**, p. 255.
19. "Commerce of the Sault Canals." A. G. BALLERT, *Econ. Geog.,* **33**, p. 135.
20. "Prospects and Problems of the Port of Chicago." H. M. MAYER, *Econ. Geog.,* **31**, p. 95.
21. "Appalachian State: West Virginia as a case study in the Appalachian regional development problem." R. C. ESTALL, *Geography,* **53**, p. 1.

CHAPTER IX

THE GREAT PLAINS

1. *The Great Plains.* W. P. WEBB.
2. *The Oregon Trail.* F. PARKMAN.
3. *The Great Plains in Transition.* C. F. KRAENZEL.
4. "Natural Vegetation of the Great Plains," H. L. SHANTZ; and "Soils of the Great Plains", C. F. MARBUT, *Annals of Assoc. American Geographer,* **13**.
5. "The Northern Great Plains as Producer of Wheat." R. E. WARD, *Econ. Geog.,* **22**, p. 231.
6. "The Oklahoma Panhandle—a Cross-section of the Southern High Plains." A. H. DOERR and J. W. MORRIS, *Econ. Geog.,* **36**, p. 70.
7. "Risk in the Central Great Plains: Geographical Pattern of Wheat Failure in Nebraska, 1931-52." L. HEWES and A. C. SCHMIEDING, *Geog. Review,* **46**, p. 375.

CHAPTER X

THE MOUNTAIN STATES

1. *California and the South-west.* C. M. ZIERER.
2. *Habitat, Economy and Society.* D. FORDE, Chap. xii.
3. "The Colorado River: Its Utilisation in South California." G. P. CURTI, *Geography,* **42**, p. 230.
4. "Recent Economic Trends in Arizona." W. V. G. BALCHIN and N. PYE, *Geog. Jour.,* **120**, p. 156.
5. "Desert Controls Illustrated by the Coachella." R. M. GLENDINNING, *Geog. Review,* **39**, p. 221.
6. "Middle Park and the Colorado—Big Thompson Diversion Project." H. A. HOFFMEISTER, *Econ. Geog.,* **23**, p. 220.

7. "Fruit Industry of the Yakima Valley." E. E. MILLER and R. M. HIGHSMITH, *Econ. Geog.*, **25**, p. 285.
8. "Man's Effects on the Palouse." W. A. ROCKIE, *Geog. Review*, **29**, p. 34.

CHAPTER XI

CALIFORNIA

1. *California and the South-west.* C. M. ZIERER.
2. "The Central Valley Project." E. EISELEN, *Econ. Geog.*, **23**, p. 22.
3. "Californian Manufacturing." J. J. PARSONS, *Geog. Review*, **39**, p. 229.
4. "Cotton in the San Joaquin Valley." D. C. LARGE, *Geog. Review*, **47**, p. 365.
5. "Recent Land Changes in the San Francisco Bay Area." A. N. YOUNG and P. F. GRIFFIN, *Geog. Review*, **47**, p. 396.
6. "Population: A Challenge to California's Changing Citrus Industry." P. F. GRIFFIN and R. L. CHATHAM, *Econ. Geog.*, **34**, p. 272.

CHAPTER XII

PACIFIC NORTH-WEST

1. *The Pacific North-west.* O. W. FREEMAN and H. H. MARTIN.
2. "Rivers as Regional Bonds: The Columbia—Snake Example." E. L. ULLMAN, *Geog. Review*, **41**, p. 210.
3. "Harnessing the Columbia River." G. B. BARBOUR, *Geog. Jour.*, **96**, p. 233.
4. "Timber Supply and Demand in the United States." E. ROSTLUND, *Geog. Review*, **46**, p. 409.
5. "The Fisheries of North-western North America." G. W. HEWES, *Econ. Geog.*, **28**, p. 66.
6. "The Washington Apple Industry." H. LEMONS and R. TOUSLEY, *Econ. Geog.*, **21**, p. 161.
7. "Irrigation in the Willamette Valley." R. M. HIGHSMITH, *Geog. Review*, **46**, p. 98.

CHAPTER XIII

THE ATLANTIC PROVINCES

1. *Studies in the Economy of the Maritime Provinces.* S. A. SAUNDERS.

2. "Settlement Patterns in Maritime Canada." B. J. BIRD, *Geog. Review*, **45**, p. 385.
3. "The Bay of Fundy Salt Marshes." B. J. BIRD, *Geog. Review*, **46**, p. 263.
4. "Population Distribution in Newfoundland." E. B. SHAW, *Econ. Geog.*, **14**, p. 239.
5. "An Introduction to the Geography of Newfoundland." G. A. MERCER, *Can. Geog. Jour.*, **36**, p. 104.
6. "Maritime Industrial Empire." B. J. McGUIRE, *Can. Geog. Jour.*, **53**, p. 124.
7. "Prince Edward Island." W. R. SHAW, *Can. Geog. Jour.*, **52**, p. 182.

CHAPTER XIV

THE LAURENTIAN LOWLANDS

1. *The St Lawrence Seaway.* L. CHEVRIER.
2. *The St Lawrence Seaway.* T. H. HILLS.
3. "The French Element in the Population of Eastern Canada." P. E. HATTERSLEY, *Geography*, **35**, p. 89.
4. "Agricultural Regions of Southern Ontario." L. C. REEDS, *Econ. Geog.*, **35**, p. 219.
5. "Population of Quebec Province." H. H. LEWIS, *Econ. Geog.*, **16**, p. 59.
6. "The Geography of Settlement in Stanstead Township, Province of Quebec." P. J. M. BAILEY, *Geography*, **41**, p. 39.
7. "Farming in Ontario." L. J. CHAPMAN, *Can. Geog. Jour.*, **51**, p. 132.
8. "The Canadian Iron and Steel Industry." D. KERR, *Econ. Geog.*, **35**, p. 151.
9. "The Expansion of the Canadian Aluminium Industry." J. W. BIRCH, *Geography*, **40**, p. 52.
10. "Mapping a Hundred Years of Change in the Niagara Peninsula." J. W. WATSON, *Can. Geog. Jour.*, **32**, p. 266.
11. "Geographical Factors and Land Use in Toronto." N. A. H. DEACON, *Can. Geog. Jour.*, **29**, p. 80.
12. *Geography in the Twentieth Century.* G. TAYLOR, Chap. XX.
13. "Windsor, Ontario." J. L. ROBINSON, *Can. Geog. Jour.*, **27**, p. 106.
14. "Quebec Water Power." B. J. McGUIRE, *Can. Geog. Jour.*, **54**, p. 219.

CHAPTER XV
THE CANADIAN SHIELD

1. *Geography of the Northlands.* G. H. T. KIMBLE and D. GOOD.
2. "The Canadian Shield and its Geographic Effects." E. L. BRUCE, *Geog. Jour.*, **93**, p. 230.
3. "The Labrador Frontier." F. K. HARE, *Geog. Review*, **42**, p. 405.
4. "Schefferville, Quebec: A New Pioneering Town." G. HUMPHRYS, *Geog. Review*, **48**, p. 151.
5. "The Railway Stimulus in Labrador-Ungava." G. HUMPHRYS, *Geography*, **42**, p. 117.
6. "Mineral Regionalism of the Canadian Shield." E. W. MILLER, *Can. Geographer*, **13**, p. 17.
7. "Settlements in the Canadian Shield." G. R. RUMNEY, *Can. Geog. Jour.*, **43**, p. 116.
8. "Wealth from the Canadian Shield." B. J. McGUIRE and H. E. FREEMAN, *Can. Geog. Jour.*, **38**, p. 198.

CHAPTER XVI
THE PRAIRIES

1. *Canadian Frontiers of Settlement.* Vol. 1, *Prairie Settlement*. W. A. MACKINTOSH and W. L. G. JOERG.
2. "Relative Decline of Wheat in the Prairie Provinces of Canada." C. W. JOHNSON, *Econ. Geog.*, **24**, p. 209.
3. "Potash Mining in Saskatchewan." *Geography*, **50**, p. 295.
4. "The South Saskatchewan River." W. EGGLESTON, *Can. Geog. Jour.*, **46**, p. 232.
5. "Alberta, Nature's Treasure House." A. J. HOOKS, *Can. Geog. Jour.*, **35**, p. 154.
6. "Manitoba, Province of Industry." V. J. MACKIE, *Can. Geog. Jour.*, **41**, p. 167.

CHAPTER XVII
BRITISH COLUMBIA

1. "British Columbia: A Study in Topographic Control." G. TAYLOR, *Geog. Review*, **32**, p. 372.
2. "The Physical Basis of Agriculture in British Columbia." D. KERR, *Econ. Geog.*, **28**, p. 229.
3. "Mining Development in British Columbia." J. F. WALKER, *Can. Geog. Jour.*, **45**, p. 114.

4. "Kitimat." G. B. BARBOUR, *Geog. Jour.*, **125**, p. 217.
5. "Kitimat, A Saga of Canada." P. CLARK, *Can. Geog. Jour.*, **49**, p. 152.
6. "The Yellowhead Pass, Canadian Rockies." R. J. C. STEAD, *Can. Geog. Journ.*, **36**, p. 51.

CHAPTER XVIII

THE NORTHLANDS

1. *Geography of the Northlands.* G. H. T. KIMBLE and D. GOOD.
2. "Plant Life in the Arctic." A. E. PORSILD, *Can. Geog. Jour.*, **42**, p. 121.
3. "Land Use in the Arctic." A. E. PORSILD, *Can. Geog. Jour.*, **48**, p. 232.
4. "Recent Developments in the Canadian North." H. L. KEENLEYSIDE, *Can. Geog. Jour.*, **39**, p. 156.
5. "The Development of Transportation in the Canadian North." C. H. HERBERT, *Can. Geog. Jour.*, **53**, p. 188.
6. "The Mackenzie Waterway: A Northern Supply Route." T. LLOYD, *Geog. Review*, **33**, p. 415.
7. "Alaska, Land of Opportunity Limited." W. J. EITEMAN and A. B. SMUTS, *Econ. Geog.*, **27**, p. 33.
8. "Populating Alaska: The United States Phase." K. H. STONE, *Geog. Review*, **42**, p. 384.
9. *The Physiography of Arctic Canada.* J. B. BIRD.
10. "Outpost Agriculture: the Case of Alaska." K. E. FRANCIS, *Geog. Review*, **57**, p. 496.

NATIONAL GEOGRAPHIC MAGAZINE

Almost every issue of the *National Geographic Magazine* contains an article on some geographical aspect or region of North America. The text of these articles is usually chatty and informal but many of the photographs are excellent. Articles which have appeared in the last few years include:

The Witchitas: Land of the Living Prairie	May 1957
River Yukon	Aug. 1957
Bay of Fundy	Aug. 1957
Intracoastal Waterway	Jan. 1958
Corkscrew Swamp, Florida	Jan. 1958
Land of Louisiana Sugar Kings	April 1958
Heritage of Beauty and History (National Parks)	May 1958

FURTHER READING

D.E.W. Line, Sentry of the Far North	July 1958
British Columbia	Aug. 1958
Bryce Canyon	Oct. 1958
The Upper Mississippi	Nov. 1958
The New St Lawrence Seaway	Mar. 1959
New Era on the Great Lakes	April 1959
Staten Island Ferry	June 1959
Alaska Proudly Joins the Union	July 1959
California's Wonderful One	Nov. 1959
I'm from New Jersey	Jan. 1960
The Night the Mountain Moved	Mar. 1960
North-west Wonderland	April 1960
Alberta Unearths Her Buried Treasure	July 1960
Craters of the Moon, Idaho	Oct. 1960
The Lower Mississippi	Nov. 1960
The Fabulous State of Texas	Feb. 1961
Washington Wilderness	April 1961
Canada, My Country	Dec. 1961
North Carolina	Feb. 1962
Henry Hudson's River	Mar. 1962
Cities of Stone, Utah	May 1962
Cape Cod	Aug. 1962
Our Changing Atlantic Coast	Dec. 1962
Arizona	Mar. 1963
Niagara Falls	April 1963
Lonely Wonders of Katmai	June 1963
Ontario	July 1963
Florida rides a Space-age Boom	Dec. 1963
Over and Under Chesapeake Bay	April 1964
Exploring America Underground	June 1964
Down East to Nova Scotia	June 1964
The World in New York City	July 1964
Chesapeake Country	Sept. 1964
Washington: the City Freedom Built	Dec. 1964
Pittsburgh: Pattern for Progress	Mar. 1965
Alaska's Marine Highway	June 1965
Pennsylvania's Amish Folk	Aug. 1965
St Louis	Nov. 1965
Wyoming: High, Wide and Windy	April 1966
California	May 1966
Parkscape, U.S.A.	July 1966
Canadian Rockies	Sept. 1966
Massachusetts Builds for To-morrow	Dec. 1966

Alaska's Mighty Rivers of Ice	Feb. 1967
Montreal goes to the World	May 1967
The St Lawrence River	May 1967
Illinois	June 1967
Great Salt Lake	Aug. 1967
Houston	Sept. 1967
Everglades National Park	Oct. 1967
The Coast of Maine	June 1968
The Canadian North	July 1968
Great Smokies National Park	Oct. 1968

INDEX

ABILENE, 93, 206
Absecon Is., 123
Acadia, 280
Adirondacks, 3, 64, 132, 291
Aircraft, 166, 192, 194, 255, 267, 269, 302, 316, 318, 333
Air masses, **21-8**
Aklavik, 29, 30, 386
Akron, 193
Alabama, 89, 137, 139, 153, 157, 181
Alameda, 252
Alaska Current, 20
— Highway, 333, 348, 353, 382, 388, 389
— Panhandle, 18, 362, 378, 383-5
— Range, 17, 379, 383
Albany, 132
Alberta, 51, 71, 98, 314, 337, 340, 341, 343, 346, 347, 348, 350, 377
Albuquerque, 217, 233
Alcan, 301, 302
Alcoa, 147
Aleutian Is., 18, 20, 378, 379
Aleuts, 378, 380
Alfalfa, 121, 122, 209, 211, 212, 221, 225, 226, 229, 231, 246, 313, 314, 347, 348, 349, 370
All-American Canal, 230, 236
Allard Lake, 302, 329
Allegheny Front, 8, 87, 117, 150
— Plateau, 8, 87, 116, 117, 170, 180
— R., 86, 180, 185, 193
Allentown, 121
Altoona, 116
Aluminium, 147, 158, 163, 167, 227, 267, 269, 301, **302**, 368, **373-4**, 375
Amarillo, 167, 213
Amerinds, 76
Amherst, 288
Anaconda, 220-1
Anchorage, 383, 385
Androscoggin R., 104
Annacis Is., 374
Annapolis Valley, 280, 282, 283, **285-6**
Ann Arbor, 191
Anthracite, 120, 350, 360
Antimony, 368
Apples, 105, 120, 152, 177, **226**, 229, 246, 251, 253, 264, 285, **286**, 297, 313, 370
Apricots, 246, 251, 370
Arbuckle Mts, 11, 151, 165

Arizona, 143, 213, 215, 221, 222, 228, 232, 234, 238
Arkansas R., 11, 151, 162, 197, 202, 203, 212
— Valley, 90, 151, 152
Aroostook Valley, 103, 106, 285
Arrow Lakes, 371, 373
Arthur Kill, 128
Arvida, 302
Asbestos, 279, 299, 367
Ashville, 158
Assiniboine R., 336, 352
Assumption Valley, 297
Astoria, 266
Athabasca Lake, 320
— R., 337, 351, 389
— Tar Sands, 351
Atlanta, 158
Atlantic City, 123
— Slope, 116
Atomic energy, 148, 267, 331
Automobiles, 188, **191**, 192, 193, 194, 255, 316, 317, 333
Avalon Peninsula, 272, 273, 280

BADLANDS, 12, 198-9, 337
Baffin Island, 319, 332, 392
Baie Comeau, 302
— Verte, 279
Bakersfield, 241, 249
Balcones Fault, 165, 197, 198, 199
Baltimore, 7, 83, 86, 121, 122, **126**, 129, 186
Bancroft, 329, 331
Banff, 359
Barkerville, 368
Barrow, 43, 332, 379
Bathurst, 286, 288
Baton Rouge, 163
Bauxite, 152, 153, 158, 163, 267, 302, 373
Bay of Fundy, 280, 281, 282, 283, 284, 285, 287
Bayonne, 129
Beauharnois, 299, 302, 307, 308
Beaumont, 165, 167
Beaverlodge, 329, 331
Belle Is., 274, 276
Belleville, 317
Bellingham, 267, 268
Bell Is., 279, 288, 315
Bering Sea, 379, 384, 391

413

Berkeley, 252
Bersimis R., 302
Bethlehem, 121, 186
Big Horn Basin, 218
Bingham, 232
Birmingham, 146-7, 180, 186
Bisbee, 232
Bismark, 37
Bison, 93, 205
Bitterroot R., 220, 221
Bitumount, 351
Black Belt, Alabama, 66, 68, 96, 137, 141, 154
— Hills, 3, 12, 49, 91, 197, 201, 210, 213
Black's Harbour, 287
Blackstone Valley, 108, 111
Black Waxy Prairies, 141, 164
Blind R., 331
Blueberries, 107, 280
Blue Mts, 17, 91, 223
Boise, 226, 227
Boll Weevil, 142, 154
Bonneville, 227, 261, 266, 369
Boston, 84, 107, 111, 112, 113, **114-15**, 126, 127
Boston Mts, 151
Botwood, 278, 279
Boulder Canyon, 236, 237
Bradley, 221
Brantford, 317
Bras d'Or, 283
Break of the Plains, 12, 197, 198, 199
Bridge Canyon, 231
Bridgeport, 112
Bridge R., 368, 372
Britannia Beach, 368
Brockton, 111
Brooks Range, 13, 379
Bruce Peninsula, 309
Bryce Canyon, 234
Buchans, 279, 288
Buckingham, 299
Buffalo, 121, 132, 133, 184, 185, 186, 188, 347
— Grass, 64, 201
Butte, 220

CACTUS, **63**, 223, 340, 364
Cairo, 88, 161
Cajon Pass, 253
Calgary, 36, 48, 338, 343, 347, 348, 350, **353**
Calhoun, 146, 157
California Current, 21, 28, 30, 46, 241
— Trail, 91
Camden, 122, 125
Canadian National Railway, 327, 330, 333, 359, 372, 375

Canadian Pacific Railway, 98, 330, 332-3, 342, 348, 353, 359, 364
— R., 203
— Wheat Board, 346
Canning, 107, 122-3, 126, 152, 158, 251, 252, 266, 267, 277, 287, 314, 368, 369, 384
Canso, 287
Canton, 192
Cape Canaveral, 161
— Cod, 5, 9, 84, 102, 107
— Hatteras, 6
— Race, 275
Cariboo Mts, 358, 368
Caribou, 57, 392
— Mts, 337
Carolina, 68, 96, 137, 139, 154, 156, 158
Carson Sink, 228
Cascades, 17, 18, 34, 59, 223, 226, **260**, 262, 263, 264, 358
Cassiar Mts, 358, 367
Catawba, 156
Catskill Mts, 117, 132
Cattle: New England, 105; Middle Atlantic Region, 117, 119, 121, 133; South, 143, 145, 150, 152, 154-5, 164; Midwest, 175, 177; Great Plains, 205-6, 210-11; Mountain States, 218, 221, 226, 228, 229; California, 245, 246, 247, 251, 254; Pacific Northwest, 263, 264; Atlantic Provinces, 280, 284, 285, 289; Laurentian Lowlands, 296, 297, 313-14; Canadian Shield, 326, 330; Prairies, 343, 347, 348; British Columbia, 370, 371, 372; Alaska, 383
Cement, 120, 317, 353
Central Arizona Project, 231, 232, 237
— City, 217
— Valley Project, 248-9
Chalk R., 331
Champlain Valley, 105
Chaparral, 60, 244, 250
Charleston (S.C.), 30, 31, 36, 52, 83
— (W.V.), 192
Chatham, 317
Chattanooga, 93, 146
Cheese, 177, 264, 296, 314, 327
Chehalis R., 258, 264
Chemicals: New England, 113; Middle Atlantic Region, 126, 133; South, 148, 158, 163, 166-7; Midwest, 182, 192, 193, 195; California, 252; Pacific Northwest, 269; Laurentian Lowlands, 315, 316, 317, 318; Prairies, 353; British Columbia, 368

INDEX

Chernozems, 71, 201, 208, 340, 344
Cherries, 177, 226, 264, 313
Chesapeake Bay, 6, 123, 126, 127
Cheyenne, 214
Chibougamau, 328, 329, 330, 333
Chicago, 89, 93, 96, 137, 173, 176, 182, 184, 185, 186, **187-90**, 342
Chilkoot Pass, 385, 388
Chinook Winds, **26**, 49, 201, 338
Chisholm Trail, 206
Chromium, 279
Churchill, 333, 346
Cimarron R., 203
Cincinatti, 88, 171, 186, 188, **192**
Civil War, 92, 93, 96, 111, 137, **138-40**, 141, 205
Clarkson, 314, 318
Clay Belt, 5, 321, **326-7**, 328, 330, 333, 347
Cleveland, 182, 184, 185, 186, 188, **192-3**, 332
Clifton, 131
Climatic regions, **42-53**
Climax, 218
Clothing manufacture, 126, 131, 190, 302, 305, 316, 317, 318
Clover, 75, 121, 122, 144, 150, 155, 175, 313, 314, 348
Coachella Valley, **230-1**, 236
Coal: Middle Atlantic Region, 120, 125, 126, 129; South, 146, 152; Midwest, 170, **179-81**, 184, 193; Great Plains, 213; Mountain States, 218, 233; California, 255; Pacific North-west, 267; Maritime Provinces, 279, 283, 287-8; Prairies, 349, 350, 353; British Columbia, 360, 367, 372; Alaska, 383; Northern Canada, 388, 392
Cobalt, 314, 328, 329
Cobequid Mts, 282
Cochrane, 321
Cod, 108, 277, 287, 368, 383
Codroy Valley, 280
Coeur d'Alene, 220, 221, 267
Cohoes, 133
Cold wall, 275
Collingwood, 313
Colonies, **79-85**, 116
Colorado, 15, 49, 178, 208, 212, 213, 215, 216, 217, 221, 238
— -Big Thompson Project, 212
— Piedmont, 72, 197, 203
— R., 3, 16, 74, 91, 164, 228, 230-1, **235-7**, 239, 253, 256, 260
Columbia Basin Reclamation Project, 226
— R., 17, 224-7, **260-2**, 267, 269, 359, 368, 371, 372, **373**

Columbus, 154, 187, 188
Commodity Credit Corporation, 143, 210
Comstock Lode, 231
Coniston, 330
Connecticut, 101, 103, 109, 112
— Valley, 9, 101, 102, 105, 107, 108, 112
Connelsville, 180
Copper: Middle Atlantic Region, 126, 129, 131, 133; South, 146; Midwest, 183, 191; Mountain States, 220, **221**, 232-3; Pacific Northwest, 269; Atlantic Provinces, 279, 288; Laurentian Lowlands, 314; Canadian Shield, **329-30**; British Columbia, 368, 376
— Cliff, 330
Coppermine, 29, 30, 33, 329, 330, 333
Copper Mt, 368
Corn: New England, 107; Middle Atlantic Region, 119, 121; South, 142, 143, 145, 150, 151, 155; Midwest, **174-6**; Great Plains, 207, 208; Pacific North-west, 264; Laurentian Lowlands, 296, 312, 399
Corner Brook, 275, 278
Cornwall, 307
Corpus Christi, 167
Cotton, 89, 96, 111, **140-3**, 151, 153, 154, 158, 162, 163, 164, 207, 212, 231, 246, 399
Coulees, 17, 224
Courtenay, 367
Cowlitz R., 259, 356
Cranberries, 107
Crater Lake, 260
Creosote bush, 63, 223, 234
Cripple Creek, 218
Crow's Nest Pass, 350, 359, 360, 367
Cultivated fallow, 208, 210
Cumberland Gap, 87, 119, 150
— Plateau, 145, 149
— R., 8, 87, 88
— Road, 86, 124, 187, 192
Cuyahoga R., 193
Cypress Hills, 337, 343

DAIRY farming: New England, 105; Middle Atlantic Region, 119, 121, 122, 133; South, 152; Midwest, 177; Mountain States, 221, 226, 229; California, 246, 251, 254; Pacific North-west, 263, 264; Maritime Provinces, 280, 284, 285, 289; Laurentian Lowlands, 296, 313-14; Canadian

INDEX

Shield, 330; Prairies, 347, 348; British Columbia, 370, 371; Alaska, 383
Dakota, 12, 37, 93, 195, 199, 207, 208, 209, 213
Dalhousie, 286
Dallas, 166
Dalles, the, 260, 261, 269
Dates, 164, 231
Dawson City, 32, 44, 385, 388
— Creek, 348, 389
Dayton, 187, 188, 192
Deer Lake, 278
Delaware, 122, 129
— Bay, 6, 122, 123, 126
— R., 116, 125, 128
Delhi, 313
Delmarva, 122, 126
Deloro, 314
Denver, 36, 48, 49, 200, 213, 214, 217
Depressions, **22-3**, 27, 37, 49, 50, 52, 103, 243, 275, 295
Deserts, **62**, 72, 223
Detroit, 96, 184, 185, 186, 188, **191**, 255, 316
D.E.W. Line, 394
Dismal Swamp, 6, 153
Dolbean, 299
Donner Pass, 91, 244, 252
Door Peninsula, 178
Douglas fir, 59, 60, 61, 216, 223, 250, 259, 264, 362, 364, 365
Drumheller, 350
Dry farming, 73, 75, 208, 224, **345-6**
Duck Mt, 336
Duluth, 173, 184, 185, 186
Dumas, 213
Durum Wheat, 345
Dust Bowl, 73, 210

EAGLE Mt, 255
Eastern Shore, 122
East R., 127, 129
Edmonton, 339, 343, 347, 348, 350, **352-3**, 389
Edmundston, 284, 286
Edwards Plateau, 197
Effective precipitation, **38-41**, 49, 59, 199, 200, 339, 347, 361, 363
Eldorado, 329, 331
Electrical industries, 112, 115, 131, 133, 190, 192, 193, 195, 302, 316, 317, 318
Elephant Butte, 217
Elizabeth, 130
Elliot Lake, 329, 331
Ellis Is., 128
El Paso, 79, 217

Ely, 232
Engelmann Spruce, 61, 216, 223, 364
Engineering, 112, 125, 126, 131, 133, 190, 252, 269, 353
Erie Canal, 89, 124, 132
Eskimos, 76, 98, 321, 378, **380**, 387, 389, 390, 392
Esterhazy, 352
Estevan, 350
Eureka, 46, 251
Evaporation, **39**, 200, 203, 222, 237, 348
Evapotranspiration, **40-1**, 199
Everett, 112, 268
Exploits R., 273, 274, 276, 278

FAIRBANKS, 382, 384
Falconbridge, 330
Fall Line, **6-7**, 121, 122, 123, 128, 154
— River, 109, 111
Farmland: New England, 105; Middle Atlantic Region, 119, 121, 122, 133; South, 143, 144, 145, 150, 151, 154-6, 160, 162, 164; Midwest, 174-9; Great Plains, 207, 211, 212; Rockies, 221; Palouse, 224; Columbia Plateau, 225-6; Great Basin, 228-31; Irrigated, 238; California, 245-9, 250-1, 253-4; Pacific North-west, 263; Atlantic Provinces, 279, 280, 284-5, 289, 296-7; St Lawrence Valley, 296; Ontario Peninsula, 311-12; Shield, 326, 327; Prairies, 340, 343; Peace R., 348; British Columbia, 365, 370; Alaska, 382, 383; North-west Territories, 388
Fayetteville, 181
Fernie, 350, 367
Fertilisers, 123, 126, 148, 159, 175, 266, 285, 287, 317, 368
Filberts, 264
Films, 254
Finger Lakes, 117, 132, 133, 178
Finlay R., 359
Fiords, 9, 18, 355, 358, 374, 384
Fishing: New England, 84, 107-8; Middle Atlantic Region, 123; California, 251, 256; Pacific North-west, 265-6; Newfoundland, 80, 271, 276-8; Maritime Provinces, 286-7; St Lawrence Valley, 297; British Columbia, 364, 368-9; Northlands, 378; Alaska, 384
Flakes, 272, 277
Flathead Valley, 221

INDEX 417

Flat R., 152
Flax, 208, 297, 348
Flin Flon, 329, 330
Flint, 191
— Hills, 210
Floods, 10, 25, 162, 317, 389
Florida Keys, 1, 6, 160
Flour-milling, 133, 195, 209, 213, 227, 269, 349, 353
Fog, 21, 46, 48, 51, 104, 128, 243, 251, 275, 284, 360, 361
Fontana, 186, 255
Forests: 55, **57-66**; New England, 104; South, 145, 146, 156; Midwest, 169; Mountain States, 216, 222; California, 244, 250; Pacific North-west, 259, 264; Newfoundland, 276; Maritime Provinces, 286, 289; Laurentian Lowlands, 297, 311; Shield, 322; Prairies, 347; British Columbia, 362-4, 365; Alaska, 382, 384; North-west Territories, 387, 396
Forestry: 58; New England, **104-5**; Middle Atlantic Region, 119; South, 146, 152, **156-7**; Midwest, 169; Mountain States, 221; California, 244, 250; Pacific North-west, **264-5**, 269; Newfoundland, 279-80; Maritime Provinces, 286; Laurentian Lowlands, **297-9**; Shield, **324-6**, 334; British Columbia, **365-6**
Forks of the Ohio, 86, 87, 193
Fort Augustine, 79
— Cataraqui, 308
— Dearborn, 190
— Duquesne, 193, 308
— Niagara, 308
— Providence, 391
— Rouge, 352
— Rouillé, 308
— Royal, 119
— Saskatchewan, 331
— Smith, 377, 389
— Vermilion, 30, 31, 32, 44
— Wayne, 186
— William, 307, 326, 333, 346, 347
— Worth, 166
Franklin, 377, 390
— Range, 385
Fraser Plateau, 358, 372
— R., 17, 357, 358, 359, 364, 369, 370, 372, 374, 375
Fredericton, 285
Freeport, 167
Freezing foods, 106, 108, 123, 158, 247, 254, 263, 266, 267, 277, 369

French Broad R., 147
French-Canadians, **80-2**, 98, 114, **292-4**, 395
Fresno, 246
Frobisher, 332, 392
Frontenac Axis, 291, 313
Frontier, 87, 88, 89, 94, 98, 119, 168, 308, 333, 353
Front Range, 212, 217
Frost, **33**, *see* Growing season
Fruit: New England, 107; Middle Atlantic Region, 120, 122, 123, 133; South, 152, 155, 160, 164; Midwest, **177-9**; Great Plains, 212; Mountain States, 221, 226, 229, 231; California, 240, **246-7**, 251, 253; Pacific North-west, 264; Maritime Provinces, 280, 285; Ontario Peninsula, 312, 313; Prairies, 349; British Columbia, 370; Northlands, 383; 399
Fur farming, 285, 324
Furs, 162, 191, 220, **323-4**, 341, 364, **387-8**
Fur trading, 77, 81, 168, **323-4**, 341, 352, 378, 388, 390

GAGNON, 332
Galt, 317
Galveston, 25, 29, 30, 32, 36, 52, 167
Gander, 273
— R., 274, 276
Gary, 185, 186, 188, 190
Gaspé Peninsula, 281, 294, 297
Gatineau, 299, 302
Genesee R., 133
— Road, 86, 132
Geneva, 186, 233, 256
Georgia, 6, 7, 96, 137, 139, 154, 156, 157
Georgian Bay, 309, 313, 318
Georgia Strait, 18, 369
Geysers, 15, 218
Ghost towns, 217, 231
Gila R., 79, 231, 236
Glaciation, **3-5**, 9, 10-11, 13, 17; New England, 102; Middle Atlantic Region, 132; Midwest, 171; Rockies, 218, 220; Columbia Plateau, 224; Pacific North-west, 259; Atlantic Provinces, 270; Newfoundland, 274; Maritime Provinces, 283; St Lawrence Valley, 294; Ontario Peninsula, 309-10; Shield, 320; Prairies, 335, 336, 337; British Columbia, 358; Alaska, 379; North-west Territories, 392

N.A. 27

418 INDEX

Glaciers, 13, 18, 220, 260, 359
Glass, 193, 252, 317
Glen Canyon, 237
Gloucester, 107
Gloversville, 133
Goats, 211
Gold, 91, **213**, 217, 218, 220, 240, 245, 279, **328-9**, 330, 364, 368, 378, 380, 382, 385, 388, 393
Golden Gate, 18, 46, 250, 252
Goose Bay, 332
Graham Is., 357, 358
Grama Grass, 63, 201, 340
Granby, 303
Grand Banks, 274, 275, 277
— Canal, 126
— Canyon, 3, 16, 233, 236
— Coulee, 224, 226, 227, 261, 266
— Falls, 278, 283
— Haven, 29
— 'Mère, 298, 301
— Prairie, 164, 347, 348
— River, 309, 310, 316
Grapes, 133, 152, 160, 177, 179, 226, 231, 246, 313
Grassland, **63**, 201, 339-40, 364, 380
Grazing, 207, 209, 210-11, 222, 228-9, 245, 264, 372, 380, *see also* Ranching
Great Bear Lake, 44, 320
— Falls, 214, 220, 221
— Salt Lake, 16, 228
— Slave Highway, 389
— — Lake, 44, 320, 333, 348, 389
— Smoky Mts, 7, 145, 154
— Valley, 18, 91, 101, 119, 120
Green Mts, 9, 101, 132
Growing season: 33, 51, 52; New England, 104; Middle Atlantic Region, 116, 122; South, 135, 140, 150; Midwest, 173, 174, 179; Rockies, 216, 218; Intermontane Plateaus, 222, 226; California, 243; Pacific Northwest, 262-3; Newfoundland, 275; Maritime Provinces, 280, 284, 289; St Lawrence Valley, 295; Ontario Peninsula, 311, 312; Shield, 326; Prairies, 338, 344, 348, 353; British Columbia, 361; Alaska, 382, 383
Guelph, 317
Gulf Stream, 34, 51, 275
Gullying, 73
Gunnison R., 212

HACKENSACK R., 130
Haddock, 108, 287
Hail, 103, 200, 209, 339, 345
Halibut, 108, 266, 368, 384
Halifax, 281, 284, 287, 288, 305, 313, 347, 351
Hamilton, 192, 305, 313, 315, 316, 317, 331
Hampton Roads, 129, 181
Hanford, 267
Hardwoods, 58, 64, 65, 104, 146, 169, 172, 286, 297, 311, 325
Harlem R., 127, 129
Harper's Ferry, 86, 119, 120
Harrisburg, 116, 119
Hartford, 112
Haverhill, 111
Hay, 150, 151, 175, 208, 211, 212, 229, 263, 264, 280, 284, 285, 286, 296, 314, 326, 330, 347, 370, 372, 383, 399
— R., 348, 389, 390
Hebron, 30, 31, 43
Helena, 220, 221
Hell's Canyon, 224
— Gate, 369
Henderson Lake, 360
Herring, 108, 266, 277, 287, 368, 384
Hibbing, 182
Hiwassee R., 146
Hoboken, 129
Hogs, 145, 175, 211, 247, 285, 296, 314, 326, 347, 370
Holland Marsh, 313
Hollywood, 254
Holston R., 147
Holyoke, 105, 108, 109, 112, 113
Hope, 358, 368, 372
Hopi Indians, 235
Hops, 226, 264
Horseshoe Moraine, 309
Houston, 129, 166, **167**, 186
Hudson Bay, 3, 20, 43, 319, 320, 321, 327, 333, 337, 359
— Hope, 372, 373
— -Mohawk Gap, 89, 115, 125
— — Valley, 85, 124, **132-3**, 168
— R., 9, 82, 84, 115, 116, 119, 127, 128, 129, 132, 133, 303
Hudson's Bay Co., 82, 96, 98, 323, 341, 352, 390
Hull, 299
Humber R., 273, 274, 276, 278, 280, 318
Humboldt R., 91, 228, 229
Hurricanes, **23-6**, 28, 36, 52, 103, 160
Hydro-electricity: New England, 109; Middle Atlantic Region, 123; South, **147-8**, 157; Midwest, 182; Great Plains, 204; Columbia, **226-7**; Colorado, 237; Cali-

INDEX

fornia, 244, 252; Pacific Northwest, 261-2, 267; Newfoundland, 278; Maritime provinces, 283; St Lawrence Valley, 298, **299-302**, 308; Ontario, 315; Shield, 320; Prairies, 352; British Columbia, 365, 368, **372-4**

ICEBERGS, 275
Icefields, 13, 358, 359
Idaho, 215, 220, 221, 225, 226, 238, 257, 267
Ile Jésus, 297
— Maligne, 301, 302
Illinois, 10, 55, 175, 181, 182, 221
— Canal, 89
Immigration, 86, 94, **95-6**, 97, 109, 131-2, 190, 191, 245, 257, 281, 289, 292, 293, 308, 316, 342, 395
Imperial Valley, **230-1**, 236, 253
Indiana, 172, 181, 190, 192
— Harbour, 185
Indianapolis, 93, 187, 188, **192**
Indian R., 6, 160
Indians, 60, **76-9**, 83, 93, 94, 98, 160, 205, **235**, 323, 378, 380, 387, 390
Inland Passage, 18, 266, 384
Inner Coast Plain, 140, 141, 154
Inner Ranges, 17, 18
International Rapids, 306, 307
Intra-coastal Waterway, 163, 167
Inverness, 287
Inuvik, 386, 389
Iowa, 55, 172, 175, 211
Iron ore: Middle Atlantic Region, 125, 129, 133; South, 147; Midwest, 170, **182-3**, 185, 193-4; Great Plains, 213; Utah, 233; California, 255; Newfoundland, 279; Maritime provinces, 288; Laurentian Lowlands, 307, 315-16; Shield, **331-2**; British Columbia, 368
— and steel industry: New England, 112; Middle Atlantic Region, 121, 125, 126, 133; South, 146, 167; Midwest, **185-6**, 188, 190, 191, 192, 193-4; Great Plains, 213; Utah, 233; California, 255; Pacific North-west, 267; Newfoundland, 279; Maritime Provinces, 287-8; Ontario, 315-16, 317; Shield, 333; Prairies, 353; British Columbia, 368
Iroquois Indians, 85
— Locks, 307
Irrigation: 17; South, 141, 155, 164; Great Plains, 203, 204-5, 211,

212; Rockies, 217, 221; Columbia Plateau, 225-7; Great Basin, 229-31, **237-9**; California, 240, 244, **246-9**, 253, 256; Pacific North-west, 261, 264; Ontario, 313; Prairies, 343, **348-9**, 353; British Columbia, 370
Island Ranges, 356, 357, 379

JACKSONVILLE, 161
James R., 83
Jamestown, 83
Japanese, 95, 241, 246, 251
Jersey City, 129
Jewellery, 112
Johnstown, 185, 192
Joliette, 297, 299
Jonquière, 299
Joplin, 152
Judith Basin, 213
Juneau, 383, 385

KAMLOOPS, 363, 376
Kanawha R., 8, 181, **192**
Kansas, 152, 166, 208, 209, 210
Kansas City, 176, 194
Keewatin, 3, 29, 43, 321, 377, 390
Kellog, 221
Kelowna, 366, 370, 376
Kemano, 373
Kenai Peninsula, 59, 379, 383
Kennebec R., 104
Kennebecasis, R., 282
Kenogan, 299
Kentucky, 10, 87, 88, 137, 139, 144, 145, 149, 150, 151, 156, 180, 181
Ketchikan, 384, 385
Keweenaw, 170, 183
Keys, Florida, 6, 160
Key West, 160
Kicking Horse Pass, 353, 359, 360
Kill van Kull, 128
Kimberley, 367
King's R., 245
Kingston, 308
Kipawa, 299
Kirkland Lake, 329
Kitchener, 317
Kitimat, 368, 373, 375
Klamath Mts, 244, 245, 250, 258.
Klondike, 91, 378, 388
Knoxville, 148, 163
Kodiak, 378, 379, 384
Kootenay Valley, 221, 359, 362, 368, 372, 373
Kudzu, 75, 144, 155
Kuskokwim R., 379, 382

420 INDEX

LABRADOR Current, 21, 31, 51, 275, 284, 295, 321
Lachine Rapids, 304, 305, 307
Lachute, 299
Lac Jeannine, 332
Lackawanna R., 120
Lake Abitibi, 327
— Agassiz, 5, 172, 335
— Algonquin, 5, 320
— Allard, 302, 329
— Athabasca, 320
— Barlow, 326
— Bonneville, 16, 228, 229
— Champlain, 101, 105, 294, 303
— Chelan, 260
— Erie, 168, 172, 178, 179, 184, 185, 193, 305, 307, 309, 310, 312, 313, 314, 315, 317, 330, 331
— Flathead, 220, 359
— Humboldt, 228
— Huron, 184, 305, 309, 321
— Lake Kenogami, 301
— Lahontan, 228
— Manitoba, 5, 335
— Mead, 237
— Michigan, 29, 89, 178-9, 184, 185, 187-9, 307
— Mono, 244, 256
— Ojibway, 5, 321, 327
— Okeechobee, 6, 159, 160
— Ontario, 133, 178, 294, 305, 305, 307, 309, 310, 312, 313, 314, 315, 316, 318
— Owens, 244, 256
— Pen d'Oreille, 220
— Pontchartrain, 162
— Roosevelt, 226
— St Francis, 307
— St John, 294, 296, 299, 301, 327
— St Louis, 307
— Simcoe, 310, 311, 313, 318
— Superior, 170, **182-3**, 184, 185, 305, 307, 316, 320, 321, 331, 347
— Tahoe, 244
— Tulare, 245
— Timiskaming, 326
— Washington, 268, 269
— Winnipeg, 5, 320, 335, 337, 352
— Winnipegosis, 5, 335
Lancaster, 121
Lanigan, 352
Lansing, 191
Laprairie, 297
Laramie Range, 217
Laredo, 167
Lassen Peak, 244
Las Vegas, 233
La Tranche, 301
La Tuque, 298, 301, 302

Laurentides, 3, 319
Lava, 16, 17, 101, 215, 218, 223-4, 319
Lawrence, 108, 111
Lead, 152, 170, 218, 220, **221**, 232, 279, 288, 329, 367, 368, 376, 388
Leadville, 217
Leather, 109, 111, 115, 190, 195, 303, 305, 317
Leduc, 350
Lehigh Valley, 120
Lenoir, 146
Lespedeza, 75, 144, 151, 155
Lethbridge, 28, 348, 349, 350
Lettuce, 160, 229, 231, 246, 251, 253, 313, 370
Lexington, 10, 149
Liard Plains, 359
— R., 359, 360, 385
Lichen, 56, 57, 58, 276, 322, 380, 382
Lièvre R., 302
Lignite, 213, 349, 350
Lillooet, 358, 372
Limestone, 120, 147, 183, 279, 288
Little Rock, 152-3
Liverpool, 286
Lobsters, 108, 277-8, 287
Loess, 11, 172, 197, 224
London, 316
Long Beach, 254, 256
— Island, 5, 9, 102, 122, 127, 128
— Lac, 329
— Range, 274
— Sault, 307
Longueuil, 302
Longview, 267
Lorain, 186
Los Angeles, 79, 90, 93, 129, 236, 246, 250, 251, **253-6**
Louisbourg, 280, 281
Louisiana, 139, 162, 166, 182, 193
— Purchase, 80, 82
Louisville, 88, 188
Lowell, 108, 111
Lunenburg, 281, 287
Lynn, 111
— Lake, 328, 329, 330, 331, 333

MACHINERY manufactures, 112, 188, 192, 194, 256, 316, 317, 318
Mackenzie Highway, 333, 348, 389
— Mts, 385, 388
Madawaska R., 315
Magnesium, 167, 329
Magog, 303
Maine, 102, 104, 106, 107, 109
Maize, see Corn
Mammoth Cave, 150
Manassas Gap, 119
Manchester, 111

INDEX

Manganese, 218, 288, 329
Manhattan Is., 84, 127, 129, 131-2
Manicouagan R., 302
Manitoba, 58, 68, 324, 325, 338, 377
Manitouwadge, 328, 330
Maple, 65, 104, 106, 276, 286, 297
Marmora, 315
Marquette, 183
Martha's Vineyard, 102
Maryland, 122, 134, 156
Mason-Dixon Line, 134
Massachusetts, 101, 109
Masson, 299
Matanuska Valley, 383
Mayo, 388
McDame, 367
Meat-packing, 166, 176, 189-90, 192, 195, 213, 250, 343, 349, 353, 374
Medicine Hat, 339, 348
Megalopolis, 123
Megantic, 303
Memphis, 163
Menhaden, 123
Menominee, 183
Mercury, 245
Merrimac R., 108, 111
Mesabi, 182-3, 331
Mesquite, 63, 64, 201, 234
Mexicans, 78, 241, 247
Miami, 36, 53, 161
Mica Creek, 373
Michigan, 10, 176, 182, 191, 221
Michipicoten, 183, 315, 331
Milk R., 337
Milwaukee, 29, 179, 188
Minas Basin, 283
Minneapolis, 163, 188, **194-5**, 209
Minnesota, 171, 176, 177, 208
Mississippi, 137, 139, 153, 156
— R., 10, 12, 13, 74, 81, 88, 89, **161-3**, 171, 182, 188, 202, 315
Missoula, 221
Missouri, 73, 96, 137, 139, 152, 169, 221
— Coteau, 12, 170, 199, 337
— Plateau, 197, 199, 202, 203
— R., 91, 171, 202, **203-5**, 220, 337
— Valley Administration, 204
Mobile, 158
Moisture Deficiency, 41
Mojave Desert, 253
Molybdenum, 218
Monadnock, 7, 9, 320
Monashee Mts, 358
Monongahela R., 86, 180, 185, 193, 194
Montana, 15, 207, 208, 209, 213, 215, 216, 219, 220, 221, 238, 359
Monteregian Hills, 294, 297
Montreal, 37, 80, 96, 288, 292, 294, 295, 296, 299, 302, **303-5**, 306, 307, 313, 347, 350, 351
Monument Valley, 234
Moose Jaw, 350
Moosonee, 333
Morenci, 232
Mormons, 229, 233, 348
Morrisville, 125, 186
Moses-Saunders Dam, 307, 308
Mount McKinley, 17, 379
— Royal, 294, 304
— Shasta, 243
— Whitney, 240
Murray Bay, 294
Muskeg, 57, 58, 320, 323, 347, 386, 387
Muskingum R., 187
Muskoka R., 315

NANAIMO, 367, 376
Nantucket, 102, 107
Napierville, 297
Narragansett Bay, 102, 111
Narrows, 128, 129
Natchez, 163
National Road, 86, 124, 187, 192
Natural gas: South, **165-6**; Midwest, 181-2, 194; Great Plains, 213; Mountain States, 219; California, 249, 255; Pacific Northwest, 267; Laurentian Lowlands, 315; Prairies, **350-2**, 353; British Columbia, 368; Alaska, 383
Navajo Indians, 235
Nebraska, 63, 68, 172, 176, 197, 202, 206, 208, 209, 210, 212
Nechako Plateau, 358, 363, 365, 372
Negroes, 78, 95-6, 127, 132, **137-8**, 153, 190, 191, 241
Nevada, 215, 221, 228, 229, 231, 232, 233, 236, 238
Newark Bay, 129
New Bedford, 107, 111
— Britain, 112
— Brunswick, 270, 277, 280, 284, 285, 286, 288, 290, 294
Newcastle, 288
New Deal, 75, 147
— Glasgow, 288
— Hampshire, 101, 106
— Haven, 112
— Jersey, 6, 122, 123
— Mexico, 213, 215, 221, 233, 238, 331
— Orleans, 28, 29, 30, 82, 88, 129, 162, 163, 166, 169, 308
— Westminster, 366, 374
— York, 7, 37, 50, 96, 111, 115, 123, 125, **127-32**, 137, 303, 347
Niagara Escarpment, 305, 309, 310, 312, 313

Niagara Falls, 133, 182, 305, 315
— Fruit Belt, 313, 318
— Peninsula, 309, 310
— R., 305, 315
Nickel, 279, 314, **329-31**
Nisei, 246
Nome, 332, 380
Noranda, 329, 330
Norman Wells, 388, 389
Northers, 27, 135, 201
North Bay, 326
— Mountain, 282, 285
— Pacific Current, 383
Northumberland Strait, 282, 287
Notre Dame Bay, 277, 278
— — Mts, 9
Nova Scotia, 9, 270, 277, 280, 283, 284, 285, 286, 287, 290

OAKLAND, 252
Oak Ridge, 148
— — Moraine, 310
Oaks, 65, 145, 152, 169, 172, 244, 250, 311
Oats, 175, 176, 208, 225, 263, 284, 285, 296, 314, 326, 330, 347, 349, 372, 382, 393, 399
Ocean Currents, 20, 31, 46, 47, 51
Ogden, 93, 229
Ohio, 172, 176, 178, 180, 181, 192
— R., 8, 86, 87, 88, 92, 119, 150, 171, 182, 188, 192, 308
Oil: Middle Atlantic Region, 125, 126, 129, 131; South, 152, 165-6, 167; Midwest, 181-2; Great Plains, 213; Mountain States, 218, 219; California, 240, 249, 252, 254-5; Ontario Peninsula, 314; Prairies, 350-2, 353; British Columbia, 368; Northlands, 380, 383, 388, 392
— refining: Middle Atlantic Region, 125, 129, 131; South, 163, 166; Midwest, 190, 193; Great Plains, 213; California, 252, 254; Maritime Provinces, 288; Laurentian Lowlands, 302, 304, 314, 317, 318; Shield, 333; Prairies, 349, 350, 351, 352, 353; British Columbia, 374; Northlands, 388
Oklahoma, 26, 137, 141, 152, 166, 208, 209, 210, 213
— City, 165, 209
Olives, 246
Olympic Mts, 59, 258-9
Omaha, 32, 91, 93, 176, 194
Onondaga Escarpment, 309
Ontario, 5, 58, 65, 286, 300, 308, 311, 316, 321, 324, 325, 326, 327, 329, 377
Orange, 167
Oranges, 160, 246, 253
Oregon, 17, 34, 41, 215, 238, 257, 258, 265, 356
— City, 261
— Trail, 90-1, 218, 257, 269
Osage Plains, 164
Oshawa, 316, 317
Ottawa R., 294, 299, 302, 303, 306, 313, 315, 331
Ouachita Mts, 11, 144, 151
Oysters, 266, 287

PACIFIC Mts, 15, 17-19
Padre Is., 12
Paint, 131, 191, 193, 375
Painted Desert, 234
Palisades, 128
Palliser's Triangle, 340, 342
Palmer, 383
Palo Verde, 231, 237
Pamlico Sound, 6
Pangnirtung, 392
Paper, 104-5, 146, 156-7, 265, 278, 286, 288, **297-9**, 301, 302, 303, 314, 333, 365-6, 374, 384
Parkland, 340, 347
Park Range, 217
Parks, 217
Parsnip R., 359
Pasquia Hills, 336
Passaic, 130, 131
Patapsco R., 126
Paterson, 130, 131
Pawtucket, 111
Peace R., 17, 337, 359, 360, 372, 373, 389
Peaches, 133, 152, **155**, 177, 226, 229, 246, 253, 313, 370
Peanuts, 122, 143, 155
Pears, 133, 226, 246, 251, 313
Pecos R., 197, 202
Pedalfers, **68**, 196, 201
Pedocals, **68**, 196, 201
Pembina Mt, 336
— Oilfield, 350
— R., 336
Pennsylvania, 179, 180, 181, 316
— Route, 86, 123
Pennyroyal, 150
Penobscot R., 104
Penokee, 3
Penticton, 376
Peribonca R., 301
Permafrost, 57, 69, 322, 323, 377-8, 379, **386-7**

INDEX 423

Perth-Amboy, 130
Petroleum, see Oil
Petrolia, 314
Philadelphia, 7, 116, 121, 123, 124, **125-6**, 127
Phoenix, 35, 222, 231
Phosphates, 159
Pick-Sloan Plan, 204-5
Pictou, 287
Pineapples, 160
Pine Barrens, 122
— Hills, 153
— Pass, 348, 360
— Ridge, 197
— trees, 57, 58, 59, 61, 64, 66, 152, 156, 169, 172, 216, 223, 244, 264, 276, 286, 297, 323, 364, 387
Pingoes, 387
Pipelines, 166, 182, 190, 314, 350-1, 374
Pittsburgh, 86, 87, 92, 96, 119, 163, 168, 180, 182, 185, 186, 188, **192-4**, 308
Plantations, 137, 139, 141-2, 154
Platinum, 245, 329, 330
Platte R., 91, 197, 199, 202, 203, 212
Plymouth, 84
Pocahontas, 181
Podsols, 69, 70, 107, 326
Pontiac, 191
Porcupine District, 328, 329
— Mts, 336
Portages, 81, 320, 332
Port Alfred, 299
— Arthur (Ont.), 305, 307, 326, 333, 346, 347
— — (Tex.), 167
— aux Basques, 273, 278, 280
— Cartier, 332
— Credit, 314
— Colborne, 314, 330
— Edward, 366
— Hope, 314
— Lavaca, 167
— Radium, 329, 331
Portland (Maine), 107, 109
Portland (Ore.), 261, 262, 264, **269**
Potash, 213, 352
Potatoes, 107, 121, 160, 177, 208, 212, 226, 229, 264, 273, 280, 284, 285, 313, 326, 330, 347, 349, 370, 382, 383
Potomac R., 8, 86, 116, 119, 126, 168
Poultry, 106, 122, 175, 226, 263, 285, 296, 314, 328, 347, 348, 370
Powder R., 213
Powell R., 366
Precipitation, **33-41**
Prescott, 307
Pribilof Is., 384

Prince Edward Is., 270, 277, 280, 281, 282, 284, 285, 286, 287
— George, 348, 359, 372, 376
— Rupert, 359, 366, 375
— Rupert's Land, 323
Providence, 108, 112
Provo, 233
Public Domain, 93, 168, 205, 215, 228, 342
Pueblo, 213, 214, 256
Puget Sound, 18, 91, 259, 263, 265, 266, 267, 268, 356
Pulpwood, 104, 157, 265, 286, 297, 325
Purcell Range, 220, 358, 367
— Trench, 220

QUEBEC, 80, 96, 292, 294, 295, 296, 299, **303**, 305, 307, 313
— Province, 58, 291, 296, 297, 299, 300, 308, 316, 325, 326, 327, 329
Queen Charlotte Is., 18, 356, 362
Quinsam Lake, 316, 368

RADIUM, 314, 393
Railways, **92-4**, 123, 124, 125, 129, 132, 163, 167, 170, 189-90, 192, 221-2, 233, 252, 268, 281, 298, 303, 314, 318, **332-3**, 342, 344, 348, 359
Railway workshops, 125, 131, 288, 305, 316, 352
Rainy R., 326
Ranching, 164, 205-6, **210-11**, 228, 245, 343, 353
Range, 206
Rankin Inlet, 330
Raton Mesa, 213
Rayon, 158, 192
Reconstruction, 138
Red Bluff, 241
— Deer R., 336, 337
— Indian Lake, 279
— Lake, 329, 333
— Prairies, 141, 164
— R., 5, 172, 195, 202, 207, 335, 341, 352
Redwater, 350
Redwoods, 59, 250
Regina, 350
Reindeer, 380, 390
Reno, 233
— Oasis, 229
Resolute, 392
Restigouche R., 282, 286
Rhode Is., 101, 109
Rice, 143, **162**, 164, 246, 247
Richardson Mts, 385
Richelieu R., 297, 303

Richmond (Calif.), 252
— (N.J.), 129
— (Va.), 158
Riding Mt, 336
Rio Grande, 12, 79, 90, 135, 164, 178, 202, 203, 216, 217
Riverbend, 299
Rivière des Prairies, 304
Roanoke, 158
Rochester, 133
Rockaway Beach, 128
Rockfish Gap, 119
Rogue R., 258, 264
Rolphton, 331
Rome (Ga.), 157
— (N.Y.), 133
Root crops, 229, 284, 296, 372
Rossland, 368
Rouyn, 329, 330
Rubber, 111, 129, 167, 191, 192, 193, 315, 316, 317, 318, 375, 396
Run-off, 40, 73, 137, 142, 148, 234
Ruth, 232
Rye, 208, 312, 347

SABINE R., 89, 167
Sacramento, 46, 243, 251
— R., 245, 248-9, 250, 251, 256, 356
Sagebrush, 62, 201, 216, 223, 364
Saguenay R., 294, 301, 302
St Anthony Falls, 194
— Catharines, 313, 316, 317
— Charles R., 303
— Clair R., 191, 305
— Elias Range, 18, 379, 383, 385
— Francis Mts, 3, 11, 151
— — R., 299
— George's Bay, 273, 276, 279
— Hyacinthe, 302
— Jerome, 299
— John, 284, 288, 305, 347
— — R., 283, 285
— John's, 30, 31, 37, 51, 272, 273, 275, 277
— Lawrence R., 5, 30, 80, 97, 291, 295, 298, 299, 303, 304, **306-8**, 315, 319, 325, 331
— — Seaway, 115, 183, 193, 302, **305-8**, 347
— Louis, 29, 30, 31, 50, 88, 153, 173, 176, 179, 186, 188, **195**, 203, 308
— Mary's R. (Ont.), 305
— — — (Alb.), 348
— Maurice R., 298, 301, 302
— Paul, 173, 176, 188, **194-5**, 342
Salinas R., 250, 251
Salmon, 266, 369, 384
— River Mts, 220

Salt Domes, 162, 165, 166
— Lake City, 222, 229, 233
— — Oasis, 229, 233
Salton Sea, 230, 240
Salt R., 141, 231
San Andreas Fault, 250
— Bernadino Mts, 253
— Diego, 30, 31, 35, 47, 48, 90, 236, 241, 251, 253, 255
— Fernando Valley, 254
— Francisco, 30, 31, 35, 46, 79, 91, 129, 241, 243, 250, **251-3**, 384
— Gabriel Mts, 253
— Gorgonio Pass, 253
— Joaquin R., 141, 245, 246, 248, 249, 250, 251
— Juan Mts, 216, 217
— Manuel, 232
— Pedro, 254, 256
Sandy Hook, 128
Sangre de Cristo Mts, 90, 217
Santa Clara Valley, 250, 251
— Fé, 79, 90, 217
— Maria Valley, 251
— Ynez Valley, 250, 251
Sardines, 251, 287
Sarnia, 314, 317, 350
Saskatchewan, 312, 325, 337, 340, 341, 343, 345, 346, 350, 377
— R. 337, 348-9, 352
Saskatoon, 339
Sault Ste Marie (Mich.), 184, 185, 305
— — — (Ont.), 305, 315, 326, 333
Savannah, 83
Sawatch Range, 217
Saw mills, 195, 221, 265, 278, 286, 297, 365, 374
Scablands, 224
Schefferville, 183, 315, 316, 328, **331**
Schenectady, 133
Schuylkill R., 119, 125
Scioto R., 88, 187, 193
Scranton, 120, 121
Seals, 278, 364, 384, 392
Seattle, 93, 266, 267, **268-9**, 383, 384
Seigneuries, 80, 292, 293
Selkirk Mts, 358, 367
Sept Iles, 305, 307, 328, 329, 331
Seward, 382
— Peninsula, 380
Share-cropping, 139, 141
Shawinigan Falls, 298, 301, 302
Sheep, 152, 211, 218, 221, 228, 246, 314, 343, 371, 372
Sheffield, 167
Shelter Bay, 332
Shenandoah Valley, 8, 119, 120
Sherbrooke, 303
Sherridon, 329, 331

INDEX

Shickshock Mts, 9, 281
Shipbuilding, 125, 126, 131, 158, 269, 288, 302, 333, 374, 375
Shipshaw, 301
Sierra Madre, 13
Silver, 92, 220, 279, 314, 329, 330, 367, 368, 388
Sioux City, 176, 204
Sitka, 30, 31, 35, 45, 378, 384, 385
— Spruce, 59, 264, 362, 384
Skagway, 384, 388
Skeena Mts, 358
— R., 358
— Saddle, 358, 364
Slave R., 389
Smog, 255
Snag, 44
Snake R., 17, 91, 216, **224-7**, 260, 261, 262, 263
Snowline, 53
Softwood, 104, 146, 157, 165, 297, 326
Soil Bank Scheme, 143, 210
— Conservation, **74-5**, 142, 148, 210
— Erosion, **72-4**, 137, 142, 145, 148, 176, 210, 211, 224, 313, 344, 396
Soils, 54, **66-72**, 140-1, 172, 196, 201, 276, 296, 311, 326, 340
Sonoran Desert, 62
Soo Canals, 184, 305
Sorel, 302
Sorghum, 143, 155, 209
Soulanges Plain, 297
South Bend, 188
— Pass, 91, 218
— Saskatchewan Project, 348, 349
Soy-beans, 143, 155, 162, 175, 313, 399
Spanish, **79-80**, 240
— Trail, 90
Sparrow's Point, 121, 126
Sphagnum, 57, 58, 276, 323, 386
Spokane, 48, 222, 227, 267
Springfield (Mass.), 112, 113
Spruce trees, 57, 58, 59, 61, 64, 216, 223, 264, 286, 297, 311, 323, 325, 362, 364, 382, 384, 387
Spur, 73
Staked Plains, 197
Standard Metropolitan Areas, 109, 124, 254
Staten Is., 128
Steel, 112, 167, 193, 307; *see also* Iron and steel industry
Steep Rock, 183, 315, 331, 333
Sudbury, 326, 329, **330**
Sugar beet, 208, 211, 212, 226, 229, 231, 297, 312, 349
— cane, 143, 160, 162
— refining, 213, 233, 288
Sulphur, 162, 165, 166

Sunflowers, 347
Susquehanna R., 86, 116, 117, 119, 120, 121, 128, 168
Sydney, 279, 283, 287, **288**, 315
Syracuse, 133

TACOMA, 267, 268, 269
Taconic Mts, 9, 101, 115, 119, 132
Taconite, 183
Taiga, 57-8, 276
Taku R., 368, 374
Taltson Lake, 329
Tampa, 161
Tanana Valley, 379, 382
Tariffs, 288, 290, 315
Tejon Pass, 244, 253
Temperatures, 28-33
Tennessee, 10, 137, 139, 144, 146, 149, 150, 151, 156, 221
— R., 8, 87, 141, 145, 146, 147
— Valley Authority, 75, **147-9**
Teton Range, 218
Texada Is., 368
Texas, 3, 64, 68, 71, 73, 137, 139, 141, 142, 162, 164, 166, 167, 199, 200, 208, 209, 211, 212, 213
Texas City, 167
Textiles, 109, **110-11**, 112, 113, 115, 120, 125, 131, **158**, 163, 166, 192, 193, 269, 302, 303, 316, 317, 318
Thames, R., 309, 310, 316
Thetford, 299
Thompson Lake, 329, 330
— R., 364, 371
Thousand Isles, 291
Thunder Bay, 326
Timmins, 328
Tin, 167
Tintic, 232
Titanium, 302, 329
Titusville, 181
Tobacco, 75, 107, 121, 122, **150-1**, 156, 158, 235, 297, 312
Toledo, 182, 184, 185, 188, 191
Tomatoes, 107, 122, 162, 229, 246, 253, 297, 312, 349
Tongass National Forest, 59, 384
Topeka, 209
Tornadoes, **26**, 201
Torngat Mts, 3, 319
Toronto, 305, 308, 311, 313, **318**, 331, 350
Tourism, 106, 108, 123, 127, 153, 161, 163, 235, 368
Trade, 115, **129**, 163, 167, **251-2**, 256, 261, 269, 277, 284, 287, 299, 303, **305**, 346, 350, 351, 352, 356, 366, 369, 375, **396**, **397**

INDEX

Trail, 368, 376
Trans-Canada Highway, 333
Transhumance, 211, 228
Trash cover, 75, 210, 225
Tree line, 59, 60, 61, 217, 244, 259, 276, 362, 387
Trenton, 125
— Escarpment, 309
Trent R., 315
Trinity R., 164
Tri-State Area, 152
Trois Rivières, 292, 298, 304
Troutdale, 267
Troy, 132, 133
Truck farming, 107, **122-3**, **155-6**, 160, 164, 229, 231, 240, 246, **247-53**, 263, 264, 289, 297
Truckee R., 229
Tucson, 231
Tuktoyaktuk, 389
Tulsa, 165
Tulsequah, 368, 374
Tuna, 251, 266, 368
Tundra, **56-7**, **68-9**, 321, 322, **323**, 362, 380, 382, 387, 391, 392
Tung nuts, 162
Tungsten, 329, 368
Turner Valley, 350, 353
Turtle Mt, 337

UINTA Mts, 15, 218, 233
Ungava Trough, 332
Union Pacific Railway, 93
Uranium, 233, 329, 331, 393
— City, 329, 331
Utah, 215, 221, 222, 233, 238

VAL d'Or, 329, 330
Vancouver (B.C.), 305, 346, 348, 350, 353, 355, 359, 361, 362, 366, **374-5**
— Is., 18, 34, 356, 357, 364, 366, 367, 368, 370, 372, 376
— (Wash.), 265, 267
Vegetables, 107, 212, 226, 229, 231, 273, 280, 312, 313, 326, 327, 328, 349, 370, 371, 382, 383, 388, 399; see also Truck farming
Vegetation types, **56-66**
Vermont, 101, 105
Vernon, 376
Vicksburg, 30, 31, 32, 163
Victoria, 30, 31, 34, 35, 45, 361, 372, 375
Virginia, 116, 122, 139, 153, 156, 180, 181, 182, 192, 221
— City (Mont.), 220
— — (Nev.), 231-2

Volcanoes, 18, 244, 379

WABANA, 279, 288
Wabash R., 88, 187
Wabush Lake, 332
Walla Walla, 91, 227
Warrior R., 146, 147
Wasatch Range, 16, 218, **227-8**, 229, 233, 332
Washington, 17, 34, 41, 59, 215, 221, 222, 224, 225, 238, 257, 258, 261, 265, 356
— D.C., 30, 31, 121, 123, **126-7**
Water-power, 108, 123, 300-2, 317, 393; see also Hydro-electricity
Waterbury, 112
Waterfalls, 4, 6, 102, 122, 132, 283
Waterways, 389
Waynesboro, 119
Welland Canal, 305, 314, 315
Wenatchee, 227, 267
— Valley, 226
Western Shore, 122
West Point, 119
Whaling, 278, 368, 392
Wheat, 93, 121, 122, 126, 145, 150, 151, 175, 176, 184, 206, **207-10**, **224-5**, 229, 240, 245, 246, 263, 284, 296, 312, 333, **343-7**, 349, 353, 371, 399
Wheeling, 86, 119, 168, 185, 192
White Bay, 273, 280
Whitehorse, 382, 384, 388, 389
White Mts, 101
— Pass, 384, 388
Wichita Mts, 11, 151, 165
Wilderness Road, 87, 150
Willamette R., 260, 261, 265, 269, 356
Williston, 213
Wilmington, 125, 126
Wind-chill, 322
Windsor, 311, 316, 317
Winnipeg, 30, 31, 32, 51, 313, 335, 339, 342, 343, 346, 347, 350, **352**
Winston Salem, 158
Winter Garden, 164
Wisconsin, 169, 176, 177, 182
— Driftless, 10, 172
Wood Mt, 337, 343
Wool, 111
Worcester, 108, 111, 112
Wrangell, 385
Wyoming, 166, 211, 213, 215, 238

YAKIMA, 227, 262
— Valley, 226, 261
Yarmouth, 287
Yarrington, 232

Yellowhead Pass, 359, 360
Yellowknife, 329, 333, 389
Yellowstone National Park, 15
— R., 202, 218
Yosemite National Park, 17, 244
Youghiogeny R., 180, 194
Youngstown, 185, 192
Yucca, 63, 201, 223, 234

Yukon Plateau, 378, 379, 382, 385
— R., 374, 379, 382, 384, 388, 389
Yuma, 35, 47, 48, 222, 231, 237

ZANESVILLE, 187
Zinc, 92, 152, 167, 213, 218, 220, **221**, 279, 288, **329**, 367, 368, 376, 388

REGIONAL REFERENCES

ALASKA, 1, 13, 18, 30, 34, 59, 76, 269, 375, 377, **378-85**, 390
Appalachians, **7-9**, 64, 65, 84, **85-7**, 89, 92, 101, 116, **117-22**, 135, 137, 144, **145-7**, 178, 185, 270, 273, 281, 289, 294, 297, 299
Arctic, Canadian, 378, **391-3**
Atlantic Coast Plain, **5-7**, 66, 68, 83, **122-3**, 135, 137, 140, 153
— Provinces, **270-90**, 300, 326

BLUE Grass Region, 87, 119, **149-51**
— Ridge, 7, 9, 86, 87, **117-22**
British Columbia, 18, 34, 59, 97, 262, 267, 277, 286, 300, 315, 325, 326, 347, 350, **355-76**, 377, 378, 384, 385

CALIFORNIA, 17, 18, 26, 28, 31, 46, 79, 80, 91, 132, 137, 143, 166, 178, 215, 230, 236, 238, **240-56**, 258, 267, 351
Canadian Shield, **1-3**, 97, 98, 170, 291, 294, 297, 299, 300, 302, 308, 309, 314, **319-34**, 354, 378, 385, 392
Cape Breton Is., 280, 283, **287-8**
Central Lowlands, **9-13**, 87-9, 170, 385
— Valley (California), 18, 32, 60, 64, 68, 91, 241, 243, **245-50**, 252
Coast Mts, 358, 360, 362, 367, 373, 379, 385
— Ranges, 17, 18, 59, 60, 240, 241, **250-3**, **258-9**, 264, 356
Colorado Plateaus, 15, 72, **233-7**
Columbia Plateau, 16, **223-7**, 263, 269
Corn Belt, 152, **174-6**, 189, 211, 312
Cotton Belt, 140, 142, 143

DEATH Valley, 47, 62, 240

EASTERN Townships, 293, 297, 299, 302, 303
Everglades, 6, 159

FLORIDA, 6, 25, 31, 33, 34, 52, 77, 79, 80, 135, 137, 139, **159-61**, 178

GREAT Basin, 16, 17, 68, 213, **227-33**, 243, 244

Great Lakes, 4, 5, 29, 30, 132, 169, 173, **177-9**, **183-6**, 191, 304, 305-6, 314, 322, 327, 333, 346
— Plains, 11-12, 15, 22, 26, 28, 30, 35, 37, 48, 49, 62, 73, 78, 89, 93, 94, 164, **196-214**, 219, 220, 339, 343, **353-4**
Gulf Coast Plain, **12-13**, 25, 26, 29, 30, 31, 36, 68, 79, 87, 92, 134, 141, 153, 164

HAY and Dairy Belt, 105, **176-7**, 208, 296
High Plains, 12, 197

INTERIOR Plateaus, 149-53
— Uplands, 358, 359, 360
Intermontane Plateaus, 15-17, 215, 219, **222-39**

LABRADOR, 3, 5, 42, 273, 277, 288, 307, 319, 321, 331, 332, 377
Laurentian Lowlands, **291-318**

MACKENZIE Basin, 9, 30, 31, 335, 337, **385-91**, 393
Manufacturing Belt, 126, **179**, 187-95
Maritime Provinces, 98, 107, 270, **280-90**, 293, 294
Middle Atlantic Region, **116-33**, 186
— South, **144-53**
Midwest, 111, 119, 126, 153, **168-95**, 203, 267, 315
Mississippi Valley, 26, 32, 66, 68, 79, 82, 90, 135, 140, 141, **161-3**, 178
Mohawk Valley, 117, **132-3**, 193
Mountain States, **215-39**

NASHVILLE Basin, 10, **149-50**
New England, 9, 25, 65, 84, 98, **100-15**, 119, 132, **288-90**, 293
Newfoundland, 43, 51, 57, 80, 107, 270, **271-80**, 286, 287, 288
Northlands, 354, **377-94**
North-west Territories, 377, 378, **385-94**

OKANAGAN Valley, 226, 261, 359, 364, 366, **370-1**

429

Ontario Peninsula, 292, 293, **308-18**, 342
Ozarks, 3, 11, 65, 89, 135, 137, 144, **151-3**, 165

PACIFIC North-west, **257-69**, 356
Palouse, 64, **224-5**, 263
Peace River District, 335, 341, 342, **347-8**, 352, 367, 368, 372, 374, 389
Piedmont, 6, 7, 75, 86, 96, 116, **121-2**, 125, 126, 127, 137, 141, 145, 154, 156, 157, 158, 203
Prairies, 22, 30, 40, 63, 71, 98, 105, 133, 189, 201, 294, 300, 312, 333, **335-54**, 374

RIDGE and Valley Province, 8, **117-22**, 145
Rocky Mountains, 13-15, 34, 41, 61, 89, 91, 196, 199, 213, **215-22**, 337, 343, **359-60**, 367, 385

Rocky Mountain Trench, 17, 220, **359**, 371

ST LAWRENCE Valley, 3, 51, 96, 288, **291-308**, 311, 320
Sand Hills, 12, 63, 68, 202, 209, 210
Sierra Nevada, 16, 17, 34, 59, 60, 61, 91, 223, 227-8, 240, 241, **243-5**, 252, 256
South, 75, 95, 111, **134-67**, 186
— -east, 143, **153-8**, 178
— -west, 143, **164-7**

WESTERN Cordilleras, **13-19**, 41, 45, 53, 62, 378, 385
Wheat Belts, 144, 207-10, 224-5, 343-7
Willamette Valley, 18, 91, 259, 262, 263, 265, 269, 356
Wyoming Basin, 15, 62, 72, 216, **218**

YELLOWSTONE Plateau, 216, 218
Yukon, 17, 33, 44, 353, 377, 378, 382, 388, 390